Medieval Worlds

Medieval Worlds

An Introduction to European History, 300–1492

JO ANN HOEPPNER MORAN CRUZ
Georgetown University

RICHARD GERBERDING
University of Alabama, Huntsville

HOUGHTON MIFFLIN COMPANY
Boston   New York

Publisher: Charles Hartford
Editor-in-Chief: Jean L. Woy
Senior Sponsoring Editor: Nancy Blaine
Senior Development Editor: Fran Gay
Senior Project Editor: Carol Newman
Editorial Assistants: Kendra Johnson, Marlowe Shaeffer
Senior Production Design Coordinator: Jodi O'Rourke
Manufacturing Manager: Florence Cadran
Senior Marketing Manager: Sandra McGuire

Cover illustration: St. Gregory writing with scribes below. Carolingian, Franco-German school, c. 850–875 (ivory).

TEXT CREDITS: p. 244: Map from *Medieval Iberia: Readings from Christian, Muslim, and Jewish Sources,* edited by Olivia Remie Constable. Copyright © 1997 University of Pennsylvania Press. Reprinted by permission of the University of Pennsylvania Press. p. 271: Map from *The Times History of the World,* ed. Geoffrey Barraclough; *New Edition,* ed. Richard Overy (London, Times Books), 1999. Used with permission. p. 358: From "In Balance," translated by George F. Whicher, *The Goliard Poets: Medieval Latin Songs and Satires.* Copyright © 1949 by George F. Whicher. Reprinted by permission of New Directions Publishing Corp. p. 384: "Something in the Pastourelle Line," translated by George F. Whicher, *The Goliard Poets: Medieval Latin Songs and Satires.* Copyright © 1949 by George F. Whicher. Reprinted by permission of New Directions Publishing Corp. p. 389:From *Perceval: Or, the Story of the Grail* by Chretien de Troyes, translated by Ruth Harwood Cline. Copyright © 1983. Reprinted by permission of University of Georgia Press. p. 393: Copyright © 1995. From *Songs of the Women Troubadours,* edited and translated by Bruckner, Shepard, and White. Reproduced by permission of Routledge, Inc., part of the Tayler & Francis Group. p. 422: Excerpt from Michael Clanchy, *England and Its Rulers, 1066–1272* (Barnes and Noble, 1983), p. 280. p. 455: "When the Days Are Long in May," from the *Lyrics of the Troubadour, Trouveres,* translated by Frederick Goldin. Used by permission of Doubleday, a division of Random House, Inc. p. 456: "Of Things I'd Rather Keep in Silence I Must Sing," poem by the Countess of Dia, from Meg Bogin, *The Women Troubadours* (Norton, 1980), p. 85. Reprinted by permission of the author.

Printed in U.S.A.

Library of Congress Catalog Number: 2002117255

ISBN: 0-395-56087-X

3 4 5 6 7 8 9 –QF-08 07 06 05 04

CONTENTS

Introduction: **The Birth of Europe and the Mentality of Medieval People**   **1**

PART I   **The Transformation of the Roman World, A.D. 100–751**   **17**

CHAPTER 1   *The Roman Foundations of Medieval Europe, 100–500*   18

CHAPTER 2   *Early Christianity: From Sect to State Religion, 30–500*   43

MAPS

PREFACE

We have written this text for undergraduate university and college students. We have endeavored to present an expansive view of medieval society and a fluid view of the changes medieval society underwent from late antiquity into the Italian Renaissance. We wanted a text that would integrate cultural and literary developments, intellectual contributions, literacy and education, the role of women, popular religious impulses, and papal perspectives, as well as the political history of kings and queens, emperors, counts, and communes. We have chosen not to directly discuss theoretical or methodological approaches to gender, race, class, post-colonialism or post-modernism. Rather, we have folded a sensitivity to these approaches into the narrative itself and into a rather inclusive treatment of topics. Women have been incorporated into the narrative at every level. Social groupings, ethnic identities, slavery, the interactions of Europeans with non-Europeans, as well as the conditions for minorities and for new groups entering Europe all find their appropriate place in our account.

We have given a good deal of attention to Islam, both as a subject in itself and as an important influence on medieval Europe. We have given broad consideration to eastern Europe, something which allows us, for example, to present a richer view of the post-Carolingian period, focusing on the new and powerful kingdoms on the European peripheries as well as the situation within the Carolingian territories. Europe is viewed with a wide lens in this text, allowing us to range from Iceland to Rusland and into the Mediterreanean. Each chapter also contains much of what is normally considered more traditional political history, but politics conceived in the round. Here we examine the ways societies organized themselves and the ways rulers adapted to changing political climates. Finally, we have placed a great emphasis on cultural conditions: literary works, religious practice, patronage, education, family and marriage, and literacy. Embedded in this cultural context are discussions of the prevailing mental frameworks within which medieval society functioned, an emerging sense of self-awareness, as well as the shift from a predominately oral culture to one that was increasingly written.

An introductory chapter gives the setting of the birth of Europe and describes the mentality of medieval people. Then the text follows a roughly chronological order, and the chapter divisions are somewhat traditional. We begin with the Roman world and early Christianity. The barbarians (Germans and others) follow, along with a chapter on the Byzantines and the Muslims who continue to inhabit the pages of this text in subsequent chapters. We have included a chapter on the early Church to provide an introduction to basic ecclesiastical information. Next come the Carolingians and the Anglo-Saxons. Chapter 8 treats the period from 900 to 1050 A.D., focusing on the fluid situation in eastern Europe, the Vikings, and the Muslims in Europe. Social, economic, and political developments in this period follow in Part III, Chapters 9 and 10. Part IV begins with the renewal of spirituality at the turn of the millennium and follows with the reformation of the Church, rising persecution, and the Crusades. We examine the bases for legitimacy for political and religious authorities, the growth in governmental institutions, and the shifting power relations of various ruling authorities in Chapter 13. Chapter 14 examines the explosion of learning from 1050 to 1200, including the shift from cathedral schools to universities, the emerging emphasis on the dialectic, and discussions of schools, curriculum, literacy, and patronage. Medieval marriage, families, children, clergy, life at the local level, social groupings from top to bottom, courtly culture, and a moneyed economy are all treated in Chapter 15. Next is a chapter on the church-state struggles in the thirteenth century. This chapter includes a political survey of Europe as well as material on the Mongol invasion and the rise of the mendicant orders. We then return to intellectual history and popular culture in Chapter 17. The last two chapters focus on economic and political crises as well as the institutional and intellectual developments of the late Middle Ages. An epilogue introduces the student to the Italian Renaissance.

There are aids for students throughout, including explanatory notes at the bottom of pages, and lists of rulers and a timeline at the end of the book. Each chapter and each section begins with introductory material, and each chapter ends with a summary. Features within each chapter give the students glimpses into primary sources from the period (Medieval Voices) and biographical information on various individuals (Medieval Portraits). Bibliographies at the end of the book give students suggestions for further reading and research.

Writing this text has been a large undertaking for both of us, and we owe thanks that we cannot hope to repay to many people. Jo Ann would like to thank John Contreni and Jean Woy for initially promoting the idea of this book. She would like to thank her colleagues Jenny Paxton, Andrzej Kaminsky, David Goldfrank, Haifaa Khallafallah, Constance Berman, Yvonne Haddad, Scott Redford, Clive Foss, and especially Bennett Hill for their interest in the project and their willingness to read all or parts of the manuscript. Parts of this book were written while Jo Ann was in Egypt and, thanks are due to Georgetown's program in Alanya, Turkey. She further wants to thank her children and her husband, Fernando, for putting up with the long gestation process involved in producing a book of this scope. Dick is deeply grateful to Ian Wood for his help with parts of the text, to Marie Adams and Gordon Stobart for making his time in the British Library possible, to John Severn for many suggestions and reactions, and to Curtis Bridgeman for providing time to work on the book by helping with the house.

We both are greatly indebted to the many reviewers whose comments and corrections have sharpened considerably our presentation: Blake Beattie, University of Louisville; Robert F. Berkhofer III, Western Kentucky University; William Delehanty, University of Saint Thomas; Katherine French, SUNY, New Paltz; Matthew Gordon, Miami University; Tia Kolbaba, Princeton University; Thomas Noble,

University of Notre Dame; Silvia C. Shannon, Saint Anselm College; Thomas Turley, Santa Clara University; and Kimberly Rivers, University of Wisconsin, Oshkosh. We are very grateful also to the people at Houghton Mifflin who helped along the way: Jean Woy, Fran Gay, Carol Newman, Jodi O'Rourke, Florence Cadran, Linda Sykes, Charlotte Miller, and especially to the skillful, gentle, and often surgical Dale Anderson. We look forward to any comments, corrections and critical suggestions that colleagues who use this text and students who study it may have for future editions.

J. H. M. C.

R. G.

TO THE STUDENT

This text is a guidebook for your journey through the Middle Ages. As you travel you will see many marvelous things. You will visit cities: ones with thousands of inhabitants and buildings full of gold and mosaics; port towns with foreign people speaking strange languages; capitals built for kings; cathedral cities built by bishops; new bustling local market towns; as well as forgotten outposts and deserted villages. You will meet people: great women who ruled empires, wrote books, founded institutions, or had mystic visions of God; warrior kings, soldiers and knights who fought bloody battles mostly among themselves but also against fierce invaders; philosophers of exquisite gentility and intellectual refinement; poets; singers; crusaders; merchants; lovers; pagans; Jews; Muslims; people mad for God who offer prayers locked in stone cells or atop pillars; and many hardworking family members leading ordinary, often precarious, lives. You will see buildings, some of unimaginable size and others of such sophistication that they stretch the material quality of stone to its architectural limits. You will watch empires come and go, economies change, armies march, fearless explorers head off into the cold Atlantic, and eager merchants travel to mysterious Asia.

You will begin to understand the material richness of medieval culture, which the few enjoyed: statues, fine clothes, pictures, fountains, tools, weapons, jewels and dazzlingly illuminated parchment books. You will think about the nature of law, family, honor, the role of women, philosophy, theology, sex, science, and love. And you will watch people and societies face enormous challenges caused by such things as migrating and sometimes dangerous peoples, famine, floods, the bubonic plague, or religious war. By the end of this journey we hope you will have come to understand the origin of many attitudes, institutions, foods, governments, languages, religious beliefs, and concepts that affect the modern western world.

The European Middle Ages themselves are, of course, fixed in the past, but their study continues to evolve. Not only do today's scholars continually discover new things about the Middle Ages, but they also, in reflecting on the problems and attitudes of our own times, pose new problems and ask new questions. This book was written both to include the best research in traditional medieval topics and to explore those elements of medieval society that reflect the changed interests of our times. For instance, as Europeans and Americans now wrestle with ideas of what makes a person American or European, so too have recent scholars explored the medieval origins of ethnic identity, asking what made a man or woman a Roman, a Visigoth, a Briton, a Spaniard, or a Pole.

Recent scholarship is greatly concerned with cultural and social history, exploring medieval marriage, children, families, and demographic history. These inquiries have produced a picture of the Middle Ages that is much more complex and much more exciting than once thought. We find that medieval societies varied greatly by time and place, and that medieval Europe was not its own closed world but quite open to outside influences. This book presents this richer, deeper, and broader view of medieval life. You will find women presented as an integral part of medieval society rather than as a fascinating afterthought. You will find that the geographical boundaries of medieval Europe presented here reflect the integral part played by societies once thought to have been outsiders. For instance, the treatment of the tenth century moves beyond the traditional focus on the disintegrating Carolingian Empire to show the vital new societies emerging in Scandinavia, Germany, eastern Europe and Rusland, the Balkans, Italy, and Spain. We cover much political history, but this is politics conceived in light of recent scholarship, that is, not as battles, dates, or deeds of kings and popes, but as the way societies in various times and places organized themselves for concerted action.

History is, at its base, the study of change set in time, and we expect that the chronological organization of this text will give you the structure you will need should you decide to explore various topics in medieval history more fully later. To help you see how a clear understanding of medieval history anchors itself firmly in time we have included timelines and chronological lists of rulers at the back of the book. To help you understand medieval peoples themselves, we have included special features in each chapter where the people of each period speak for themselves (Medieval Voices) or where we describe a contemporary individual in some detail (Medieval Portraits).

J. H. M. C.

R. G.

Medieval Worlds

~

The Birth of Europe and the Mentality of Medieval People

Why study the Middle Ages? Out of the many reasons, perhaps two deserve attention as we begin. First, even today European culture not only thrives on the continent of Europe where it was born, but has transported itself far beyond. European influence is felt not only in the former colonies, but today it penetrates even to places Europeans never controlled. Why should someone who lives as far away from Spain as Santiago, Chile, speak Spanish or someone as far from the British Isles as Hiroshima hum U2's latest hit? Whether one would like to preserve or emulate European culture or to unbalance its dominance by emphasizing the merits of other cultures, it is necessary to understand how European culture came to be. The search for this understanding brings us to the world of medieval Europe. The particular culture we now call "European" emerged in the early Middle Ages (500–900) and grew up during the high (900–1300) and later Middle Ages (1300–1500) before it came to dominate much of the world in the modern period.

Second, medieval history has an intrinsic fascination. It is simply worth knowing on its own. It is much like visiting a foreign land. When we venture into the medieval world, we find some things deceivingly familiar, but many others that seem completely alien. As in our own modern societies, we find people of every complexion, profession, and ability, but whose sense of the past, underlying assumptions about how to act toward each other, and religious expectations were vastly different from our own. This is largely because they lived before the modern revolutions in science, technology, and politics. For example, medieval culture was largely oral rather than written, especially in the early Middle Ages. So ceremony and memory were far more important, and the visual arts served different functions than they do in modern societies. Religion, too, directed and justified medieval lives to a much greater degree than it does most modern communities. Although medieval people gave birth, grew up, fell in love, married, worked, entertained themselves, faced death, and died all in ways we might recognize, still they experienced and perceived the world in a fundamentally different way from modern people. So before we describe the history of their world, it is important to examine some of the ways they viewed themselves.

"MIDDLE AGES"

People living between 500 and 1500 certainly did not perceive themselves as medieval or living in the "Middle Ages." The words "Middle Ages" are loaded with modern meaning. They and words such as "Dark Ages," "barbaric," "monkish," "popish," "feudal," "honor," "Germanic," and "Gothic," just to name a few, are encumbered with more meaning, usually negative, than their proper definitions bear. But how can two simple little words like "middle" and "age" be loaded?

Middle means to be in the middle or to be between. The word makes the middle ages an age between two others. Such a term would obviously not be used by medieval people themselves. How could it be? They considered themselves then, just as we consider ourselves now, to be at the end of history, not between any ages. The term Middle Ages was coined in Latin, *Medium Aevum,* by Christoph Keller, a German professor, in 1688. It was used to describe the supposedly somber and Gothic age between the glorious ancient period and the resplendent rebirth of classical ideals in the Renaissance. The term makes our study of the period seem like a trip through a curiosity shop—dark, dusty, and out of the mainstream. "Middle" implies that the medieval period has less relevance, located, as it was, between two ages of mankind's splendid march through time. The word is loaded, but we shall use it. We have no other.

An age is a unit of time; it has a beginning and an end. The word age makes us ask when the Middle Ages began. A common answer to the question used to be that the early Middle Ages began when the Western Roman Empire "fell" and the year A.D. 476 was often used. Obviously, serious historians did not mean by this that anything as complicated as a change in age for a significant part of the western world happened in one single year, but 476 was used as a convenient signpost. As we shall see, the transition from ancient to medieval culture was a complex phenomenon that happened in different places at different times and affected people's lives in different ways.

We would be wise not to narrow our view of the birth, death, or development of the Middle Ages to specific points, when any one particular government died or came to life, nor to any one place. Events that took place as far east as China, as far west as Iceland or Greenland, as far south as Ethiopia, and as far north as Norway all influenced what we call the European Middle Ages. And Europe itself is viewed expansively in this text, ranging from the western Atlantic seaboard eastward across the considerable expanse of eastern Europe to the city of Constantinople, the Black Sea and the Dnieper River, and then south into the Mediterranean and north to Scandinavia.

TIME

Medieval Europeans viewed time differently than we do today. For most medieval people, waking hours began at daybreak and ended at dusk,* unless one could afford candles, was in a religious order and awoke early for divine service, or did not mind stumbling in the dark or the moonlight when perhaps returning home from the alehouse. Day and night were divided into twelve hours each, but the length of the hours varied with the length of the day.† In the summer, when the day was longer, so were the day-light hours. In the winter, it was the opposite. The only time day and night hours were of equal length was on the equinoxes.

Sundials and sand and water clocks calculated hourly divisions. Muslims also used astrolabes (instruments that measure the altitude of the sun and stars), and they commonly measured the daily change in the length of a shadow to determine the hours of prayer.

Monasteries and cathedrals needed sundials and water clocks to calculate the hours of the Divine Office,‡ which derived from Roman divisions of the days and the Jewish hours of private prayer. The first office was matins, also called vigils, celebrated almost anytime in the middle of the night. After matins came lauds, at dawn, followed by prime during the first hour of the day, terce (the third hour of the day), sext (the sixth hour of the day), nones (the ninth hour of the day),§ vespers (in the evening) and compline (at nightfall). Most people measured time by these liturgical hours, which were announced through the day by church bells that began to be used throughout Europe by the fifth and sixth centuries.

By the fourteenth century, bells began to regulate working hours in some towns, although people ordinarily did not work according to strict schedules. The fourteenth-century statutes of the Parisian leather-softeners noted that they were to work from dawn to dusk, or "until such time as one can only just distinguish a citizen of Tours from one of Paris." In the countryside, people paid more attention to seasonal changes than to the hours of the day.

In the Middle Ages time was not a commodity, as it often appears to be today. Time, it was thought, belonged to God. Given as a gift to all people, time began with God and was dominated by Him. For this reason, medieval churchmen were uneasy with the idea of selling time. Usury, charging interest for lending money over time, was an example of man profiting from selling what did not belong to him. This religious understanding of time shifted by the end of the Middle Ages, as

---

* Recent research, however, suggests that premodern people commonly woke up after midnight for as long as several hours before returning to sleep.

† The division of days into equal hours was not unknown, especially in the Islamic world. In Europe by the thirteenth century there began a gradual shift toward measuring hours by equal lengths. This became the norm with the introduction of mechanical clocks in the early fourteenth century.

‡ The daily round of religious services performed in Christian churches.

§ Gradually, in the course of the Middle Ages, "nones," which was originally the ninth hour of the day and the time of the main meal (around 3 p.m.) crept forward to mid-day, to become our "noon." "Sext" was then dispensed with.

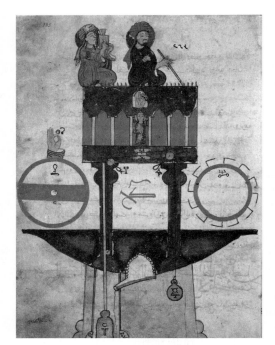 

Keeping Time: A Thirteenth-Century Islamic Water Clock and a Fourteenth-Century Sandglass
Waterclocks with elaborate mechanisms that struck equal hours were common in the Middle East and North Africa as early as the eighth century. Water clocks, however, were not well suited to northern climes, as the water froze in the winter. Sandglasses also measured equal hours but only for brief periods of time. They do not seem to have been common in Europe before the fourteenth century. The illustration on the right shows a Jewish teacher in his school in Germany using a sandglass to measure classtime. *Water clock: Dagli Orti/Library of Topkapi Museum, Istanbul/ The Art Archive; Sandglass: The British Library, London/The Bridgeman Art Library.*

merchants began to treat time as a valuable commodity.[1] Time and travel equaled money. Time could be bought and sold.

The mechanical clock was invented sometime between about 1270 and 1330, most likely by 1300, changing dramatically the measurement of time. Clocks were introduced rapidly throughout Europe in the fourteenth century.[2] They were expensive to build and maintain, and at first they were not much more efficient than older types of time-keeping devices. They had to be reset two or three times a week by reference to a sundial and usually required a specially appointed overseer.

However, the mechanical clock allowed people to divide the day into equal hours, independent of the movement of the sun, although some early mechanical clocks continued to be adjusted to measure variable hours. With the mechanical clock also came an increased effort to regulate the time of urban workers, and clocks themselves became objects of pride to territorial lords and town governments.

Yearly Calendars

The year was calculated according to the Julian calendar. In 45 B.C., Julius Caesar established the solar year of 365¼ days as the official basis of the Roman calendar, with January 1 serving as the beginning of the new year. Since the Julian year was not entirely accurate (the length of the year had been overestimated by 11 minutes), by A.D. 1000, the dates of the seasons were off by one week. By 1582, the year of the Gregorian reform of the calendar, they were off by ten days.

A further problem was the difficulty of dating any given year. The Roman tradition was to count year one from the date of the founding of the city of Rome, about 753 B.C. by modern reckoning. Romans also named their years after the terms of office of their leading officials, the consuls, and later, the emperors. By the year A.D. 1050, medieval people counted the date of the current year in a variety of ways—from the date of creation (calculated from 5508 to 3761 B.C.), the foundation of Rome, the birth of Christ (variously calculated), the accession of Diocletian or the Era of the Martyrs (A.D. 284), the conversion of Constantine (A.D. 312), the Spanish era (beginning January 1, 38 B.C.) or in terms of indictions,* the year of the reigning king or pope, or the latest flood, plague, or eclipse. Jews and Muslims, of course, had their own ways of reckoning years. Jewish tradition dates the creation of the world to 3761 B.C. at which point the Hebrew calendar takes its start; the Muslim lunar calendar starts in A.D. 622, the approximate date of Muhammad's migration (*hegira*) from Mecca to Medina.

The evolution of the Christian calendar was long and contentious. The most significant medieval calendar innovation was made by Dionysius Exiguus, a Scythian monk who settled in Rome sometime in the 490s and was the first to record years from the date of Christ's birth (*anno incarnationis Domini* = A.D.). His method was adopted slowly in the Christian world, first in the seventh and eighth centuries among the Anglo-Saxons, then in the eighth and ninth centuries in France and Germany, and in the tenth century in Rome. Although modern chronologists agree that Dionysius missed the actual date of Christ's birth by four to seven years (that is, Christ appears to have been born anywhere from 4 B.C. to 7 B.C.), his starting point eventually became the standard for much of the Western world.

Even when medieval people agreed to begin counting with the year of Christ's birth, there was no uniformity in determining the first day of the year. Some parts of the Christian world started the new year on January 1 or September 1 (old Roman dates) or even July 9 (the Armenian calendar); some started on December 25, the date chosen to celebrate the birth of Christ. Others began the new year on March 25, the date of the annunciation, when the angel Gabriel announced to

---

* During the late Roman Empire, the administrative practice of grouping years into fifteen-year cycles called indictions began; this practice carried over into the Byzantine empire.

Mary that she was carrying the Christ child. Still others preferred to begin the new year with Easter, which is, however, a moveable feast.*

Of course, most medieval individuals would not have known very clearly what year it was, but they did know the seasons of the year, which had shaped the pattern of their lives and the unceasing round of work associated with each quarter from time immemorial.

The Week

Another pattern of great antiquity was the seven-day week. Medieval calendars had weeks of seven days patterned on the ancient practice of assigning days to the seven observable planets (including the sun and the moon), no doubt reinforced by the biblical account of creation in seven days. However, it was not until Emperor Constantine (A.D. 312–337) that the seven-day week was made official. The Romans named their days after the sun (*sol*), moon (*luna*), Mars, Mercury, Jove, Venus, and Saturn. The Germanic words for *sol* and *luna* give us Sunday and Monday, while the Germanic gods and goddesses Tiw, Woden, Thor, and Friga give us other day names. Roman Saturn is still recognizable in Saturday. The day could begin at sundown, midnight, sunrise, or even noon depending on local custom.

The Month

The month is a natural astronomical division; the twelve months with which we are familiar were an early Roman development, based ultimately on ancient Mesopotamian practices, that reached its present form under Caesar Augustus. For official and ecclesiastical purposes, the Middle Ages followed a complicated Roman system for numbering the days of the months, based on three fixed days—Kalends, Ides, and Nones. Alongside this system (which began to disappear after the eleventh century), the custom developed of naming days according to the feasts of the ecclesiastical calendar. Depending on local observances, January 21, February 26, and November 11 might be known as the days of Saints Agnes, Dorothy, and Martin. Debts and rents were usually due on St. Michael's Day or Michaelmas (September 29). Markets were held on feast days ("feriae," hence our term "fairs"). The summer fair at Troyes was held on the Tuesday after the fortnight of St. John's Day. The Sorbonne opened, not on November 12, but on the day after St. Martin's feast. January 1 was not the New Year but rather, the day of the circumcision of the Lord. Besides Christmas and Easter, popular festivals were Epiphany (January 6), Pentecost (the seventh Sunday after Easter), Corpus Christi Day (Thursday after Trinity Sunday, which was the eighth Sunday after Easter), All Saints' Day (November 1), and St. Nicholas' Day (December 6).

---

* Fixing the date of Easter, the date of Christ's resurrection, proved to be particularly difficult and led to debate and much calculating among Christians. The biblical account reveals only that it took place during the Jewish Passover holiday. The Jewish calendar is based on lunar months, causing Passover to occur on different days each year according to the solar calendar. Therefore the date for Easter changes each year, and other religious dates are moveable in relation to the date of Easter.

The medieval Christian attachment to an ecclesiastical calendar, marked by saints' festivals and religious holidays, reached its height in the twelfth and thirteenth centuries. The subsequent reappearance of pagan festivals (for example, New Year's or May Day) and the use of consecutive numbered days of the month, which first appeared in the twelfth century and became prevalent by the fifteenth century, gradually diminished the importance of the ecclesiastical calendar. From the twelfth century on, medieval calendars were organized by days and months and illustrated by seasonal occupations and the appropriate astrological sign.

HISTORY

The medieval view of history was different from that of the modern view. The three major religions of Judaism, Christianity, and Islam are eschatological; that is, they are directed toward the end of mankind and the Last Judgment. They are also sometimes apocalyptic, that is, revelatory, unfolding divine secrets regarding the coming, perhaps catastrophic, end. Jewish expectations centered on the arrival of the Messiah who would combat the devil, the Antichrist, or Gog and Magog, redeem Jerusalem and build a new Temple. Early Christian writers had a somewhat different scenario. They described a sequence of events that included a supreme battle against the Antichrist, the return of Christ (expected shortly), the establishment of a glorious, messianic kingdom on earth, and the Last Judgment, to be followed by the end of the world. The duration of this messianic earthly kingdom was debatable but was usually thought to be 1,000 years.*

By the fourth century, however, Christianity had become the official religion of the Roman Empire, and the second coming of Christ (and the end of the world) were no longer so evident and perhaps also less desirable. Augustine, saint and Church father, writing in the early fifth century, devised the historical framework that most influenced the medieval world and sought to counteract expectations of a blessed age within history. In his *City of God,* Augustine wrote that the world was to last through six ages. The first age lasted from Adam to the Flood, the second from the Flood to Abraham, the third from Abraham to David, the fourth from David to the Babylonian Captivity of the Jews, the fifth from the Captivity to the birth of Christ, and the last, from the birth of Christ to the Last Day. In all, the world would last approximately 6,000 years. Augustine suggested that there would be an interval of about 1,000 years from the first coming of Christ to the loosening of the Devil for 3½ years, during which brief time the Antichrist would reign. For Augustine, the coming of the Antichrist passed immediately into the Final Judgment, the second resurrection (of the body), and an eternal kingdom in which there shall be no death. Some medieval writers, however, returning to the early Christian tradition, envisioned the time following the Antichrist as a real historical period during which a new age of peace and the presence of saints would prevail.

---

* The Qur'an tells a somewhat similar story: the disintegration of family, society, and economy, the coming of a beast and of Gog and Magog, with the coming of Jesus as a sign of the hour.

The Last Judgement, Sculpted in Stone   This tympanum, dated to about 1115 A.D., is sculpted over the south portal of the church at Moissac, a priory belonging to the Cluniac order of monks. Moissac was a way station for pilgrims going to Compostela in Spain (Chapter 11). The carving shows Christ as judge of the universe, sitting in triumph amid symbols of the Evangelists and with the twenty-four elders of the Apocalypse. As pilgrims entered the church it reminded them of the coming of the Last Judgement. *Ruggero Vanni/Corbis.*

Augustine was to have enormous influence throughout the Middle Ages. While he may have succeeded in convincing his fifth-century contemporaries that the second coming was not imminent, his chronology of the Last Judgment was to bedevil medieval society, particularly from the twelfth century on, when expectations of the end of the world began to build.* Expectations of the end became common at the time of the Crusades, and especially when the western Christians lost their strongholds in the Holy Land in the thirteenth century (see Chapter 12). The Antichrist was variously identified with German emperors or with Muslim rulers in the East, but as disillusionment with the papacy grew by the end of the thirteenth century, the idea that the pope might be the Antichrist began to seem reasonable, and predictions circulated that suggested that the papacy would pass away, giving way to a new order of spiritual men or at least to a reformed papacy in a new age.

Augustine influenced the medieval view of history in other ways. He turned away from the traditional Roman sense of history as cyclical and secular and pro-

---

* Although there is evidence that some individuals expected the world's end around the year A.D.1000 (see Chapter 10), the evidence for such expectations becomes even stronger by the twelfth and thirteenth centuries.

claimed history as a progressive revelation, marked by the frequent intervention of God (see Chapter 2). History became miraculous—a proof of God's working in the world—and miracles became history. Although Augustine argued that there were really only the miracles of creation and of Christ's resurrection, he also saw God's hand working through history in the astonishing victory of the Christian church over pagan Rome and in the miraculous healing experiences of individual Christians in his bishopric in North Africa. For Augustine, God performed wonderful acts that were not contradictory to nature but rather illustrated the hidden workings of God within a nature that was all, potentially, miraculous.

Not all medieval commentators agreed with Augustine. Some divided miracles into those that were natural and those that were against nature, but nearly all medieval thinkers saw miracles as signs of God's concern for Christians. Lives of saints, in particular, were punctuated by miracles during their lifetimes as well as after death. In this regard, it is important to keep in mind that, in the Middle Ages, the dead, whether saintly or not, were considered actively present in the afterworld, in their tombs, through parts of their bodies, and even through physical objects they had touched. As one historian has put it, the dead in the Middle Ages were simply in an older age bracket. In the cult of martyrs and saints that evolved in the early Middle Ages, we can find one of the fundamental characteristics of the medieval mind—the idea that heaven and earth are not separable, and that the dead can act as protectors of the living. It is for this reason that Dante, the great Italian poet writing at the beginning of the fourteenth century, could chronicle his journey through Hell, Purgatory, and Paradise in his *Divine Comedy* as though it were real. And it is for this reason that Dante's contemporaries could believe his account. As a result of this mental framework, much of the history of the Middle Ages is the history of saints* and miracles.

Christian history is salvational. The minds of medieval men and women focused to a great degree on their prospects in the afterlife. The severity of the contrasts between Heaven and Hell, and the irremediability of that demarcation at the Last Judgment led, gradually, to the idea of purgatory—an intermediate place where sins could be purged in expectation of ultimate salvation. This idea of purgatory, which emerged as a fully developed concept in the twelfth century, was incorporated officially into Christian teaching at the Council of Lyons in 1274. In preparation for the afterlife, men sought to follow God's will. But how is one to interpret God's will? If man's sinful and material nature clouds his mind, how can he apprehend truth? Independent of the mystical truths of divine revelation, there were two paths by which God was known to medieval minds. The first was through scripture, and thus scriptural interpretation was of foremost importance in the medieval intellectual tradition. A second "book" through which truth was manifest was the "Book of Nature." As one twelfth-century monastic author (Hugh of St. Victor) put it, "This entire perceptible world is as a book written by the finger of God . . .

---

* Some of the most characteristic figures in the Middle Ages are saints such as St. Benedict, St. James of Compostela (the patron saint of Spain), St. Denis (patron saint of the Capetian kings of France), St. Francis of Assisi and St. Catherine of Siena (both patron saints of Italy), St. Thomas Becket of England, and St. Patrick and St. Brigid of Ireland.

and individual creatures are as figures within it . . . to make manifest the invisible wisdom of God."[3] Thus, everything visible might have spiritual significance beyond its material reality; it might be "read" at different levels.* For example, another medieval writer could look at a nut and see Jesus: "The green and fleshly sheath is His flesh, His humanity. The wood of the shell is the wood of the Cross on which that flesh suffered. But the kernel of the nut from which men gain nourishment, is His hidden divinity."[4]

This central, spiritual concern led medieval thinkers to imagine that there was an eternal recurrence of spiritual events, even in the midst of a progressive view of history. Thus, the central events of sacred history are constantly reenacted. The exile of the Hebrews from Israel to Egypt is reenacted in the Babylonian exile, in Christ's journey to Egypt as a child, in individual exiles, and in the exile of all humankind from its heavenly homeland. Thus, King David prefigures Christ; Abraham's sacrifice of Isaac prefigures God's sacrifice of His Son; the Temple of Solomon prefigures Heavenly Jerusalem. Numbers also acquire spiritual significance. The number two symbolizes the two natures of Christ (human and divine); three symbolizes the Trinity; four the world (with the four corners of the inhabited world); nine is a multiple of the Trinity; while twelve, the number of the apostles, symbolizes a mix of the divine and human (3×4)—the nature of the universal Christian Church.

In the modern world, individuals are less inclined to seek spiritual significance in the world around them. We demand scientific and provable truths based on "reality." The medieval sense of reality was different from ours, however. In the early Middle Ages there was little distinction between the miraculous and the mundane, and the sense of context was very different. Nor was there much sense of history beyond what was offered in annals, saints' lives, and epic warrior stories. For example, one of the oldest surviving medieval epic poems is *Beowulf* (see Chapter 7). The author (or authors) clearly understood the poem's cultural context, but the modern scholar cannot quite place the story. Was the warrior-hero Beowulf real, legendary, or mythical? Is the historical memory of the poem earlier (7th century) or later (10th century)? Does it represent a Scandinavian, Anglo-Saxon, or English Viking milieu? We are not sure. This kind of historical opacity is typical of the early Middle Ages when documents were rare, the world was seen as either good or evil with very few ambiguities in between, and communal values tended to overshadow the needs of individuals. Thus the historian's view is sometimes a limited one.

Although this contextual confusion began to change in the eleventh and twelfth centuries, when literacy expanded, documents became more common, and a more specific sense of context emerged, it is still difficult to separate history from legend or myth. "Historia," in Latin, means "story," and this is what medieval people expected. Medieval chroniclers and historians wrote or recited stories in an entertaining style, highlighting the heroic, romantic, and legendary aspects without close

---

* In today's scholarly world, the study of levels of meaning and symbols is called the study of semiotics— the study of signs. Humberto Eco, who has written extensively on semiotics, has also written a novel, *The Name of the Rose,* that functions as a commentary on medieval symbolism, where the mystery surrounding several deaths turns on the function of apocalyptic signs.

attention to documentary proof. The ordinary educated individual in thirteenth-century Britain, for example, would have believed that Brutus, the great-grandson of Aeneas, legendary founder of Rome, first colonized Britain. Brutus, who was supposed to have killed his father and mother, left Italy and followed a prophetic dream "that beyond the setting of the sun, past the realms of Gaul, there lies an island in the sea, once occupied by giants but now empty. . . . A race of kings will be born there from your stock and the round circle of the whole earth will be subject to them."[5] Thus British imperialism was born, based on a myth! Eventually, in the medieval version of British history, King Arthur, the son of Uther Pendragon, conquered the British Isles and all of western Europe (except Rome, where he was forced to turn back home to deal with treachery). Other legendary figures, who may never have existed, or whose exploits were romanticized or distorted, include Tristan and Isolde, Yvain, Percival, Richard the Lion-Hearted, Pope Joan, Lancelot, Siegfried and Brunhilda, Robin Hood, and Richard III, as well as a great many saints. Occasionally, voices rose in disbelief regarding some of these figures and their exploits, but in general these legends were the stuff of history. Every emerging national group in medieval Europe traced its foundation to a legendary history, whether it was Brutus in England, Aeneas (and the Trojans) in Italy, a remnant of Alexander the Great's army in Germany, or King Friga, descendant of Priam of Troy, who supposedly led the Franks to Europe. It is therefore fair to conclude that medieval people accepted a more generous concept of reality than most moderns do.

SPACE

Medieval people were not only open to believing the legendary, they were also more open to believing in extrarational phenomena. As Carolly Erickson puts it, in her book *Medieval Vision,* "they saw more than we do." In particular, they placed a great deal of importance on vision and the visionary. The act of seeing was not simply a physical act; it had a spiritual dimension. And light was viewed, not simply as corporeal, but as the most sublime reality, that is, the reality most representative of the divine on earth.

This emphasis on light is seen in the interest medieval scientists and craftsmen had in optics (see Chapter 17): They came close to pronouncing the quantum theory of light, produced a sophisticated mathematical system of measuring the color spectrum, detailed the working of the eye, invented eye-glasses and the pin-hole camera, and developed a theory of perspective that influenced Renaissance artists. Light was equated with reason. It was commonplace among medieval writers to argue that man was more rational than animals because God had placed man's eyes above his other sense organs. (Dogs, for example, have ears higher than their eyes.) According to Bartholomew, an Englishman writing in the thirteenth century, the eyes were the token of the soul, more important than all other senses.[6] Light symbolized good and darkness evil; Hell was dark and Heaven full of light. And blindness was the most horrible of disabilities, signifying not only a loss of vision but also of reason and, possibly, of God's grace.

Thus, Gothic cathedrals were constructed with large, stained glass windows so as to let in as much light as possible. The mystical experience was described in terms of light, an experience of illumination. The sensitivity to the visionary was profound. It is a constant device in literature, most eloquently expressed in Dante's *Divine Comedy,* where light metaphysics pervade the work. Much of medieval literature uses the imagery of a dream vision. *Piers Plowman,* a fourteenth-century critique of English society, is presented as a dream, as is Dante's great work. Common titles of medieval works are: *The Vision of God, The Mirror of Priests, The Mirror of Love, The Fire of Love, The Eye of the Clergy,* and so forth. Nicholas of Cusa, a late medieval philosopher, mystic, and cardinal of the Church, described the essence of God as "absolute sight, whence all sight springeth. . . . the true Unlimited Sight, beyond all comparison more perfect. . . . seen by every person that seeth, in all that may be seen, and in every act of seeing."[7] As Carolly Erickson notes, "The profound truths of the Middle Ages were to be grasped through the education of the eyes."[8]

Nicholas of Cusa, in addition to his mystical writings, wrote a work entitled *On Learned Ignorance* in which he envisioned a physical universe that was finite but unbounded, with no absolute center. Therefore, he hypothesized, the earth must move, "even though we do not perceive this to be the case. For we apprehend motion only through a certain comparison with something fixed." Moreover, the earth, viewed from the sun, would look like a star; and God, Nicholas suggested, had most likely placed inhabitants on other stars as well as this one.[9]

The views of Nicholas of Cusa anticipated Copernicus as well as modern physics and astronomy, but they were not the views held by most medieval thinkers. Their ideas came from the Greeks, who believed that the earth was an immobile globe in the center of a spherical universe. A circumference of fixed stars bound this universe. Below the stars, seven other celestial bodies (the sun, moon, and five planets) traveled. The sphere of the fixed stars rotated from east to west every twenty-four hours, carrying with it the seven celestial bodies, which moved in the opposite direction. All of this circled around the earth, which, at the center, was the heaviest and the most imperfect part of the universe. God, the prime mover, caused the motion of the universe. And most medieval thinkers, again influenced by the ancient Greeks, believed that there were intelligences that moved the spheres in accordance with God's desire. Man, although in the center, was furthest from God—a lowly creature to whom, nonetheless, God had deigned to send his Son.

This vision of the universe includes a spherical earth. Although there were occasional cosmographers in the early Middle Ages as well as, most likely, some ordinary individuals who believed that the world was flat,[10] most medieval people thought of the earth as a globe. "Most educated people throughout [medieval] Europe knew the earth's spherical shape and its approximate circumference."[11] The ancient writings of Ptolemy, Plato (the *Timaeus*), and Aristotle, all introduced by the twelfth century, described the earth as a sphere. Portraits and sculptures of medieval emperors, symbolizing universal rule, showed them holding the ball of the earth, while the motto of Rome, proclaimed by twelfth and thirteenth-century guidebooks and written on coins, was "Rome, head of the world, holds the reins of the round globe (orb)." Early medieval mapmakers referred to the earth as a sphere, a globe, or an orb. The Vikings, who explored the coast of Newfoundland and perhaps even further, did not think they were going to fall off the edge of the world. Neither did a Muslim sailor named Khashkhāsh who embarked on an expedition into the Atlantic in the ninth century, returning with riches, nor some Genoese merchants who, in 1291, sought the east by going west. (They, however, did not return). Dante, when he (fictionally) reached the first circle of Paradise, looked back to a spherical earth; Thomas Aquinas, in his *Summa Theologiae,* argued that the earth was spherical, and Pierre d'Ailly, a French intellectual of the fourteenth century, stated that it was possible to circle the globe. When Christopher Columbus was negotiating with Isabella and Ferdinand in Spain in 1492, he encountered difficulties getting support for his westward voyage, not because people thought the world was flat, but rather because, knowing it was round, they thought his calculations of the distance were too optimistic. (They were right, and he was wrong.)

Medieval people worried, however, about the inhabitants of the other side of the world and those who lived below the equator. Cosmas Indicopleutes, a sixth-century Egyptian traveler and merchant turned monk, wrote on topography and berated the pagans for believing in what were called the Antipodes—a continent in the southern hemisphere. He believed that the tropics were too hot to be passable, and that humans did not exist there. Nor could they exist on the other side of the earth (which, in Cosmas's ideosyncratic opinion *was* flat) because they would have to walk with their heads downward. Others argued that there was too large an expanse of water to cross, and to have humans on the other side of the earth possibly not descended from Adam and Eve was theologically impossible.

Knowledge about the eastern and western limits of the known, inhabitable world was more speculative than reality-based. Medieval maps showed giants, headless creatures, dogheaded people, and devilish creatures in the more exotic regions of Asia, Africa, and the far north. The Atlantic was full of mythical islands—St. Brendan's Isle, the Fortunate Isle, Brasil, Antilla—all of which suggested to medieval explorers that real lands were to be found by sailing west. In the east, besides spices and gold, they expected to find the earthly paradise, where Christian writers had placed it in the seventh century. For many medieval writers, the great rivers of the earth flowed from paradise. Generally, medieval mapmakers oriented their maps toward this terrestrial paradise in the east rather than toward the north, although they understood that a spiritual rather than a physical journey was required to arrive there. This mixing of spiritual and physical geography is typical of the Middle Ages, where maps showed Jerusalem, the city of Christ's resurrection, as the center of the world, and cathedrals were built on an east-west axis so that the high altar would point toward Jerusalem.

THE BODY

This intermingling between the spiritual and the physical is also evident in the way medieval people perceived the body and the soul. The soul (*anima*) was thought to be lodged in the heart, and was sometimes portrayed as a grain. Spirit, an ethereal

Evesham Mappa Mundi c. 1390   This large oval world map was made in England. It is oriented to the Asian East, with Paradise above India at the top and Jerusalem in the center. England, which is enlarged and the most detailed part of the map, is the large island along the bottom. The Fortunate Isles are to its right (off the coast of Africa), and Ireland is along the western edge, below England. *Bibliotheque Nazionale, Florence/Scala/Art Resource, NY.*

breath from God that breathed life into man, was the mediating force between the body and the soul. Spirit entered through the mouth and nostrils and intermingled in the heart with the flow of blood. There it fed the soul and then circulated throughout the body, through the lungs, the left ventricle, and the arteries.

Blood, it was thought, circulated mostly separately from spirit—through the right ventricle and the veins and was primarily responsible for digestion. It was also subject to corruption, particularly if the various humors in the body were not balanced.* Overweight people, it was believed, had blood that corrupted more quickly. Drinking too much wine could have a similar effect. Frequent bloodletting was a remedy for such corruption, although doctors warned against bleeding individuals who were too weak, too ill, too young, or too old. It was thought that women, through their menstrual cycles, had a natural means of sloughing off corrupt blood that made them healthier and less in need of bloodletting.

Medieval medicine tailored treatment to the individual, since disease was considered to stem from internal corruption or an imbalance of humors (see Chapter 17). Today some treatments seem irrational, such as when animal products like cat's dung, wolves' dung, mouse droppings, serpents' skin, lizards, or urine mixed with food were prescribed.[12] Magic and astrology were also practiced. On the other hand, medieval physicians made perceptive diagnoses of rabies, epilepsy, hernias, and arthritis, along with some very practical prescriptions. They treated patients with herbs, diet, and surgery. And medieval attitudes toward mental illness, which included recommendations for music, rest, understanding, "busy thoughts," and sunshine, were sufficiently advanced that they have been praised in modern medical journals.

SUMMARY

Critical attitudes and methodologies were not entirely absent from medieval perceptions of the universe, the human body, time, or history. However, the medieval attitude's mixture of the critical and credulous, the novel and the traditional, the spiritual and the physical sometimes makes comprehension difficult for the modern student. It is helpful to keep this in mind as we begin our journey into the foreign territory that we call "The Medieval World."

NOTES

1. For evidence of this cultural shift in perceptions of time, see Yves Renouard, *Les Hommes d'affaires italiens du Moyen Age,* new ed. (Paris, 1968); and Jacques Le Goff, "Merchant's Time and

---

* Medieval doctors and surgeons accepted a theory of humors (or bodily fluids) that had evolved in ancient times. Health (both physical and psychological) was a matter of balancing four humors: blood (which was hot and moist), phlegm (cold and moist), black bile (hot and dry), and cholera or yellow bile (cold and dry). Each individual acquired at birth a particular mixture of these humors; this explained human temperaments. For example, the sanguine person had an excess of blood, the melancholic an abundance of black bile.

Church's Time in the Middle Ages," *Time, Work, and Culture in the Middle Ages* (Chicago: University of Chicago Press, 1980) 29–42. Gerhard Dohrn-van Rossum, *History of the Hour: Clocks and Modern Temporal Orders,* trans. T. Dunlap (Chicago: University of Chicago, 1996) argues that this shift is not so obvious and that ancient sources suggest a more long-standing perception of time as a commodity.

2. Carlo Cipolla, *Clocks and Culture 1300–1700* (New York: W.W. Norton, 1978), 39. For the diffusion of public clocks, see Gerhard Dohrn-van Rossum, *The History of the Hour,* trans. T. Dunlap (Chicago: University of Chicago Press, 1996) 157–172 where he documents nearly 500 mentions of first references to public clocks in towns from 1300 to 1450.

3. Hugh of St. Victor, *Eruditionis didascaliae* VII, cap. 4; *Patrologia Latina,* vol. 176, col. 814.

4. Adam of St. Victor, "Dominicaé intra octavas nativitatis domini" in *Patrologia Latina,* vol. 196, col. 1433B-1434A. quoted in Émile Mâle, *The Gothic Image: Religious Art in France of the Thirteenth Century,* trans. Dora Nussey (New York: Harper & Row, 1958) 30.

5. Geoffrey of Monmouth, *The History of the Kings of Britain,* trans. Lewis Thorpe (New York: Penguin, 1966) 65.

6. *On the Properties of Things: John Trevisa's Translation of Bartholomaeus Anglicus De proprietatibus rerum: a critical text,* gen. ed. M.C. Seymour, vol. 1 (Oxford: Clarendon Press, 1975) 111–112, 178.

7. Nicholas of Cusa, *The Vision of God,* trans. E.G. Salter (New York: Ungar, 1960) 8, 54.

8. Carolly Erickson, *The Medieval Vision: Essays in History and Perception* (London: Oxford University Press, 1976) 46

9. Nicholas of Cusa, *On Learned Ignorance,* trans. Jasper Hopkins, II, 12 (Minneapolis: Arthur J. Banning, 1981) 116–121.

10. As J.B. Russell points out, there are still people today who believe that the world is flat, and they are not all members of the International Flat Earth Society. Russell, *Inventing the Flat Earth: Columbus and Modern Historians* (Westwoood, Conn: Praeger, 1991) 4.

11. Russell, *Inventing the Flat Earth,* 2

12. C. H. Talbot, *Medicine in Medieval England* (London: Oldbourne, 1967) 42.

PART I

~

The Transformation of
the Roman World,
A.D. 100–751

CHAPTER 1

~

The Roman Foundations of Medieval Europe, 100–500

Very skillful historians, tucked away in libraries and universities for the last two hundred years, have examined the Roman Empire from every possible viewpoint. They have chopped it up and extracted its economic, political, social, cultural, military, religious, architectural, artistic, geographical, and even climatic characteristics in various and often brilliant attempts to explain it. But they have never quite managed to do so completely. It is remarkable that a city, not obviously endowed by nature more than many other ancient cities, managed in a little over two hundred years to conquer almost all the civilized Mediterranean world. Not only did Rome's political rule outdo in time and space anything the Mediterranean world had seen before or has seen since, but also Rome's religious, legal, and literary culture influenced, if not dominated, medieval Europe long after the Roman Empire vanished. Thus it is little wonder that we cannot point with certainty to the reasons for Rome's remarkable accomplishment. Ancient Rome remains a wonder, perhaps the greatest wonder, of western history.

Roman civilization lasted about a thousand years, from roughly 500 B.C. to A.D. 500. Only its last two or three centuries, the ones that were the immediate antecedent of the Middle Ages, are of direct concern to us here. We shall, by way of background, hurry through Rome's first seven centuries in a few paragraphs providing largely a summarizing political account and then slow down to examine more fully the last years of this civilization whose influence the Middle Ages could not avoid and whose legacy still haunts even us. In many ways it is difficult to draw a clear line between the late-Roman and the early-medieval eras. Although direct Roman political rule ended in western Europe shortly before A.D. 500, much of the governmental structure that had existed in the late empire continued into the Middle Ages, albeit now without a Roman emperor in the West. In addition to the late empire's politics, its art, language, urban and rural living conditions, status of women, public education, philosophical thought, law, and religion also formed important bases for life in Europe's early Middle Ages.

EARLY ROME: FROM REPUBLIC TO EMPIRE

Tradition has it that in 509 B.C., a group of Roman nobles overthrew Tarquin the Proud, the last of the Etruscan kings who had ruled over their city, and established a republic. This sounds like a substantial alteration, but in fact the structure of their body politic changed very little.

The Roman Republic (509–31 B.C.)

At the top of the Roman government was an elected executive. Under the monarchy this obviously had been a king, usually the designated heir of the former king and elected for life by the people. In the Roman Republic, the head of state was called a consul and was chosen for a term of one year. The Romans elected two consuls to govern simultaneously; they shared the power by ruling on alternate days or months and by dividing certain functions between them. The executive, be it a king or consul, had two primary responsibilities: religious and military. The middle layer in this governmental structure was the Senate. Throughout Roman history, the senators were for the most part the highly born, wealthy, great landholders. During the Republic, the Senate was the real seat of power. The theoretical source of all authority, however, lay in the lowest of the three levels of government, the assembly. All Roman citizens were members of the assembly, and it is often useful to view it as the army called together for civilian political purposes, at least in the early days of the Republic when citizen-soldiers rather than professionals still comprised the military. The assembly passed the laws, which usually meant confirming the recommendations of the senators, and elected the governmental officials, including the consuls.

When the Roman aristocrats expelled King Tarquin and began to set up their republic, Rome was a prosperous but rather unimportant city-state with little international weight. Some 150 years later, however, the Romans controlled all of central Italy. By 264 B.C., they held most of the Italian peninsula. By 202 B.C., they had added the western Mediterranean and by 45 B.C. their legions, governors, senators, and magistrates ruled the whole Mediterranean and much of what we call the Middle East, that is, they ruled most of the western civilized world.

As Rome's authority grew, the nature of its political apparatus changed. Political power began to shift to the leaders and factions that best knew how to cater to the immediate needs of the assemblies and the armies. The leaders were the great war heroes and dictators (Marius, Sulla, Pompey, and Caesar) who, often with the cheerful approval of the lower classes whom they skillfully manipulated, assumed more and more of the reins of government. Their grab for power, however, plunged the Roman world into almost constant civil war. By the first century B.C., the Roman Republic was dying.

The Early Empire (31 B.C.–A.D. 192)

With the rule of Octavian (31 B.C.–A.D.14), whom the Romans soon called Caesar Augustus, many of the changes that had been taking place during the late Republic became formalized. Augustus took credit for ending the civil wars and bringing peace at long last. The system that he and his backers established is usually called "the principate" from the Latin word, *princeps*, or "first citizen," the title that he preferred, although today he is most often called emperor. The principate, at least in its earlier years, is often described as a joint rule between the *princeps* and the Senate, since that ancient body retained many of the important functions of government albeit now under a permanent single ruler.

The principate lasted with some changes for about 200 years, that is, from the reign of Augustus until the death of the emperor Commodus in A.D.192. These two centuries form the Golden Age of Rome, the *Pax Romana*. The most Romanized parts of the world, the great cities and their lands that bordered the Mediterranean, enjoyed a peace and security that lasted so long that it almost came to be regarded as the normal state of affairs. Obviously wars of conquest and protection went on along the frontiers of the empire, but these were wars as wars should be: safely far away, providing magnificent sources of booty and slaves along with enduring economic and political opportunities for Romans. The Mediterranean had never been richer. Trade, agriculture, communications, manufacturing, and building all burst forth and poured their riches into Rome. The staid brick city-state on the Tiber had become the glistening marble capital of the world.

As long as the Roman Empire continued to enjoy the fruits of territorial expansion, Augustus' system worked and worked well. But the years of rapid expansion were over by the late first century B.C., and through the ensuing generations the advantages the expansion had brought to the Italians began to dwindle. The Roman Empire ceased to expand in the early second century A.D. and thereafter began to contract slightly.

The empire showered wonderful political and military positions along with breathtaking riches upon the Italians who controlled Rome's political apparatus. Their position gave them important advantages over the rich who lived in other parts of the empire. But when the expansion stopped, so too eventually did its attendant boon for the Italians. Slowly but surely non-Italians began to acquire economic and military stature equal to or exceeding that of the powerful Italian families. Another readjustment in the political system reflecting these new circumstances became necessary, a readjustment that would make the Roman government more cosmopolitan.

The Crisis of the Third Century

By the time of Commodus' rule certain political changes had occurred that could cause serious trouble for Rome if there were not strong leadership at the top. For one thing, that vital class of senators that had established and run the Republic had been transformed from a group with real decision-making power into a group of officials, competent and loyal perhaps, but with less and less experience and ability in real political leadership in their own right. Second, the need for border defense was becoming ever greater. The threat at the borders demanded not only good leadership at the top but also caused the military to gain more and more political influence. Third, the structure of the government was becoming more centralized, making local authorities less capable of intelligent local rule and more dependent on the central government. As a result, if the central government was weak, the provinces would suffer in ways they had not in earlier times. All of these problems were long-term ones that would increase right to the end of the Roman Empire.

During the reigns of the Severan emperors (A.D.193–235), we can see certain events that indicate that the nature of imperial government was changing significantly. One change was the militarization of the Roman state. Although from the days of the late Republic the army had played an increasingly important role in Roman politics, it was now making its way into the workings of the Roman state as well. For example, soldiers increasingly took over jobs such as those of tax collectors and judges that formerly had been held by civilians.

The Roman Empire was also becoming controlled less by Italians. By the time of the Severans, the emperors were no longer Italians and many high officials—generals, imperial advisors, and the like—also did not trace their roots to Italy. The Roman senatorial families had lost control both of the Roman Senate and even the high posts in their own city as the urban government of Rome fell under an imperial official called the Prefect of the City, who was often not a local. The normal military recruit also was increasingly drawn from the less Romanized provinces, giving the Roman army a much less Roman makeup. And in A.D. 212, with a measure now called the Antonine Constitution, the emperor Caracalla (A.D. 212–217) extended full Roman citizenship to all males in the whole Empire, excluding only the very poorest freemen.

In A.D. 235 the army murdered the last of the Severans, Severus Alexander (A.D. 222–235), along with his mother, Julia Mamaea, who had been the real ruler during his reign. The resulting succession crisis was not short lived as the others had been. This time the chaos lasted some fifty years as the army put up and then murdered twenty-five different emperors; only one died a natural death. The mid-third century was a low point for the once smug and secure Mediterranean. A seemingly endless procession of invasions, foreign wars, civil wars, loss of territory, piracy, and brigandage, topped by a plague from the east, caused great suffering. With the civil unrest came economic troubles, as they almost always do. Agricultural production and manufacturing declined. The imperial treasury was always empty, prompting the government to raise the already suffocating taxes. Gold and silver went out of circulation, a good indication that trading activity, especially long-distance trading activity, had plummeted. And just to dampen an already cheerless situation, Rome's only truly civilized and organized foreign enemy, the ancient Persian Empire to the east, enjoyed a splendid revival. In A.D. 260 the Persians actually captured the Roman emperor, Valerian (A.D. 253–260). Imagine the shock to the Romans; no Roman emperor had ever been captured by mere foreigners.

The chaos of the third century brought the principate to an end in the same way that the civil wars of the first century B.C. had ended the Republic. Gone now were even the remnants of Augustus' joint rule with the Senate; power was concentrated in the hands of an autocratic emperor. The chaos and economic hardship brought about significant social changes. Society was becoming more stratified according to wealth. Roman society had obviously always been stratified according to wealth, but now the divisions became increasingly rigid and legally defined. Severus formally established legal differences between the classes. The upper stratum, the senators, wealthy businessmen, provincial rich, military officials, and the like were termed *honestiores* and granted a different status before the law from the lower stratum, whose members were called the *humiliores*. This was not all to the advantage of the rich. Certain of the *honestiores* were forced to take on provincial and municipal positions without pay and to bear some of the expenses associated with those positions. The population as a whole was becoming tied to a certain place, fixed to a certain job, and anchored in a certain social level. Social mobility became even rarer than before. This rigidity was not just the usual situation where free peasants were forced to sell their lands during hard times and become immobile tenants of large landholders, but artisans, manufacturers, certain officials, and even merchants were also anchored in one place. Of course, the bureaucracy needed to manage all this grew and became increasingly expensive. And, as we have said, it was increasingly dominated by the army.

THE REFORMS OF DIOCLETIAN AND CONSTANTINE

In A.D. 284 an emperor emerged who with a sweeping reorganization was to make a desperate attempt to put things right. This was Diocletian (A.D. 284–305), and he and his successor, Constantine (A.D. 306– 337), were indeed successful enough in the measures they took to be given credit for providing solutions that lasted for over 100 years.

Diocletian established the famous Tetrarchy, or four-person rulership. He divided the Empire into four huge parts, assigning a different emperor to each. He created two senior emperors with the title of augustus and two junior emperors, called caesars, each responsible to an augustus. Collegiality, or sharing rule between or among colleagues, was an ancient principle of Roman government, dating from the very beginning of the Republic. Many emperors before Diocletian had designated colleagues with the words "augustus" and "caesar" used as official titles for them. But Diocletian's actions were different in that he attempted to regularize joint rulership with his sweeping geographical division of the Empire.

Diocletian carved up the whole Roman Empire into new geographic units (see Map 1.1). The old system had large provinces and these were now redivided into many smaller ones. Because they were much smaller, they were both easier to administer internally and less likely to be large enough to be used as a power base for rebellion against the central government. Eventually the provinces were grouped under twelve dioceses*, and these in turn under four main parts, later to

---

* The term "diocese" was also later used to describe the geographical jurisdiction of a Christian bishop. The Church's dioceses, however, were much smaller than the imperial ones described here.

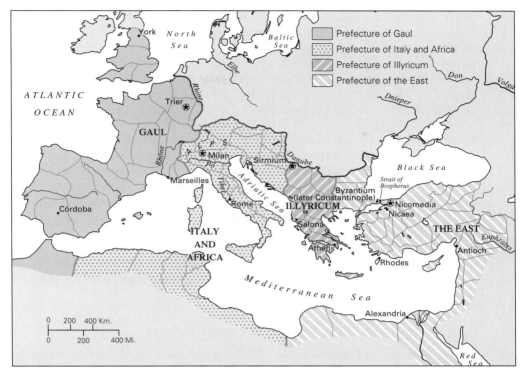

Map 1.1   The Roman Empire under Diocletian c. 300 The map shows the four great prefectures of Diocletian's tetrarchy. Note that the principle residences of the emperors (designated by a star within a circle) are much closer to the borders than is Rome.

be known as prefectures, each with its own emperor, its own principal residence, its own army, and its own borders.

The result of all this change was truly remarkable; by A.D. 298 the Mediterranean was again bordered by lands at peace, and with Diocletian as the senior augustus, the empire was once again united. This is not to say that the Roman Empire was not faced by huge and perhaps unsolvable problems. But now at least it had reorganized itself to confront them.

The Problem of Local Government

The government of communities away from the center became an increasingly painful thorn in Rome's skin. The empire's administrative apparatus was based in the cities; local urban governments formed the lowest level of the imperial regime. A city was usually governed by a *curia,* or city council, whose officials, the *decuriones* or *curiales,* in addition to local responsibilities, represented the imperial government, collected the imperial taxes, and provided their assigned allotment of recruits for the imperial army. City officials served without pay and often were forced to make up financial shortfalls from their own funds. For this and for other reasons, they often had to be forced to serve.

The health of the empire suffered from this system of local government in two important ways. First, it obviously lay itself open to corruption. The onerous requirements and forced service brought along all sorts of corrupt means of avoiding them. The local government often worked for the advantage of local factions and families and this also brought corruption.

Second, the combination of local and imperial government meant that too much local control was exercised far up the imperial hierarchy. The involvement of a huge and increasingly top-heavy central bureaucracy in the making of local decisions is obviously extremely inefficient, but it has another less obvious but more insidious effect: It destroys local initiative. Communities would take on only those projects that had central approval, or more frequently, those supported by imperial funds, rather than initiating projects actually dictated by local needs. The eyes of local leaders, too, tended more than was healthy to turn toward careers up the bureaucratic chain, and decisions were made with that goal rather than local considerations in mind. As a result, local mechanisms were no longer healthy enough or responsive enough to cope with the increased threat of foreign invasion and with the other problems of the late empire.

The Problem of Frontier Defense

As long as there had been civilization around the Mediterranean, and possibly even before, there had been movements of peoples from the north and from the east toward its shores. Two Roman frontiers, the long Rhine-Danube border in the north and the border against the Parthians and then the Sassanian Persians in the east, stood as barriers to these movements. These two borders demanded special effort by the Romans to defend, especially after the chaotic years of the third century. Although in the third and fifth centuries many foreign peoples crossed the empire's borders, in the fourth century they did so far less frequently. The borders were secure in large part because of the measures that Diocletian and Constantine instituted to improve the defenses.

With the new tetrarchy, the principal residences of the four emperors were are all in good strategic positions, each much closer to some troublesome border than Rome had been. Their geographical positions meant that the central commands could react to an invasion more quickly and more effectively. Diocletian improved the mobile striking forces stationed at some distance back from the border. These could be used to reinforce the troops stationed along the border when they were under attack. He also instituted huge building projects of permanent defense works along the borders and doubled the number of units defending them. And even the morale and the effectiveness of the military as a whole improved, largely because of the new effective central leadership.

The Problem of the Economy

Although Diocletian and Constantine took some drastic governmental steps to help the empire's economy, their efforts only had short-term and limited success.

They instituted a major reform of the coinage, imposed price controls with severe penalties for their violation, and started huge building programs supported by governmental funds. These were obviously forceful steps, but not very effective ones economically. More effective for the economy were the benefits of the political and military stability that their reigns engendered. But the fundamental economic maladies of a chronic shortage of labor, declining agricultural production, and dwindling trade continued to eat away at even the once plumper portions of the Empire's economy, especially in the West.

The Problem of the Government's Size

As the responsibilities of the imperial government grew, so too did its size. The increased expanse of the imperial government required greatly increased revenues, and in response Diocletian instituted a huge and fundamental regularization of the tax system. His system was based on a thorough census of the Empire. He instituted a complicated universal land tax called the *annona,* based on the measure of land's productive value and on the *caput,* a unit of labor, a "man-day." The *annona* existed alongside certain traditional indirect taxes. The universal obligation to pay these taxes was a striking innovation; previously the nobility and others of privilege had been exempt. They were no longer. The *annona* could be paid in kind, that is, paid in goods not necessarily in money. Diocletian's reform of the taxes did, of course, increase revenues but it also greatly exacerbated the rigidity in the social structure. Now even more than before, landholders required their tenants to stay where they were to produce the tax, and the position of merchants and artisans also continued to become less flexible.

The Problem of Loyalty

The chaos of the third century is violent testimony to the fact that many parts of the political structure were not loyal enough to the central government for the well-being of the empire. Diocletian's solution to this problem was to become a god, or more technically, the earthly vehicle through which Jupiter acted. He was called *Jovius,* "Jupiter-like," and his personage became holy, shrouded from mere mortals by the mystery of a complicated court ceremonial. In fact, his public appearances became extremely rare and were occasions for public celebration. His chamber became sacred and his edicts expressions of divine will. *Dominus,* "Lord," became the normal form for addressing him. Rule by god or god's representative is called theocracy, or sometimes Caesaropapism. A certain amount of theocracy had always been present in Roman rule, increasing as Rome's rule became more imperial. But divine authority and imperial pomp to the degree Diocletian used them were not Roman; they were much more characteristic of the ancient civilizations of the Middle East.

Did it work? Was the theocracy believed? Yes. The eastern parts of the Roman Empire had for centuries exhibited a tendency toward worship of the emperor. Often this was worship of his *genius,* or guiding spirit, rather than the man himself, but nonetheless statues to rulers as early as the Divine Augustus and even the Divine Julius abounded. Even the privileged, who perhaps knew Diocletian personally or for other sound reasons doubted that this very human, low-born, military figure from Dalmatia had somehow gained a sacred majesty, went along with it. Perhaps they did so with a wry smile or perhaps not, for a system that preserved peace and order also preserved their prosperous places high in its structure.

The greatest of the persecutions the Christians suffered came in A.D. 303 under Diocletian. For this reason Diocletian became the personification of the wicked emperor for the Christian Middle Ages. The reason that this persecution was particularly grave lies in the nature of Diocletian's rule. If the state bases a good deal of its call for loyalty on religion, then disagreement in religion becomes very close to disloyalty to the state. Again this idea is not new with Diocletian's era, but since imperial rule had now become far more theocratic, religious dissent became far more treasonable.

The Problem of Succession

The tetrarchy's system for succession was theoretically simple. When an augustus died or retired, his subordinate caesar was to move up to the senior level and a new caesar would be appointed. In A.D. 303 Diocletian took ill and in A.D. 305 he took the unheard of step of "retiring," forcing the other augustus, Maximian, to step down as well. Constantius and Galerius were promoted to augusti and two new caesars were appointed. But this beautiful system soon broke down. When Constantius died in A.D. 306, the old nemesis, armed struggle for succession, returned, and by A.D. 310 there were five proclaimed augusti and no caesars. What went awry? Once again, there was a crisis in loyalty and one that illustrates certain principles useful to keep in mind when we come to examine succession in the Middle Ages.

In A.D. 305, when Diocletian and Maximian retired and Constantius and Galerius moved up, Constantius' son, Constantine, and Maximian's son, Maxentius, were both passed over in the appointment of the new caesars, ignoring hereditary succession. Both sons would eventually rebel. Hereditary succession seems like nonsense in modern democratic systems that hope to choose by election the most capable person for a vacant position. But having a less capable leader is far less of an evil than is the horror of civil war, and if the passed-over heir of a former leader is in a position to make an armed bid to claim what is "rightfully" his, hereditary succession quickly becomes far from nonsense. Both Constantine and Maxentius were in such a position and, as events proved, both let loose the dogs of war.

On the other hand, nonhereditary succession had worked very well and without crisis for most of the Republic and had also provided the empire its avowed most capable leaders, the five Good Emperors. But in those cases, the abstract idea of loyalty to the state as state or the institution of emperorship as institution had been long established and was strong enough to command allegiance. More readily understandable to less sophisticated minds than abstract notions of loyalty to state or institution is the personal loyalty commanded by a particular leader. The bonds of personal loyalty were basic to Roman society where almost every adult male was either a client, i.e. subordinate, to some patron who looked out for his interests or was himself a patron who controlled and protected a number of clients. In Rome's political life, the conflict between concrete loyalty to a person and abstract loyalty to an institution had been in play at least since the days of the late Republic. Increasingly, personal loyalty won out as the expedient of having a good leader, especially in times of crisis, seemed far more valuable than the long-term good of the institution. In the early fourth century, to their separate supporters, Constantine, Maxentius, and others each seemed best able to ensure advantage, and in this way immediate politics, fierce personal loyalty, and, most probably, greed were obviously far more important than preserving some newly formed, abstract means of succession. We also note that the supporters of these contenders were mostly from the less Romanized parts of the empire. Those with deeper Roman traditions, senators, Italians, or imperial bureaucrats, tended not to support them.

Diocletian spent an eleven-year retirement at Salona, with only one brief return to politics. What he witnessed from his seclusion could not have pleased him: succession crises, the return of civil war and increasing disorder, and even the persecution of his own family. The great reforming emperor died in A.D. 316.

Constantine (A.D. 306–337)

Through these turbulent years of succession crises, Constantine was moving up. In A.D. 306 he was declared augustus by his father's troops in far-off York, England, although legally at this point he only reached the rank of caesar. In A.D. 308 he officially became an augustus; in A.D. 312 with his defeat of Maxentius at the famous battle of the Milvian Bridge on the edge of Rome, he became the senior augustus; and at last in A.D. 324 sole emperor. He was a moody man, some say of limited intelligence, and despite the fact that more is known about him than about the other rulers of the Late Roman Empire, in many ways he remains an enigma to historians. Since he was the first Roman emperor to embrace Christianity, he became a great hero to Christian authors and they wrote much about him, lauding his great Christian works and his great Christian virtues. For this reason, he became the favorite of all the Roman emperors bar none in the Middle Ages.

Constantine had been trained at the court of Diocletian where he saw and absorbed firsthand the lessons of theocratic and autocratic rule. His own theocracy, however, would come to have a significant difference from Diocletian's: His would be Christian. In many ways Constantine combined the Roman state with the Christian Church, although there is much disagreement among historians about why he did so. Some believe that he sincerely pursued Christian purposes in his statesmanship while others question whether he was exclusively, or even traditionally, Christian.

Between A.D. 324 and A.D. 330, Constantine established the Roman imperial residence in the small Greek city of Byzantion on the Bosphorus. He named his capital "New Rome" and set about a building program to make it truly imperial. The city was soon named for him, "Constantine's City," or Constantinople. The establishment of Constantinople as the seat of the imperial government reflects trends that developed in the late empire. It made good military sense. The city is both easily defended and sits poised between Rome's two most troublesome borders. It lies in the Greek world and is thus far less "Roman" than Rome itself or most of the other principal late-imperial residences. It is an eastward-looking city, reflecting the fact that now the primary economic engines of the empire churned in the great cities of the East and not in the West, where a debilitated agriculture and reduced trade were increasingly less able to support a bustling urban economy. And it was a Christian city. Constantine wanted it to be "the Christian Rome" and, indeed, it was.

Constantine's building in his New Rome was magnificently imperial, consciously imitating old Rome. There were palaces, arsenals, warehouses, and governmental buildings of impressive grandeur but, significantly, no pagan temples. The old Roman urban traditions of grain and circus were also brought forth afresh on the Bosphorus; Constantinople had its public dole and its Hippodrome.

Constantine's final years were spent largely at peace. The Goths were repelled in A.D. 332 and the Persians remained quiet. His reforms of the government were largely in line with those Diocletian had begun. He expanded the field army, enlarging the mobile force. He separated the civil from the military bureaucracy. The chief military commanders reported directly to him. In the end, the battered prestige of the empire and of the imperial office was amazingly restored.

THE FOURTH AND FIFTH CENTURIES

The effects of the autocracy of Diocletian and Constantine, their militarization, regimentation, and, perhaps, Constantine's Christianization, were meant to preserve the Empire. In large measure, they worked, if not perfectly or permanently. The fourth century comprised a period in which the quality of Roman life on all levels of the social ladder was better in general than it had been in the third century or would be in the fifth. Despite the fourth century's military defeats, its bitter conflicts between pagans and Christians, and its civil wars, at the end of the century the empire was still intact. At least it seemed so to contemporaries (see Medieval Voices).

The Last of Constantine's Family

Constantine returned to the principle of hereditary succession with dangerous enthusiasm. His saintly status among Christian writers seems more than slightly misplaced given that he had potential rivals from his own family killed, including his eldest son and heir. Nonetheless, when he died in 337, three of his sons were alive and capable of succeeding him; unfortunately, none was the clearly designated successor. After years of squabbling and civil war, two emerged to split the Empire; in 353 it was again united under the third son, Constantius II (324–361). Constantius was a good general and spent the majority of his reign campaigning on the borders. In most important matters he followed Constantine's policies. In 356 he closed all the pagan temples and confirmed the ban on public pagan sacrifices. The last member of Constantine's family to rule was a cousin of the direct line called Julian (361–363). He is known to history as Julian the Apostate. Julian, a product of the most elegant late antique education, found Christianity crude and lacking, preferring a mystical, pagan, Neoplatonism (see Medieval Portraits).

MEDIEVAL VOICES

Ammianus Describes the Empire

Ammianus Marcellinus, a former high-ranking military official from Antioch living and writing in Rome c. 390, has this to say about the Roman Empire in the late fourth century:

And now [the Roman people], tending toward its old age, and sometimes gaining victory by means of its name alone, has come to the quieter parts of its life. So the venerable city, after humbling the proud necks of unbridled peoples, and after bringing forth laws (the eternal foundation and restraint of liberty), like a virtuous, wise, and wealthy parent, has entrusted the right to rule her inheritance to the Caesars, as if to her own children. Now for some time, on the one hand the tribal and centurial assemblies have been at peace and there have been no contests for votes, . . . and on the other, throughout all the regions of the earth, as many as there are shores, she is accepted as mistress and queen; everywhere the white hair of her senators is revered with authority and the name of the Roman People is respected and honored.

Source: The Books of History, XIV, 4–6.

The Beginning of the End

In the last decades of the fourth century, peace and stability started to make their exit from the Roman world, slowly at first but then at a trot. New problems along with the ones Diocletian and Constantine confronted and to some measure overcame would now begin to get the best of the Romans.

Cooperation at the highest levels between East and West became increasingly rare, something that made other problems more difficult to solve. From the days of Diocletian and his short-lived tetrarchy we find an increasing divergence between the two sections. The East had long been far richer, and the location of Constantine's new imperial city clearly indicates that it also had become the dominant political part. After Constantine's family left the throne, the two parts would only rarely be united under one emperor.

The rule of Valens, emperor in the East from 364 to 378, signals another trend: the threat of powerful barbarians* eager to make their homes in Roman lands. To decrease the danger from the Visigoths, Valens took the expedient of offering them settlement in Roman territory, but by 377 they had been so mistreated by the Roman officials that they revolted. Valens' successor, Theodosius I (379–395) was

---

* The word "Germanic" can often be found instead of "barbarian" to describe these non-Mediterranean peoples. Both terms carry inappropriate connotations. "Germanic" suggests an ethnic unity that did not exist and "barbarian" carries unfair notions of cultural inferiority. Barbarian is used here and by it we mean simply "foreign."

MEDIEVAL PORTRAITS

Julian the Apostate (333–363, emperor from 361)

Julian was a nephew of Constantine and cousin of Constantius II, Constantine's son and successor. Constantius, always fearful lest some other member of Constantine's family unseat him, had Julian's father lynched when Julian was five years old. As a boy, Julian was given a pious Christian education, but he showed a decided preference for classical paganism, especially in its mystical and Neoplatonic form. He was a bright child and grew to become a very talented military commander and administrative reformer.

In 355 Constantius created Julian caesar for Gaul and Britain, and he soon gained the devotion of his troops because of his successful generalship and his simple and austere way of life. Constantius grew jealous but died in 361 before it came to full civil war between the two emperors.

As sole emperor, Julian was to rule only nineteen months after Constantius's death before he himself was killed on a campaign against the Persians in 363. It was, however, a year and a half of startling reversal in imperial policy. In many of his reforms, Julian acted from a sincere conviction that Christianity was a corrupting influence eating away at the true morality and education preserved in pagan Greek traditions. Thus he reduced the ostentatiously Christian imperial court of his predecessors in favor of a more austere regime. He reinstated the lands and privileges of the pagan temples and priesthoods while eliminating those that the Christian clergy had enjoyed. He removed Christian teachers from the schools and allowed exiled Christian bishops to return to their cities in the hopes that they would cause rivalries and thus weaken the Church. Although intelligent, articulate, and clear-headed, he was also mystical, believing in oracles and miracles, and passionately committed to ancient pagan rites. His reign was too short and the Christian tide too far advanced for him to have much lasting effect beyond the revitalization of some pagan intellectual circles in the more Hellenized parts of the Empire. With him died the last pagan Roman emperor.

forced to take barbarian settlement a significant step further. He allowed the Visigoths to settle as a federated people. This meant that they not only lived on formerly Roman territory, but did so under their own government with their own kings and without Roman officials. The step stopped their plundering, but the Visigoths' separate political status meant that they never became part of the Roman state, a dangerous development for a state having increasing trouble commanding loyalty. Barbarians living on former Roman territory will become more and more the rule, and although it solved some problems, it created others.

Under Valentinian II (emperor in the West 375–392) we read another important signpost: The emperor was not the real ruler. The head of the military, now called the Master of the Soldiers, held the actual power. Arbogast by name, he was of Frankish descent. Throughout the last century of the Roman Empire in the West, barbarian military leaders would control not only the "Roman" armies but also the western imperial state. Arbogast was so much in control that when Valentinian was found dead in 392 (a murder in which there are reasons to suspect Arbogast's hand), the Frankish leader ruled on, appointing a certain Eugenius in the West, who reigned as his puppet.

Meanwhile long-reigning Theodosius in the East had had enough. In 394 he moved his armies into the West, defeated Arbogast and Eugenius, and became sole emperor. A short five months later he died of illness in Milan. With him died single rulership of East and West. Never again in all its history would the Mediterranean be united under one government. Although obviously this permanent political division did not mean that East and West suddenly sprang in opposite directions, nonetheless the political end of the *Mare Nostrum,* or "our sea," as the Romans called the Mediterranean, is a significant descent toward "Rome's fall."

Over the next hundred years as official Roman rule in the West neared its end, we find the West increasingly following its own path, diverging more and more from the East. The East, richer and more urban, was by the beginning of the fifth century more Christian, better defended, and had a far more unified and more stable central government that was lodged in the splendid and well-fortified capital city of Constantinople. Here centralized, imperial rule could and did work effectively. In the East the Roman Empire, in a reduced and increasingly Greek form, continued for another millennium. The West, on the other hand, poorer and more rural, was much easier prey to foreign attack. As the barbarian threat increased during the course of the fifth century, local loyalty turned in panic to anyone who could provide protection. This decreased even further the central government's ability to protect the borders, and in the process the Roman political structure crumbled in the very part of the Mediterranean world it had first conquered.

The Child Emperors and Regents

When Theodosius died in 395 his elder son, eighteen-year-old Arcadius (395–408), became emperor in the East and his younger son, eleven-year-old Honorius (395–423), assumed the throne in the West. They, in turn, were also succeeded by children. Children on the thrones meant, of course, that for long stretches of the new century it was not the emperors themselves but adult advisors and regents who actually ruled. Regencies are often periods of weak rule in which intrigues, jealousy, rivalry, and even wars flare up as various figures contend for the power the ruler is too young to exercise. The most powerful of the regents were of two types: First, the military leaders, the Masters of the Soldiers, most of whom like Arbogast before them were of barbarian extraction; and second, women, the mothers and sisters of the reigning children. These regents were people of strong personalities, almost always far more capable than the actual emperors even after they had become adults.

Capable as the military masters may have been, more often than not, they used their skill and position for ends which were not particularly Roman. Personal aggrandizement or even dynastic ambition too often motivated them. Stilicho, for instance, a Vandal and chief advisor to the young Honorius in the West, wanted his son to marry the emperor's half sister, Galla Placidia, so that his grandson could become emperor.

The imperial women, on the other hand, had no diverging dynastic or national motives and they were often truly remarkable rulers. Their sex gave them certain advantages over the males of their families, who tended to be rather flaccid. Being women they were not treated from infancy as potential or actual divine rulers as were their divine brothers and sons, and consequently their personalities did not suffer the warping effects of such treatment. Their political skills also seemed far more highly honed since the usual simpler male means of direct authority and the whole world of military command were closed to them. In Chapter 3 we shall see the finest example of female imperial rule as we watch the remarkable career of Galla Placidia, half sister of the child emperors Arcadius and Honorius.

Thus the first decades of the fifth century thundered on with young or weak characters on the imperial thrones, and the high imperial politics largely attempting to secure Roman advantage by pitting one body of powerful barbarians against another. The Romans employed various means: They paid out heaps of gold as subsidies to the barbarians, they offered them land and federated status, and they even seduced their leaders with the prestige of high imperial positions and titles. None of it worked, at least not for long. By mid-century it was all over for the once proud mistress of the world but the tumult.

The Good Shepherd Mosiac from the Tomb of Galla Placidia in Ravenna   Galla Placidia (died 450), who had been an imperial hostage, general's wife, barbarian queen, and "empress" of the West for twelve difficult years (see Chapter 3), is commemorated by a magnificent tomb in Ravenna, which still stands and bears some of the most dazzling mosaics of the age. Christ is not represented here as a simple shepherd, but as an imperial figure, dressed in gold and purple and holding a golden septre. *Michael S. Yamashita/Corbis.*

The Transformation of the Roman Empire

Historians are coming more and more to see that for most people, that is, for those who were not senators, masters of the soldiers, or emperors, and for those who were fortunate enough not to live in a city during a barbarian sack or be in the path of an invading army—what was once called "the fall of the Roman Empire" did not have as great an effect as once thought. Although some parts of the high classical culture, that is the glorious architecture, the magnificent art, the exquisite poetry and literature, the remarkable political structure, and the sophisticated intellectual and legal life did "decline and fall," other parts changed only in form, not in quality. It is thus far more common to talk today of the transformation of the Roman Empire than of its "fall."

By the middle of the fifth century, only Italy along with some parts of both Gaul and Spain were under the control of the Roman emperor in the West. Even in this territorial remnant, it was not the reigning Roman emperors but either their barbarian Masters of the Soldiers or other influential barbarian leaders who exercised real control. It was they who put up the rapid succession of candidates for the throne.

Romulus Augustulus (475–476) is often considered the last reigning Roman emperor in the West. But he actually was a usurper, installed by his father, Orestes, using his army of barbarians, and never officially recognized by the emperor in the East. His reign was in any event short lived and once again we see that the real power was the barbarian military. Orestes' soldiers had naturally expected to be rewarded with Italian land for their help in installing Romulus Augustulus. Orestes failed to deliver and the barbarians under their leader, Odoacer, killed Orestes in 476 but spared the boy emperor. They sent him into retirement and his fate is unknown.

A barbarian king, Odoacer, now ruled the Western empire, or what little was left of it. Roman imperial government thus ended in the West, certainly not with a bang and not even with much of a whimper.

CONTINUITIES AND CRISES IN THE WEST

The changes in the high politics by no means meant that Roman life, Roman culture, or even Roman government suddenly ended for most people living in the West. Indeed, much of what had been a part of the ancient Mediterranean civilization went on affecting the lives of most people.

The Continuation of Roman Language

With their language, the Romans made almost a clean sweep of the areas they controlled in the West. Despite the fall of the central Roman government, the terrifying invasions of barbarians, and even the fact that all of the former imperial West came to be ruled by German-speakers, nowhere, except in one part of insular

Britain and here and there along the Rhine border, did a German tongue come to be the language of the people. In every other part of the West, the people went right on speaking the language they had been speaking when the Romans ruled them. Those languages were, for the most part, either some form of Latin or a language heavily influenced by it. Even today one must scratch to find more than a dozen words of Gothic origin in Spanish or Italian, and even in French, spoken where the German-speaking Franks ruled for centuries, only about 300 modern words trace their origins to Frankish. Most of the rest of French vocabulary is Romance—that is, based on Latin.

The Continuation of Roman Rural Life

There are many ways in which we are correct to view the ancient culture as urban and the medieval as rural. But for most people in both periods (in fact, for most people in all of history) life took place in the countryside, and here especially there was no drastic change with the decline of Rome. In both the early Middle Ages and in the late empire, most people lived as most people in many developing countries do today: just this side of hunger. Under the Romans as well as under medieval kings, almost all income of rural households was taken up in rent or taxes and in procuring food and shelter; very little remained for anything else. With the population teetering on the brink like this, any unbalancing event, a bad crop-year, war, drought, harsh winter, or anything that raised the cost of food, even slightly, could cause real and wide-spread misery.

We have seen the increasingly military nature of the Roman state. As long as the armies were far away, successfully fighting foreigners, and well supplied, the major economic effect they had upon the poor was the heavy taxation the poor bore in order to support them. But in the late imperial period, the armies that crossed the interior of the empire were both larger than in earlier times and increasingly poorly supplied. This led to "requisitioning" whereby the military units would simply take what they needed from the local farms. Theoretically the farmers were to be reimbursed by the government but rarely did this occur. As far as we can tell, this evil diminished somewhat in the early Middle Ages when armies become smaller, campaigns shorter, and military activity generally confined much closer to home.

Heavy taxation, depredations by the military, and the depletion of nutrients in the soil after centuries of use caused many people simply to abandon their land. For an economy based on agriculture, this became a huge problem, one attacking the foundations of Roman life. The government did what it could with legislation and tax incentives to bring abandoned land back under cultivation. Sometimes abandoned land was given to those who would farm it; at other times the government tried to force its owners to put it back into production. But despite these efforts weeds rather than wheat continued to grow.

The Continuation of Roman Aristocratic Life

Even if we consider for a moment the lot of the upper classes, those who stood to lose the most from the Roman government's collapse one might think, we find that at least some of them actually welcomed the change to barbarian rule and that others carried on their privileged and elegant lives largely as before. We have the famous report from Salvian, a Christian priest from Marseilles, writing in the middle of the fifth century, who, as a part of his praise for the virtues of the barbarians as opposed to the decadence of the Romans, said that Romans living in places now governed by barbarians had no desire to return to imperial government. Sidonius Apollinaris, writing at about the same time, has left us an account of a charming "house party" with friends. It is hard to imagine a description of life in a country villa that would be more Roman.

The Continuation of Roman Ties of Loyalty

It is safe to characterize medieval society as one in which the ties of personal rather than abstract or institutional loyalty bound society together. In the Middle Ages aristocratic warriors pledged loyalty to the person of the king by name, as did lowly peasants to their lords. Even though the Roman citizen felt the tug of an abstract loyalty to the state, a type of loyalty akin to modern patriotism, the ties of personal loyalty also root themselves deeply in Roman soil. In traditional Roman society, every male was bound to someone more powerful than he was by the personal ties of *obsequium,* a term best translated as obedience or respect. The man holding the higher position was the patron, the one holding the lower, the client. The ties were not official, but they were universal and extremely powerful. The client was reckoned as part of the patron's following, and it was normal for him to call his patron "lord." The patron was obligated to assist his clients with help in matters of the law and with a financial aid called a *sportula,* often a cash payment. For poor clients, the handouts from their patrons were by no means boons but necessary for their survival. It is difficult to overly emphasize the importance of clientage in most people's lives. It was part of the daily routine for clients to gather before dawn at the door of their patron to pay their respects and receive the *sportula.*

The Continuation of the Economic and Legal Status of the Poor

The economic and legal status of the lower classes in the late empire also endured into the Middle Ages. Roman society in its very early days was made up of many small landholders who were full citizens. By the time of the late Empire, however, most of the agricultural land formed part of huge estates owned by great landholders, the greatest of whom by far was the emperor himself. For the most part, gone was the yeoman farmer and gone too were the brigades of slaves who had worked the great estates in the days of the late Republic, when the empire was expanding and slaves were relatively cheap. Now most farmers were tenants, farming someone else's land in return for rent, a share of the produce, labor services, or some combination thereof. As the empire became longer in the tooth, the status of the peasants worsened. The development did not happen everywhere at the same time, but by the reign of Constantine we can see huge numbers of half-free peasants, called *coloni,* so bound by the tax registers that they could not move. They are obviously the antecedents of the medieval serfs, and although the obligations and requirements will take on different forms when we arrive in the early and central Middle Ages, the sorry lot of the peasant will have changed very little from the days of the late Roman Empire.

The Continuing Plight of the Cities

As the Western economy contracted in the late empire, so too did opportunities for those whose lives depended on economic exchange. The small traders seem to have been badly hurt, although some could now make a living supplying the ever-increasing Roman armies. The government reacted, making membership in the craft guilds obligatory and requiring the status to be passed on to the members' children. The intention was to insure that goods would be produced and distributed and that financial obligations would be met. But the regulations did not work. Their real effect was to restrict the mobility of this class and thus make it less able to respond to economic conditions.

The physical conditions for all but the rich in the splendid ancient cities were anything but splendid. In Rome itself most streets were not paved, and in the city center only two, the Via Sacra and the Via Nova, were wide enough for two carts to pass. Very few dwellings had running water, and fewer still a connection to the sewers. The sewer systems of the great Roman cities were a marvel, but they were inadequate. The stench in the streets was appalling. Even the wonderful, public latrines were not often used by the poor. The streets were crowded and noisy. They were also very dangerous, even more so by night since there were no streetlights. The protection offered by the public authorities was useless, and those who could afford it never went about without the accompaniment of armed retainers. The emperor Marcus Aurelius (161–180) banned all carts in the cities of the Empire to the night hours in order to lessen the congestion during the day. Tired urban residents complained of noise and insomnia.

The rich lived in wonderful urban houses, often with running water, indoor latrines, a spacious center courtyard and reflecting pool, all lavishly done out in costly furniture and artwork. Most of the population, however, was crowded into stuffy multistory tenements with no comfort facilities and poor ventilation. Cooking and heating were done with charcoal, and the fact that many lived high above the streets meant that the slop pails were emptied with somewhat less than desirable frequency. Furniture was sparse: a table, benches, and a pallet for sleeping.

Medieval towns were small and built within walls for protection, but already in the late empire the towns were shrinking and building walls. Many Roman cities depended upon imperial good fortune for their health. But with the crises of the third century and the constricting of the empire in the fourth and fifth, the cities suffered. Their walled areas comprised from 25 to 50 acres, a situation that indicates their populations were already probably no more than 5,000 people. The great cities of the East and the city of Rome remained in better physical shape, but for most, especially in the West, it was a different fate.

This is not to say that all urban building stopped. It certainly did not. As the empire in the West neared its end, however, the costs of large public buildings were borne more and more by private patrons than by the government. Whereas the early empire witnessed the construction of amphitheaters, public baths, or municipal law courts, the rich of the late empire were more likely to fund the building of churches. Some of these were architecturally every bit as impressive as the more secular buildings of the earlier period.

We notice a change in the sculpture and the decorative arts. Obviously Christian subjects became more common, but even the works treating secular themes became more transcendental and symbolic. As the future seemed less and less bright, Roman thoughts withdrew from the here and now and Roman artists presented even their secular heroes as having contact with the beyond. This will become more pronounced in medieval art.

The Continuation of the Great Landed Estate

Another characteristic of the Middle Ages is that those who ruled lived in the countryside whereas the powerful in the ancient Mediterranean culture were city-dwellers. But a very important group of locally powerful people began to live in the countryside long before the barbarian kings set up rule in the West. In the late Republic and early empire much of the agricultural land was owned by absentee

The Nave of the Basilica Santa Maria Majore in Rome, Constructed about 440 The basilica was a common architectural form employed by the late antique Christians for their important church buildings. The word "basilica" comes from the Greek meaning "the king's (house)" and was used by the Romans to designate important assembly halls built for judicial, political, and commercial purposes. The Christians adopted both the word "basilica" and its grand style to designate an assembly hall for Christian worship. *Archivo Iconographico, S.A./Corbis.*

landlords who resided in fashion in the cities and managed their great rural estates through subordinates. But the villa, or country home, originally used chiefly to escape temporarily the heat or occupational demands of city life, became in the late empire the principal residence of many great landholders. The villas themselves became magnificently appointed, decked out with splendid mosaics, lavish furniture, and spacious apartments. In far-off and chilly Britain and in the other northern regions of the Empire, it was common for them to even enjoy a toasty, under-the-floor central heating system.

Whereas the towns in the late western empire withered, the villas blossomed. They were becoming more self-sufficient. The great estate had been the means of agricultural exploitation in the East since time immemorial and ever since its introduction to the West during the Republic it had, by necessity, displayed a certain degree of economic self-sufficiency, processing crops and manufacturing certain tools and other items *in situ*. But many of the late-imperial great estates of Britain and Gaul have left archaeological remains of glassworks, forges, and workshops, all indicating a much greater amount of manufacturing and self-sufficiency than had been normal in earlier times. In the late empire the estates also became more self-contained legally and more self-reliant for protection. Many obtained an exemption from the jurisdiction of the local authorities and thus the landlords began to exercise some of the roles of government on their estates. The villas, too, began to fortify and to seek other ways to provide themselves with safety. Since, as we have seen, local imperial government was largely urban, the ruling class on the rural estates managed to escape many of the restricting obligations laid upon their social equals living in the towns. The rural estate-owners grew in power and importance and, obviously, in many cases it was they who evolved into the great landlords of the early Middle Ages.

Continuity in the Status of Women

Another important matter that remained relatively constant throughout the late Empire and beyond was the position of women. This is because women moved in the private, not the public, life of Rome, and the conduct of private lives does not seem to have changed greatly. The fact that the women's realm was not public is also the reason that they are almost hidden from us; private lives do not generally find their way to the contemporary written sources unless they impinge in some way upon the public sphere. There are, nonetheless, certain things concerning the female half of the Roman people that we can see and some of these glimpses are surprising.

There does not seem to have been a war between the sexes, probably because the domain of each was so demarcated from the other's that neither felt the other as a threat. When on occasion men did cross the gender boundary and partake in activities from the feminine side, they were labeled as soft and degenerate. By the same token, a woman would be accused of moral laxity, usually sexual transgression, if she ventured into the male domains of the public sphere. This is not to say that women were excluded totally from public life, or that men were from the private. But acceptable direct female participation beyond the home seems to have been limited largely to public benefaction, mostly funding local buildings, and to religious duties. Both of these were a vital part of late Imperial public life. A woman who exercised political control did so through her connections with a male member of her family who held office.

We have no direct indication from the Roman women themselves of what they thought of men, since Roman women wrote neither material for publication nor other types of sources that would be likely to be preserved. It is clear, however, that Roman men considered women inferior to themselves. Their often irritating condescension criticized the female's supposed lesser ability to act in the male sphere. Women were said to be less strong physically, less able to reason, and less constant of purpose. In the days of the Republic, when upper-class males were fiercely engaged in public life, the public rights and status of women were in sorry condition indeed. They were a legal nonentity, totally part of the legal personality of their fathers or husbands. A woman could not inherit, she could be divorced on the whim of her husband, and she had little or no recourse to legal redress of any grievance. But in the imperial period, as the men found less and less satisfaction in public life with its huge bureaucracy and its increasingly theocratic nature, and as they began to look more and more to matters private for a sense of fulfillment, the condition of those in charge of private life, that is, women, ameliorated significantly. Women came to possess more public dignity and often an independence in their own right. By Hadrian's rule (117–138) women could inherit and pass on land. Private portraits picture women by themselves, and the women of the imperial family were featured on the coins, albeit less frequently and later in their reigns than were the men. In the iconography of gravestones and of official monuments, including the coins, women had always been associated with the domestic virtues: health, fertility, modesty, beauty, loyalty, and faithfulness and this does not change. But as the men retreated into the private sphere, they also came to laud these virtues, and the image of their female defenders took on a new dignity in the masculine world. Nonetheless, despite these significant improvements, the realm of women remained with only rare and magnificent exceptions largely as it had been, the private one. In the late Roman Empire, as in the early Middle Ages, women did not often venture into public life and thus did not come often enough into the light of history to satisfy our curiosity about them.

Continuing Poor State of Public Education

With education, too, it has been fashionable among scholars to worry about when the classical educational system "died out" and learning retreated behind the thick walls of medieval monasteries. The truth is that for most people in the Roman Empire as well as in the early Middle Ages learning was never very much alive. In the high empire in the city of Rome, many children from the lower classes learned some form of halting reading and computation, but they never progressed beyond that. The first years of education were conducted in the home under parental guidance. Upper-class Romans often purchased Greek slaves to educate their young

A Roman Coin from cir. 112–115 A.D.   This coin depicts Plotina, wife of the emperor, Hadiran on the obverse (the front) and the goddess, Vesta, on the reverse. Coins were an important means of imperial propaganda and most showed images of the emperors. The fact that the empress and a female goddess are represented here is a sign of the importance of imperial women. *Araldo de Luca/Corbis.*

children. Elementary schools were private affairs, where the teachers subsisted on the modest fees paid by the pupils' parents. The fees, modest as they were, nonetheless prohibited most poor children from attending. The instruction was appalling, mostly repetitive drilling of the three Rs with frequent application of the cane all conducted in dismal surroundings. There were no school buildings as such; the teacher simply gathered his pupils where he could, usually somewhere in the open in the noisy streets.

Wonderful education did exist in the late empire, but it was limited to the wealthier classes. We have no evidence that the emperors took any interest at all in elementary education except to provide certain tax concessions for elementary teachers in order to encourage the spread of the profession. They do seem to have taught throughout the empire, sometimes even in remote villages. Imperial interest in education concentrated on the upper levels. Diocletian appointed professors in many cities, Julian established a type of university in Constantinople with a permanent staff, and the imperial families and others of the high nobility often sent their sons to Rhodes or to Athens, to the Lyceum and the Academy. Those lucky enough to partake in this education received exquisite training in the classical disciplines of rhetoric and philosophy. Although literary creativity in the late empire seems to have found its home with the Christian writers writing on Christian subjects rather than with the traditionally pagan ones, the classical techniques and material were nonetheless being taught and learned, albeit by a very few. This too continued into the early Middle Ages.

The Continuing Realm of Thought

In the world of ideas, the late Roman Empire was also the direct antecedent of the early Middle Ages in the way its intellectual climate molded the Christianity that it passed on. By the time of the late empire the two great Hellenistic philosophies, Stoicism and Epicureanism, had been superseded by a vigorous new interest in Plato, but Plato with an important twist. Plato had called upon the world of ideals beyond this one largely in order to create the good citizen; his was a public and political morality. But, as we have seen in the late empire, public political life too often offered little fulfillment to thinking Romans. The Stoic's call to duty rang increasingly hollow in a world where political freedom had been sapped by huge bureaucracies and far-away imperial powers. Out of the teachings of the Stoics and Epicureans and the worldview of the Neopythagorians, Plato returned. The most important thinker, but certainly not the only one, in the creation of the Neoplatonism was Plotinus (205–270), who had studied at Alexandria but who lived most of his productive years at Rome. Neoplatonism taught people not how to be good citizens but how to use their intellect to put themselves in touch with the world beyond. It was a powerful new force, intellectually sophisticated, and one that merged what we would call religion with philosophy. Its approach was contemplative rather than active and its morality private. Significantly, Plotinus studied under Ammonius Saccos, also the teacher of Origen, the third century's most important Christian theologian.

From the time of Constantine onwards we see in the pagan writers a concentration on the values and the ideas of the past. It was these men of late antiquity who put the classical texts in the form that the early Middle Ages would know them. They were the editors and commentators whom the scholars of the early Middle Ages would study. They include the fourth-century grammarian, Donatus (who, incidentally, was a teacher of the Christian writer, Jerome) and the Neoplatonist, Macrobius. Much of what the early Middle Ages knew about ancient learning came from a fantastic and florid summary written by Martianus Capella in the early fifth century.

While pagans looked backward, the Christian writers looked ahead. Intellectual life concentrated more and more at the imperial court, itself since the days of Constantine an increasingly Christian center, and in the Church itself. These were the only institutions that saw both a need for the higher learning and had the resources to support it. It was the Christians who provided answers deemed most useful in solving the problems that troubled intellects in the late empire. In their writings vitality was anything but sapped, and it was they more than any other intellectual force that carried the late Roman Empire into the Middle Ages. About them we shall have much to say in Chapter 2.

Roman Law and Its Legacy

Roman ideas of law, that is, how law is created and how it governs, are often held up as the greatest of Rome's legacies to succeeding ages. The heyday of Roman law came in the late Republic and early empire, when Rome had accumulated both a splendid body of law and a huge cadre of sophisticated jurists who knew how to wield it. Romans were convinced that law was the cement that bound their society together and allowed it to function. Especially during and after the age of Cicero (died 43 B.C.), Roman jurisprudence became infused with a good deal of Greek philosophical thinking allowing the highly trained jurists to apply not only the letter but also the spirit, or abstract principles, of the law. By the time of the late empire, however, this juridical sophistication had become greatly simplified. Gone were the great jurists of Cicero's day, and the simpler needs of the rural provinces demanded a simpler code. Consequently the exercise of Roman law became much more concrete, less abstract, and far more dependent on following specific precedent or edicts. This later law is now known as Roman Provincial or Roman Vulgar (from *vulgus,* "the people") Law. It is the law which lies at the base of much of the Emperor Theodosius's code, published in 438, and which entered into the early middle ages in the codes of the early medieval kings. Although Rome's earlier, more sophisticated jurisprudence was reissued in the 530s by the Emperor Justinian, it lay largely dormant in western Europe until the eleventh and twelfth centuries.

Summary

The Roman Empire's political life began about 500 B.C. and lasted in the West for about a thousand years. Roman civilization, however, long outlasted even this seemingly eternal political control. During their Republic, about the first 500 years of the Romans' political history, they laid the basics of their law, economy, literature, art, philosophy, and social and military structure. Republican officials were replaced by emperors, who ruled over Rome's "golden age" in the first and second century A.D.. But even then, Roman society was showing signs of dangerous rigidity. The third century saw economic crisis, civil wars, and the first of the "barbarian invasions." With the reforms of Diocletian and Constantine in the late third and early fourth centuries, the rigidity deepened: The imperial government became more theocratic, the military came to dominate even more of civil life, and economic and legal measures bound ordinary people to their fathers' occupations and positions. The generally tolerant ancient paganism gave way to monotheistic Christianity, which sought greater religious uniformity. By the end of the fourth century, Roman rule was permanently divided between the Eastern Empire, centered in Constantinople, and the Western Empire, centered mostly in northern Italy. Roman political rule would survive in the East, but in the West it continued to deteriorate until it vanished toward the end of the fifth century.

Direct Roman political rule may have ended in the West, but Roman civilization refused to give up its grip on Europe. Rome's imperial political structure may have fallen to barbarian kings and its ancient buildings become magnificent ruins or quarries of already-hewn stone for Christian churches, but much of Rome—its language, agriculture, aristocratic life, clientage, the life of the peasant, urban conditions, the great landed estates, the status of women, public education, philosophical thought, and law—would endure to become important parts of the lives of medieval men and women. Christianity, the religion of Romans in their late empire, was the most important carrier of their intellectual and artistic culture into the early Middle Ages. Our attention will now turn to the beginnings of this religion in Chapter 2.

CHAPTER 2

∾

Early Christianity: From Sect to State Religion, 30–500

By the end of Roman political rule in the West, Christianity had become the dominant Roman religion. It began as a small, almost unnoticed sect in the Roman province of Palestine and grew to become the Empire's only official religion. A plausible historical explanation for Christianity's seemingly surprising rise to dominance can be found by examining several of its early characteristics: its valuable Jewish heritage, its concept of an afterlife, a visible proof of truth of its teaching in the miracles it claimed, its appealingly simple way of life, and its very effective organizational structure.

Christianity changed a great deal during its rise to prominence; the official imperial religion differed greatly from its beginnings as a simple, humble sect. It developed a new relationship with the Roman state, a more philosophically sophisticated theology, and a richer liturgical life. After a period of antagonism toward Christians, the Roman state eventually made the Christian Church an integral part of itself. The Christians developed a systematic theology, not only through careful thinking and writing, but also often through violent settlement of disagreements among various Christian groups. The growing Church established its sacred text, recognized its authoritative thinkers, now called the Fathers of the Church, and formed the way ordinary Christians would live and worship. All of this was a huge accomplishment and a huge legacy for the Middle Ages that followed.

THE BEGINNINGS OF CHRISTIANITY

Christianity is based on the teachings *about* Jesus, not the teachings *of* Jesus, and so it is with the history of his life. To our knowledge he left no writings. To our knowledge, he left no direct instructions to those he knew that either his life or his teachings be written. We do, however, have a group of very early sources treating both his life and his teachings. But the historian, as opposed to the theologian, encounters a problem at the very beginning of the study of Christianity. Our knowledge is limited almost exclusively to what we can learn from the Gospels and other early Christian writings. The historian must exercise special caution when using these sources which were written for religious, not historical, purposes.

The Sources

Very few surviving early non-Christian sources mention either Christ or the first Christians. The Church was too small to warrant much attention from anyone beyond those who by chance knew a Christian directly, and the pagan world at first could not distinguish between Christians and Jews. In the early second century, about fifty years after the first Gospel was written, we do find a few brief mentions of Christ and Christians by important pagan authors. Suetonius (d. after 118), Pliny the Younger (d. cir. 112) and Tacitus (d. 117) all mention them. The works of the very pro-Roman Jewish author, Josephus, who wrote about 95, contain a brief allusion to James, "the brother of Jesus who is called the Christ" and a short description of the life of Jesus, his condemnation under Pilate, his crucifixion, and his resurrection. But in this non-Christian account, there are textual problems since at this point the manuscript of Josephus' work was edited by a Christian.

Not only modern historians but the people of the Middle Ages knew the life of Christ and the beginnings of their religion almost exclusively through the Gospels—the first four books of the Christian New Testament. Three of them, Matthew, Mark, and Luke, contain much information in common. Biblical scholars term these three the synoptic Gospels, from the Greek word for "the same view." Mark is the oldest of the synoptics and the authors of the other two seem to have read and used Mark's gospel along with other sources when writing their own. Their use of Mark explains in great part why the three have similarities. The Gospel of John, which is more spiritual and theological than the synoptics, was written at about the same time perhaps by John the disciple of Jesus or perhaps by someone who knew John the disciple.

Thus our prime sources about the life of Jesus were written within about fifty years of his death by people who perhaps knew him, but certainly by people who knew people who knew him. If this is beginning to sound slightly second hand, we may wish to consider two points. First, throughout most of our study of the Middle Ages we shall be very grateful indeed for narrative sources this chronologically and personally close to their subjects; most ancient and medieval history was written from a much greater distance. Second, all the Gospel writers could have talked to people who were actually on the spot and, while perhaps not eyewitnesses themselves, their position is certainly the next best thing. Because these are not historical books but religious ones (and for other serious reasons) many historians have grave reservations about their use for writing history. Even the most hesitant, however, will concede that we are probably on a safe historical footing in concluding the following four things from them about the life of Jesus:

1. He was born about 4 or 5 B.C.* and grew up in Nazareth in Galilee, although the Gospels contain almost nothing about the first thirty years of his life.
2. He was a Jewish teacher, well versed in the Jewish sacred writings. Christ's teaching, however, does not indicate influence of the formal theology of the Rabbinical schools (as, by contrast, the language of Saint Paul does). On the other hand, he also shows no evidence of zealous Jewish patriotism.
3. He attracted a small following of local Galileans.
4. He was crucified by the Jewish and Roman authorities in Jerusalem about A.D. 30.

When we move beyond these, we leave the realm of history and enter religion, but it was for religious reasons, it must be remembered, that the Gospels were written.

The Life of Jesus

Of all their provinces, the Romans had the most difficulty controlling Palestine. It was always a trouble spot. Guided by their proud and ancient religion, the Jews walked their own path. They alone won legal exemption from the requirement that all peoples subject to the Romans participate in the Roman state religion. The northern part of their territory, the hill country of Galilee, varied ever further from what the Romans wanted; it was the region's outback, its "wild west," so to speak, an area especially popular with outlaws, malcontents, and zealous Jewish rebels. It was here in Galilee that Jesus grew up and performed the majority of his teaching. It was here too that he attracted his original followers, all of whom were Galileans. They were neither rich nor in any way influential, and some even lived on the wrong side of the law. When Jesus was about thirty-three years old, he made his second (or perhaps his only) trip to Jerusalem where he was arrested, tried, and crucified by the Jewish and Roman authorities.

The First Christians

It is very difficult for the historian to see the early Christians. Once again we are dependent mostly upon the New Testament, and here we encounter the same methodological problems that occur when using the Gospels to see the life of Jesus. We are on far safer historical grounds reconstructing what the first Christians believed than we are trying to assess what they did. Since the New Testament was written by members of the early Church, historians sometimes subject their work to "form" or "text" criticism in order to decipher what was important to them. For example, John the Baptist is mentioned more times in the New Testament than anyone other than Peter, Paul, and Jesus himself. This is taken to indicate the early Christians' concern with baptism and acquiring new members. One theory has it that the apostles organized themselves rather like an academy at Jerusalem and preached and taught in the rabbinical style, that is, they made the early Christians

---

* Jesus' birth is now placed in 4 or 5 B.C. and not at the turn of the first millennium because the sixth-century monk, Dionysius Exiguus, who developed our system of dating years consecutively from Christ's birth, miscalculated slightly.

study and memorize the standard doctrines. If this was the case, the written version of the teachings in the later books of the New Testament would accurately reflect what the first Christians taught. In addition, the epistles of Saint Paul found in the New Testament are the earliest of its books, and most scholars agree that at least seven of them are indeed the work of the great apostle himself. Taken together, and despite our problem of using religious sources for historical purposes, the New Testament does contain much that is historically probable about the beliefs of the first Christians, their lives, and their early Church.

From the earliest days, Christians have believed that the man Jesus was the long-awaited Jewish messiah, the "anointed one" or "the Christ," from the Greek word meaning anointed. He was sent from God to save the human race. For many Jewish thinkers, the salvation that the messiah would bring was the Jewish people's return to a healthy social, political, moral, and religious standing in God's eyes. But for Christians, Christ's salvation was almost wholly otherworldly. They believed that Jesus was more than the messiah; that he was God Himself in human form, that he had risen from the dead after his crucifixion, ascended into heaven, and that he would come again to earth at the end of the world. Their teaching viewed this life on earth as a preparation for the life in the hereafter and salvation as acquired only by loving Christ, being faithful to him, and following what they said he had taught.

Although Christianity had great appeal to the poor, the early Christians were largely urban and middle class. The epistles are addressed to churches in cities, not in the countryside, and in them Paul addresses the problems of the urban middle class: goods, marriage, clubs, care of widows, and houses. They seem to have been simple people; many were tradesmen who traveled a great deal. Some of this travel, like that of Saint Paul, was undertaken for missionary purposes, but much of it was conducted in the normal course of doing business in the Roman Empire. Thus when the first Christians appear in cities other than Jerusalem, they are found in the sections of those cities inhabited by Greek-speaking merchants, artisans, and other foreigners.

Their religious life, too, seems to have been a simple one, free from the elaborate ritual of the state religion. There was no sexual license, temple prostitution, or frenzied rites often found in the other cults. Local Christians formed themselves into a small community, or assembly (*ecclesia*), led by officials called elders (presbyters) who were in turn assisted by servants (deacons). At first there was no formal priesthood. The community worshipped together, often ate together, and looked out for each other. The Christians' worship, too, was simple. They sang and prayed the Jewish Psalms, performed baptism, and partook in a common meal called *agape,* or "feast of love." The First Epistle to the Corinthians shows us that at a very early date the ritualistic eating of bread and drinking of wine had a holy significance.

What we know about the occupations and social status of the very early Christians fits very nicely with where we find them geographically. The churches to which the Epistles are addressed, with the exception of the one in Rome, are all located in Greece and Asia Minor. The major Roman road across Asia Minor, the one used by merchants and tradesmen, passes through Antioch, Tarsus, Laranda and the Cicilian Gates, Philomelium, Pisidia, Apameia, Laodicea, the Maeander valley,

A Third-Century Wall Painting from the Catacomb of Saint Callistus in Rome This painting shows early Christians sharing a meal. One of the reasons Christianity spread rapidly was the close and sharing nature of the early Christian communities. Eating together was an important part of early Christian life. *Pirozzi/AKG London.*

and then runs past Tralles to Ephesus. It is no surprise that these are the places we first find Christians.

THE CHRISTIANS CONQUER ROME

From the perspective of the Romans, Christianity was just one of several new cults that came from the East and spread across their empire in the Republican and early Imperial periods. Despite the fact that some of these religions became quite popular, traditional Romans were often very disapproving of them. The Roman historian Tacitus who wrote in the first century A.D. says this about Christians:

> These were the people called Christians by the mob and hated for their abominations. The originator of the name, Christus, was put to death by the procurator, Pontius Pilate, in the reign of Tiberius. For a time the horrible superstition

was suppressed, but it tended to break out again, not only in Judaea, the source of the mischief, but in Rome, whither all that is monstrous flows and finds a ready welcome.

Tacitus, Annals XV. 44.

The Mystery Religions

The mystery religions form a category of these new cults in which Christianity is sometimes included. They are so called because their initiates entered a closed community of believers by means of certain rites or "mysteries." There were many of them about: the cults of Serapis; Cybele, also called The Great Mother; Isis; and Mithra, a Persian god, to name the most important ones.

These mystery religions, Christianity included, had many similar characteristics. They came from the East. They were universal, not limited to a particular ethnic group or social station. They had a private and personal nature rather than the civic and public one the traditional Greek and Roman pagan religions had. And they offered the initiate the promise of a good afterlife. From these characteristics we can see that these cults struck the same sorts of chords in the Hellenistic mind as did the reigning philosophies: Epicureanism, Stoicism, and Neoplatonism.

The most widespread of the mystery religions in the Roman Empire before the triumph of Christianity was Mithraism, the cult of "The Unconquerable Sun." Mithra is often depicted killing a bull, the source of life, and this depiction conveys the idea of life through death. The cult practiced many "mysteries" of holy eating and drinking and espoused highly ethical behavior. The believer was judged worthy of the afterlife based on his conduct in this one. Although it originated in Persia, it spread westward and was especially popular in the Roman Army. The Emperor Aurelian (270–275) contemplated making Mithraism the state religion but died before he could do so.

Reasons for the Spread of Christianity

Christ's life and death seem originally to have caused no stir except in the lives of his few followers and with those Jewish officials concerned about him directly. The origins of Christianity were humble to say the least and took place in an area cut off from the main centers of Roman political and cultural life. How then did this strange, little, out-of-the-way, Jewish sect grow to become the only official religion of the whole Roman Empire and, of course, from there become the dominant faith of the European Middle Ages? It is a question of great historical interest and one not easily answered.

Most modern attempts to answer the question are still dependent, at least for the basic direction of their analyses, on the guiding hand of Edward Gibbon, even some two hundred years after the publication of his book.[1] Believing Christians will, of course, conclude that Christianity's surprising triumph was due to God's plan, but since Gibbon was not a believing Christian, he rejected religious answers and looked for historical ones. He organized his answer in five causes, and we shall use them as our guide, adding thoughts he did not consider.

The Jewish Heritage Religious appeal is usually based on two things: holiness and antiquity. Often these are the same because something that is very old frequently takes on a holy or mystical quality. As we have seen, Jesus and his immediate followers were Jews, and the early Christians saw Jesus as the Messiah, or savior, whose coming was promised by ancient Jewish teaching. Thus although Christianity was a new religion, it nonetheless had an instant claim to a very old and very holy history. The Christians retained much of the Jewish concept of God and much of the Jewish idea of the religious life.

The early Christians, like the Jews around them, were absorbed by their religious life. In good Jewish tradition, they were also inflexible; that is, they were convinced that only they had the true religion and they would not compromise. Without this uncompromising nature, there was a large danger that the Christian God would find just another perch on Olympus among all the other gods, and that Christians would merge into the dominant religious culture, simply emphasizing different matters.

But Christianity was not Judaism, and while it inherited much of value from the Jews, it also changed its inheritance significantly. Judaism was an ethnic religion, limited largely, though not exclusively, to those who were born Jewish. The Christians, on the other hand, after a bit of internal squabbling over whether they should, began zealously to seek converts from other peoples. Their most important early missionary to non-Jewish peoples was Saint Paul, who was only partially of Jewish blood. The words of his letters to Christian communities record his teaching: "There is neither Jew nor Greek . . . for you are all one in Christ Jesus." Christianity also did not take on the great mass of Jewish religious requirements, its rituals, rites, laws, language, and especially its painful requirement for male circumcision. These all had acted to dampen the enthusiasm of potential converts to the Jewish faith, but Christianity was free of them and consequently was far more appealing.

The Promise of Eternal Happiness In general, the ancient pagan religions did not promise much of a life after death. Greeks and Romans had grim views of "shades" wandering shadowy paths of Hades, and although the mystery religions held out bright prospects, Christianity emphatically promised eternal happiness to its faithful. This obviously had great appeal for people all up and down the social ladder but especially for the miserable standing on the cold and soggy bottom rungs whose poverty ensured they had no part in the joys of this world. A faith that invited them to feast of eternal joy in the life after death certainly did more than catch their passing interest. It also had a stick to go with this carrot. The ideal of Hell, too, spurred conversions, especially by Christians who worried about the souls of their friends or relatives.

The Proof of Miracles The New Testament is awash with miracles. Our purpose here is not to comment on whether or not the miracles actually happened but to note that from the very beginning of the faith, Christians have been convinced that the miraculous was a usual part of Christian life. The early Church claimed for itself and its followers all sorts of miraculous happenings: visions, prophesy, healing, raising from the dead, and especially the casting out of demons. As we shall see right to the end of this book, miracles remain a central part of Christianity and we shall have much to say about them later in their medieval context. The Bible calls miracles "signs and wonders" and this phrase reveals their most important character. More important than the actual miraculous occurrence itself is the perception that a miracle is a concrete sign from heaven of the truth of Christianity. Other religions also claimed miracles; they were not an exclusively Christian phenomenon. But the Christians convinced potential converts of the power of their faith by showing them where the Christian God had wondrously intervened into the workings of the world.

The Christian Way of Life   Although the great Roman nobles like Tacitus or Pliny complained about the "abominations" of the Christians, it does seem, on the contrary, that they led simple and moral lives. There were neither financial advantages nor any gain of political or social influence by becoming Christian; in fact, just the opposite resulted, oftentimes bringing on suffering or even martyrdom. Many of Christianity's early converts had been "outlaws and sinners" but once they became members of the Church, they shed their tawdry ways. As we said, its simple ritual and communal way of life were a welcome change from the cold and official temple cults. Christianity was a very private and ethical religion, two characteristics that, as we saw in Chapter 1, were common to many ideas that were gaining popularity in the Roman Empire. In sum, Christianity represented what may be termed "the democratization of morality." The usual view of the moral life in the ancient world was that it was a noble thing and only attainable in a truly exemplary form by people of stature and refinement. Christianity, however, preached humility, and its moral heroes were fishermen, farmers, and women from the lower classes.

The Organization of the Early Church   The Christian Church developed an organizational structure that proved to be very effective for its years in the ancient world as well as in the Middle Ages. It did not come about at once; it was not designed but grew up along with the Church. But by the time late antiquity gave way to the Middle Ages, the Church's organization was firmly in place, and although some things about it would, of course, change thereafter, its basic structure never altered.

At first there was very little organization. A Christian community was led by its presbyters, and these were assisted by deacons, some of whom were women. There were no other officials. Originally, too, the various communities looked to the Christians at Jerusalem for guidance in most matters. About the year 100, officials called bishops, or "overseers," appear. The formal priesthood developed more slowly, coming to light between 150 and 200.

The real genius of the organization was the office of bishop, and in the nature of this official we can find many of the reasons for both the Church's early success and its organizational stability in the Middle Ages. It was a strong office; the bishops held real authority. They maintained the discipline, spoke for the community, and kept the doctrine and practice pure by expelling those who would not conform and by a mechanism called "conference," which meant making all important decisions by conferring with other bishops.

For these and other reasons, the little cult began to attract converts, slowly at first, but then in greater numbers. By the year 100 there were Christian communities in almost all the major cities of the empire, and in the second century the Church grew to the point where the Roman officials were forced to deal with it.

The Post-Apostolic Church

Any religious organization faces many recurring problems: financial, moral, political, and organizational. Not least of these is the need to rein in disagreement. Religion by its nature seems to breed speculation, and once divergence in belief appears, splinter groups with competing organizational structures soon follow. Disagreement from the accepted belief, or heresy as Christians call it from the Greek word "to choose," was a problem that plagued the Christian Church in its beginnings and throughout its history. When the original apostles in Jerusalem died, the Church lost its only body with enough authority to quell disagreement. In many of the ensuing disputes, it was impossible to foresee which group or idea would win out to become orthodox and which would be labeled as heretical. Thus the Christian writings that survive from the period after the apostles died show a great concern with authority. The question simply stated is, "Who has the authority to say what true belief and proper practice are?" It was largely the office of bishop that kept dissent under control. The authoritative nature of this office along with a clear means of appointing one, and only one, official successor to a vacant episcopal post helped ensure that the post-apostolic Church was not fatally rent by dissent.

The Reaction of the Roman State

At first the Roman authorities ignored the Christians; they considered them just another Jewish sect, and as such they fell under the Jewish exemption from the obligation to participate in the state religion. As Christianity spread farther and farther from Jerusalem and more and more non-Jews became Christian, the authorities became aware that Christians were not Jews and consequently their refusal to worship the official cult became a breach of Roman law. Nonetheless, for the first two hundred years of the Christian era, the Roman government seems to have troubled itself only occasionally with Christians, and then usually when incited to do so by the Jews who, more than did the Romans, felt the new sect a threat to their ways.

In the third century matters changed. Christians were now present in great enough numbers and had spread themselves to enough major cities that the Romans could no longer simply pretend they did not matter. This is the century of the persecutions when, for various, mostly political reasons, the Romans tried to force Christians to participate in the state religion under penalty of death. (See Medieval Portraits.) Most of the persecutions took place in the eastern part of the Empire because that was where most Christians lived. Although most persecutions were

MEDIEVAL PORTRAITS

Vibia Perpetua, Early Christian Martyr

Perpetua was a young, wealthy woman who lived in Roman Carthage in northern Africa in the late second century. In 203 she, along with four companions, was imprisoned by the Roman authorities and later thrown to beasts in the arena because she was a confessed Christian. Written accounts of her life and sufferings soon began to circulate, and she became a famous and influential martyr for the Faith. In these accounts much of her story is told in the first person, based on a diary she may have written in prison. If these first-person versions are authentic, they contain one of the very rare surviving examples of an ancient text written by a woman. Some of them seem to have been edited by the famous theologian, Tertullian, who was a contemporary of Perpetua's and born at Carthage. She was also the subject of a sermon by Saint Augustine of Hippo, a city not far away.

The story of Perpetua's faith, arrest, and martyrdom was an inspiring example to early Christians. She was only twenty-two years old when arrested and was nursing a baby. The tender image of the young mother only heightened her representation of innocence. When arrested, she and her companions were still candidates for baptism, and the fact that they bravely had themselves baptized while in prison served to emphasize the strength of their faith. Even the following short excerpt makes clear how Perpetua exemplified the Christian virtues of uprightness, humility, charity, and faithfulness in suffering.

> Every one then left that dungeon and shifted for himself. I nursed my baby, who was faint from hunger. In my anxiety I spoke to my mother about the child, I tried to comfort my brother, and I gave the child into their charge. I was in pain because I saw them suffering out of pity for me. These were the trials I had to endure for many days. Then I got permission for my baby to stay with me in prison. At once I recovered my health, relieved as I was of my worry and anxiety over the child. My prison had suddenly become a palace, so that I wanted to be there rather than anywhere else.

Source: H. Musurillo, trans., "Life of Saint Perpetua," in Mary R. Lefkowitz and Maureen B. Fant, *Women's Life in Greece and Rome* (Baltimore, Md.: Johns Hopkins University Press, 1982) 266.

sporadic and local affairs promulgated by local Roman officials, there were some exercised throughout the Empire. The first came in 202 under the Emperor Severus, another in 250 under Decius, and the most famous, "The Great Persecution" of Diocletian in 303.

The persecutions were failures if we assume that their intention was to root out Christianity. In fact, in creating martyrs, they actually strengthened the Church by providing it with heroes. Martyr is the Greek word for witness, and obviously the ultimate witness of one's faith is to die for it. Many died horrible deaths and in so doing provided examples of the strength of the faith for others.

Martyrdom, however, had its dangerous side for the Church authorities as well. Although a snarling lion, a threatening sword, or crucifixion would seem to be things Christians would seek to avoid, many in fact actively sought ways to become martyrs. Actively seeking martyrdom, or any form of religious fanaticism, complicated the lines of religious authority for the established Church by offering a direct way to heaven without the Church acting as "the vessel of salvation," that is, without the Church acting as the necessary means through which Christians must seek to be saved. Many prohibitions against actively seeking martyrdom written by early Christian leaders have survived. These clearly demonstrate that although the martyrdom was revered, the Church nonetheless sought to control it

With Constantine's victory over Licinius in 323–324, the official persecutions of the Christians came to an end. With Constantine's official toleration and imperial favor, the number of Christians exploded during the fourth century. It is a reasonable estimate that during Constantine's reign, Christians comprised about one fourth of the Empire's population. By the end of the century, in the reign of Theodosius I (379–395), they were so much the majority that the emperor issued edicts intolerant of the pagans. The little cult from Galilee had done it. Despite its obscure beginnings and despite official persecutions, by the 320s it had become the religion of the imperial family and by the 390s the official religion of the whole Roman Empire. The Christians had conquered Rome.

ROME CONQUERS THE CHRISTIANS

Christianity's conquest of the late Roman Empire, that is, its acquisition of official status, marks a division in the history of the religion. The end of the persecutions and its newfound respectability did not bode a wholly rose-tinted future for the Church. In many ways the low-born sect that preached humility would actually suffer as its bishops now began to exercise influence over powerful officials of the Empire. In fact, for many analysts the change is so great that they see the shift from ancient to medieval Christianity here rather than some two centuries later with the political end of the Empire in the West and the advent of the barbarian kingdoms. The early Church had gathered the sacred texts, established the basic organizational structure of the Church, and developed the fundamental forms of its worship. The Church of late antiquity would work out its relationship with the state, adopt a different and more liturgical form of life for the ordinary believer, and develop a far more sophisticated body of theology, refining both its ideas of the good Christian life and of the nature of Christ. In other words, the Church would become far more institutionalized. The reasons for these fundamental changes are, broadly speaking, two: Christianity's new official status and the obvious delay of the *parousia,* or Christ's second coming.

As the emperors publicly espoused the Christian faith, Christianity not only became tolerated, but fashionable. No longer were its converts largely limited to the lower and middle social orders, but now the great, the educated, the rich, and the powerful flocked to be baptized. The effects of this movement on the religion were enormous. Many of these people represented ancient families whose cultural and educational traditions included the best the late Roman world had to offer. They were not likely to remain spellbound by a simple and humble cult that offered little intellectual and cultural refinement. Consequently along with its official status, Christianity increasingly developed an intellectually respectable and philosophically sophisticated theology. It is now among the Christians that we find the best philosophical minds of the late antique world and its most creative writers.

The writers of the New Testament seemed to promise that the *parousia* would occur quickly. Thus the biblical and the post-apostolic Church had little need for permanence since it was assumed that the end of the world lay in the immediate future. As the centuries rolled past, however, the Church saw that its role on earth was to last much longer than it had once thought. In the middle and especially in the late empire, the Church became a much more hardened and permanent institution, adopting those qualities that would give it a lasting existence on earth.

The Relationship of Church and State

From the reign of Constantine forward, the narrative sources most helpful in describing the relationship of the Roman state and the Christian Church were almost all written by Christian authors. The first and most influential was Eusebius, bishop of Caesarea from 314 to 340. Narrowly escaping the persecution of Diocletian, he went on to be made bishop of Caesarea and it was he who wrote the first ecclesiastical history we know of. His book covers the events up to the year 324.

Eusebius' *Ecclesiastical History* is important in many ways. In it he began the tradition in Christian histories of quoting sources and documents. This practice has preserved for us much important historical material that would have otherwise been lost. His is a type that sees history as the evidence of God's hand in human affairs. For instance, it was divine providence that created the Roman Peace of the first century in order that Christianity could spread. His great hero is Constantine, who as heir to the promises made to Abraham, acts out his part in God's script for the history of the world. The point cannot be emphasized enough: As Europe's intellectual life in the Middle Ages fell more and more under the exclusive purview of the Church, the fact that history was read, written, and deemed important is due in large part to the idea that it is the concrete record of God's actions. History in this sense becomes an extension of Scripture, concrete and observable, in contrast to theology, which is abstract and systematic.

Although most of what we know about Constantine and his relationship to the Christians comes from Eusebius's history, we do have other sources. The Theodosian Code, a compilation of Roman law issued in 438, preserves a great set of legal documents from Constantine's reign. We have some inscriptions carved in stone monuments and a pagan history written by Zosimus in 410. Zosimus was very pagan, very anti-Christian, and very hostile to Constantine. We also have enough of Constantine's official letters, speeches, and edicts that it is possible to trace some aspects of his own intellectual development in them. Some, as evidenced by their turgid and long-winded style, seem actually to have been drafted by the emperor himself.

Constantine had a direct connection to Christianity's humble nature in that his mother, Helena, herself a Christian, was of modest birth. She is often said to have been a barmaid and was concubine or perhaps wife to Constantine's father. There is, however, scholarly controversy about whether her son, a prince of the blood, adopted his mother's humble religion in his youth or came to it gradually over the course of his career.

The Christian sources report that Constantine had a significant encounter with Christianity in 312 at the famous, but misnamed, Battle of the Milvian Bridge, a bridge across the Tiber on the outskirts of Rome. The decisive part of the battle actually took place a good distance to the northwest of the bridge along the Flaminian Way. Before the battle, as the story goes, Constantine saw the words "In this sign thou shalt conquer" written in the clouds above a cross. He then commanded his soldiers to paint a Christian symbol on their shields and consequently soundly defeated his rival, Maxentius. Despite the fact that the story is recounted by Eusebius in his *Life of Constantine,* it does have a rather legendary ring to it. How much of Christianity he adopted at this point is difficult to say; it may not have been an advantageous political move on his part this early in his rule. Most influential people were still pagans and this was especially the case with the high military officials. The Roman coins minted for eight years after the battle still honor Hercules, Mars, Jupiter, and the Unconquerable Sun, something a zealous Christian emperor surely would have stopped. Despite the difficulties of interpreting the famous story, it is nonetheless important for us for two reasons. First, Christ plays the unmistakable role as war-god, a role he will play with distressing frequency throughout the whole of the Middle Ages. Second, Constantine's actions both before and after the battle indicate his need to propitiate his new divine protector. This idea of giving something to Christ so that he confer earthly advantages in return will also recur in the Christianity of the early medieval rulers.

Whether or not we assign Constantine's perception of a Christian sign in the clouds and his consequent conversion to history or to enthusiastic writing by Christian authors, the period of the battle and its immediate aftermath do mark a turning point for the new religion and its relationship with the Roman state. After 312 Constantine began to support the Church financially, he extended certain privileges to the Christian clergy, and he returned much of the Church's confiscated property. It is also at this time that the first Christian bishop seems to have become a part of the imperial court, Bishop Hosius of Cordova. His presence at court is an important harbinger of politics to come. As with most "dividing lines" in history, we should be careful not to regard the reign of Constantine as an impermeable barrier. Christianity had long been present in the imperial family before him, significantly in its women. Emperor Gallienus (253–268) had a Christian wife, the Empress Salonia, and Diocletian's wife and daughter were both Christians. Paganism also lingered in imperial circles long after Constantine's reign. There was still a large and influential pagan party at Constantinople late in Constantine's reign. Even at the end of the fourth century the pagan Themistius was governor of

Constantinople, "The Christian Rome," and tutor to a son of Theodosius I (379–395), the very emperor who closed the pagan temples and forbade pagan worship. But even if Constantine's reign is in some ways an artificial dividing line, it does indeed mark a turning point for the medieval historian, since the people of the Middle Ages certainly saw him as the first Christian emperor.

In 313 we find another famous "dividing line" marked by what has become known as the Edict of Milan. In this edict, which survives in two different versions, Constantine and Licinius, the emperor in the East, declared toleration for all religions equally and granted the Church legal status under the law. This edict was not important for the West since Constantine had already gone further than its provisions in his relationship with the Christians there, but for the East it was important and novel. It should have meant the end of the persecutions of the Christians and seems an obvious bid for their political support. But war soon broke out between Licinius and Constantine. Constantine is the unabashed hero of the Christian authors reporting these conflicts since Licinius reverted to persecuting Christians. In 324, after years of intermittent war, Licinius fell and Constantine, the "first Christian emperor," now ruled the whole empire.

Through all of this we see the bond between church and state tightening more and more. Constantine began to favor Christians in high offices and to use them increasingly as advisors at the imperial court. He built church buildings all over the Empire, including the first basilica of Holy Wisdom at Byzantium; confiscated pagan temple treasuries; restored confiscated properties to the Church; refurbished church buildings; and granted tax concessions to the Christian clergy. In 316 he acted as a judge in a dispute in the Church in North Africa where a divergent group of Christians called the Donatists had taken firm root. Again in 325 it was he who summoned the great Church Council of Nicaea to deal with the heresy called Arianism. This council, as we shall see, had to settle a sophisticated theological question concerning the nature of Christ, but also of great concern to the emperor was the preservation of unity within the Church, now an important part of the Empire. The increasing convergence of Church and state meant that ecclesiastical issues became political ones and vice versa. Not only were Christians becoming important Roman officials, but important Romans were becoming Christian.

Between 324 and 330 Constantine built his new imperial capital at Byzantium on the Bosphorus. His wars with Licinius had taught him the strategic importance of the place, and it was geographically far more sensibly located within the empire than was Rome. The new capital in the East meant that the Roman government was now in that part of the empire that was most heavily Christian, and the architecture of the city reflects the Christian influence. "New Rome," soon to be named Constantinople, sported Christian churches. Significantly, Constantine built no pagan temples there; the old Roman gods were all but vanquished from New Rome.

Christianity and the Roman state continued their new partnership under Constantine's successors. His third son, Constantius II (337–361), who succeeded him as emperor in the East, openly espoused a heresy called Arianism, the very one that Constantine's Council of Nicaea had been called to settle. We find Arian bishops replacing orthodox ones in several dioceses, and they appear at the imperial court. Constantius' brother, Constans, who ruled the West (337–350), supported the orthodox party and served to keep Constantius' Arian policies somewhat in check. Nonetheless, it was during the reign of Constantius II that Ulfilas, a convinced Arian bishop, set out on his mission to the Goths, the dominant barbarian tribe living to the north and northwest of Constantinople. Ulfilas had been born among the Goths and spoke their language. He translated the Bible into Gothic and provided them with a Gothic creed which was Arian in its theology. His efforts helped the barbarian peoples living in the Balkans and around the Black Sea to take up Christianity in its Arian form. The fact that they espoused a different type of Christianity from that practiced in the Roman West had important political and social consequences for the history of the early Middle Ages as they moved across the frontiers of the empire and established their states on formerly Roman soil in the fifth and sixth centuries.

The Christians lost influence in the imperial government for a while under the short reign of Constantius II's successor, Julian (361–363). Julian favored paganism in a mystical Neoplatonic form, but his reign was short, and the Church soon regained its former position. By the end of the century it was unthinkable that the emperor would not be a convinced Christian. Theodosius I (379–395) was just such a pious ruler. So closely had the Roman state become bound to the Christian religion that Theodosius thought it prudent to quickly put down any divergent Christian movement or doctrine. He even ordained the death penalty for certain heretical sects. In 394 he closed the pagan temples and forbade pagan worship throughout the empire. The pagan persecution of the Christians had long been over, and now the long Christian persecution of pagans was beginning.

Our brief look here at the Christians and the Roman state in the course of the fourth century has shown the high politics becoming increasingly Christian. As we look ahead to the fifth century, we see the parallel development in the opposite direction; that is, we see the Church becoming increasingly political. Obviously the important clergymen learned to use the government to get their way in ecclesiastical matters, but more significantly the common people found themselves turning more and more to the Church with matters they had formerly brought to the state. This development was much more pronounced in the West than in the East. With the foreign invasions, civil wars, economic problems, and the shift of the imperial government eastwards to Constantinople, the Roman government in the West was no longer the effective organ it had been. Often its structure was in chaos, its coffers empty, and its leaders absent. The local church, on the other hand, with its strong sense of community and its strong leadership, appeared in a more stable position than did the government. Consequently we find bishops providing food for their cities' poor, repairing buildings, organizing municipal services, and even building defenses. Ordinary people would now turn to their bishop to settle their disputes where they had formerly brought them before a governmental court.

The Church not only fulfilled local political functions but began to play much of the role of the national government as well. In the mid-fifth century, in 451, we find shrewd Pope Leo I (440–461) concluding a treaty with the Huns when they, under their famous leader, Attila, threatened to wreak destruction on Italy. Three years latter we also find Pope Leo I treating with the Vandals when they attacked. By the year 500, Church and State at both the local and the national levels had become closely entwined, and it would be some six hundred years before they would begin to slowly seperate from each other.

The Heresies

After Constantine's reign the theological need was not so much to defend the faith against nonbelievers as to preserve its unity against heresy, or false Christian teaching. Consequently, Christians once again direct their theological works to Christians rather than outsiders. Most of the controversy was Christological, that is, concerned about the nature of Christ, and broadly speaking, most of it dealt with two heretical propositions. First, that Christ had no human nature, the position maintained by the Monophysites, Cathars, and Manichaes, to name the most famous groups. And second was the proposition that Christ did not have a fully divine nature, the position of the Arians. Most of these groups espouse various forms of "dualism," or the contention that reality is made up of two antagonistic parts, a material world, usually seen as evil, and a spiritual world that was of a higher order and good. Orthodox Christianity sees both the material and the spiritual as created by God and represented in the unified human and divine nature of Christ, and therefore both as good.

Beginning in the second century, many Christians followed a form of metaphysical dualism called Gnosticism. The Gnostics, Greek for "those who know," believed in the saving power of knowledge revealed by God. This knowledge was usually secret and passed with great care to the initiate. It had the power to save by returning the soul of the believer, or knower, from the evil material world to the holy spiritual one. In Gnostic theology, the material world was not created by God, who is good, but by a demiurge, who made the world either by accident or out of evil. Christ's nature, too, is only divine and he merely passed through a human appearance rather than becoming truly human, as orthodox Christianity teaches. Although certain parts of Gnostic thinking can be found in pre-Christian thought, it first appears as an organized sect among the Christians. It went on to heavily influence the third-century Persian religion called Manichaeism and much of it survived into various later Christian heresies in the West. It was a powerful influence.

Another heresy, Arianism, attracted many adherents, some of whom were extremely influential. Constantine's sister, Constantia, and his third son and successor in the East, Constantius II (337–361), both openly espoused it. Despite the fact that the orthodox party won out at Constantine's great Church Council at Nicaea in 325, the heresy continued to flourish. In the fourth century, Arian bishops intermittently replaced orthodox ones in several important sees and some cities experienced two bishops simultaneously, one orthodox and one Arian.

In the fifth and sixth centuries, the Monophysite teaching that Christ was wholly divine and not "corrupted" by a human nature became popular in the East. Many important Christians, including some bishops of Alexandria and Antioch were Monophysites. Although the heresy was condemned in 451 by the famous

Council of Chalcedon, it continued to thrive, finding large followings in Syria, Egypt, and Ethiopia, eventually producing separate Coptic, Armenian, and Jacobite (Syrian) churches.

Disagreement among Christian groups was widespread in the late Roman Empire and was not always purely or even primarily caused by disagreement in doctrine. Regional feelings, imperial support for one party or the other, local politics, and economic differences could all affect the strength and destiny of a group and its teaching. The Donatists, for example, established a separate church organization in North Africa around Carthage in the fourth century. Much of their popularity was due to local resentment of Rome and its officials along with social differences between the more rural Donatists and the more urban orthodox Catholics. Despite many Roman attempts at repression or reconciliation, the Donatists lasted until the Arab conquest of North Africa in the seventh century. With great support from the Emperor Theodosius, the Church managed to achieve doctrinal harmony with the Arians, at least officially on orthodox terms at the Council of Constantinople in 381. But even given the official agreement, the heresy continued to exist among the barbarian peoples then living outside the empire to the north around the Black Sea. They would carry it with them as they invaded western Europe in the fifth century where the Arian Church would again come into conflict with orthodox Christianity. The Coptic Church in Egypt and Ethiopia is still Monophysite today.

Lives of the Ordinary Christians

By the time the fifth century ended, most ordinary people living in the Mediterranean lands of the Roman Empire were Christians. There were still large pockets of followers of other beliefs, but for the most part Christianity had become the Roman religion. As the great senatorial families began to exercise their traditional roles in local leadership through the position of bishop, so too the bonds of ordinary people's loyalty were tugged more and more toward the Church. Less and less was it the local citadel, municipal buildings, or pagan temples that elicited the patriotism and pride of the local denizen, but now more and more it was the church building, usually endowed by the munificence of a rich local family.

Ironically, if naturally, the humble sect from Galilee developed on two increasingly divergent levels. As the mighty of the empire became Christian, and Christianity increased its need for cultural and intellectual sophistication in order to satisfy them, its theology, the liturgy of its worship, and its leadership fell from the grasp of fishermen and tent makers and was restricted to the Empire's privileged. Theirs was a splendid life of pomp, politics, administration, comfort, and erudition all carried out in an overly polished and artificial Latin increasingly less comprehensible to ordinary Christians. At the other end of the social ladder, the mass of the faithful found their religious life in the quiet comfort of routinized worship and festival.

The ways that ordinary Christians worshipped, too, had changed by the late empire. By the year 400, the language of Christian worship in the West had shifted from Greek to Latin. As we saw, early Christian worship was rather simple, consisting of readings from sacred texts, singing the Jewish Psalms, praying, and eating together. But as the Church became hierarchical and then became the vehicle of official Roman religious life, Christian worship became more formalized and dependent upon holy and mysterious actions performed by priests. What began as the *agape,* or love feast and a real meal, very quickly (before the mid-second century) became a ceremony, the eucharist, embodying the ancient theology of thanksgiving and sacrifice. The eucharist became the center piece of Christian worship and was surrounded by a complex of prayers, responses, hymns, rites, and readings that we group under the heading, liturgy. Laymen were not competent to conduct the complicated liturgy; it demanded a highly trained formal priesthood. The Christian priesthood grew up during the second century and by the late empire it already had a long history behind it. The conduct of worship was in the priest's hands, and ordinary lay people participated in most of it by observing and reciting certain assenting responses.

The Cult of the Saints

As Christ, the humble Galilean, came more and more to resemble a far-off and majestic emperor of heaven, ordinary people focused their religious devotion more and more on a palpable and accessible protector of their interests: the local saint. The saint, a holy and mysterious figure from the past, had earned the right through her or his virtuous life and perhaps martyrdom to enjoy immediate admission into heaven at death. Even though saints were not normally of humble birth themselves, ordinary Christians felt a great affinity for them because they were human and perhaps more importantly, local, and thus close to and interested in the ordinary Christian's human life. The saints' ability to direct God's power was their most important property; this was the reason Christians, both humble and not so, prayed to them and became devoted to them. The saint could ask God to heal, protect, cause a good harvest, or cause any number of other earthly benefits. They were especially interested in the places that housed what they had left behind on earth, their relics. Relics could be parts of a saint's body, clothes, or other intimate possession. At the same time as bishops began to take on the functions of Roman secular officials, the saints began to usurp the functions of those officials' erstwhile ancient gods. The two developments rest in the same historical causes.

The Church of the elite, while practicing a religious life different from that of the people, was nonetheless very aware of its responsibility to them. Many sermons and homilies aimed at the populace survive. These with simpler ideas and in simpler language sought to explain the more complicated mysteries and tenets of the religion. Many lives of the saints were written in order to preserve and promote them as focal points for Christian devotion.

Not all saints' lives and sermons were aimed at the ordinary lay person. The saint also had a vital role to play in sophisticated Christian metaphysics. He or she formed an important metaphysical link between the material world and the spiritual realm that lay beyond it. This is why the saints' graves became particular points of devotion. In the spiritual world, the dead and the living are both part of the same Church. Although the Church of the common folk and of the educated elite may have been different in many ways, the saints and their relics helped to unite both with the world beyond.

THE FATHERS OF THE CHURCH

When the thinkers of the Middle Ages looked back to the beginnings of their religion, they saw almost nothing of ordinary Christians, except for those few who had become saints and had their lives written or their images preserved in stone or mosaic. But they were very aware of the teachings of the great theologians who lived between the time of the apostles and the end of Roman rule in the West. This is the age of the Fathers of the Church, and the study of their lives and their teaching is now called patristics. It is not necessary to be a specialist in patristics to understand the history of thought in the Middle Ages (although it would help), but it is necessary at least to recognize the origin of questions that often occupied medieval thinkers. As they wrestled with important problems, they turned to the authorities of the patristic age for clarification and support of various theological positions. The Fathers formed a level of authority second only to the Bible in the intellectual life of the Middle Ages; we find their works read, studied, and extensively quoted in every age of the medieval period.

Patristic Thought

There are three major tenets of Christianity that seem to recur as troublesome and difficult to accept. First is its view of the Godhead in three persons: Father, Son, and Holy Spirit. Unless handled very expertly, this can quickly appear as polytheism with three separate gods. Second is the view that God created the physical world. For those who see the physical world as basically evil, or at least as comprising evil, and many Christians have tended to view it this way, it is difficult to see how a good God could have created it. And third, the Christian doctrine that Christ was both true God and true man is a difficult proposition. It is much easier to grasp Christ as purely divine than it is also to make room in him for a truly human nature. It was largely these three problems that concerned patristic thinkers, and it was the Fathers who developed the great body of systematic Christian theology in seeking solutions to them.

The fact that the patristic age developed systematic theology is another sign that the Church was settling in for the long duration. The apostles and the other Biblical authors had written their works for people who were already Christian, for "those that have eyes to see." But in the second century, as Christianity came under fire from nonbelievers, it became necessary to defend, in Greek "to apologize," the new sect to the outside world. The great apologists, people like Aristides (before 138), Justin Martyr (c. 100–165), Tertullian (c. 160–225), and Minucius Felix (c. 200), produced some marvelous theology as they defended the Christians against accusations of incest, cannibalism, and drunkenness by explaining the religion and its practices to Greeks and Jews.

The most important centers of Greek patristic thought were Cappadocia, the heavily Christian section of Asia Minor; and Alexandria, the great Hellenistic city on the western edge of the Nile delta in Egypt. These produced the Greek Fathers, complicated and mysterious men like Basil, Gregory of Nyssa, Gregory of Nazianzus, Clement of Alexandria, Cyril, and Origen. It was they who, using the philosophical concepts of the Platonic notion of reality, developed Christianity's theological vocabulary and described its intricate vision of the nature of the Divine. These men laid the foundations of Christian theology, and the medieval thinkers used their works and quoted extensively from them. For most of the Middle Ages, access to the Greek Fathers was limited by availability of Latin translations since the ability to read Greek died out in the Latin West, even among the most learned. The Latin Fathers, on the other hand, men like Tertullian, Ambrose, Jerome, and especially Augustine of Hippo, presented no language barrier to the West and their influence on medieval thinking was enormous.

Ambrose (c. 339–397)

Ambrose was born into a Roman aristocratic family in Trier, in what is now southwestern Germany, son of the Roman Praetorian Prefect of Gaul. He enjoyed an excellent classical education and began his adult life as a lawyer, working his way up the ladder of Roman officialdom. In 370 he was appointed governor of Aemilia-Liguria, in northwestern Italy, with his administrative center at Milan. In 374 his ecclesiastical career began, and as typical for a man of his rank and position in the fourth century, it began at the top. He was elected bishop of Milan, despite the fact that he was not yet a priest, nor even baptized. Ambrose was still a catechumen, or candidate for baptism. But in short order he was both baptized and ordained and then assumed the episcopacy.

In 375, a year after Ambrose's election, the Emperor Valentinian I died, and his four-year-old son, Valentinian II, became emperor in the West with his seat at Milan. This meant that the imperial court lay within Ambrose's diocese and that Ambrose was the emperor's bishop. Much of Ambrose's importance for the Middle Ages comes from the example he set as the brave bishop who stood up to secular power when he considered it to err morally. Ambrose stood up to no less a power than the imperial one. He managed to force the empress, Justina, young Valentinian II's mother, to abandon her demands for a church for Arian soldiers of the imperial guard by barricading himself and some of his clergy in the building and refusing to surrender it. A famous debate between Ambrose and Symmachus, one of the last aristocratic pagans of the city of Rome, broke out because Symmachus wanted to restore a statue of the pagan god of victory to its traditional place in the Roman Senate House. Ambrose strongly objected and managed to force Valentinian to disallow the restoration by threatening to withhold the sacraments from him. Ambrose is more famous for standing up to Theodosius, the powerful Eastern emperor. When some rioting Christians burned down a synagogue, Theodosius ordered it rebuilt at the Church's expense, but Ambrose objected. Ambrose actually withheld the sacraments from Theodosius because of a massacre the emperor had ordered at Thessalonica until he had humbly done penance for the crime. These actions set a strong example for later medieval ideas that sought to demarcate the Church's authority from the emperor's authority, ideas that were always much stronger in the West than they were in the East where Church and state were much more tightly fused.

Ambrose provided another important example in that he brought to the episcopacy many of the characteristics of stable, Roman, bureaucratic administration. He

Bishop Ambrose of Milan (339–397)
This mosaic of Ambrose, the powerful bishop of Milan and friend and mentor of Saint Augustine, was completed within a hundred years of his death. It shows the bishop dressed as a Roman aristocrat and may be a good representation of his actual appearance.
Scala/Art Resource, NY.

did much to propel the change in the nature of the bishop's position from one of wise and *ad hoc* leader of a city's Christian community to one of an authoritarian, powerful, efficient, and increasingly legalistic local official.

His intellectual influence on the early medieval Church was also immense, not least because of the great personal influence he exercised on Augustine. He was fluent in Greek and thus introduced much Eastern thought into the West. He fostered monasticism. His sermons, letters, and moral and theological tracts were cherished reading throughout the Middle Ages, and some of his hymns still form popular parts of Christian worship.

Jerome (c. 342–420)

Unlike most other great figures in the early Church, Jerome never held high ecclesiastical office. He was a scholar, a rather quiet and personally timid man. He too came from a privileged background and was educated at Rome. Even as a young man he preferred the ascetic life and he traveled extensively, visiting Christian monks and hermits in Syria, Palestine, and Egypt, sometimes remaining for years secluded in remote areas. He also visited the great cities of Antioch, Constantinople, and Rome, where in 382 we find him working as secretary to Pope Damasus.

In 386 he settled into the monastic life near Bethlehem, were he remained until his death in 420.

Jerome was an inspiring intellectual, possessed of a powerful mind, a love of learning, and a passion for elegant expression. He was a master of dialogue, often the form used by ancient thinkers to express important ideas. His love for literature posed a profound problem of conscience for him since most literary works were pagan and thus dangerously devoid of Christian content. This inner conflict found expression in his famous dream where he appears in heaven and is accused of being a Ciceronian and not a Christian.

Jerome wrote an immense amount: history, biography, translations into Latin of important Christian Greek theology, tracts against heretics, and wonderful letters. His most important achievement, however, was his Latin translation of the Bible, known as the *Vulgate*. By the late fourth century, several Latin versions of the Bible were in circulation in the West, but they varied greatly among themselves and were not of satisfactory quality. To remedy this sorry state, Pope Damasus asked Jerome to take on the formidable task of producing a Latin Bible. The result was a masterpiece. In a style falling happily between the erudite polish of the Ciceronian idiom and simple, everyday language, Jerome's Latin moves in marvelous cadence with stunning lexical precision and yet preserves a clarity that makes it easily readable without offending the ear of most intellectuals. His achievement shows his enormous literary skill. Christianity is a very bookish religion: The inspired word of its God is a book, the Bible, and Christ himself is called "the Word" in the Gospel of John. Jerome's wonderful sensitivity to the meaning of words meant he was able to move beyond mere translation to transpose the holy book and holy Word of a neareastern people into the language and culture of the West.

Augustine of Hippo (354–430)

By far the most influential of the Latin Fathers was the intense Augustine of Hippo. A prolific writer, the ink flowed from his quill almost as freely as the emotions flowed from his soul. The force of his intellect, the power of his personality, and the infectious nature of his literary style turned the Christian world in the West decidedly Augustinian. It is no exaggeration to claim that Augustine of Hippo governed the way most learned people in the West thought for over 1000 years. He is still, in the early twenty-first century, required reading in most courses of Christian theological training. Why was it that this bishop of a medium-sized, North African town to the west of Carthage came to have such immense sway?

Augustine is often credited with the synthesis of Christian dogma and Greek, that is Platonic metaphysics. Indeed his works, even his seemingly most personal ones, seethe with Greek thought. Even though the Greek Fathers before him, and especially Origen, had merged Biblical theology with sophisticated Greek thinking, they had done so in the Greek language and in the systematic, cerebral fashion of philosophers. Augustine wrote in Latin and he was not a philosopher in the systematic way that, for instance, Aristotle and Origen had been; Augustine was first and foremost a pastor and bishop. His primary concern was not philosophical systems but the salvation of his flock (see Medieval Voices). His theology and philos-

MEDIEVAL VOICES

Saint Augustine of Hippo Talks to God

The Confessions, *a title best translated as "Acknowledgements" or "Openly Declared Truths," is Augustine's spiritual and intellectual autobiography. In startling personal language, he agonizes over how he came to profess Christianity. The purpose of his book is not simply to be a record, but as a good bishop and pastor he seeks to prevent others from making his mistakes and to help save their souls.*

I now wish to call to mind the foulness I have transacted and the carnal corruptions of my soul, not because I love them but so that I may love you, oh my God. For love of your love I do it, reflecting upon my most wicked ways in bitterness of my recollection, that you may grow sweet to me, oh sweetness never false; happy and carefree sweetness. And I gather myself together out of that dissipated state in which I was torn to pieces. While turned from you, the one, I faded away into the many.

At a certain point in my youth, I burned to take my fill of hell and I dared to run wild in various and shady loves, *my beauty wasted away*, and I stank in your eyes, pleasing myself and desirous to please the eyes of men. . . .

Source: Augustine, *Confessions*, II-1.

ophy are exquisite bastions of Christian orthodoxy, but he expresses them in a personal and often tumultuously emotional way. For instance in his *Confessions,* he addresses God as "you," as if he were talking personally to some great teacher, friend, or master. A shockingly revolutionary idea for its time and one that continued to strike chords in the medieval mind which, as we shall see, came more and more to regard lines of authority not as abstract loyalty, but as extremely personal. Augustine's was a theology not merely of the mind, but a philosophy wrung through agonizing human experience.

Augustine saw mankind as suffering, enslaved to evil. This differs greatly from the classical conception where, except for the intervention of fate, mankind was largely in control of its own destiny. For Augustine mankind has a sort of free will; it can choose to do good, but it is so enslaved to evil that it cannot do good without God's help. This help, called "grace," forms a basic part of Augustinian thought. Augustine is taken up with this concept and never tires of relating how poor, miserable mankind is driven to incredible depths of suffering by its pride, greed, passions, and lust for power. Obviously this too is a precocious blueprint for the view of ordinary earthly life in the Middle Ages.

A fascinating aside about Augustine, more important for historians perhaps than it was for medieval thinkers (indeed they may not have noticed it in his work), is that Augustine fundamentally changed the conception about how history moves. The ancient concept, such as found in Thucydides or Livy, was that history moves in recurring cycles. Augustine, however, saw human history as the unfolding of

God's grand plan for mankind and as such it was teleological or goal-directed. For him, history did not move in cycles but in a straight line. This idea forms part of our modern notion of progress.

The Church Fathers and Women

There is an element of misogyny in patristic thought that in many ways is difficult to explain. Tertullian especially rails against the female sex. Eve is portrayed as an agent of the devil and Jezebel too is pulled from the Old Testament and used as an example of woman's evil nature in patristic writing. The position of women in all societies of the ancient world was decidedly inferior to that of men. Sometimes their lot was abysmal, as in classical Greece, and sometimes they fared somewhat better, as in Greece's heroic era or in the late Roman cities, but never did they approach anything resembling equality with the males. Patristic teaching, however, goes further than simply reflecting women's inferior social state; women were pictured as evil. This can appear all the more surprising since many central figures in the New Testament, in the history of the early Church, in the imperial family, and among the Christian saints and martyrs were women. Christian women served as deacons and were indispensable to the fortunes of the Church as endowers of buildings and influential figures at court.

Obviously a huge dichotomy exists between the practice of the ancient Church, which relied upon women and obviously loved and valued them, and much patristic teaching. The problem with females for much of patristic thought, as it would be for many medieval writers, is the obvious fusion of the female with earthly human life. It is women who give birth, and more importantly from a male perspective, it is the female who provides carnal pleasure. Both of these tie mankind (malekind) to this world and distract him from the next. If the physical world is viewed as evil, then the ties that bind mankind to the physical are also evil. But even in the orthodox Christian view of the physical world as good, anything from it that diverts attention from the spiritual performs an evil function. The distinction between the "evil" which this view of female nature entails and the women themselves can be difficult to explain and to understand. Patristic writing reflects the difficulty.

The Vessel of Ancient Culture

It is no coincidence that our words "cult" and "culture" share a common root. For the Middle Ages, Christianity was not only the era's nearly exclusive religious cult, but it was also the purveyor of a good deal of its common culture and almost all of its high, or literate, culture. By the mid-seventh century most literate people in Western Europe were clerics, and Christianity thus became the nearly exclusive vessel which freighted ancient literary culture into the Middle Ages. To the secularly minded, the importance of Christianity's function in the cultural sector rivals or perhaps exceeds its religious one.

It is in many ways a miracle that ancient secular literature survived at all: Christians were not always the most sympathetic custodians of such writings. Works that did not espouse the truths of Christianity could be at best considered a waste of time and at worst downright dangerous. Before the invention of the printing press, for a work to survive it had to be copied so as not to be dependent upon the vagaries of one or two storage places. Despite many warnings about the dangers of ancient pagan literature, the works were nonetheless copied by Christians. The fact that Christians did so was due in great part to the influence of very few people, men like Boethius and Cassiordorus (see Chapter 3) and especially Benedict of Nursia (Chapter 6).

Summary

As the European Middle Ages began, the Latin West was soundly Christian. The ancient Church had established its holy texts, delineated the forms of Christian worship, developed a sophisticated and systematic theology, and created an organizational structure that not only governed Europe's religious life but also performed many of what we would call political functions.

What began as a small Jewish sect grew to become the official Roman religion. The route to official status was not without disagreement. Christians often disagreed among themselves and created many divergent groups. Those whose ideas did not win out were often repressed or even persecuted. Out of these disagreements and with the aid of the Fathers, the Church developed the basic precepts of Christian teaching and practice. As the Church grew, it began to take on many of the functions formerly performed by the Roman state. When the barbarians arrived to rule the former Roman West, they saw no difference between Christian culture and Roman culture nor between Christians and Romans. Christ had become the Roman God.

NOTES:

1. Edward Gibbon, J. B. Bury, ed., *The Decline and Fall of the Roman Empire*, vol. I (New York: Heritage Press, 1946) 348–381.

CHAPTER 3

∼

Barbarians Enter the Empire, 275–640

I n the year 370 most people living along the Mediterranean felt secure. The
troubles of the third century were now a misty hundred years in the past.
Granted, their world had changed: the old Roman gods had given way to a new
Christian one; taxes were higher; and the splendid new buildings were mostly privately funded religious ones rather than publicly funded civic ones. But in general,
life was as it should be: peaceful, prosperous, and Roman. But even as "their sea"
peacefully washed the Romans' shores, storms brewing in the north and east were
about to change the Roman world forever.

The agents of change were peoples the Romans called German, although the
peoples themselves did not perceive any such overarching ethnic unity. The Germans were living in northern Europe, largely between the Elbe and the Oder Rivers
when the Mediterranean peoples first learned about them. By the first century A.D.
the Germans inhabited lands from the lower Rhine all the way to the northern and
western shores of the Black Sea.

The movement of these peoples into the Roman Empire in the fifth and sixth
centuries used to be called the barbarian invasions, but now historians generally
prefer words such as migration, accommodation, and transformation to describe
the process. Long before the fifth century, many barbarians were already living
within the empire. They were there as slaves, as soldiers in Roman armies, and as
settlers invited by the Roman government to help protect the borders. All the barbarians who eventually established kingdoms on Roman soil had actually at one
time or another been invited to settle within the empire as "federated peoples."
They had received subsidies from the Romans as well as provided troops. Although
the movement of the barbarians was by no means lacking in battles and bloodshed,
much of the settlement was done peacefully in accordance with treaties and other
accommodating arrangements worked out with the Romans. Their inclusion in the
late Roman world changed it. The most fundamental change disrupted the political structure, but we shall also find much in early medieval thought, art, religion,
and social values that can be traced to them.

MIGRATING PEOPLES: POLITICAL DISRUPTION

The barbarians were not originally grouped into clearly defined large tribes. During the migrations, the large political units, or tribes, by which they are usually known—Franks, Goths, Vandals and so on—were really made up of smaller units that either joined together or went their own ways depending on the needs of the times. The leader of one of these smaller units the Romans called a *rex* (king), if he held his position largely by birth and a *dux* (war-leader) if he were chosen for military purposes. These Latin terms, however, carry very Roman ideas with them and often do not accurately convey the nature of the authority exercised by a barbarian king or war-leader. A king, and rarely a queen, owed his or her position to more than just royal birth; real political and military ability were usually also required.

The migrations in the fifth century were different from earlier ones because the barbarians governed their own large political units on formerly Roman soil. It was in their reaction to Rome and in the process of establishing their kingdoms within the Empire that they formed themselves into the large political units often called the barbarian tribes. We shall first watch the various peoples as they enter western Europe and establish themselves politically, and then examine in somewhat more detail the societies within two of these new kingdoms: the Ostrogothic one in Italy and the Frankish one in northern Europe.

The Visigoths

Early in the third century, Gothic peoples were living along the shores of the Black Sea. For reasons that historians do not fully understand, but that probably had to do with the need for more food, the Goths banded together politically into two large groups and began to raid the Roman Empire. The larger and more powerful of the two was formed by those living on the western side of the Gothic area and later became known as the Visigoths. The smaller of the two is commonly called the Ostrogoths. In the third century, the Visigoths overran and settled Dacia, a Roman province on the north side of the Danube, now Transylvania in modern Romania. The Emperor Aurelian, in about 275, withdrew the Roman army and administration from Dacia and left it to the Visigoths, thus making the Danube once more the border of the Empire. The Ostrogoths, on the other hand, did not yet settle on imperial land but continued to dominate the land to the north of the Black Sea, which is now part of modern Ukraine.

The situation changed very little for about 100 years. Here, as in most places attached to the Romans and their sea, the fourth century ticked off its years in comparative peace. Meanwhile, however, something was happening on the steppes of Asia or perhaps in China. Historians are not sure what it was, but it caused the Huns, the most feared of all the barbarian peoples who invaded Europe in the early Middle Ages, to move westward. In 370 the Huns conquered the Ostrogoths in Ukraine and six years later fell upon the Visigoths in Dacia, throwing them into panic and turmoil. Trapped, hungry, and desperate, the Visigoths, along with some Ostrogothic refugees, moved south to the banks of the Danube and begged the

---

MEDIEVAL VOICES

The Roman Historian Ammianus Marcellinus (c. 330–395) Describes the "Invasion" of the Visigoths

Yet when the report crept widely among the other tribes of the Goths that a race of men never before imagined [the Huns] had arisen from a hidden fold of the earth and, like a blizzard from high up the mountains, was shaking and destroying whatever was situated in its path, the greater part of the people, who, worn out by lack of necessities, had deserted Athanaricus, were looking for a home removed from all knowledge of the barbarians. Deliberating at length about what seat to choose, they decided that the safe haven of Thrace would be fitting for them for two reasons: because it had very rich grazing land and because it was cut off by the full flooding of the Danube from their fields [in Dacia]which now lay open to the thunderbolts of foreign Mars.

Therefore under their leader, Alavivus, they occupied the banks of the Danube, and sending envoys to Valens, with humble petition begged to be taken in, promising that they would both live peacefully and would furnish auxiliaries, if circumstances required. . . . Accordingly, having obtained by the emperor's permission the opportunity of crossing the Danube and settling parts of Thrace, they were ferried across for some nights and days placed by companies in boats, on rafts, and in hollowed tree-trunks. Some, on account of the overcrowding, struggled against the force of the water and tried to swim, but many were swallowed by the river, by far the most dangerous of all, being swollen then by frequent rain.

Source: History, XXXI, 3, 8 to 4, 5.

Roman emperor, Valens, to take them into the safety of the Roman provinces south of the river. The emperor agreed, largely because he saw the possibility of many Gothic recruits for his armies. Then in a frantic operation, complete with makeshift boats and rafts, the Romans ferried the Visigoths across the treacherous lower Danube into the Balkan provinces. Such was the nature of one of the major barbarian "invasions" (see Medieval Voices).

The settlement of the Visigoths did not go well. With no precedent for settling a whole people quickly in Roman lands, a great deal of friction resulted. It seems, too, that the local Roman officials saw the chance for quick money by demanding payment from the Visigoths for supplies the imperial government had meant them to have without charge. On August 9, 378, a mere two years after the Visigoths' hasty crossing of the Danube, it came to a major confrontation between the two sides at the battle of Adrianople. The barbarians gained a complete victory, the Romans a complete disgrace. The Visigothic horsemen stampeded across the Roman infantry inflicting death and havoc. Two thirds of the Romans were killed, including Emperor Valens himself.

This battle is a famous one. The Roman historian, Ammianus Marcellinus, has left us a detailed account of it. It is prudent, as we try to understand medieval history, not to make too much of battles. Despite the way they are often treated, they are more apt to represent the symptoms than the causes of important historical change. Adrianople, too, points up several important characteristics of the period.

The Goths were successful on the battlefield at Adrianople not so much because of their own superiority but because of poor Roman coordination or even downright ineptitude. To many minds, Valens got what he deserved at Adrianople. At the very moment when the men of his army were feeling Gothic swords in their throats, another huge Roman army under the command of Gratian, emperor in the West, was on its way from Italy to help the eastern Romans. Valens knew of Gratian's approach and purposely engaged the Goths before Gratian could arrive so that he would not have to share the glory of victory. Most experts speculate that the Goths would not have prevailed against a combined Roman force. This would come to be the way of many barbarian incursions; that is, they were not of sufficient military strength to overwhelm a coordinated Roman resistance, but the Romans were all too often incapable of the requisite coordination.

Although the Visigoths defeated the Romans at Adrianople, they were unable to follow up their victory and take the nearby capital, Constantinople. This too was to become a theme of warfare for the coming age. The Romans had much more success against the barbarians when they avoided large battles and instead used their forts and cities as well-defended points from which to wear the enemy down, largely by preventing them from obtaining adequate supplies. Such tactics do not make dazzling reputations for heroic generals and emperors, but they do eventually force even warlike migrating peoples at a vulnerable distance from dependable supplies to negotiate. Although the Goths ravaged Thrace and Macedonia for two years after the battle of Adrianople, they eventually came to negotiate with the Romans and settle down on allotted lands.

And finally, we see in Adrianople the role of food. Peoples constantly on the move have a desperate need for food since planting crops and fattening animals requires staying put. The friction between Goth and Roman that led to the battle came about because the Goths needed food. According to Ammianus, the barbarian request to settle in Thrace was based in large part on the fact that Thrace had good grazing land. Food was a constant problem for nearly all the barbarian peoples, and it is no coincidence that it was the breadbaskets of the Empire— Africa, Italy, and southern Gaul—that attracted them.

In 395 the Visigoths took a new step: they elected one king—the inscrutable Alaric—to command many of the various groups. This is a major political step indicating that the Visigoths were organizing themselves into a larger political unit. This new structure was a reaction to the fact that they now faced a large and organized enemy, the Romans, rather than the smaller and varying confederations of other barbarian peoples that had threatened them before.

Alaric's position was different from earlier Visigothic leaders'. Not only was he now head of a much larger political group, but he also had to operate within the world of Roman imperial politics. Although settled within the Empire, the Visigoths did not have enough land to support themselves and thus lived from imperial subsidies given in return for providing troops. The system did not function without pressure, and Alaric continued to lead raids against the Romans in order to coerce them to give up more. He also skillfully took advantage of the mounting tension between the eastern and the western imperial governments, playing one off against the other and making agreements with both.

This sort of political maneuvering brought the Visigoths to western Europe. In the autumn of 408, when the western government reneged on a major agreement to provide subsidies, Alaric led his Visigothic forces into Italy and marched on Rome. For the next two years they marched here and there in Italy trying to force the imperial government to honor its treaties. The Romans for the most part simply held out; they avoided any huge pitched battles and managed to withhold the supplies the Visigoths desperately needed. Alaric's situation was becoming dire; with such small success in Italy, he tried to lead his people from southern Italy to Africa, but the attempt was foiled. He could force nothing from the emperor, Honorius, secure in Ravenna in the midst of its swamps. Some of his own Goths were now beginning to desert. In the end, Alaric turned back to the city of Rome and on August 24, 410, after a full siege, the Goths broke in and sacked, burned, looted, and pillaged the eternal city for three days. The mountains of loot Alaric's warriors carted away probably cemented their loyalty to him for a while, but the sack did nothing to solve their long-term problems of obtaining adequate land and food, or in lieu of them, at least subsidies and imperial recognition. He again turned south in another attempt to reach Africa, but died before he could fulfill his plan.

Even with the great king's death, the Visigothic nation held together and chose his brother-in-law, Ataulf (410–416), to succeed him. Since the emperors were seemingly never going to provide the Visigoths the land and subsidies they needed in Italy, Ataulf led his people across the Alps and into Gaul in 412. Honorius's policy of nonconfrontation had worked; the Gothic menace had disappeared into Gaul.

Gone perhaps they were, but the effects of the Visigoths' Italian campaigns would linger. Because the very heart of the Italian western empire had been ravaged by the barbarians, the imperial government pulled in troops from the provinces north of the Alps. This action left those provinces vulnerable, the Rhine frontier fatally weak, and the British Isles emptied of Roman legions. Although in one way or another Italians would always be a force to reckon with for the northern Europeans, never again would Italy control the north to the degree it had done for the previous four centuries.

Even more profound were the psychological effects on the Romans. Mere foreigners had sacked the eternal city. The astonishing event called into question not only assumptions of the permanence and stability of the Roman world, but also, since that world was now officially Christian, assumptions about the role of the Christian God in human history. As we saw in Chapter 2, many fourth-century Christian writers saw the Roman Empire as a visible agent in God's plan for spreading the Gospel. But since the ancient seat of that empire was now vulnerable and open to sack, had not the Christian God deserted it? Or worse still, did the event not call into question the truth of what the Christians said about their God? The Visigothic sack of Rome caused Augustine to answer these questions in his monumental book, *The City* of God*. Here he argues, using Platonic thinking, that God's

---

* "City" is the traditional word used in translating Augustine's title into English. Today, words such as "state," "nation," "politics," or "government" come closer to Augustine's meaning.

plan is far greater than human history and stands outside it while also acting through it. *The City of God* details Augustine's vision of divine and human history. Using the concepts of the Earthly City and the Heavenly City, Augustine charts the successes of God's chosen people through the Old Testament and the rise of the Christian Church in contrast to the failures and defeats of the pagans. The struggles and successes of Israel and of Christianity, however, are but faint reflections of God's plan for mankind. Although the Kingdom and Church of God on earth exhibit elements of the Heavenly City, they should never be equated with it. It exists outside of history and beyond this temporal world. Augustine's book, which shows that God works through and above human history, will become the basis for most medieval political theory.

The Visigothic campaigns in Italy also brought to the forefront a most remarkable woman. The contemporary sources treating women are frustratingly rare, but Galla Placidia (390–450) led a life of movielike adventure and was a person of too much importance to hide. She was not a Goth, but the strong-minded daughter of Theodosius I (379–395) and sister of the emperor, Honorius (393–423). In 410, while her brother sat snugly in Ravenna, Galla Placidia had the misfortune to be at Rome. Being quite a prize, she was carted off by the Visigoths and dragged around Italy with them. Even with Alaric's death she was not returned to her brother, but taken by Ataulf into Gaul. Ataulf wanted to ally himself with the imperial family, and the headstrong sister of the emperor married him in 414.

Ataulf's policies in Gaul were much the same as Alaric's had been in Italy. He joined his army to various confederations, both imperial and barbarian, in return for what subsidies and other rewards he could acquire. But a permanent solution still alluded him and his people. In 415 they moved into Spain, where they fought the Vandals and their allies, the Alans, on behalf of the Romans and destroyed those peoples' newly established kingdoms. During these campaigns Ataulf was murdered, and his successor, Wallia (416–419), traded Ataulf's young widow, Galla Placidia, to the Romans for grain, restoring her to her brother, Honorius.

The Romans soon forced the Visigoths to return to Gaul by withholding food supplies. In 418 they recrossed the Pyrenees and were officially allowed to settle a huge area of Aquitaine. They made Toulouse the center of their new kingdom and finally began a much more settled, although by no means peaceful, life. Instead of destroying the great farms of their new homeland, the Goths moved in. They were the first of the barbarian peoples to begin to live like Romans.

The kingdom of Toulouse was not to remain the center of the Visigothic state. Under their kings Theoderic II (453–466) and his successor, Euric (466–484), they again established themselves in Spain. It was here, south of the Pyreness, that the Visigoths would rule until they collapsed in the face of the invading Muslims early in the eighth century.

The Vandals

About all that lingers now in European culture of the Vandals is their name. This name, which once described one of the most powerful of the barbarian peoples, is now applied to hoodlums who destroy for the thuggish delight of it. So little remains because the Vandals only passed through western Europe, albeit often justifying the modern use of their name as they went.

On New Year's Eve 405 the Vandals, along with other barbarian groups, crossed the frozen Rhine near Mainz. Gaul was in such a state of turmoil and the Roman forces were so thin that the Vandals and their allies had little trouble. The barbarians split up and burned a wide swath. Mainz, Trier, Reims, Amiens, Arras, and Tournai were all sacked. The usual barbarian problem, the need for food, kept them on the move. In 409 they easily invaded Spain and by 411 they had established several kingdoms on the Iberian Peninsula. These Vandalic kingdoms in Spain, however, hardly lasted two decades and were replaced by the Visigoths.

It was in the rich grain-growing regions of North Africa that the Vandals set up their state and looked menacingly across the Tyrhennian Sea at Rome, just as the ancient Carthaginians had done. In many ways the Romans, often through their own ineptitude, were themselves responsible for this new threat in the home of their ancient foes. The Romans had vacated the Rhenish border, allowing the Vandals to cross unopposed in 406; a Roman usurper had allowed them into northern Spain in 409; the Roman use of the Visigoths against the Vandals in Spain united the smaller Vandalic Iberian kingdoms into a more powerful force. And now as the Vandals were about to take the final step in their long migration, they would be invited to do so by a rebellious Roman commander in Africa.

That Roman commander was named Boniface, and to understand his actions we must dip into imperial politics, at whose center we find none other than Galla Placidia. She was then ruling the Western Empire as regent for her rather weak-minded son, Valentinian III (425–455). In 428 and 429, she sent Roman armies to Africa against the rebel Boniface, causing him to turn to the Vandals for help. Boniface offered them ships for their crossing and land in Africa. Their king, Gaiseric (428–477), accepted, and in May 429, they embarked.

The Vandalic conquest of Africa took thirteen years and was the most destructive barbarian conquest of the entire century. Nothing was sacred. Gaiseric made and broke treaties, looted churches, burned, sacked, and tortured, or so the Roman sources claim. By 442, he had his way, obtaining official treaties from the Romans recognizing his rule in Africa and betrothing his son, Huneric, to Emperor Valentinian's daughter.

Although the Vandalic state was located in Africa and fell to the Eastern Roman Empire after only 100 years, it nonetheless offers a good example of how events outside Europe affected the formation of early medieval European culture. Even though African grain no longer fed Rome and Italy to the degree it had done during the heyday of the empire, the Vandals now nonetheless controlled it. Their rule in Africa weakened the Italians' hand when dealing with those who controlled the grain-producing areas of Gaul. Also, the Vandals had a very large and very dangerous navy, which they used to attack Palermo on Sicily in 442 and to sack Rome itself in 455. The Vandalic kingdom became a ubiquitous danger in a way other kingdoms were not. The Mediterranean was no longer exclusively the Romans' sea, and with their shores threatened from Africa, they were less free to deal with the barbarians north of the Alps.

The Burgundians

While the Vandals were still in Spain, the Burgundians, who had migrated from the Baltic region, were settled as a federated people along the middle Rhine with their capital at Worms. They, like most of the settled barbarians, made a bid for more land. They attacked the Roman province of Belgica Prima, but in 436 the Roman commander in Gaul, Aetius, engaged the Huns to stop them, and the Huns certainly did. It is said that 20,000 Burgundians along with their king, Guntiar, were slaughtered, bringing their kingdom at Worms to an end. These are the events so heroically celebrated in the famous thirteenth-century German epic, *The Niebelungenlied*.

In 443, remnants of the Burgundians were settled in southeastern Gaul along the Rhone with capitals at Lyons and Geneva. They behaved much like the other federated peoples, at times serving the Romans with their military forces or, if it suited them, allying with the Romans' enemies. They grew to be a major force in Gaul. After a short adherence to Arianism, they became Catholics. The Frankish king, Clovis I (481–511), married a Catholic Burgundian princess, and with this union the Catholic faith entered the Frankish royal house. In the 530s the Burgundian kingdom was conquered by the Franks and became one of the three Frankish realms.

The Huns

The Huns were an Asiatic people, physically smaller than the other barbarians. When this "people never before imagined appeared out of a hidden fold of the earth," as Ammianus wrote in the late fourth century, their name became synonymous with terror. As we saw, they attacked the peoples living around the Black Sea and soon became enmeshed, as did all the barbarians, in imperial politics. For the first half of the fifth century they generally raided and extorted huge sums from the eastern Romans, while devastating various peoples in the west in the employ of the western Romans. At the same time they established a centralized monarchy and subjected peoples from the Black Sea to the Rhine border. The most famous of their great kings was, of course, Attila, the "scourge of God."

To western eyes, Attila did not posses regal physical qualities. He was short and squarish in stature, his head was too large, his nose too flat, and his beard only a few wispy stands. He also had a habit of rolling his eyes. We know more about Attila than the other barbarian kings because the Roman historian Priscus, part of a delegation sent to Attila in 448, has left us an engaging account. Attila was then at the height of this power and very eager to extend it still further. Once again, his excuse came from the Romans themselves.

The long-ruling but intellectually feeble emperor, Valentinian III, had a sister who outshone him in every way, Augusta Honoria. She seems to have equaled the enviable talents and iron will of her mother, Galla Placidia. Imperial women were politically dangerous because they could become the wives of ambitious men who use the marriage to make claims of legitimacy for the throne either for themselves or their sons. Once a believable claim to the throne was established, these men attracted powerful, politically discontented followings. In 449 Augusta Honoria actually made such a move: She took an ambitious lover and plotted the overthrow of her brother. The plot was discovered, her lover was executed, and she was quickly and forcibly betrothed to a very respectable and politically safe senator, no potential usurper. But the palace had obviously underestimated Augusta Honoria. The most powerful political figure of the time was Attila, and Augusta Honoria did not shy from turning to the ferocious king of the Huns for help. She sent off an embassy stating her case, and Attila leapt at the chance to take up her cause.

In 451 Attila amassed a huge army of Huns and his other subjects and invaded Gaul, which he claimed was Augusta Honoria's portion of the empire. His reasons for doing so were not all based on the convenience of a palace intrigue. In 450, Theodosius, the eastern emperor, had ceased paying subsidies ("gifts") to Attila, and Attila probably realized that his usual attacks on the East were no longer likely to yield him much. The Vandals, too, had been sending gifts asking for his aid against the Visigoths. Some Burgundians and Franks joined the Hunnic force at the Rhine. On April 7, 451, this huge barbarian army took the city of Metz. Attila's invasion caused Aetius, the Roman ruler of northern Gaul, to do a complete about-face in his usual policy. Obviously the only force capable of stopping the Huns was Aetius' old enemy, the Visigoths. They too realized the threat, and a combined force met the Huns near Châlons-sur-Marne in the famous Battle of the Catalaunian Plains. The Huns were defeated but not destroyed, perhaps because Aetius assumed he would again need them to contain the Visigoths. Attila then turned south and in 452 invaded Italy. He devastated the important ecclesiastical city of Aquilea, near Venice, and it never recovered.

The dreaded king of the Huns was not to conquer Italy. In fact, the end of his life and that of the Huns' huge empire was very near. The story that he was dissuaded from attacking Rome because of the personal entreaties of Pope Leo I is probably just that: a story. Leo, along with two important Roman senators, did indeed meet with Attila just south of Lake Garda, but an outbreak of plague in Attila's army and the arrival of an army from Constantinople did more to turn the pagan Huns around than did the pope's requests. And once again we see the chronic barbarian problem: The Huns were short of food. They withdrew from Italy.

A year later Attila was dead, and the Hunnic empire quickly fell apart. It had been too short lived to develop any lasting cohesive political structures, depending almost entirely on the ruthless abilities of its kings. The subject peoples quickly threw off Hunnic rule, and the Huns themselves settled down on the Hungarian plain. Their place in the formation of early medieval culture is important, although indirect. As we have seen, it was they who helped push the Visigoths into Roman territory and they whom Aetius largely used to curb the ambitious Visigoths in southern Gaul. It was also they who kept the various other peoples subject to their short-lived empire in check. Both these actions had an important retarding effect in the spread of barbarian influence across the empire in the fifth century. The resultant slower pace of barbarian incursion was far more conducive to the merging of the Roman and the barbarian; it allowed the barbarians to absorb more of what they might have otherwise destroyed had their advance been a quicker one.

TWO KINGDOMS IN THE WEST: OSTROGOTHS AND FRANKS

The heart of the late Roman Empire of the West saw the establishment of two large barbarian kingdoms: the Ostrogothic in Italy and the Frankish in Gaul (see Map 3.1). Two different barbarian peoples settled and ruled large parts of Italy, first the Ostrogoths in the fifth century and then the Lombards in the sixth. We shall save the late-arriving Lombards for Chapter 7. Several barbarian peoples settled in Roman Gaul, but it was the Franks who established the dominant political structure.

Ostrogothic Italy

In the aftermath of the breakup of the Huns' empire, many barbarian peoples once subject to them were uprooted, splitting apart. Among these were two groups of Ostrogoths who came to settle in the Balkins. In 471, Theoderic became king of both groups. This Ostrogothic king was a very Romanized barbarian. He had spent about ten years at Constantinople as a hostage and thus knew well the ways and the culture of the Roman Empire from the inside. He soon extended his authority over more of the Ostrogoths and then forced the eastern emperor, Leo II (473–474), to grant them lands in Macedonia. Here they settled and remained until 489. Theoderic was awarded great Roman status, achieving the rank of *magister militum praesentalis,* that is—leader of the troops attached to the emperor himself, and he was even made consul.

Despite Theoderic's assumption of high Roman titles, his loyalties remained firmly with his people. Several times he besieged Constantinople, although he never took it, largely because the eastern Romans were able to cut off his food supply. The eastern emperor, Zeno, obviously wishing to put some reassuring distance between this dangerous friend and Constantinople, occasioned the Ostrogothic invasion of Italy. He did so by commissioning Theoderic to expel and replace Odoacer, the barbarian chieftain who had recently deposed Romulus Augustulus, the last reigning Roman emperor in the West.

Thus it was that in 489 Theoderic led his army into Italy and for three years tried to dislodge Odoacer from Ravenna. In the end, in February of 493, he tricked Odoacer with a false treaty and, once admitted into Ravenna, deposed him and soon had him murdered.

Theoderic set up a very Romanized state in Italy, which he ruled until his death in 526. He kept the military side of the government in the hands of his Goths, making them a ruling military elite. The Goths, as Arians, also remained separate from the Roman Church; they had their own Arian ecclesiastical structure, bishops, and buildings. For their support, the Goths appropriated Roman land and took one third of the taxes for themselves. While the Goths controlled the military, the Italians ran the civil government and kept their cultural and religious life on its late Roman course. With the exception of Gothic counts, who governed the various districts of the kingdom, old Roman families held the other high offices, both in Church and state, and continued to conduct matters as they thought Romans

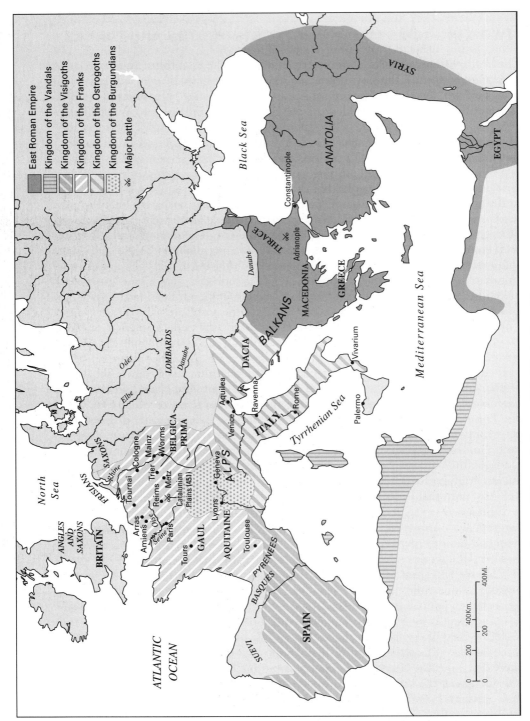

Map 3.1   The Barbarian Successor States c. 500 A.D.   By the year 500 all the territory of the former Roman Empire in the West was under the control of barbarian rulers.

should. In fact, under Theoderic, who was a very tolerant ruler, Italy seemed more Roman than it had for quite a while. In many important Italian cities he constructed new public buildings and baths, and repaired the city walls and aqueducts. This last was especially important for Ravenna itself, situated as it was in the midst of swamps. He reinstituted the old Roman practice of providing cheap grain to the poor and of entertaining them with circus games. The whole apparatus of government, courts, districts, cities, and municipalities remained. He issued royal edicts in the imperial manner. It seemed as if there was a Roman revival in Italy: Theoderic's government was certainly better and more secure than the official imperial government had been in its last years.

Theoderic crafted a sort of hegemony over the other barbarian states, reflected in his treaties and marriage alliances. His sister married the king of the Vandals in an agreement meant to reduce the African threat to Italy. One daughter married Sigismund, king of the Burgundians. Another daughter married Alaric II (484–507), king of the Visigoths. After Alaric died, Theoderic virtually ruled the Visigothic kingdom until his death as protector and regent for his grandson, the young Visigothic heir, Amalaric. Another people, the Alamans, were dependent upon him for protection against the increasing power of the Franks, and he himself married the sister of the Frankish king, Clovis I (481–511). Theoderic's rule was peaceful and reasonably prosperous, but within ten years of his death, the eastern emperor, Justinian I (527–565), sent an army that would destroy the Ostrogothic kingdom and retake Italy for the empire.

Theoderic's kingdom may have been short lived, but its importance for early medieval civilization was immense. Perhaps because of Thoderic's own personal fondness for Roman ways and culture, or perhaps because of his government's need for the talents of the deeply entrenched and well-educated Italian upper classes, Ostrogothic Italy was responsible for preserving a remarkable amount of western Europe's classical heritage. Theoderic enjoyed the services of two extraordinarily talented men, Boethius and Cassiodorus, who by themselves were responsible for preserving much of the written culture of the ancient world.

Boethius (ca. 480–524) was born into an Italian senatorial family. He had a fine education and achieved an exquisite mastery of Greek, something rare for someone from his period living in the West. He was consul in 510 and beamed with pride when his two sons, still infants, were also appointed to hold this most honorific of Roman offices. He served as Theoderic's chief advisor, but was later accused of treason by the king, imprisoned, and executed.

Boethius was to become one of the most popular authors for all the Middle Ages. He translated Aristotle's introductory works on logic into Latin, and his translations, called the "Old Logic," constituted what Europe knew of Aristotle until the great philosopher's other works on logic and his scientific works appeared in the West in the twelfth and thirteenth centuries. C. S. Lewis called Boethius "the divine popularizer," and indeed he wrote a best seller while waiting to be executed. It is called *The Consolation of Philosophy* and became one of western Europe's favorite books. It was translated into Old English by King Alfred, into Middle English by Chaucer, and into modern English by Queen Elizabeth I. In the book, Philosophy is personified as a woman who appears to Boethius while in prison; she convinces him of the value of philosophical meditation for proving God's nature and existence and for understanding man's goal of true happiness. It is a marvelously clear and persuasive justification for philosophical inquiry as well as a comfort in the face of death.

It is difficult to overly emphasize Boethius' importance for the intellectual life of the Middle Ages. His original works on education, philosophical inquiry, the Trinity, and other theological matters were much copied and read in the centuries that followed his own, and his translations of Greek works, especially Aristotle's, provided medieval thinkers with the Latin vocabulary needed in much of their philosophical writing.

Cassiodorus was born about 490 into one of the Italian senatorial families. His father had served Theoderic and he followed in the paternal path. Cassiodorus, as opposed to Boethius, long outlived Theoderic; he served the great king's successor, Athalaricus, as praetorian prefect and even held influential positions in Constantinople under Justinian. When he returned to Italy in the 550s, he retired from public life and established a religious community at Vivarium on his family's estate in Calabria. Here he created one of the world's great libraries. His work at Vivarium set an important monastic precedent for scholarship and the copying of manuscripts, something that was later to influence the Benedictine order.

Cassiodorus was a prolific author, and his writings were as important as the monastic precedents he set at Vivarium. Although many Christian leaders often displayed biting hostility toward the study of pagan literature, Cassiodorus in his *Institutes of Divine and Secular Letters* managed a union of secular and Christian studies such that Christians of good conscience could include the secular as a basic part of a Christian education. Cassiodorus showed how the methods, the approach, and above all the elegant and precise use of language employed by the ancient pagan authors were models for Christian scholarship, even if their pagan content was to be disregarded. As a result, many of the classical world's most important works were copied and thus preserved by Christian monks. Cassiodorus was also influential in bringing the study of the seven liberal arts into the Christian tradition. His study of the Psalms became famous for its allegorical exegesis, and he wrote many histories, including a twelve-volume history of the Goths, which has not survived.

The Franks

The Ostrogoths' great rivals to the north were the Franks. As far back as we can see them, that is, as far back as the Romans and Greeks tell us about them, they had been living in northern Europe. They were not grouped into one official Frankish tribe, but as with the other barbarians, they belonged to much smaller groups that would join constantly changing confederations. By the fifth century we find them living in two places, grouped together under two names. The Salian Franks inhabited an area in what is now the Netherlands, and the Ripuarian Franks, bearing a Latin name for "dwellers along the bank," lived upstream on the banks of the Rhine, in the area of Cologne.

The Franks, too, began to move south, although we do not know whether problems of food supply were the reason. As they came to face the Romans, their political confederations became much larger and more permanent. The study of Frankish political structure revolves around one family, the Merovingian, which provided the Franks with their kings for three hundred years.

Childeric I is the first of the Merovingians to emerge out of the mists of legend into history, although he is not visible in overly sharp focus. He died in 481; we do not know when he was born. He ruled from Tournai, a city located in modern Belgium.

Childeric is hardly mentioned by Frankish authors, but in 1653, near Tournai, a Frankish grave was accidentally discovered containing goods of such splendor that it was obviously a king's burial place. Among the treasure was a gold ring bearing Childeric's name in Latin. There were weapons, his battle axe, his spear, a strange metal horse's head, jewelry, a mounted crystal ball, gold and silver coins, and even three hundred gold cicadas with their wings inlaid with garnet sewn to a cloak. This insect would adorn the vestments of the French monarchy right down to Napoleon.

The quality and the artistic motifs of these objects are not matched by those found in less grand Frankish graves of the period but reflect the style of objects worn by the wealthy in Roman society, in Italy and in Constantinople. Yet there is no evidence of Christianity. It is difficult to know what to make of this. On the one hand, the very Roman grave goods make it seem that Childeric, the Frankish king

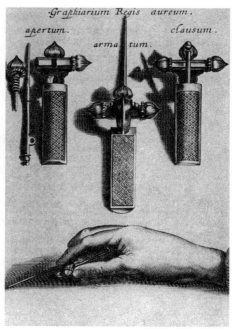

Objects Buried with an Early Frankish King Jean-Jacques Chifflet, a seventeenth-century physician with an antiquarian's passion, has left us careful drawings of the grand objects found in the grave of the Frankish king, Chilperic I (died 481). *Private Collection/The Bridgeman Art Library.*

at Tournai, saw himself as the successor of Roman power in northern Gaul. On the other, the lack of any indication of Rome's religion could indicate that Childeric was still very barbarian in his culture.

Childeric's son, King Clovis I (481–511), was the real architect of the Frankish kingdom. In 486 he and his warriors moved southward to defeat Syagrius who led an outpost of Roman authority centered at Soissons. It was something of a marvel that this small band of Salians and not the far more powerful Visigoths or Alamans became the barbarian masters of northern Gaul. In 496 Clovis defeated the Alamans in a battle that is traditionally taken as the occasion for his conversion to Catholic Christianity. His most important confrontation came, however, in 507 when the Franks, moving farther south, crossed the Loire and defeated the Visigoths. Although it would take the Franks another twenty-five years to reduce Visigothic control of southern Gaul, Clovis' great victory had begun the process.

In 511 Clovis' kingdom was divided among his four sons, legitimate and illegitimate alike, in reasonably equal portions. This was in accordance with Frankish inheritance custom that pertained not only to dividing kingdoms among kings, but estates among nobles, and farms among farmers. In the second half of the sixth century, the kingdom based at Paris began to play the politically dominant role among the Franks. It was here in the upper Seine and Oise basin that the Frankish center of power would remain until the eighth century when the Carolingians, the royal family that would succeed the Merovingians, moved it eastward.

For about fifty years, from the 560s to the second decade of the seventh century, the Frankish kingdoms suffered almost continual civil war as the grandsons of Clovis fought back and forth, contesting and begrudging this or that piece of territory, privilege, or store of booty. Civil war can be extremely destructive for any society. In an early medieval kingdom, however, it not only caused suffering and physical destruction, but because it shifted and confused the bonds of loyalty between the warriors and the kings, it attacked the very sinews that bound the political structure together.

The Frankish kings had two primary responsibilities; contemporary sources make no doubts about it. They were to win battles against foreign foes and keep the internal peace. Without the cooperation of the noble families of their kingdoms, they could do neither. The nobles in turn were equally dependent upon their king; without him to lead and to settle disputes, they too found their position undermined, either by foreign enemies or by the ambitions of each other.

The kings kept the nobles' loyalty through distribution of "largess"—that is, through rewards of land and money. Foreign war was a good source of both, and thus as long as the Frankish kingdoms expanded against foreigners, the system worked well. Except for the fifty years here in question, and contrary to what the Carolingians were wont to say about their Merovingian predecessors, the Merovingian era showed a remarkable degree of political stability. Nonetheless, if the kings could not get what they needed from outside the Frankish lands, they would war among themselves.

The need for a king in keeping the internal peace also helps to explain the fierce loyalty the Franks displayed to the Merovingian family. To such a powerful warrior nobility with so many potential contenders, the throne had to be unquestionably out of reach. The fact that no Frank other than a legitimate Merovingian could be king was the block preventing the ambitious from breaking the internal peace and clawing Frankish society apart in pursuit of royal power.

Toward the end of the sixth century the number of Frankish kingdoms became fixed at three, as each of three areas developed a permanent political system centered on its own royal court. Paris became the center of the western realm, known as Neustria. Reims and then Metz became the center of the eastern kingdom called Austrasia, and the old Burgundian kingdom formed a third Frankish realm until it fell under the Neustrian kings in the mid-seventh century. It was at these royal courts that the kings performed their function for keeping the internal peace by settling disputes. An elaborate legal system grew up, based largely on Roman models. We still have many of the royal documents, called *diplomata,* which record the outcome of those disputes.

By the time the Frankish kingdoms entered the seventh century, they had all the markings we would call medieval. The political structure was based on the cooperation between crown and nobility expressed in terms of personal loyalty. The Frankish warriors had become a rich and powerful landed Christian aristocracy. And the realm had a highly organized ecclesiastical structure. The cult centers and holy places were endowed with land for their support and for the upkeep of their buildings, and many were attached to thriving monasteries.

From 613 to 623 all of Francia was united under one king, Clothar II (613–629), the king of Neustria. It is indicative of the relationship between a king and the nobility that in 623 the nobles of the eastern kingdom, Austrasia, requested that Clothar give them his young son, Dagobert, as their king. In other words, they wanted their own royal court in their own lands. In 629 Clothar died and Dagobert moved to Paris, assuming control of all three kingdoms as his father had done. But once again in 633 he in turn was forced to send his son, Sigibert III (633–651), to rule in Austrasia.

The rule of Dagobert I (623–638) is often held up as a high point in Merovingian power. After him, it is said, the old royal family's power dwindled to the point where the later Merovingian rulers are called the "do-nothing kings" and real power supposedly passed to the leading family of the nobility, the Pippinids, soon to be known as the Carolingians. This dismal view of the later Merovingians comes largely from sources written by Carolingian authors who wanted to glorify the new dynasty by belittling the older one. The less exciting, but more trustworthy late Merovingian sources, however, show us the legitimate Merovingian kings still settling disputes, holding court, and leading armies to keep the realm safe (see Medieval Voices). Their real demise belongs to the eighth century and the shift in the economic center of gravity to new lands along the Rhine and beyond, lands which the Carolingians controlled. We shall examine the Carolinian era in Chapter 6.

BARBARIAN CULTURE IN A LATE ANTIQUE WORLD

The historian's eyes strain to see what life was like for the barbarians as they entered the confines of the former Roman Empire of the West and established their kingdoms. Five or six types of information tell us about them in the fifth and sixth

MEDIEVAL VOICES

A
Contemporary
Hagiographer
Describes a
Powerful
Queen

*After the death of King Clovis II (638–657), his wife Queen Balthild
ruled as regent. She later became venerated as a saint, and an account of
her life was written very shortly after her death. In the following its author
describes her period of rule. Note the emphasis on counsel with the great
nobles, the political role of bishops, and the praise she receives for
maintaining peace.*

At God's command, her husband, King Clovis, went forth from his body
leaving a lineage of sons with their mother. In his place after him, his son,
the late King Clothar, took the throne of the Franks. [His father had then left him] also with
the excellent princes Chrodbert, bishop of Paris, Lord Audoin, and Ebroin, mayor of the
palace, along with other great nobles and very many of the rest. And, indeed, the kingdom of
the Franks was maintained in peace. Then indeed a little while ago, the Austasians peacefully
received her son Childeric as king in Austrasia by the arrangement of Lady Balthild and with
the advice of the great nobles. The Burgundians and the Neustrians were united. And we believe that with God guiding, and in accordance with the great faith of Lady Balthild, these
three kingdoms kept the harmony of peace among themselves.

Source: Life of Lady Balthild, ch 5.

centuries, but each is limited in some way and none is as revealing as we would like
it to be.

The Sources

Archaeology is very helpful for some places but for others almost no use at all. For
Ostrogothic and Longobardic Italy, for instance, archaeologists have uncovered
many revealing artifacts, but for Visigothic Gaul, the archaeological finds are almost negligible. In Frankish Gaul, generally the more southern areas are richer in
archaeological information, but since progressively fewer barbarian inhabited the
south, the information is less helpful for our specific purposes. In addition to many
graves, which often contain revealing possessions of the deceased, the outlines of
cities, towns, and even villages have survived here and there, along with, in some
extraordinary cases, the foundations of buildings and some of the structure.

In almost all the barbarian kingdoms, the kings issued law codes, some very
shortly after the kingdoms were established, and many of these codes have survived.
With thoughtful treatment, these "barbarian codes," as they are called, can be a
very good source of information about how the barbarians lived. In fact, even the
consideration of the problems involved in using them for historical purposes reveals
a great deal about the barbarians and especially about their relations with the Romans. A law code is what historians call a normative source, meaning a work

written to describe how society should be rather than how it actually was. The historian seeks to uncover what went on in addition to ideas of what should have gone on, and thus the first problem in the historical use of the barbarian codes lies in their very nature as law. This problem is offset somewhat by the type of law the barbarian codes contain. They are, for the most part, precedent or customary law; that is, their various sections reflect specific wrongful acts that actually occurred and the penalties actually levied upon the guilty person. By very careful analysis both of the various acts and of the severity of the penalty prescribed for each, we can deduce certain things about what and whom barbarian society thought important.

The histories written by authors living in the barbarian kingdoms form another important source of information about the barbarian way of life. Even though these historians wrote largely to support some cause of their own times, they can be used with thoughtful analysis.

The Romans, either commenting on the barbarians beyond their borders or reacting to their new masters once they had settled within the empire, have also left us information about how the barbarians lived. Romans living during or near the time of the migrations have left us poems and narrative works describing their reactions to the barbarians, and these, too, are helpful.

Other written sources—records, decrees, poems, saints' lives, treaties, canons of Church councils, and letters—all occasionally help. But most of these, and indeed all the written sources, are aristocratic in outlook, reflecting little interest in ordinary people.

Ethnic Identity

The invaders do not seem to have had any concept of themselves as "Germans" in a broad sense, and even ideas of being Frankish or Visigothic developed slowly, only becoming reasonably firm once they came into frequent contact with the Roman Empire. Ethnic identity was generally connected to much smaller groups and was far more dependent upon the consciousness of shared traditions and allegiances than upon any physical or even linguistic characteristics.

Nonetheless, in the early years of the barbarian kingdoms, in the fifth and sixth centuries, ethnic identity had real meaning. We have seen the famous dual state of Ostrogothic Italy, where the Goths controlled the military and the Italians the civil government. The Barbarian codes, too, were issued in the name of various ethnic groups: Visigoths, Salian Franks, Ripuarian Franks, and Burgundians. The codes also provided for different treatment of their own people as opposed to other peoples or the "Romans;" that is, the mostly Celtic people whom they now ruled and who were subject to Roman law. This principle—where a person is subject to the law of her or his people, rather than to the law of the territory in which he or she lives—is termed (rather strangely in English) "the personality of the law." Under the personality of the law, for instance, an Italian and an Ostrogoth could each be subject to a different legal system for certain legal matters even though they might be living as neighbors.

Over the generations and through the centuries, however, the ethnic distinctions between those living in the same area faded and the personality of the law, too, gave way to a "territoriality." By the late eighth century we find that formerly ethnic words like "Frank" and "Roman" had taken on territorial meanings in the sources. Even the lower classes, most of whom were not descendents of the invaders, slowly began to consider themselves "Gothic," "Frankish," or "Burgundian," depending upon where they lived.

The Countryside

It was hunger that drove the barbarians into Roman territory, and although their lot improved once they arrived and settled, rarely if ever did the lower classes find a way of life that approached comfortable. The yields from their crops were miserable, often as low as only two or three times the seeds they planted, whereas modern yields commonly reach thirty times seed. Living with starvation as an ever-present threat, the all-too-common natural disasters, plagues, severe winters, drought, or bad harvests caused immediate and widespread abject misery (see Medieval Voices). The practice continued whereby these wretched poor gave themselves in servitude to a person with means in a final desperate maneuver to find some form of protection and support.

Not every year was an agricultural disaster, of course, but even normal conditions do not seem to have allowed farmers to accumulate much wealth. Archaeologists have found the remains of an early medieval village in northern France, about three miles south of the modern city of Douai. The village lasted for about 200 years and then was abandoned. While it lasted, it raised meat for the Merovingian kings, an occupation that probably provided this village with a better living than many others. Even so, what the archaeologists have found bespeaks poverty. In addition to remains of the domesticated animals, the digs have uncovered some nails, knives, combs, four belt buckles, three rings, scissors, a wooden pestle, and some fragments of pots and glass. All of it showed very poor quality, sorry rewards indeed for two hundred years of toil.

The Towns

Those in the towns fared somewhat better than the country dwellers. By the end of the empire, large numbers of towns in Europe were situated in defensible locations and sported walls. Under the barbarian rulers many of these continued their existence and maintained their defenses. Increasingly the towns took on a more local and more clerical character. Long-distance trade continued to shrink throughout the fifth and sixth centuries, although it never disappeared. The local rulers were for the most part now settled on their estates in the countryside, abandoning the towns, which became increasingly the haunt of the Christian clergy. The public buildings of antiquity, the baths, courts, temples, theaters, and governmental structures, gave way now to ecclesiastical ones: churches, monasteries, baptistries, and chantries. Not just the architectural appearance, but the human atmosphere in the town had a particularly churchly whiff to it. The Church's leading officials were now the town's most important denizens. Members of these officials' staffs— priests, monks, nuns, canons, deacons, and others who performed ecclesiastical

MEDIEVAL VOICES

Gregory of Tours (d. 594) Describes a Famine in Gaul in 585

Gregory, bishop of Tours, a city in central Gaul, describes the misery that a bad harvest would bring to ordinary people.

In this year a great famine oppressed nearly all of Gaul. Many people made bread from grape-seeds or the blossoms of hazelnut trees, and some used dried roots of ferns ground into powder with a little flour added. Many cut the stalks of the grain and did likewise. There were also many who, having no flour at all, gathered various grass and ate them; they became swollen, and died. Many people at that time wasted away from hunger and died. The merchants so exploited the people, that they sold a measure of grain or half a measure of wine for a third of a gold piece. The poor sold themselves into servitude in order to obtain some food.

Source: Histories, VII-45.

functions—along with the many who earned their living by providing the clergy with goods and services all squeezed into the cramped space within the town walls.

The principal figure in the larger towns was the bishop. Administratively he was responsible for all the ecclesiastical institutions within his diocese, and that could be a huge geographical area. In northern Europe, for instance, a bishop's diocese was usually coterminous with the ancient Roman *civitas* as established by the reforms of Diocletian. This meant it usually included some sort of major, or almost major, urban center along with the smaller towns, villages, and countryside round about. In the ordinary life of ordinary people, the bishop loomed far larger than the king. In the very early days of barbarian settlement there was some confusion as most of the newcomers were Arian Christians and not Catholic, and the Arian Church had its own organization. But by the second half of the sixth century, Arianism was all but dead in Europe and the Catholic bishops reigned uncontested over their churches (see Medieval Portraits).

It was not the bishop's administrative position but his spiritual one that placed him in the thick of ordinary life. A local area's actual protector and provider in the usual and tangible sense was its patron saint. It was the bishop who was the saint's living representative to the people and their representative to the saint. As such, not only did the bishop direct all the liturgical functions due the saint, the chanting, praying, and commemorative worship, but also all celebratory ones. For ordinary people the highlights of the festive year were the processions, often splendidly staged on saints' days. The clergy would parade in their finery through the town, blessing, singing, reading Scripture at this or that station, often bearing some relic of the saint in a sacred container as they went. The event was cause for great celebration and it drew not only the townspeople but people from all over the diocese. For most, partaking in the feasting, drinking, and dancing was a more immediate

Avitus, Bishop of Vienne c. 490–c. 519

The career of Avitus of Vienne provides us with a good example of the central position of an early medieval bishop. He was born into a Roman senatorial family in the area controlled by the Burgundian kings; his father was the bishop of the important city of Vienne. In 490 when his father died, Avitus became his successor as bishop. This sort of near familial right to an episcopal see was typical of the age and the area. Avitus' family was nearly an episcopal dynasty. In addition to his father as bishop, he was the godson of another bishop of Vienne, Mamertus, and a close relative of Sidonius, bishop of Clermont.

Vienne was one of the favorite residences of the Burgundian kings. When Avitus became bishop, the reigning king, Gundobad, adhered to the Arian heresy. His son, Sigismund, who succeeded him in 516, adopted Catholicism before becoming king, and although Avitus probably did not convert him, he was, as Catholic bishop, very influential in the literary life and court politics of the new king's reign. He is, for instance, probably responsible for the formal letters of state that Sigismund sent to the Eastern Roman emperor.

Avitus owes his importance not just to his privileged birth and position, but, as with many of his contemporary bishops, also to a good deal of native talent and ability. He was a reasonable theologian, a poet, and a master of rhetoric. His great learning impressed King Clovis, the Burgundians' powerful Frankish neighbor. All these political, literary, and scholarly pursuits he conducted while living the model of a Christian ascetic life.

lure than the solemnities themselves. These grand occasions cemented hearts and loyalty not only to the saint and his or her churchly apparatus, but also to the town as focal point of local pride and local identity. The center of attention in all this was the bishop, who not only led the celebrations in the good times, but also ordered the requisite prayers and processions to beseech the saint in the all-too-frequent droughts, diseases, bad harvests, or military sieges.

The Christian clergy were forbidden to marry, but if already married they were also forbidden to divorce their wives upon entering holy orders, although once they were ordained, conjugal sexual life had to cease. Consequently the bishop's wife could also be an important public figure in the life of the area. We know of one who directed the artists who created the holy images inside an important new church.

The Family

As far as we can tell, the barbarian family was a tightly knit and rather large social unit. The interests of the family came first, and its social, economic, and legal well-being determined the nature of much behavior on the part of individuals. Indeed, the individual did not seem to exist with the barbarians in ways Romans were used to. For instance, in the Barbarian codes, part of the penalty adjudged for a crime is paid by the perpetrator's family to the victim's; the individual plays far less of a legal role than in either the Roman or in modern legal systems. In the codes we can also see that the family was held responsible for the debts and obligations of the individual. Marriage, too, was an agreement between families, as it had been in certain forms of Roman marriage. In barbarian society, the *mundium*, a Latinized German word meaning responsibility for protection and support of the bride, passed from her father's family to her husband's.

We know frustratingly little about the nature of the barbarians' marriage practices during the period of their migrations and while they were settling in during the first few centuries of their new life in western Europe. We know that the Frankish kings had several wives simultaneously and do not seem to have abandoned the practice until the seventh century, despite the fact that by then they had been Christian for a century and a half.

In Roman society the bride's family had to provide the groom's with a large gift (the *dos*) in order to conclude a marriage, whereas in barbarian practice, it was the groom who had to "pay" for a bride. This can mean that barbarian culture valued women more than the Roman did. In some circumstances in some of the early barbarian law codes, the penalty for harming a woman is three times that for injuring a man, something that may also indicate a high status for women. Divorce practices, on the other hand, in both societies greatly favor the man.

The legal status of barbarian women in general was more restricted, with a more limited ability to own and inherit property than for Roman women. Women everywhere did not enjoy a full legal status but were considered under the guardianship (the *mundium*) of some male, either a father, husband, or some other male relative, or failing these, sometimes they fell under the legal protection of the king. In the late empire women increasingly were able to own and inherit property in their own right. Barbarian women, however, did not enjoy these rights until the barbarian kingdoms were reasonably well established. This development most likely reflects increasing Roman influence in the legal systems of those kingdoms.

The family was the social unit responsible for keeping the peace. Ruffians were slowed in their plans for crime and violence by the threat of retaliation from the family of the victim. Vengeance on the part of kin for injuries suffered by a relative was a universal obligation. The system did not necessarily lead to long-lasting, bitter, and escalating blood feuds, although these certainly did happen. The certainty that injury would result in vengeance caused both families, the victim's and the perpetrator's, to find ways to reach a settlement. According to what is reflected in the barbarian codes, we assume it was rather common for the disputants to seek out someone wise in the law to render a decision settling the dispute. That person was often the king's legal representative. The codes are full of various amounts of compensation, or *wergeld*, a monetary sum that the guilty must pay for various crimes according to the status of both the victim and the guilty. According to *The Law of the Salian Franks,* the compensation was divided into three parts: the *fredus,* paid to the king or his representative for the rendering of the judgment; the *faidus,* paid to the male relatives of the victim upon whom the obligation for vengeance would have fallen; and the *debitum,* paid to the heirs of the victim, male, female, and children alike.

In matters of inheritance, too, the family took precedence over the individual's ability to choose who would inherit property. There were no wills, and the order of inheritance is carefully laid out. The children come first; if there are no children, then the father and mother; if no father or mother, then brothers and sisters; if no brothers and sisters, then sisters of the mother; if no sisters of the mother, then sisters of the father; and if no sisters of the father, then the nearest relative on the father's side. There is a rather unexpected prominence of female heirs in this system, something that has not yet been adequately explained.

Not only did the individual bow to the family in matters of marriage and inheritance, but barbarian ideas of ownership also calculated the interests of the family to a greater degree than do modern ones. Again, according to the Salian code, not all land was totally alienable. Totally alienable property is property that its owner can dispose of as he or she wishes. It can be sold, willed, traded, mortgaged, or given away to anyone the owner pleases. The code speaks of a type of land it calls *terra salica*, land that can only be passed on to male heirs; it could not be sold or otherwise disposed. The practice is called entailment and is found elsewhere, as, for instance, among the ancient Spartans. It is done to ensure the long-term stability of the family; no single person in the string of generations can sell entailed land and thereby shortchange the family's future.

Summary

The barbarians penetrated the Roman Empire for the most part desperate and hungry, only to be manipulated through the complicated Roman politics of food and subsidies. Although their wars often lacked any kind of grand strategy, they were not undertaken simply for love of plundering and destruction. The Romans knew how to turn the barbarians on each other, dangling land, food, and high positions in the Roman military as rewards. These very politics and the increasing inability of the Romans to mount a coordinated defense meant that the barbarians did prevail politically. Roman imperial might gradually receded from the West during the fifth century as the barbarians established their own kingdoms within the Empire. By the year 500, every part of the West once ruled by the Romans was under the control of the barbarians, and in parts of Europe, especially in the northwest, the political system, culture, economy, and the way of life for aristocrats and ordinary people alike were now influenced by the new arrivals.

CHAPTER 4

∿

Two Eastern Mediterranean Empires:
Byzantines and Arabs, 300–800

To the southeast of the geographic center of western Europe, two neighboring civilizations began to form at about the time western Europe entered its Middle Ages. The heart of one, the Byzantine, lay on the Anatolian plain in that part of the Mediterranean world formerly called Asia Minor, now modern Turkey. The core of the other, the Muslim Empire, would eventually come to lie on the great Mesopotamian plain in what is now modern Iraq.

Although throughout the Middle Ages either of these civilizations could be at war with parts of Europe, they also exercised profound influence on the West in peaceful ways. They buffered Europe against invasion; taught it new forms of architecture, science, and medicine; and preserved and transmitted to it knowledge of the ancient past. The Byzantine Empire was the direct heir of the eastern half of the Roman Empire and its capital remained in Constantine's city. Muslim civilization arose in the Middle East and eventually dominated peoples from Spain to India and beyond. It developed traditions very different from those either of western Europe or the Byzantines. In this chapter, we shall watch these influential neighbors of the West as they build their great civilizations, taking their histories to about the year A.D. 800.

BYZANTIUM: A NEW ROME

"Byzantium," "The Eastern Roman Empire," and even the general word "Greek" are all used to describe that civilization which had its capital at Constantinople, now the Turkish city Istanbul. Byzantium's influence on Europe went far beyond its role as buffer state. Byzantine monks Christianized the eastern half of Europe and in their studying and copying of texts, they were responsible for preserving much ancient learning. The Byzantines, under their emperor Justinian, codified the great corpus of Roman law, and when Justinian's code spread across Europe in the twelfth century, ideas of Roman law changed forever the nature of most of Europe's important institutions. Byzantine political theories, too, would find fruitful soil in Europe, blossoming into ideas of universal empire and theocratic kingship and providing Europe with its models for royal ceremony and royal and imperial dress. Their alluring supply of luxury goods—silks, spices, brocade, and objects of intricate workmanship—drained western Europe of gold and silver. Their coin, the solidus or byzant, was Europe's international monetary standard until about 690. Their highly symbolic art had a huge influence on European art; even in far-away Ireland scholars find the direct influence of artistic models from Constantinople. The Byzantines also taught Europe how to place a huge dome over a quadrangular space, enabling European architects to create many of their finest buildings.

The Beginnings of Byzantine History

The Byzantine Empire was actually, although not consciously, founded by Constantine the Great (306–337) when, on November 4, 328, he consecrated his New Rome on the site of Byzantion. It was splendidly placed for defense, wedged onto a peninsula between the Sea of Marmara and a small bay called The Golden Horn. With mighty walls constructed across the landward side of the peninsula, the city would stand largely unassailable for over a thousand years. Constantine himself may have traced out the city's dimensions: It was to be five times as large as old Rome and in its verdant freshness, much more splendid. There were important pagan astrological considerations and important pagan officials in the founding ceremonies on that day, but soon the city became officially Christian.

Throughout the fourth century Constantinople continued to gain in importance. By the end of the reign of Theodosius I (379–395), it was clearly the most important city in the Empire, reflecting both the continued vitality of imperial fortunes in the East and their decline in the West. Even at the end of the fifth century when, as we have seen, the West had fallen to the control of barbarian kings, the East retained its imperial structure, albeit in an ever more eastern form. Although there was increasingly less unity between the East and the West, the barbarian kings in the West did nonetheless recognize the emperor at Constantinople as their overlord. More uniting than this formal political bond was the membership of both halves of the Mediterranean world in the Christian Church. But this too began to crack. Rivalries between the pope in Rome and the patriarchs of the great eastern cities along with political jealousy and theological disagreement split the Church. During the reign of Emperor Zeno (474–491), a long and serious schism between the eastern and western Churches broke out. The split lasted thirty-five years and would be followed by many others.

The Theocratic State

Depictions of Byzantine emperors bore an obvious resemblance to depictions of Christ. Both were seated in resplendent mosaic majesty, emanating golden glory, immutable, permanent, almighty, all-just, and all-wise. The Byzantines saw their realm as Christ's kingdom on earth and saw Christ, not the emperor, as its ruler.

Following sound Platonic conceptions, the emperor was considered Christ's earthly and visible shadow. Consequently all that the emperor did, ate, touched, slept in, inhabited, decreed, wore, held, sat upon, rode in, and all with whom he associated had to be fashioned to resemble heaven.

His palace was called the Sacred Palace and resembled a church, the house of God. It was a dazzling warren of reception halls, parade grounds, gardens, offices, barracks, baths, and living quarters. Everything was done to make the emperor's residence holy. Its walls were hung with icons, sacred images of sainted or divine figures, and its rooms housed holy relics, fragments of the true cross or the rod of Moses, for example. His daily routine and the imperial court etiquette were more like Christian ritual or a mysterious and holy drama than the workday of a ruler. Audiences with him were not meant to be conferences, but epiphanies, "showings" of his divine presence. The emperor dressed in the holiest manner with clothes resembling the sacred vestments of the Christian clergy. His jeweled and silken clothes had to befit not only his own sacred nature but also the particular occasion in which he participated. The long procession through the city at an emperor's coronation transformed his person, originally clothed as a hero in gleaming armor, through a series of changes to his new nature as Christ's vicar appropriately robed. On Easter Sunday he would appear surrounded by twelve apostles, his body clothed in white bands and his face made up deathly white. This was not court theatrics, but reality itself: theology made tangible, visible, and as beautiful and holy as humanly possible.

In an atmosphere where the spirit is real and the flesh a mere shadow of it, theological disagreement is difficult to separate from political disloyalty. Heresy becomes treason and treason is heresy. The eastern provinces of the Byzantine Empire chafed the most under the yoke of the central government, and their political dissatisfaction was often accompanied by religious dissent.

The Reign of Justinian (527–565)

Justinian's rule began before his actual reign for he not only engineered the accession of his predecessor and uncle, Justin I (518–527), but he also controlled his uncle from behind the scenes. In 518 he brought about a reconciliation with the western Church, ending the thirty-five-year schism.

In 522 he met Theodora. They soon fell hopelessly in love and she became his mistress. Historians have difficulty assessing the personality of this powerful woman and the relationship she had with Justinian because the major sources of information about them are the histories written by Procopius, a highly placed military advisor and bureaucrat. In most of his works, Procopius shows himself to be an intelligent, skillful, and truthful, if a bit traditional, historian. But he had a decided distaste for the imperial couple and the central government in general and he let his venom flow in a work now called *The Secret Histories,* which was not published until after Justinian's death.

Theodora's status as Justinian's mistress did not long satisfy her (see Medieval Voices). They married in 525, forming what seems to have been a real partnership. The splendid and famous mosaics of the imperial couple in the chancel of the

MEDIEVAL VOICES

An
Ostrogothic
King Writes to
the Empress
Theodora

The following is taken from a letter written in 535 to Theodora, wife of the emperor Justinian, by Theodahad, King of the Ostrogoths in Italy. Here it is revealed that the empress has asked the king to inform her before he sends any request to the emperor. It is obvious that the king has complied with this and her other wishes.

Now I have received Your Piety's letters with the gratitude always due to things we long for and have gained with most reverent joy your verbal message, more exalted than any gift. I promise myself everything from so serene a soul, since in such kindly discourse I have received whatever I could hope for. For you exhort me to bring first to your attention anything I decide to ask from the triumphal prince, your husband. . . . Hence it is that, advised by Your Reverence, I ordained that both the most blessed pope and the most noble Senate should reply without any delay to what you saw fit to request from them. . . . For it is my desire that you should command me no less in my realm than in your empire through the medium of your influence.

Quoted by Cassiodorus in his *Variae*.

Source: Lynda Garlan, *Byzantine Empresses. Women and Power in Byzantium A.D. 527–1204* (New York: Routledge, 1999) 35.

church of San Vitale in Ravenna makes it clear that this woman was a partner in rule. In 527 they were crowned co-emperor and co-empress to reign along with Justin I. A few months later, when he died, they ascended to rule, she at Justinian's side. The new emperor was forty-five years old, a man of ambition, vision, broad learning and culture, seasoned experience, and (naturally) many enemies. The new empress was also talented and ambitious. She is known to have made governmental decisions, carried out policy in Justinian's name, and been one of his closest and most trusted advisors.

Theodora was a convinced Monophysite, a rather startling religious position for the empress. Monophysitism was a form of religious dissent that became widespread, especially in the eastern provinces. The name comes from Greek words meaning "one nature." The Monophysites maintained that Christ had only one nature, the divine, not two simultaneously, human and divine, as orthodox Christian theology maintains. Theodora's strong sympathy for this teaching performed a real political function. It was very easy for the central government to alienate the eastern provinces by any measure perceived as anti-Monophysite. Egypt was particularly sensitive and particularly important to Constantinople as it was a major source of grain. On the other hand, any movement seeming to favor the Monophysites would cause dangerous discontent in the orthodox parts of the empire. It was thus more than convenient for Justinian to have a Monophysite empress. He could

The Empress Theodora (c. 500–547)   This beautiful mosaic was created in
the church of San Vitale in the eastern Italian city of Ravenna about the time
Theodora died. It represents a real likeness of the empress, wearing crown,
imperial robes, and much jewelry. She is carrying a chalice, her expensive
gift to the church. *Scala/Art Resource, NY.*

openly and strenuously espouse an orthodox position knowing that Theodora
would discreetly temper its effects on the Monophysites.

Security of the borders was Justinian's first concern. From 527 to 531 he was at
war with the Persians. In 532 he concluded an "Everlasting Peace" with them by
agreeing to pay them 11,000 pounds of gold annually. Although never called tribute, it was, however, nothing but. He accomplished much with imperial gold.
Huge subsidies flowed to keep the barbarians calm and to promote the loyalty of
various cities within the empire. Added to these were extravagant games and huge
building projects. He built magnificent churches and lavished them with exquisite
decoration, the holiest of relics, and other appointments.

The tribute, subsidies, and other projects meant that the central government had a great need for revenue. Justinian entrusted the imperial finances to a talented, efficient, incorruptible, but personally distasteful man from Caesarea, John of Cappadocia. John introduced new taxes, led a campaign against inefficiency and corruption, and decreased governmental expenditure, especially in the army. None of these was a recipe for popularity and, coupled with his personal debauchery, they soon made him the most hated official in the Empire. Nonetheless, the imperial finances improved.

Justinian's most enduring legacy was his project to organize and reissue the whole written corpus of Roman law. The project was immense, not only in the huge amount of material to be organized, but also in the intellectual effort and broad learning needed to accomplish it. Once again, Justinian found a person capable of the task.

Justinian appointed Tribonian the director of the commission to reissue and update the older Roman legal codices. His accomplishments were truly remarkable. Written law based on abstract principles and expressed with precise language is one of the most important legacies of the Roman Empire. Many types of enactments in Rome's legal history had the force of law: resolutions of the Senate, measures passed by the assemblies, edicts of the emperors, and the decisions and learned opinions of judges and legal specialists, all available in many written forms burdened with chaos, imprecision, repetition, and contradiction. There was no standard authoritative reference work. Justinian set out to create one, and Tribonian and his commission accomplished it with remarkable speed and accuracy. The result, referred to as the *Corpus Juris Civilis,* the "Body of Civil Law," or sometimes less accurately as "Justinian's Code," made both the application and the teaching of law more ordered and efficient in the Byzantine Empire. It lay largely unused during the European Middle Ages until the eleventh and twelfth centuries, when it was taught in the Italian city of Bologna. From here it spread rapidly as Europeans began to recognize the value of Roman civil law in regulating the new political, economic, and social conditions of their times.

Not all was efficiency, organization, and divine beauty in Justinian's Byzantium. His fiscal and legal reforms obviously displeased those who had benefited under the old systems, and discontent showed its ugly and violent head, often in the capital city itself. The Byzantine Empire was dominated by the city of Constantinople, and happenings in that great city's urban life greatly influenced the imperial politics.

A large part of Constantinople's politics took place at the race track, the famous Hippodrome. Here the horseracing teams were supported by organized factions of mostly young spectators, named for their identifying colors, the Blues and the Greens. The circus factions, as they are usually called, are infamous in Byzantine history because they often rioted in their enthusiasm for their own racing team and in antipathy to the fans of the others. Their rowdiness often burst forth on the streets and especially in the theaters. Emotions ran high; successful chariot drivers became national heroes and statues of them were placed next to those of the emperor. Both men and women were fans and fiercely loyal members of their faction. The factions' leaders were officials appointed by the emperor and entrusted with important responsibilities of public entertainment and imperial ceremony. It was important for the emperor to appear at the races. Here he received the cheering of his subjects or heard their complaints. All the major cities of the empire had their Blues and Greens as well.

The urban life of faction and Hippodrome was more than merely an exciting and often violent sporting event. Since the races were financed from imperial coffers and the emperor appointed the factions' leaders, this public entertainment continued the long Roman tradition of diversion for the urban populace. In this way an important part of the sporting, emotional, and ceremonial life of the capital city merged at the racetrack. The emperor himself opened the first day of the races each season. The magnificent imperial viewing box was set high atop splendid columns with its own passageway to the Sacred Palace. Often the public punishment of criminals took place here as well.

In a famous attempt to suppress the excesses of the circus factions, Justinian almost dealt his own regime its deathblow. On January 10, 532, the Blues and Greens were brawling in the Hippodrome after the races. Justinian sent in troops to quell the violence, arrested leaders from both sides and condemned them to death. The factions demanded their release. Tension mounted. Days later when the emperor faced his subjects in the Hippodrome he was met with cries of "Nika! Nika!" ("Win! Win!"), and the mob poured out of the arena into the streets. For five days and nights they rioted and burned. The Senate House, the law buildings, public baths, and churches all crumbled in ashes. They demanded the dismissal of John of Cappadocia and of Tribonian. Justinian agreed. They rioted more. He offered them a complete amnesty. On they went. They demanded a new emperor, and when Justinian in panic planned to flee the capital, according to Procopius, Theodora intervened. With heavy use of troops, many of them foreign mercenaries, the mob was penned up in the Hippodrome and 30,000 killed. Thus by the strong will of the empress the Nika Rebellion, as it is called, was quelled, but not before much of the capital lay smoldering.

Things did eventually return to normal. John and Tribonian were reinstated, and Justinian began a huge rebuilding program, the most spectacular part being the reconstruction of the great basilica of Hagia Sophia. Even the sophisticated urban dweller felt more than a slight tingle of awe upon entering this, the most magnificent of Constantinople's churches. Justinian had ordered the components and the workmen from all parts of the Empire and obviously spared no expense. The result was a wonderful display of colors and columns, all of the richest marble and porphyry and assembled with consummate skill. The upper portion of the interior, a surface area estimated at about four acres, was covered completely in glittering golden mosaics carrying various patterns in red, green, and blue. Even more sparkling was the huge cross of jewels on a background of stars spread across the dome. It was that dome that most mystified the beholders who have left us their descriptions of it. Its dimensions are gargantuan: 107 feet across and 160 above the floor. All around its base it is pierced by a row of windows so that it does not seem to rest on its supports but rather to be suspended from heaven itself like a great protecting shield. The glitter, the color, the windows, the jewels, the polished stone created a symphony of dancing light. The furniture too evoked the divine: the altar of gold and precious stones and the solid-silver iconostasis rising some fifty feet and bearing mystifying icons of angels, apostles, and the Virgin. How could heaven be more beautiful? When in 537 Justinian entered his completed masterpiece, he is reported to have said, "Solomon, I have outdone thee."

Justinian was the last of the Latin-speaking emperors; indeed, not only his language but his concept of empire looked westward. The relative domestic tranquility following the suppression of the Nika rebellion and the peace he had concluded with Persia allowed him to take up another project of remarkable proportions: the reconquest of the West.

Justinian had a brilliant young general, Belisarius, who proved more than capable of the daunting task. We know a great deal about him because his secretary (and most enthusiastic fan) was none other than Procopius. In the summer of 533, Belisarius set sail from Constantinople, under the proud gaze of the emperor, with 5,000 cavalry and 10,000 infantry on a fleet of 500 transports and nearly 100 war ships—a huge military undertaking. Within six months, the Vandalic kingdom in Africa, Sardinia, Corsica, and the Balearic Island, were once again part of the Roman Empire. By 540 so too was most of the Italian peninsula (see Map 4.1).

In 549, probably because of fear and jealousy on the part of Justinian, Belisarius was relieved of his command in Italy, which passed to Narses, a seventy-one-year-old eunuch and the most influential of the imperial courtiers. Although Procopius makes no secret of his distaste for the fat little man who replaced his hero, Narses also proved himself a brilliant general and by 554 he had subjugated the whole of the Italian peninsula, which he ruled for the next thirteen years. In 551, the southern part of Spain was also rejoined to the Empire. The Mediterranean was once again a Roman lake.

Map 4.1   The Roman Empire Under Justinian c. 550   After Justinian's reconquests, the entire shore of the Mediterranean, with the exception of the northwestern corner, was once again under Roman control, if only for a few years.

Justinian is justifiably remembered as the greatest of the early Byzantine emperors, but his spectacular successes took their toll. The conquests, the subsidies, the building projects, and the administration of the reconquered West stretched the Empire's resources beyond what it could sustain. Justinian's successors were left to try to pay for what he had spent, and they were not very successful.

Troubled Times (565–610)

Justinian's successor, Justin II (565–578), stopped paying the annual tribute, and war with Persia resumed. In 568 a new and formidable enemy appeared as well in Italy: the Lombards. They set up a kingdom centered on Pavia and two independent duchies at Spoleto and Benevento. Although the Lombards managed to dislodge huge portions of Italy from Byzantine rule, they suffered from internal disunity, and consequently were not able to take it all; a large part of the peninsula still remained within the empire. It is a sad comment on Byzantine rule in Italy to note that the Lombards found it in poverty and disorder. Part of the blame for the dilapidation can be placed on a serious outbreak of the bubonic plague, the Black Death, in mid century, but the prolonged conquest of the peninsula and the rules of Belisarius and Narses had apparently not benefited the locals.

In the next thirty years the empire's troubles worsened. The Persians at one point pushed westward to Chalcedon, which lies directly across the Bosphorus from Constantinople. Avars and Slavs overran the Crimea and the Balkans. Troubles arose between the emperor and patriarch of Constantinople and the pope in Rome. Dissention, civil war, and internal conflict seemed to spew forth everywhere. Blues butchered Greens, a civil war broke out in Palestine, and just when the empire could take no more of this internal bloodletting, the emperor Phocas (602–610) launched another persecution of the Jews with the result that Christians and Jews slaughtered each other with distressing zeal.

Rebuilding: The Rule of Heraclius (610–641)

Although the problems continued after Phocas's death, and some even became worse, Byzantium was to recover. The Emperor Heraclius led an amazing revival. He did away with many relics of the Roman Empire. For example, to increase efficiency he made the language of government Greek, the actual language of the empire, rather than Latin, and he greatly decreased the late Roman practices of using subsidies to buy the favor of foreign peoples and of depending on foreign mercenaries for defense.

By 629 Heraclius had reconquered most of the lands that had fallen to the Persians and dealt them such a military defeat that they would not have time to regroup and rebuild before the new danger in the Middle East, the Arabs, would finally bring them to their knees. Even so, his last years were not happy; what he had regained from the Persians he lost to the Arabs. But the core of the empire held firm and this smaller but more efficient Byzantium was stronger and more secure than it had been.

The Muslim Advance (641–700)

The Arabs swiftly cut away huge portions of the empire. First they took the eastern Mediterranean coast; then in 642 Alexandria fell, giving them Egypt; and by the end of the century they had taken Carthage, ending Byzantine rule of North Africa.

The Byzantines reacted by securing both their remaining western provinces and all-important Anatolia. Under Constantine IV (668–685), the seemingly invincible Arabs were finally checked. The struggle was dangerous; in 674 the Arabs besieged Constantinople itself, but the empire was ready. In fact, the Byzantines achieved so much success that the Arabs were forced to pay tribute in 679.

The easiest and most direct route for the Muslims to enter Europe, and therefore the route most dangerous to the Europeans, lay across the heartland of the Byzantine Empire. But Byzantium had stood firm, and the Muslim advance had been checked. The Europeans realized that they had been saved and by whom and were grateful. The Franks, the Lombards, the Slavs, and others sent embassies to Constantine's court requesting peace and friendship, and in 680 the eastern and western churches managed a joint agreement condemning Monophysitism.

The reorganization of this smaller, but stronger, Byzantine Empire continued apace in the late seventh century. Justinian II (685–695 and 705–711) undertook

The Byzantines Use Greek Fire   It was during the siege of Constantinople in 674 that we first hear of the use of Greek Fire, an oil-based liquid (the exact formula is no longer known) pumped or hurled at an enemy ship. When set aflame, it was nearly impossible to extinguish. Greek Fire became a valuable and secret weapon of the Byzantines. This illustration is taken from a thirteenth-century manuscript now in the Bibliotheca Nacional, Madrid. *Biblioteca Nacional, Madrid/Institute Amatller D'Art Hispanic, Barcelona.*

a huge project to resettle whole segments of the empire's Slavic population into Anatolia. Whole communities and villages, an estimated three quarters of a million people, were moved to new homes. This, along with other developments, caused a fundamental shift in the political center of gravity in Byzantium's most important lands. The dominance of the great landholders was greatly decreased in favor of the small farmers. As citizens, these farmers had military responsibilities and they made loyal soldiers, often constituting effective local militias.

The communities formed by the small farmers administered much in common. When land fell vacant, it was reassigned by decision of the community. There were often common woods, pastures, and fields, the rights to which were regulated by the community. Even livestock was often held in common. This may have resulted from the common nature of the imperial taxes; they were levied upon the community, which divided the obligation up among its members. The government was clever at finding ways to make the peasants pay. If someone reneged or ran away, his share of the obligation had to be met by the others of the village. Communities obviously had strict rules against such shirking. This organization resulted in increased production as well as population. Although the criminal law still subjected peasants to the same sorts of punishments as slaves, and although their obligations to the community may not have been greatly less than a tenant-farmer's to an aristocratic landlord, it does seem that the system gave them a valued degree of independence and self-respect.

Iconoclasm and End of the Western Provinces (717–751)

In 730, Leo III (717–741) issued the Iconoclastic decrees. Iconoclasm was Byzantium's most notable form of religious dissent. The name comes from Greek words meaning to break images. The iconoclasts objected to the veneration of icons, or sacred images. They had serious theological support for this opposition, not least of which came from Old Testament prohibitions against idolatry. Byzantine iconoclasm spread in the seventh and eighth centuries largely because of concern that Christians were investing pious but false trust in icons to protect them against disasters, especially against the advances of the Islamic armies. Leo declared that all images were to be destroyed immediately and the venerators of icons persecuted. The reaction in the West was firm. Pope Gregory III (731–741) sternly condemned iconoclasm and promised excommunication for anyone who harmed a sacred image. He also sent an official statement of his position to the emperor, telling him to keep out of theological matters.

Relations between East and West had often been thorny, but this breech over iconoclasm only deepened the division between the two. By the eighth century, most of Byzantium's western provinces that had not been conquered either by the Arabs or the Lombards were in fact under local rule and imperial only in name. The popes at Rome exercised more political control in non-Lombard Italy than did the emperors from Constantinople. In 751, Aistulf, king of the Lombards, took Ravenna signaling that effective Byzantine political control of the West was now at an end.

The World's Emporium

From its perch on the Bosphorus, Constantinople controlled the brisk trade between the Mediterranean and the world outside. As early as Justinian's reign, Byzantium's commercial dominance was secured; it had even captured the ports on the Black Sea and thus controlled the trade to Russia and the Scandinavian lands beyond. The great city's market, the famous Mese, was ablaze with alluring luxury goods from places even the sophisticated Byzantines found hard to picture. Exquisite porcelain and silks, many embroidered and all in wonderful colors, purple (especially purple), pale green, violet, and peach came from China. From Persia came carpets in exciting designs and colors; blue was a favorite. From India came tantalizing spices and sparkling precious stones. Ships from the West, from the Adriatic, Genoa, Amalfi, and Marseilles, crowded the harbor and greedily gathered these wonders for transport to Europe.

Constantinople owed its commercial dominance to more than just its geographic setting and political control, although these were certainly the major factors. The Byzantine currency, the byzant, or solidus as Europe called it, was trusted everywhere. This coin remained the monetary standard in Europe until the end of the seventh century. Constantinople's skillful artisans also manufactured many highly sought-after wares. Its own tapestries, dyed skins, inlaid bronze and silver work, religious artifacts, leather goods, and the like excited buyers as much as the imported goods did. And then in the mid-sixth century, two monks appeared in the city with cocoons of the silk worm. The worms were carefully bred and soon the imperial government sported an extremely lucrative monopoly of native silk production. Byzantium no longer depended on the long and expensive journey to import the luxurious fabric from China.

The commercial activity required a great deal of careful supervision. The government controlled almost every aspect of trade and manufacturing. Cloth and fish merchants were told how much they could buy. Weavers were required to use the state-owned dye works. Some purple dye they could not use; it was reserved for the emperor. Yellow soap was also reserved for imperial use. Work at certain hours and on certain days was prohibited. There were even pub hours: They had to close at 8:00 P.M. to inhibit undue merrymaking and noise. Goldsmiths could not hold more than a pound of unworked gold at one time. The government often stipulated which supplier could be used and set the price of the goods. The visits of foreign merchants were strictly limited, usually to three months, and they could live only in certain areas, usually outside the walls. Punishments for infractions of any of these rules were severe and had a shaming public nature to them.

The government seemed to snatch up revenue in any way it could. It owned vast imperial estates and other properties, and the Byzantines were famous as avaricious and thorough tax collectors. They levied a poll tax, inheritance taxes, and a ten-percent tax on all imports, something that created both a healthy income and a healthy smuggling industry. But most of the income came from the onerous land tax, which fell mostly upon the poor; aristocrats were exempt both from it and from the poll tax.

The Reign of a Woman: The Empress Irene

Emperor Leo IV (775–780) concluded a marriage with an Athenian woman of unremarkable lineage that seemed to bring no obvious advantages to the imperial family. She is said to have been wondrously beautiful but disastrously ambitious, ruthless, capable, and deceitful. Ironically her name was Irene, the Greek word for peace.

Once in the Sacred Palace she dominated her husband and after his death acted as regent for their young son, Constantine VI (780–797). Since the days of Leo III, the iconoclasts had taken over many extremely important positions in the imperial government and Church. Irene, a passionate venerator of images, began to support those who shared her view. She reinstated the veneration of the Virgin Mary, allowed monks exiled by the iconoclasts to return to their monasteries, and began to purge iconoclasts from their positions. The result was uproar, rebellion, and trouble in the army.

She caused a rebellion against her son, in the course of which she had him blinded. When he died from those wounds, she took over the throne, becoming the first woman to rule Byzantium not as regent or coruler, but in her own right. She may have held the throne, but it was not a secure seat. In a bid for popularity she executed a drastic tax cut, something the government could not afford. The effort backfired. Aware citizens recognized the measure as grandstanding, and the army in the east voiced loud concerns about the government's ability to meet the military payroll.

Because a woman occupied Byzantium's throne, Europeans considered it vacant. On Christmas day, 800, the pope crowned the Frankish king, Charlemagne, Roman Emperor, and the fact that there was no emperor in Constantinople was very likely a factor in the pope's motivation. Two years later, Charlemagne's ambassadors appeared in Constantinople with an offer of marriage for Irene. She may have been inclined to accept. She desperately needed support, and an uncultured barbarian could not be too awfully difficult to control as husband. But the idea was abhorrent to the Byzantines. It was not only unbelievable arrogance on the part of the Franks, but sacrilege. The proposal came to nothing, and soon a palace coup sent Irene into exile.

Everyday Life

Much like the Roman Empire before it, Byzantine culture was urban; it flourished in the great cities of the eastern Mediterranean and especially in Constantinople itself. Gold seemed to be everywhere at a time when payment in kind was becoming the rule in Europe. Its culture was rich, sophisticated, hierarchical, permeated by religion, and tightly controlled. Tight building codes were enforced for the good of all: no balconies nearer than ten feet to the neighbors, no blocking of the neighbor's view. Teaching valuable skills to foreigners was strictly forbidden. The trades, weights, measures, and prices were all regulated by an army of state officials. Laws stipulated requirements for clothing, public gatherings, worship, working, and the evening's activities.

Women in Byzantine society, especially married women, seem to have enjoyed a reasonably high status. Wives were not kept from the public lives of their husbands. Although the sphere of women was still primarily the private one of children and household, they could own and manage property. Children often took the family name of their mothers. A reflection of the position of women in general is seen in the role of the empresses at the top of the social scale. They often performed the usual political functions of regents for young or incapacitated male relatives, but many had great power in their own right. The empress's presence was required at many important ceremonies and she often carried out imperial policy. In a charming story, the Emperor Theophilus needed a ship and having found a suitable vessel, asked who the owner was. The reply came that his wife owned it; the emperor had had no inkling.

Life in Byzantium was permeated with religion. The erudite bishop, Gregory of Nyssa (c. 330–c. 395), was amazed to overhear theological arguments on the street corners among waiters and hawkers. "If I ask the price of bread," he wrote, "I am told that God the Father is greater than God the Son." Although official festivals, ceremonies, saints' days, and worship in the great basilicas formed a large part of the people's religious practice, Constantinople was also a notorious hotbed for the underbelly of religious life: palm-reading, fortune-telling, magic, and sorcery. The area around the Hippodrome was especially rank with such practitioners, and they were extremely popular. The difference between prayer and incantation or between priest and magician was often blurred. Just as the most highly placed and most powerful often sought spiritual solutions for what we would consider earthly problems, so too those at the less respectable end of the social scale often looked for answers from these less respectable spiritual sources.

Reverence for the Past

Intellectual life in Byzantium did not place great value on new ideas; rather Byzantine scholars (just as European scholars of the period) showed a profound reverence for the past. Ancient, especially biblical authority, not creativity, was the guide of intellectual activity. The Byzantines were great editors and commentators; their goal was to reproduce the truths of the past, adding appropriate comments of awe, reverence, and explanation. The influential theologian John of Damascus (c. 675–c. 749) actually boasted that there was nothing new in his book, although serious analysts certainly find much profound originality in his work. The fact that the creative element was absent more than we might expect in such a great civilization does not mean that there were not Byzantines of great erudition. There certainly were, and to them we owe an unamortized debt for having preserved and edited much of the Greek, Roman, and Christian past they so revered.

MUHAMMAD AND THE RELIGION OF ISLAM

In 570, just five years after the death of Justinian, in a recently vitalized Arabian commercial town lying half way down the western edge of the Arabian peninsula very near the coast of the Red Sea, a child was born who would grow to affect the religious and political life of the Near East, the Mediterranean, and then the world beyond. That town was Mecca, and the child was Muhammad, messenger of Allah.

Arabia Before Muhammad

Traditional Arabian society was based on loyalty to the clan and tribe. This loyalty was expressed by a sense of common ancestry and an allegiance to local gods. The tribe was a very strong social unit, usually holding pastures, water sources, and even livestock in common. It was ruled by a sheikh or group of sheikhs. The sheikh was usually the head of a prominent family, elected by his peers. His power depended upon his wisdom, generosity, and ability, and he was often advised, and also often greatly constrained, by a council of elders. A sheikh ruled by judgment or arbitration rather than by command; ideas of commanding kingly authority or of public coercive power were not part of the tribal system. Public discipline was maintained by mutual accountability for criminal activity largely through the fear of vengeance on the part of a victim's kin. As was often true in Europe in the early Middle Ages, the obligation to seek vengeance was closely bound to the concept of honor. As a result, Arabian men were often warriors.

Most Arabian towns grew up in the western part of the peninsula along the trade routes. The government in these towns was an adaptation of the tribal system. Here each clan still had its council, but an oligarchy of privileged commercial families developed, greatly limiting or even supplanting the position of the sheikh. The new wealth created new social distinctions, straining the traditional tribal culture. Still the political ethos remained nomadic, with authority resting in clans and not in public institutions.

The towns also contained significant settlements of Christians and Jews. Medina, for instance, had a large Jewish population. In the towns, too, writing, literature, ideas of monotheism, and new conceptions of social and moral norms were beginning to take root—all important ingredients in the culture of Mecca and Medina in which both Muhammad and Islam grew.

The wars between the Byzantines and the Persians in the sixth century caused the traditional trade routes that led from the Mediterranean to the east across Mesopotamia to become too dangerous. As a result, the route running north and south along the western side of Arabia between Damascus and Yemen became increasingly important. This route passed through Mecca, a small market town with an important religious center. Mecca's holy site was the Kaa'ba, a cube-shaped building that housed many sacred images and a sacred black stone embedded in its walls. Early in the sixth century the traditional guardians of the Kaa'ba were replaced by the Quraysh tribe, under whom Mecca attained a preeminent position in northern and western Arabia. The thriving city's urban patriciate was aggressive and exercising obvious talent in self-governance and cooperative rule, valuable skills indeed for ruling the great empire that would shortly be theirs.

The Life of Muhammad

Muhammad was born in Mecca in 570. Orphaned when he was only six, he was raised by his clan. As a young man he became the successful manager of the business affairs of a widow, Khadija, whom he married. They had several children, the most important of whom was his daughter, Fatima (see Medieval Portraits). When Muhammad was about forty years old, he began to receive divine revelations in which he was commanded to preach and so he began his religious calling.

Muhammad did not want to create a new religion, but to return to the faith of Abraham, which he thought Jews and Christians had perverted over the centuries. He espoused total submission to the greatness of Allah, the only God. In fact, the name Islam means "submission" to one Supreme God. His teaching directly opposed the polytheism of much of traditional Arabian society and denied the Christian concept of the Holy Trinity. He was fortunate to have the complete support of his wife, Khadija, who first backed him in trade and then affirmed his revelations and religious calling.

Muhammad made little headway in Mecca. He was often subjected to ridicule, ostracism, and even persecution, especially after his wife and his uncle died. His fortunes changed, however, in 622 when he and his followers left Mecca for Medina. This migration to Medina is called the *Hijra* and would become the starting point for the Islamic calendar. Muhammad's Islamic community in Medina came to be called the *umma,* a complicated word that indicates the community of the faithful. The idea of community was and remained extremely strong in Islam and the converts' ties to the *umma* transcended those to tribe and clan. Their new religion also separated them from Medina's other inhabitants.

Islam is often described as a union of arms and religion, the sword and the Book. Indeed, the sword entered Islam very early on when Muhammad realized that without defeating the Meccans, Islam would never flourish. In January of 624, he and his followers ambushed a Meccan caravan at Badr, defeating a large defending force. When he finally captured Mecca in 630, his position opened the way for him to extend his influence over much of the Arabian peninsula. He did so through a mixture of propaganda, diplomacy, religious conversion, and military conquest. In Mecca the Kaa'ba was cleared of the stone images and became Islam's most holy site: According to Muhammad, it had been founded by Abraham. By the time Muhammad died in 632, his authority over Arabia was uncontested and Muslim warriors had begun to push into Syria.

Muhammad's authority within the community was that of Prophet, Apostle, and Messenger of God. He is, according to the Qur'an, the greatest of the messengers of God, greater than the Old Testament prophets and Christ. Contrary to what some medieval writers thought, Muhammad did not claim divine status and did not ask to be worshipped by Muslims. He also never claimed to perform miracles. Instead, he provided an example of righteousness, trustworthiness, compassion, and piety.

MEDIEVAL PORTRAITS

Fatima (d. 632), Daughter of Muhammad

Fatima became the most important of Muhammad's children more because of what she was than because of what she did. She never held important political office nor did she write important Muslim works. She lived a devoted, pious, and upright life and became an inspiration to all Islam, and because of her important position in Muhammad's family, she became a central figure in the teachings of the Shia.

Fatima was the daughter of the Prophet and his first wife, Khadija, who had been instrumental in supporting him in his early years. She married Ali (d. 661), her father's cousin, and their two children, Hasan and Husayn, lived to be the only surviving legitimate grandsons of Muhammad. Fatima died almost thirty years before her husband. She was very devoted to her father and died from grief and suffering seventy-five days after he did. She is said to have undergone many injustices at the hands of her husband's political rivals in the period between Muhammad's death and her own.

Since Shi'ites trace the line of legitimate Muslim authority through the Prophet's earthly family, it is among their traditions that Fatima is especially honored. As early as the seventh century, hymns and invocations were addressed to her, and we have records of prayers to her from the tenth. The following is an excerpt from one:

> Peace be with you, O you who were afflicted with trials by the One who created you. When he tested you, he found you to be patient under affliction. . .
>
> Peace be with you, O mistress of the women of the worlds. Peace be with you, O mother of the vindicators of humankind in argument. Peace be with you, O you who were wronged, you who were deprived of that to which you were entitled by right. . . .*

The medieval literature about her emphasizes her virtues as guiltless victim and her patience in suffering. Her life is portrayed as one of endurance, rather than one of action. As such, she became the archetype of the suffering mother and devotional focus for the political quietism that has characterized much of Shi'ite history.

* Gavin R. G. Hambly, *Women in the Islamic World* (New York: St. Martin's, 1999) 72.

Muhammad was a reformer not only in religion but also in cultural practices. For example, he condemned exploitation of the weaker members of society and especially the abuse of women and children. In contrast to pre-Islamic customs, he condemned infanticide and discouraged divorce, while at the same time giving women a narrowly defined right to divorce. A Muslim man is legitimately allowed to have more than one wife, up to four, if they can be treated equally. Muhammad promoted equitable relations between spouses and the right of women to inherit. He also insisted on charity and social justice.

Islam adamantly insists on the oneness of God and rests on five obligatory practices, or pillars. All Muslims are expected to: 1) profess the belief that "There is no god but Allah and Muhammad is the messenger of God"; 2) pray five times a day, facing Mecca; 3) perform alms, 4) fast during the month of Ramadan; and 5) make a pilgrimage to Mecca at least once in their lifetime if they can afford it.

Muhammad proved himself an inspiring leader. He combined total religious devotion with a clear-sighted and practical political sense. His authority was far greater, his rule far more effective, and his followers far more loyal than had been the case with any sheikh. He combined political and religious authority in his own person, acting as military commander, lawgiver, ruler, and religious leader. He left no provision for the leadership of his organization after his death. His successors were called caliphs, meaning "Successors of the Prophet." They were originally picked from among his closest companions. The caliph did not have the same authority as Muhammad: for instance, a caliph was never a lawmaker; he could only apply the law. Nonetheless with the strong leadership exercised by Muhammad and the caliphs who followed him, Islam took root and it would quickly come to rule a very large part of the civilized world.

The Sources

The Qur'an, Islam's holiest book, was collected and organized after Muhammad's death during the caliphate of 'Uthman (644–656). It contains the holy word of God as revealed to Muhammad by the archangel Gabriel at different times during his preaching career. Its primary emphasis is the unity of God and the need for mankind's total submission to God's will (see Medieval Voices). It is consequently very concerned with piety and morality and lays out vivid images of the joys of heaven or the suffering that awaits in hell. Many of its ideas are found in earlier Arabian, Jewish, and Christian teaching, but Muslims see the Qur'an as completing and restoring these earlier revelations to the pure word of God. It is important to note that in Muslim belief Muhammad did not "write" the Qur'an, but he was rather the instrument through which Allah made his word known.

The rapid expansion of Islam within a few generations of Muhammad's death brought Muslims into situations for which the Qur'an gave little guidance. The idea then became current that not only the Qur'an, i.e., the inspired word of God, but anything Muhammad said or did carried authoritative weight. A body of "traditions" grew up, known as *hadith,* that contained a great amount of material concerning Muhammad's life and teachings. As Muslim scholars admit, not all *hadith* is authentic; much was added since Muhammad's death and not all for disinterested reasons. Among the more trustworthy of *hadiths* were those that can be shown to have originated with A'isha bint Abu Bakr, Muhammad's favorite wife and daughter of Abu Bakr, the first caliph. A'isha, who was eighteen when Muhammad died, passed on information regarding religious ritual, marriage, inheritance, dowries, and much more. She was consulted on political matters and her authority often was preferred to that of any of the first four caliphs.

In addition to *hadith,* a written biographical tradition for Muhammad, the *Sira,* developed. Here he became the subject of heroic tales that sang his military victories for the Faith in tribal fashion, giving him a treatment much like the one

MEDIEVAL VOICES

The Qur'an
Describes
Islam

The Qur'an presents the word of God in such an engaging way, easily understood, compellingly believable, and with such simple and dignified eloquence that it seems to prove a power greater than a human one had produced it. Its rhymed prose became a model for the developing Arabic language and the traditional idea that the purveyor of such a beautiful and holy book, Muhammad, was unlettered added to this "miracle of the Qur'an." It is arranged into 114 chapters of 6000 verses largely in order of decreasing length.

In the Name of God, the Merciful, the Compassionate. Praise belongs to God, the Lord of all Being, the All-merciful, the All-compassionate, the Master of the Day of Judgment. Thee only we serve; to Thee alone we pray for succor. Guide us in the Straight Path, the path of those whom Thou hast blessed, not of those against whom Thou are wrathful, nor of those who are astray. (Q1: 1-7)

Surely God's friends—no fear shall be on them, neither shall they sorrow. Those who believe, and are godfearing—for them is good tidings in the present life and in the world to come. (Q10: 62-4)

Give thou good tidings to those who believe and do deeds of righteousness, that for them await gardens underneath which rivers flow; . . . and there for them shall be spouses purified; therein they shall dwell forever. (Q2: 25)

True piety is this: to believe in God, and the Last Day, the angels, the Book, and the Prophets, to give of one's substance, however cherished, to kinsmen, and orphans, the needy, the traveller, beggars, and to ransom the slave, to perform the prayer, to pay the alms. (Q2: 177)

Source: Michael Cook, *The Koran. A Very Short Introduction* (Oxford: OUP, 2000) 8–11.

Christian hagiographers were wont to give their saints. Here he was not only God's messenger; he was also a wonder-worker.

Women in Islam

The Qur'an portrays women as representatives of spiritual freedom and moral responsibility. It calls only one woman by name, Mary, the mother of Jesus. Even though it does not name them, women are strong figures in the Qur'an. The wives of Lot and Noah serve as warnings about the consequences of disobedience. The Queen of Sheba is the royal equal of Solomon and rules in her own right. The wife (Sara) and concubine (Hagar) of Abraham are portrayed as strong positive examples. Other women too, for instance, the mother of Moses and the wives of the Prophet, are presented as moral models and exemplary individuals. In telling the story of Adam and Eve, the Qur'an lays no particular blame on Eve as does the Old Testament. Here both Eve and Adam sin and the fault is Satan's.

The relatively high status of women in the Qur'an and in early Islamic history did not survive Islam's political and military successes. The effects of the Persian and Byzantine cultures upon the expanding Islam, along with a certain tension resulting from its view of marriage as patriarchal, helped to all but exclude Islamic women from public life and increasingly to restrict their freedom. Although a number of early Islamic women, such as Khadija, Muhammad's first wife, were able to arrange their own marriages, and one, A'isha, became a prominent political leader, by the eighth century, Islamic women were increasingly subject to the restricting conditions of polygamy and seclusion. Only a man could be a caliph, and although occasionally a woman could exercise earthly authority as sultana or queen, her position was rarely secure.

AN EMPIRE RISES FROM ARABIA

Within the 100 years from 632 to 732, Islam overran most of the Western civilized world (see Map 4.2). The reasons for the breathless speed of the Muslims' success

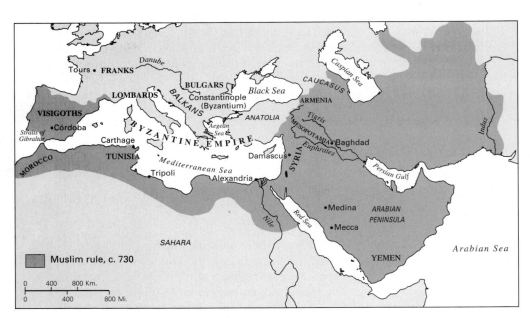

Map 4.2   The Muslim Conquests c. 800   As is obvious from this map, the Muslims most direct route into western Europe from their heartlands in Arabia, Syria, and Mesopotamia lay through Anatolia and the Balkans. The dogged resistance of the Byzantines, however, closed this access to them.

are many. Their major obstacles, the Persians and the Byzantines, were, as we have seen, exhausted from fighting each other. The Muslims initially conquered many peoples who were the overtaxed or the religiously oppressed subjects of the Byzantines or Persians, and thus their resistance to the Arab advance was not great. They met no serious resistance in their sweep across Africa and when they got to Gibraltar, they were actually invited into Spain to help one side in a local war. But all these factors, which are external to Islamic society, do not provide a totally satisfying explanation. There was something about the Muslims themselves which made them so startlingly successful.

Early Muslim Leadership

One factor in the Muslims' success was the quality of their leadership; Muhammad was followed by a series of remarkable caliphs. The lives of the first two, 'Abu Bakr (632–634) and 'Umar (634–644), were austere examples to their followers and devoid of the material trappings and comforts usually associated with mighty rule. With them, Islam was true to its name, "total submission." The fact that the dedicated life personified by the Prophet and the early caliphs was enthusiastically adopted by their followers was another important factor in Islam's early success. 'Umar took measures to ensure that this Islamic purity would not be diluted by contact with conquered peoples. He forbade the Arabs occupying Palestine and Syria to settle down among the locals, keeping them instead a separate and mobile force. Consequently the Arabs developed into a ruling caste, separate, above, and supported by the indigenous populations.

Under 'Umar's successor, 'Uthman (644–656), Muhammad's son-in-law from the Meccan clan, Bani Umayya, the rush of conquests continued. By 647, they had moved across northern Africa and taken Tripoli. Armenia fell in the same year and by 653 they had taken all of Persia up to the Indus River and had pushed northward to the Caucasus Mountains.

Even amid these successes, all was not well. 'Uthman attempted to impose a greater centralization of power. He reduced the independence of provincial governors, controlled the finances from Medina, and produced a definitive version of the *Qur'an*. For many, this centralizing policy was an unwelcome change. 'Uthman was also beset with complaints that he unfairly favored his own clansmen, the Bani Umayya, with the most important and lucrative offices of the Empire. In the last half of his reign, he was plagued with almost universal rebellion; it was not so much the conquered peoples who revolted, but the Arabs themselves. In fact, he was assassinated by Arabs who felt betrayed by him.

The next to be proclaimed caliph was Ali (656–661), Muhammad's cousin and son-in-law who was married to his daughter Fatima and was a member of Muhammad's own clan, the Bani Hashim. He dismissed all of 'Uthman's appointees, except Mu'awiya, the ruler of Syria, who was protected by a powerful and loyal army. A bloody but indecisive civil war was the result, and then Ali, too, was assassinated. Ali had two sons by his wife, Fatima. These two, Hasan and Husayn, were thus grandsons of the Prophet and considered his only legitimate heirs. Hasan was immediately proclaimed caliph, but so too was Mu'awiya. Faced with the prospect of certain and continued civil war, the two brothers retired to political seclusion in Medina. Their followers, however, stayed active, forming a separate sect of Islam. They are known as *Shia*, the Arabic word for "following." Shi'ite Muslims, although persecuted by the Umayyads and driven underground, never lost their sense of legitimate succession. They are led not by caliphs, but by Imams. Ali is considered the first Iman and all others must be directly descended from him. Modern Iran is a Shi'ite nation.

Mu'awiya (661–680) established his capital in Damascus. For the next eighty years Umayyad caliphs came to power in reasonably orderly succession, bringing much needed stability to the empire. Although the old days of rapid conquests were over, the Umayyads steadily chipped away at the Byzantines. With daunting regularity they sent their armies into Anatolia and their fleets into the Aegean. By 672 they were fifty miles from Constantinople, and in 674 they began their famous siege of the city itself. The Byzantines, with help from the Bulgars and from the newly discovered "Greek fire," a napalm that water could not extinguish, managed to ward them off. In the West, on the other hand, the Muslims overran Carthage in 698, ending Byzantine rule of Africa.

The movement of the capital from Medina, the city of the Prophet, to Damascus lessened the legitimacy of the caliphs' rule somewhat. They began to behave more like kings than warriors and community leaders, as had the earliest caliphs. They settled in, governing through a council of sheikhs, and taking over much of the Byzantine and Persian administrative machinery. But for all this, the caliphs were still successors of the Prophet and heads of Islam.

The Abbasid Revolution

Just as the history of the ancient Roman Empire can be seen as a steady progression of becoming less Roman, so too as the Arabian Empire accommodated itself to the lands it ruled, it became less Arabian. The Umayyads' empire was Arabian, governed by a great, tax-exempt, Arabian warrior-elite. But a large Muslim commercial class, the *Mawali*, grew up in its cities. As Muslims, the *Mawali* paid only the religious tithe, but as non-Arabs, they were second-class citizens. They became rich, and with their increasing wealth, they were increasingly resented. As is often the case with dissatisfied factions, they found a religious focus for their discontent, many becoming members of the *Shia*.

As the wars of conquest ended, the function of the Arabian warrior elite lost its importance. Its aloof and privileged position was becoming increasingly less justified by the current nature of the empire. The conquered populations, too, were changing. Over the generations Arabic replaced the indigenous languages in almost all the territories west of Persia, and the peoples gradually began to convert to Islam. These changes, coupled with the resentment of the *Mawali* and the natural discontent felt by local peoples for a far-away, conquering, and taxing central government, eventually united various elements in a successful overthrow of the Umayyads. All Umayyad claimants to the caliphate were killed, with one exception.

'Abd al-Rahman survived by fleeing to Spain across North Africa in an adventure worthy of the Arabian Nights, to become emir in Cordoba and to create a Umayyad breakaway state in Spain.

The new dynasty, the Abbasids, came to power in 750, claiming descent from the Prophet's paternal uncle and calling for a return to early Islam and the practices of the Prophet. Their second caliph, al-Mansur (754–775), built a new capital for the empire. He chose a site near ancient Babylon, a village called Baghdad, and in so doing shifted the center of Islamic rule from Syria to Mesopotamia. In their new setting the caliphs adopted the highly ceremonial, aloof, and theocratic rule typical of Persian culture. No longer residing in the simple houses of Medina or the palaces of Damascus, they were now luxuriously and firmly anchored in a brilliant royal complex, resplendent with costly furniture and decoration, staffed by a cultured and permanent bureaucracy, and far from view of the ordinary Muslim. The caliph now claimed to rule by divine mandate, attempting to unite both temporal and spiritual authority into one absolute rule.

The Abbasid revolution represents the social and political maturing of Islam. It was no longer a lithe adolescent, flush with the headiness of Allah's rapid conquests; it was now an adult, already with more than a century of its own history and beset with the problems of established rule. The Abbasid Empire replaced the older Arab warrior elite with one reflecting a peaceful society based on agriculture, a thriving urban life, and a growing cultured class. Merchants, bankers, landowners, jurists, teachers, and religious scholars along with the military and governmental officials now began to occupy positions of privilege. It was faith in Allah rather than national origin that permitted membership. Spain, Morocco, and Tunisia all broke away from direct Abbasid control, yet until the Mongols seized Baghdad in 1258 Abbasid rule, however fragmented, saw a great flowering of Islamic civilization.

Life under the Abbasids

From very early in Islamic history, the Arabs had devoted themselves both to the study of the Qur'an and other holy books and to the study of jurisprudence. The greatest scholars were therefore linguists, grammarians, exegetes, and legal experts. Under the Abbasids, works in Latin, Syriac, Coptic, Sanskrit, and Persian along with some in Greek were all translated into Arabic. As Islamic scholars came increasingly into contact with these other cultures, they felt new influences in the study of Islamic theology, namely an increased interest in logic and philosophy. This intellectual flowering was not limited to theology; geography, mathematics (algebra and geometry), medicine, alchemy, literature, and Islamic law all advanced under Abbasid rule as well.

In contrast to the scholarly approach, many religious Muslims began to take up the interior way of mysticism. The Islamic mystical path is called Sufism and, like other mystical movements, it seeks to know God through direct encounter. Sufism developed early; many Sufis were among the early opponents of the Umayyads, rejecting Islamic imperialism and the distractions of the material world. Throughout the ninth and tenth centuries, Sufism spread across Arabia, Syria, Egypt, and Iraq and later grew to be a mass movement within Islam.

Many of these intellectual, literary, and mystical achievements later influenced western Europe. For instance, Islamic poetry shaped the rise of romance and of troubadour poetry in Europe. The Islamic use of Hindu numbers (including the concept of zero) brought "Arabic" numerals to Europe. A scientist in optics, al-Kindī, influenced European ideas of the anatomy of the eye and the working of light. And the writings of Ibn Sina (Avicenna), the "Great Commentator" on Aristotle, were instrumental in causing Europe's scholastic renaissance in the eleventh and twelfth centuries and later.

Muslim rulers generally treated minorities, nonbelievers, lower classes, and outcasts far better than did Christian rulers. One minority with special status were the *Dhimmi*, the "People of the Book", that is, Christians and Jews who did not convert to Islam. The *Dhimmi* paid taxes but only very rarely suffered persecution. They were allowed to practice their religion, enjoyed normal property rights, suffered no major vocational prohibitions, were exempt from mandatory military service, and sometimes held high positions at court.

Although most labor in Islamic society was done by free or semifree peasants, Muslims did own slaves. There were domestic slaves in the more comfortable households, and northern European slave women were prized as concubines. Muslim armies from early Abbasid times were filled with slave soldiers: Africans, Turks, Khazars, Slavs, Greeks, and Yemeni, who sometimes rose to high ranks. Slaves were

Islamic Coin from Year 79 (698–699 A.D.)   In keeping with the Islamic prohibition, the coin bears no human likeness. The center of the obverse (the front) carries the Arabic inscription: "There is no god but God alone without companion" and around it "In the name of God." The reverse (the back) displays quotations from the Qur'an. *The British Museum.*

used for particularly undesirable work: They toiled in the mines, rowed in the fleets, and did such thoroughly unpleasant jobs as draining swamps or extracting salt. Some large-scale agricultural slavery existed, and these slaves were often black people purchased from sub-Saharan Africa. The Qur'an recommended freeing slaves, and they could ransom themselves. Women slaves were freed if they bore sons.

Since Islam ruled the great cities of the Middle East and sat astride the trade routes to the orient, it had a bustling commercial life. The Muslims were very good sailors; as early as the eighth century we find them not only along the African and Indian coasts, but also in East Asia. Their ships returned laden with the most wonderful goods: silks, paper, ink, peacocks, saddles, cinnamon, slave girls, tiger skins, panthers, or coconuts. Thousands of Muslim coins from the seventh through the tenth centuries have been found in Scandinavia and along the Volga. The earliest known Swedish coins used Muslim weights, and Arabic words are found even in early Icelandic literature, indicating trading contact with that far-off outpost of European culture.

Summary

Early medieval Europe was bounded to its east and south by two great civilizations. Between the early fourth and late eighth century, a New Rome formed itself astride the Bosphorus, bridging Europe and the Near East. It was to prove itself a powerful, dynamic, highly cultured society that would endure as long as European medieval civilization. In many important ways, Europeans in the early Middle Ages felt strong influence from the Bosphorus. Byzantine gold, in the form of subsidies skillfully dangled and proffered, directed much of their politics even into the sixth century. The Europeans used Byzantium's coins, hired its artists, copied its architecture, and scrambled to purchase its luxury goods. Most barbarian kings in the West recognized the overlordship of the Byzantine emperor. As Byzantium's direct political control over parts of western Europe dwindled and then disappeared in the eighth century, and as its propensity toward iconoclasm strained its relationship with the Church in the West, its direct influence on Europe waned. But in the very period when it was retreating geographically, it stood as bulwark against Europe's would-be invaders, especially blocking the Muslims' most direct path into the West.

In 633 the Muslims advanced out of Arabia to absorb the Persian Empire and to reduce the Byzantines to such proportions as to make the Mediterranean largely their own lake. We can attempt to explain their success by three factors: 1) the weakness of their enemies, brought on by relentless wars with each other, 2) their welcome by the local peoples subjugated by unpopular rule of Byzantium and Persia, and 3) the nature of Islam itself. Early Islam brought unity to the Arabs. It provided them with an invigorating self-confidence. Allah was unquestionably the true and only God and he was obviously on their side. Their faith promised them eternal rewards that were easily understandable and delightful. Their toleration of conquered peoples made their new subjects less likely to revolt. But primarily it was both their startlingly unquestioning obedience to the will of Allah (Islam) and their austere discipline in carrying out that will that gave them their early success. With the end of the conquests, when obedience and austerity took a back seat to the requirements of established rule, their unity broke down along with their ability to expand farther. As we shall see, (Chapter 14), their cultural achievements were to have far-reaching effects on the intellectual and scientific history of medieval Europe.

PART II

~

The Early Middle Ages, A.D. 751–910

CHAPTER 5

~

The Early Medieval Church
in the West, 500–800

It is common for historians to talk about how the Christian Church carried ancient culture into the Middle Ages. Indeed, it would be difficult to exaggerate the cultural role of early medieval Christianity. Although there were strong secular elements of culture that were not derived from the Church, for much of the medieval period and for most Europeans, Christian teaching guided morals, philosophy, art, and education, and set many of the rules governing the family. The Church's immense influence was not limited to these matters; much of medieval law, politics, economics, and at times even warfare was conducted according to Christian precepts.

The ancient world had brought the Church into being, provided it with its sacred texts, worked out most of its theology, developed its fundamental forms of worship, and given the institution its basic structure. The Middle Ages would change none of this appreciably; the period would, however, greatly expand the Church, giving it a more complex institutional structure, a broader geographical area, and a greater role in society. In this chapter we shall view the Church in the years roughly between A.D. 500 and 800. After an explanation of its structure, we shall watch it expand both geographically as it converted pagans and heretics, and culturally as it extended its spiritual control into important aspects of everyday life.

POPES, PRIESTS, MONKS, AND NUNS:
A SPIRITUAL HIERARCHY EMERGES

The early medieval Church in western Europe was a spiritual hierarchy. The head was the pope in Rome. Next came the archbishops, whose area of authority was the archdiocese, or province, comprising several dioceses. The archbishop was also a bishop, usually the bishop of the most important diocese in his province. In the actual workings of the Church, the crucial figures were the leaders on the next level:

the bishops. The bishops exercised great authority over the property, priests, and other ecclesiastical personnel of their dioceses. Priests who were in turn assisted by deacons and other personnel normally led the churches in the diocese. The popes, bishops, priests, deacons and others, were the secular clergy, that is, the clergy whose function it was to work in the world (Latin *saeculum*) for the salvation of other peoples' souls.

In addition to the secular clergy, the Church had another huge body of clerics who formed the regular clergy because they followed a monastic rule (Latin *regula*). These were the monks and nuns. They did not do God's work in this world but cut themselves off from it, usually by living in a monastery, in order to seek their own salvation. Although they often prayed for those living beyond the monastery, their own lives took place almost exclusively within it. Their avowed purpose may have been to flee this world and its evils, but in fact their institution, monasticism, became a central part of the medieval world.

The Pope

In rank, the pope is no more than a bishop, the bishop of the city of Rome. In position, however, he is far more; the pope claims what is called "primacy," or first place, among all the bishops of the Church. Recognition of Rome's primacy took centuries to build. At first, Rome had no more ecclesiastical standing than did the late Roman Empire's other leading cities: Constantinople, Antioch, Jerusalem, and Alexandria, whose bishops were called patriarchs. The patriarchs of the East never fully acknowledged Rome's claim to primacy, but in the West it came to be universally recognized. This primacy was founded in two ways: practically and spiritually.

On the practical side, the prestige and historical tradition of the city of Rome greatly strengthened the pope's authority. The West was accustomed to taking orders from Rome. Rome had long set literary, cultural, political, military, and social standards, and it seemed quite natural that its bishop should also hold first place in the Church. Rome, too, had a history of good bishops. Damasus (366–384), Leo I (440–461), and Gelasius (492–496) for example, had shown practical sense in administration and had supported the thinking that became recognized as orthodox in the early Church's many theological disputes. Thus the leadership at Rome was both generally competent in administration and not tinged with heresy, as other bishops, even some of the great patriarchs, too often were.

The spiritual supports for Rome's primacy were more important than these impressive practical ones. By the doctrine called apostolic succession, bishops traced their spiritual ancestry back to the apostles. The pope, as bishop of Rome, traced his to Saint Peter, seen as the first bishop of Rome. Since according to interpretation, Christ had made Peter first among his apostles, it followed that Peter's successors should be first among the other bishops. In addition, Rome claimed to have the actual physical relics of both Saint Peter and Saint Paul. According to tradition, both were buried in Rome. Thus Rome had a special connection with the two most important apostles. By the time Gregory I assumed the papacy in 590, the primacy of Rome was well on its way to being universally accepted in the West.

Even though the early medieval popes held primacy in the Church's hierarchy, their ability to influence churches in various parts of northern Europe varied greatly by time and by region. Some parts, namely England and Germany, were often more responsive to papal influence while the Frankish and Spanish churches at times walked a more independent path.

The Bishops

In the sixth and seventh centuries throughout the West the position of bishop remained a very powerful one. The Church continued the tradition from the earlier centuries of its history (see Chapter 2) of attracting powerful men to the episcopacy. Bishops served at the imperial court in Constantinople as early as the reign of Constantine, and soon thereafter they began to influence the barbarian kings in western Europe. For example, we have a long letter of advice from Remigius, bishop of Rheims (c. 438–c.533) to Clovis, the first important Frankish king; Avitus, bishop of Vienne (490–519), advised the early Burgundian kings; and Isidore, bishop of Seville (600–636), counseled the kings of Visigothic Spain.

The power of the bishop rested on many foundations. First, and most importantly, it was spiritual. He was the duly recognized official of the Church responsible for the salvation of souls within his diocese. He was the keeper of the relics of the local saint and responsible for all the festivals and ceremonies that the saint's honor required. For these reasons, the people perceived him as their spiritual protector and were often fiercely loyal to him. On the other hand, they would also blame him if they were beset by any plague, drought, or other indication of divine displeasure.

Second, the bishops almost always came from powerful families. The situation in southern Gaul in the sixth century clearly illustrates this. The famous author and historian, Gregory, bishop of Tours (573–594) came from an ancient and wealthy Gallo-Roman family which had for generations held the sees at Tours and Langres almost as a familial right. Gregory was powerful enough to defend the interests of his city against the king's local representative and even stand up to the king himself (see Medieval Voices).

Third, a bishop could gain a great deal of local prestige from his influence at the royal court. For the royal governments, the Church was a valuable source of learned officials capable of advising the king, keeping records, drafting laws, concluding treaties, composing documents, or conducting embassies. In the seventh and eighth centuries, bishops regularly attended the royal courts. A young man from an important family could begin his career as a secular administrator or military leader at court and later receive a bishopric as the crown of his career. In this way the royal court installed loyal men in local positions that mattered. By the same token, to have influence at court certainly raised the local prestige of a bishop.

Fourth, the bishop's local secular functions brought him a good deal of authority and influence. In Byzantine Italy as well as in the newly established barbarian kingdoms, bishops assumed more and more of the traditional functions of local government. In some cities the bishops and their ecclesiastical officials were virtually the only effective government. The Church had literate leaders and an effec-

---

MEDIEVAL VOICES

Bishop Gregory of Tours (573– 594) Tells of Confronting King Chilperic I

Bishops in the early Middle Ages had become very powerful figures, able to resist even kings. At the trial of Bishop Praetextus of Rouen, Bishop Gregory of Tours stood up for Praetextus and bravely confronted the king, although in the end the king had his way and exiled Praetextus The following is Gregory's own account of what he said to King Chilperic.

I replied, "You do not know whether I am unjust; for He to whom the secret places of the heart lie open, knows my conscience. What the people cry in false shouting when you insult me is nothing because everybody knows that these things came from you. It is therefore not me but you who are indicated in their disapproval. Why should I say any more? You have the law and the canons. It behooves you to study them diligently. If you do not carry out what they order, may you know that the judgment of God hangs over you."

Souce: Histories, V.18.

---

tive and established organization. It also had a regularized system for training successors and a usually peaceful means of passing on authority. It was almost natural that it assume the role of the fading, or in places nonexistent, civil government. In many cities the bishop ran the civil administration, settled local legal disputes, and provided for public building projects, education, poor relief, care of the sick, burial of the dead, and even repair of the city walls and defense of the population. Spiritual duties aside, a bishop's earthly responsibilities often made him the most important figure in the city.

Fifth, in the barbarian kingdoms the Church was quickly becoming the single biggest landholder after the king. In fact, by the seventh century, three quarters of the land the Church was ever to own was already in its possession. Much, if not most, of the Church's land in a diocese fell under the control of its bishop. In a society where land was almost the only source of wealth, being a landlord on this scale meant that the bishop exercised a great deal of authority. It was the sort of authority that spread well beyond his cathedral church and its urban surroundings into the countryside.

Within his own ecclesiastical organization, an early medieval bishop was nearly an absolute ruler. Originally all the lands of the diocese were the possession of his cathedral church, and he was their absolute administrator. There were some standards for the division of the church's income, but these were so general that they placed no real strictures on the bishop's plans for its use. Even the development of the parish churches, whose lands slowly came to be considered their own possessions and not those of the episcopal church, did not really affect the bishop's power. The bishop usually still held the best Church lands, he exercised certain administrative authority over the parishes, and he had rights to a portion of their incomes.

No early medieval governmental official had so much power over his bureaucracy as did the bishop over his. The clerics were totally dependent on him; he ordained them, he promoted them, and he saw to their maintenance. Discipline was also entirely in his hands. A priest could not leave the diocese in which he was ordained. In other words, he could not escape his bishop's authority by means of transfer.

By the beginning of the seventh century, the episcopacy had established itself as a closed and powerful caste that was aware of its position and acted accordingly. Complaints against a bishop could only be heard by a court made up of other bishops. The bishop as a powerful, absolute, and efficient administrator presented alluring political possibilities, which did not escape the notice of the secular authorities. In the records from the end of the seventh century, we find increasing mention of such abuses as simony, the naming of two bishops for one diocese, and secular interference in episcopal elections, all of which indicate that the episcopacy was being drawn into secular politics.

Since the bishop was such an important figure, choosing people to fill the position was a matter of great interest to many parties. "Episcopal election," as the choice of a new bishop is called, was always a complicated matter. Officially, the people and the clergy of a diocese chose a new bishop, but in fact other powerful people usually made the choice. These could be influential local families; powerful ecclesiastical figures, that is, other bishops, archbishops, or the pope; or the political powers, most often the king. Since the kings normally reserved the right to approve the choice of bishops within their kingdoms, they could exercise great influence over the episcopal elections. Their influence here varied from time to time and from place to place just as their ability to exercise the royal will varied in other matters.

The Priests

We know far less about priests in the early Middle Ages than we do about popes and bishops. Some priests were wonderfully educated and have left us collections of learned sermons and letters. On the other hand, we also hear many complaints about priests' illiteracy and sloth. Christianity began as a religion of the city and it took many centuries for it to establish a pervasive network of parishes in the countryside. Generally speaking, the more urban and more Romanized parts of Europe had such a system earlier than did parts where there were fewer cities and where Roman influence was less deeply rooted. For instance, we still hear of pockets of paganism in rural Gaul in the late seventh century. The system of priests and parishes in most parts of what is today Belgium, the Netherlands, western Germany, and parts of northern France was not established until the eighth century, under the early Carolingians, and it was not established in much of Germany east of the Rhine until the ninth century.

The nature of the priesthood obviously varied greatly from place to place. In the cities a priest was likely to be an important figure, administering the parish church, its personnel, and its dependent churches, along with a great deal of land. He probably came from an important family and enjoyed an adequate education. A rural priest, on the other hand, could have been as poor as his parishioners and incapable of reading the Scriptures and conducting the mass properly.

The Deacons and Other Officials

The deacon held the lowest place in the "major orders," that is, in the upper ranks of the Church's hierarchy (bishop-priest-deacon). The deacon was charged with important liturgical functions, the most important of which was the reading or chanting of the Gospel. He also exercised important nonliturgical duties such as the distribution of alms to the poor. The diaconate could be a life-long occupation or a preliminary step on the way to the priesthood.

A large, early medieval church, especially the seat of a bishop, had a staff of other clerics. Documents speak of subdeacons, door-keepers, exorcists (healers), lectors, and acolytes, to name the ones usually officially included in the "minor orders." They exercised various liturgical, administrative, and practical functions in aiding the priests and deacons and in the running of the church.

The Monks

Monks were awakened by a bell about two in the morning. Without a word and without much thought, for the routine was nightly and ancient, they arose from their beds and filed into the church. Young, old, senior, junior, abbot, prior, each knew his appointed place; the only sounds were the shuffle of sandals on the stone floor, the rustle of garments, and an occasional cough. Then it began. In their singing voices, their holy voices, they intoned as they did every night, the words *Domine, labia mea aperies* "Lord, open thou my lips," words from the Psalms. With their holy music wafting upwards to disappear behind the cold stone and the timbers of the ceiling, the monks thus began another day. This day, like all their days, they would be organized around seven appointed occasions for ritualized prayer, called the monastic "hours." Distributed at set times round the clock, the monks would fill such hours with the ritualistic praying of appointed Psalms, much of it set to beautiful music.

Like the Christian secular clergy, Christian monasticism had its origins in the ancient world, specifically in Roman Egypt in the latter half of the second century. It began slowly, but then in the third and fourth centuries it attracted increasing numbers of people eager to flee the world. Its attractive power was much like that of the popular philosophies of late antiquity, Stoicism and Epicureanism, which also provided people with a private means of coping with a frustrating public world.

Early written accounts of monastic life in Egypt and then in Syria and Palestine provided it with its first heroes, women like Saint Paula (347–404) and men like Paul of Thebes (died c. 340) and especially Saint Antony (c. 251–356). Jerome and Athanasius, both influential Christian leaders, wrote about these early heroes from the East and consequently helped both to spread the movement and to present inspiring examples of valiant struggles against the temptations of this world. The *Life of Saint Anthony* by Athanasius (c. 296–373) was a particularly influential work, both in the East and the West. It not only served as a model for other saints' lives, an extremely important genre of medieval Christian literature, but Anthony's absolute resistance to any physical temptation and his heroic combat against spiritual evil inspired many who sought the monastic life.

Christian monasticism spread first throughout the East, where Christianity itself first spread, and then came to western Europe probably in the fourth century. The most influential center of early western monasticism was founded by Honoratus (c. 350–429), the future bishop of Arles, on the island of Lérins, off the southern coast of Gaul, in about 410. By the mid-fifth century, Lérins was the most important monastic center in southern Gaul, and its abbots and monks were sought after as bishops for cities and as abbots for monasteries throughout the region.

The Nuns

Christian female monasticism also began in Egypt in the second half of the third century, although it does not seem to have been as widespread as the male version. Saint Augustine (354–430) speaks of visiting (or more accurately of not visiting) convents of nuns and Saint Jerome (342–420) established both male and female institutions in Jerusalem. In Europe, the movement found its significant beginnings along with the monasteries for men in southern Gaul. John Cassian (c. 360–435) established monastic houses for men and women in Marseilles in the first decade of the fifth century, and in the early sixth century, Caesarius (470–542) founded an important monastery for women in Arles, where he was bishop, and wrote a rule directing its way of life.

The nunneries, like the monasteries, became rich and important landowners, and consequently the abbesses became important local figures. They were often great ladies or even queens who had retired to a monastic life of seclusion. The nunneries, as opposed to the monasteries, could not cut themselves off completely from the opposite sex since all Christians needed to receive holy communion, which only priests could administer, thus the practice of establishing "double monasteries" developed. Here a monastery for men and one for women would form two parts of the same institution. The two were geographically near to one another and often led, not by an abbot, but by an abbess.

Benedict of Nursia and the Benedictine Rule

The most advanced form of the monastic life for the Christian is to live absolutely alone. Living alone in constant prayer and contemplation is seen as the best way to renounce the world, battle its temptations, and purify oneself for God. This is called living "in the desert" or "in the wilderness," although it can be done anywhere absolute ascetic solitude can be found. Its practitioners are called anchorites or hermits (see Chapter 11). The eremitical ideal also generated powerful propaganda that circulated widely in the form of written accounts of inspiring heroes who lived without companions in trees, on the tops of pillars, or in the snake-infested crags of the Egyptian desert. Often, according to these accounts, they survived on a single loaf of bread for forty days and battled demons of unimaginable ferocity. Although the monastic ideal was always to be alone with God (hence the word "monk," from the Greek *monachos,* someone who lives alone), it was in practice almost impossible. Holy men who tried to live alone soon attracted followers, and there was a tendency for some of those seeking to flee the world and to deny its pleasures to take matters to enthusiastic limits. Self-mutilation and starvation were dangerous and unacceptable means of expressing monastic zeal. The Church found it difficult to prevent the excesses, as indeed it found it very difficult to guide, perhaps control, any sort of religious fervor espousing a personal and direct link to heaven. An obvious need arose to regulate the monastic life and to preserve its ideal of holy solitude without the dangerous practices that came from actually living alone. The problem then became how to live alone together, or how to organize a community of monks.

Several early attempts were made to lay out a rule for monastic life both in the East and in the West, but the one that came to dominate Europe was written by the Italian, Benedict of Nursia (c. 480–c. 550). Although his intentions were modest enough, his *Rule* not only became one of Europe's most widely read books but it also came to regulate Western monasticism, one of the most important institutions of the entire Middle Ages.

Unfortunately little is known about Benedict himself. He was born at Nursia, educated at Rome, and began his monastic life about A.D. 500 by living alone in a cave near Subiaco. He soon attracted a following and was thus confronted by the problem of having anchorites live together. According to tradition, he divided his followers into twelve groups of twelve men, each under the leadership of an abbot, or spiritual father, whom he appointed. In 525, he and a few of his followers moved to Monte Cassino where he established his famous monastery. Benedict's sister, Scholastica, also founded a convent for women a few miles away in Plombariola. It was at Monte Cassino that Benedict wrote his famous *Rule* and where he died in about 550.

Why was *The Rule of Saint Benedict* so successful? Other monastic rules existed, some quite similar to Benedict's. The Benedictine *Rule* owes its success to a number of factors, some political, some geographical, and some stemming from the marvelous nature of Benedict's work itself.

There were several worldly causes for its success. The Irish came to appreciate St Benedict's work very early on and used it along with the rule of their own hero and missionary to the continent, St. Columbanus (see Medieval Portraits). Thus it spread through many European monasteries where Irish influence was felt. The Anglo-Saxon monasteries, too, adopted it, for one reason because Pope Gregory was held in high esteem among them and he made mention of Benedict's *Rule* in his writings. The great expansion of Western monasticism in the seventh century came in northern Europe. Powerful political families were founding monasteries here, often for other than strictly monastic reasons, and many of these houses experienced the spiritual influence of the Irish or Anglo-Saxons; consequently, they spread the Benedictine *Rule*. The Carolingian kings of the Franks and their ancestors before them also promoted Benedict's *Rule*. Under their early patronage, it spread to many important monastic houses and then with the official imperial reforms of the Carolingians in the early ninth century, it became the nearly exclusive guide for monasticism in western Europe.

There were religious reasons for its success as well. Benedict's *Rule* beautifully balanced the spiritual ideal of living in the wilderness with the practical situation of living in a community. It was strict in its discipline, but not overly so. Its daily routine and its way of life were demanding, but did not include excesses or demand what normal human beings could not achieve. It also directed that the wayward

MEDIEVAL PORTRAITS

Columbanus (c. 543–615), Irish Missionary to the Continent

Columbanus, an Irishman from Leinster, became the most famous of the early medieval Irish missionaries to the continent. He was educated at the Irish monastery at Bangor. As he was nearing fifty years old, like many fervent Irish Christians, he felt the compulsion to make a *peregrinatio*, or journey of exile for Christ. Thus he and several followers abandoned their homeland and in about 590 settled in a remote area of Merovingian Burgundy, a kingdom then under the rule of King Childebert II (575–596) and his mother, the powerful Queen Brunhild. Under royal patronage, he founded two monasteries, one at Annegray and the other at Luxeuil. In about 613 he had a falling out with Brunhild and the reigning King Theuderic II (596–613) because he refused to baptize Theuderic's illegitimate children. Forced out of Burgundy, he settled in northern Italy where, with royal patronage from the Lombard King Agilulf (590–c. 615) and Queen Theudelinda, he founded the influential monastery at Bobbio. Several of his writings survive: a rule for monks, some letters, and a penitential, or guide for assigning penance to sinners for certain sins. In 643, a monk at Bobbio named Jonas wrote an account of Columbanus' life that forms the basis of most of what we know about him.

Columbanus was known for his strict asceticism, passionate faith, and unbending will. Although he operated under the protection of royal patronage, he was not afraid to stand up to royal authority when he deemed it right. He also stood up to the pope. He wrote letters to Pope Gregory I using learned arguments to defend certain Irish practices that disagreed with Roman usage. He also argued against Arians at Queen Thodelinda's court. His monastery at Luxeuil went on to become instrumental in the spread of the Rule of Saint Benedict in the Frankish realms, and Bobbio collected one of the most significant libraries in all of Europe in the early Middle Ages.

monk be forgiven and allowed a fresh start. The *Rule* shows its genius in two other important ways. First, its precisely structured daily routine, with round-the-clock requirements for liturgical prayer, made it difficult for the monks to forget the religious purpose of their monastic life by becoming sidetracked with the cares of building a healthy or successful institution. A monk's day included labor, be it physical work or study, but the importance of a monk's labor was never allowed to overshadow his spiritual duties. Second, the *Rule* defined an extremely practical and effective type of authoritarian leader, the abbot (see Medieval Voices).

"Abbot," a late Greek word for "father," was chosen by Benedict for the title of a monastery's leader. The abbot is to act as the monks' spiritual father. His office is imbued with a traditional, unquestioned patriarchal authority, but since the authority is paternal, it is to be balanced by a father's love. Although the abbot's word is final, he is to make all important decisions after consulting with his monks. Benedict describes how the abbot should balance discipline with forgiveness, adopt different techniques for guiding monks with different personalities, and set an example in all things with his deeds not just in his words. At first glance this may

MEDIEVAL VOICES

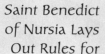

Saint Benedict of Nursia Lays Out Rules for Monastic Living

The following excerpts are taken from The Rule of Saint Benedict, *a work that came to be the almost exclusive guide for the important institution of monasticism in western Europe, after the reforms of the Church carried out under the Carolingians in the early ninth century.*

Chapter 2. What the Abbot Should Be Like

An abbot who is worthy to rule a monastery ought to remember by what title he is called, and justify the title of a superior by his deeds. He is believed to hold the place of Christ in the monastery, since he is called by His title as the apostle says: "*Ye have received the spirit of adoption of sons, whereby we call, Abba, Father.*" . . . [Romans, 8:15]

Therefore when anyone takes up the title of abbot, he should govern his disciples by a twofold teaching, that is, let him show all things good and holy by his deeds rather than by his words. . . . Let not individuality be made the deciding factor by him in the monastery. Let not one be loved more than another, unless he finds him to be better than the other in good deeds and in obedience. Let not a person of good birth be placed above one coming from servitude unless another reasonable cause exists. . . . In his instruction the abbot ought always to keep to the guide in which the apostle says: *Explain, beseech, and then reprove.* . . . [2 Timothy 4:2]

Chapter 8. The Divine Office at Night

In winter, that is from the beginning of November to Easter, in accordance with reason, wake-up must be at two in the morning so that, as sleep will continue to slightly past midnight, [the brothers] may arise already having digested.

Chapter 29. Whether Brothers Who Leave the Monastery Ought To Be Taken Back Again

If a brother who by his own fault leaves the monastery wishes to return, let him first promise all amends for the fault on account of which he departed and let him be received into the last place so that thereby his humility may be proved. But if he leaves again, up to the third time, let him be taken back in the same way knowing that after this every opportunity of return is denied.

Chapter 48. Concerning Daily Manual Labor

Idleness is the enemy of the soul. And therefore, at fixed times, the brothers ought to be occupied in manual labor and again, at fixed times, in prayerful reading.

seem like pious naivete, but the office of abbot as laid out by Benedict stood the test of time and proved itself over the centuries to be an effective one for leading those who pursued an extremely difficult way of life.

The *Rule* defines the other important officers of the monastery and describes the various parts of the monastic life: eating, sleeping, working, prayer, singing, reception of guests, clothes, living quarters, the monastery's organization, and its ideals. In all, it shows Benedict's perceptive balance between the ideal and the practical.

Friction occurred between the regular and secular clergy. The bishop often exercised much more control over the monasteries within his diocese than the monks and their abbots wished. The bishop had certain traditional ceremonial and visitational rights in the monasteries, but many bishops found it easy to expand these to the point where they controlled both internal and external monastic policies. The bishop often exercised the same sort of administrative authority over the monasteries' wealth as he did over that of his parishes. His permission was needed to found a monastery or to sell any monastic land, and he sometimes exercised great influence in the election of the abbots. The monasteries often appealed to Church councils or to powerful nobles and the king for aid in containing the bishops. The appeals could result in edicts that declared the rights of monasteries to conduct their own affairs and elect their own abbots, but these measures could not always be enforced.

THE GROWTH AND EXPANSION OF THE CHURCH

Throughout the early Middle Ages until the time of the collapse of the Carolingian empire in the mid-ninth century (see Chapter 7), the Church saw a dramatic expansion. It expanded geographically, reaching vast new areas of northern and eastern Europe. It expanded locally, spreading Christianity from the urban centers into parts of the countryside where it previously had exercised little influence. And it expanded organizationally, with both the regular and the secular clergy performing more functions.

Pope Gregory I (590–604)

Pope Gregory I, called "the Great," played an important role in all the ways the Western Church grew. He is known as "the father of the medieval papacy" for good reason: He was a man of solid ability and great foresight, and he greatly strengthened the position of the papacy. As with most leaders of the early medieval Church, Gregory was born to privilege; he was the son of a Roman senator and heir to vast estates. As a young man, about age 33, he was made Prefect of the City, the senior governmental official for the city of Rome. As prefect he seems to have learned a great deal about practical administration in a difficult time, for the Rome he administered, as all Italy in the mid-sixth century, had suffered badly in the wars between the Goths and the Byzantine armies.

Gregory gave up his governmental career and sold his lands. He used the proceeds to help the poor and to establish monasteries. He is said to have founded seven, six in Sicily and the famous monastery of Saint Andrew in Rome itself. In 575 he entered Saint Andrew's as a monk, but was soon assigned duties outside the monastic community. In about 578 or 580, Pope Pelagius II sent Gregory as papal ambassador to the court at Constantinople. Gregory's six years in New Rome, beleaguered as it was by the problems of the eastern part of the Empire, were enough to convince him that New Rome would provide little enough help for Old Rome. In 585 or 586, Pelagius sent a new ambassador, and Gregory returned home to re-enter Saint Andrew's where he became its abbot.

Pope Gregory the Great (590–604) This striking picture of Gregory illustrates a twelfth-century French manuscript that contains his letters. Gregory is seated here "in majesty," a seated pose with knees apart and used throughout the Middle Ages to depict figures of great authority. Note he is wearing the palium. *Bibliotheque Nationale, Paris/Giraudon/Art Resource, NY.*

Soon his monastic life was again interrupted, this time by the death of Pelagius in 590. The clergy and people of Rome elected Gregory as their next bishop—that is, as pope. Tradition has it that Gregory did not want to be pope, and that he even tried to appeal to the emperor not to confirm his appointment. But once installed, he proved himself to be one of the most capable men ever to hold the position. His actions as pope indicate not only his own remarkable ability but also the changing nature of both the papacy and the Church as a whole.

The situation at Gregory's accession was grim. Byzantium's newly won political hold over Italy was slipping. The Lombards had come across the Alps in 568 and quickly established a large kingdom in northern Italy centered on Pavia as well as two independent duchies farther to the south at Spoleto and at Benevento. They were not able to conquer the other Byzantine cities of Italy, such as Rome, in large part because they frequently fought among themselves. But shortly before Gregory's election they managed to stop quarreling and consequently presented a new and ugly danger to Rome. While the Lombards were destroying the countryside, choking off Rome's trade and food supply, a plague broke out, the same bubonic plague that would return to spread death and dread in the late Middle Ages. Rumors and stories darkened the panicked city: Spirits stalked the streets and a great dragon was seen rising up out of the Tiber. Living and sanitary conditions quickly deteriorated, and although Constantinople did send some troops and supplies, it was clear that if Rome was to survive, it had to do so largely on its own.

Gregory got the grain shipments coming from Sicily again, food distributed to the poor, the aqueducts repaired, the dead buried, other sanitary measures organized, the city's defenses rebuilt, and the garrison trained. It was he and not the Byzantine authority in Ravenna who appointed governors for some of the Italian cities and who concluded an agreement with the Lombards in 592–593. In short, the pope fulfilled many of the important functions traditionally exercised by the government.

Gregory made no explicit claims for papal primacy, but his international activities certainly extended papel authority far beyond Rome. He sent letters to the Church in Africa to help counter heresy there. He requested the help of the Merovingian Queen Brunhild in rooting out simony in the Frankish church and even stood up to the Byzantine empress when she requested certain relics. He used his considerable administrative ability to organize the management of the papal estates, putting them on a sound fiscal path and using much of their proceeds for relief of the poor. And in 596, he sent about forty missionaries, monks from Saint Andrew's, to the British Isles.

Despite the papacy's growing social, economic, and political influence, the basis of its power was the perception on the part of its adherents that it exercised real spiritual authority. Similarly, Gregory's spiritual contributions rather than his practical ones had the greater historical effect. Gregory was the first pope who had been a monk and his enthusiastic support of monasticism helped establish this important institution in the religious life of the West. As noted earlier, his support of Benedictine monasticism was one of the major reasons why Benedict's rule came to dominate. Gregory was a prolific and highly influential author. Many of his sermons, letters, and other works survive. In all of these, while exuding a confidence in the correctness of his interpretation of older Christian works, especially Augustine's, he helped to solidify certain important Christian doctrines. He insisted on clerical celibacy, then slowly becoming the ideal, if not always the practice. His explanations of Augustine promoted the doctrines of Purgatory and the sacrifice of the mass, perhaps the two single most important teachings of the Church that led to its worldly power. These defined the Church as the "vessel of salvation"—that is, God's vehicle for bestowing salvation on mankind. Purgatory was the state or place where the departed soul did penance not completed before death for forgivable sins he or she had committed while living. A person still living could pray for departed loved ones and arrange that masses be said for them asking that they be released from purgatory into heaven. Thus the sacrament of the mass, which only a priest could perform, became not only necessary for the living but also beneficial for the dead. Medieval men and women were assured that without the Church and its sacraments they could not get to heaven, and this assurance that the Church kept the keys to heaven formed the foundation of their allegiance to it.

Gregory wrote a type of how-to manual for bishops with his popular and influential book, *Pastoral Care*. Its picture of heaven and earth is essentially Augustine's, but expressed more simply and more clearly. Here were clear moral guidelines and practical advice for leadership, now adapted to the new situations of society in the period after late antiquity. Even the title of this book is an indication that most of what Gregory did and wrote was in some way connected to his concern to save souls. He saw this as his primary responsibility as pope and he considered it the same for all the other secular clergy.

Dionysius the Pseudo-Areopagite

Although Gregory's theology was soundly based on that of Augustine of Hippo, he did promote some important refinements. He came to espouse the theories of a mystical theologian now called Dionysius the Pseudo-Areopagite. Dionysius had worked out a detailed vision of heaven and earth as a continuous hierarchy with God at its pinnacle. This hierarchy extended downward through the powers and angels of heaven to the more highly placed (kings, nobles, bishops, and the like) and then the less exalted humans on earth.

This cosmic view is basic to medieval thought in two important ways. First, it is a vivid display of the continuum of the here and the hereafter; heaven and earth form a unit. In the medieval mind the spiritual was as real as was the material; it was every bit as present, concretely frightening as well as actually comforting, and always more important. There was a material quality to matters spiritual, and this "angelology" of Dionysius showed that matter and spirit were united in one cosmic picture. Second, it was a hierarchy. God had instituted his whole creation in a dazzling series of levels, assigning all things and all people to their proper places. It was characteristic of the Middle Ages to see the divine purpose for one's life in patiently performing the role proper to an assigned level; it was dangerous to advocate changing. Or put another way, such a hierarchical view of the cosmos justified the wealth and privilege of those born to them and also showed how it was divine plan that the poor not strive to rise above their luckless lot.

The Geographical Expansion of the Early Medieval Church

When Gregory the Great held his solid rein over the papacy at Rome, most of the Roman world was already Christian; but Europe north of the Loire and east of the Rhine was either only nominally and scantily so or was still unconverted. Much of barbarian Europe followed the Arian heresy, and other parts were still devoted to Celtic, Germanic, or other pagan gods. If we include Scandinavia, the Church would require another 500 years to anchor itself firmly throughout western Europe, and parts of northeastern Europe were still pagan as late as the fourteenth century. As the Church expanded, it not only spread Rome's religion to areas previously little touched by anything Roman, but it also spread Roman culture. With the geographical expansion of the Christian Church, Rome's cultural boundaries greatly expanded into many areas never controlled by its political empire.

By Gregory's days the process of converting northern Europe had only begun. With the large exception of the reconversion of Britain (see Chapter 7), the seventh century saw no significant extension of Christianity into new areas. Conversion activity concentrated on areas already nominally Christian or ones under the political control of Christian rulers. This concentration was due in large measure to the fact that the Christian kingdoms themselves, notably the Merovingian kingdoms, had ceased to expand. A famous example of someone performing this type of internal expansion was the great Aquitainian missionary Amandus (died c. 675), who was active in mid-century both in the south of the Frankish kingdoms in Aquitaine and in the north of their realms in the area east of the river Scheldt, now in modern Belgium. By the end of the century, however, Christianity was again pushing outward.

In 698, two rich Frankish noble women, Plectrud and her mother Irmina, founded a monastery on one of their family's estates at Echternach on the River Sûre, now in modern Luxembourg not far from the old Roman capital at Trier. Echternach quickly became an active missionary center and remained one of western Europe's most important monasteries throughout the Middle Ages. Its foundation indicates how the Church spread to northern Europe in four important ways.

The Lion, Symbol of Saint Mark the Evangelist   This illustration is taken from a manuscript produced about 690 called *The Gospels of Saint Willibrord* or *The Echternach Gospels*. The startling rampant lion is an example of Irish artistic influence. Irish missionaries played an important role in the spread of Christianity on the European continent if the seventh and eighth century. *Bibliotheque Nationale.*

First, we note the role of women. Christian women played a crucial role in the expansion of the Church not only by founding important monasteries, like Echternach, but also by exposing the pagan political leaders whom they married to the faith. For example, the pagan king of Kent, Ethelbert (c. 565–616) had a Christian wife before his conversion, as did the Frankish king, Clovis (481–511). In fact, Gregory of Tour's account of Clovis' conversion has him call Christ ". . . the God whom my wife, Queen Clothild, professes. . . ." When a pagan king took a Christian queen, she and her chaplains served as important examples of Christian practice in a pagan land. Through her the king gained a certain familiarity with the ideas that would be preached to him later by the missionaries who came to convert him and his kingdom.

Second, we note the role of missionaries from the British Isles working on the continent. The first abbot of Irmina's and Plectrud's new monastery was Willibrord (658–739), a noble Anglo-Saxon from Northumbria. Largely through his efforts, the greater part of Frisia was brought into the Church. Willibrord was one of many famous Anglo-Saxon missionaries who expanded the Church into most of Germany in the eighth century. Thuringia, Franconia, Saxony, Bavaria, and Hesse all became fruitful fields for their missions.

Third, Echternach reminds us of the crucial role of secular politics in the geographical expansion of the Church. In 689, only one year before Willibrord's arrival in Frisia, the Franks, under their leader Pippin II, had taken from the Frisians all their lands south of the Rhine except for the area around Utrecht. It was in the territory still controlled by the Frisians that Willibrord and his companions arrived in 690. Their reception was hostile. Although they were Anglo-Saxons, to the Frisians they preached the religion of the hated Franks. The missionaries quickly and wisely retreated south of the Rhine to seek out Pippin. Here the welcome was warm. Pippin realized these zealous missionaries could serve as extremely effective instruments for Frankish expansionist politics. Gods were tribal property, and to Christianize the Frisians was to bring them into Frankish culture in a very important and concrete way. On the other hand, the advantages in a relationship between priest and politician did not all flow in one direction. Willibrord's short stay in Utrecht had taught him the hopelessness of missionary endeavor without political protection, and consequently he now limited his work of conversion almost exclusively to those parts of Frisia controlled by the Franks. The two powers needed each other. Most successful early medieval missionary work, in the British Isles as well as in continental western Europe, was done under the protecting arm of some interested political power.

Fourth and finally, we note the role of Rome. In the summer of 691, after only six or seven months on the continent, Willibrord made his first trip to Rome. Such a trip was usual for almost all the great missionaries of the eighth century. Often the reasons for such a journey seem purely religious, as they do here with Willibrord's first trip. The pope granted him the usual aids for missionaries: relics and status as a papal emissary. Relics were necessary for founding churches and Rome's official blessing added great spiritual weight to his endeavor. A Frisian mission, blessed by the pope and organized by his emissary, spread Rome's influence. The established churches of Spain and Merovingian Gaul, which had assumed the local lands, organization, and practices of the local Church of late antiquity, had also assumed a rather national character, obeying the dictates of their kings and national councils of bishops. Although these churches also acknowledged the pope's leadership, they did not show the degree of Roman influence that the mission fields did. The new areas were mostly German, and from the beginning, strong ties bound them to Rome.

But the hand of politics is often not far from the road to Rome. In 695, Willibrord again made the long and difficult journey to the Eternal City. This time Pippin sent him. The Frankish leader wanted Pope Sergius (687–701) to create an archdiocese based at Utrecht and to make Willibrord its archbishop. An ecclesiastical province comprising all of Frisia with its own archbishop would ensure that the area would not fall under another archbishop outside Pippin's influence. With Willibrord as Frisia's archbishop, Pippin would have great influence in the way the Church was to be organized in this area new to Frankish control. Rome's hierarchical structure of archbishop, bishops, and priests with their defined dioceses and parishes would help ensure that the conversion of Frisia to the Frankish God would have the institutional underpinning to make it permanent. The pope agreed and Willibrord began his work.

As the eighth century progressed, other new areas of northern Europe were won for the Church. Willibrord was followed by the famous Saint Boniface (680–754), another Anglo-Saxon. Boniface also worked hand in hand both with Pippin's family, specifically with Pippin's grandson also called Pippin (741–768) and with Rome. Boniface established the ecclesiastical organization in the greater part of what is now the Netherlands and northwestern Germany, along with helping with important reforms of the Frankish Church (see Medieval Voices). The Church was also pushing southeastwards from the Frankish heartlands into the areas of the upper Rhine and beyond. Here the missionary work was not carried on by the Anglo-Saxon allies of the Pippinids, but by native representatives of the neighboring Frankish churches. By the end of the century most of northwestern Europe, with the exception of Scandinavia, had become Christian. Most of the area also owed allegiance to the Franks. It was no coincidence.

The Local Community

The pervasive parish structure of the high Middle Ages with its carefully defined geographical boundaries, complex organization, and maze of legal prerogatives, was not yet present in the seventh and eighth centuries. But parish life was none the less beginning to influence important aspects of life in the local communities. The Church required all Christians to be baptized, attend mass on Sundays and on the important festivals in the Church year, belong to a parish, and to be buried in it.

In many ways the Christianization of northern Europe meant providing structure and identity to Europe's local communities. The Church was the organization more than any other that brought people together to conduct affairs in common, to hear news, to worship, and to celebrate. In this way the church building became the community's gathering place and the visible symbol of its cohesion.

The Church was also the usual vehicle for the relief of the poor. In many places in the early Middle Ages, it was customary for a table to be set up in front of the

MEDIEVAL VOICES

A Contemporary Hagiographer Describes the Dangers of Missionary Work Without Political Protection

At the end of his long career of organizing the German and Frankish churches, Saint Boniface (680–754) returned to missionary work among the Frisians. At Dokkum, in northeastern Frisia, he and fifty-three companions were attacked and killed by pagans.

A vast number of foes armed with spears and shields rushed into the camp brandishing their weapons. In the twinkling of an eye the attendants sprang from the camp to meet them and snatched up arms here and there to defend the holy band of martyrs (for that is what they were to be) against the insensate fury of the mob. But the man of God [Boniface], hearing the shouts and the onrush of the rabble, straightway called the clergy to his side, and, collecting together the relics of the saints, which he always carried with him, came out of his tent. At once he reproved the attendants and forbade them to continue the conflict, saying: "Sons, cease fighting. Lay down your arms, for we are told in Scripture not to render evil for good but to overcome evil by good. The hour to which we have long looked forward is near and the day of our release is at hand. . . ." And addressing himself like a loving father to the priests, deacons, and other clerics, all trained to the service of God, who stood about him, he gave them courage, saying: "Brethren, be of stout heart, fear not them who slay the body for they cannot slay the soul, which continues to live forever. . . ."

Whilst with these words he was encouraging his disciples to accept the crown of martyrdom, the frenzied mob of pagans rushed suddenly upon them with swords and every kind of warlike weapon, staining their bodies with their [the missionaries'] precious blood.

Source: Willibald, "The Life of Saint Boniface," C. H. Talbert, trans. in Thomas F. X. Noble and Thomas Head, eds., *Soldiers of Christ* (Pennsylvania State University Press, 1995) 135–136.

Church door and the clergy to distribute food to the needy from it. The Church made provisions for taking care of the sick, widows, and orphans. The church building also offered physical sanctuary. If a fugitive managed to get inside a church, he could not be captured or harmed while he remained in it. Gregory of Tours relates the story of an unfortunate who tripped while dashing through the church door. The refugee's pursuer lopped off his foot with a sword. When accused of violating the church's sanctity, the swordsman replied that while most of his victim had indeed been within the church, his foot was still sticking out the doorway.

THE CULTURAL CONSEQUENCES OF CHRISTIANIZATION

The early Middle Ages saw the Church come to play an increasing role in the ordinary lives of Europeans. Obviously the way they exercised their religion would change after conversion to Christianity, but so too would other fundamental parts of life such as marriage practices, education, care of the poor, and the focus of local social life.

Marriage

Although the Church exalted chastity as the most desirable practice for Christians, it also recognized marriage as a Christian state and slowly became the recognized authority regulating this important aspect of most people's lives.

The barbarian view of the family extended to more distant relatives, differing from the late Roman view. Consequently the Church in the barbarian kingdoms extended the degrees of consanguinity within which it forbade marriage. These and other regulations of churchmen found secular legal force in the decrees and laws of the barbarian kings in the seventh and eighth centuries. For instance, Kind Liutprand of the Lombards (712–744) issued a law forbidding marriage between first cousins, saying that he does so because he was requested to by "the bishop of Rome, who is head of the churches." In the ninth century, the influential Bishop Hincmar of Rheims (c. 806–882) included matrimony among the sacraments, that is, among those sacred ways in which God confers his grace to humans.

The Church's increasing regulation of marriage generally helped the status of women. Christian marriage was deemed a lifelong partnership, and consequently the relative ease of divorce in the Roman world was all but stopped by the Church. The Church's insistence on monogamy and sexual fidelity also greatly curtailed the open practices of polygamy and concubinage. The legal status of women was generally better under the Romans than under the barbarians, but the increasing Christianization of marriage helped to offset women's legal decline somewhat.

Education

Education in Europe's early Middle Ages fell almost exclusively into the control of the Church, and the Church would maintain its influence largely undiminished for well over a thousand years. Organized secular education was dying out in the sixth century; although in the larger cities of Italy and southern Gaul it managed to linger longer than elsewhere. These cities continued to enjoy literate administrative classes, but in most of Europe reading and writing had become luxuries, usually practiced only by the men and some women who could afford other expensive delights, or by the servants and slaves of such people trained to do written work.

A revival of schools of sorts was to come, but it appeared in the Christian monasteries and cathedrals, not in a secular setting. It happened all over Europe: in Visigothic Spain after the conversion of King Reccared from Arianism in 586; in the great monasteries of Ireland in the sixth century; in Northumbria in the seventh and eighth centuries; and in northern Gaul and Germany in the eighth and ninth centuries. These Christian institutions taught Christian learning. Their language was indeed Latin, but it was not the florid literary Latin of late antiquity, but the much simpler Latin of the Bible, and especially of the Psalms. The students were destined mostly for careers in the Church. Although some girls were educated in the nunneries, most pupils were boys and from the more affluent levels of society. As, however, the practice whereby monasteries took in oblates, that is, young children given by parents to a monastery for a life of service to Christ, became more common, some offspring of more modest families also learned to read and write.

The consequences of the Church's assumption of education were enormous. In such an environment, literary production took on decidedly Christian directions. Theology, liturgy, sermons, lives of the saints, and hymns became the means of literary and creative expression. The uneducated masses came into contact with literary themes and written work almost exclusively in the churches. Here they would hear sermons, hymns, beautiful prayers and liturgy, and exciting tales of the spiritual battles of the Church's heroes, the lives of its saints. Much of this was written in a simplified Latin that the unlettered could either understand or that could be translated on the spot by the reader into whatever vernacular his audience spoke.

By the early eighth century, another stream in western Europe's education flowed alongside the Christian one. As long as the Church perceived a major danger from the classical pagans, it was naturally hostile to the great pagan authors of antiquity. But as European society in general became more Christian, the classical pagans ceased to be an object of the church's concern and its attitude toward ancient literature consequently changed. No longer were the great ancient authors begrudgingly tolerated in order to exploit their linguistic ability, as reflected in Jerome's and Augustine's attitude toward them. Now classical literature in both its language and its contents was seen as a good in itself. Virgil never completely replaced the Psalms as the textbook from which medieval students learned to read and write. But more and more, purely classical study was creeping into the schools, especially in northern Europe where the vestiges of the classical world were far fainter and therefore the study of its achievement more fascinating. This stream would grow into an actual "renaissance" of classical learning in the eighth and ninth centuries under the Carolingian kings.

The Local Saint

Loyalty to the Church's heroes, its saints, and veneration of their relics formed a vital part of early medieval life. Gregory the Great insisted that the altars in new churches contain relics as one of the means of making a place of worship holy. It was thought that the saint would take a special interest in the place that held her or his relics and consequently would channel God's power through them to cause miracles. Relics were a link in the continuum of heaven and earth; they were matter that evidenced real spiritual power. They came to be highly prized; the afflicted poured into the churches that held important relics, seeking the saint's help for healing and other forms of spiritual aid for earthly woes.

Gregory the Great's teaching concerning the veneration of saints and their relics reveals that these things were not simply aspects of medieval "popular" religion. It is sometimes said that the uneducated classes believed in and even needed the often fantastic stories of what these relics could perform, whereas the educated higher clergy only saw them either as a kind of advertising ploy used to convert or convince the masses or as a means to attract them for financial gain, since cult centers of the saints generated money the way any popular attraction does. But Gregory's teaching was based on Augustine, and his own view of the cosmos in Dionysian terms provided a highly sophisticated metaphysical framework into which saints and their relics fit as a natural part. Although the educated seemed not to have believed miracle stories that were not properly authenticated, for them as well as for the uneducated, the material and the spiritual worlds existed shoulder to shoulder.

Thus the parish—its building, its clergy, the dead buried near or in its church, and especially its patron saint—became the focus of many parts of daily life, both urban and rural. The Church as a whole, its popes, the king, and even Christ were a long way off, but the parish was in the midst of normal life. The local clergy acted as the conduit through which the written culture reached the people. The local clergy also sanctioned the important milestones of normal life, guided and aided in the settlement of minor disputes, and in the end sent the soul off to the next world and buried the body.

Summary

The early Middle Ages saw the Christianization of northwestern Europe. The expansion not only brought a huge geographical area into the western Church, but in many ways the Church provided structure and identity to Europe's communities. Gregory the Great (590–604), both in his actions as pope and in his writings, played a key role in the process. Monasteries, although in theory not concerned with the fortunes of this present world, nonetheless often formed important bases for missionary activity. Women from noble families sometimes founded these monasteries and, with their marriages to pagan kings, introduced the faith to the courts of their new husbands. Missionaries from the British Isles worked to convert large sections of northern Europe, establishing close ties to the papacy and setting up the diocesan and parish structures. The missionary work was almost always carried out with the support of some expanding Christian political power. The missionaries needed its physical protection, and the secular authority benefited from the Church's role in extending the culture of the conquerors into their new lands. By the end of the eighth century, northern Europe, with the exception of Scandinavia, had become Christian.

In addition to its geographical growth, the early medieval Church expanded into important areas of European life. It began to regulate certain aspects of Christian marriage. It shaped education and learning. The local parish began to become the focus of ordinary social life. Its local saint offered spiritual and material protection; he or she could both help save the soul and protect the body against disease, famine, flood, war, and other material disasters. The local church served as the contact point between the world of learning and those who could not read. Even its building offered physical sanctuary and protection when dangers, all too present in early medieval life, loomed large.

CHAPTER 6

❧

An Early Medieval Empire in the West: The Carolingians, 600–900

On December 25, 800, in the great Basilica of Saint Peter in Rome, Charles, king of the Franks and king of the Lombards, was crowned Roman Emperor by Pope Leo III amid all the heavenly pomp of the Christmas mass. This Charles, known to history as Charles the Great, or Charlemagne, was the most famous ruler of his family, a family known now as the Carolingians and one that would rule most of western Europe for about 200 years.

Carolingian society, both in its royal government and in its organization at the local level, retained much from the Merovingian age that had preceded it (see Chapter 3). But not all was the same. Charlemagne is sometimes called "the father of Europe" and the Carolingian era "the first Europe," and there is a good deal of truth in both these phrases. Now for the first time the German-speaking peoples living east of the Rhine became politically and culturally integrated parts of western Europe, ceasing to be only partially conquered or intermittent sources of tribute. The power, influence, and amount of activity exercised by the royal government also greatly increased. This increase was more a change of degree than one of type. The Carolingians were war-leaders and they secured the loyalty of the Frankish ruling elite by the same means the Merovingians had done (and all early medieval barbarian kings did), and many of those means came from war and its booty. The difference with the Carolingians was that they had greater military success than all but the very early Merovingian kings, and consequently they rebuilt and deepened royal influence over a much greater area. And too, their culture was now more "European." The Carolingian cultural centers were in northern Europe and not in the great cities near the Mediterranean. Carolingian culture spread literacy as the Church spread (see Chapter 5) and showed greater Roman influence in its liturgical, literary, and artistic life than had late Merovingian culture. The Carolingians' legacy would long outlast their political empire, an empire that would clearly show signs of its own demise some short seventy-seven years after Charlemagne's imperial coronation. Their literary and cultural achievements as well as their political ideals of empire would continue to influence and inspire Europeans throughout the Middle Ages.

THE RISE OF THE CAROLINGIANS

When referring to the time before Charles Martel (714–741), it is usual to call this family the Pippinids, that is, the descendents of Pippin rather than Carolingians, which means descendents of Charles. We first see the Pippinids in the early seventh century as important local nobility serving the Merovingian royal family, the only family that could provide a legitimate Frankish king. By the early seventh century there were two Frankish kingdoms, Neustria in the west with its political center around Paris, and Austrasia in the east with its political center between the rivers Meuse and Rhine. The Pippinids lived in Austrasia.

The Beginnings of the Family

The Pippinids' lands lay between the Meuse and the Moselle rivers. Their geographical position, perhaps more than any other single factor, was responsible for the family's early rise to prominence under the Merovingian kings (see Map 6.1). Their lands lay in the northeastern part of Austrasia, where they could reap the political and economic benefits of the great Frankish expansion to the north and east into Frisia and Thuringia in the seventh century. Their road to imperial power was certainly not foreseen in their early years, but historical hindsight helps us to uncover several factors crucial to their rise.

The first powerful leaders of the family we know of were Pippin I (d. 639) and his wife, Itta. In 613 Pippin was instrumental in helping Clothar II (584–629), king of Neustria, to invade Austrasia and end the regency of Queen Brunhild, whom the local nobility resented. Clothar rewarded Pippin with power and influence at court for his help. Pippin also married well; his union combined Itta's extensive inherited properties with his own vast estates. Advantageous marriages would be a happy recurrence in the family and an important factor in its rise.

Pippin's son, Grimoald I, who led the family for the middle decades of the seventh century, saw his position as the most important nobleman in Austrasia officially recognized with the title Mayor of the Palace. Mayor of the Palace was an ancient and traditional office in most of the barbarian kingdoms, but among the Franks it grew to become a position second only to the king's. The Pippinids from Grimoald I onwards held this office in Austrasia almost as hereditary right. It is important to remember, however, that they were mayors because they were important; they were not important because they were mayors. Their real power lay in their vast landed wealth and the skill with which they moved in the Merovingian political world of family, faction, war, and religion.

In the 650s, Grimoald tried to place his own son on the Austrasian throne. His coup, however, had only short-lived success and the legitimate Merovingian line was restored. Both Grimoald and his son were executed. Grimoald's fall pushed the family from the political limelight for about twenty years until his nephew, Pippin II (d. 714) assumed control.

Pippin II also married well; his wife Plectrud was heir to a great deal of land, largely in what is now Luxembourg. As we saw in Chapter 5, Plectrud founded

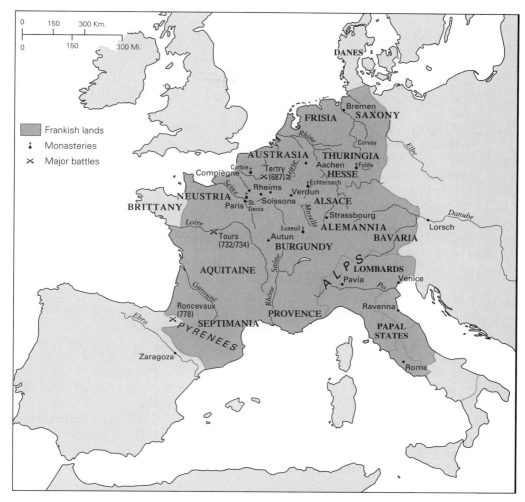

Map 6.1   The Frankish Lands c. 800   The map shows the vast area of the Franks' political control. Much of this was often only nominally Frankish; they had great difficulty controlling the peripheral areas such as France south of the Loire and southwestern Germany.

Willibrord's important monastery at Echternach, and Pippin supported Willibrord's Frisian mission. Founding and controlling important monasteries and influencing important bishops were practiced by the family as far back as Pippin I and Itta. Although such control was a normal part of politics for all the early medieval royalty and nobility, the Pippinids were particularly adept, or perhaps lucky, at it. The control of important religious institutions was another factor in the family's rise.

Pippin II was the first of the family's leaders to make significant political inroads into Neustria. He won an important battle over the Neustrians at Tertry in 687 and came to be recognized as the principal member of the Neustrian royal court. Still, the Pippinids did not yet permanently control Neustria and its powerful nobility.

Charles Martel (714–741)

Pippin's death created a struggle for power within the family. At first, his wife, Plectrud, ruled as regent for her infant grandson, since the couple's sons were dead. Even though she was one of the early Middle Ages' most politically talented and powerful aristocrats, she had the misfortune to be opposed by a shrewd and ambitious rival. This was Charles Martel, Pippin's son by another wife, or perhaps concubine, named Alpaida. By the time of his father's death, Charles was an adult and an experienced warrior. Plectrud and her young grandson were no match.

Charles Martel secured the control of Frankish politics for the family, whom we may now call Carolingians. Charles forced the family's treasure from Plectrud and successfully defeated the Neustrians, Frisians, and Aquitainians. After 723 he faced no significant challenge to his control.

Charles Martel not only controlled the whole Frankish realm under the titular rule of the Merovingian king, but he also became the most powerful political figure in all of western Europe. The internal peace and unity he provided meant that the Franks grew more powerful and influential in the international arena. His successful military campaigns brought large numbers of Frisians, Alemans, Thuringians, Saxons, and Bavarians under Frankish domination. His most famous victory against a foreign foe came in 732 when he defeated the Muslims near Tours (see Chapter 8). This famous battle did not end the Muslim threat; he had to fight them again several times. In the course of these wars, he strengthened Frankish rule over Burgundy, Aquitaine, and Provence, gaining a more secure access to the Mediterranean.

When the Merovingian king, Theuderic IV, died in 737, the Frankish throne remained vacant for nearly six years and was not reoccupied until two years after Charles' death. To rule without a king was unheard of. The fact that Charles and then his heirs could do so is strong testament to the Carolingians' powerful position.

Pippin (741–768)

Charles Martel died on October 22, 741, and was succeeded by his two sons. The elder, Carloman, became mayor in the east, governing Austrasia, Alemannia, and Thuringia. The younger son, Pippin, became mayor in the west, controlling Neustria, Burgundy, and Provence. In the beginning the two brothers cooperated closely and for good reason. As so often happens with succession of power, the death of Charles Martel occasioned the resurgence of much regional independence. The Aquitainians, Alemans, Saxons, Gascons, and Bavarians all revolted, and it took the two mayors some eight years to restore a semblance of their father's former authority over the outlying areas. To bolster their position against these potential dangers, Carloman and Pippin reestablished the legitimate Merovingian line. Childeric III (743–751) was recognized as king in 743. He was the last Merovingian to reign.

In 747, Carloman left his son and his authority to Pippin's care and retired to the monastic life at Rome. By 749, Pippin's political problems north of the Alps were ameliorating somewhat, but on the Italian side of the mountains the pope's problems with the Lombards were increasing. The Byzantine emperor was too preoccupied with the Arabs and the Avars to lend much support to his Italian subjects. This meant that throughout the eighth century prudent popes looked elsewhere for protection. The pope's need would bring him to the Franks.

The Carolingian mayors had long possessed the qualities of Frankish royal authority; they ruled in all but name. This condition was obvious to their contemporaries and some sources—though not the official legal documents—refer to them as kings. But kings they were not, and thus they lacked the vital attractive power for political loyalty that only royal status could provide. Pippin sent envoys to Rome asking Pope Zacharias (741–752) the famous question whether it was right for a king to rule without having any royal power. The pope answered that he who actually has the royal power should be king. In 751, Pippin deposed Chilperic III, tonsured him, and sent him packing to a monastery. Then in a holy and elaborate ceremony in the traditional Merovingian seat of Soissons, he had himself proclaimed king by the traditional assembly of Frankish warriors along with the bishops. The deed was done; the new dynasty was born, but it was startlingly novel and a risky step.

In 753 and 754, the new royal family's alliance with Rome received a very strong confirmation. Pope Stephen III (752–757) crossed the Alps to personally ask for Pippin's help against the Lombards and in another ceremony the pope himself anointed the former mayor as King of the Franks along with his wife, Bertrada, as queen. Anointing is a holy ceremony taken from the Old Testament. It shows, among other things, that the king is God's choice. The bond between pope and Pippin was a powerful one.

Once king, Pippin crossed the Alps in 755 and eased the pope's position by defeating the Lombards. The consequences of Pippin's actions here were to play a role in the history of Western Europe well into the twentieth century. Pippin established what became known as the Papal States, a large slice of central Italy in a diagonal belt from Venice and Ravenna in the north to south of Rome. This area was established and protected by Frankish arms and at its head was the pope. Its creation directly involved the papacy in political governance. Never again could the popes make important decisions without considering the political needs of the Papal States.*

The famous "Donation of Constantine" appeared about this time, lending spurious legitimacy to the popes' position as rulers of much of Italy. Although this document was a forgery, it was widely considered genuine until the fifteenth century. In it, the Emperor Constantine was said to have conferred on Pope Sylvester I (314–35) primacy over the great patriarchs of the East along with political rule over the provinces of the West, which, of course, included Italy. Leo IX (1048–54)

---

* In the nineteenth century, most of the Papal States were finally undone, and in the twentieth, the Italian dictator, Mussolini, formally concluded the treaty acknowledging their reduction to the Vatican City and a few other small holdings.

is the first pope known to have used the Donation to support the papal position, but thereafter it became quite influential until its falsity was exposed.

Both as mayor and king, Pippin was a strong ruler. His rule relied on the mutual advantage gained from cooperation between the crown and the powerful nobility, as did all early medieval barbarian kings. Pippin relied heavily, although not exclusively, on the Austrasian nobility, whom he now placed in positions of authority throughout the Frankish realm. The aristocracy's loyalty required periodic grants of land and money, which came in large part from foreign wars. In addition to his campaigns against the neighboring German tribes, Pippin attempted to bring independently minded Aquitaine and the other areas south of the Loire more firmly under Frankish royal control. To do so he had to campaign there almost every year from 760 to his death in 768. When he died, the position of his new dynasty was secure.

Charlemagne (768–814)

When Pippin died, his kingdom was divided according to Frankish usage between his two sons, Charles, the elder one, whom we call Charlemagne, and the younger brother, Carloman. Charlemagne seems to have been an impressive king: intelligent, hardworking, aggressive, ruthless, and blessed with seemingly limitless energy. His physical appearance was striking; he was a big man, over six feet tall with a bit of a belly, but according to his biographer, Einhard, his voice was thin, hardly fitting his physique. He was convivial, to say the least, and partook in the raucous aristocratic pastimes—horsemanship, hunting, food, drink, and women—with great gusto. He was particularly fond of great slabs of roast meat and was greatly disturbed in later life when his doctors forbade them. He was learned, fluent in Latin, and knew some Greek. He loved to read but never learned to write.* He was a seriously religious man and deeply concerned for the spiritual well-being of his kingdom.

Charlemagne inherited the north, west, and east: Bavaria, eastern Austrasia, Thuringia, Hesse, Frisia, western Neustria, and western Aquitaine; Carloman the center and the south: Alemania, western Austrasia, Burgundy, eastern Neustria, and eastern Aquitaine. The two royal brothers did not always cooperate. When the Aquitainians revolted in 769, Charlemagne moved south with an army against them, but Carloman refused to help. It was probably a good thing for the dynasty that Carloman died in 771. His warriors immediately pledged their loyalty to Charlemagne, despite the fact that Carloman left an infant son and possible heir.

Charlemagne greatly expanded the extent of the Frankish rule. He first turned his attention to Italy where he put an end to the kingdom of the Lombards. In 773 when the Lombard king, Desiderius, was again threatening the lands of the pope, Charlemagne crossed the Alps, besieged Pavia, and within a year deposed him. He then assumed the title, King of Lombards, for himself. He also took the opportu-

---

* In the Middle Ages, not all readers could write; writing was a specialized art practiced especially by scribes, some of whom could not read very well.

nity to travel southwards to Rome and to solidify his relationship with Pope Hadrian I (772–795).

Charlemagne's great German foe, the Saxons, proved far more resistant. It took the Frankish king over thirty years (772–804) of nearly annual campaigns, all of them bloody, to subdue them. The most famous campaign came in 785 when the Saxon leader, Widukind, surrendered, and Charlemagne forced Christianity on him and on many of his people. The hostilities continued, however, and Charlemagne used many tactics trying to end them. In 794 he deported thousands of Saxons; in 797 he gave orders that every third household be moved; in 798 he removed 1,600 of their leaders. But his most effective instrument for peace with them was the Church. In 781 he established the huge diocese of Bremen, again on the Roman model, and the process of bringing the Saxons into the culture shared by the Franks deepened. By 804, Franks and Saxons were largely at peace.

The Lombards and Saxons were not the only target of Charlemagne's ambitions. In 778, he crossed the Pyrenees and moved south into Spain, stopping just short of Saragossa. On his return, his rear guard was attacked by the Basques near Ronceveaux. The battle became extremely famous, forming the basis of the *Song of Roland,* one of the most important works in medieval French. In 778, Charlemagne also deposed Tassilo, duke of the Bavarians. In the following year he defeated the Bretons. In 791, he led his army down the Danube into the territory of the Avars, and in both 808 and 810 he marched north against the Danes.

Charlemagne did not conduct this yearly campaigning simply out of a robust love of battle and the military life. War formed a vital part of the early medieval political system. An early medieval king had three basic responsibilities: to fight foreign foes, keep the internal peace, and to represent his people to God. War is what kings should do and they must do it well. Charlemagne personally commanded most of his reign's major military campaigns. He was a magnificent warrior, a large part of being a magnificent king.

On Christmas Day, 800, Charlemagne received the title of emperor from the pope, adding a new, imperial dimension to his rule. Being Roman emperors carried certain advantages for the Carolingians, but we must be careful not to make too much of their new status. It is true that the title was by no means empty. It had been duly conferred by the pope, and Charlemagne used it in many of his official documents. It certainly lent a higher level of legitimacy to a dynasty whose royalty only went back one generation and to a usurper at that. The title was in some ways an apt description of Charlemagne's position in the year 800, but in other ways it was not. He ruled more of western Europe than anyone had before him and he would soon conquer the Saxons, a task that had stumped even the ancient Roman emperors. But the land of the Franks, the heart of his empire, was not the ancient, urban, sophisticated Mediterranean coast. Charlemagne's subjects lived for the most part on their rural estates carved out like dots of cultivated land in the great northern European forest. Their world was local; few traveled or knew much more than their plot or what they learned in their local church. Even in the towns, wolves could be a worry.

The title also meant, at least in some western eyes, that the ruler of western Europe now had a status equal to that of the emperor in the East. Charlemagne had

MEDIEVAL VOICES

An Edict of Charlemagne Describes Proper Religious Observance

In 789, Charlemagne issued a set of royal decrees known as the Admonitio Generalis. *They are drawn largely from the acts of councils of the Church and show clearly how important Charlemagne considered proper religious observance to be for the well-being of his realm. The following is part of the introduction.*

Considering with the salutary judgement of a pious mind, together with our bishops and counsellors, the abundant clemency of Christ the King toward us and our people, and how necessary it is not only to render unceasing thanks to His goodness with all our heart and voice, but also to devote ourselves to His praise by continuous practice of good works, that He who has conferred such great honors on our realm may vouchsafe always to preserve us and it by His protection.

Source: Roger Collins, *Early Medieval Europe, 300–1000,* (London: Macmillan, 1991) 284.

frequent diplomatic dealings with Byzantium and at one point actually proposed marriage to the Empress, Irene (see Chapter 4). His own subjects and their neighbors may have considered Charlemagne Roman emperor, but the proud Byzantines scoffed. In their eyes there was only one Roman emperor and he, or in this case she, ruled from Constantinople, not from Aachen. In many important senses, the Easterners were correct. Charlemagne's new title certainly did not change the basis of his rule. He was not the distant theocratic monarch in the style of the Byzantines or the late-antique Romans, nor did he head an elaborate and well-established bureaucratic state. He was and would remain a Frankish king.

On the other hand, ideas of emperor and empire were certainly larger than the concepts of king and kingdom and these ideas accurately reflected the fact that Carolingian rule now extended far beyond their kingship of Franks and Lombards. The idea of empire also contained a strong sense of universality, that is, that people living in many different regions belonged to the same political body. But for Charlemagne, the universal nature of his title, Roman Emperor, came not from uniting his far-flung subjects in a Roman community, but in a Christian one. The empire as the community of Christians was an important idea that could be used to bind all the various ethnic peoples to a Frankish king. The Frankish nobility did not encourage any "melting pot" in which other peoples would come to consider themselves culturally Frankish; the Franks remained very keen to distinguish who was a Frank and who was not. But Christianity offered an intellectual bond common to all, and the great king took concrete and lasting measures to spread and strengthen the faith (see Medieval Voices).

THE ROYAL ADMINISTRATION

Charlemagne governed, as did all the early medieval kings, through the ties of personal loyalty. The most important royal officials were the counts. They managed the local districts for the king, recruiting the army, collecting his taxes and rents, and dispensing his justice. Usually they were members of local noble families, but in the areas less thickly settled by Franks, they were likely to be from the Austrasian nobility, that is, natives of the ancestral homeland of the Carolingian family imposed upon the locals. A count's district was often coterminous with the ancient Roman district and with the diocese of the Carolingian bishop.

Along those frontiers of the kingdom that faced threatening foes, the Carolingians usually established marches. A marcher count, or margrave, (*Markgraf* in German, *marquis* in French) often became a much more powerful figure than the other counts for a number of reasons. Marches were larger than interior counties and much more military in nature because of their function as protector at the border. Since a march was usually new territory, the margrave was not as encumbered with traditions and limitations to his authority as were other counts and he was likely to own a great deal more land within the march. The marches, too, were farther from the royal court and thus less often under direct royal scrutiny. In a sense, the Pippinids had been marcher lords in the Merovingian kingdom. Because of their powerful positions, Margraves were often a danger to the central government.

Other officials included dukes, military leaders often placed over a large amount of territory such as a march or several counties, and kings, who were Charlemagne's sons and heirs. In 781, Pope Hadrian anointed Charlemagne's son, Pippin, king of Italy and Pippin's three-year-old brother, Louis, was made king of Aquitaine. In 800, Charles Junior (as opposed to Charles Senior, or Charlemagne) was anointed king of Neustria. These subkingships served many purposes. First, they performed the function of coregency in helping to secure the succession. When the old king died, the succession was settled because the heir was already a king and already ruling. We shall find this among many dynasties throughout the Middle Ages. The Capetians, who succeeded the Carolingians in France, are especially noted for it. Second, the establishment of subkings created courts loyal to the central government for the local nobility of the various regions. Here the nobility decided regional policy and settled their disputes. And third, having Carolingian kings on the spot bound the local nobility to the Carolingian family more closely and more personally. Subkings were usually placed over areas particularly prone to independence from the central government.

Alongside these lay officials existed another whole system of ecclesiastical ones. These men were often from the same families as the counts and dukes. The most important were the bishops and archbishops, who, as we saw in Chapter 5, were not only rich and powerful local officials, but also often influential members of the royal court. Around the Carolingian kings, and exercising much influence on them, we find the abbots of the great monasteries: Fulda, Corbie, Luxeuil, Echternach, and St-Denis, to name a few. Such abbatial influence at court was new with the Carolingians and reflected not only the growing power and wealth of the monasteries but also the Carolingians' long-standing use of monasteries to help secure the family's influence on the local level.

In addition to these officials, Charlemagne used the famous royal emissaries, the *missi dominici*. These worked as a pair, one lay and one clerical, usually a count and a bishop. They would set out to investigate alleged abuses by local officials, to carry new royal decrees, or to settle disputes. They reported their activities and findings directly to Charlemagne.

Carolingian government, like all early medieval royal government, was not primarily financed by taxes. There were taxes, especially on commerce, and they did provide both income and a bothersome source of dispute. But a king was supposed to support himself and his government from the revenue of his own lands, the royal fisc. The Carolingians had a huge fisc, some of it their ancient familial holdings, mostly where modern Belgium, Luxembourg, and western Germany now are; some of it the remnant of the Merovingian fisc, mostly in the area around Paris; and some of it acquired through conquest or real-estate transactions. When a Frankish king, either the Carolingian or the early Merovingian, made arrangements to divide his kingdom among his heirs, close attention was paid to arranging the borders such that the fisc was fairly divided. To a royal heir, both the expanse of the kingdom he was to inherit and the amount of fiscal land it was to contain were matters of great importance.

Kings also had the right to "visit" certain nobles and ecclesiastical institutions for a certain period. The noble or abbot was responsible for feeding and housing the king and his retinue during these visits. The system was obviously another means of financing the court and it usually put an unwelcome strain on the host who saw his stores of food and wine disappear down the royal gullet and his feed and firewood vanish. The royal court was itinerant not just for financial reasons; it needed to move throughout the realm for political reasons as well. Because of the personal nature of their rule, kings could never be absent too long or too far from those whom they supposedly controlled.

When compared to the government of ancient Rome or to those of the high Middle Ages, the Carolingian seems rudimentary. Its binding force was personal loyalty. We find the early Carolingians bound in ties of *amicitia*, a political friendship, to their *leudes*, or men. Powerful lords gathered around themselves a group of warriors who were rewarded to retain their loyalty. The pledging of loyalty, which had begun as a private form of agreement between two people, became more regularized, more legally defined, and official under the Carolingian kings. It permeated all levels of the aristocratic structure and grew to be the form of expression for the binding force that held the government together. The Carolingian sources use the word *vassus* to designate the subordinate person in such an agreement; the lord is often called the *senior*. The lord would ensure the loyalty of his *vassus* by gifts: usually land, but sometimes also an influential position or money. In return the vassal would provide his lord with certain services, mostly military, and obey the lord's will. The gifts were originally not hereditary, but during the ninth century it became the rule to consider them so. One of the services due a lord was "counsel," the offering of advice. No king or lord would undertake much of importance without taking counsel with his followers. This was not so much to receive their advice as it was to insure the support of those without whom undertakings of any scale could not be carried out. Counsel was a vital political mechanism and it will remain a part of government throughout the Middle Ages.

The relationship between lords and vassals, often called "vassalage" by modern analysts, formed a complex network with many layers. The specific obligations and requirements varied by time and locality. The direct vassals of the king himself (the *vassi dominici*) had a special status and could be used as royal agents. Vassalage formed an important part of Carolingian and all subsequent medieval politics.

THE CAROLINGIAN CULTURAL REVIVAL

Although ancient Rome's political influence north of the Alps retreated with the establishment of the barbarian kingdoms, Roman cultural influence continued and even expanded geographically as the Church expanded. For the Franks, some of this Roman influence came directly across the Alps with a flow northward of books, objects of art, architectural ideas, and scholars from Italy, but much of it came indirectly from Ireland and England (see Chapter 5). The reinvigorated study of Latin; the copying of classical and early Christian texts; the writing of history, philosophy, and poetry; Roman influence in art and architecture; and reenlivened liturgical and theological discussions all received new life under Carolingian rule. Carolingian scholars searched, analyzed, and then applied the ideas they found in the works of recognized authorities in solving the great problems of their own day. In addition to the Bible and some Byzantine works, these authorities were for the most part Christian and pagan Romans.

The Scholars

The reinvigorated intellectual activity developed under Pippin II, Charles Martel, and King Pippin, but its great flowering came under Charlemagne and his son and successor, Louis the Pious (814–840). Historians call the movement the Carolingian Renaissance, and its effects on the subsequent history of Europe even outdid those of the family's splendid, but short-lived, political empire.

Although by Charlemagne's time the movement was well underway, he did not simply flow with its stream but took an active part in increasing it. He was deeply concerned about the spiritual well-being of his subjects; a proper and effective means of salvation must be available for the many peoples of the empire. This in turn meant that the clergy must be educated and able to read and understand certain important religious books along with being able to teach, preach, and properly perform the complicated Christian rituals, the chanting, the liturgies, and especially the mass. To this end he issued decrees, set standards, and supported a system of schools for the education of the ordinary clergy and often lay people as well.

He gathered around him the most famous scholars of the age from both Frankish and non-Frankish lands. Their collective scholarly activity is now known as the

Palace School. The most prominent figure among them was Alcuin (c. 735–804), from York in England. Charlemagne met Alcuin in Italy and later asked him to join his court. Alcuin became Charlemagne's chief advisor in educational and religious matters. He made Boethius, Augustine, the Latin grammarians, and Cassiodorus important objects of Carolingian study. In 796, he retired from the court to become abbot of Saint Martin's monastery at Tours, where he carried on his scholarly work in the monastery's library and school.

Charlemagne's court boasted other famous scholars. Einhard (c. 770–840), a learned Frank who had been educated at the monastery in Fulda, joined the court in 791 and became a valued advisor and close personal friend of the king. Charlemagne's conquest of the Lombards made northern Italian scholars even more available to him. Peter of Pisa, a deacon and literary figure, joined the court and is reported to have taught Charlemagne "grammar," that is, Latin and Latin literature. Paul the Deacon (c. 720–c. 800), an Italian poet and historian, also studied and wrote in the Frankish kingdom from 782–786. From the Visigothic kingdom came the court's leading theologian, Theodulf of Orleans (c. 750–821). He was a biblical scholar as well as a poet, and hymnist ("All Glory Laud and Honor" is his). He promoted the production of illuminated manuscripts—that is, manuscripts richly decorated and illustrated with paintings and gold leaf.

These scholars conducted a vigorous intellectual life, albeit often besmirched with that tiresome personal pettiness too often found among academics. Many of their letters, poems, tracts, histories, legal documents, and commentaries have survived. After the 790s, many of the leading intellectuals established residences in the important monasteries and episcopal centers, thereby spreading their activities throughout the realm.

The Schools and the Scriptoria

In many ways the most important work of the Carolingian Renaissance did not take place among the famous authors, but in the schools and the scriptoria, that is, the "writing rooms" where manuscript books were copied. The parishes often had a sort of elementary school that could teach the rudiments of reading to young children, both rich and poor. Their success often depended on the ability of the parish priest, and this as we saw (Chapter 5) varied greatly. The more advanced schools formed part of the cathedrals and monasteries. Here, too, the vital activity of copying manuscripts took place. For the most part monks were the scribes.

Although Dhuoda, who wrote in the early 840s, is the only known female Carolingian author (see Medieval Voices), there were many literate women in the Carolingian world. The most visible were members of the high nobility, but there were others as well. Both teachers and pupils in the schools in the nunneries were women, and there is mention of girls attending the day schools of the monasteries. In some places nuns also copied manuscripts.

Scribal activity under the Carolingians was truly remarkable; the number of texts they copied and the number of copies they made ensured the survival of many important works. They copied not only the standard religious works—the Bible, liturgical books, works of the fathers, sermons, letters, canons and the like—but a

MEDIEVAL VOICES

Dhuoda of Uzés Writes a "Handbook" for Her Son

One of the most revealing reflections of Carolingian conditions in the mid-ninth century was written between 840 and 843 by Dhuoda, wife of Bernard of Septimania, to her son, William. In elevated Latin and showing her considerable learning, Dhuoda offers advice that is almost entirely spiritual to a young son about to be entangled in very dangerous politics. The reader immediately senses the inseparable mixture of the next world with advice for living in this one and the fact that loyalty was a guiding theme. Her husband, Bernard, was executed by Charles the Bald for treason and the same end may have come to her son, William, the sixteen-year-old lad for whom she wrote the following.

He who fears the Lord honors his parents. You, my son, honor your father and constantly pray for him so that you may become old in years on this earth and so that you can live a long time. . . . Be obedient to your father in every useful endeavor and follow his judgment. Support his old age, if with God's help you come to this, and do not grieve him in his own life and neither spurn him when you become strong. . . . Do not be unmindful that dangers befell the sons of Eli, who disregarding the orders of their father were disobedient and because of this received a bitter death.

Moreover, hold to Charles [the Bald] whom you have as lord, since, as I believe, God (and your father, Bernard) in the beginning of your youth chose his flourishing strength to be served by you. . . . Serve him not only so that you are pleasing in his eyes, but also be fit in your perception for both your body and your soul. Hold a pure and constant loyalty to him in all useful endeavors.

If God someday leads you to fulfillment so that you merit being called to be among the great nobles offering counsel, consider carefully what, when, to whom and how you can offer worthy and fitting words. Act with the advice of those who prepare a loyal action for you for your body and your soul.

Source: Dhuoda, *Liber Manualis* from Book III.

great deal of ancient secular literature as well. In fact, over 90 percent of the ancient Roman texts we now possess survived because of the work of Carolingian copyists. One reason the Carolingian copies survived is that they were written on velum or parchment, substances much more resistant than the ancient papyrus to mice, insects, mildew, rot, and the other insidious weapons of time. Anyone who enjoys reading Virgil or Catullus owes gratitude to the Carolingians. And by a quirk of history, we also owe our modern lowercase script to Carolingian scribes. They developed a new script, the famous Carolingian minuscule; clear, roundish, attractive, and easily legible, it was a great improvement over older scripts, especially over the Merovingian ones. In the fifteenth century, the first printers fashioned their fonts for printing ancient Latin texts on the script they found in what they thought were the ancient Roman manuscripts. Those manuscripts, however, were not ancient Roman but Carolingian, and the script the printers imitated was Carolingian minuscule. Our modern script is derived from those first printed ones.

Art and Architecture

The themes treated in Carolingian intellectual and literary life also found expression in visual forms. An artistic renaissance accompanied the written one and it too showed great influence from both antique and contemporary Rome. The art was luxurious, reflecting the patronage of the king, the nobility, bishops, or the rich monasteries, and much of it was religious, reflecting the same purposes expressed in the intellectual life. Its style was European, combining Celtic, Germanic, Byzantine, and Roman elements.

The artistic renaissance came in many forms: painting, book production, ivory carving, mosaics, metal work, and architecture. It of course showed great variety in the various geographical sections of the huge empire and in various purposes for which it was created.

Most extant Carolingian painting survives in manuscripts. The interior walls of important building were also decorated with paintings but these have almost all vanished. In Carolingian work, gone are the gaunt, abstract figures of the seventh and early eighth centuries; now they are rounder, fleshier, more real—that is, much more Roman. The paintings portray important scenes: Bible stories, coronations, the dedication of important churches, or episodes from the lives of the saints. Their imagery and symbolism are often extremely sophisticated since they were often placed to accompany complicated texts in the manuscripts. Many paintings were also didactic in purpose, that is, intended to help teach people who could not read.

Certain things received special artistic attention, and not surprisingly they were the very things that conformed to Charlemagne's purposes. Liturgical books were lavishly decorated during the period. Altars were often ornamented with stone and ivory carving and magnificent metal work. Ivory carving, which had disappeared since the antique period, enjoyed a revival under the Carolingians. The facades of monastic churches were richly decorated, especially the western façade, which contained the principal entrance. Liturgical vestments were produced with consummate skill and extravagant expense. These could sport woven silks, pearls, thread wrapped with gold, intricate floral patterns, and lace.

Much Carolingian construction was of wood, and some splendid churches and palaces were wooden. These were mostly in the very northern parts of the empire. North of the Alps the ordinary buildings were usually wooden: houses, barns, sheds, and workshops. These wooden buildings have all disappeared.

Parts of some of the more important stone and brick buildings, however, have survived, and chief among these are the churches. With the Carolingians, church architecture took on a new and larger scale. In form, most of the great episcopal and monastic churches harken to Rome, as may be expected. Their plans follow the ancient Roman form of the basilica, consisting primarily of one huge, long, principal room called the nave. The nave had aisles running along each side and separated

Influence of the Carolingian Renaissance on Manuscript Illustration   The two illustrations above show the dramatic change in style that occurred with the Carolingian Renaissance. The picture on the left is taken from *the Gundohinus Gospels,* produced at Fleury between 751 and 754. Note how abstract and stiff the figures are. The picture on the right is taken from *the Aachen Gospels,* produced about 810. Here the figures are roundish and much more lifelike. The later manuscript presents its illustrations far more in the artistic style of the ancient Romans.   *Gundohinus Gospels: Bibliotheque Municipale, Autun, France; Aachen Gospels: Cathedral Treasury, Cathedral, Aachen/AKG, London.*

from it by a row of columns. The great churches in the city of Rome provided examples of basilicas to the northerners. In the latter eighth and early ninth centuries, the Carolingians built basilicas in the form of a T with a huge transept crossing the nave at the eastern end. The monastic church at the Abbey of St-Denis, near Paris, which was consecrated in 775 in the presence of Charlemagne, seems to have been the first transepted basilica built since the ancient period. The basilican form focused attention on the main altar, which was usually placed at the meeting of the nave and transept. Although the basilica became almost standard with the Carolingians, some of their most famous churches were not basilican. The palace chapel at Aachen is a magnificent octagonal building, showing influence from Byzantine Italy. Charles the Bald built a similar chapel at the royal residence in Compiegne, north of Paris.

Church architecture adapted to its new setting. The Carolingian period saw a flourishing in the veneration of relics and consequently the churches were equipped with impressive crypts, that is, with a level below ground to house the tombs and the relics of the saints. The crypt at Fulda, which still exists, is a good example. They also built impressive towers, often on each side of the west facade. This allowed for the construction of a second-story floor between the towers providing a platform from which the king or other important personage could view the liturgical observances taking place below in the nave. From this level between the towers, people outside the building could see the dignitary. This type of structure still stands at the monastic church at Corvey.

The Carolingians also adapted Roman examples of palaces to fit their own needs. The Roman palaces the Carolingians knew were in the cities of Italy. Their urban setting reflected the urban and fixed nature of Roman administration. The Carolingian royal courts were itinerant, and the Carolingian aristocracy was based in the countryside. Thus the Carolingian kings had several residences and all of them were rural. Even Charlemagne's great residential complex at Aachen was in a rural setting. At Lorsch, in modern Germany, a monumental Carolingian arch still stands, recalling the triumphal Arch of Constantine in Rome in its form. It is now called the Gate House and was probably the entrance to an important burial place.

The Revival After Charlemagne

The reign of Charlemagne's son, Louis the Pious (814–840), saw an increase in intellectual and artistic activity. Under him such noted scholars as Rabanus Maurus and Amalarius of Metz continued the scholarly work, and a great monastic reform was undertaken under the leadership of Benedict of Aniane (d. 821). Benedict attempted to reinvigorate monastic practice by emphasizing a standard liturgy, prayers for the dead, and a uniform following of the Benedictine Rule. He is sometimes called the second founder of the Benedictine Order. Under Charlemagne's grandson, Charles the Bald (841–877), John Scotus Eriugena (c. 810–877), an Irishman, and the most original thinker of the movement, devised a philosophical scheme that attempted to reconcile ancient Neoplatonic ideas where reality "emanates" throughout the world from a source called "the one," with Christian ideas where reality does not emanate but was created by God.

Except for Eriugena's work, the Carolingian Renaissance is often criticized for being intellectually weak because of its lack of original thought. This is not a useful criticism. The Carolingians did make original contributions in philosophy and theology, the study of law, the writing of history, and the uses of poetry. It is true, however, that the bulk of their work was not new. But the Carolingians were not seeking intellectual novelty; their goals were, as we have seen, educational and religious revival, and in both they succeeded admirably. It was not until the twelfth century that medieval people began to strive for the "new"; tradition and authority are the early medieval guiding forces, not fragile, untested novelty. The famous scholars, teachers, and scribes of the Carolingian Renaissance provided the intellectual tools to help correct and strengthen the religious observance, the morality, and the efficiency of clergy and laity alike. In so doing, they carried out Charlemagne's purpose for the whole movement: the saving of souls.

THE LATER CAROLINGIANS, 814–911

Although the religious and intellectual life of the Carolingian Empire saw its high-point under Charlemagne's son and successor, Louis the Pious (814–840), the Empire's politics became decidedly less happy. Once again political expansion stopped and internal dissension broke the unity that Charles Martel, Pippin I, and Charlemagne had so successfully built. Now, too, a new and terrifying foreign foe appeared: the Vikings, skilled raiders and conquerors from the north.

Louis the Pious (814–840)

At the time of Charlemagne's death in January of 814, Louis was his only surviving legitimate son, and the crown and imperial title passed to him without a hitch. He had been king in Aquitaine since he was three and had also been made co-emperor with his father in 813. Louis was a warrior-king, personally leading his armies, a ruler with a majestic sense of empire, and, as his sobriquet "pious" proclaims, one deeply concerned about the spiritual welfare of his realm. He made great use of the imperial title and worked tirelessly to insure the permanence of empire in the West. Despite Louis' skillful and sometimes ruthless efforts to maintain unity and consensus among various regions and factions, the empire as his father, Charlemagne, had known it did not outlive him.

Louis used many methods to try to keep the empire united. Although Aachen remained his usual residence, he also frequented the traditional Merovingian haunts in the Seine-Oise basin around Paris. He held a Carolingian housecleaning at court upon his succession. Almost all of Charlemagne's entourage was replaced with Louis' own loyal followers, many of whom were from Aquitaine. He sent his sons as subkings to important parts of the empire: Pippin to Aquitaine and Lothar to Bavaria. In 816, he held his own recoronation at the Merovingian ecclesiastical center of Reims where Pope Stephen IV (816–817) consecrated him and his wife, Irmengard, as emperor and empress. This ceremony was not only public testimony of the empire's sacral tie to Rome, but a declaration that imperial rule should pass to Irmengard's offspring, thereby lessening any contention from Louis's illegitimate half-brothers and nephews, all of whom were also Charlemagne's progeny.

Nevertheless, for most of the last half of his twenty-six year reign, the empire was plagued with civil war among Louis and his royal sons. The causes of the troubles were manifold, but prime among them was the fact that the empire had ceased to expand. Without the boons of money and land from foreign war, the nobility within the empire found reasons to war among each other by championing one prince or king against his royal relatives.

Louis hoped to arrange for a peaceful succession as early as 817, only three years into his reign. At the traditional annual assembly of the king and nobles he announced provisions for the succession. This *Ordinatio Imperii* stipulated that the bulk of the empire along with the imperial title was to be left to his eldest son, Lothar, giving his other sons subkingdoms and making them subordinate to their brother. Trouble erupted immediately. Nobility dissatisfied with their lot in general or because Louis's ecclesiastical reforms had dampened their ability to control Church offices or confiscate Church property began to gather around the disgruntled princes, who became rallying points for rebellion. Matters took a decided turn for the worse in 823 when Louis' second wife, Judith, gave birth to a son, Charles, the future Charles the Bald. In 829 the inheritance was redivided to make room for the royal newcomer. Judith was not about to let her son slip from power because of his adult half-brothers, and she had powerful supporters eager to help insure the empire would be divided in Charles' favor.

From about 830 onward, the brothers and half-brother were almost constantly leading factions at war among each other and against their father. In 833, Lothar actually dislodged his father from the throne for about a year, but Louis regained it to rule until his death in 840.*

It was not until 843, three years after Louis' death, that Charles and his two surviving elder half-brothers, Lothar and Louis, agreed upon a division of the empire and managed to conclude a peace, albeit not a long-lasting one, the famous Treaty of Verdun.

The Treaty of Verdun split the Carolingian Empire into three huge sections. Charles, known as Charles the Bald (840–877), gained the western section, roughly most of what is now modern France. Lothar (840–855), who also inherited the imperial title, gained the central portion: the old Carolingian heartlands between the Meuse and the Moselle, most of Burgundy, and Carolingian Italy. Louis, known as Louis the German (840–876), obtained the eastern portion, roughly most of what is now modern Germany. The settlement brought only temporary peace; a great deal of war ensued among the brothers. The division recognized in the Treaty of Verdun seems to reflect tensions in European politics more deeply seated and of longer term than just those that surfaced during Louis' reign and its aftermath. At many times in European history right into the twentieth century, international conflict can be seen as roughly organized on the geography laid out in the Treaty of Verdun—that is, its western portion battling its eastern portion over its center.

The End of Carolingian Rule

The strongest of Louis' three heirs was the youngest, Charles the Bald. Until the last few years of his reign, the western Frankish kingdom remained strong. His was a brilliant court, and in his realm the Carolingian intellectual life continued with notable vitality. With the deaths of his half-brothers, Lothar in 855 and Louis the German in 876, Charles managed to absorb their portions and briefly to unite the empire under his single rule until his own death in 877.

It was not the divisions *per se* of the Carolingian Empire that ended its political control; divisions and subkingdoms were a normal part of Frankish politics. It was rather the civil wars in which the Franks turned upon themselves. When faced with

---

* In 842, an alliance between Pippin and Charles against Lothar found expression in the famous Oaths of Strassbourg. These contain the oldest surviving written examples of the early German and early French languages.

Charles the Bald (823–877) This picture from a Carolingian Bible made in Tours shows Charles the Bald seated under a canopy in imperial majesty in a very ancient Roman fashion. Note the very non-Roman presence of monks in audience with the emperor. *Adam Woolfit/Corbis.*

a new wave of foreign threats, the royal Carolingian governments were so divided and weakened, that they were not able to mount effective resistance against the invaders (see Chapter 8). The Vikings began their incursions in 787 in England and then soon shifted to the continent. In the south the Muslims moved against Italy, invading Sicily in 827. Somewhat later, in 895, in the east, the Magyars from the Hungarian plain began troubling the Germans.

After the death of Charles the Bald in 877, Carolingian political control saw a rapid decline. The center kingdom was itself subdivided several times, and in all the Carolingian realms the extent of effective royal rule was greatly reduced. Louis the Child (899–911) was the last Carolingian to rule in the East; in the West it was Louis V (986–987). Other families would now rise to kingship, leading western Europe's defense and eventually its renewed expansion. Their story will be told in Chapter 10.

CAROLINGIAN LIFE

From the mid-seventh century on, western Europe seems to have experienced a general economic expansion, accompanied by an increase in population. As western Europe became slowly but steadily richer and more populous, more land was brought under cultivation, some improved agricultural techniques found wider use, and trade expanded. The economic expansion helped people on all levels of Carolingian society, but those on its lower levels still lived for the most part in appalling poverty.

The Aristocracy

The very few lived very well. Huge amounts of land and riches became concentrated in the hands of only about twenty-seven great families and in the possession of the important ecclesiastical institutions. The great among the Carolingians seemed to have been awash with gold, bedecked in finery, and comfortably ensconced in many fine new buildings. For instance, Charlemagne's friend and later biographer, Einhard, enjoyed expansive and lavish quarters at the royal palace in Aachen and fine residences at the monasteries and estates he controlled or owned (see Medieval Portraits). Northern Europe has long seasons of cold and damp, and yet the rich stayed dry, somewhat warm, and well fed. Very few rooms in the great buildings were heated—in a monastery, for instance, usually only one—but the records speak of the cartloads of firewood used for heating. The monastic *scriptoria*, the writing rooms, were not heated and thus manuscript production often shut down for the winter because fingers were too numb to write. The method of heating was usually as simple as building a firepit in the center of a room and allowing the smoke to escape through a hole in the ceiling, although there were some chimneys. Lighting was very expensive and even the rich seemed to have reserved wax candles largely for lighting the sanctuaries of the churches. Darkness was for sleeping, and the well off nestled comfortably at night under sheets, warm blankets, and eiderdown. We even know of a type of counterpane designed so it could be snatched off the bed and worn as a sort of bathrobe when it was necessary to get up at night. Monks could wear these when attending the night offices. The rooms of the rich were decorated with curtains and tapestries, and important people even had portable beds so as not to be without the familiar comfort on their official journeys. Aristocrats also had silver dishes, spoons, and knives, along with pottery and some glassware, although this last item was rare and expensive.

Fine clothes and gold jewelry, much of it exquisitely worked and some showing Byzantine influence, were marks of the rich. Aristocrats also bathed. It was the Carolingian custom to bathe and change clothes on Saturday. Monks bathed far less often, since abstaining from such pleasure was an ascetic (if not olfactory) plus.

The male aristocrat's days were filled with official duties, estate-management along with hunting and warfare in their seasons. A great cleric would add liturgical and ecclesiastical duties to the list. Legal processes—trials, preparation of documents, ordeals, or advising on matters of tradition and law—consumed a good deal

---

MEDIEVAL PORTRAITS

Einhard (c. 770–840) Frankish Nobleman, Royal Counselor, Abbot, Biographer, and Scholar

---

Many of the noted scholars whom Charlemagne gathered around him into the "palace school" during the 780s came from areas that he ruled but that were not Frankish. Einhard, however, who joined the court in 791, was a true Frank. He was born and grew up a Frankish noble in the heart of Germany, in the Main Valley. He spoke the East Frankish language and was educated in the school of the monastery at Fulda, a monastery to which his family had probably donated land and where he acted as scribe for the abbot. Some examples of his handwriting have survived. At Charlemagne's court, he became a friend and advisor of the king. He continued in favor at court under Charlemagne's son and successor, Louis the Pious (814–841). Under Louis, he was entrusted with the education of the king's' eldest son, Lothar (d. 855) and reached the height of his literary production. In 830, he and his wife left the life at court. Now sixty and in poor health, he settled at Seligenstadt, a monastery he founded near his native lands and where he died in 841.

Einhard was an extremely well-educated man. Beginning in the school at Fulda, he studied not only the Bible, the Latin Fathers, and other sacred texts, but also many important authors of the ancient pagan classics. He was small physically and often teased because of his size, but of unconquerable energy and he won the trust and respect of those around him, especially of Charlemagne himself. Although Einhard married and never became a priest or a monk, Louis nonetheless made him "lay abbot" of many monasteries as a reward for his faithful and valuable service. He took his responsibility for these monasteries seriously and effected many improvements in their physical and organizational conditions while also using some of their produce, as was his right, to support his own quite luxurious life. He was a tireless worker at court, not only fulfilling his diplomatic duties but also often seeking to direct the high politics by letters of entreaty to Louis and his sons.

In addition to his letters, Einhard wrote learned and theological tracts. His most famous work, however, is his *Life of Charlemagne*, one of the most remarkable biographies of the Middle Ages. Written in the 820s and modeled on the ancient secular biography of Augustus by the second-century author, Suetonius, Einhard's is the first known biography written since the ancient period that has a secular figure as its subject. In it he gives a close personal picture of the powerful Frankish king and emperor who had been his own close personal friend.

---

of aristocratic energy, since the settlement of disputes was a primary way that the government attempted to maintain the internal peace.

The female aristocrats of the Carolingian age, as in other periods, were occupied mostly in managing the private and familial sphere. In this era as well, we have descriptions of them doing the spinning and weaving. It was they who raised and educated the children. They taught the boys until they were sent off either for book learning in order to become clerics or for training in hunting and warfare. The girls were kept until they were married, something that could happen in their early teens. Some great women were highly educated, and many became nuns and abbesses, especially in later life, directing some of the kingdom's most important and richest ecclesiastical institutions. Others, women such as Plectrud, Dhuoda, and Judith, were very powerful and active in the realm's high politics. The fact that the title "countess" appears at the end of the ninth century may well indicate that it was becoming more typical for aristocratic Carolingian women to be active in the traditionally male spheres. Carolingian women could and did inherit, control, and pass on lands, and these were often huge estates. Even when married, they retained ownership of their own property. We frequently find both husband and wife signing the documents that transfer land.

In a world where the spiritual was considered more real than the visible, where the saints hovered near their earthly remains ready to help with their miraculous powers, where the interventions of the almighty God who had created the world were recorded as extraordinary but natural events, it is little wonder that those holding high ecclesiastical positions were every bit as important, if not more so, than the lay aristocrats. In fact, there was often little difference between them. Both came from the great families, both had their private wealth and private followings, and both often carried on the same sort of daily routine. Clad in silks and finery, perched upon soft cushions, the prelates, both bishops and abbots, like their lay counterparts were wont to eat lavishly and entertain themselves by listening to delightful music or poetry—often amorous poetry. They also enjoyed hunting, war, fine horses, and sex. Needless to say, an important position in the Church was an alluring plum for a family, and many an aristocratic father maneuvered to get one for his son. Once obtained, every effort was made to pass it on to another family member. With time, the distinction between the Church's lands, which the prelates administered, and their familial land, which they owned, often became confused. Unless the higher authorities were keen and able to stop ecclesiastical land from falling into private hands through this sort of legal confusion, the great families grew even richer. Many abbots led more than one monastery—Alcuin, for instance, had at least four and Einhard six. The heads of some monasteries were not even monks. Some were "lay abbots," and other houses had a nominal abbot but were really under the authority of the monastery's advocate, or defender. Under Charlemagne's strong leadership, these practices seem to have been held more in check than they were under the other Carolingian monarchs. Under Louis the Pious, the great monastic reforms of Benedict of Aniane made matters more forthright and spiritual in many of the empire's abbeys, but by the end of the ninth century the abuses had returned.

The Townsfolk

Towns were the homes of merchants, artisans, bureaucrats, and professionals. The Carolingian epoch had many towns and the documents list the people who populated them: goldsmiths, silversmiths, shoemakers, fishermen, fullers, saddlers, parchment makers, carpenters, turners, harness makers, polishers, sword makers, tinsmiths, sculptors, bronze workers, painters, and iron workers.

These last were very rare; only the very great employed them. Iron was scarce, expensive, and much in demand. Its most spectacular use was in the making of arms. The Franks were fine sword makers, and their lethal wares were prized even at the eastern end of the Mediterranean.

Most of the merchants and artisans served the needs of the aristocracy; there was not anything like a mass market for their goods, and consequently most Carolingian towns were small. Italy and the Mediterranean coast still boasted some cities, but in northern Europe there were only towns, including ones that are now great cities, like Paris. These housed between 4,000 and 7,000 people. They nonetheless performed vital functions providing for the itinerant royal courts, the episcopal cathedrals, the law courts of the counts, and they were the seat of local markets, fairs, and community celebrations.

Most Carolingian trade was local, but some merchants did conduct trade over long distances. Many of these merchants were Jews. Jews were not persecuted under the Carolingians; they seem to have been welcomed, most likely because of the economic benefit their commerce brought. Luxury goods were procured from the East through the Mediterranean, and in return the Franks exported local products. In addition to swords, the merchants conducted a flourishing trade in slaves, obtained in the Slavic lands (hence our word "slave") and sold mostly to the Muslims. Charlemagne took steps to regularize the system of weights, measures, and the coinage, all of which indicate an increasing volume of long-distance trade.*

The Peasants

The Carolingian peasantry lived close to the edge; from what we can tell, their lot was better than the Merovingian peasants' had been, but they were still haunted far too frequently by the terrible fear of starvation. Shortages caused hardship for the wealthy, but for the poor, any sort of adverse change, natural or man-made—flood, plague, drought, severe cold, epidemic among the livestock, earthquake, war, or devastation—could easily cause misery, hunger, disease, and death.

Some peasants fared better than others. According to one of Charlemagne's edicts, if a peasant owned more than four "manses" of land (about 130 acres in total), he was liable for military duty. Some conditions of land use allowed peasants ample opportunity to farm for their own profit and even to sell their surplus. At the other end of the scale, however, many people had absolutely no steady means of support. Carolingian roads were dangerous, full of beggars, outlaws, and the desperately poor. These massed around the doors of churches and monasteries where alms, that is, leftover food, small gifts and perhaps coins, were distributed to them. They presented a huge problem that was never solved.

Food depended on the season; storage was difficult. The greatest worries appeared in late winter and early spring before the growing began. The peasants

---

* It is an interesting aside for English-speakers to note that Offa, the contemporary Anglo-Saxon king of Mercia, adopted Charlemagne's system of coinage, and, as pounds, shillings, and pence, it lasted in England until 1970 when the British government decimalized it.

consumed mostly grain, that is bread, gruel, or beer, and garden vegetables, beans, peas, onions, lettuce, parsnips, cabbage, carrots, beets and others, along with some dairy products and whatever else they could glean from the wild. Very rarely did a Carolingian peasant ever eat meat, although the sources make frequent mention of the *vivaria,* or fish ponds.

Every class of Carolingian society knew its cups; no one, country folk or towns-folk, was very far from a beckoning tavern. Although all drank, frequently to excess, it was the wealthy who produced and enjoyed the wine. Grapes require consider-able labor, and new vines require four to five years before they yield. The poor could neither hire labor, wait the requisite years, nor devote land to the process. Grapes had long been grown in western Europe, especially in Italy and Spain, but north of the Alps viticulture increased greatly as the monasteries spread. Much con-tinental wine was sold abroad; England was a particularly thirsty market. Thus many vineyards were planted near the rivers so that the wine would be near to water transportation.

The peasants' garb was as simple as their lives. They wore a rough, loose gar-ment, pulled in at the waist with a belt. Their shoes were heavy, their legs wrapped with narrow strips of cloth, and their heads usually covered by a hood. The hides of both domestic and wild animals were used to make the leather.

By modern standards, Carolingian crop yields were abysmally low. Today a farmer can expect to reap between twenty-five to thirty berries of grain for every seed planted; a Carolingian farmer could expect from about two to four. Without enough manure to fertilize the fields, they were left fallow every second or third year to restore the nutrients. Even so, the soil often quickly wore out. The draft an-imals were, of course, oxen, not horses; oxen eat grass but horses eat the precious grain in addition to grass. In some places the *carruca,* or deep plow, was used. Al-though it required a team of four oxen to pull it, it could turn the heavy, wet, northern European soil making deep furrows, something that the scratch, or sim-ple plow, used in the sandy soil of Mediterranean lands, could not do. The deep plow greatly cut down the amount of hand labor needed to prepare the soil, but it was very expensive since some of its parts had to be made of iron.

A peasant's lot was almost unbelievably hard. Most of the work was long and dif-ficult and done by hand. Men worked the fields; Carolingian women usually did not. Most tools were wooden and simple, although a water-powered mill, at least, usually ground the grain.

Heaped on top of the hardships inherent in the nature of the work, were those inflicted by the landowners. Some peasants did own their own land; these lived mostly in the south of France, Italy, and Germany. Most, however, did not, but worked someone else's in one of various servile statuses. Although some were slaves, most lived in some sort of semifree legal status, using the fields of a landlord in return for rents, service, a share of the crops, or a combination of the three. The exactions were oppressive, to say the least, causing the elite to live in comfort and the peasants to find little comfort in their lives. Their houses were huts, which they often shared with animals. They had earthen floors and very simple wooden furniture.

Many great estates in the Carolingian era came to be organized on a bipartite system. In this system, peasants were granted the use of one part of the estate's land in return for their labor, working the other part that was retained by the landlord. Modern analysts call estates organized like this "manors." Recent theory suggests that the bipartite manor was not as widely spread as once thought. It would seem it was largely confined to areas where the Carolingian royal estates were concentrated, that is, north of the river Loire and then in northern Italy after Charlemagne's assumption of the Lombard kingdom in 774. The conditions of "land holding," that is, the legal and financial arrangements under which peasants used a landlord's land, were often complicated and varied greatly throughout western Europe. Many peasants did not live on the manors, but owned or rented other lands. Land freely owned by a peasant is called an allod.

Imagine lives that varied by season but never by year; houses that were little more than rain shelters, drafty, filthy, and cold; a diet bland beyond boredom; and survival itself forged in a horrifying world of spirits, unpredictable nature, and sudden disease, all amid the terrors of the deep forest and the night. The recourse to the tavern and the church is of little surprise. A head numbed by the comfort of spirits and a soul comforted with spiritual promise were welcome buffers. And things were to become worse before they would get better.

In the period after the crumbling of strong Carolingian royal government, roughly from the death of Charles the Bald in 877, not only did the high culture, the Church, and the central governments suffer, but so too did the peasants. With the decrease in the power of royal governments came a corresponding decrease in their ability to keep out foreign invaders, offer royal justice as an alternative to local armed conflict, and curb the rapaciousness of local landlords. When power at the top crumbles and falls, it usually falls on the masses.

Summary

The family known as the Carolingians first appeared as important local nobility living between the rivers Meuse and Moselle in the early seventh century. By skilful politics, successful warfare, and advantageous marriages they rose to become the most politically prominent family in western Europe by the time of Charles Martel (714–741). Pippin (741–768) became king of the Franks in 751, and Charlemagne (768–814) added the title of emperor in 800. Dissention among Charlemagne's grandsons, however, caused the empire to be divided into three parts with the Treaty of Verdun in 843. The continuous wars among the Carolingian kings and their rivals, both Frankish and foreign, caused the family's political decline in the later ninth century.

Even though other families would take over the political control of western Europe, what had been accomplished under the Carolingians was remarkable and enduring. Vast new areas to the north and east in what is now the Netherlands and Germany were conquered and Christianized and thus became a political and cultural part of western Europe. Northern Europe's ties with the Roman church were strengthened, and Roman cultural influence, largely in Christian form, flowed northward. The Carolingians actively supported a movement of cultural reawakening now called the Carolingian Renaissance. Under their rule, famous scholars exchanged ideas, wrote theology, history, and poetry. Europe's literary past was copied onto new manuscripts and preserved. Schools were established in the monasteries and cathedrals, and Europe's religious life in its theology, liturgy, and monastic practice was revitalized. Art and architecture flourished and even a new and legible script developed. Western Europe's agriculture improved, population increased, and economy expanded. The Carolingians ruled over "the first Europe" as under them for the first time the western political, cultural, and economic center of gravity crossed the Alps and came to rest in the north.

~

CHAPTER 7

The British Isles: Celts, Anglo-Saxons, and Vikings, 407–980

The English Channel severs the British Isles from the rest of Europe. For centuries this twenty-six miles of water seemed to form a huge gulf between Britain and the continent. But with the spread of Roman Christianity, early medieval Britain returned to Europe and came to form a solid part of European culture just as it had under the Romans. In this chapter we shall examine the origins of medieval England, concentrating on two periods: During the seventh century, the conversion of the Anglo-Saxons to Christianity when the roots of a good deal of England's European culture were planted; and the late ninth and early tenth centuries, when the bases of much of England's national political structure were established. This history will reveal that the cause of England's differences is not "the Channel." England's differences are due more to its internal development than to its separation by water.

Before beginning it will be useful to define some geographical terminology that can be confusing. Many islands make up the British Isles, but two are much larger by far than the others: Ireland to the west and Great Britain to the east. These names are geographical, not political, terms; the political divisions on the British Isles have changed greatly over the centuries. In modern times, "British" means any subject of the United Kingdom, but in the Middle Ages it meant only the Celtic peoples who lived in the British Isles. In modern times, "English" means someone from England, a political division of the United Kingdom covering most of the southern part of the island of Great Britain. In the Middle Ages, the English were the Anglo-Saxons and their descendents, who settled southern Great Britain. The English were Germans, not Celts. The Scots were a Celtic people who originally inhabited northeastern Ireland. Many Scots crossed the Irish Sea to settle parts of what is now Scotland. It is from the name of these early Irish immigrants that Scotland gets its modern name. "Irish" in both its modern and medieval senses means someone from the island of Ireland.

England differs physically from the other parts of Great Britain. It is mostly, although certainly not totally, lowland with fertile, heavy, wet, clay soil meant for heavy plowing. Scotland and Wales are more mountainous and their lighter soil is more suitable for grazing and occasional light plowing. England, as opposed to Scotland and Wales, is a continuation of the great northern European plain that begins far to the east in the Slavic lands and sweeps westward through northern Germany, Denmark, the Benelux countries, and northern France. In its physical features, there is a much greater difference between England and Wales than there is between England and Flanders, the part of the European continent closest to it.

THE EARLY ANGLO-SAXONS, 407–597

In the course of the fifth and sixth centuries, groups of German peoples settled the southern part of the island of Great Britain, killing, displacing, and assimilating the native inhabitants. These Germans brought with them the language, the culture, and the social and political institutions that set the foundation for what would eventually become the medieval kingdom of England.

Hinged Clasp from the Sutton Hoo Burial Ship   The treasure ship buried near the East Anglian town of Sutton Hoo is one of the most magnificent discoveries from the early Anglo-Saxon period. It is now usually considered to be the funerary monument of King Redwald of East Anglia who died about 620, although it could be from one of his successors. To serve as a funerary monument, the ship was pulled from the river to the top of a bluff, a height of 100 feet, and then buried in a trench. The king was placed in the center of the ship in a huge coffin and surrounded by a great amount of treasure and a great number of valuable objects, Christian and pagan alike. This intricately worked clasp was among them. The grave remained untouched until its discovery in 1939. *The British Museum.*

The Arrival of the Anglo-Saxons

In 407, Constantine III removed the Roman field army from Great Britain as part of his attempt to gain control of the western empire. Without the formidable prop of its military, Roman rule quickly faded from the British Isles. By 440, many small and independent British kingdoms were often warring with one another and unable to present an effective united resistance against outsiders. In the course of the fifth century, outsiders arrived piecemeal from both Ireland and from the European continent. At first they were only looking for plunder, but eventually they sought areas where they could settle. The most significant of these newcomers are usually loosely called the Anglo-Saxons, a term that is used to describe several north German peoples including the Angles, the Saxons, and the Jutes. There were others in the mix also: Frisians and Franks, to name just two. The Angles settled mostly in the north, in what would be called Northumbria and Mercia; the Saxons mostly in the middle and west; and the Jutes largely in Kent in the south. Most of the land in England was settled by the Angles, and thus the whole German area on Great Britain became known as "Angle-land," or England.

Historians used to view the Anglo-Saxon "invasion" as a tumultuous event for the natives of Great Britain. They now see it differently. First, the process was more gradual than the word "invasion" might imply. Second, there were Saxons in Britain even in Roman times. The Romans had brought them in to help defend Roman lands against British revolts and against outsiders. These Saxons invited their kinfolk from the continent to join them. Third, the old view that the Germans drove the British wholesale from England into Scotland, Wales, and Ireland now seems an exaggeration since historians now see evidence of assimilation between the British and German peoples. None the less, there was conflict enough.*

Early Anglo-Saxon England

By the end of the sixth century, the Anglo-Saxons had come to dominate England politically and had created larger political units within it. It was traditional to speak of this period as the Heptarchy—that is, as a system of seven kingdoms, but the new political units can be viewed more accurately as confederations of smaller tribes than as kingdoms, and there never was a neatly established system of seven. Early medieval rule is not nearly as territorial as it would later become; the kings surrounded themselves with a band of powerful warrior-aristocrats and saw their authority exercised far more over peoples than over carefully defined sections of territory. An important contemporary document called the Tribal Hidage, composed in the late seventh or during the eighth century, lists thirty-four different tribes living south of the Humber and includes an amount of land for each. The fact that these lands were grouped under many tribes shows that peoples rather than borders comprised the political units and that the kingdoms were not static.

* The High Middle Ages found in this struggle between the British and the Anglo-Saxon invaders the setting for one of its most important legends: King Arthur and his knights were supposedly true British defenders against the invading Germans.

The structure of the various early Anglo-Saxon kingdoms varied greatly, with some enjoying a greater effectiveness of royal authority than others.

The relationship among these kingdoms was usually hostile and always complicated as loyalties shifted. It used to be thought that some of the kings would rise from time to time to a kind of imperial status and rule in a superregional kingship with the Anglo-Saxon title, *Bretwalda*. It is now thought that the *Bretwalda* did not exist, and it is more accurate to speak of hegemony exercised by various kings over the others at various times.

THE CONVERSION OF THE ANGLO-SAXONS TO CHRISTIANITY, 597–730

Christianity had been widespread in Roman Britain, but as Roman culture waned in Britain, Christianity suffered although it did not die out. The arriving Anglo-Saxons were not faced with a strong church with powerful bishops as the Franks had been in Gaul. It is hardly surprising that Anglo-Saxon society, led as it was by a warrior aristocracy, was not quick to adopt the religion of a subservient and defeated British population. The British church remained the strongest in the highland areas where the Anglo-Saxons did not settle, in Wales and northern Britain.

The most logical source for Christian influence on the Anglo-Saxons would seem to have been the Frankish Church, geographically close, culturally advanced, and supported by the Merovingian kings. Although the Franks did have a hand in the process of converting the Anglo-Saxons, the major impetus came from two other sources: the far-off papacy and the Irish. The conversion of the Anglo-Saxons is not simply the story of a people changing its religion. It is far more the story of how England rejoined the culture of Europe.

The Papal Mission to England

The pope who sent the mission to England was none other than Gregory the Great (590–604). Gregory had long been an enthusiastic supporter of monasticism (see Chapter 5) and he chose the monk, Augustine,* then prior of Saint Andrews, to lead this mission. Augustine and his fellow monks set off in 596. With forty people in the party, it was a huge undertaking for its day. It was also a huge adventure for them to leave cultured Rome and travel across western Europe to far-off, dangerous, and mysterious Britain. It was obviously more of an adventure than Augustine wanted, for he wrote letters along the way to Gregory asking permission to turn back. Gregory replied with encouragement, insisting that the mission go forth. The

---

* This Augustine is known as Augustine of Canterbury and is not to be confused with Augustine of Hippo (see Chapter 5).

pope also arranged for a good deal of Frankish support for Augustine and his group. In the summer of 597, they reached Britain. Aethelbert, the powerful king of Kent, came out to meet the strange visitors on the Isle of Thanet at the mouth of the Thames. He received them in the open air rather than in a building in order to avoid whatever magic they might be able to work. King and missionaries then retired to Canterbury, Aethelbert's royal seat.

Aethelbert was no stranger to Christianity; he had a Christian wife, Bertha, daughter of the Merovingian king of Paris. Nonetheless Aethelbert was not converted by Bertha and her Frankish chaplain, but by Augustine and the Romans. The Anglo-Saxons probably resisted Frankish Christianity to avoid an act of political subservience. Rome, on the other hand, was far away and well removed from English politics.

Aethelbert was the dominant political figure in southern England, and with his conversion the faith began to spread rather rapidly to those whom he politically influenced. Although it took centuries for Christianity to completely penetrate the countryside, within about ninety years of Augustine's arrival, the English kings and aristocracy had accepted the new faith. Even so, the process was neither smooth nor steady.

Augustine and his successors established the new English church on the Roman model as best they could. The Anglo-Saxon political structure was neither administrated from towns nor were the Anglo-Saxon towns the sorts of commanding urban centers where Rome usually established its bishops. Nonetheless, the English church set up its ecclesiastical organization centered on them. The practice actually helped some urban areas whose primary function now became to serve as ceremonial and administrative centers for the bishops.

The Roman liturgy was also adopted, although it is not clear how quickly and to what degree this came about. It also became the custom for the Archbishops of Canterbury from the time of Augustine onwards to receive from the pope himself the pallium after their consecrations.* Roman organization, Roman liturgy, the use of the pallium, the reciprocal giving of many costly gifts between England and Rome, and the importation of Roman books and personnel all indicate the strong papal influence in the English church.

The Irish Mission to Northumbria

At the same time as Christianity was spreading from its Roman mission across southern England, it was also reintroduced north of the River Humber. Here, however, it came from Ireland. Irish Christianity differed in several ways from Roman practice.

The very beginning of Christianity in Ireland is lost to the historian's view. It had probably spread to the island from Roman Britain during the fourth century, for

---

* The pallium was a thin stole worn during the performance of certain liturgical functions and it carried great prestige.

the first missionaries to Ireland we know of, Palladius and Patrick, came in the fifth century and are said to have come not only to convert but to administer to Christians already on the island. They established a normal Roman episcopal and diocesan structure, but for most of Ireland this soon changed. Ireland had no significant towns, and Irish society was almost totally rural; its political centers were the rural homes of its tribal chiefs and clan leaders. Thus the diocesan structure, based in a town, did not fit. By about 615, the monasteries and their strong abbots had become the centers of Irish Christianity. In fact, Irish monasteries are known to have had bishops living in them, subject to the abbot or abbess, in order to perform the liturgical functions reserved for bishops. Here, as elsewhere in medieval Europe, the monastery was a very political animal. It was closely bound to the ruling families of the various Irish tribes, the abbot most often being a close relative of the tribal ruler. The monasteries were also a means by which the great families could increase the land they controlled.

Both by its geographical position and by its monastic nature, the Irish Church was isolated from continental Christianity and for a while at least, tended to tread its own path. Some of the differences caused the Irish to have a surprising influence on medieval life, both on Great Britain and on the continent. They also reveal important aspects of early medieval life in general.

Irish monks were known for their austerity and their enthusiasm. They sacrificed every physical comfort, satisfying their physical needs only to the point that would allow health and survival. Their zealotry in prayer, sometimes conducted submersed in freezing water, and in penance gained them a broad reputation and much respect. Anglo-Saxon and continental Christians were eager to listen to and much influenced by these men "mad for God." Ireland itself became known as "the island of saints."

Irish monasteries also gained reputations as great centers of learning. The Irish were accomplished Latinists, and Greek also formed part of their education at a time when it was all but untaught in western Europe. They became talented copyists and illustrators, creating splendid manuscripts, the most famous of which is *The Book of Kells,* probably produced in the monastery of Kells in County Meath about the year 800.

The institution of *peregrinatio,* pilgrimage, had a magnetism for the Irish. Irish monks set off in boats, sometimes not knowing where or if they would land. The pilgrimage was undertaken in order to cut every tie to this world in the search for God. The Irish pilgrims indeed traveled far from hearth and kin; Saint Brendan is even said to have sailed to North America. More believable, if nautically less daring, were the travels of two other famous Irish saints. Saint Columba (cir. 521–597) crossed the Irish Sea and established the important monastery of Iona on an island near Scotland. From here he supervised much of northern Ireland and converted much of western Scotland. The other, Saint Columbanus (543–615), ventured much farther afield. He established the influential monastery of Luxeuil in Frankish Burgundy and ended his years in northern Italy. These pilgrimages, while exhilarating religiously, were frightening physically. In medieval life, only one's own people, lord, family, village, friends, laws, and customs offered protection. To leave

The Chi-Rho Monogram Page from the Book of Kells   This beautiful illustration represents the first two letters of Christ's name in Greek, chi and rho. The Greek letters were a common way to write the name Christ in medieval Latin manuscripts. The Book of Kells was produced in Ireland about 800. It is lavishly illustrated and a clear example of the care and expense expended by monks in copying important religious books.   *Trinity College, Dublin/Art Resource, NY.*

them was to be at the mercy of forces terrifyingly unknown. But such was the quest for God for many Irish monks.

The Irish held to a different form of monastic tonsure. Instead of shaving the head so that the remaining hair formed the shape of a crown, as was usual for European monks, the Irish shaved the whole front half of the head, leaving a half moon of hair on the back of the scalp. This was anything but a minor difference in early medieval society where outward appearances were thought to reflect the more important and the more real inner and spiritual status.

By far the most important difference between Irish and Roman religious practice was the difference in the calculation of the date of Easter. Since the date of Easter is based on the lunar, not the solar calendar, it is a "movable feast." This means its date, not its day of the week, changes each year. The two methods of calculating Easter did not always yield different dates, but they could produce dates as much a month apart. Not only would Easter then be celebrated at different times, but so too would Ash Wednesday, Lent, Holy Week, Pentecost, and all the other observances dependent upon the date of Easter. This had a great effect not only on the clergy but also on everyone else. Much daily routine depended on the ecclesiastical calendar, and those following Celtic dates might be feasting at Easter while those on the Roman calendar were still fasting for Lent (see the Introduction to this book).

It was the Irish who first converted the north of England to Christianity. As in most places in early medieval Europe, the progress of missionaries was greatly dependent upon royal favor. In the 620s under King Edwin (617–633) and his wife, Aethelberga, Roman Christianity made important, but temporary, inroads into Northumbria, but Edwin's kingdom lapsed officially into paganism with his defeat and death in battle at the hands of pagan invaders in 633. In 634, King Oswald (634–643), head of another royal family, managed to regain Northumbria. In Bede's account of the decisive battle, Oswald, like Constantine and Clovis before him, commanded his troops to pray to Christ for victory and indeed he won. Encouraged by the heavenly help, Oswald began to convert Northumbria. He had been brought up and educated in the faith by the Irish monks of Iona, thus it was not from Kent and the Romans but from Iona and the Irish that he summoned missionaries to spread the type of Christianity he knew. This also had the political advantage of avoiding any kind of dependence on Kent, a powerful rival kingdom.

From Columba's monastery at Iona, Oswald brought Aidan (d. 651) to be his chief missionary. Aidan established his base in the Irish fashion at a monastery on an island, Lindisfarne, off the east coast of Northumbria, from which he made many missionary journeys into the Northumbrian hinterland. Lindisfarne became an important center of learning, and its ecclesiastical importance actually eclipsed Canterbury's for several decades in the mid-seventh century. England's most powerful kings were now the Northumbrians and the fact that they were Lindisfarne's earthly patrons had more than a little to do with its years of heavenly glory.

The pagan Mercian king, Penda, killed Oswald in battle in 643, and the Northumbrian throne eventually passed to Oswald's brother, Oswy (643–670). Oswy could do little more than buy the Mercians off until he finally defeated them in the decisive battle at Winwaed in 656, where Penda fell. The defeat of the Mercians allowed the Northumbrians to send their missionaries south of the Humber. But by 679 the Mercians were again strong enough to defeat the Northumbrians and thus contain their influence largely to Northumbria itself.

The Synod of Whitby (664)

Amid these political machinations, the most famous event of Oswy's reign occurred: the Synod of Whitby in 664 (see Medieval Portraits). The event was given lasting renown by Bede's colorful account of it. Both Roman and Irish missionaries were active in northern England during Oswy's rule, and he called the synod to decide which practice his realm should follow. The Roman side was represented by Wilfred, soon to become bishop of York. According to Bede, Oswy was convinced to declare for the Roman practice when Wilfred pointed out that Saint Peter, its champion, held the keys to heaven.

Other considerations, however, may have been afoot. Irish practice was losing in the British Isles. In fact, in 633 a large section of southern Ireland itself had adopted

MEDIEVAL PORTRAITS

Hild (614–680), Abbess of Whitby

Hild was a princess of the Northumbrian royal family, grand niece of King Edwin (617–633), related to both King Oswald (634–643) and King Oswy (643–670), and her sister was married to Aethelhere, king of the East Angles. For thirty-three years she led the life of a married noblewoman during which she was converted to Christianity by Paulinus. When her husband died, she became a nun and lived the religious life for another thirty-three years. After a short stay with her sister in East Anglia, she was recalled to Northumbria by Bishop Aidan and eventually put in charge of a small monastic community in Hartlepool. In 657, she founded the famous double monastery at Whitby and here she stayed until her death which came in 680 after a long illness.

The double monastery comprised institutions for both men and women living in strict separation, and in Anglo-Saxon England they were typically under the control of an abbess. Rich and powerful Anglo-Saxon widows, who often long outlived their warrior husbands, often took up the monastic life and continued to exert great influence by ruling such institutions. One indication of Hild's importance is that fact that the famous Synod of Whitby (664) was held at her monastery while she was abbess. During the proceedings she supported Colman and the Celtic rite, but eventually came to follow the Roman practice. Her reputation and her influence were immense. Christians not only from Northumbria, but also from all over England visited her monastery. While she was abbess she taught no fewer than five future bishops and many priests. Through their influence, and thus through hers, many new double monasteries were founded.

the Roman ways. And more importantly for Oswy, not only would his own kingdom most likely remain religiously divided if it continued in the Irish practice, but his efforts south of the Humber would be hampered if the natives saw the Northumbrians as bringing a divergent form of the faith. The queen, too, played an important role. Oswy's wife, Eanfled, had been brought up in Roman practice, which she continued to follow at her husband's court. Once again, a queen introduced religious change to an important royal household. The Synod of Whitby remains an important signpost of the increasing cultural unity of England along with its increasing openness to European, in this case Roman and papal, influence.

Bede and the Anglo-Saxon Renaissance

The events in the century or so following the Synod of Whitby show the close connection between Roman Christianity and the emerging culture of Anglo-Saxon England. The Irish practice continued to fade, and many important Irish ecclesiastical leaders actually left England and settled in Scotland. In 668/9 Pope Vitalian (657–672) consecrated a Greek, Theodore of Tarsus (668–690), as archbishop of Canterbury and sent him to England along with two other influential leaders, Hadrian and a Northumbrian nobleman and monk, Benedict Biscop (628–690).

Archbishop Theodore did much to establish the lasting structure of the English Church. He organized the dioceses, established the parishes, installed bishops, called councils, and promoted schools. He was a shrewd and much respected leader. In the Synod of Hereford (672), which he led, he had a lasting influence not only on the English Church but on English medieval history in general. This synod drew the lines of the English dioceses, making them huge, in the continental fashion. Huge dioceses would lead to powerful bishops and not to the much meeker British version of the office. A powerful episcopacy was to become a real force in English history throughout the Middle Ages.

Benedict Biscop became the abbot of the monastery in Canterbury and then founded the two influential Northumbrian monasteries, Wearmouth (673/4) and Jarrow (681/2). Biscop made the astounding number of five journeys to Rome during his lifetime, bringing back many relics, paintings, Roman glassworkers, and especially books. He was an avid supporter of Roman liturgy and even brought the archcantor from Saint Peter's in Rome to teach the Roman chant at Wearmouth and Jarrow.

All of this brought about a cultural flowering now called the Anglo-Saxon or Northumbrian Renaissance. The high point of their manuscript production is represented by the almost unbelievable *Codex Amiatinus*. This huge Bible, whose pages measure 27½ x 20½ inches, is the oldest extant copy of the Latin Vulgate. It is calculated that it took the skins of over 1,500 calves to make the vellum for this and two other volumes like it. This masterpiece of calligraphy in the Mediterranean style was made at Wearmouth and Jarrow as a gift for the pope. In 716, old Abbot Ceolfrith bravely set out for Rome to deliver it, but he died en route.

Northumbrian art of the period represents a fusion of Celtic and Roman styles both in sculpture and in the decoration of manuscript books. The famous *Lindisfarne Gospels*, produced a little before 698, is a good example. The decoration on the pages is almost wholly Celtic in style whereas the full-page portraits of the Gospel writers are Mediterranean.

More remarkable even than the production of splendid books was the flowering of learning. There in distant Northumbria far from its original home, Latin learning blossomed. Northumbria became the most learned place in Europe, and the most famous exponent of its learning was the remarkable Bede.

Bede (672/3–735), a local lad from County Durham, was given by his parents at age seven as an oblate to Abbot Benedict Biscop to be educated for the monastic life at Wearmouth. Oblates were children given by pious parents to monasteries to be reared and educated by the monks in order to became monks themselves. Bede was to spend his whole life in Wearmouth and Jarrow; we know of his venturing forth on trips only twice, once to Lindisfarne and once to York. And yet, there on the world's edge with virtually no personal experience of it, amid other scholarly monks and especially amid his beloved books, Bede became Europe's most learned man. He wrote biblical commentaries; tracts on spelling, on Latin grammar and poetic meter; saint's lives; original poetry; tracts on astronomy, cosmography, and the reckoning of time; letters; and theology. His works were famous within his own lifetime, and his influence, not only in England but in all Europe, has been immense (see Medieval Voices). It is largely through his works that western Europe

MEDIEVAL VOICES

Bede
Describes a
Meeting of
Christian and
Pagan Priests

The following passage from Bede's Ecclesiastical History *describes the meeting of Christian and pagan priests called by King Edwin of Northumbria in 627 to determine which would be the religion of his kingdom. The story is beautifully told and allows the modern reader a valuable glance into the nature of early medieval religion and kingship.*

. . . [Paulinus] spoke in a rather familiar voice [to the king], "You have escaped the hand of the enemy whom you feared because the Lord granted it; behold, you have gained the kingdom which you desired because the Lord bestowed it. Be mindful that you do not delay to do the third thing you promised. . . . If hereafter you would be willing to follow His will which He has preached to you through me, He, delivering you from everlasting torments of evils, will make you, along with Himself, a participant of His eternal reign in heaven."

When the king heard these words he responded that he both ought and wished to take up the faith which he was teaching. But he said that he would confer concerning this with the leaders, his friends, and with his advisors so that if they were willing to think the same things as he did, they could all be consecrated at the same time to Christ in the font of life. He therefore held a council with his wise men and asked each of them in turn how this teaching, which was unheard until that time, and how this new worship of the Divinity, which was being preached, seemed to them.

. . . Another of the king's nobles giving his assent quickly added, "The present life of men on earth," he said, "seems to me to be such (looking to compare that time which is uncertain to us) as if when you are seated at dinner with your Ealdormen and thanes in wintertime with the hall made cozy by its fire in the middle but with the winter winds of rain and snow raging everywhere outside, a sparrow should come and fly very quickly through the house, entering through one window and leaving through another. In that time in which it is inside, it is not touched by the winter's storm, that very small space of peace is a digression for a moment. Quickly returning from winter into winter the sparrow slips from your eyes. Thus the life of men is visible for an instant; but we certainly do not know what follows or what precedes it. Wherefore if this new teaching has brought us something more certain, then certainly it seems we must follow it." The other nobles and counselors of the king having been divinely moved added things similar to these.

Source: Ecclesiastical History, II-13.

came to use the Dionysian dating system, that is, the dating of years sequentially from the year of Christ's birth.

His most famous work for modern readers, although medieval readers were more interested in his religious writings, is his *Ecclesiastical History of the English People*. Most of what we know about medieval England up to the year 664 comes from this book. It is so skillfully constructed and so clearly and engagingly written that it is difficult for the reader to remember the sketchy nature of Bede's sources. It is for good reason that Bede has come to be called "the father of English history."

THE STRUGGLE FOR POLITICAL CONTROL, 730–974

By the time the Mercians defeated the Northumbrians in 679, the political situation in England had evolved into one in which three powerful kingdoms dominated the others: Northumbria, Mercia, and Wessex. These three lived with each other in an uneasy equilibrium for the next fifty years, but then a long struggle for political control of England emerged, first among the Anglo-Saxon kingdoms and then against the Vikings (see Map 7.1).

The Mercian Hegemony (730–825)

The power of the kings of Mercia had been growing steadily, if not without occasional setbacks, since the days of Penda, and they dominated English politics from about 730 to 825. When Bede was writing in the 730s, all the kingdoms south of the Humber were subject to Aethelbald (716–757), the king of Mercia. Aethelbald's more famous successor, Offa (757–796), probably lost Kent but nonetheless retained the dominant position in southern England. Offa had close connections to Charlemagne; in fact, he was most likely in some sort of subordinate position to the great Frankish king, receiving subsidies from him. In the early ninth century, however, Mercia experienced a rapid succession of kings who were probably not related to each other, a good indication that the throne did not pass peacefully and that there was a good deal of internal war.

In 825, a weakened Mercia fell victim to Egbert of Wessex (802–839), and immediately the warriors of Kent, Surrey, Sussex, Essex, and East Anglia changed sides and declared their allegiance to him. In 829, Egbert conquered Mercia itself and in 830 even defeated the Welsh. Briefly at least, Egbert had control of most of Britain south of the Humber. In the same year, Wiglaf of Mercia (827–840) regained his kingdom, probably with Egbert's blessing, since we know there were strong and friendly relations between the two. But the terrifying new danger from across the North Sea was already beginning to spread its misery. The real end of Mercian power did not come from domination by Wessex; it came in the long ships.

Anglo-Saxon England and the Vikings (830–871)

The Vikings seemed to explode from their homelands in Norway and Denmark to raid and eventually to settle all over northern Europe (see Chapter 8). Most of the Viking settlements in England were Danish; most of the ones on the other British islands were Norwegian. Dublin, for instance, was originally a Viking settlement.

Viking warriors comprised the upper class of their society, a class that knew the glittering social value of gold, silver, jewelry, wealth, and luxury goods of all types. These items not only made the leaders rich but, more importantly, displayed their elevated status to others—the lavish rewards for their followers, the decorations for their halls and their feasts, and the jewels to beautify their women, all in dazzling testimony to their own greatness. The warriors were hungry for such goods and they plied the cold northern seas to get them by trade or by plunder. The ship's company, about forty men, under its own leader was the Vikings' basic tactical unit. It was versatile, skilled, hungry, vicious, and effective. The plundering raid was at first the quickest way to riches, but with larger armies the Vikings could demand tribute of the natives and eventually ownership and rule of the foreign lands.

The first famous attack of the Vikings in England was their sack of Lindisfarne in 793, although the Danes had raided English land before. At first the Vikings were not overly interested in England; the pickings were fatter elsewhere, especially on the Frankish coast, and the resistance there was less fierce. In the 830s, however, they increased their plundering of England and after 835, Viking armies came every year.

Map 7.1 Great Britain in the Anglo-Saxon Period, 600–900 During much of the Anglo-Saxon period, a large portion of what would be England in the high and late Middle Ages was under Danish control. As the Anglo-Saxon kings gradually reabsorbed this Danelaw, they were able to organize it for the benefit of their own royal power.

Sometimes the Vikings would attack successfully, but sometimes the English would defeat them. The military methods, aspirations, and way of life of the warriors of both peoples were very similar in the eighth and ninth centuries. Both understood heroic warfare and the search for easy plunder.

In England, the Vikings' hit-and-run plundering changed with the campaign of 850–851, after which they formed bases in England itself. In that year, *The Anglo-Saxon Chronicle* records that the heathens, as it calls the Norsemen, spent the winter on the Isle of Thanet, which lies at the mouth of the Thames. The Viking armies were now bigger; the *Chronicle* claims that 350 ships were part of the storming of London in 851. Here, as often with numbers in medieval sources, it is probably best to consider 350 as synonymous with "very many." The situation for the English was very dangerous; no part of the British Isles was safe. The terrifying ships appeared suddenly as if from nowhere and their fearsome occupants would plunder, kill, rape, burn and then disappear again as mysteriously as they had come. Nor was the terror limited to the coast. Once disembarked, the Vikings could move inland with a horrible speed.

The Defense of Alfred the Great and His Successors (871–974)

Egbert's grandson, Alfred the Great, king of Wessex (871–899), kept Wessex from becoming a Viking kingdom. It was from Wessex that the Anglo-Saxons would eventually regain their lands and in the process establish much of the political structure for the united England of the high and later Middle Ages.

For 865, *The Anglo-Saxon Chronicle* reports "a huge heathen army" arrived and wintered in East Anglia. The East Anglians "made peace"—that is, they paid off the Vikings handsomely, as did the Northumbrians in 866 and the Mercians in 868. The Vikings had the run of England and were extracting huge sums in tribute.

Alfred came to the throne of Wessex in 871 just as a second huge heathen army arrived. He seems to have been a model early medieval king—that is, intelligent, pious, decisive, and fiercely loved. That last means, of course, brave, successful in battle, and ruthless. Only a month after taking over, he was forced to fight the Vikings; battles occurred at Reading, Ashdown, Wilton, and other places. Alfred "made peace"; he could do nothing else. The Vikings wintered in London. The Anglo-Saxon situation was grim.

By 876, the Vikings had moved from demanding tribute to taking and ruling English territory. The part of England they controlled came to be called the Danelaw, and the first stage of its establishment occurred in Northumbria. In 876, they dislodged their puppet king there and established their own kingdom, centered at York. From there they ruled the south and west of Northumbria and made trouble farther to the south. Alfred had to make peace again.

In 877, the Vikings settled in eastern Mercia. Alfred paid them huge tributes and sent them hostages. In January 878, they invaded Wessex and caught Alfred completely off guard since winter was not the campaigning season, and most of his men had been sent home. Alfred was now on the run. To this bleak period belongs the famous, if fanciful, story of how when Alfred was hiding incognito in the marshes of Somerset and had begged shelter from a swineherd, the lowly peasant's wife upbraided the king of Wessex for allowing the cakes to burn on the hearth. It would seem that the royal fortunes could have nowhere to go but upwards from suffering the scoldings of a swineherd's wife, and indeed 878 does seem to have been Alfred's low point. With the return of spring, he gathered his followers and struck. The Anglo-Saxons won a miraculous victory over the Vikings at Edington, and with their aggressive follow-up, they actually forced the Danish king to accept Christian baptism.

The victory at Edington was by no means decisive, but the Vikings did turn back eastward to East Anglia and set up rule there. A third Viking army had also landed in England in that year, but discouraged by the news from Edington, it quickly departed to ravish the continent. By 879, the Danes controlled Northumbria, East Anglia, and the eastern parts of Mercia. But Wessex was still in English hands.

"Making peace" was obviously not an optimal way to deal with the Vikings, and Alfred set about making Wessex secure from their threats. He established a system of fortifications called burhs, strategically placed fortified locations, some refurbished, some newly established. Some were military forts, but the more remarkable were much like walled towns. Alfred placed them so that most people lived within twenty miles of one. The burhs became an important part of English life. Not only did they form an effective defensive system against the Vikings, but many became centers for trade and administration and greatly helped in the revitalization of English town life. Unlike the defensive points on the continent established for protection against the Vikings, many of which were in the hands of the local nobility, the English burhs were under royal control. They comprised an important part of the strength of English royal power.

Alfred also reorganized the military. Alfred's army comprised both his aristocratic men at arms and the ancient Anglo-Saxon *fyrd*, or militia. Alfred divided the army in two and alternated the military service in three-month periods, putting one half on duty at a time while allowing the other half to stay home to perform the agricultural work. He built ships so as to take on the Vikings in their chief military advantages of surprise and mobility, and he made increasing use of thegns, members of a growing military class who, along with their retainers, made a profession of war. The result was an effective military, nicely under royal control.

When the third Viking army returned to England in 892, Alfred was ready. For four years the Vikings tried to overrun Wessex from their bases all along the Danelaw, but to no avail. Alfred's defenses held.

The kings who succeeded Alfred, Edward the Elder (899–924), Aethelstan (924–939), Edmund I (940–946), Eadred (946–955), and Eadwig (955–959) gradually regained the Danelaw, some by conquest, some by peaceful means. Edward came very close to governing nearly all of England's diverse populations, and in 937, Aethelstan defeated a combined force of Scots and Norsemen from Dublin at the famous battle of Brunanburh. Aethelstan's stature was such among Europe's kings that he married one daughter to Otto I of Germany and another to the powerful duke of the Franks.

The new royal organization established in the old Danish territory was based on Alfred's beginnings and used the shire as the royal administrative unit. In charge of the shire was the king's representative, the ealdorman. He conducted the king's business and held the shire court. With the passing generations, the loyalty of the shire's nobility became more and more anchored in their various localities as they acquired more landed possessions and became less directly dependent on the king. Nonetheless, the system of shires helped the late Anglo-Saxon kings to enjoy a very strong position compared with their continental counterparts. In England, too, it was the king, and not the local nobility, who controlled the system of defenses against the Vikings. The retaking of the Danelaw provided the English monarchs with new territory where the local Anglo-Saxon nobility was not so firmly entrenched. The English crown was well organized: it had its system of burhs, the shires, the *fyrd*, and even an important national tax, called the Danegeld, levied to support defense against the Danes.

This is not to say that England's kings were without the usual medieval problem of competition from powerful local nobility. Especially under Edgar (959–975), the great ealdormen sapped the royal authority. The local courts were taking the administration of justice from the king's courts and the appointment of important officials fell more and more under local control.

ANGLO-SAXON SOCIETY

A constant theme in the study of Anglo-Saxon society is its great variety. Added to the diversity of invading peoples lumped together under the term Anglo-Saxon is a great diversity in the type of land they settled and the great differences in their political histories. Even so, some general conclusions can help draw a picture of how the Anglo-Saxons lived.

The Peasants

The lot of the Anglo-Saxon peasant, as most peasants, was a difficult one. The invading Anglo-Saxons in the fifth and sixth centuries were largely free peasant farmers, called *coerls* in Anglo-Saxon. Although the newcomers subjected the native British, they seem to have eventually intermingled with them. By the time of King Alfred, the sources reveal no legal distinctions among the peasantry based on race.

Where the land was most fertile, the peasants tended to live in villages. Much of the arable land was owned in strips, long narrow fields, with no physical boundaries separating them from their neighbors'. The village life allowed for forms of cooperation: the sharing of draft teams of oxen, equipment, and the common use of pastures, woodlands, and marshes. There were individual homesteads as well. These tended to be located on the poorer land.

Documents from the seventh century show that a coerl owed several obligations to his king. He was obligated to serve in the *fyrd* and to work on the construction and repair of bridges. He owed the king a "food-rent," an exaction originally to support the king when he traveled and calculated according to the amount of land the coerl owned. The food-rent does not seem to have been oppressive.

A slow change, visible in the late seventh century, brought a change in the legal status of much of the peasantry. By the late ninth century, many coerls were living in a semifree legal status. They were personally free in that they could not be bought and sold, but they were subject to their landlord, who exacted rents and tolls from their land and who also had certain legal rights to fine and seize them. There were also slaves, peasants with no legal freedoms at all, and ceorls could own them. The growth of the semifree status in the peasantry resulted from the growth in the amount of land owned by the nobility. The peasants came to be grouped in a variety of legally defined categories. Most were personally free but tied to the land and under heavy obligations to their lords. But not all suffered: One legal category of peasant, the *gemeat*, also called the "free man" or "sokeman," was quite well off. He owned a comfortably sized farm and was often close in status to the lower nobility.

A large part of Anglo-Saxon life was directed by the Church and revolved around the parish. Alfred's reign only saw the beginnings of the great parish system. Christianity began in the towns and took centuries to set its roots firmly in the countryside. The local churches and their clergy were supported by the local peasantry; the parish owned land and lived from its income by making exactions on the peasantry just as the secular landlords did. In addition, all Christians were theoretically obligated to set aside one tenth of their income for support of the Church beyond the parish and especially for relief of the poor. This English tithe dates to the days of Archbishop Theodore when it was in the form of private almsgiving. In the course of the tenth century, it became a legal obligation dictated by secular law. Those on the king's land suffered under another ecclesiastical due called church-scot, or Peter's Pence. This, like the tithe, could be paid in kind. It was originally an alms payment delivered by the king to the pope, but the burden was soon passed to the peasantry and calculated according to the size of the peasant's land. It is likely that these ecclesiastical dues often went uncollected, especially in hard years.

As is usual in history, it is very difficult to see the public lives of the ordinary early medieval women. Ordinary women, unlike queens, noble women, great abbesses, or the men, do not often make clear appearances in the documents. With the spread of the Church's ideas of the sanctity of marriage and its condemnation of concubinage and divorce, the legitimate wife's status within the marriage climbed considerably, and her position became much more secure.

Since among the Anglo-Saxons, as well as among the British, kinship and the family were the basic organizational units of society, the role of women had central social importance. This had both a good and a bad outcome for the individual female. Since political and economic power was brokered among families, royal or humble, women were often pawns used to seal agreements by being given in marriage. As such they were considered under the legal control of their fathers or husbands. But late Anglo-Saxon charters reveal that this process granted women significant economic and legal protections. In some cases at least, a woman had the right to accept or reject the suitor. When she accepted one, she was legally entitled to material guarantees in the form of both money and land.

The Nobility

The most important members of the early Anglo-Saxon nobility were the warriors in the immediate company of the king. A royal companion formed part of an institution found among Germanic peoples everywhere in the early Middle Ages. The secular literature of the early Middle Ages, in particular the Old English epic, *Beowulf*, reflects the ideals and the way of life of the king and his companions. The ideals governing their conduct are termed "heroic," and the early Middle Ages in the British Isles are often called a heroic age. The epics tell glorious tales of great battles, fantastic acts of heroism, and colorful evenings in the great halls, where the king and his companions ate, drank, and sang their military exploits and those of their ancestors. Heroic ideals are characterized particularly by the bond of fierce personal loyalty between a lord, usually a king, and his men. The men are dedicated to protecting and avenging the king, and he in return is expected to show great personal valor and wonderful generosity toward his men.

This royal military household was the origin of many of the officials of the early Anglo-Saxon royal governments, and in most of England the companions of the king evolved into the most important members of the land-owning noble class. The king rewarded his companions with grants of land and by this along with other means, the nobility became less dependent on the king and, as we have seen, richer in their own right. As landlords, they fell heir to many of the royal exactions from their lands traditionally due the king. With time they increased these rents and dues, and the coerls on their estates suffered a harder lot.

The greatest of the Anglo-Saxon nobility were the ealdormen. They were originally the king's representatives in charge of managing his interests in a region and leading the local *fyrd*. As they slowly became more independent of the king, they evolved into local leaders of their districts and often became powerful enough in their own right to oppose the king. Thus in some places, the king installed a new official, the shire reeve or sheriff, as the royal representative. Although the institution of sheriff had its beginnings in the late Anglo-Saxon period, the sheriffs experienced the high point of their authority in the twelfth century.

The peasants' toil supported not only the political and cultural life of the aristocratic males, but it also provided a rich and varied public life for many upper-class women as well. These women, in Anglo-Saxon England as on the continent, queens and others of the high-born, often finished their public lives by "retiring" to a nunnery, often one that they had founded. With these retirements, it is always difficult to evaluate the relative importance of private religious motives, which we cannot see very well, as opposed to public and therefore more obvious political ones. Still, it seems that in these societies where warring aristocratic husbands usually died much younger than their wives, important women were often packed off to religious retirement in order to prevent them from passing on dangerous legitimacy to new husbands or to future offspring.

Not all important women gave up politics for the prayer book. Aethelflaed, daughter of King Alfred and sister of King Edward the Elder, is a good case in point. She was married to Aethelred, the ealdorman of English Mercia. Aethelred died in 911, but instead of taking up the veil, Aethelflaed continued in public life, helping to complete the construction of the system of burhs that her father had begun. She was also instrumental in helping Edward reconquer huge portions of the Danelaw. The fate of her daughter, Aelfwynn, however, was more typical. When Aethelflaed died in 919, her position passed to Aelfwynn, but Edward quickly dislodged her and seems to have sent her off to a convent in Wessex (see Medieval Voices).

Intellectual Life

By the reign of King Alfred, English high literary life was no longer what it had been in the glorious days of Bede. Learning and teaching on the lower levels were suffering as well. Priests were often so badly educated that they could not perform

MEDIEVAL VOICES

An Early
Eleventh-
Century
Anglo-Saxon
Marriage
Contract

This marriage agreement was contracted in Old English between a bridegroom, Brihtric, and the bride's father, Godwine. The families are quite wealthy, much money, land, and other possessions go to serve as guarantee for the woman. Note that none other than the king and the archbishop of Canterbury witnessed the agreement and that the bride's father kept a copy of it.

Here in this document is made known the agreement which Godwine made with Brihtric when he wooed his daughter; first, namely, that he gave her a pound's weight of gold in return for her acceptance of his suit, and he granted her the land at Street with everything that belongs to it, and 150 acres at Burmarsh and in addition 30 oxen, and 20 cows, and 10 horses, and 10 slaves.

This was agreed at Kingston in King Cnut's presence in the witness of Archbishop Lifing and of the community of Christ Church . . . and whichever of them shall live the longer is to succeed to all the possessions both in land . . . and in all things. Every trustworthy man in Kent and Sussex, thegn or ceorl, is aware of these terms.

And there are three of these documents; one is at Christ Church, the second at St Augustine's, and the third Brihtric has himself.

Source: Kevin Crossley-Holland, ed., *The Anglo-Saxon World* (Oxford, 1987 reprint) 261.

simple liturgical duties properly. Alfred obtained scholars from the Carolingians, set up schools to train the priests, began to restock England's monasteries with books because the Vikings in their lunge for a monastery's wealth often burned them, and he issued a law code.

More remarkable than any of these for an early medieval warrior king was Alfred's own involvement in the literary activity. He devised a list of the four books "most necessary for all men to know," and then, because most of his important subjects did not know much Latin, he himself either translated or supervised the translation of the works into Old English. These works were: 1) Pope Gregory I's *Pastoral Care,* 2) Boethius's *The Consolation of Philosophy,* 3) The first fifty Psalms from the Bible, and 4) Bede's *Ecclesiastical History of the English People.* Both the nature of the books and Alfred's own comments in his introduction to his translation of Gregory's *Pastoral Care* clearly show once again how very practically early medieval kings viewed their religious responsibilities. The well-being of Alfred's subjects in the here-and-now was dependent upon their proper preparation for the hereafter. These works were also all Latin-based. The only English work in this very English king's list was by Bede, who although Anglo-Saxon, was steeped in Rome's culture. Alfred's reintroduction of learning and ecclesiastical reform put England's intellectual life on a firmer footing for the future.

Summary

In the course of the fifth and sixth centuries, Germanic peoples conquered and settled most of the southern part of the island of Great Britain. Their settlement was often violent, and the native British suffered both death and displacement, although some were assimilated into the society of the conquerors. The Anglo-Saxons, a term used loosely to describe all these Germanic invaders, established kingdoms of various sizes throughout southern Britain. In the course of the seventh century, they adopted Christianity in its Roman organizational form. Their conversion more than anything else turned the culture of the British Isles to that of continental Europe. In fact, in the late seventh and early eighth centuries, one of their kingdoms, Northumbria, blossomed into one of Europe's most important cultural centers.

From the eighth to the tenth centuries, England witnessed a struggle for political control. This was waged first among the Anglo-Saxons themselves, but then against the Vikings. These conquerors from Denmark managed in the course of the ninth century to establish their rule over all of England except for part of Mercia and the kingdom of Wessex. After King Alfred the Great came to the West Saxon throne in 871, the tide began to turn and over the next 120 years the Anglo-Saxon kings regained their lands.

Anglo-Saxon society was originally one of largely free peasants owning their own lands. By the time of the Viking invasions, however, this had changed, and many were now semifree peasants subject to a land-owning nobility. The cultural bases for Anglo-Saxon society were laid both in the period of the conversion to Christianity and in the period of struggle with the Vikings, especially under the rule of King Alfred. It was also during this struggle that many of England's political institutions took the basic form they would keep into the central and even into the high Middle Ages.

CHAPTER 8

~

New Influences: Vikings, Arabs, and Peoples of the Steppe and Eastern Europe, 800–1000

The ninth and tenth centuries were unsettled times in Europe, as Arabs, Vikings, and Magyars attacked from every direction. Venturing from Scandinavia, Viking ships ranged from the Arctic to the Mediterranean, southeast to the Black and Caspian Seas, and west across the Atlantic to North America. Everywhere the Vikings went they raided and traded. And where they landed (Ireland, Iceland, Greenland, Newfoundland, England, Normandy, Belorussia and the Ukraine), they often eventually settled.

The Arab conquest of Spain in the eighth century and of Sicily in the ninth and tenth centuries made Muslims a dominant presence in the Mediterranean and brought Islam into southern Europe. The Islamic takeover of the Mediterranean was among the most important developments in medieval Europe. Unsettling as these conquests were, they were of great value in opening Europe to intellectual, economic, and technological influences from the Middle East.

The movements and influences of peoples in eastern Europe, including the Eurasian steppe, are less well known: Avars, mentioned in Chapter 6. Slavs who spread into the Byzantine empire and throughout eastern Europe; Bulgars, whose newly established state* of Bulgaria threatened Byzantium; Khazars, whose empire dominated the steppe from the seventh century to the tenth; and Magyars (or Hungarians) who ravaged Europe from the early tenth century until their defeat by the Germans at Lechfeld in 955.†

---

* The "states" created by nomadic groups such as the early Bulgars were indeterminate territories controlled by a military that exacted tribute. Still organized tribally, they had not yet developed such centralizing elements as a bureaucracy, taxes, public spaces, a centralized church, mints, or greater economic specialization.
† None of these peoples of the Steppe were a single ethnic group. A dominant ethnic group with a tradition of common origin usually masked a polyethnic mix of peoples. Successful warriors attracted men from other ethnic groups. For example, some "Slavs" may have been Avars who assimilated Slavic culture; Huns may have incorporated Goths into their "unit"; Magyars seem to have been joined by tribes of Khazars.

Although Europe suffered significant disruptions from these attacks, these same conquerors and marauders also crafted some of the best defended and most dynamic kingdoms of the tenth and eleventh centuries.

SLAVS, BULGARS, KHAZARS, AND MAGYARS: TURMOIL IN THE EAST

Slavs and Bulgars

The Slavic peoples* enter recorded history in the sixth century, at which time they were already scattered over the Danubian plains, around the Dniester river and extending into southern Poland, and west of the middle Dnieper. They seem to appear with the disappearance of those Germanic tribes who had moved across the Danube and into the Roman Empire (Chapter 3). Archaeological remains show a culture with rich agricultural resources, an iron technology, extensive trading links, trading towns and fortified strongholds by the eighth century, and numerous small villages located in scattered, difficult-to-reach areas. Slavic agrarian communities were, however, vulnerable to nomads moving west from Central Asia. Between the sixth and eighth centuries, the Slavs expanded further, either subjugated by, allied with, following, or fleeing the Huns, Avars, and Bulgars. Increasing population and the wealth of other regions also prompted their migrations (see Map 8.1).

The movement of Slavic peoples is difficult to trace. In general, however, Slavs moved into the Balkans, Dalmatia, peninsular Greece, and the Peloponnese in the sixth and seventh centuries, weakening the Byzantine Empire's hold on Greece. Byzantium lost its frontier on the Danube, lost Macedonia, and nearly lost western Greece (Chapter 4). These southern Slavs were later to become Croats, Macedonians, Slovenes, and Serbs. West Slavs—Bohemians (Czechs) and Slovaks—moved up the Danube into central Europe. Other West Slavs (including Polish tribes) spread northwest as far as the Elbe River, forming a frontier with the Germans in the west, while the eastern Slavs (linguistically divided by the sixteenth century into Great Russians, Ukrainians, and Belorussians) expanded up the Dnieper River into northwest Russia and northeast as far as the river Don and the upper Volta. Other Slavic groups remained in the lower Danube and consolidated around leaders who united warriors and different tribal elements. All were initially pagan, practicing polygamy and cremation rites for the dead and believing in a variety of gods and demons, including vampires.

In the seventh century the Slavs in the lower Danube area were invaded by Bulgars, a nomadic Turkic group in a line of succession that included the Huns, Avars, Khazars, Magyars, and Pechenegs. The Bulgars moved into the Black Sea region and separated into groups, one that settled in the middle Volga region, others scattering to various territories, and another that migrated west to the mouth of the Danube, expanding along the western shore of the Black Sea and into modern-day

---

* "Slav" is a linguistic term that refers to a common language; it may include a variety of peoples.

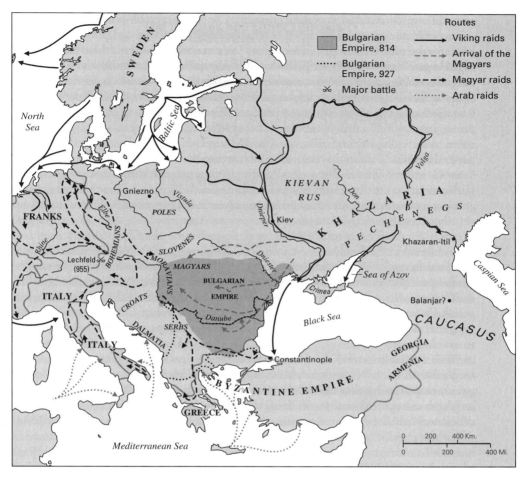

Map 8.1   Europe and Western Asia c. 900   This map shows the movement of Vikings, Magyars, and Arabs within and around Europe at the turn of the tenth century. The greatest powers in eastern Europe were Khazaria (soon to be defeated by the Kievan Rus), Greater Moravia (destroyed by the Magyars moving west), Bulgaria, and Byzantium, although Byzantium was seriously threatened by the expansion of Bulgaria into the Balkans and to the doorstep of Constantinople.

Hungary. From there they invaded Byzantine territories in the Balkans. Over the next two centuries the Danube Bulgars dominated but also assimilated with the Slavs already settled in these areas. From that strategic perch the Bulgar rulers (called khans) and nobles threatened the center of Byzantium. As pagans, the Bulgars also aggressively persecuted and martyred Christians.

From the seventh century to the ninth, Slavs in the middle Danube basin created Moravia, a kingdom that struggled for autonomy between the Carolingian rulers of East Francia and the Bulgars to the southeast. Archaeologists have uncovered a developed culture with fine jewelry, iron and pottery production, towns, churches, fortifications, and palaces. In an attempt to strengthen his position between Franks and Bulgars, the Moravian ruler reached out to Constantinople in 862 and sent for Orthodox Christian missionaries. The leaders of the mission were two Slavic monks who were brothers, Cyril (d. 869) and Methodius (d. 885). They were scholar-teachers, fluent in Slavic and Greek. It was their great contribution to create a Slavic alphabet with which they translated the Byzantine liturgy, the Greek Psalter, and the Gospels into the Slavic tongue. This dialect (a generalized literary Slavic called Old Church Slavonic) became the liturgical language for Bulgars, Serbs, Macedonians, and East Slavs as well. Although it has been disputed, it is likely that Old Church Slavonic was also intelligible to West Slavs. As such, it is an early example of the use of a "barbarian" (neither Greek nor Latin) language for Christian religious texts in the West.*

Despite these contributions (and despite Methodius's ecumenical attitude toward the western church and papal support of his mission), the Moravians expelled Methodius's disciples after his death, turning to missionaries and bishops who used Latin rather than Slavonic. The Croatians, Slovenes, Czechs, Poles, and Slovaks also accepted Roman Catholic rather than Byzantine Orthodox Christianity. In general by the late ninth or early tenth centuries, their rulers were baptized, although paganism remained strong among the populace even as late as the twelfth century.

The West Slavs were dominated, willingly or unwillingly, by the power of the Frankish and then the German empires. Both Bohemia and Poland consolidated into princely states in the tenth century, for the most part supported by an emerging Roman Catholic ecclesiastical hierarchy and, to varying degrees, pulled into the German orbit. The Polish princely dynasty gained an autonomous Catholic archbishopric at Gniezno in the year 1000 in cooperation with the German emperor, although Poland insisted on its independence from the German empire (see Medieval Voices). Bohemia was far less able to remain independent of German authority. Other tribes of pagan western Slavs whose names have been nearly obliterated in history—Lusatians, Obodrites, Veletians, Wends—were overrun by Germans, Poles, or Czechs and converted by force. These peoples, despite efforts at unification led by the Veletians and Obodrites, were doomed to defeat.

Among the southern Slavs, conversion from paganism to Christianity occurred slowly and was not forced. Churches in Croatia alternatively looked to the Franks and then the Byzantines for support, finally settling into the Latin sphere of ecclesiastical influence by the early tenth century. The Serbs, located more inland than the Croats, did not become the object of missionary efforts until well into the ninth century when both Bulgarians and Byzantines sought to control and convert them. Serbia remained within the Orthodox Christian orbit, and the division between Croatia and Serbia was to mark a lasting division between the Orthodox and Catholic worlds. The Croats, Slovenes, and Serbs began to form states, with the Croats retaining their independence well into the eleventh century.

In 865, the Bulgarian Khan Boris was baptized an Orthodox Christian, a strategically crucial and sensational conversion for the Byzantine Church. The Bulgars

---

* In the East, biblical and liturgical texts had been translated into a variety of languages, including Syriac, Armenian, Persian, Georgian, and Ethiopic.

MEDIEVAL VOICES

A Tenth-
Century
Report on
Poland

Around 965 a Moorish Jew, Ibrāhīm Ibn Ja'kūb, traveled throughout northern Europe, perhaps as far west as Ireland and east to Prague and possibly Cracow. His report (perhaps sent to the caliph at Córdoba) is the earliest documentary evidence relating to Poland. Originally written in Arabic, parts of it were later translated into Latin.

As far as the realm of Mesko [Mieszko I of Poland] is concerned, this is the most extensive of their [Slav] lands. It produces an abundance of food, meat, honey, and fish. The taxes collected by the King from commercial goods are used for the support of his retainers. He keeps three thousand armed men divided into detachments . . . and provides them with everything they need, clothing, horses, and weapons . . . The dowry system is very important to the Slavs . . . When a man possesses several daughters or a couple of sons, the former become a source of wealth, the latter a source of great prestige.

In general, the Slavs are violent and inclined to aggression. If not for the disharmony among them, caused by the multiplication of factions and by their fragmentation into clans, no people could match their strength . . . They are specially energetic in agriculture . . . Their trade on land and sea reaches to the Ruthenians [Rus] and to Constantinople. . . .

The lands of the Slavs are the coldest of all. When the nights are moonlit and the days clear, the most severe frosts occur . . . When people breathe, icicles form on their beards, as if made of glass . . . They have no bath-houses as such, but they do make use of wooden huts. They build a stone stove, on which, when it is heated, they pour water. They hold a bunch of grass in their hands, and waft the steam around. Then their pores open, and all excess matter escapes from their bodies . . . Their kings travel in great carriages, on four wheels. From the corners of the carriage a cradle is slung on chains, so that the passenger is not shaken by the motion. They prepare similar carriages for the sick and injured . . . The Slavs wage war with the Byzantines, with the Franks and Longobards [Lombards], and with other peoples, conducting themselves in battle with varying success.

Source: "Relatio Ibrāhīm ibn Ja'kūb de itinere slavico, quae traditur apud Al-Bekrī," T. Kowalski, ed., Monumenta Poloniae Historica, new ser., vol. 1 (Cracow, 1946) 145–151, partially translated by Norman Davies, God's Playground: A History of Poland, vol. 1 (New York: Columbia University Press, 1982) 3–4. © 1982 Columbia University Press. Reprinted with the permission of the publisher.

accepted the Byzantine liturgy in the Slavonic tongue; many of Methodius's disciples, exiled from Moravia, moved into Bulgaria as missionaries, and in 893, a final pagan revolt of the nobility was crushed. The establishment of a Christian ecclesiastical hierarchy, monasteries, and a Slavonic literary culture strengthened royal authority, albeit not without bloodshed. The Bulgarian state, under Boris's son Symeon (r. 893–927), experienced a golden age for art, literature, and architecture. It also expanded further into the Balkans, annexing Serbia and threatening the gates of Constantinople. Symeon, a remarkable scholar-ruler, marched on Constantinople six times from 896 to 924 but never captured it. He took, or claimed to have been given, the title Emperor of the Bulgars and the Greeks. Symeon's death ended the most serious Bulgar threat to Byzantium; by the end of the tenth century, Byzantium was on the verge of conquering Bulgaria.

The eastern Slavs were slower to convert to Christianity than the Bulgars or than other Slavs, partly because of their remoteness from urban Christian centers and partly because, in the early years of the Rus state, they were led by pagan Viking warriors. After several fits and starts, Bulgar and Byzantine missionary activity among the eastern Slavs became more concerted by the end of the tenth century; old Church Slavonic, following the Bulgar tradition rather than Byzantine Greek, became the liturgical language of Rus.

Khazars and Magyars

In the seventh century a nomadic group in the lower Volga region established a little-known but important empire, Khazaria. The Khazars were predominantly a Central Asian Turkic tribe, closely related to the Bulgars. The Khazar Empire ranged from Kiev to the Sea of Azov and from the Middle Volga to the Crimea and Caucasus; it subordinated a number of East Slavic tribes and defeated and divided the Bulgars. Khazaria offered a military bulwark to the advance of Arab armies, preventing Arab conquests that might have reached eastern Europe and would have threatened Byzantium from the north. D. M. Dunlop notes that it is a matter of great importance that at "the moment when the victories of Islam brought the Arabs to the Caucasus barrier, they met the Khazars, then vigorous and expanding."[1] The Arabs first attacked Khazaria in 642 but were defeated disastrously in 652. Subsequently the Khazars, with a paid, standing army of some 12,000 men, overran Georgia and Armenia and intruded into the Byzantine political sphere. From 722 to 737 a second Arab-Khazar war ensued, with devastating setbacks on both sides. Despite this, the Khazars held firm. Had they not contained the Arab armies beyond the Caucasus mountains, Europe might have evolved very differently.

The Khazar kingdom also provided a protected trade route for long-distance merchants, allowing goods to be transferred from China to Europe and from the Baltic to the Mediterranean. The Khazars supplied the Abbasid caliphate with furs, and they were the main supplier of Slavs to the slave markets of the eastern Mediterranean.* They bred horses, raised sheep, fished, and cultivated rice and millet as well as vineyards. They controlled silver and perhaps gold mines in the Caucasus region; and they promoted town building, particularly that of their capital Itil, founded near the mouth of the Volga. The Khazar beg, or king, and kagan (the two formed a kind of dual rulership) drew income from the tribute of conquered territories and from tithes on trade goods such as slaves, honey, wax, swords, amber, ivory, falcons, and furs. In about 715, a Muslim army took the Khazar city of Balanjar, reaping so many coins (300 dinars per soldier) as to suggest the enormous wealth of the Khazar Empire.

Finally, by converting to Judaism sometime between the early eighth and ninth centuries, the Khazars present an even more remarkable face to the historian. The

---

* The word "slave" derives from the Slavic origin of tens of thousands of individuals sold in the markets of the Mediterranean and Middle East in the ninth, tenth, and eleventh centuries.

conversion of the Khazars to Judaism is possibly linked to the persecution of Jews in Byzantium in the early eighth century, when they were forced to convert or emigrate; it might also be related to the merchant character of Khazaria, which attracted long-distance Jewish traders. The decision might have been politically strategic, allowing the rulers of Khazaria to avoid pressures to convert to Islam or to Greek or Roman Christianity. While some Khazars retained their Turkish pagan religion, the kagan, beg, and all the highest officials became adherents of Judaism. This circumstance attracted more Jewish settlers, since they were protected. At its height, Khazaria was a remarkably diverse and tolerant empire, with nomads, townspeople, and farmers; Christians, pagans, Jews, and Muslims; Arabs, Turks, Finno-Ugric speakers, Iranians, Slavs, Greeks, and Palaeo-Caucasian peoples, all part of an aristocratic and mercantile warrior society dominated by Judaized Turks.

Khazaria eventually collapsed. It was weakened in the second half of the ninth century by internal, possibly religious, strife, by the break-off of rebellious Khazar tribes who joined the Magyars (see next section), and by a coalition of peoples (including the Byzantines) who attacked Khazaria. Trade competition from the Bulgars on the middle Volga and from the increasingly wealthy Islamic state of Transoxiana weakened the kingdom further. In addition, the growing power of a polity called Kievan Rus threatened Khazaria. Around 965 the Kievan Rus ruler, Sviatosláv, defeated the Khazars, taking their major cities and fortifications. Khazar peoples scattered through eastern Europe, the steppe, and further east.

The Magyars* were a group of Finno-Ugric-speaking nomadic peoples who lived near the upper Volga and drifted south between the Don and the Dnieper in the ninth century. At first the Magyars were allies (or tributaries) to the Khazars, but relations became strained. Around 860 the Magyars moved toward the Lower Danube and began to raid into the west. In 895, the Magyars, strengthened by tribes of rebellious Khazar warriors, were almost destroyed by the combined forces of Pechenegs,† Byzantines, and Bulgarians. The Pechenegs carried off Magyar women and children and devastated their homeland—a loss that burned deeply into the consciousness of medieval Hungarians. Having lost their families and some of their armed forces, perhaps as many as 400,000 to 450,000 Magyars and Khazars migrated to present-day Hungary where their settlement resulted in the permanent division of the Slavic peoples, separating the South Slavs from both the West and East Slavs.

From Hungary, the Magyars began to raid Italy, central Europe, and eastern Germany in an effort to regain wealth and prestige, seek wives, capture slaves, and extend their homeland westward. In short order they defeated the king of Italy, occupied parts of the Balkans, destroyed Moravia, and defeated the east Franks, thereby ending nearly a century and a half of Carolingian efforts to dominate the middle Danube. They devastated Bavaria until a truce was signed and raided

* Magyars were also called Hungarians from their association with the Bulgar-Turkic "Onogur" tribes. A merger of these two groups may have taken place at the end of the ninth century.
† The Pechenegs (also called the Patzinaks) were a Turkic nomadic peoples who crossed the lower Volga moving west in the ninth century. After attacking the Magyars they settled along the Dnieper where they threatened both Rus and Byzantium. In the eleventh century they were forced further west by the Rus and then almost completely destroyed by the Byzantines in 1091.

The Crown of St. Stephen of Hungry
Although often said to be the crown presented to King Stephen I in 1001 by Pope Sylvester II, this crown was probably sent in the 1070s by the Byzantine Emperor Michael VII to the Hungarian King Géza I. The gold, gems and enamels in the crown are typical of the Byzantine style. In accepting this crown, Géza was rejecting claims of papal lordship over Hungary. According to tradition, it has been worn by every Hungarian king up to the time of the last Hapsburg emperor. In U.S. hands after World War II, the crown was returned to Hungary by President Carter. It rests presently in the Hungarian National Museum. *Mgyar Nemzeti Galeria, Budapest, Hungry/The Bridgeman Art Library.*

eastern Germany in search of yearly tribute. With their borders secured and hegemony established over the middle Danube, small mobile units of Magyars raided from Rome and the southern tip of Italy to Saxony, reaching as far west as Spain and the mouth of the Loire River on the Atlantic coast. Hungarian raiders were difficult to defeat as they used light cavalry, attacking with cascades of arrows from horseback and tempting the heavier Germanic cavalry to break ranks. Their raids created a climate of fear; they massacred the adults, burned villages, and took the young with them. Finally, in 955 an expedition was completely overcome by Otto I, king of Germany, at the battle of Lechfeld; the Hungarian military commanders and their Byzantine advisors were hung. With this defeat and Otto's subsequent establishment of manned marches along his eastern borders, the Hungarians settled down under the Árpád dynasty to produce one of the largest medieval kingdoms of eastern Europe.

Eastern Orthodox Christianity had been gradually making inroads among the Magyars. In the second half of the tenth century, however, the foreign policy of the Hungarian ruler turned toward the German Empire and western Christianity. This culminated in the decision of King István (Stephen I, 975–1038), called the Apostle of Hungary, to receive a crown from Pope Sylvester II in the year 1000. He consolidated control over the country by defeating other leaders, establishing ten Roman Catholic bishoprics and numerous monasteries, and converting the pagan Hungarians to western Christianity by force if necessary.

Hungary quickly took on the trappings of western European culture—elaborate public buildings, cathedrals, Latinate clergy, monasteries, laws, royal fortresses, coinage, military training that replaced light cavalry arms with the heavy sword of western Europe, and an increasingly powerful nobility. Nomadic traditions gave way slowly to a more settled agrarian life. Royal government benefited from a wealthy trade and market economy that attracted German and Muslim merchants and the beginnings of urban settlements. Despite some pagan revolts and a continuing, strong attachment to their past, the Hungarians settled into the orbit of European kingdoms, strengthening their economy (in agriculture, animal husbandry, trade, and mining) and their commitment to king and church until the thirteenth century, at which time the Hungarians (along with the Rus) bore the brunt of the Mongol invasions.

THE VIKINGS: RAIDERS AND TRADERS FROM THE NORTH

Almost exactly one century earlier than the first Magyar raids, the Vikings* attacked from the north. Although there had been earlier attacks, the Viking assault on the monastic community of St. Cuthbert on Lindisfarne Island in 793 shook much of Europe. Tidings reached Charlemagne's court, where Alcuin of York reacted with impassioned letters, writing, "Lo, it is nearly three hundred and fifty years that we and our fathers have inhabited this most lovely land, and never before has such terror appeared in Britain as we have now suffered from a pagan race, nor was it thought that such an inroad from the sea could be made. Behold the church of St. Cuthbert spattered with the blood of the priests of God, despoiled of all its ornaments; a place more venerable than all in Britain is given as a prey to pagan peoples . . . What should be expected for other places, when the divine judgment has not spared this holy place?"[2]

Alcuin's remarks were prophetic. Both West and East suffered from the assaults of these pagan Vikings. Although contemporaries like Alcuin attributed Viking onslaughts to divine judgment, modern scholars seek to understand the role that Viking culture and technology had in their expansion overseas. Although Alcuin stressed Viking destructiveness, modern scholars are more balanced in their assessments of the Viking impact.

Viking Raids

The raid on Lindisfarne was only one of a series of raids that included the island of Iona, the west coast of Scotland, and islands off Ireland. The raiders were probably

---

* The term "viking" was used by the northmen themselves and appears to mean "raiders," although it might also signify "the men from the Vík," the traditional pirate-infested Víkin region (the fjords south of Oslo and the southwest coast of Sweden). The Franks most often referred to the Vikings as heathen (*pagani*) or northmen. The Anglo-Saxons described them as "haethene men," while Arabs called them *al-Majus* (wizards, heathen) and Germans called them *ascomanni* (shipmen). In the East, they were Rus or Varangians. It is sometimes difficult to determine whether any particular group of Vikings were Danes, Swedes, or Norwegians—all of whom shared a basic unity in languages and customs.

Vikings already based in the Orkney and Shetland islands. The attacking groups were smallish, numbering in the hundreds, but the numbers were belied by their destructiveness, particularly against vulnerable churches and monasteries, some of which (like Whitby Abbey in northern England) were completely destroyed. By 799, Viking groups were raiding Aquitaine, and Charlemagne was concerned enough to strengthen his defenses, as was King Offa in England. After 830, the attacks became bolder and the Viking fleets larger; they began to attack port towns and to sail up the rivers of Ireland, England, and Francia. For the year 884, a Frankish chronicler wrote, "there did not exist a road which was not littered with dead, priests and laymen, women, children and babies. Despair spread throughout the land, and it seemed that all Christian people would perish."[3]

Viking attacks on towns could be devastating. In western France, Rouen was burned and the townspeople killed or carried off. Bordeaux was burned and de-populated, as was Orléans. The two principal northern ports of the Carolingians, Quentovic in Francia and Dorestad in Frisia, were attacked at the end of the eighth century. Archaeologists who have dug in these two ports, which are now so thoroughly erased from historical memory, suggest several reasons for their disappearance, vulnerability to Viking attacks being one. Settlements along the Loire were hard hit. Rural depopulation and economic disruption is more difficult to document, but large parts of Aquitaine and of Flanders became dangerous to inhabit. Peasants accordingly sought protection inland or near fortified castles. In 844, the Vikings took Seville briefly from the Arabs. By 851, they wintered in England for the first time, camping at the mouth of the Thames. They were prevented from taking all England only by the spirited, sometimes desperate defenses of King Alfred of Wessex (see Chapter 7). In the second half of the ninth century Vikings occasionally attacked Spain and North Africa, wintered over in the Rhone delta, and plundered Pisa and other coastal Italian cities, although they continued to concentrate their attacks on western Francia and the British Isles. (See Map 8.2).

Sometimes the Vikings could be staved off by huge payments. An 845 attack on Paris was averted by a tribute of £7,000 in silver. In all it is estimated the Franks gave £44,000 of precious metal to the Vikings in the ninth century, while the Anglo-Saxons expended £150,000 in silver. Although Alfred tried to build a navy to defend England, generally neither the French, the English, nor the Irish had defending fleets. They depended instead on landed fortifications—bridges, town walls, coastal, and river forts—which they rebuilt or built anew. By about 920, Vikings had settled throughout northwestern Europe, most notably in northern England, eastern Ireland, and in Normandy (Chapter 10) where they provided a bulwark against further raids of their own peoples.

This explosion of raiding and colonizing bedeviled not only western Europe and the Mediterranean but also, beginning in the 830s, the East where Vikings sailed, raided and traded down the Don, the Dnieper, and the Volga, arriving in the Black Sea, the Caspian Sea, Constantinople, the eastern Mediterranean, and as far afield as Baghdad. These Vikings (called Rus or Varangians) were mostly of Swedish origin. Their presence is indicated by graves, scattered artifacts, coin hoards, and runes, and by the commentaries of Byzantines and Arabs. By the first half of the ninth century, some settled along lakes and rivers in the upper Volga region,

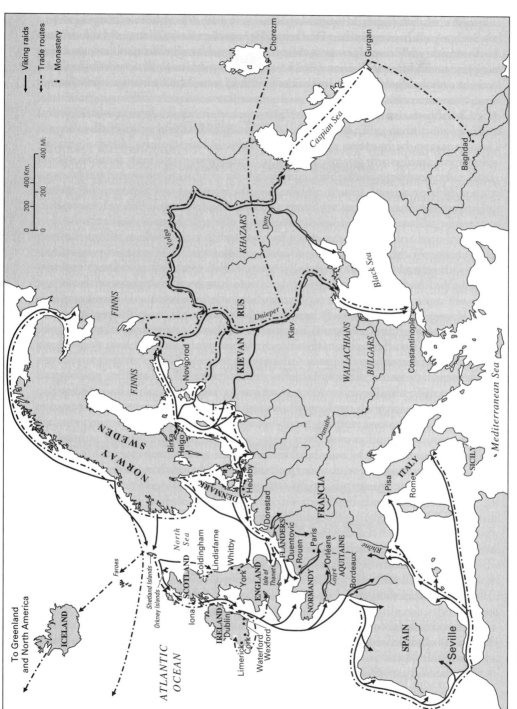

Map 8.2 Viking Raiding and Trading Routes c. 1000 A.D.   The Vikings ranged west across the north Atlantic as far as Newfoundland and east as far as Chorezm and Baghdad. They sailed along the Atlantic coasts of Europe and around the Straits of Gibraltar into the western Mediterranean. The Vikings mostly went by water, although they had to portage at places on the Dnieper and Volga Rivers and travel overland to Baghdad and Chorezm.

especially around what was to become Novgorod. By the early tenth century, they had moved south to Kiev on the Dnieper, among the East Slavs. They gained wealth from trade, imposed tribute on local populations, and raided extensively. In 860, possibly in 907, and again in 941 they attacked Constantinople, exacting tribute and trading privileges and establishing a diplomatic relationship, confirmed by treaties in 907 and throughout the tenth century.

Kiev, already a Slavic settlement, gained greater power under the leadership of Rus who claimed to be descendents of a ninth-century Viking leader named Rurik. These Rus were to give their name to Russia. In 945, Ígor, ruler of Kiev, was killed, leaving a young son, Sviatosláv. For nearly 20 years Kiev, now a state of considerable size, was governed by Ígor's wife Olga as regent. According to the *Rus Primary Chronicle*, she was a formidable ruler. She led attacks against enemy tribes, established trading posts, collected tribute, converted to Greek Orthodox Christianity, and negotiated in person with the Byzantines over trade restrictions. Her son Sviatosláv (r. 962–?972), a pagan ruler, defeated the Khazars, devastated parts of Bulgaria, and was able to command tribute from peoples as far away as the Finns in the north and the Wallachians in Romania. His son Vladimir (r. 980–1015) first adopted a mixture of pagan gods. Subsequently he may have explored Judaism, Islam, and Western and Greek Christianity. In or about 988, he was baptized into Greek Orthodox Christianity. This centralizing Kievan state was to be a unique cultural combination of East Slav, Scandinavian, Khazar, and Byzantine elements.

The Causes for Viking Migrations

Why did Vikings leave their homelands in such large numbers and to such dramatic effect? A combination of explanations has been offered. Dudo, a Norman chronicler writing about 1020, saw overpopulation (and sexual overindulgence) as a primary cause. "These people . . . live in outrageous union with many women and there in shameless and unlawful intercourse breed innumerable progeny. Once they have grown up, the young quarrel violently with their fathers and grandfathers, or with each other, about property, and if they increase too greatly in number, and cannot acquire sufficient arable land to live on, a large group is selected by the drawing of lots according to ancient custom, who are driven away to foreign peoples and realms."[4] Adam of Bremen, writing about 1075, blamed the poverty of the land. Modern scholars agree that overpopulation was a problem, though spurred perhaps less by overindulgence and more by a warming climate and (contrary to Adam of Bremen) a growing agricultural and pastoral economy.

Technological developments, particularly in shipbuilding, were crucial. We know from rock carvings as well as from the recovery of ancient ships that Viking warships evolved significantly by the eighth century. They were slender, built from thin overlapping oak planking, with full-length decking, fully oared, with closeable oar-ports and a mast that could be easily lowered. The ships had square sails and a steering oar (called a *styra*) at the stern's right side (hence the term starboard or steerboard); they rode high in the water and could be beached easily. Their design allowed them to plane on the water, not unlike a modern powerboat. Reaching speeds of over ten knots, they could, with luck, cross the Atlantic in four weeks time.

The growing demand from Khazars, Byzantines, Arabs, and western Europeans

A Tenth-Century Viking Ship   The Gokstad ship, which is currently housed in the Viking Ship Museum outside Oslo, was crafted at the end of the ninth or beginning of the tenth century and excavated in Norway in the 1880s. Masterfully built, it was 23.3 meters long and 5.25 meters broad amidships, with 32 oars and the ability to carry a crew of 70 men. It was made of oak and used primarily for ceremonial purposes. It may also have been a royal burial ship. Clearly visible is the thin planking that allowed Viking ships to sail into shallow waters. The excavation also recovered round yellow and black shields that would have been fitted along the sides of the ship. *Viking Ship Museum, Bygdoy, Norway/Werner Forman/Art Resource, NY.*

for furs, falcons, ivory, slaves, and probably iron ingots attracted Scandinavian adventurers, as did the prosperity of Carolingian France and Anglo-Saxon England and the silver coins of the Middle East. According to a tenth-century work, *Meadows of Gold* by al-Mas'ūdī (a famous Arab historian and traveler-geographer), the Viking Rus carried merchandise to Spain, Rome, Constantinople, and Khazaria and back. One of the more exotic items found in a Viking trading center (at Helgö, near modern Stockholm) is a sixth- or seventh-century bronze figure of a Buddha from northern India. Scandinavian homes began to be filled with luxury goods, foreign objects, and a variety of beautiful things that may have created a growing demand for wealth.

A further incentive was slave trading. Scandinavian society was based on extensive slave holding. As Carolingian markets for slaves declined, raiding became a major source for obtaining slaves. The Vikings opened up slave trading with Islamic Spain and the Middle East, garnering great wealth; Dublin became a major slaving port where the Irish and other peoples from the British Isles were taken by the hundreds to be sold and transported elsewhere. The *Annals of Ulster* records a plunder of Ireland in 951 in which Vikings captured 3,000 men with booty of cows, horses, gold, and silver. A twelfth-century Irish scribe wrote "Many were the . . . women and modest . . . maidens . . . and gentle, well-reared youths and brave warriors, whom they carried off into oppression and slavery over the broad green sea. Alas! many were the bright eyes filled with tears and dimmed with grief and despair at the separation of father from son and mother from daughter, brother from brother, and kindred from race and tribe."[5]

Anyone aspiring to leadership in Viking society required a reputation that was trumpeted in song, story, and on rune-stone monuments. Reputations were built on far-flung adventure, the glory of successful raids, and the accumulation of wealth. Such adventures attracted youthful leaders who needed to be generous with booty to reward followers and consolidate their positions. The resulting geographical and social mobility might well have made this the great "Age of Ambition" for Scandinavians.

According to the sagas,* quarrels and vendettas were also very much part of Scandinavian society. It was not uncommon for an individual to be pushed into exile by rivalries and family feuds. The sagas also suggest that some Vikings left Scandinavia to seek freedom and in reaction to centralizing tendencies toward kingship that they disliked.

Viking Culture and Society

The Vikings were, as one Irish writer put it, "a valiant, wrathful, purely pagan people." They were polytheists, with gods similar to those of other Germanic peoples. Odin was the god of power, poetry, and battle and lord of the dead. Ravens were his emissaries. He encouraged battle, which was further encouraged by belief in Valhalla, the heaven-like hall of the slain. Vikings believed that Valkyries, warrior-like women, conducted fallen warriors from the battlefield to Valhalla, where they were served food and drink. The god Thor, with his mighty hammer, governed the weather and fought evil. Freya was the goddess of love and fertility and, at times, a source of great conflict. The Vikings practiced sacrifices to their gods, including the occasional human sacrifice.

Viking society was class based, dominated by a warrior elite, with farmers, poorer freemen, freedmen, and a large slave population. The slave, or thrall, had a rough life and a legal position similar to a farm animal. Smaller farms might have three to four slaves, while larger farms used upwards of thirty.[†] Scandinavian society was rich, with many middle level families and some very wealthy individuals. Pagan Vikings were sometimes buried with their boats and other provisions for the afterlife; very rich burials (often in mounds) honored those who were socially prominent.

---

* Sagas are narrative tales in vernacular prose; the saga is a literary form somewhat between an epic and a novel. Sagas tell the story of heroic individuals from kings to well-to-do farmers, under circumstances that range from legendary to historical. The largest body of saga literature was written down in Iceland in the thirteenth and fourteenth centuries.

† Slaves did not disappear in Scandinavia until the fourteenth century.

Women in Scandinavian society could enjoy high status and independent authority. Evidence exists for female poets and prophetesses, and one of the sagas, the *Laxdoela Saga* (written in the thirteenth century, but based on oral traditions reaching back to the tenth century) was written or recited for a female audience. Women had a measure of equality in marriage, with the right to divorce; they could also inherit lands, and royal blood could pass through the female line. At times they accompanied men on sea voyages, although mostly for trade or resettlement. Occasionally a woman might travel great distances on her own. In the ninth century, Auðr, widow of Óláfr, the Norse king of Dublin (853–871), sailed to Iceland with her grandchildren and with twenty men to help her; she appears to have brought her Christian beliefs with her. Women are often mentioned as important persons in the sagas and on rune stones. In *Eirik's Saga,* for example, a central character is Gudrid, a woman of exceptional beauty and talent. She moved to Greenland with her father, married Thorstein Eiriksson (Leif Eiriksson's brother) and, after his death, married Thorfinn Karlsefni from Iceland. Together they joined Leif Eiriksson's expedition to Vinland, where Gudrid gave birth to the first known European born in the New World—Snorri Karlsefnisson. Gudrid was a Christian and great-grandmother of Icelandic bishops.

The Christianization of the north began in the early ninth century when Pope Paschal I sent a mission to Scandinavia. Viking attachment to paganism was strong, however, and conversion was a prolonged affair. Anskar, bishop of Bremen and the "apostle of the north," was the most successful of the ninth-century missionaries, but he had ups and downs and failed to convert any Scandinavian rulers. One hundred years later (around 960), King Harold Bluetooth of Denmark converted, according to the story, when a priest carried a red-hot iron in his hand without harm. Around 1000, two Norwegian rulers, Olaf Tryggvason and Olaf Haraldsson, brought Christianity to Norway, aggressively forcing the population to convert. Olaf Skotkönung was the first Christian king of Sweden in the early eleventh century, but Christianity progressed slowly through pagan Sweden. Icelanders, under pressure from Olaf Tryggvason but apparently of their own free will, agreed at their assembly, the Althing, to accept Christianity around 1000. They then carried Christianity with them as they peopled Greenland.

Impact of the Vikings

For centuries the Viking reputation was that of a ferocious and destructive people. This view was based largely on Latin texts written by Christian clergy who abhorred these pagan people. An example of the stories told by clergy is that of the nuns of Coldingham. In 870, according to the tale, an army of Danes landed in Scotland and headed south toward Coldingham in northern England. "Seeing no hope of flight," the abbess Ebba and all her nuns "slashed off their noses and upper lips to confront their would-by rapists with a line of ghastly, bleeding virgins. The horrified Danes burned the convent, and the sisters victoriously achieved the status of martyrs."[6] Tales like this were used to promote martyrdom in the face of pagan attacks. The Irish described Viking brutality dramatically in a twelfth-century retrospective Virgilian lament: "In a word, although there were an hundred hard-steeled iron heads on one neck, and an hundred sharp, ready, cool, never rusting, brazen tongues in each head, and an hundred garrulous, loud, unceasing voices from each tongue, they could not recount or narrate, enumerate or tell, what all the Irish suffered in common, both men and women, laity and clergy, old and young, noble and ignoble, of hardships and of injury and of oppression, in every house, from those . . . pagan people."[7]

The Vikings, however, celebrated their own bloodthirstiness, as the Viking poet Egil Skallagrimsson boasted to an earl's daughter toward the end of the tenth century (written down in the early thirteenth century):

> I've been with sword and spear
> slippery with bright blood
> where kites wheeled. And how well
> we violent Vikings clashed!
> Red flames ate up men's roofs,
> raging we killed and killed,
> and skewered bodies sprawled
> sleepy in town gate-ways.[8]

Whether Vikings were more willing to kill unarmed people than other medieval warriors is difficult to judge. Perhaps their reputation comes as much from their paganism, the suddenness and unpredictability with which they appeared, and their success in battle as it does from any greater viciousness.

In recent times the negative reputation of the Vikings has been supplemented (and sometimes supplanted) by a more positive portrait based on archaeological finds, the study of Viking sagas, a greater appreciation of the variety and extent of Viking activity, and less objection to their paganism. Archaeological discoveries, in particular, have revolutionized our understanding of the Vikings. One such discovery comes from the English city of York. From 867 until 954 (when its king, Erik Bloodaxe, was expelled by the English), York was the capital of the Viking Kingdom of Yorvik. In 1976 the York Archaeological Trust, excavating one of the medieval streets, discovered a row of tightly packed timber-built shops and houses for industrial workers, craftspeople, and traders, all built in the mid-tenth century and all well preserved. The layout suggests that the Viking city of York was an expanding and well-planned city[9]—a city of crafts (with leatherworking, woodworking, jewelry production, bone and antler products, weapon making, bronzeworking, manufacture of coins and ingots, and textile production) and of trade, with exports from as far away as Asia. These excavations also show that the Vikings used ice skates (with bone blades), played board games, and insulated the walls of their houses.

The most important Viking craft was metalworking. Viking craftsmen worked in bronze, silver, gold, and iron, but it was the availability of iron and the superior ability of Viking blacksmiths that gave Vikings a technological edge. Scandinavians extracted iron from bog deposits in southern Norway and Sweden and applied their metallurgical skills, including the manufacture of steel, in small furnaces that they had been working for centuries. Indeed, by the end of the twelfth century, they had

Viking Tools These blacksmith tools came from the grave of a wealthy Norwegian Viking. Blacksmiths enjoyed high status in Viking society. They produced iron cooking utensils, farm implements, and weapons such as axes, spear blades and high quality sword blades, some of which were forged by pattern-welding. This grave collection includes the anvil that the blacksmith used. *(University Museum of Cultural Heritage—University of Norway, Oslo.*

invented the blast furnace, allowing for mass production. Excavations throughout Scandinavia have uncovered Viking sickles, scythes, knives, and other iron objects for everyday use. Ready access to iron made it possible for less wealthy warriors to have iron weapons, shields, and helmets.

Technology gave the Vikings an edge in war. Their ships were more mobile than those of their opponents, could range further, and could transport horses as well as men. They were among the first in Europe to use stirrups and bridles and were as comfortable with horses as they were with ships. Vikings were also masters of fortification. Tenth-century military camps in Denmark had regular, timbered barracks for as many as 5,500 men. They used iron tools to timber forts, construct catapults, and build bridges.

Not all Viking enterprises were destructive. Within Scandinavia, they constructed bridges, causeways and canals, cleared roads, and built towns. Adam of Bremen described Jutland around the year 1075: "Wherever there is an arm of the sea it has very large cities."[10] Southern Norway and Sweden saw the development of port towns, some of which, such as Birka in Sweden, were briefly very wealthy. In areas where the Vikings settled they often revived towns and cities. The revitalization of York is one example, and the Viking seizure of Normandy at the beginning of the tenth century led to a flourishing city at Rouen, fueled by booty, trade, and tribute. They also established towns for the first time in Ireland, at Dublin, Waterford, Wexford, Limerick, and possibly Cork.

Some areas explored and settled by the Vikings were previously unpopulated or lightly populated, such as Iceland, the Faröe Islands, and Greenland. Norwegian Vikings found their way to Iceland before the end of the ninth century, and by the mid-tenth century waves of immigrants from Norway and the British Isles had taken all the habitable farming land. Iceland is notable for its long-enduring representative government founded on annual meetings of the leading farmers at an assembly called the "Althing." Here laws were declaimed, disputes settled, markets held, and social ties strengthened.

Vikings from Iceland, under the leadership of Eirik the Red, settled southern Greenland by about 985, bringing Christianity with them. Greenland supported a pasture economy as well as the hunting of fish, seals, whales, narwhals, walrus, bears, birds, caribou, and reindeer. Exports from Greenland were luxury items— furs, ivory from walrus and narwhal, hunting falcons, whale products, and, perhaps the most exotic of all, live polar bears, one of which was presented to the Pope in the 1050s. Perhaps as many as 3,000 to 7,000 people lived in Greenland at the height of its prosperity in the thirteenth century. By the early sixteenth century this community had died out or disappeared, for reasons that are still unclear.

Viking sagas tell of the discovery of a land called Vinland, first sighted by Bjarni Herjolfsson when his ship went off course around the year 1000 (see Medieval Voices). The sagas relate that Leif Eiriksson made the first planned visit to this area in the north Atlantic; subsequently others explored from Baffin Island to Newfoundland and the St. Lawrence Seaway. The initial impulse for these trips was most likely the search for shipbuilding timber and iron deposits, since neither Iceland nor Greenland had adequate resources of either. It was not until the 1960s, however, that Dr. Helge Ingstad and his wife discovered the remains of a Viking settlement or way station on the northern coast of Newfoundland, at L'Anse aux Meadows, thereby confirming the reliability of the sagas. In fact, it is likely that Greenlanders visited these western lands fairly regularly. The sagas report, however, that the indigenous peoples, called "Scraelings" (wretches) by the Vikings, were hostile, making any permanent settlement precarious.

In the Viking world, the tenth and eleventh centuries saw the unification of territories under Christian kings, first in Denmark where Harald Bluetooth's (958–987) control over his kingdom allowed him to build forts and to command impressive military forces. The short-lived kingships of two rulers (Olaf Tryggvason (r. 995–1000) and Olav Haraldsson (r. 1015–1028)) in Norway laid the foundation for a united, independent, and Christian Norwegian state by about 1050, but not until after a brief (1028–1035) period of Danish control under King Canute. King Canute of England(r. 1016–1035) who ruled Norway, Denmark, and much of England as one empire had created, even if briefly, the largest state of the day. And finally, Olof Skötkonung (995–1022), also a Christian ruler, united the two largest kingdoms in Sweden. These expanding royal authorities produced national coinages at the end of the tenth century, and national conversions to Christianity through the late tenth and eleventh centuries, although paganism in Scandinavia (and

MEDIEVAL VOICES

The Viking
Discovery of
America

The Graenlendinga Saga, written prior to 1200 and no longer extant in its original form, describes the late tenth-century Viking discovery of the New World by the Icelander Bjarni Herjolfsson. According to this account Bjarni, while sighting the New World, did not land on it.

Bjarni was a man of much promise. From early youth he had been eager to sail to foreign lands; he earned himself both wealth and a good reputation, and used to spend his winters alternately abroad and in Iceland with his father. He soon had a merchant ship of his own. . . .

Bjarni arrived in Iceland . . . in the summer of the year that his father had left for Greenland. The news came as a shock to Bjarni, and he refused to have his ship unloaded. His crew asked him what he had in mind; he replied that he intended to keep his custom of enjoying his father's hospitality over the winter—"So I want to sail my ship to Greenland, if you are willing to come with me."

They all replied that they would do what he thought best. Then Bjarni said, "This voyage of ours will be considered foolhardy, for not one of us has ever sailed the Greenland Sea."

However, they put to sea as soon as they were ready and sailed for three days until land was lost to sight below the horizon. Then the fair wind failed and northerly winds and fog set in, and for many days they had no idea what their course was. After that they saw the sun again and were able to get their bearings; they hoisted sail and after a day's sailing they sighted land.

They discussed amongst themselves what country this might be. Bjarni said he thought it could not be Greenland. The crew asked him if he wanted to land there or not; Bjarni replied, "I think we should sail in close."

They did so, and soon they could see that the country was not mountainous, but was well wooded and with low hills. So they put to sea again, leaving the land on the port quarter; and after sailing for two days they sighted land once more.

Bjarni's men asked him if he thought this was Greenland yet; he said he did not think that was Greenland, any more than the previous one—"for there are said to be huge glaciers in Greenland."

They closed the land quickly and saw that it was flat and wooded. Then the wind failed and the crew all said they thought it advisable to land there, but Bjarni refused. They claimed they needed both firewood and water; but Bjarni said, "You have no shortage of either." He was criticized for this by his men.

He ordered them to hoist sail, and they did so. . . . They sailed now for four days, until they sighted . . . land.

The men asked Bjarni if he thought this would be Greenland or not.

"This tallies most closely with what I have been told about Greenland," replied Bjarni. "And here we shall go in to land."

They did so, and made land as dusk was falling at a promontory which had a board hauled up on it. This was where Bjarni's father, Herjolf, lived . . . Some time later, Bjarni Herjolfsson sailed from Greenland to Norway and visited Earl Eirik [Hakonarson], who received him well. Bjarni told the earl about his voyage and the lands he had sighted. . . . There was now great talk of discovering new countries.

Source: Approximately 850 words translated from *The Vinland Sagas: The Norse Discovery of America*, trans. by Magnus Magnusson and Hermann Palsson. (New York: Penguin, 1965) 51–54. Copyright © Magnus Magnusson and Hermann Palsson, 1965. Reprinted by permission of Penguin Press, The Penguin Group (UK).

especially in Sweden) continued to overlap with Christianity into the twelfth century.

The Vikings also held Normandy, where, as Normans or Northmen, they created a powerful, French-speaking kingdom by the eleventh century. These Normans conquered England in 1066 and spawned the Guiscard family that began the conquest of southern Sicily and Italy in the same decade.

ARAB CONQUESTS IN THE WESTERN MEDITERRANEAN

When Viking adventurers rounded the coast of Spain in 844 and again from 859 to 862, harassing the coasts of Spain, the Balearic Isles, and North Africa, they more than met their match. Arab armies and navies successfully contained the Viking raids and never allowed them to inflict on Islamic territories the kind of damage that Francia, the British Isles, and the East Slav hinterlands endured. This was partly due to the extensive nature of the Arab conquests and the strength of the kingdoms they established in the western Mediterranean between the eighth and tenth centuries.

The Conquests

The Arab conquerors rose out of the Arabian peninsula in the early seventh century. As Chapter 4 explains, Muslim armies quickly conquered the Middle East and threatened the Byzantine Empire. In the late seventh century, the Byzantines and the Khazars prevented the Arabs from taking Anatolia or the Caucasus and lower Volga regions, while the Byzantines also resisted an Arab attempt to take Constantinople in 716. As a result, the Arabs could not enter Europe along those paths.

The route by which the Arabs entered Europe was, therefore, across North Africa and then through Spain and Sicily. Their march across North Africa was not an easy one. They were harassed by Berbers and by Byzantine imperial authority. Only gradually did the Berber tribes convert to Islam and the isolated Byzantine cities and fortresses fall. The Arabs took Carthage, the last Byzantine stronghold in North Africa, in 698.

Muslim attacks on Sicily were relentless over an extended period of time (from 652, the date of the first naval raid, to 753, after which there was a respite until 800). They appear to have been part of an overall strategy of dismantling the Byzantine empire, which then governed Sicily and parts of southern Italy. Until the ninth century, the Muslims gained enormous booty but no footholds in Sicily, which continued to be a refuge for those displaced from North Africa, a base for the Byzantine navy, and a potential capital should Constantinople be captured. The conquest of Spain in 711, on the other hand, seems to have been the result of a raid that, almost inadvertently, toppled the Visigothic kingdom.

Spain fell quickly for reasons that are unclear. After a series of raids on southern Spain, two Arab expeditionary forces landed in 711 (see Medieval Voices). They

MEDIEVAL VOICES

The Arabs Invade Spain in 711

The Chronicle of 754, the only surviving, somewhat contemporary chronicle in Spain, offers the most credible account of the Arab invasion of Spain. It was written by a Spanish Christian.

In [A.D. 711] which was the fourth year of the rule of Justinian II [of Byzantium] and year 92 of the Arabs, and when al-Walid I was in the fifth year of his rule as Caliph, Roderick [king of Visigothic Spain] violently usurped the crown with the support of leading members of the nobility. He reigned for one year. He gathered the full strength of his army to face the Arabs together with the Moors sent by Musa [Musa ibn Nusayr, governor of the Magrib], that is Tariq ibn Ziyad [governor of Tangier] and the others who had for long been raiding the province assigned to him and despoiling many cities. That was in the fifth year of Justinian II's rule, year 93 of the Arabs, the sixth of al-Walid, and [712]. Roderick met and joined battle with them on the hills behind Tarifa, and was killed in the fight together with the whole Gothic army as it fled. . . . In this way Roderick lost both the crown and his realm in the general destruction caused by wicked rivalries . . . .

In [711], the fourth year of the rule of Justinian II and year 92 of the Arabs, and the fifth year of al-Walid's rule, while Spain was being laid waste by the aforementioned invaders and was being devastated by the fury not only of the enemy but also of internal dissent, Musa himself crossed the strait marked by the pillars of Hercules. . . . Altogether pitiless, destroying everything as he went, Musa reached the royal city of Toledo. He separated off the areas around it by offering deceitful peace, and beheaded certain noblemen . . . when they tried to escape from Toledo. Thus by famine and by leading people into captivity Musa depopulated not only the further parts of Spain, but also the nearer parts as far as Saragossa, a most ancient and splendid city for long up till now, by the judgment of God laid open to the sword. He speedily burned fair cities, sentenced noble and leading men of the time to be tortured, and had children and nursing mothers beaten to death.

Source: From "The Chronicle of 754," in Colin Smith, *Christians and Moors in Spain: Volume 1, 711–750* (Warminster: Aris & Phillips, 1988). Reprinted with permission at Aris & Phillips Ltd.

first defeated the army of the Visigothic king Roderic, who did not survive, and then took Córdoba. The second army entered Toledo, the capital, and executed many of the nobility. The Visigoths, as an elite Germanic peoples ruling over a much larger Hispanic population, were clearly vulnerable. They had centralized the kingdom, politically and religiously, making conquest easier once their leadership was destroyed. The Visigoths also had internal divisions—a kingdom that might have been split between Roderic in the south and a King Achila toward the Pyrenees, as well as other rivalries. It is also possible that some on the Spanish peninsula welcomed the Visigothic overthrow. The Visigoths were notoriously intolerant of Spain's Jewish population, and their treatment of the Jews worsened as the Arabs drew closer, culminating in a decree in 694 that enslaved all Jews in perpetuity, expropriated their properties, and required that their children be raised as Christians. Their lot, under Arab rule, improved considerably.

Muslim Spain

The Arabs subjected most of Spain to their rule, exceptions being the mountainous areas of the north and northwest (Asturias-León) and the Basque country. The terms they offered towns and strongholds were attractive, given the alternatives. In a surviving treaty of 713 offered to Tudmir, a Visigothic ruler of several towns in the southeast, the terms were as follows: Those who surrendered and entered into a covenant with the Prophet would not be killed, taken captive, or separated from their women and children. Tudmir would retain his kingship; his subjects would not be molested in their religious practices; their churches would not be destroyed, and they were to pay an annual tribute.[11] Those who resisted, for example at Zaragoza in 712, were killed.

Spain was to become an Umayyad stronghold when, after a 749 revolt against the Umayyad caliphs in the East, the sole surviving Umayyad heir escaped across North Africa and appeared in Spain. Within two years most of Spain was under the rule of 'Abd al-Rahmān I (756–788), who broke away from the newly installed Abbasids in Baghdad, giving himself the title of emir (a military rather than a religious title). The Umayyads, governing from the city of Córdoba, oversaw a cultural revival in Spain that reached its zenith in the tenth century and was to strongly influence Christian Europe. Manufactures in textiles, leather crafts, gold and silver (among others) flourished. The Umayyad rulers were great builders, creating impressive mosques, palaces and gardens and a huge navy. They patronized men of learning, attracting scholars from as far away as Persia; they built schools and collected books, with the Caliph al-Hakam II (961–976), for example, building up a royal library of 400,000 volumes. To have a library became a sign of prestige for well-to-do households.

The royal court at Córdoba became a center for Islamic religious orthodoxy and for scientific learning. Greek writings in astronomy, logic, and mathematics, translated into Arabic under the Abbasid caliphs, became available in Spain. The Abbasids had access to Persian and Indian astronomy and mathematics, which also made their way to Spain. In addition, Spanish Muslims were interested in philosophy, grammatical and philological studies, geography, chemistry and botany, poetry, history and wisdom books, and Islamic law. Within this scholarly mix Muslim women could be teachers, librarians, secretaries, copyists, reciters of poetry and the Qur'an, and even occasionally doctors and lawyers.

The Umayyad court was liberal with respect to Jewish communities. Jewish scholars were welcomed at court, and Córdoba became a center for Jewish study of the scriptures, the Mishnah (the collection of Jewish laws), and rabbinical commentaries. Poetry, medicine, diplomacy, and financial and public administration were arenas for Jewish endeavor in a society where their religion was tolerated and their communal life preserved.

Christians, while not absent at the Umayyad court (and sometimes holding prestigious posts), were less welcomed as time went on. They were not allowed to

Prayer Hall of the Great Mosque at Córdoba   'Abd al-Rahmān I (756-788), the first Umayyad ruler of Islamic Spain, originally built this great mosque. Constructed on the site of the Christian church of San Vicente, it was a large hall with parallel rows of pillars and arches. The rounded, double arches are made of alternating red brick and white stone. The columns were reused from Roman buildings, but the overall architecture is reminiscent of the seventh-century Umayyad mosque in Damascus. Although it was significantly expanded over the next 200 years, the original architectural style was largely maintained. *Adam Woolfit/Corbis.*

build new churches or ring church bells; their priests and bishops were not accorded respect; and any Christian denunciations of Muhammad invited martyrdom. As a result, Christian–Muslim relations were uneasy. Christianity became entrenched in rural areas and in monasteries, particularly as Arab culture attracted townspeople and increasing numbers of Christians converted to Islam by the end of the tenth century. Those who remained Christian often took up Arab customs and are called Mozarabs. Eventually Latin was banished and Christian children went to Arabic schools, although Latin probably never went out of use completely among Christians in the south. Despite its loss of prestige, Christianity possibly remained the religion of the majority in a religiously diverse peninsula.

The Arabs maintained themselves by using Berber mercenaries and slave soldiers, many of them pagan Slavs from eastern Europe. They mounted annual military expeditions into the Christian kingdoms and allowed pirates to use their ports to attack shipping in the Mediterranean. They built navy bases and fleets of ships with which they harassed the southern French and Italian coasts into the tenth century and overran Sicily and the Balearic Isles by 902. Yet they never seemed seriously to consider annexing further territories on the European continent. This leads historians

to suspect that the army that reached Poitiers sometime between 732 (the traditional date) and 734 and was defeated by Charles Martel was not an army of invasion but simply a raid (see Chapter 5). As such, the significance of the Christian
victory has been exaggerated. In addition, Charles Martel's victory occurred simultaneously with the Arab-Khazar wars of the 720s and 730s and the Arab-Byzantine
struggles. In all three cases the Arabs found their paths blocked. In European history, however, it has been Charles Martel who has been given credit for this feat.

Henri Pirenne, the great early twentieth-century Belgian historian, argued that
the Islamic conquest of North Africa and Spain closed Mediterranean trade to Europe. One result, he proposed, was that the weight of European civilization shifted
from the Mediterranean toward the north and was soon centered on the Carolingians, who were reduced to a more primitive economy and divorced from Roman
roots. In Pirenne's famous words, "without Mohammed Charlemagne would have
been inconceivable."[12] Subsequent research suggests that the Carolingian economy
was not as primitive as Pirenne thought and that trade between East and West,
while sometimes disrupted, was never completely cut off. Trade routes shifted to
eastern Europe and through Khazaria, although trade between Byzantium and the
Arabs never ceased. Arab traders could be found in Sicily and in Italian ports such
as Bari, Amalfi, and Naples, while Viking traders were also active in the Mediterranean. Spain benefited from the growth in caravan routes along North Africa and
from trade coming up from sub-Saharan Africa. When Crete fell to the Muslims in
827 and Sicily followed between 840 and 902, the Mediterranean did indeed become an Islamic lake, but one that was open to the free flow of commerce. Demand
from the West for spices, silks, jewels, and perfumes meant that silver escaped to the
East, but the goods flowed in, while eastern demands for raw materials, slaves, and
Frankish swords meant that the flow of specie was not just one-way.

The Struggle for Sicily and the Mediterranean Coast of Europe

The struggle for Sicily was a long, drawn out, terrible conflict between the Byzantines and various Islamic forces. The population of Sicily suffered throughout from
raids, massacres, famine, fire, and enslavement. By 842, Arabs from North Africa
had conquered the western end of the island. In 843, they took Messina and were
able to prevent the Byzantine navy from passing into the western Mediterranean.
Only in 878 did the ancient town of Syracuse fall, with the massacre of its inhabitants and the burning of the city. By 902, Muslims controlled most of Sicily, and
Byzantine authority had become a thing of the past.

Simultaneously with the raiding, invading, and enslaving of Sicily, Arab fleets
took the island of Crete and sailed up the Adriatic, taking Brindisi, Taranto, and
Bari and threatening the Venetians. In 846, an Arab fleet entered Rome through
the Tiber River and pillaged the church of St. Peter. By the mid-ninth century Arab
incursions throughout Italy were pervasive. In 891, a Muslim force settled near
Nice and advanced into the Alps, controlling the passes between Italy and France
and occasionally attacking the areas of Piedmont and Provence and inland as far as
the upper Rhine. A combined counteroffensive on the part of Louis II of France
and the papacy thwarted more extensive incursions, as did a revived Byzantine

effort to protect southern Italy. By 915, the Byzantines had forced the Arabs out of central Italy, but raids continued against Calabria, Lombardy, and Naples. It was not until 961 that Crete was retaken by the Byzantines and not until 972/3 that the Muslims near Nice were expelled.

Sicily, on the other hand, remained firmly in the grip of Arab governors, and many Christians became vassals or slaves to Muslim military landowners, although the degree of oppression meant that revolt was always close to the surface. The Muslims also fought among themselves, as Berbers and Arabs, Sunni Muslims and Fatimid Shi'ites jockeyed for power. In the second half of the tenth century, Byzantine forces tried to wrest Sicily from Muslim hands, but continuing Arab raids on the coasts of Italy and Provence and the Adriatic coast of Greece and Dalmatia kept the Byzantine Empire, as well as the West, on the defensive.

Under Muslim rule, Sicily benefited with the introduction of Persian-style irrigation systems and rich crops of cotton, hemp, oranges, and lemons. The Arabs also introduced sugarcane, silk, and papyrus cultivation. And Sicily was naturally rich in timber, fishing, vineyards, grains, cattle, slaves, and mineral resources. Thus, despite the constant violence and the growth of fortified towns, Sicily could support a wealthy elite and a scholarly milieu. Sicilian Islamic scholars concentrated on traditionalist scholarship—the recitation and study of the Qur'ān and hadīth, Islamic law, and theology. There were Islamic philologists, grammarians, poets, and doctors, although very little of their work has survived.

It was the growing sea powers of Pisa and Genoa that first seriously put Sicilian Muslims on the defensive. Then civil conflict within Sicily after 1040 resulted in one of the rivals inviting the Normans onto the island in 1061. Thirty years later the last Muslim stronghold capitulated, and Sicily became the last great conquest of the Vikings.

Summary

From the eighth century to the end of the first millennium, movements of peoples into and around Europe caused enormous destruction. Francia, England, Ireland, and the East Slavs suffered particularly severely from Viking attacks. Arab invaders destroyed the Visigothic kingdom in Spain and caused years of warfare in Sicily and around the western Mediterranean. Lightning raids of the Magyars terrorized tenth-century Europe. And in eastern Europe, Slavic settlements as well as the Byzantine Empire were threatened by Bulgars, Khazars, and Magyars.

In the aftermath of these migrations and conquests, however, kingdoms arose. In Hungary, the Magyars settled down after 955 to produce one of the largest, most populous kingdoms of Europe by the twelfth century. The West Slavs consolidated political power in Moravia and, in the wake of its destruction by the Magyars, shifted their political power centers to Bohemia and Poland, both of which became medieval kingdoms of great importance. The Bulgarian kingdom, although threatened by the Rus and absorbed for a while by Byzantium, emerged once more as an independent kingdom from the twelfth century until its take-over by the Ottoman Turks. The Viking states of Denmark (including much of England at one point), Norway, Sweden, Iceland, Normandy (including England after 1066), and Kievan

Rus ringed Europe. Finally, the Arab kingdoms of Sicily and Spain offered Europeans a taste of wealth and culture. They provided models of effective administration with diplomatic and mercantile ties that linked the West with trade routes and cultural influences as far away as India and Persia.

These kingdoms provided a bulwark against further destructive raids. Their growth also went hand in hand with their Christianization—or, in the case of Spain and Sicily, their conversion to Islam. Religion and ruler worked together to protect cultures that were increasingly open to trade, learning, and cultural assimilation. The tenth-century peasant farmer in Aquitaine, threatened by raids from Vikings, Arabs, and Magyars alike, may not have appreciated the extent to which the cultures of these peoples were to enrich and inform subsequent generations. We, however, can see further.

NOTES

1. D.M. Dunlop, *The History of the Jewish Khazars* (Princeton: Princeton University Press, 1954; repr. Schocken Books, 1967), p. 46.
2. *Two Alcuin Letter-Books,* ed. Colin Chase from BM Ms. Cotton Vespasian A XIV (Toronto: Pontifical Institute of Mediaeval Studies, 1975) 53–54.
3. *Annales Vedastini (The Annals of. St. Vaast),* ed. B. von Simson, MGH Scrip. rer. Germ. in U.S. 12 (Hanover 1905, reprint 1979).
4. Dudo, "De Moribus et Actis Primorum Normanniae Ducum," *Patrologia Latina,* vol. 141, col. 620 (Paris: J.P. Migne, 1880).
5. *Cogadh Gaedhel re Gallaibh,* ed. Todd, vol. 48, (London: Rolls Series, 1867) 42–43, quoted in Alfred P. Smyth, *Scandinavian Kings in the British Isles, 850-880* (London: Oxford University Press, 1977) 159.
6. As described in Jo Ann McNamara and Suzanne F. Wemple, "Sanctity and Power: The Dual Pursuit of Medieval Women," in *Becoming Visible: Women in European History,* ed. R. Bridenthal and C. Koonz (Boston: Houghton-Mifflin, 1977) 102–103.
7. *Cogadh Gaedhel re Gallaibh,* quoted in David M. Wilson, *The Vikings and Their Origins* (New York: McGraw-Hill, 1970) 70.
8. Quoted in Else Roesdahl, *The Vikings,* from *Egil's Saga,* ch. 48 (London: Allen Lane, 1987) 145–146.
9. Peter V. Addyman, "Excavating Viking Age York," *Archaeology,* 33 (1980): 15–22.
10. Adam of Bremen, *History of the Archbishops of Hamburg-Bremen,* trans. Francis J. Tschan (New York: Columbia University Press, 1959) 187.
11. *Christians and Moors in Spain,* vol. 3: Arabic Sources, ed. and trans. Charles Melville and Ahmad Ubaydli (Warminster: Aris & Phillips, 1992) 11.
12. Henri Pirenne, *Mohammed and Charlemagne* (New York: Barnes and Noble, 1955), 234.

PART III

~

The Quickening of Europe, 900–1050

CHAPTER 9

❦

Land and People

B etween the eighth and late tenth centuries, few areas in Europe were unaffected by the armed movement of pagan or Muslim peoples. Although Europeans fought, fled, suffered, and survived, society did not collapse. In fact, the opposite happened. Changes occurring in the tenth and early eleventh centuries set the stage for a transformed Europe, as new influences flowed in, older institutions changed, and new institutions developed.

Between 900 and 1050, population grew, towns developed, and trade expanded. In the countryside new lands opened up; there was greater mobility, fewer slaves, and the expansion of a freer—albeit still servile—peasantry. The peripheries of Europe, although wracked by invasions and unsettled conditions, began to form into territories ruled by dukes (duchies), counts (counties), or kings (kingdoms). The Carolingian empire, already fatally weak by the year 900, eventually gave way to Capetian kings and lesser lordships. In part because of the weakness of the Capetians, Roman imperial authority, conferred by the papacy, was in German hands by the year 1000.

The mounted warrior became a more common sight in Europe, while castles and other fortified sites mushroomed in response to internal and external threats. Islamic Spain, perhaps the most sophisticated culture in Europe in the tenth century, began to retreat in the face of aggressive Christian rulers and warriors. Throughout Europe more and more individuals began to assert lordly power, laying the foundations for new social hierarchies, new political authorities, and reinvigorated Christian institutions. Gradually, over the next five hundred years, Europe shifted from a regional backwater to a global leader, as its armies, peoples, culture, and politics moved toward a hegemonic role in the world. The remainder of this volume will tell the stories involved in this growth and analyze the reasons behind such dynamism. Part III focuses on the transitional period of the tenth to the mid-eleventh centuries. Chapter 9 examines the economic, social, technological, and demographic developments, while Chapter 10 describes the changing political and religious landscape.

POPULAR CONCEPTIONS OF THE MIDDLE AGES

Before addressing the historical trends of the years from 900 to 1050, we will examine three common conceptions about the Middle Ages. The first is the label "Dark Ages," which is sometimes used to describe medieval Europe. Another common view is that medieval society was based on a feudal "system," a prevailing order that dominated western Europe with the decline of the Carolingian Empire. The final conception, common not only to people in the twenty-first century but also to medieval authors, is the notion that medieval society was tripartite, with rigid divisions between three social groups—clergy, knights, and peasants.

Middle Ages: The "Dark Ages"?

In a 1942 article in *Speculum,* Theodor Mommsen speculated that "the notion of the mediaeval period as the 'Dark Ages' is now destined to pass away for good."[1] Mommsen's prediction was wrong. Reference to the "Dark Ages" is still common among nonacademics, while popular histories, such as William Manchester's *A World Lit by Fire,* perpetuate a portrait of the Middle Ages as an uncultured, pathetic period.

The idea of a "Dark Age" was an intellectual construct crafted by Renaissance thinkers. In the 1340s, Francesco Petrarch (1304–1374) was the first to characterize the times following Rome's decline as a period of *tenebrae* (darkness, shadows). It was a time of "stupid sleep," of "barbarian obstinacy," an age when no one with any culture could be found. In the sixteenth century, Rabelais, the great French humanist, wrote about the Middle Ages: "The times then were dark, reflecting the unfortunate calamities brought about by the Goths who had destroyed all fine literature; but through divine goodness, in my own lifetime light and dignity have been restored to the art of letters."[2] This pejorative branding of the Middle Ages became an orthodoxy among Renaissance thinkers who rejected many aspects of medieval culture—its literature, pedagogy, Latin style, and its links with German (Gothic) culture. In doing so, they sharpened the contrast between the Middle Ages and their own time, thereby privileging their own contributions.

By the 1700s, Enlightenment thinkers saw the Middle Ages as even more detestable than Renaissance humanists had supposed. But it was the "barbarity" of medieval Catholicism that disturbed Voltaire and others more than the "barbarity" of the medieval Latin tongue and learning. Voltaire concluded, "It is necessary only to know the history of that age in order to scorn it."[3] Although nineteenth-century romantics revived interest in the Middle Ages, presenting a more positive view of its literature and religious manifestations, academics continued to discuss, and even to title their books, the "Dark Ages." George Adams in his *Civilization during the Middle Ages,* first published in 1894 and reprinted in 1966, described the Middle Ages as "a transition age," "not primarily an age of progress," popularly recognized as "the 'dark ages'—so confused and without evident plan that its facts are a mere disorganized jumble, impossible to reduce to system or to hold in mind."[4]

This notion has given way slowly. Twentieth-century historians, in detailing the dimensions and achievements of the Middle Ages, applied the term "Dark Ages" particularly to the early centuries, from 500 to 1000, usually making an exception for the Carolingian period. In current research, however, the term refers not so much to the supposed barbarity of the period, but to the fact that since written documentation for the period is sparse, historians cannot "see" what happened as clearly as they can for other periods.

Feudalism: An Evolving Construct

The concept of "feudalism" or a "feudal system" is traditionally associated with the Middle Ages, and especially with western Europe between the tenth and twelfth centuries.[5] Feudalism has been defined in various ways. Legally, it is a form of property rights where a landholding (fief) is held in return for certain obligations. Definitions of feudalism include the property relationship between lords and vassals, in which land is given to a vassal in exchange for military service and obedience (homage) to a lord. Another component of feudalism is the personal relationship between a lord and his armed followers, although such personal ties extend back far into the European past, predating medieval society in general and feudal property laws in particular. Personal loyalty to a lord or chief was an ancient value of heroic societies, both Roman and Germanic, which continued into the Middle Ages.

This alliance of lord and vassal might be within a centralized, hierarchical state. Or it might occur in a political framework where power is fragmented and treated as a personal possession, and public power is weak. An additional, socioeconomic approach to feudalism emphasizes the subservience of peasants to their lords in terms of justice, land tenure, and labor or other services. The classic definition, provided by Marc Bloch in his influential book *Feudal Society* (1940), is fairly broad. Feudalism, he wrote, included: "a subject peasantry; widespread use of the service tenement instead of salary . . . the supremacy of a class of specialized warriors; ties of obedience and protection which bind man to man and, within the warrior class, assume the distinctive form called vassalage; fragmentation of authority—leading inevitably to disorder; and, in the midst of all this, survival of other forms of association, family and State." More generally, he concluded, feudalism is "a kind of network of dependent ties."[6]

The confusing variety of ways in which feudalism has been defined, the ferocity of the debates over what is or is not feudal, as well as a growing number of regional studies showing variable features of feudalism or no feudalism at all, have suggested to some that "feudalism" is not a helpful concept in describing the Middle Ages. In 1974, Elizabeth A.R. Brown published an article entitled, "The Tyranny of a Construct: Feudalism and Historians of Medieval Europe,"[7] in which she detailed the ambivalence with which historians have used the term. She suggested that the term be dropped. This attack on "feudalism" was followed, in 1994, by Susan Reynolds' *Fiefs and Vassals: The Medieval Evidence Reinterpreted,*[8] which argued for separating out the evolving concept of feudalism, which is mostly post-medieval, from the social and political realities of the medieval period.

As Reynolds and others have noted, the word feudalism derives from the medieval word "feu" or "feudum," the fee or fief, viz. land or a revenue source granted in return for services. The use of the term spread in the eleventh and twelfth centuries. A twelfth-century Italian law book entitled *Books of Fiefs* described the law as it related to fiefs. This body of property law was then studied in medieval universities alongside Roman law. For the most part it was university-trained lawyers who introduced the terminology of fiefs and vassals into the legal documents of the late Middle Ages and the legal histories of the sixteenth century. By the eighteenth century, "feudalism" had emerged as an overarching concept primarily associated with the Middle Ages, sometimes designating a system of laws, or a system of government, or a system of labor exploitation. French Enlightenment thinkers and revolutionaries thought that feudalism continued into their times, identifying it with the oppressive customs and legal restraints that pressed on eighteenth-century French peasants and with the long-standing aristocratic social and legal privileges that precluded equality. It was part of the burden and propaganda of the French Revolution to abolish "the feudal regime." A fully developed concept of feudalism, however, is a product of nineteenth-century thought. It is especially associated with the ideas of Karl Marx, who described feudalism as an economic mode of production, in which lords exploited serfs, that characterized the thousand years between ancient slave societies and modern capitalism. In contrast to the Marxian emphasis on feudalism as an economic system, twentieth-century English historians, in particular, have identified feudalism with a military contract system in which land is offered in exchange for military services.

If "feudalism" is a modern construct, it is nonetheless true that fiefs were a common form of property holding throughout parts of medieval Europe. There were also vassals and lords, and, although the term "vassal" becomes uncommon by the eleventh century, lords continued to have dominance over others who owed them homage, loyalty, and, usually, military service. While there may not have been a systematic pattern of lords enfiefing their vassals (or faithful men), and the ceremonies of homage may have been irregularly practiced (they are certainly irregularly recorded), it is still the case that medieval society was dominated by lordship, military dependents (or retainers), and wealth derived from landholdings that were used to support the cost of military expeditions.

By the tenth and eleventh centuries, public oaths and ceremonies defining these relationships were common (see Medieval Voices). But the relations between lords and vassals were often unpredictable and cannot be made to fit a single model. Warriors who fought loyally for a lord might be rewarded with fiefs (lands with attached obligations) and might expect to serve (or have others serve) in the military in exchange. They might also have land free of obligations (called *allods*); sometimes they received wages or room and board rather than land. It was, moreover, often difficult to enforce loyalty from one's "vassals" and common enough for vassals to refuse to do homage. In Burgundy, in 960, the duke was not able to force many of his vassals to swear fidelity. The dukes of Normandy, in addition to depending upon vassalage to build a power base, looked to kinship ties. And when William the Conqueror put together an army in England in 1085 to combat a possible Danish invasion, he used

MEDIEVAL VOICES

The Count of Flanders Signs a Charter of Agreement, Accepts Homage, and Bestows Fiefs and Offices	*This twelfth-century account of election, homage, and enfiefment reflects traditions that extend back into previous centuries. In 1127, Count William of Normandy was nominated to became the Count of Flanders by the king of France and the barons of France* and Flanders. Among the various citizen groups who agreed to accept (or elect) him were the leading men of the small port of Aardenburg. They did so, however, only after William agreed to lift some financial burdens and restrictions on their liberty. The excerpt begins with their demands, after which the chronicler, Galbert of Bruges, provides a classic account of the feudal ceremony of homage and enfiefment.*

We [the men of Aardenburg] . . . will proceed on our part to elect the newly chosen count of Flanders, but on this condition, that you will . . . completely free us and the inhabitants of our vicinity from [military] expeditions about which we have not been consulted, and do away with the evil exactions of the barons and the new tolls which were levied recently and contrary to the customary law of the land . . . and also on condition that our farmers secure the liberty of going out and pasturing their flocks on the land . . . without . . . evil payment. . . . Concerning all these things, we beg your approval, lord king, and concession and confirmation from the new count, so that he may confirm by oath all those things that we have written down in this charter and that have been announced in the hearing of all. . . .

And when the charter had been read through in the sight of all, the new count took an oath to confirm it and to grant honestly and fairly and without reservation everything they had demanded from him. And then throughout all the rest of the day those who had formerly been enfeoffed by the [previous] count did homage to the [new] count, receiving now in the same way their fiefs and offices and whatever they had held before rightfully and lawfully. [The next day] homages to the count were again performed; they were carried out in this order in expression of faith and loyalty. First they did homage in this way. The count asked each one if he wished to become wholly his man, and the latter replied, "I so wish," and with his hands clasped and enclosed by those of the count, they were bound together by a kiss. Secondly, he who had done homage pledged his faith to the county's spokesman in these words: "I promise on my faith that I will henceforth be faithful to Count William and that I will maintain my homage toward him completely against everyone, in good faith and without guile." And in the third place he swore an oath to this effect on the relics of the saints. Then the county, with a wand which he held in his hand, gave investiture [i.e. bestowed fiefs or offices] to all those who by this compact had promised loyalty and done homage and likewise had taken an oath.

Source: From *The Murder of Charles the Good, Count of Flanders,* by Galbert of Bruges, trans. by J.B. Ross, pp. 204–207. © 1960 Columbia University Press. Reprinted with the permission of the publisher.

* With the death of the previous count of Flanders, the king of France became the direct lord of the county.

mercenaries. In early eleventh-century Germany, the nobility might be officials of the king, but not vassals, while their military retainers were bound servants, not loyal dependents. Nor did the eleventh-century kings of Germany see themselves as tied to their subordinates but rather as autocratic, exalted rulers. In other areas of Europe, for example Scandinavia, Scotland, Ireland, Poland, and Hungary, the evolving political structures and military forces developed from tribal associations rather than from the bond between lord and vassal.

Despite these differences and difficulties, one can still characterize much of European society in the period from the tenth through the twelfth centuries in terms of the relative weakness of public power and the practice of lordship, with all its strengths, weaknesses, and various strategies.[9] Thomas Bisson argues that, by the tenth century "lordship was becoming more and more common, . . . progressing at the expense of what may be called public obligations." With the decline of Carolingian authority, there was a dramatic increase in the number of warrior elites and landowners jockeying for power. Increasingly, individuals became subordinate to one another, castles were built, and dependent landholdings (fiefs) grew alongside dependent, nonfree labor (serfs). "Never had there been so many lords in Europe; never again would so many people seek or expect to be lords."[10] This striving for power, with its attendant violence, was a messy affair, and it ran its course differently in different areas of Europe. But in large parts of western Europe between the tenth and fourteenth centuries, it did produce a society dominated by fighting, landowning lords (*seigneurs*), their armed followers, and numbers of dependent peasants. These characteristic power relationships are what is meant when the words "feudal" or "feudalism" are used in this textbook.

The Three Orders: An Ideal Type

Another common construct, deriving from what medieval writers themselves said, divides medieval society into three orders: those who prayed (*oratores*), those who fought (*bellatores*), and those who worked (*agricultores*). This was the way King Alfred characterized English society in the ninth century. This tripartite model gained in popularity by the eleventh century. In the 1020s, two powerful Frankish bishops exalted the three orders in response to change in their time. Bishop Gerard of Cambrai saw royal power declining under the French Capetian dynasty. He witnessed unheard-of attacks against bishops by coalitions of lower clergy and laity. His contemporary, Bishop Adalbert of Laon, was likewise concerned with the ineffective monarchy. He disliked monks advising the king and spreading pious ideals among the warrior aristocracy. Both prelates, in conservative reaction to changes they abhorred, pictured an ideal world where social orders were not confused. "On earth," Gerard noted, "some pray, others fight, still others work." Adalbert echoed this idea, "since the beginning, mankind has been divided into three parts . . . men of prayer, farmers and men of war . . . each is the concern of both the others."[11]

This tripartite scheme took hold of the medieval imagination. It flourished as an ideology in the twelfth and thirteenth centuries. In this theory, there is no room for change. Bernard of Clairvaux, in the twelfth century, insisted that it was a sacred order, with every man assigned his task by the will of God.

This mental construct was an ideal in a society where rank ordering was common in everyday life, and especially so among the elites. But it ignored the social transformations taking place; it ignored the growing number of townsmen—merchants, craftsmen, and manufacturers; it ignored the divisions between rich, middle levels, and poor peasants; it ignored the social and geographical mobility of society; and it ignored women. As expressed by Bernard of Clairvaux, it was also an implicitly Christian order that excluded Jews, Muslims, and other non-Christians. A more sophisticated, secular, and realistic description of the social orders comes from the writings of Honorius Augustodunensis, a twelfth-century author with a tongue-tying Latin name![12] In his *Mirror of the Church,* Honorius described a preacher's audience as consisting of lords, then knights, the rich and the poor, merchants and peasants, and finally, the married, where, as Georges Duby puts it, "women wormed their way in among society's representative figureheads."

These three constructs (Dark Ages, feudalism, and the three orders) convey a picture of a hierarchical, static, and uncultured society, when, in fact, especially from the tenth century forward, medieval Europe was a time of expansion, mobility, and growing sophistication.

RURAL SOCIETY: LIFE AT THE LOCAL LEVEL

From ninth and tenth-century Europe there exist so few written deeds (charters), from only a handful of locales, that we can barely begin to guess the landholding patterns. In the eleventh century there was a rebirth of the written word; charters survive from around Europe, and they begin to reveal land tenure patterns and to tell us something about life in the countryside. Rural life revolved around villages and hamlets in much of England, France, Germany, Poland, and Hungary and elsewhere, while individual farmsteads were common in northern lands, mountainous regions, some Mediterranean islands, and newly cleared areas.

Village life was communal; peasants had to work together to survive, prosper, and protect themselves. Famine, marauders, and other dangers were omnipresent, and in the face of these dangers, mounted warriors were often able to enforce subservience from peasant communities in exchange for a measure of protection. Although Europe had seen mounted warriors in late Roman, Merovingian, and Carolingian armies, in the ninth and tenth centuries mounted warriors became more central to Europe's defense. The resultant proliferation of castles and of land tied to military obligations that occurred in parts of western Europe gives this period its distinctive feudal flavor. At the same time slavery, although still practiced in mid-eleventh century Europe, diminished as slaves gave way to serfs.

The Village

As noted above, the village was the main form of rural life and the focus of most rural society in large parts of Europe. Villagers depended upon one another and tended to allocate resources on a communal basis. Gardens and arable lands were parceled out in ways we do not yet understand, and sometimes draught animals and tools were shared. Householders were allocated plots for growing grain and meadowlands for pasturing livestock, although farmhouses had their own nearby gardens where vegetables and textile plants (flax and hemp) were grown for the individual household. Villagers would also, usually, have rights in the wastelands, waterways, and woodlands (to hunt, fish and trap, keep pigs, collect firewood and plants), although Europe's woodlands shrank substantially from the tenth century on. They worked together to build homes, churches, roads, and bridges.

Within the village, most peasant families were nuclear; it was uncommon for extended kin (cousins, aunts and uncles, brothers and sisters) to live under one roof or on one plot of land. Two, at most three, generations shared a living space. Death rates were high; a child's chance of survival probably ranged around forty to fifty percent.

One of the great accomplishments of the tenth and eleventh centuries was land clearance. Charters allow us to follow, step-by-step, the progress of clearance and settlement of new villages and homesteads. Whether achieved by dyking the sea, draining swamps, or felling timber and tilling soil, reclaimed land was given or leased to the peasant farmers who had done the work. They often kept, freely, one-half the property they had cleared and paid rent for the other half, which remained in the hands of the entrepreneurial lord or the partnership of individuals or institutions that had provided the land and perhaps the tools.

The opportunities open to enterprising peasants were balanced by the constant threat of ecological disaster. Although food production was rising, famines were a periodic occurrence, and no expansion of available land was sufficient to protect against epidemics, floods, and fires. Radulfus Glaber, a wandering Benedictine monk who wrote toward the beginning of the eleventh century, described a three-year famine that punished Europeans in the early 1030s: "Some time later a famine began to ravage the whole earth, and death threatened almost all the human race. . . . This dearth pressed hard upon all the people; rich men and those of middling estate grew pallid with hunger like the poor, and the brigandage of the mighty ceased in the face of universal want. If food for sale could be found, the seller was free to raise his price at will. . . . After men had eaten beasts and birds, under the pressure of rampant famine they began to eat carrion and things too horrible to mention."[13]

The possibilities for disaster and the recurrent dangers of invasion, along with the decline of effective kingship in parts of western Europe around 900, encouraged or forced many peasant families to seek safety from those who were better armed, while it encouraged warriors to protect themselves by building castles and controlling the surrounding countryside. Thus, in parts of western Europe—most notably in the heartland of the Carolingian Empire, in parts of northern Italy, and to some degree in southern England, two other rural institutions emerged—the castle and the manor.

The Castle and the Manor

Charlemagne had used the *mansus*—a large rural farmstead—as an administrative unit. These Carolingian manors controlled fields worked by slave or semifree labor. They also had limited rights (the right to impose rents, for example) on peasants on free farms nearby (see Chapter 6). Between the ninth and the eleventh centuries the large estates characteristic of Carolingian Europe were, to a very great extent, cut up and redistributed in smaller plots. This fragmentation of landholding coincided with the virtual disappearance of public power. In the wake of this disintegration, Europe began to sprout castles and small family farms.

Some castle builders were long-standing aristocrats in a neighborhood. Others were mounted warriors who secured land free of obligations or, increasingly in parts of western Europe, as fiefs. The importance of these mounted warriors derived from the military necessity of employing them in battle. In an age when centralized authority was weak and unable to train and coordinate phalanxes of infantry soldiers, the more individually trained horseman became crucial. Although infantry forces never disappeared (and horsemen could become infantry by dismounting), nonetheless the mobile cavalry force (combined with fortifications for defense) was the most effective way of combating outside incursions. The introduction of the stirrup and of horseshoes sometime prior to the ninth century enabled mounted soldiers to be more effective in battle. In addition, large landowners, in Francia in particular, began to breed larger, faster horses from captured Arab and Berber stock; these animals were able to carry heavily armored men into combat. Counts, dukes, and kings who needed these small but effective mobile forces, supported the warriors (*milites*—knights or soldiers) with gifts of land and moveable goods, such as horses, livestock, equipment, furniture, and jewelry, and expected, in return, homage and loyalty. Sometimes warriors who felt they needed stronger protection gifted their lands to a lord in exchange. Even in England, where a central political authority survived and grew in the tenth century, rulers more and more tied their mounted warriors to land and then insisted on services being attached to that land. Many warriors (whether enfiefed or freely owning their lands) built castles. And as the military demands on their time extended through the year, it became less possible for them to engage in seasonal agricultural work. The more professional they became, the more they depended on others for sustenance.

The interactions that ensued between lords of castles (castellans) and peasant farmers produced a large measure of internal violence. The castellans, protected by fortifications and their own retainers, wanted a "high standard of living supported by revenues extorted from those in no position to refuse their demands."[14] The peasants, some of whom had risen from servile status while others were of free origin, did not have the resources to secure weaponry and war-horses. Sometimes peasant families voluntarily gave up free title to their land in exchange for protection during raids or for food during famines. For the most part, peasants had little choice. As a result, a pattern of dominance emerged that was based on the manor (the home of the local lord), where the custom of the manor* (from the peasant point of view, usually the bad custom of the manor) governed peasant lives.

---

* The "custom of the manor" included the traditional duties expected from those attached to the manor as well as the usual rights and normal practices of the manor lord. Custom often had the force of law. A common practice, for example, was the requirement that serfs work several weeks per year on those manorial lands whose crops went directly to the lord. This custom offered little or no benefit to the serf, beyond the protection he expected from a lord.

The manor, with a central house and outbuildings, was usually fortified. Its economy was based on income from direct demesne land (i.e. land cultivated directly by the lord with the use of labor services or wage labor), indirect demesne (land owned or rented and worked by peasants who owed the lord certain dues), a woodland whose access was controlled by the lord, and various attached villages. The peasants in those villages were often subject to the lord's courts and his seigneurial authority over their person; they might be constrained by his monopoly of the mill, oven, or brewery and by other customs of the manor (such as the need to pay the lord in order to marry a daughter or send a son to school). The more classic kind of manor required peasants to perform various labor services.

This description of the manorial economy, while typical, does not correspond to the reality of all peasant lives in the Middle Ages. First, manor houses did not exist in many areas of Europe. In other sections of Europe, especially in Germany and southern France, peasant holdings were largely allodial—free from services or money rents. Where manors did exist, they might consist of small, scattered plots rather than a compact estate. In general, however, where there were manorial landlords, they sought to exert economic pressure on the peasantry—by demanding special labor services, rents, fines, or payments in kind, or by requiring that they use (and pay for) equipment owned by the lord. Even as this manorial form of servitude took shape, however, peasant communities began to find ways to subvert it.

Slaves, Serfs, and Freemen

Merovingian and Carolingian estates had depended upon slave labor in the household and, to some extent, in the fields. The disorders of the ninth and tenth centuries, the decline in public power, and the opening up of frontier settlements created opportunities for slaves to become freemen and for peasants to resist heavy labor services. By the eleventh century, slaves were disappearing from western Europe (although not from eastern Europe, Muslim Spain, or Scandinavia). In Carolingian and Capetian archives, forty percent of royal acts mention slaves between 814 and 935, under twenty percent do so from 935 to the 1030s, and only 1.5 percent do subsequently.

The reasons for this shift are unclear, but the increased demand for labor is clearly part of the answer. Some have argued that the developing technologies, particularly the spread of the water mill, made slavery less crucial. Others have argued that the gradual impact of scripture enhanced the status of all men and incited lords, for Christian charity, to free their slaves. There may also have been a slow process of intermarriage between the servile and the freeborn that resulted in less clear-cut categories.

While slavery diminished, a slow, difficult-to-document and not very consistent pattern developed throughout Europe of reducing peasants—both recently freed slaves and independent peasantry—to the status of serf. By the eleventh century, many peasants, particularly in France and England, were subordinate to a lord. This status became inheritable rather than voluntary. Serfs could, in theory, depend upon their lord for protection, but they were often burdened with dues and fines, with bad customs they did not wish to bear, and with a social stigma that was difficult to erase.

Complaints were generally ineffective, and legal appeals of serfs, which occurred in courts controlled by the lord, rarely found redress. Sometimes the only recourse the subject peasantry had was to revolt. This they did, for example, in Normandy in 997, forming "parlements" or self-governing assemblies and demanding access to woods and waters. The Normandy uprisings were not successful. Wace, a twelfth-century French poet, in his *Roman de Rou* described the reaction of the Count of Evreux to executing peasants by boiling them in lead or roasting their limbs, a description that may have been exaggerated although undoubtedly believed by his audience. In northern Italy, the peasants who formed rural communes to obtain exemptions and freedom were generally more successful. In 1050, for example, the abbot of Nonantola gave his tenants a charter promising not to imprison them or to destroy their houses without legal process.[15]

These village communes soon began to exercise autonomous authority over common resources. They were part of a movement throughout Europe to build new forms of authority and to exercise independence. They became intertwined with another movement, the Peace of God movement, which will be examined in Chapter 11. The ideas of liberty, community, and freedom from abuse implied in these movements were to percolate through the Middle Ages into the modern world.

ECONOMIC REVIVAL: TECHNOLOGY, TOWNS, AND TRADE

Between the years of Carolingian rule and the middle of the eleventh century the economies in Europe witnessed various advances that have sometimes been obscured by accounts of invasions, destruction, fragmentation of authority, and feudalism. Gradually, the acreage of cultivated lands increased, as did the efficiency of agricultural and manufacturing tools. Population, while still vulnerable to wars, famine, and undernourishment, began to climb. Towns grew in size and number, and trading networks expanded, pushing back Islamic forces in the Mediterranean and strengthening the economy of the northern seas.

Land, Population, Technology, and Wealth

Medieval Europe had no land shortage, and between 900 and 1050 it expanded its available agricultural base. Forests may have naturally receded in the warming climate that prevailed between 800 and 1200. Land leases describe large areas reclaimed from woods, swamps drained, waters channeled, and valleys repopulated. The Po River valley in northern Italy, which was scarcely plowed in the early eighth century, was cleared, dammed, and irrigated by the tenth and eleventh centuries. Irrigation methods used in Syria and Egypt were transferred to Spain earlier and to Sicily by the tenth century where they fed valleys in Valencia and outside Palermo, making them rich indeed. The people who lived in Flanders (modern-day Belgium and the tip of northern France) drained land, built dykes, and reclaimed land from the sea. The frontiers of eastern Europe attracted German-speaking settlers, who carved out areas for towns and founded urban markets. By the twelfth century the marshy fens of eastern England were being drained, and everywhere the heavily forested regions of Europe receded. The Arab conquerors of Sicily cleared the island of timber, taking the wood to North Africa to build ships. Whereas in tenth-century England forests were feared and encounters with wolves expected, by the 1200s it was difficult to find the larger timbers needed for many buildings.

This land clearing went hand in hand with population growth. By the tenth century population was growing, though more rapidly in some areas than others. Parts of Spain, northern Italy, and southern France had particularly high population densities. In eastern Europe, some cemetery excavations suggest population increases of four percent per year, while recent research suggests a sevenfold population increase in Polish areas from 800 to 1100. Urban population densities were highest on the Mediterranean littoral of Europe—in Byzantium, Spain, and Sicily. Constantinople had perhaps 200,000 people; Córdoba, the largest city in the West in the tenth century, had perhaps 300,000 (although some estimates are higher); and Palermo, in Islamic Sicily, may have reached 100,000 inhabitants.[†] In the much less heavily populated north, the Viking city of York (England) grew to over 10,000 people. Further evidence of population growth comes from the genealogies of aristocratic families, where we see families with numerous sons (the documents tend not to mention daughters). In addition, the growing number of people making pilgrimages and entering monasteries suggests a demographic expansion.

Many reasons exist for such a population climb. The gradual cessation of Viking raids, the relative peace in eastern Europe after the defeat of the Magyars, and the pushing back of the Islamic frontiers (thereby reducing the ability of Arab raiders to capture and enslave Europeans) provided a measure of peace and breathing space for growth. In the East, the growing wealth of the Byzantine empire seems to have attracted immigration. In the West, slavery, common in Merovingian and Carolingian times, diminished. As former slaves moved from the lord's household onto their own lands, they had greater incentives to bear children as well as greater capacity to be productive.

Demographic expansion was also related to an increased food supply. The expanded lands for growing and grazing diminished the forests but promoted food production. The yield from fields increased—from a very feeble grain to seed ratio of 1.5 to 2:1 in Carolingian times to 6:1 by the thirteenth century.[*] The Arabs also introduced new crops, while the growing concentrations of population allowed for specialization—wine regions in France and Italy, silk in Spain and Sicily, sheep breeding in Spain and England. These changes meant healthier diets, fewer famines, more produce, and perhaps better distribution of surplus produce in years of famine.

---

* This produced a yield, in England, of six to eight bushels of grain per acre, in contrast to up to eighty bushels of grain per acre today.
† In comparison, Baghdad at this time may have had a population of perhaps 2 million and Cairo 500,000. All such numbers for this time period are, of course, guesstimates.

Rising food production owed something to more and better tools. The Arabs in Sicily extracted greater amounts of iron and lead from the island. The Vikings, who extracted iron from bog deposits in southern Norway and Sweden, also enhanced Europe's supply of iron. New furnaces with forced draughts, run by waterpower, increased the efficiency of metal refining. This meant that metal was available not only for weapons but also for the cutting edges of plows, scythes, axes, and many humble farm implements. The village smithy became an increasingly common sight. By 1050, iron agricultural technology had significantly increased the ability of Europeans to alter their environment.

Along with expanding iron production, the productive use of water as an energy source increased. The water mill, although available in Roman times, was more useful in northern Europe where rivers and streams abound and flow all year. As northern European soils came increasingly under the plow, water mills appeared everywhere (see Map 9.1). By the beginning of the ninth century, the estates of

Map 9.1 Water Mills in England, 1086 This map marks the numerous (5,624) water mills that were recorded in the Doomsday Book, a survey of the resources of England commissioned by William the Conqueror in 1086. On one river alone, the Wylye in Wiltshire, there were thirty mills along just ten miles of the river. A number of these mills can still be seen.

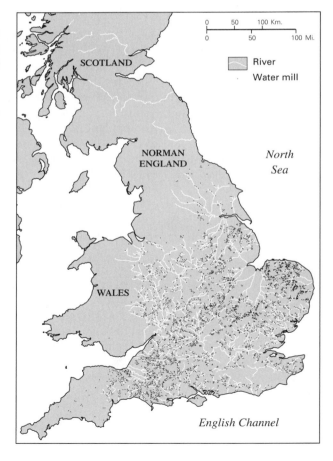

Saint Germain-des-Prés outside Paris had over 80 mills; the Domesday Book, compiled in England in 1086, recorded a total of 5,624 water mills. Most of these mills were used to grind and sieve flour (thereby relieving women of hand grinding), but some, employing a somewhat different mechanism (the cam) to produce different motions, forged iron, treated hemp, sawed timber, crushed olives, smashed hops, ground pigments, turned lathes, fulled cloth, and tanned hides. By the end of the twelfth century the windmill appeared in selected sites, thereby adding wind power to the waterpower that was energizing Europe.

Other technical innovations that enhanced agricultural output were the heavy wheeled plow, the horse collar, iron horseshoes, the harrow, and the three-field system. The heavy plow was probably introduced from Slavic lands; it spread throughout northern Europe by the seventh century. The heavy plow dug deeper into the soil and then turned it over, thus increasing the flow of nutrients. With its wheels the plowman could cover greater distances and regulate the depth of a furrow. It eliminated the need for cross plowing and led to the invention of the harrow, which, by being drawn across the field, smoothed the earth, mixing seeds and soil.

Ox teams traditionally pulled plows. In the classical period it was not feasible to use horses to pull heavy loads; ancient collars pressed against their jugular veins, forcing their heads to rear back. By the ninth century, a padded, rigid horse collar appeared in Europe, perhaps first in Norway. This collar, a forerunner of the modern horse collar, exerted force against the animal's shoulders rather than the neck, thereby increasing by more than tenfold the horsepower available for pulling loads. Iron horseshoes, with iron nails, began to be used in Europe by the ninth century. They were being manufactured for the English king in the eleventh century and mass-produced by the twelfth century. Iron horseshoes extended the wear of a horse's hooves and, along with the newer collar, made the horse a more practical draught animal. As a result of these changes, horses, which can move faster and

The Bayeaux Tapestry Illustrates Early Agricultural Practices   The Bayeux tapestry, most likely woven in England by women embroiderers, was produced in the aftermath of the Norman conquest of England in 1066. It is long—over 230 feet in length—and tells the story of the conquest from the Norman point of view. Along its edges are scenes from everyday life. This is the first image we have of a harrow (an instrument that breaks up and smooths the soil to prepare it for planting). One peasant leads the horse and harrow, while another follows behind casting the seeds. *Michael Holford.*

cover more ground, gradually replaced oxen, although the process took hundreds of years and the shift was never complete.*

The agricultural cycle in late Roman times had depended upon a two-field system. The light, dry soils of the Mediterranean were left fallow every other year to restore fertility. Thus, half the arable land was unplanted every year. The heavier soils of northern Europe seem to have allowed for a more efficient rotation. Beginning around the eighth century, the three-field system was introduced, in which only one-third of the arable land lay fallow each year. This shift, which increased productivity, worked in part because of more and better fertilizers. More farm animals were available to fertilize the fallow, and marl, a carbon-rich soil, was rediscovered as a fertilizer in Carolingian times.

Technological innovations also occurred outside the agricultural sector. In industrializing areas, particularly in Flanders, the manufacture of textiles moved out of the household into something akin to factories. A two-person, horizontal treadle-operated loom replaced the one-person vertical, hand-operated loom. Mills for fulling (the process of beating cloth to make it thicker and softer) sprang up, and the dyeing process became more specialized. The shift was also from a female-dominated activity to a male-dominated profession. The new looms took wool imported from England or from Spain and produced woolen cloths that were larger and wider. By the thirteenth century England was exporting 50,000 sacks of raw wool each year, or the equivalent of shearings from 6 million sheep. The growing sophistication of the textile crafts supported a mercantile elite and a proletarian kind of underclass (dependent upon a wage of only pennies for each cloth woven) in towns like Ghent, Ypres, and Bruges in Flanders. It also produced particularly fine wools. These wools were in demand in the fairs of northern France, the newly emerging towns of Germany, throughout the Mediterranean, and as far east as Palestine. In a treatise (composed around 1070 in northern France) entitled *The Conflict between Sheep and Flax,* the author paid tribute to Flanders for producing "cloths which appeal to lords."[16] As a result, Flanders was well on its way to becoming one of the most important urban areas in Christendom. Other textiles that were beginning to be produced included silk (in tenth-century Sicily and Spain and in northern Italy and Paris by the eleventh century), fine linens, and eventually cotton (introduced into Sicily by the Arabs). For those who could afford linens and cottons, living conditions improved from wearing fabrics that were more washable than woolens. The merchants marketing these finer textiles built fortunes that, in some cases, enabled them to move into the knightly class.

Trade benefited from new seafaring technologies. Technological and navigational innovations in shipbuilding and sailing took place from the seventh century on. In the Mediterranean, ships were still mostly galleys propelled by oars that gave them maneuverability and speed (sometimes up to seven to ten knots), although they had very low sides and swamped easily. Such ships could not venture, without great danger, into open water and tended to hug the shores. Gradually ships powered by sail or by a combination of sails and oars became common. The square sails

---

*Oxen and bullocks were still being used for farm work in Europe in the twentieth century.

used in ancient times were supplemented by the triangular lateen sail common in the Indian Ocean. Maneuvered by steering oars near the stern, these ships were able to sail closer to the wind. The hull was rounded, and the keel was shallow. Even with these improvements in maneuverability, however, seafaring on the Mediterranean was never easy. Currents were dangerous; the North African coast was treacherous, with shallow, low-lying coasts; and the winds were unfavorable much of the year. In response sailors used standard routes that took them as close as possible to friendly islands and accessible shores. In contrast, travel in the northern seas (the Atlantic, the North Sea, and Baltic Sea) was often out of sight of land. By the year 900, however, the Vikings had become experts at tracking their latitudinal position, using sun compasses, following the North Star, and paying attention to patterns of currents, waves, and winds, as well as bird and fish migrations.

Demographic expansion and technological innovation went hand in hand with newfound wealth. Perhaps as many as 1,000 hoards of gold and silver objects have been discovered in Scandinavia as well as perhaps 85,000 silver coins, mostly from the tenth century. Georges Duby has argued that the seizure of treasures by Viking raiders and the tribute demanded from western rulers liquidated reserves of wealth that had been hoarded in churches and palaces, thereby stimulating the circulation of silver. Even more important may have been the flow of silver (and then gold) from the Islamic world, first into northern and eastern and then into southern Europe, in payment for timber, furs, and slaves. In the tenth century, when North

A Viking Sun Compass for Determining Latitude   The Vikings used a nearly semicircular wooden bearing dial to measure the shadow of the sun. This allowed them to determine the four points of the compass and the declination of the sun (and therefore latitude). This single surviving example was discovered in Greenland in 1948. Its use precedes the use of the compass in southern Europe by two centuries. For more on this sun compass and on other Viking measuring instruments, see the website *eti@ddf.dk* and the research done by Erik Torpegaard. *Erik Torpegaard.*

Africa was united under the Fatimid caliphate in Cairo, gold from Nubia and West Africa (Ghana) moved north into Spain and Italy as well as into Byzantium. By the eleventh century silver mines opened in Germany and Bohemia. German rulers also exacted large tribute payments from Slavs on their eastern borders. The result was a monetary explosion. As early as the 830s, Byzantine rulers dramatically increased their minting of bronze coins. From about 950 to 1100 mints and coinage rapidly diffused throughout Europe. England, for example, had 70 mints by the year 1000, and the silver *denarius* (penny) minted there penetrated Scandinavia and eastern Europe.

By the eleventh century, Europeans no longer simply traded for Islamic gold; they reached aggressively into Islamic cities and territories. The poem *El Cid Campeador,* written in the first half of the twelfth century but reflecting the career of Rodrigo Díaz de Vivar in the eleventh century, stresses the riches he obtained from raids and conquests. The wealth of Spain became a magnet for Frankish soldiers. The spoils they gained from booty and tribute went to enrich the nobles and the church. Catalonia, in northeast Spain, for example, showed unmistakable signs of expanding wealth, growing population, and developing culture.

Throughout Europe, people were using these and other monies to invest in stone churches and castles as well as in trade and towns. Radulfus Glaber remarked on the rebuilding of churches: ". . . men began to reconstruct churches, although for the most part the existing ones were properly built and not in the least unworthy. But it seemed as though each Christian community were aiming to surpass all others in the splendor of construction."[17] Large-scale building of churches, cathedrals and monasteries allowed wealth to filter down to master masons, carpenters, pavers, tilers, brickmakers, plasterers, quarrymen, and many unskilled laborers. The growing wealth of Italian ports, such as Amalfi on the west coast or Venice on the east, can be gauged by the charters of merchants buying land in neighboring territories, the building up of town lots, and the growing references to stone churches and townhouses.

The tenth and eleventh centuries were a time when social mobility was possible, despite a general prejudice against someone of lowly rank reaching too high a position. A well-to-do merchant, risen from a craft status perhaps, might imagine his child or grandchild parlaying riches into a noble ranking. It was possible for a serf or slave to gain his freedom and then gain capital, as wealth began to provide an entrée into society. Men who could amass wealth through military success or through expanded landholdings rose to the ranks of counts and created for themselves genealogies that obscured their humbler backgrounds. Even in the rarified, elite atmosphere of Constantinople, people from diverse and unprivileged backgrounds (Armenian, Arab, Slav, Khazar, Bulgar, Rus) rose to positions of power. Both the Roman and the Orthodox churches were avenues of social mobility. Some children were able to take advantage of expanding educational networks to learn Latin or Greek and to enter the clergy where advancement depended in part on patronage and family connections but also in part on talent. Although there were constraints on social mobility, medieval Europe had no caste system.

In addition, geographical mobility was common. It is a mistake to imagine medieval people tied to the land. While some villagers, poorer townsmen, and proba-

A Late Tenth-Century Anglo-Saxon Stone Church –St. Lawrence at Bradford-on-Avon   This is one of the best preserved Anglo-Saxon church buildings in England. It was most likely built at the end of the tenth century to house the relics of St. Edward, martyr and king of England from 975–978. The surviving portions of the building include a nave, chancel and a north portico. The small original windows survive. The building is tall, narrow and dark inside; it would have been lit up with candles to supplement the sparse exterior light. The interior was possibly plastered and painted with images. This church is one of many stone churches built in western Europe at the turn of the millennium. Most of them, however, do not survive or survive with significant alterations. *John Heseltine/Corbis.*

bly very many women may have lived and died close to home, many people were on the move—traveling on pilgrimage, trading long-distance, going to market, migrating from rural to urban areas, or moving to newly cleared lands. The growing labor population, with its mobility and flexibility, allowed medieval men (more than women) to take advantage of expanding economic opportunities.

The Origins of Towns

Scholars have long been aware that the tenth and eleventh centuries were a time when people planted towns throughout Europe. But the reasons for this development (which is fundamentally new, although some towns were on old Roman sites) have been obscure and much debated. Henri Pirenne argued, in the 1930s, that eighth and ninth-century Europe was economically primitive, with towns functioning as ecclesiastical centers but with no vital economic functions. He postulated a connection between rising seigneurial power and urban vitality. Tenth-century towns, he argued, were the result of fortified castle-palaces, erected by feudal lords, around which merchants eventually settled in order to gain protection. These merchants eventually attracted artisans. The motive force, Pirenne believed, was

Venetian and Viking shipbuilding, which attracted adventurous vagabonds and runaway serfs to the ports and to commercial capitalism.

Others point to Byzantine influence on Italian towns. Some have argued that the Jews held a monopoly on trade at this time and those Jewish communities became the nuclei for town revivals. Many historians, while not emphasizing the role of Jewish merchants, agree that town origins are to be found in merchant market settlements from the ninth century onwards. Recent theories focus on the role of free peasants and artisans moving into towns, making them centers of production and distribution prior to taking on any public character. In some of these towns, peasants may have been marketing goods at sites that were also traditional, sacred places of assembly. In fact, Europe's urban revival at the turn of the millennium is due to all of these factors and more.

A quick survey around Europe suggests a variety of origins. Towns in early eleventh-century Germany formed mostly around the sites of bishoprics but also around monasteries and royal palaces. Many of these had markets that received imperial privileges in the tenth century; they were also enhanced by an impressive wave of building projects that dramatically changed the face of these urban centers. In Islamic Spain, where perhaps five percent of the population lived in cities over 5,000, urbanization was due to a combination of factors: industry (glasswork, textile manufacture, and arms and leather production), commerce, learning, and agricultural marketing. In eastern Europe, towns such as Cracow, Wrockaw and Vienna emerged from periodic markets and fairs, promoted by long-distance trade and royal authority. Bohemia, in particular, had several flourishing urban centers. Prague developed as a center for the slave trade, becoming one of the most important markets in Europe. Other west Slav towns were strongholds, cult centers, and sites of craft production. The Bulgar kingdom created some of the earliest new urban centers, modelled on Byzantine towns.

As the Rus gained in power to the east, towns also developed around fortified sites associated with particular Rus princes. In Italy, the port cities of Venice, Amalfi, and Bari grew due to their strategic locations and the protection and privileges they received from Byzantine authority. Amalfi also provided an entrée for many Middle Eastern and North African goods. Other cities (Naples, Salerno, Taranto, or Brindisi in Italy, Ragusa on the Dalmatian coast, and Arles, Sens, Autun, or Mâcon in Gaul) were of ancient Roman or pre-Roman origin. Pavia, in northern Italy, grew because of its administrative and legal importance to the German empire and to Lombard lawyers as well as its strategic location near the Po River and alpine passes. Rome survived and grew because of its importance to the Catholic Church. Towns like Hedeby (in Denmark), Birka (in Sweden), and York (in England) were Viking trade centers where individuals could buy or order made an array of goods.* Al-Tartushi, a tenth-century Arab merchant from urbanized Spain, was impressed, describing Hedeby as "a large town at the end of the world

---

* In these faraway climes one could find oriental textiles and garments, Frankish swords, Frisian pottery, imported glass from the Rhineland, Lappish jewelry, Irish slaves, and British tin. Artisans living there manufactured leather clothes and footwear, soapstone cookware, glass beads, objects made of bone, jewelry of jet, amber, gold, and silver, wooden furniture, iron and bronze weapons, and repaired ships.

ocean." Medieval towns, like Hedeby, had few public buildings and very little of the public character of Roman towns. They evolved mostly as centers of production and distribution, and their expansion tended to be the result of the opening up of trade routes and an expanding rural economy.

The Geography of Trade

Prosperity and growing trade in the Mediterranean, the northern seas, and the Black Sea influenced Europe's economy. In the ninth century the Mediterranean was an Islamic lake, dominated by Muslim navies from Spain, North Africa, Sicily, and the eastern Mediterranean. This naval superiority promoted commercial prosperity. Jewish and Arab merchants from Cairo developed trading and banking networks across the southern Mediterranean, offering cheap money, checks, and deposit banking. The gold currency of the Muslim and Byzantine worlds (the gold dinar and bezant) spread throughout Spain and Italy, gradually introducing a gold standard into the West. Revived Byzantine towns and ports around the Black and Aegean Seas offered growing opportunities for foreign merchants. New industrial centers throughout the Mediterranean manufactured silk, linen, and cotton textiles. Carpets, wool cloth, even gold cloth, leather-work and paper manufacture, swords and gold and silver jewelry were produced in Muslim and Byzantine workshops and sold throughout the Mediterranean.

Islamic connections between East and West facilitated the spread of tropical and subtropical plants. The introduction of irrigation techniques and technologies from the Levant made it possible for lemons, limes, oranges, apricots, date-palms, melons, grapefruits, and even pistachios, once grown in the Middle East, to be transplanted to Spain. Muslims introduced the cultivation of rice and sugar cane as well, making Spain the most diversified agricultural economy in Europe by the eleventh century. Middle Eastern vegetables, such as carrots, eggplant, artichokes, and parsnips, previously unknown in the West, now supplemented the peas, beans, onions, and cabbage that were the staple of western agriculture. Hardier forms of wheat grew in North Africa, Spain, and Sicily; viticulture expanded around the Mediterranean; and olive oil was produced everywhere in great quantities. The novelty of some of these foods is apparent from the response of Rashi, an eleventh-century Jewish scholar from Troyes, who was asked about eating rice on Passover. He answered, "It is permissible to eat rice on Passover, since rice is not one of the five species [of grain], the dough of which turns to leaven. Even in accordance with the report that in the country where rice is grown it is pre-cooked, it is permissible nevertheless."[18]

In the eleventh century, however, Muslim North Africa began to break up. Political upheavals, and consequent political weakness, made North Africa, with all its wealth, an attractive target for nomads. Bedouin and Berber tribes sacked cities and destroyed agriculture. The slaves and mercenaries who had provided administrative manpower and manned Muslim navies revolted in Egypt, weakening Egypt's hold over Syria and making it impossible for Egypt to reassert its authority over the western part of North Africa (the *Maghreb*). The rulers of Egypt, the Shi'ite Fatimids, were, in any case, oppressive, religiously intolerant, and disliked throughout North

Tenth-Century Cavalry and Infantry in Islamic Spain   This image comes from a Mozarabic manuscript of the tenth century. "Mozarab" is the name given to Spanish Christians who lived under Islamic rule. The image shows Muslim warriors, one of whom is an archer, on horseback. Mounted archers were common in Islamic armies; it was not a skill mastered by Christian cavalry forces. The Asiatic bow, and smaller rounded shield are characteristic of Islamic arms. The equipment displayed in this image was lighter and the soldiers had less armor than would have been the case for Christian cavalry units. *Biblioteca Nacional, Madrid/Laurie Platt Winfrey, Inc.*

Africa. By 1050, North Africa had broken into three separate Muslim principalities. In this state of political confusion, Muslim territories around the Mediterranean were vulnerable to the reviving power of the Latin West, particularly the navies of Venice, Pisa, and Genoa, and the growing Christian armies in Spain and Italy. It was not long before the Pisans and Genoese took Corsica and Sardinia and breached Muslim strongholds in North Africa. Simultaneously, Frankish, Spanish, and Norman warriors captured Toledo in Spain, all of Sicily, and parts of southern Italy from the Muslims.

The Christian West moved into the power vacuum left by the Muslims. This happened in part because the economic prosperity of the Mediterranean over the previous two centuries had strengthened the towns, armies, and navies of southern Europe. Italian merchants raided and traded along the coasts of North Africa, eventually becoming the backbone for the shipping industry throughout the Mediterranean. Southern European prosperity promoted overland trade, so that, gradually, the passes over the Alps and rivers such as the Rhone, Po, Seine, and Danube began

MEDIEVAL VOICES

A Jewish Responsum from the Eleventh Century

Rabbincal responsa *were public documents that were sent to talmudic scholars for an opinion. They usually derived from difficult local court cases. The scholar would provide technical analysis and a legal opinion. The form of a* responsum *was normally in terms of question and answer. The following response from the* Sefer Hadinim *(an eleventh-century rabbinic text of R. Judah haCohen of Mayence) offers evidence for the violence and precariousness of life for eastern European Jews in the eleventh century. It also testifies to the Jewish sense of communal responsibility, to the continuation of slave trading in Prague, and to travel between Poland and Byzantium. The text is concerned with a young Jewish orphan who had been brought up by relatives in the southeastern Polish town of Przemyśl. He grew up and married and then he passed away only one month after the marriage. The question was whether the widow was free to remarry; the answer depended upon whether or not the young man had a living brother.*

Question: [At the funeral a] member of our community named A, happened to be there. As the people were sitting around the dead body, A began to inquire whether or not the deceased had had a son or a brother. One of the mourners then said to A. 'He was our relative. There were two brothers. When the war broke out in Poland, captors from Przemyśl apprehended us and led us with tied hands into the field. The boys were also taken captive, were tied, but were abandoned and thrown into the field. When we were being led away we saw them lying in the field, moaning and whimpering. We then saw an acquaintance, a Pole, and asked him to take the boys home and care for them. We promised him that when, with the help of Heaven, we succeeded in gaining our freedom, we would honor him greatly and reward him handsomely. He then complied. . . . Subsequently I was miraculously saved from captivity. I returned to the Pole and he handed over this boy to me, saying that his brother had died. Some time later, however, we heard that Gentiles had bought a Jewish boy for sale at Prague, and that the boy claimed he had been taken captive in Przemyśl. A Byzantine Jew then redeemed him. . . . Subsequently an emancipated slave . . . came from Byzantium and said that he had seen the boy in Constantinople.' Is the widow permitted to remarry?

Answer: The statement of the Pole was legally acceptable as valid testimony, and thus established the fact that the boy's brother had died. The widow is therefore permitted to remarry. The subsequent vague statements cannot invalidate the fact thus established.

Source: Irving A. Agus, *Urban Civilization in Pre-Crusade Europe,* vol. 1 (New York: Yeshiva University Press, 1965) 104–105.

to bear more and more goods into and out of the interior of Europe. In addition, the Byzantine Empire, which might have cut off western expansionism and taken advantage of Muslim naval weakness, was itself going through political upheavals and was greatly diminishing as a naval power. It is also possible that the growing population of Europe combined with advancing technologies gave Europe an edge over Muslim sea power. And finally, the revival of trade in the northern seas had prepared northern Europeans to move into the Mediterranean.

As we saw in Chapter 8, Viking trade routes out of the north were extensive. But the Vikings were not the only long-distance merchant-traders in northern Europe. By the eleventh century, English merchants might be encountered in France, Germany, Flanders, Italy, and elsewhere in the Mediterranean. In the trading towns of Sweden and Norway, there were Frisian, Saxon, and, occasionally, Arab merchants. The Slavs were sometimes merchants, although in eastern Europe, according to Arab reports, there was always a mix of Rus, Slav, Jewish, and Muslim merchants. Jewish traders were especially common in Germany and eastern Europe; they also dominated some of the long-range routes around the eastern Mediterranean as well as routes to Spain. Ibrāhīm ibn Ja'kūb, the Jewish merchant from Muslim Spain (see Chapter 8), noted when he traveled through Mainz in 965, "It is extraordinary that one can find at Mainz, at the extreme end of the West, perfumes and spices that only take their birth in the deepest end of the East, such as pepper, ginger, cloves . . . brought from India."[19] The strength of Jewish trading networks in the eastern Mediterranean grew in the ninth and tenth centuries, helped by the Khazar Empire (see Chapter 8), which attracted Jewish merchants and opened routes into Asia. Long-standing Jewish mercantile settlements in southern Europe (Italy, Spain, and especially southern France) sent immigrants into northern France and the Rhineland areas. New Jewish communities sprang up there in the late tenth and eleventh centuries, often attracted by privileges granted by a bishop, count, or king. By 1100 these communities had spread over urban areas and smaller villages from Hungary to Poland to the Rhineland to England (see Medieval Voices).

Summary

The period from 900–1050, which straddled the first millennium of the Christian era, was a transformative period of recovery. In response to outside incursions and internal instability, some of the characteristic institutions that historians have traditionally associated with feudalism (knights, lords, manors, and serfs) began to emerge. Castles and mobile cavalry forces began to dot the countryside. At the same time, however, new technologies, the opening of lands, and the introduction of new foods led to an increasingly diversified countryside. Trade and population grew despite wars and natural disasters. The ensuing wealth helps explain the marked growth in towns, while the extent to which that growth was market-based becomes less surprising. It also helps explain the investments in churches that so struck Radulfus Glaber.

By the second half of the tenth century, with Muslims, Magyars, and Vikings all beginning to settle down, Europeans could stabilize their communities and strengthen political power. The form that this was to take eventually produced, not so much a new empire, as a collection of nation-states. This process of political consolidation, which is the subject of the next chapter, began to take place first on the peripheries of Europe rather than in the center. It involved, to a great extent, those very invaders who had recently been so threatening.

NOTES

1. Theodor Mommsen, "Petrarch's Conception of the 'Dark Ages,'" *Speculum,* 17 (1942): 226–227.
2. Samuel Putnam, trans., "The Letter Which Pantegruel at Paris Received from His Father Gargantua," *The Portable Rabelais* (New York: Viking Press, 1946) 263.
3. Voltaire, "Remarques pour servir de supplement a l'Essai sur les moeurs," ed. Theodore Besterman, *Essai dur les moeurs et l'esprit des nations,* vol. 2 (Paris: Garnier Frères, 1963).
4. George Burton Adams, *Civilization during the Middle Ages,* rev. ed. (New York: Barnes & Noble, 1967) 6–7.
5. Classic works on medieval feudalism include: Joseph R. Strayer, *Feudalism* (Princeton: Princeton University Press, 1965); Marc Bloch, *Feudal Society,* trans. L.A. Manyon, 2 vols. (London: Routledge and Kegan Paul, 1961); F.L. Ganshof, *Feudalism,* trans. P. Grierson (London & New York: Harper 1964); and, more recently, Jean-Pierre Poly and Eric Bournazel, *The Feudal Transformation 900–1200,* trans. C. Higgitt (New York: Holmes and Meier, 1991).
6. Marc Bloch, *Feudal Society,* trans. L.A. Manyon, 2 vols. (Chicago: University of Chicago Press, 1964) 173, 442.
7. Elizabeth A.R. Brown, "The Tyranny of a Construct: Feudalism and Historians of Medieval Europe," *American Historical Review,* 79 (1974) 1063–1088.
8. Susan Reynolds, *Fiefs and Vassals: The Medieval Evidence Reinterpreted* (London: Oxford University Press, 1994).
9. A recent work on Bohemia from 1050 to 1200 (Lisa Wolverton, *Hastening Toward Prague* (Philadelphia: University of Pennsylvania Press, 2001), however, has argued that leadership rather than lordship is a more appropriate characterization of power relations in medieval Czech lands.
10. Thomas N. Bisson, "Medieval Lordship," *Speculum,* 70 (1995): 747–749.
11. Georges Duby, *The Three Orders: Feudal Society Imagined,* trans. Arthur Goldhammer (Chicago: University of Chicago Press, 1980) 5.
12. Described in Georges Duby, *The Three Orders,* 251.
13. John France, ed. and trans., *Rodulfi Glabri Historiarum Libri Quinque* (Oxford: Clarendon Press, 1989) 187–198.
14. Jean Dunbabin, *The Making of France 843–1180* (London: Oxford University Press, 1985) 146.
15. Rodney Hilton, *Bond Men Made Free,* (New York: Viking Press, 1973) 77.
16. Georges Duby, *The Early Growth of the European Economy,* trans. H.B. Clarke (Ithaca: Cornell University Press, 1974) 239.
17. *Rodulfi Glabri Historiarum Libri Quinque,* 115–117.
18. Irving A. Agus, *Urban Civilization in Pre-Crusade Europe,* vol. 1 (New York: Yeshiva University Press, 1968) 308.
19. André Miquel, "L'Europe occidentale dans la relation arabe d'Ibrahim b. Ya'qub," *Annales: E.S.C.,* 21 (1966): 1059–1060.

CHAPTER 10

~

Rulers and Religion

Chapter 9 discussed the social and economic shifts that revitalized Europe between 900 and 1050. In the wake of invasion and disorder, political structures also underwent dramatic changes. The status of political authority in tenth- and eleventh-century Europe is not always easy to discern. People of all classes and regions had a new freedom of movement; new sources of political legitimacy had arisen, but Europe lacked guiding models for the emerging power structures. And the historical evidence is fragmentary. Historians, for example, question the degree to which Carolingian institutions survived the invasions. Some argue that there was a fundamental discontinuity and fragmenting of political power. Others argue that unifying aspects of the Carolingian world, such as the public authority of the count, were still operating in a diminished form, for example in Aquitaine and parts of northern France. Historians generally agree, however, that within the old Carolingian imperial borders public power was disintegrating, to be replaced by local powers based on land, castles, military might, commerce, or the church.

Alongside this political fragmentation of Carolingian territories, new or strengthened kingdoms emerged on the Christian frontiers. Imperial power changed from the hands of weak Carolingian rulers into the more vigorous hands of east Frankish (German) rulers. In central and eastern Europe new states formed with a growing central power that, despite ongoing struggles for the kingship, were to prove enduring. The Atlantic seaboard and north-south frontiers also saw the formation of powerful kingdoms such as those in Normandy, Anglo-Saxon England, the Scandinavian countries, Islamic Spain, and Sicily. In Italy, which benefited from the revival of commerce, the newly forming authorities were closely connected to towns. Byzantium, which had been under siege sporadically since the seventh century, went on the offensive and rebuilt itself.

In the Christian parts of Europe, strong links with the church were essential in this process. Christian or newly Christianized rulers promoted monastic and liturgical reforms and invested in centers of learning. They fostered strong relations with bishops and promoted missionary activities. Some rulers, such as Alfred of England, Otto III of Germany, Stephen I of Hungary, and Robert II of France, were renowned for their piety. Hand in hand with the church, the state system that has dominated Europe until today began to form in this period. It did so, however, in an atmosphere in which the Day of Judgment seemed near and popular movements were pushing for religious reform. In some areas (Germany in particular), ecclesiastical reform and political authority would eventually clash. The result, as we will see in Chapter 11, would be to question the authority of the state and throw into doubt the mutually beneficial nature of church-state partnerships.

POLITICAL FORMATION ON THE CHRISTIAN FRONTIERS

The years 900 to 1050 saw the formation of new or strengthened states* on the peripheries of Europe, in precisely those areas that had suffered most from Viking attacks, Muslim invasions, and Magyar raids (see Map 10.1). In Bohemia, Poland, and Hungary, tribal structures weakened as *duces* (dukes), successful warlords, emerged. These ducal authorities gave way to princely leaders (Boleslav I of Bohemia, Miezko of Poland, and Stephen of Hungary) who turned to the Catholic Church for support in state-building against traditional pagan and tribal structures. These princes mounted armies that could stand up to the Germans, while they also intermarried with the German nobility, thereby establishing a degree of parity and stability in relation to the German Empire. They built fortresses and governing hierarchies that cut across tribal bounds but depended upon a free noble class and subordinate peasantry. Poland built an independent and powerful state with imperial ambitions under Kings Miezko I (c. 963–992) and Bolesław I Chrobry (r. 992–1025), who, in 1024, received a royal crown from the pope. The alliance of crown and Catholicism (Miezko formally placed his kingdom under the papacy) enabled the Poles to act independently from the German imperial ecclesiastical hierarchy and to establish the Piast dynasty, which lasted until 1370. Bohemia was to emerge as a united kingdom under German imperial overlordship with Latin bishoprics at Prague and in Moravia. The Přemyslide dynasty under Boleslav I (r. 935–972) and Boleslav II (r. 972–999), based in Prague, imposed taxes, minted coins, and expanded eastward, creating a strong central authority. Hungary, also united under a single crown—first Duke Géza (r. 972–997) and then King Stephen (r. 997–1038)—gobbled up Croatia, Slovakia, and Dalmatia, becoming the greatest and most powerful of the eastern European states. In all three countries, however, the nobility or the freemen retained the privilege of confirming the succession to the crown, a significant source of instability in eastern Europe.

* "States" in this period were territorially unified polities that existed over several generations. They had a single ruler who was either centrally located or who moved around, and they had a small ruling elite. A rudimentary administrative system and an ideology that enhanced their religious and political legitimacy served the rulers of these early medieval states.

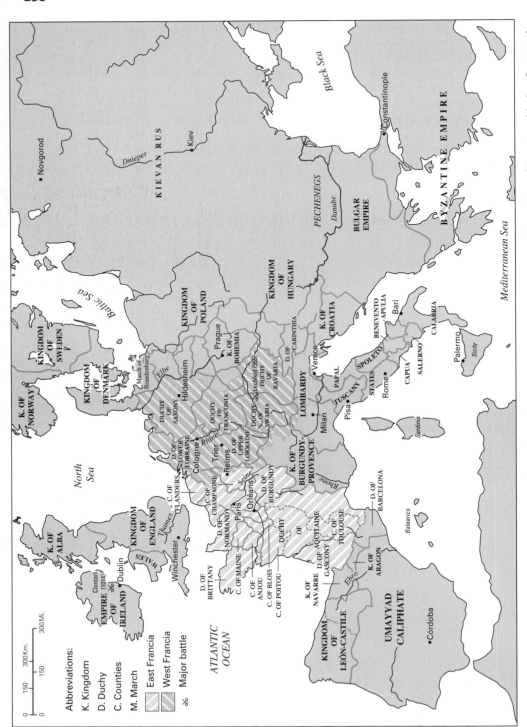

Map 10.1   Tenth-Century Europe from the Atlantic to the Dnieper River and the Black Sea   The political boundaries of Europe at this time fluctuated. Therefore these boundary lines are somewhat approximate. Nonetheless one can see that tenth-century Europe was surrounded by larger frontier kingdoms while the center, including central Italy, was more fragmented.

Rus (centered on Kiev), a principality of Slavic tribes governed by a Viking-derived dynasty, developed remarkably in the tenth and early eleventh centuries. Economically linked with the northern seas, Byzantium, and the Muslim east, Kievan Rus expanded militarily and demographically at the end of the tenth century. Vladimir (r. 980–1015), later St. Vladimir, who converted from paganism to Greek Orthodox Christianity in 988, married an extraordinarily high born Byzantine princess. Both marriage and conversion enhanced his prestige, making it easier to develop alliances with the newly Christianized rulers of Bulgaria, eastern Europe, and Scandinavia, and to bring Byzantine culture to the court at Kiev. Under Vladimir's direction, a stone palace complex and a royal Church of the Mother of God (with mosaics, paintings, and marble) were constructed. Vladimir controlled this Rus state in association with the elite and townsfolk of his kingdom, most of whom were forced into Christian baptism. In addition, he pushed Rus control westward, built over 500 kilometers of earthen and brick fortifications at defense lines and around towns, and maintained bands of mounted warriors against nomadic Pechenegs. The relative peace of his rule protected trading networks, artisan crafts, and developing towns (some eighty to ninety small to medium centers, with larger centers, for example, at Novgorod), giving the Rus polity remarkable economic vitality. His son, Iaroslav (d.1054) oversaw a cultural and religious flowering, modeled on Byzantine practices. Literature and liturgies, civil and ecclesiastical codes, monumental architecture, paintings, mosaics, oral sagas, court and city schools, monasteries, and libraries became part of Kievan culture. Parallels with Constantine the Great and saintly stories associated with Vladimir promoted an ideology in which the ruler of Kievan Rus, backed by the church, was now seen as the *tsar* or caesar of the Rus.

But the stability of this state was short-lived. Rus rulers divided the kingdom among their sons, and their defeat of the Khazars destabilized the eastern steppe, opening it to attacks by Turkish nomads who soon blocked Kievan routes to the south and east. By the end of the eleventh century, the power of Kievan Rus had fragmented, with power devolving to more local leaders.

Just to the southwest of Rus was the now well-established state of Bulgaria (Chapter 8), soon to be threatened by a revived Byzantine Empire. Byzantium had struggled with iconoclastic emperors in the eighth and ninth centuries (Chapter 4) and had barely survived the invasions of Arabs, Slavs, Bulgars, Rus, Khazars, and Magyars from the seventh through the ninth centuries. Its wealth had greatly diminished, while its educational, literary and artistic capacities had nearly disappeared. But Byzantium survived this period of trouble, stabilized in the ninth century, and began to rebuild. Some late Roman institutions managed to survive, especially the church, the imperial court, and the tax system. A reorganized army defended Byzantine borders more ably, helped by an influx of several thousand Kurdish and Armenian fighters. The Byzantine economy also appears to have rebounded, producing higher state revenues, a growing population, and expanding trade in a variety of luxury and craft productions. The Byzantines had to relearn almost from scratch the late Roman legal codes compiled by the Emperor Justinian and to pull together scattered manuscripts and teachers in whom expertise in a variety of subjects still resided.

Eleventh-Century Church of Holy Wisdom in Novgorod   This cathedral was constructed under King Iaroslav (d. 1054) around 1050. It is similar to but smaller than St. Sophia Cathedral in Kiev, which was begun a bit earlier. Whereas this cathedral has six cupolas, the cathedral at Kiev had thirteen. Both cathedrals replaced earlier wooden churches and were constructed with the aid of imported Byzantine builders. The Kievan cathedral was considerably damaged in the Mongol invasions; St. Sophia of Novgorod has survived in better shape despite serious damage done by the Germans in World War II. *Diego Lezama Orezzoli/Corbis.*

By the tenth century, a stronger Byzantium went on the offensive, enlarging its boundaries to match its pre-seventh-century period of greatness. Between 919 and 1027, Byzantium was ruled by three imperial usurpers who were military leaders and two legitimate emperors (one of whom was the scholar-emperor Constantine VII, r. 944–959). They pushed the imperial frontier east into Syria and Palestine, retook Crete, asserted dominance over Armenia and Georgia, stabilized the Byzantine presence in Italy, and first neutralized and then completely defeated the Bulgars. These successes were due to a variety of factors—the now fractured Islamic Abbasid state, the confusion of competing forces on the Italian peninsula, and the ability of the Byzantines to play Bulgars, Rus, and Pechenegs against one another on the Danube and along the Black Sea. Basil II (r. 976–1025), who was a military genius, strengthened the empire internally by preventing independent peasant farms from falling into the hands of wealthy nobility, which would have endangered the imperial tax base and the ability of the empire to recruit soldiers. Buttressed by a strengthened navy and a series of successful land campaigns, Constantinople emerged once more as a cultural and educational center. Beginning toward the end of the eighth century, private education was once more available. Eventually a palace school, legal training, and schools of grammar and rhetoric attached to churches surface in the documents. Civil servants and clergy benefited from this learning, although much of it was traditional and limited by the tedious antique style required and the limited audience for literature. Confidence in their religious orthodoxy and belief in their chosen, God-protected status also buttressed the Byzantines.

In order to maintain this reinvigorated and expanded empire, however, the Byzantines had to be ready to fight on four fronts—in the east, in Italy in the west, in the Balkans-Danube-Black Sea area, and along the Mediterranean coast. With the death of Basil II, whose devoted attention and rapid responses to the military situation had been so successful, the empire began to weaken. Tensions between the imperial bureaucracy and the military, successive revolts within the empire, and a series of mediocre rulers between 1025 and 1057 (most of them consorts of the royal princesses) set the stage for decline. By 1050, the Seljuq Turks began their very first raids into the eastern Byzantine empire, while the Normans in southern Italy reduced Byzantine holdings to a few fortresses, and the Pechenegs bedeviled the Danubian frontier. The years between 900 and 1050 saw medieval Byzantium at its height of power, but it was a position that could not be sustained.

In Scandinavia, the tenth and eleventh centuries saw the unification of kingship under the auspices of newly baptized kings (Chapter 8). In all three kingdoms, the drive toward unification gained authority from the Church, but rulers had to confront rival contenders for the throne and the constant opposition of local aristocrats. Scandinavian kings gained the upper hand by dominating the expanding Catholic hierarchy, by issuing regular coinage (stamped with emblems of their authority), by the sanctifications of their coronations and assertions of hereditary claims to the throne, by creating administrative extensions of their authority, and by leaning on their role as lawmakers and allying with national assemblies.

The same drive toward unity can be traced in the Celtic fringe of Europe. Scotland reacted to pressure from the Vikings. From the mid-ninth century on, the Picts and the Scots combined into a united kingdom of Alba. The kings of Alba became a significant force in the north of the British Isles; by the eleventh century their descendents ruled a larger, more united Scotland. The process by which this occurred is largely lost to the view of historians and cannot now be reconstructed. As a result, most Scottish histories pick up the story with the kingship of Malcolm Canmore (1054–1093) and the impact of the Norman invasion on Scotland. But Scotland should still be on the list of regions on the Christian frontiers that began state-building around the millennium.

Ireland's fragmented political landscape of high kings, province kings, and local kings coalesced in the tenth century into a single kingship symbolized by the royal seat at Tara. Although it was a highly contested kingship, the tenth and eleventh centuries were the time when the Irish most nearly achieved a nationally supreme monarch. Brian Boru (r. 1002–1014), the great "national" hero of Ireland, arose from the south to defeat the most prestigious of northern royal families—the Ui Neills (O'Neills). In 1005, he was completely in command of the south and able to carry out a royal tour of the north without challenge. The title he gave himself was Emperor of the Irish. Boru was killed in the battle of Clontarf (1014), where nevertheless his forces won against a coalition of Vikings, men from Dublin, and Leinstermen. His great-grandson Muirchertach Ua Briain became king of Dublin in 1075 and king of Ireland from 1088 to 1119. This trend toward a central monarchy, however, was cut short by the intervention of the English in the twelfth century.

Along the Atlantic coastline, the counts of Flanders had benefited from growing wealth based on the wool trade. They promoted economic growth by building dikes, draining and clearing land, protecting the wool industry, pasturing sheep on their private demesne lands, and patronizing urban growth and expanded trade networks. By the mid-eleventh century, Count Baldwin V (1037–1067) had become one of the great state-builders in Europe. Dynamic growth from internal colonization and military expansion meant that the count could depend upon a substantial military force from those who owed him military service or from mercenaries. Aristocrats who held castles (who could have become a disruptive force) remained loyal to the count, taking oaths of fealty and presiding over public courts. Although the count of Flanders did homage to the king of France, generally the county functioned independently, with a high degree of hierarchical and social development and the beginnings of a central bureaucracy under the count's authority.

Normandy was similar to Flanders, although its growing towns (Caen, Rouen, Bayeux) were less industrialized, and its ducal authority more centralized. Normandy emerged from the takeover of northwest France by the Vikings in 911. These Vikings (called Normans) were proud, ambitious warriors who, although gradually Christianized and acculturated to the French, were still Northmen, and among the most ferocious warriors in Europe. Their leader by 1050 was Duke William. William's highly successful marriage to Matilda of Flanders strengthened his position, as did the deaths of his enemies (King Henry I of France in 1051 and Count Geoffrey of Anjou).

William was also helped by the rise of a new Norman aristocracy whose power depended on land, dependent vassalage, and loyalty to him. One of Normandy's peculiar strengths, due perhaps to English influences, was the degree of judicial centralization. One law (ducal law) governed the territory. The duke's control over his vassals was very real, as was his authority over the Church. No castles were immune from the duke if he wanted to occupy them; nor could they be built without his permission. The duke, who also presided over church synods, appointed abbots and bishops. William worked with Church leaders to establish peace and to reform the Church—all done, however, under ducal supervision. A revived, reformed, powerful, and intellectually attractive Church that owed much to William gave him backing. He was also the beneficiary, according to Eleanor Searle, of a kinship network that used predatory family strategies—marriage, the "elimination" of rivals—and the identity of a warrior elite to construct a centralized political community based on cooperation. As a result, the duke of Normandy was a chosen leader who controlled a formidable army with a history of success in battle. This consolidation of authority set the stage for the conquest of England in 1066 (see Chapter 13).

Further south on the Atlantic coast of Europe the Spanish peninsula had come under the control of the remarkable Umayyad house of Córdoba (Chapter 8).* In

---

* The narrative history of tenth-century Islamic Spain is sketchy. Many documents were destroyed in the Christian conquest; Arabic texts that remain are scattered and difficult to read, and many surviving Latin monastic, diocesan, and county charters are unedited.

929 the emir 'Abd al-Rahmān III (912–961) declared himself caliph. His caliphate, supported by a powerful slave bureaucracy and a formidable army, occupied parts of North Africa and kept the small Christian kingdoms in the northern part of the Spanish peninsula on the defensive. For the remainder of the tenth century, the caliphate of Córdoba was ruled forcefully. Roger Collins concludes that, "At the end of the first millennium A.D., what may have looked like a stable pattern of political relationships had been created in the peninsula. The Caliphate of Córdoba, a formidable Mediterranean power . . . had risen in prestige, military strength and physical magnificence throughout the course of the tenth century."[1]

In the eleventh century, however, a Christian invasion of Islamic Spain began as those in the north joined forces around the combined state of León-Castile (see Map 10.2). Another power base began to develop in Catalonia, reaching into Languedoc and, in the twelfth century, unifying with Aragon (Chapter 13). As these more powerful Christian kingdoms emerged, Frankish warriors, European merchants, papal legates, and pilgrims from across the Pyrenees* penetrated the peninsula in growing numbers. The possible material gains and spiritual benefits derived from attacking Muslims attracted Frankish soldiers to the peninsula. Christian monks and priests from Islamic Spain moved north to refurbish or establish anew monasteries and ecclesiastical estates on the frontiers. Increasingly the Catholic Church in Spain and religious leaders in Europe focused on a restoration of Christendom in the Spanish peninsula.

At the southern tip of Europe, Arabs had captured Sicily by the early tenth century (Chapter 8), but their kingdom, and its flourishing culture, did not last. By the end of the tenth century, Sicily fragmented into warring cities. A declining Arab North Africa, hurt by Berber raids and Fatimid misrule, weakened Arab rule in Sicily. In 1030 the Byzantines, with an army of Rus, Normans, and Norwegians, tried to retake parts of the island. They did not succeed, but their efforts opened the way to naval attacks from northern Italian ports and to Norman mercenaries who had established a foothold in southern Italy. The Norman conquest of Sicily in the mid-eleventh century produced one of the most centralized and sophisticated states in all of Europe, altered the balance of power in Italy and in the Mediterranean overall, and laid the foundation for European expansion into the East.

This belt of mostly Christian states protected the core of Europe but also made it difficult for any single center of power (like the Carolingians) to emerge.

ANGLO-SAXON ENGLAND AFTER ALFRED

England is not normally thought of as a peripheral kingdom, but in the tenth and eleventh centuries England was just that. Although subject to increasingly

* Pilgrims were attracted to the relic-shrine of St. James of Compostela. St. James the Elder (Santiago), brother of St. John and one of Christ's apostles, was thought to have preached in Spain. The discovery of what was claimed to be his bones, buried in northwest Spain, occurred at the beginning of the ninth century. By the early eleventh century, his fame had spread, particularly as he was thought to have miraculously accompanied Christian warriors to battle against the Muslims.

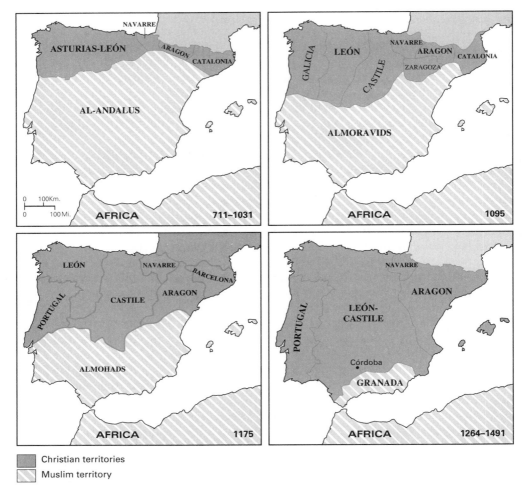

Christian territories
Muslim territory

Map 10.2   Shifting Frontiers Between Muslim and Christian Territories in the Spanish Peninsula, 711–1491   Notice the geographical expansion of the kingdoms of Castile and Aragon and the emergence of the kingdom of Portugal as the Christian frontier pushes south. Only the kingdom of Navarre, where the Basques live, was not absorbed by the three emerging kingdoms. Granada, which was in Muslim hands in 1491, was conquered by Queen Isabella of Castile and King Ferdinand of Aragon in 1492.

destructive Viking attacks in the ninth century, the victories and diplomacy of King Alfred (Chapter 8) set the stage for a more stable, united kingdom between 899 (Alfred's death) and 1066 (the Norman Conquest).

In 954, the last Scandinavian king of York, Eric Bloodaxe, was expelled, and the English experienced a generation (955–980) of comparative stability and freedom from invasion. They used this time to advance religious reform, to invest in riches and relics, and to promote learning. The coronation of King Edgar in 973 displayed an exalted view of royal authority, emphasizing its divine quality and the king's status as the natural governor of the church. The English also used the occasion to receive submission from seven Welsh and Scottish kings.

In 978, Alfred's great-great grandson came to the throne. He is known to history as Aethelred the Unready (978–1016). Although "Unraed" more properly means "No-counsel" or "Evil counsel," all of these sobriquets are to some degree apt. Aethelred's reign saw the revival of Viking attacks—this time with professional armies trained at massive, barrack-like camps in Scandinavian territories. These powerful new armies were nearly unstoppable. They exacted huge tributes from the English. Their campaigns were harsh, marked by the burning of the town of Oxford, for example, and the unusually brutal murder of the archbishop of Canterbury. The Danegeld, formerly collected for defense against the Vikings, now became a regular and heavy tax that helped to ruin many small farmers who were forced to sell their lands and assume servile status.

In 991, King Svein Forkbeard of Denmark began a conquest that resulted in the English nobility acknowledging him as king in 1013/14 ; Aethelred fled to Normandy. After much jockeying for royal authority among four contenders, Cnut (1016–1035), Svein's son, assumed the English throne, followed by his sons Harold (1035–1040) and Harthacut (1040–1042). Cnut was the first ruler of a united England and master of a North Sea empire comprising Denmark, Norway, England, and parts of Sweden. He is remembered as a good ruler of England and an especially pious Christian king, generous to the English Church and its Anglo-Saxon clergy. His government combined Anglo-Saxon traditions of loyalty to the king with Scandinavian traditions of freedom from authority. The result was successful in Cnut's lifetime, although it enabled his leading men to command enormous power.

In 1042 the Anglo-Saxon line of kings was restored to the throne with the coronation of Edward the Confessor, Aethelred's only surviving son, brought from exile in Normandy. Edward spoke French and was wont to favor his Norman friends. As his soubriquet implies, he was a pious man, but he was not a strong ruler. His reign saw the growing power of the family of Godwine, the earl of Wessex, who was, in many ways, England's real ruler. On the western border the Welsh took advantage of Edward's weakness. Gruffydd ap Llywelyn, in alliance with an Anglo-Saxon earl and a Norwegian fleet, united Wales. Gruffydd (1057–1063) is the only Welsh king ever to rule all of Wales and the first king since Cadwallon to threaten the west of England. Meanwhile war broke out in Scotland between Malcolm and Macbeth—the legendary conflict recreated in Shakespeare's *Macbeth*. This was the constellation of powers in the British Isles in 1066 when Edward died and Godwine's son, Harold, became king. Harold was to be the last Anglo-Saxon king of England. In that famous year—when Halley's Comet was seen in the skies— Harold held off a Norwegian invasion but fell to the invading army of William, duke of Normandy, who claimed Edward's throne.

ITALIAN POLITICS, THE PAPACY, AND ROME

Whereas the wealth of most European rulers derived primarily from land, economic power in Italy was more mercantile. Italy had urban traditions that had survived invasions and changes in political leadership, and it had the additional complication of Rome, dominated by the papacy and exercising both religious and political power within the peninsula. Italy was never a united political power, but its wealth, its aspiring sea powers, and Rome's international importance made Italy unique.

Northern and Central Italy

The tenth century was dominated by the struggle for control, mostly in northern Italy, of four Frankish families (Spoleto, Friuli, Ivrea, and Tuscany) with established dynasties in Italy, some with imperial aspirations. Added to the mix was the intermittent intervention of other outsiders (Hugh of Provence, the German emperors, Lombards and Byzantines from southern Italy, and Magyar, Muslim, and Norman invaders). This decentralized peninsula did not produce a feudal society, however. Italian society revolved around urban centers rather than counts and counties. Rulers and bishops were urban-based; the lord-vassal relationship was never the norm, and peasants were more often sharecroppers than serfs. It was the cities, more than mounted warriors, that became the bastions of resistance to invasion and the center of a struggle for rights and privileges, particularly in northern and central Italy.

Prior to the eleventh century, civic activity was sporadic, with occasional protests and infrequent consultations among town citizens. In the eleventh century, associations of citizens in the cities and rural villages became more organized, gathering strength from a revitalization of parish life and the ability to use legal and commercial means to negotiate specific privileges and freedoms. As a result, varieties of associations and new forms of purposeful self-government took hold in parts of eleventh-century Italy. Because information is scanty for this period, it is not possible to detail this transformation. Generally, however, the *boni homines* (the wealthier citizens, both nobles and merchants) of an urban territory were elected to a permanent council. This council then gradually increased its authority against the local count or bishop. The earliest recorded communal council was in Pisa by 1085. In Milan, citizens rose in revolt against the archbishop in 1035, resulting in an alliance between knights and citizens in 1045, evolving gradually into a communal government by the 1080s. Venice, which started out under Byzantine authority with rulers (called doges) who asserted nearly absolute power, overthrew the ruling dynasty in 1032, placed a more malleable doge in power, hemmed him in with two (and then more) councilors and established a commune by the twelfth century. These communal polities were fundamentally new and quite complex, allowing urban leaders to use legal, political, religious, and commercial networks to further their interests. But this struggle for independence also came up against the authority of the emperor as well as the papacy, two powers whose own clash was played out, in part, on the Italian peninsula.

In 961, the archbishop of Milan led the Italian bishops in calling Otto, king of Germany, south to protect the rights of the Church against harsh treatment at the hands of the king of Italy, Berengar II (950–961). The ensuing German hegemony over Italy was to shape European politics and the evolution of nation-states in Europe from this time until, some would argue, the twentieth century. The immediate impact was to give greater stability to Italy and, slowly, to extract the papacy from the crossfire of warring factions to which it had been subjected in the tenth century.

The tenth century was a time when the papacy was sold, and popes were murdered, mutilated, and mated. Early tenth-century Rome was the victim of the rising power of Roman nobility, particularly of the Crescenti family. Theodora, a member of that family, and her daughter, Marozia, according to a sensationalist tenth-century writer, were each the mistress of a pope, while Marozia was the mother of Pope John XI (931–936) and the murderer of Pope John X (914–928). In 991, the bishop of Orléans hurled accusations at individual popes (John XII, "a traitor, wallowing in lust," Leo VIII, "the neophyte," Boniface VI, "the monster").[2] "Oh unhappy Rome," he continued, "who brought our forbears the splendid light of the Father, and in our own time spread monstrous shadows, what an object of infamy you will be to future generations! . . . What is this, most reverend fathers? By what dispensation are we to believe that the first of the churches of God, which has been raised up to Heaven and crowned with honour and glory, has been thus flung in the mud. . . . This city . . . is now put up for sale to all comers, and dispenses its justice according to the quantity of money needed."

Or, as the monastic reformer, William of Dijon, put it in 1030, "If the brook is warm at its source, it stinks however far it flows."[3] The German emperors, joined in the mid-eleventh century by a host of reforming clergy, spearheaded an institutional and religious reform of the papacy in the second half of the eleventh century (see Chapter 11).

Norman Italy

Southern Italy and Sicily remained, for the most part, outside both German and papal spheres until the mid-eleventh century. The warring powers in this area at the beginning of the eleventh century included a resurgent Byzantium, a small but relatively stable group of Lombard principalities (Salerno, Capua, Benevento, Naples), Islamic rulers in Sicily, and Arab enclaves in southern Italy. In the end, however, it was the Normans who gained control of these regions. Norman adventurers, led by eight (out of the twelve) sons of Tancred de Hauteville, first appeared in the region as mercenaries for both the Byzantines and the Lombards. Soon they were given land, and they captured strongholds. From these bases they accumulated titles and ventured out to fight, usually successfully. In 1059, Pope Nicholas II made Robert Guiscard (the sly) Duke of Apulia and Calabria. Robert, one of Tancred's sons, was described by Anna Comnena, a Byzantine princess and historian, as "a Norman by birth, of obscure origin, with an overbearing character and a thoroughly villainous mind; he was a brave fighter, very cunning in his assaults . . . absolutely inexorable, diverting criticism by incontrovertible argument. He was a man of immense stature . . . he had a ruddy complexion, fair hair, broad shoulders, eyes that all but shot out sparks of fire. . . . With such endowments of fortune and nature and soul, he was . . . no man's slave, owing obedience to nobody in all the world."[4] In 1058, Robert repudiated his wife and married Sichelgaita, the sister of the Lombard prince of Salerno. Sichelgaita, described as an amazon of a woman, as "a second Pallas, if not an Athene" by Anna Comnena, fought at his side in battle, wearing armor and wielding a sword. She also bore Robert at least ten children.

By 1071, Robert captured Bari, the last Byzantine port in southern Italy. He and his younger brother, Roger de Hauteville, then finished the conquest of Sicily. Marching under a papal banner, they had already taken Messina in 1061; in 1072, they captured Palermo, allowing Roger to claim the island as its count. While Robert Guiscard welded southern Italy into a political unit, Roger governed Sicily. These two talented and fearsome Normans and their descendents gave southern Italy and Sicily political and administrative unity, a measure of peace, and the foundation for a cultural and legal revival. On the other hand, the Norman conquest devastated towns, disrupted economies, and resulted in the massacre of many inhabitants. For those cities that survived (and some thrived), the Norman rulers governed in a heavy-handed way, enforcing their rights to tolls, customs, and judicial fines. And they were quick to react negatively to any signs of civic organization or demands for communal rights. As a result, Barbara Kreutz has called the history of the towns of southern Italy in the eleventh century the history of a failed experiment.[5] When Robert Guiscard died in 1085 at age 70, still fighting Byzantium, his tomb read, in part, "Hic terror mundi Guiscardus" (Here lies Guiscard, the terror of the world). Although Norman authority ended with the twelfth century, the foundations for a powerful thirteenth-century state, governed by the Emperor Frederick II (Chapter 17), were in place.

FROM EAST FRANCIA TO THE GERMAN EMPIRE

We move now into the northwestern part of the European continent to look at the kingdoms that emerged from the disintegrating Carolingian state. As the Carolingian Empire dissolved, it divided into two major parts (East and West Francia), separated by language, customs, and different political experiences. East Francia (which evolved between 919 and 1056 into a German kingdom) was ruled by a series of able and successful men. These rulers overcame Magyar and Slavic threats on the eastern borders and Danes in the north, kept the western French weak and on the defensive, and commanded the imperial throne by 962.

In 911, Louis the Child, ruler of East Francia, died, ending the Carolingian line of rulers in the East. Louis's reign had been a low point in the exercise of royal power, and his weakness had enabled *duces* (regional leaders long suppressed by the Carolingians) to reemerge. When he died, the Aleman, Saxon, Bavarian, east Frank, and Swabian leaders chose ("elected") a non-Carolingian, Conrad I, duke of Franconia as ruler. Thus, in contrast to the Italians, who looked for protection to their cities and their bishops, or the French, who sought protection through counts descended from Carolingian counts, the East Franks reverted to their duchies in the face of invasion and insecurity. These duchies were to dominate German political life for the remainder of the Middle Ages.

Conrad I's reign (911–918) was not a success, a fact that he recognized on his deathbed when he passed over his own family and named Henry I of Saxony as his successor. Henry, called the Fowler for his habitual hawk hunting, laid the foundation for a power base in northeastern Germany. The German Empire that emerged was perhaps the greatest and certainly the longest lasting—it technically ended only in 1806—of the three German reichs of modern times. Henry's success rested on his alliance with the dukes (who became his vassals), friendly relations with western European kings, supportive relations with the Church, and military successes. In 929, he and Charles the Simple, king of the West Franks, formally agreed on a separation of East and West Francia when they crafted a treaty of friendship and recognized each other's independence.

Otto the Great (r. 936–973), son of Henry and his wife Matilda (see Medieval Portrait), led the German kingdom* to imperial status. His military victories and ruling strategies shaped what by the twelfth century was called "The Holy Roman Empire." Otto's many achievements include the defeat of several internal rebellions, success against Danish, Slav, and Magyar invaders, expansion of the cavalry in an army that was until then mostly infantry, and the establishment of newly fortified burgs, similar to those created by Alfred the Great. Otto I extended his empire eastward, establishing marches (military zones) on the Slavic borders, supporting missionary activities and new episcopal centers. Otto's long-term policy toward the Slavs was to dominate them through missionary bishoprics, permanent garrisons, and forced tributes and tithes. The Slavs, however, did not take kindly to Christianization or to absorption into a Saxon lordship and revolted frequently.

In 951, Otto made the first of three trips to Italy. On this trip he was crowned king of the Lombards and Franks at Pavia. In 955, he slaughtered a Magyar raiding party at Lechfeld in the most significant victory of his reign, ending any prospects for Magyar domination over the Slavs. At the moment of victory, Otto's troops raised him on his shield and declared him emperor. Seven years later (in 962), Pope John XII crowned him emperor in Rome, although Otto's chancery never claimed the title *Roman* emperor.[†] Eventually even the Byzantine emperor was forced to recognize his imperial authority, to partition southern Italy with Otto, and to offer a Byzantine princess, Theophano, in marriage to Otto's son and heir.

Otto shaped an empire in which there was no division between church and state. He appointed abbots, bishops, and archbishops and summoned them to synods. They, in turn, supplied him with hospitality and with the greatest part of his army. Increasingly he picked his bishops and abbots from clergy attached to the royal chapel, depending upon them for administrative and diplomatic expertise. Given the difficulty of securing support from dukes and even his own kin, Otto relied more and more on churchmen. Otto also fostered schools and scholars in these imperial churches. While monasteries continued to promote learning and the

---

* The first use of the word Teutonic kingdom ("regnum Teutonicum") appears with Otto I. Previously the German *regnum* was called the East Frankish kingdom.
† The German chancery adopted the title Roman emperor in 982, in the reign of Otto II.

MEDIEVAL PORTRAITS

Matilda, Mother of Otto I

Matilda, the second wife of Henry the Fowler, was born around 895 and died in 968. She was descended from Widukind, the great Saxon leader who fought Charlemagne. She and Henry had five children, all before she was thirty years old. Hrotsvitha of Gandersheim, in her *Gesta Oddonis,* composed in 965, says of her, "His wife ruled with him [Henry]; famous far and wide; No woman in the kingdom could ever compare to her. No one could surpass her in her mighty merits."*

Her son, Otto I, became emperor, and her daughter, Hedwig, married Hugh Capet. But her family sympathies rested with her second son, Henry, to whom she gave active support in rebellions against his brother. In a pardon issued to Henry in 941, Otto included his mother. Over time, Matilda became a support to Otto, particularly after Henry's death, and when Otto spent the majority of his time in Italy in the 960s, Matilda was left in charge of the kingdom. It was popularly believed that her prayers and piety were instrumental in Otto I's safe return from his Italian forays. She was also thought to have prophesied the deaths of her son Henry and her grandson and to have expiated her husband's sins with her prayers. As the mother of Otto the Great, himself a quasi-divine ruler, her saintliness and prophecies helped legitimate and sanctify the Ottonian line.

In her widowhood Matilda used her dowry to found convents and monasteries and to lavish alms on them. Her powerful position, extensive resources, and extravagant giving was viewed critically by her son Otto, who kept her movements and donations under surveillance. She was also criticized throughout her life for her rich, regal attire, which some thought sat poorly with her piety. In protest, at one point, she resigned her inheritance.

Matilda survived two sons and a grandson. When she died, she was buried beside her husband and venerated as a saint from the moment of her death. Two lives of Saint Matilda were written within forty years of her death. She was later canonized.

Matilda is emblematic of a large number of powerful Saxon women in this period. Many Saxon aristocratic and royal wives outlived their husbands and children and commanded huge resources. They founded thirty-six convents in Saxony alone between 919 and 1024 and placed huge tracts of lands into the hands of the Church. These convents protected women and their inheritances. They saved unmarried daughters from promiscuity and protected young widows from remarriage and childbirth. They also provided a retreat for women to learn to read, participate in the liturgy, play instruments, write, and to participate in a literate and creative culture.

* Katharina Wilson, trans., *Hrotsvit of Gandersheim: A Florilegium of Her Works* (Rochester, N.Y.: D.S. Brewer, 1998) 101.

MEDIEVAL PORTRAITS

Hrotsvitha of Gandersheim, a Learned Canoness and Activist Author

In 1494, a German humanist scholar named Conrad Celtis discovered the writings of a tenth-century German nun named Hrotsvitha of Gandersheim. His discovery of this unknown Saxon's writings was greeted with skepticism and considered by some a forgery. But Hrotsvitha was quite real—a noble canoness in the imperial abbey of Gandersheim whose dates (930s–1000) are somewhat conjectural. Her literary output, in Latin, consists of eight legends, six plays in rhymed prose, two epics (one on the deeds of Otto I, the other a short history of Gandersheim), and a short poem on the apocalypse. Her works emphasize Christian martyrdom, conversion, and eremitic solitude. She was influenced by Byzantine hagiographical models and by classical literature, particularly the plays of Terence. The resulting dramas are hagiographical and somewhat idiosyncratic in their depiction of aberrant behavior. One of her plays, *Calimachus,* features a pagan youth seducing a married, chaste Christian woman, Drusiana, who dies rather than succumb to him. On Drusiana's deathbed, Calimachus is tempted to engage in necrophilia and is himself killed just in time by a poisonous snake. Christ, however, appears and resurrects him from the dead, converting him to Christianity; Drusiana is also resurrected and rejoins her husband.

Hrotsvitha called herself the "Forceful Voice of Gandersheim." She dealt with strong themes: paganism, sorcery, homosexuality, multiple fornication, necrophilia, Christian persecution and martyrdom, all with a sense of humor and a strong Christian didacticism. She constantly shows young Christian women overcoming more powerful men with truth and virtue. In an age of Viking and Magyar incursions and Muslim slave trade, her dramas may have reflected tenth-century realities.

production of manuscripts, imperial bishoprics, such as Cologne, Trier, Hildesheim, and Mainz, became centers of a more practical kind of Latin learning that trained men to become imperial administrators and ecclesiastical activists (see Medieval Portrait. To solidify this imperial church power base, the tenth- and eleventh-century German emperors gave legal immunities and huge territories to churches and monasteries, anchoring the monarchy's hold over the kingdom via the ecclesiastical structure.

This close working relationship with the Church rested on a vision of the emperor as a quasi-priest, anointed by God directly, and responsible for the well-being of the Church, including even the appointment of the pope. During one of its heights of power, under Otto III (r. 996–1003), the German emperor established his imperial seat at Rome and placed his own candidate, Gerbert of Aurillac, on the papal throne (see Medieval Portrait). With roots in the legends of Charlemagne's Empire as well as memories of the classical Roman Empire, the emperor wore a red cope and crown similar to the garb Constantine was supposed to have worn; he carried a golden orb to symbolize his worldly dominion; and shouldered a mantle with signs of the zodiac and the apocalypse (symbolizing the priesthood in Jerusalem). His crown, with its octagonal shape, represented the octagonal walls of Jerusalem

MEDIEVAL PORTRAITS

Gerbert of Aurillac (Pope Sylvester II)

Gerbert of Aurillac, born about 945, was of obscure parentage from Aquitaine. He was given as a child to a Cluniac abbey, where he learned his Latin. In 967, his abbot sent Gerbert to Catalonia, where he mastered arithmetic, astronomy, and music. He encountered Arabic numerals, the abacus, a large body of classical texts as well as translations from Arabic scientific treatises. He may well have seen an astrolabe. His subsequent career took him to Germany, as tutor to the young Otto II, and then to the Reims cathedral school to study and teach logic, rhetoric, the classical poets and historians, as well as the quadrivium (arithmetic, music, geometry, and astronomy).

While at Reims Gerbert introduced new musical practices—establishing pitch and playing the organ. In astronomy he designed an instrument (the precursor to the telescope) for viewing the heavens and a wooden sphere for demonstrating celestial circles and constellations. After eight years at Reims, the Emperor Otto II made him abbot of St. Columba of Bobbio in northern Italy. After a tumultuous tenure as abbot (with quarrels over territorial holdings), Gerbert fled and was immediately given the very difficult task of helping save the imperial throne for a child, Otto III. His fidelity to the Ottonians was not rewarded with a bishopric at that time (perhaps due to his humble background).

Returning once more to Reims, Gerbert was instrumental in the transfer of power in West Francia to Hugh Capet in 987. He became Hugh's secretary and expected to be appointed archbishop of Reims. His disappointment in being passed over led to a fight over the archiepiscopal throne that resulted in a papal excommunication of both Hugh Capet and Gerbert. Gerbert fled to Germany. There he cultivated a mentoring friendship with the young, new Emperor Otto III, who eventually appointed him archbishop of Ravenna and, in 999, pope. Gerbert of Aurillac took the name Sylvester II, reminding Christians of the legendary partnership between Constantine I and Pope Sylvester I. An activist pope, Sylvester II worked to extend imperial and papal influence in southern Italy and against Byzantium. He was instrumental in establishing the Roman Church in Hungary, Poland, and Norway, and he supported Otto III in his vision of a revived, Christian Roman Empire. Gerbert died in 1003, one year after the emperor whose cause he had championed so vigorously.

and the chapel at Aachen; the twelve stones on each side of the crown represented the twelve tribes of Israel; and in a painting of Henry II, it was placed on the emperor's head by God himself. The emperor's scepter with its eagle was the Roman sign of victory. The Holy Lance (supposedly the lance that pierced Christ's side at Calvary) was borne in front of him (Byzantine fashion) like a standard. With his sword, a staff scarcely distinguishable from a bishop's crosier, ring, anointed status, and salutation of *Sieg und Heil* (Victory and Salvation), the emperor was, according to Archbishop Aribo of Mainz, the representative of Christ, with sovereignty over the Church as a *ministerium* imposed by God. With the death of Henry II, the last Ottonian ruler, in 1024, the crown passed to the Salian emperors (Conrad II, Henry III, Henry IV, and Henry V) who identified themselves further with the

Church and with Christ. From their exalted position they placed a heavy hand over German dukes and counts, demanding obedience. They insisted on recognition of their position as overlords from the Polish and Bohemian kings. The bishops, whose authority and wealth grew significantly, supported the emperors' autocratic style. Together the king-emperors and the bishops shaped an imperial administration and together they promoted the concept of a quasi-divine, royal authority, guarantor of the Church, crowned by God and sustained by Christ. Bishop Benzo of Alba forcefully lauded the sacramental status of the German emperor in a panegyric to Henry IV:

> God walks before His anointed and prepares for him an accumulation of victories. All the world awaits him as though he were the Redeemer; the crowds, going to meet him with palms and branches, open the gates of the towns to him. . . . Next after God, O Caesar, thou art King, thou art emperor . . . Vicar of the Creator . . . he [the emperor] has been raised by God's favour to a position of great sublimity and exalted above all powers and laws of all kingdoms.[6]

The Salian emperors also consolidated the kingdom, working to centralize it, to make it more functional with royal administrators and a legalistic basis.

Portrait of Emperor Otto III Framed by a Mandorla This image of the glorification of the Emperor Otto III (983-1002) is found in a book of gospels made in Germany about 990. Otto is surrounded by kings and clergy as well as by symbols of the four evangelists. His power comes directly from God's hand as he sits enthroned, holding the orb of the world in his right hand. The almond-shaped frame around Otto is called a *mandorla*. It usually contains a sacred person and was most commonly reserved for Christ. This image illustrates the divine qualities attributed to the Ottonian emperor. *Cathedral Treasury, Aachen, Germany/Foto Marburg/Art Resource, NY.*

Despite all this, however, the authority of the emperor within the empire was problematic. In the first place, the three kingdoms under imperial rule (Germany, Burgundy, and parts of Italy) were quite separate. Imperial power derived from an itinerant, personal rule that depended very much on how well the German ruler related to the nobles, bishops, and abbots. Unlike French kings, who succeeded by inheritance and without election, the dynastic and hereditary rights of German kings, especially of the Salian kings, were asserted but not necessarily agreed to. Before they could be crowned, German kings needed the agreement of, and eventually election by, the majority of leading secular and ecclesiastical princes. There was only the most rudimentary administration and no capital city. Most diplomatic errands and administrative tasks were done by clerics from the king's chapel or, increasingly, by servile knights bound to the king's service called *ministeriales*. Governance was sporadic; the emperor's justice was available only to the aristocracy; and political, diplomatic, and military issues were usually handled at periodic assemblies of the leading nobles. The German ruler's strongest control was exercised over the ecclesiastical structure of his kingdom.

The emperor's reach exceeded his grasp. By the mid-eleventh century a number of factors weakened the empire. German forces saw serious military defeats by Muslims in southern Italy and military setbacks on the Danish and Slav borders in the 980s. In 983, a large Slav uprising essentially marked the end of German expansionism in the East for several generations. In the 1050s, unsuccessful campaigns were waged against Hungary coupled with further defeats by the West Slavs. The German army, small but powerful with its iron-mailed soldiers (the medieval equivalent of modern tanks) intimidated opponents but did not bring them to battle easily. The army, drawn largely from military attached to the larger churches, depended upon the emperor's close relations with ecclesiastical leaders. German military dependence upon bishops and abbots became problematic when leaders of ecclesiastical reform began criticizing the emperor and calling for a separation of the Church from lay society. Gradually whole bishoprics (often including cities) gained immunities from royal control, while reformed monasteries began to look to the papacy rather than to the crown for protection. Particularly under a regency after the death of Henry III (1056) and before Henry IV reached adulthood (1065), imperial lands were disbursed, and the nobility began to build castles, declare peace, distribute justice (or injustice) without appeal, intermarry without royal assent, and expand their holdings as independent territorial rulers. Henry IV's turbulent reign (Chapter 11) did not succeed in putting the nobility back in their place. By the end of the eleventh century, it was clear that solidification of authority in the German Empire was a territorial affair of the higher aristocracy and that the emperor had limited rights. The German Empire was a collective enterprise, in which the nobles as a group gained the lion's share of control over the resources, including the ecclesiastical resources, of the kingdom.

A further factor in the changed circumstances of the emperor's position, which made the German emperor a very different ruler from Charlemagne, was the rise of independent kingdoms and territories throughout Europe. All of these counterweights made imperial lordship of any kind over Europe tenuous. The Italians acknowledged it when they were forced to, or when it was convenient. The Danes were themselves too imperialistic in the eleventh century to acknowledge German authority, and parts of eastern Europe were only sporadically under German dominance. Strong, independent kings, dukes, or counts ruled in England, Normandy, Flanders, Anjou, Aquitaine, Hungary and Spain. By the eleventh century, West Francia (or France), once an integral part of the Carolingian Empire, was fully independent. The Capetian kings of France backed away from submitting decisions to German-dominated synods or to the German emperor altogether. And because the French king was anointed, with a long-standing independent relationship with the papacy, and, to some degree the inheritor of Carolingian authority, he was able to stand alone.

LATE CAROLINGIAN AND CAPETIAN FRANCE

By 911, the West Frankish Kingdom (Neustria) was a shadow of its former greatness—severely affected by Viking invasions and slow to recover. In the period covered by this chapter, the last directly descended Carolingian rulers governed the West Franks, intermittently losing the kingship to the rising power of the counts of Paris, the first of whom was Odo (r. 888–898). The county or duchy, rather than the kingdom, became the effective political unit. By around 950 the royal vassals of Carolingian times had ceased to exist, replaced by military dependents attached to local powers. The duchies of Aquitaine, Normandy, Brittany, Burgundy, Gascony, and the counties of Toulouse, Champagne, Flanders, Blois, and Anjou all spun out of the control of the French monarchy, building their own power bases by exerting control over free landholders and independent castellans. At the end of the ninth century there were twenty-nine separate territories within West Francia; by the end of the tenth century, the number had risen to fifty-five.[7] The decentralized nature of Frankish society in the tenth and eleventh centuries meant that the job of protection fell to counts and castellans and their military retainers or "knights." In this unsettled and dangerous time, peasants lost their freedom and military profession became a sign of status. As a result, France became the most highly feudalized, albeit somewhat chaotic, area in Europe.

The following famous story provides a commentary on the weakness of the French crown. In 911, Charles the Simple made a treaty with Northmen who had been ravaging the Seine and Loire river basins. The treaty gave these Northmen, led by Rollo (eventually Count of Rouen), control over territories that now compose part of Normandy. In return, Rollo agreed to swear loyalty to Charles, be baptized, and defend the territory against other Vikings. Dudo of St. Quentin tells what happened:

> The bishops said to Rollo, unwilling to kiss the foot of the king: "Whoever receives such a gift, ought to seek the foot of the king for a kiss," And he [said]: I will never bend my knees to anyone, nor will I kiss the foot of anyone. Therefore, swayed by the prayers of the Franks, he ordered a certain soldier to kiss the foot

of the king. The soldier, immediately grabbing the king's foot, carried it to his mouth, and, standing making his kiss, he made the king fall on his back.[8]

Whether or not this presumptuously independent act actually occurred, the legend was current among the Normans who certainly believed that it did.

By 987, the last remaining directly descended Carolingian king of West Francia (Louis V) died in a hunting accident, leaving no heir. With the kingship vacant and its power substantially diminished, and with the East Frankish Empire in the hands of the Ottonians, French bishops crowned Hugh Capet, count of Paris, as king of France—almost 100 years after his ancestor, Odo, had first claimed the French throne.* But Hugh's reign (987–996) remained precarious despite alliances with the Anglo-Saxon King Aethelred, with Otto the Great of Germany, and with Normandy. Within two years, the archbishop of Reims and the duke of Lorraine, both of Carolingian blood, revolted.

Hugh was followed by three long-lived but ineffective rulers, Robert II "the Pious" (996–1031), Henry I (1031–1060), and Philip I (1060–1108). They governed the royal demesne in the Ile de France, an axis of land between Paris and Orléans. Their lordship over other Frankish, Flemish, Norman, Breton, Provençal, Aquitainian or Gascon counts and dukes was more theoretical than real. And yet, they retained sufficient prestige and leverage to prepare France for a successful expansionary policy in the twelfth and thirteenth centuries.

It was the practice of tenth-century West Frankish kings to recognize no superior, not even the emperor. One reason for this singular status was the anointment of the Capetian kings, at Reims Cathedral with the same holy and miraculous oil that was allegedly used at Clovis' baptism.[†] The Capetians shored up their status by developing a good working relationship with the Church. Robert II "the Pious," in particular, promoted ecclesiastical reform and projected the image of a monk-king and miracle-worker. His piety was presented as in marked contrast with his third wife, Queen Constance (1005–1032), who was portrayed as a volatile, angry, even heretical woman. This identification of the king with the holy man, while upsetting to some nobles and bishops who favored warrior-kings, gave the Capetians a distinctive religious charisma. Although none of the symbols that one associates with French kings—the banner of the oriflamme (a red-gold banner that, in legend, had belonged to Charlemagne), the *fleur de lis* (identified with the Virgin, whose flower is the lily), Capetian burial at St. Denys (which symbolized the connection between saint and king), or the title "Most Christian King"—are yet in evidence in the eleventh century, it would be premature to conclude that they were not there. We do not yet know the process whereby France became the familiar France of the *fleur de lis,* centered on Paris, protected by St. Denys, with a sense of Christian superiority. The attachment of the Capetians to these symbols and to Carolingian epic traditions such as *The Song of Roland* helped preserve the exalted sense of French kingship, even in the midst of limited geography and resources.

---

* After the coronation of Hugh Capet, historians tend to speak of the kingdom as France because of its continuity with the modern French state.
† The first mentions of Reims and the miraculous oil are not, however, until about 1130.

RELIGION AND SOCIETY

The emerging Christian powers described above gained prestige and power by working with Church leaders. This relationship worked to promote missionary bishoprics and monasteries on the fringes of pagan eastern Europe, monasteries on the Muslim-Christian frontiers of Spain, and royal ecclesiastical estates in the German Empire that provided men of arms and of learning to the emperor. In all cases, however, the state was the dominant partner, and it was therefore not surprising that the values of lay society were mirrored in the Church. This state of affairs gave rise to complaints from the clergy. Clerical concerns about worldliness spread through sermons to the laity, and gradually a desire for reform built up.

Monastic Reform in the Tenth Century

The invasions of the ninth and tenth centuries left the monasteries of Europe in ruins, and many of the surviving houses passed, for protection, to the control of lay lords. A council of bishops at Soisson in 909 complained,

> our abbeys have been burned and destroyed by the heathen, plundered of their possessions, reduced almost to nothing. And if in some of them there seems still to remain a few traces of outward form, within them no customs of regular discipline now abide . . . against all authority of the Church they are subject to rulers who are not of their household, who come from the world without. Through poverty, through malice, and especially through this enormity of directors unfit to hold office, our religious are living in irregular manner, forgetful of their profession, occupied in worldly business. And more. In monasteries dedicated to God and holy Religion, lay abbots are living with their wives, their sons and their daughters, their armored guards and their dogs![9]

Just as strong men threatened by invaders strengthened and centralized their rule, sometimes setting aside tradition and prior authority, so too did a vanguard of monks respond to this crisis by strengthening monastic life. The most famous of these tenth-century monastic reforms was that of Cluny.

In the last decade of the ninth century an aristocratic young man, Berno, founded a monastic cell at Baume, in Burgundy, where Norsemen had recently wrecked an abbey. The Benedictine regimen he and his monks followed was one of constant prayer, silence, and ascetic privation. In 910, William, the duke of Aquitaine, called Berno to establish a monastery on his lands at Cluny. Its charter, traditional in many respects, was unique in stressing that the only authority over Cluny was spiritual. It reads, in part:

> I give [the above-mentioned lands] on condition that a Regular Monastery be established at Cluny in honor of the apostles Peter and Paul; that monks shall form a congregation there living under the rule of St. Benedict; that they shall for ever possess, hold and order the property given in such wise that this honorable house

shall be unceasingly full of vows and prayers. . . . May they have as protectors the Apostles themselves, and for defender the Pontiff of Rome. . . . It has pleased us to set forth in this testament that from this day forward the monks . . . at Cluny shall be wholly freed from our power, from that of our kindred, and from the jurisdiction of royal greatness, and shall never submit to the yoke of any earthly power.

This promise of independence from lay authority was a commitment that Cluny made stick.

Cluny was blessed by a series of strong, saintly abbots, as well as by the numbers and importance of its benefactors. Three powerful abbots ruled Cluny between 926 and 1044—Odo from 926 to 944, Majolus from 954 to 994, and Odilo from 994 to 1044. They gained papal support for their autonomy from lay and from clerical interference. They attracted patrons such as the king of Burgundy, the king of France, and the German emperor, as well as gifts from numerous socially mobile individuals who had taken advantage of the dislocations of the time and now sought the stability and legitimacy represented by Cluny. Cluny was soon rich in buildings, agricultural lands, churches, and dependent monasteries reformed under its leadership. Cluny received the right to coin money and exemption from taxes. In 1016, the pope confirmed Cluny's privileges, extending them to all its dependencies. By 1050, Cluny had become an order, with codified rules and privileges and with hundreds of dependent houses ranging from southern Italy to Ireland. Cluniac monks lived a life governed by ritual and regulation, whether praying, learning, singing, going to bed, washing, or eating. Even when captured by Vikings or Muslims, Cluniac monks continued to practice their discipline—saying the psalter or observing silence in the face of impending death.

Cluny was not the only monastic reform movement of the tenth century. In the German-speaking areas, monastic reform was associated with the monastery of Gorze, an eighth-century foundation that had fallen into disrepair. A group of reformers led by John of Gorze and Einold, archdeacon of Toul, retrieved it from lay hands, and reendowed and reformed it in the 930s. Gorze monks were called upon to reform other monasteries, but unlike Cluny, these houses retained their autonomy. Gorze reformers received patronage from bishops and rulers alike and did not seek the independence, based on papal protection, prized by Cluny. Gorze-reformed houses emphasized schools and education, an aspect that Cluny was less concerned with, as it was based in an area already well-supplied with cathedral schools.

Both Gorze and Cluniac reforms influenced a tenth-century monastic revival in England. Gorze's model of episcopal and royal support for reform was repeated in England where King Edmund (r. 939–946) initiated a reform movement, kings Edgar and Edward the Martyr (r. 975–978) continued it, and monastic bishops like Dunstan, archbishop of Canterbury, carried it out. They promoted an ascetic monastic reform movement while simultaneously working to create schools, educate clergy, and inform the laity through sermons, homilies, and their own exemplary lives. In 964, a great council at Winchester commissioned the founding of monasteries throughout England, most of which were managed by reforming bishops. Perhaps eight years later another great council convened at Winchester, this time to standardize the usage of monasteries by accepting the great document of the English reform movement—the *Regularis Concordia,* drawn up under the authority of Archbishop Dunstan. The presence of monks at Winchester from Fleury (reformed by Cluny) and monks from Ghent (associated with Gorze) symbolized the two strands of continental reform coming together in an English context.

Millennial Expectations Around the Year 1000

The tenth-century monastic reform movement promoted liturgical reform; better, more accessible schools; and preaching in the vernacular to a wider audience. Although there are occasional vernacular sermons and prose religious writings from the continent, the bulk of vernacular literature from this period is Anglo-Saxon. Two large collections of homilies, scattered anonymous homilies, and the works of two great English preachers—Aelfric of Eynsham (c. 950–c.1010) and Archbishop Wulfstan II of York (d. 1023)—testify to the power of the preached vernacular. The primary, if not the overriding focus of this literature is the afterlife, the Day of Judgment, and the coming end of the world. Archbishop Wulfstan, for example, began his "Sermon to the English" (1014) by exhorting his audience to "recognize what the truth is: this world is in haste and is drawing near the end, and therefore the longer it is the worse it will get in the world. And it needs must thus become very much worse as a result of the people's sins prior to the advent of Antichrist; and then, indeed, it will be terrible and cruel throughout the world."[10] A late tenth-century Anglo-Saxon collection called the Blicking Homilies includes an Easter homily on the apocalyptic signs of the end of the world:

> Let us consider how great a terror will come upon us created things, in this present time, when the Judgment draws near; and the revelation of that day will be very terrible to all. . . . In that day heaven and earth and the sea, and all the things that are in them will pass away. . . . And in that day heaven will be folded up like a book; and in that day the earth will be burned to ashes; and in that day the sea will dry up; and in that day all the power of the skies will be turned and stirred. And six days before this day, marvellous signs will occur every day. At noon on the first day, there will occur a great lamentation of all created things, and men will hear a great noise in the skies, as if an army were being assembled and set in order there; then a great bloody cloud will arise from out of the north and obscure all the sky; and after the cloud will come lightning and thunder all day; and in the evening bloody rain will rain down. . . . Then all men will see how it will be at this world's end. Then they will flee to the mountains and hide because of the sight of the angels; and then they will call to the earth and beg it to swallow and hide them, and will wish that they were never born.[11]

These sermons suggest an eschatological urgency to Christian teaching.

Anglo-Saxon poetry is also full of depictions of the Judgment Day and the afterlife, some of it quite explicit, as in Eynewulf's *The Last Judgment, The Judgment Day,* and his *The Descent into Hell.* In other poems the concern is implicit, as in *The Wanderer*'s meditation on life's fleeting quality.

Concern for the afterlife was also common on the continent where it was expressed in new forms of drama—re-creations of events between Christ's crucifixion and his resurrection. These liturgical dramas were initiated at Gorze but soon popularized around Europe. The theme of the Harrowing of Hell (in the popular *Gospel of Nicodemus*) and numerous sculptures and manuscript illuminations of Hell and devils all suggest a European society preoccupied with the possibility that the world might soon end. Many medieval writers, as mentioned in the introduction, focused on the coming of Antichrist. These apocalyptic concerns, ironically, occurred simultaneously with growing economic prosperity, political reconstruction, signs of religious revival, investments in building new churches, and efforts to establish new bishoprics and extend the Christian message.

Summary

The years from 900 to 1050 were a formative period in the growth of Europe. Increasingly freed from invasion, Europeans began to invest in towns and cities, stone buildings, the reclamation of lands, and territorial control. In the political arena, as even the remnant of Carolingian public power faded, new forms of order emerged. The kingdoms that took shape did so despite military setbacks, administrative immaturity, recalcitrant nobility, and dynastic struggles. They formed the nucleus for an order based on the sacred and on heredity, wealth, and loyalty in which slavery was increasingly a thing of the past and loyalty to a lord (and especially the king) a harbinger of the future. It was also a society where counts, dukes, kings, and emperors patronized religious institutions as part of their efforts to legitimate newly emerging forms of power; in the process they also sometimes promoted religious reform. These efforts at reform, spread throughout Europe by ascetic monks, reforming bishops, and Christian kings, set the stage for a far more aggressive Christianity in the beginning of the second millennium.

NOTES

1. Roger Collins, *Early Medieval Spain: Unity in Diversity, 400–1000* (New York: St. Martin's Press, 1983) 266.
2. Eleanor Duckett, *Death and Life in the Tenth Century* (Ann Arbor: University of Michigan Press, 1968) 120.
3. Rodulfus Glaber, *The Life of St. William*, ed. N. Bulst, trans. John France and Paul Reynolds in *Rodulfi Glabri Opera* (Oxford: Clarendon Press, 1989) 282–283.
4. *The Alexiad of Anna Comnena*, trans. E.R.A. Sewter (New York: Penguin, 1969) 54.
5. Barbara Kreutz, *Before the Normans: Southern Italy in the Ninth and Tenth Centuries* (Philadelphia: University of Pennsylvania Press, 1991) 157.
6. Benzo of Alba, *Liber ad Heinricum IV, MGH, Scriptores,* XI (Hanover: Kraus reprt., 1963), 605, 608.
7. Geoffrey Barraclough, *The Crucible of Europe* (Berkeley: University of California Press, 1976) 94.
8. Dudo, "De Moribus et Actis Primorum Normanniae Ducum," *Patrologia Latina*, vol. 141 (Paris, 1880) 650–651.
9. Duckett, *Death and Life in the Tenth Century,* 195–196.
10. *Anglo-Saxon Prose,* ed. and trans. Michael Swanton (Lanham, Md.: Rowman & Littlefield, 1975) 116–117.
11. *Anglo-Saxon Prose,* 67–68.

PART IV

❧

Reformation and Renewal, 1050–1200

CHAPTER 11

~

Religious Revival and Reform, 1050–1200

By the mid-eleventh century, as the economic and political developments described in Chapters 9 and 10 transformed Europe, demand for religious reform was growing. Around the turn of the millennium, many Europeans seem to have become more interested in their spiritual well-being. This may have been in response to fears of the end of the world, or due to a desire for answers in the midst of change, or perhaps in reaction to the domination of the Church by newly emerging secular rulers. Individuals also turned to religious pursuits to escape worldliness and wealth and to expiate sinful acts. As a result, the number of pilgrims traveling to shrines increased, as did the number of individuals entering monasteries or becoming hermits. Peace movements and reforms of the papacy, ecclesiastical hierarchy, and monasteries were organized, all of which profoundly affected the course of European history. A revived papacy asserted claims of superiority over the political sphere and strengthened the Church's role in society. Out of this context of religious renewal, however, heresy was to become more evident and the persecution of minorities more severe.

A REBIRTH OF CHRISTIAN FERVOR

Many Europeans around the year 1000 looked for better order and for God's will in the world they inhabited. But too often they found that princes were not protectors and priests preyed on people as much as they prayed for them. In their sermons and in their written charters, contemporaries complained about the changing times, expressing upset over conflicting standards and the injustices of leaders. In the confusion of that world and concerned for their salvation, individuals expressed greater religious fervor and, increasingly, demanded religious reform.

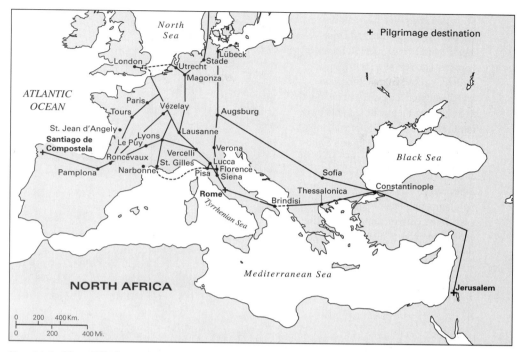

Map 11.1 Three Pilgrimage Destinations, c. 1030   The three major pilgrimage destinations in the eleventh century were Santiago de Compostela in northwest Spain, Rome, and Jerusalem. Of these, Santiago de Compostela was the more recent; the bones of St. James were discovered in the ninth century, and the cult was popular by 1000. The route to Santiago de Compostela went through a number of towns (Le Puy, Tours, St. Gilles, and Vézelay) that were also relic centers, and then struck out across the mountains and valleys of northern Spain. The routes to Jerusalem were still largely overland. Of the three pilgrim destinations, Rome was the most accessible and the most visited.

The Geography of Salvation: Pilgrimages, Relics, and Penance

The eleventh century was a great age for pilgrimage. At the end of the tenth century an overland route to the Holy Land opened up. As a result of Byzantine conquests in the Balkans, Asia Minor, and parts of Syria, and the conversion to Christianity of the king of Hungary, it become possible for large numbers of people—noble and common, clerical and secular, men and women— to travel entirely by land from western Europe to Jerusalem (see Map 11.1). There they sought the Holy Sepulchre and sites where tradition held that Jesus had walked. In 1009, the autocratic (and perhaps mad) Caliph al-Hākim destroyed Christian churches, including the church that stood over the place where the Holy Sepulchre was. The ensuing outrage provided added motivation for Europeans to journey eastward. Radulfus Glaber, the itinerant monk from Burgundy, wrote in the 1030s that people of every nation were filling the roads to Jerusalem.

St. James Portrayed as a Pilgrim to His Own Shrine   This early four-teenth-century statue of St. James of Compostela as a pilgrim is from Toulouse in southern France. It was highly unusual for a saint to be identi-fied as a pilgrim traveling to his own tomb. He carries a staff for walking and for defense; the staff was also symbolic of the wood of the cross. His cap is decorated with shells, which are common on the beaches near Santiago and became the symbol associated with this pilgrimage. The wide brimmed hat also provided protection from sun and rain. These statues were common in churches that were on the pilgrimage route. *Roger-Viollet.*

Simultaneously, the developing powers of León-Castile and of Catalonia and Aragon opened northern Spain to pilgrims who wished to visit the shrine of St. James (*Santiago* in Spanish)* in Compostela in the northwest corner of Spain. James, nicknamed *Matamoros* (Killer of Moors), was a military saint and protector of Christian knights, and Christian need for protection was enhanced with the suc-cessful sacking of Compostela by the Muslims in 997. The appeal of St. James says a great deal about the religiosity of the age, for the rigor of this pilgrimage (across mountains and rushing streams, hot by day and cold by night, with scarce drinking water) often brought death and sickness to pilgrims.

Rome was the oldest Christian pilgrimage center in Europe, and it was more ac-cessible, physically, than either Jerusalem or Santiago of Compostela. Rome was the location of the tombs of martyrs, the papal seat, and the home of the relics† of Saints Peter and Paul. Richard, abbot of St. Vanne, explained its appeal in a sermon he preached after visiting Rome in 1026:

---

* St. James was the first of the twelve apostles to be martyred. He was beheaded by Herod in 44 A.D. Some-time around 813 a tomb was discovered in Spain at a place called Compostela. Miracles associated with that discovery convinced the local bishop that the body was that of St. James.

† The term "relics" applies to the material remains of saints or martyrs, as well as to objects that have been in contact with them. The relics of Peter and Paul were their bodies that had been buried in Rome. The only relics associated with either Christ or his mother were objects (such as the cross) that they touched or parts of their body (hair, mother's milk) that they discarded while alive.

The city of Rome, the capital of the world, is rendered more special by the most glorious triumphs of the holy apostles Peter and Paul. Thither flock daily the races and peoples with devotion of heart, to plead with the holy apostles to hear their prayers, either by compunction of faith, or by grief for sins, or in hope of the more abundant life of heaven.[1]

Pilgrimages broadened one's awareness. People began to understand that Jerusalem was home to Jews and Muslims and ruled by Islamic powers. Thousands saw the extent to which the customs of Greek Christians differed from the West. Pilgrims to Rome could contrast the holiness of the city with its observable worldliness, and travelers to Compostela saw a need for military aid to expand Christian authority in Spain.

Hospices, bridges, roads, churches, and monasteries were built and rebuilt along the pilgrim routes to facilitate travel. Relics of saints were discovered and venerated along the way. On the road to Compostela in 1037, the monastery at Vézelay in France announced that it had Mary Magdalene's relics, while in 1010, the head of St. John the Baptist surfaced at St. Jean d'Angely.

A fervor for relics grew throughout Christian Europe. Relics of the Virgin Mary had begun to be particularly popular; the most celebrated was at Chartres, which claimed to have her tunic. Relics embodied spiritual power and worked miracles. Oaths were made on them. The foundation and consecration of new churches required a relic, and as the Church expanded demand grew. Relics attracted offerings and were therefore a source of revenue. As a result, relics were discovered, transported, traded, bought, and stolen.

With relic centers multiplying and travel becoming more commodious, thousands went on pilgrimage. In 1026, William, the count of Angoulême, left France for the Holy Land with "an army of pilgrims," described as the largest group to date. In 1033, another mass pilgrimage set off to the East. Medieval chroniclers report that in 1064 over 10,000 Germans headed toward Jerusalem.* Although we have no detailed records (and no way of estimating the numbers) of the thousands who traveled to shrines near and far, we know that pilgrimages appealed to nobles, bishops, and knights as well as to the poor and middle-income individual. Women were not prevented from going on pilgrimage, and two of the earliest accounts of such journeys are by or about women.†

It is difficult to fathom the reasons for such dramatic religious outbursts. Medieval writers tended to be uninterested in analyzing motives. Modern historians have argued that it was caused, in part, by a growing emphasis on penance. From

---

* Medieval chroniclers lacked a modern sense of numerical precision. Their numbers are usually rounded, mostly exaggerated, and quite undependable. This estimate means that an impressive number of Germans went on pilgrimage.

† Extant in an eleventh-century manuscript from Montecassino monastery is a late fourth-century pilgrimage account written by Egeria, a prominent, pious Christian from Spain, possibly a person with imperial connections, writing for her "sisters." The "Life of Melanie the younger" describes Melanie's pilgrimage in the early fifth century. For the importance of women in the early stages of pilgrimage to the Holy Land, see E.D. Hunt, *Holy Land Pilgrimage in the Later Roman Empire A.D. 312–460* (Oxford: Clarendon, 1982).

the ninth through the eleventh centuries, the idea grew that a person could be pardoned from sin by visiting a sacred shrine. As a result, clergy began to impose pilgrimage as a penance. Then, as the conception of purgatory developed,* so did the belief that pious actions, such as visits to saints' tombs, could increase one's chances for entering heaven. In addition, there may have been a developing psychology of fear rooted in intensifying apocalyptic beliefs that the world was old and would soon end. None of these ideas could have had much impact if itinerant preachers and greater availability of books had not made them more accessible.

Victor and Edith Turner, in an anthropological analysis of pilgrimage,[2] suggest that being a pilgrim enhanced one's moral standing and freed one from "homegrown ills" and the conflicts of daily life. Pilgrims might also experience a brief, perhaps exhilarating sense of community that transcended time and was independent of social status. All pilgrims were one of a crowd, engaged in a ritually satisfying and richly psychological event. Absorbed into the flow of penitential rhythms, pilgrims vicariously experienced the sufferings of Christ. Finally, medieval Europeans tended to equate sinfulness with sickness, sanctity with health. As a result, many local relics and religious centers were centers of healing to which people were drawn in the expectation of miracles.

The Peace and Truce of God

Another aspect of the religious revival in which relics played a crucial role was a widespread peace movement. From the 980s until well into the twelfth century, peace movements occurred sporadically, beginning in France and developing in parts of Spain, Flanders, and Germany. Bishops, monastic communities, and laity banded together to contain attacks on ecclesiastical rights and property and to curb violence against unarmed members of society—actions that were all too common in medieval Europe and, with the decline of Carolingian power, had escalated in former Carolingian regions. Participants swore oaths to preserve peace, sanctified by the presence of relics and presided over by the clergy. This was often done in open fields, before crowds of witnesses.

In its early stages, participants called this movement the Peace of God. It was essentially an ecclesiastical effort to resolve conflicts using legal means, spiritual injunctions, and the power of relics rather than violence and feuds. Since the preservation of peace had been traditionally the responsibility of kings, it was an essentially new development when the Church, through its bishops, began to offer protection for churches, clerics, peaceable persons (especially the poor), and their possessions. The Church began to discipline, even to excommunicate, disturbers of the peace. By extending the privilege of clerical inviolability to lay people, the Church attracted support for this movement. For much of the eleventh century, masses rallied for the cause of peace at periodic church councils throughout the old

---

* By the twelfth century, purgatory had become a more clearly delineated aspect of the afterlife. It was a place of expiation, separate from hell but usually somewhat hellish, where a person could, through active penance, work toward entrance into paradise.

Carolingian territories in what can only be described as a widespread religious movement.

By the mid-eleventh century, the Church promoted a more institutionalized form of this peace called the Truce of God. Certain time periods, e.g. Wednesday to Monday, were set aside for peace between all Christians. By 1054 in Narbonne, a council of clerics and laity (both noblemen and commoners) met to confirm both Truce and Peace, concluding that "no Christian shall kill another Christian, for whoever kills a Christian undoubtedly sheds the blood of Christ."[3] After Narbonne, the peace movement lost some of its popularity, although there were revivals in the early twelfth century.

The ideals of the Peace and Truce of God movements extended to new ideas of religious sanctuary, including the protection of merchants and peasants selling goods in the immediate area surrounding a church. Many traditional markets in France still today are located on sites in the vicinity of a cathedral or parish church where arrests for debt or seizures of one's person were forbidden. The spread of new priories along the routes towards Compostela also led to the creation of villages described as *salvamenta* or *sauvetés* laid out near those churches and protected as spiritual sanctuaries. These new villages were part of the expansion into previously uninhabited areas of western Europe already discussed in Chapter 9.

These peace movements embodied many of the central concerns of the eleventh century—the importance of relics, the growth of ecclesiastical authority, the focus on armed soldiers (as violators of the peace or, alternatively, as enforcers of the peace), and the involvement of the masses. In particular, they may have opened men's eyes to the potential for harnessing public opinion to the Church's goals of reform and, by the end of the eleventh century, the Crusades. When Pope Urban II called for a crusade in 1095, he did so in the context of a renewal of the Peace of God.

Hermits and Anchorites

The eleventh century also witnessed the growth of eremitism, which is the desire of individuals to live apart from society as hermits. Becoming a hermit had been a religious option in the East since the third century and in the West since about the sixth century (see Chapter 5). These men and women possibly wanted a more contemplative, more studious, less materialistic, unmarried, or more isolated existence; and perhaps they did not have the resources to enter a monastery. Between the sixth and the eleventh centuries, such hermits were few. This changed dramatically in the eleventh century, at which time contemporaries felt they were being overrun by recluses. Numerous men and women sought poverty, prayer, and ascetic simplicity and, according to their own testimony, rejected a society of increasing wealth, worldliness, and busyness. Their values derived from scripture, early Christian literature, and the earliest monastic rules. Some historians have seen these pious individuals as revolutionary in their rejection of wealth, family, and social ties, opening up new possibilities for relationships between men and women and between the human and divine.

A cleric named Rainaud (d. 1104?) described his reasons for becoming a hermit in a letter to Bishop Ivo of Chartres:

When you mentioned the model of the primitive church to which, as you truly say, I wish to cleave, I rejoiced and with all my heart I thank you for your watchful attention, but good father, as scripture testifies and as I have learnt from your own teaching, the model of the primitive church is no more nor less than the life of the apostles and the disciples shaped by gospel teaching; the life of those to whom it is said "if any man will take away thy coat, let him have thy cloak also", . . . this manner of perfection can, by your own testimony rarely or ever be kept within monasteries and this I reckon is because the poverty which the poor Christ preached is kept out of them as far as possible.[4]

This conscious imitation of the *vita apostolica* (the life thought to have been led by Christ's apostles) suggests that many recluses had access to the written word, if not directly then through hearing preachers or talking with those who could read.

Theoretically, anyone could become a hermit, but practically speaking the movement attracted the wealthy and not the poor, who were already leading lives of deprivation. Despite their radical change in lifestyle, these hermits were not always intent on leading a solitary life of strict seclusion. They often brought companions with them into the wilderness and organized communities. These communities, however, shunned the ornate building style and corporate wealth of many monasteries, the monastic preoccupation with the liturgy, and its tendency toward immersion in daily cares and property concerns. Hermits engaged in manual labor, charitable acts, and prayer, sometimes maintaining a simple liturgy.

The two most prominent communities of hermits were in Italy: Camaldoli, that was mother-house to an eremitical order, and Vallombrosa, a hermitage that eventually became a monastery, notable for its isolation and the severity of its discipline. Peter Damian (1007–1072), one of the great Italian reformers of the eleventh century, joined another group of recluses at Fonte Avellana in the Apennines, where he became a propagandist for a particularly severe life of fasting, solitude, and self-flagellation.

The role of women in hermitages was a problem, whether their numbers were small (as in Italy) or larger (north of the Alps). Were they to govern themselves or be governed by men? How much could the sexes mix? How cloistered were the women to be? At first a popular solution was double houses, one for the men and another for the women. Over time, however, communities of female hermits became more cloistered, and increasingly separated from the men while at the same time more controlled by them. One eremitical order that attracted both men and women and did conform to this pattern was Fontevrault in northern France, established about the year 1100 by Robert of Arbrissel, a hermit-preacher from Brittany. Placing the women in one community, he appointed a prioress as head and established an adjunct community of monks to provide material and sacramental support. This double monastery was governed by a woman, and had its own order of dependent priories.

For some women, the greatest freedom rested in seeking solitary confinement as anchorites—living virtually entombed in cells attached to churches, monasteries, city walls, even old gates. Both men and women became anchorites, but female anchorites (called anchoresses) were more common by the twelfth century. Locked in for life, they differed from hermits in that they took vows of permanent stability (they could not travel or change their location). They were immured (imprisoned within walls, usually with only a small window to the outside world) by a bishop who performed the Office of the Dead, proclaiming a kind of symbolic "death." Anchorites needed community support—alms, food and clothing—to survive. They returned value to their community by acting as counselors, sometimes as schoolteachers, and as a channel to God for the community. One of the better known anchoresses is Christina of Markyate (1096/98–1160), born in England to a prominent Anglo-Saxon family. The eremitical movement of which Christina became a part seems to have been popular among Anglo-Saxons in the wake of the Norman conquest. In Christina's case, her family refused to honor an early vow of virginity she had made and tried to force her into marriage. Christina sought freedom by hiding for four years in the cramped closet of a hermit's cell. Eventually her family broke off the betrothal, and she was able to live out her life enclosed.

Cluniac Expansion

Expressions of religious fervor (pilgrimages, peace movements, and retreats into hermitages or anchoritic cells) occurred alongside an expansion and renewal of monasticism. Although several monastic reform movements occurred prior to the year 1000 (Chapter 10), it was the growth of Cluniac monasticism that dominated the eleventh century. Cluny grew in wealth, numbers, and influence under the leadership of Abbot Hugh (d. 1109), who ruled for sixty years. Hugh had an exalted idea of his spiritual responsibilities for all Christians, not just for the monks of Cluny. He willingly and diplomatically mediated between popes and secular rulers. Contemporaries described him as a model of piety and wisdom and a powerful orator and administrator; they also believed he had a gift for reading the minds of others.

Under Hugh, Cluny built the largest church in Europe, not to be surpassed until St. Peter's was rebuilt in Rome in the sixteenth century. The community of monks at Cluny rose to over 300 in number, while the number of houses adopting Cluniac or related customs grew rapidly, from approximately 160 to possibly as many as 2,000. At the end of his life, Hugh wrote that Cluny had established communities "not only in this region, but also in Italy, Lorraine, England, Normandy, France, Aquitaine, Gascony, Provence and Spain" (see Map 11.2).[5]

Cluniac monasteries were not isolated from society. They formed bonds with local landowners and rulers through gifts, necrologies (lists of names of the dead for whom they prayed), confraternities, and patronage networks. They promoted peace movements and lobbied for justice under God's laws. Popes and councils extended to Cluny the ancient privilege of sanctuary, which allowed anyone fleeing authority to seek safety there. And perhaps as many as 100 Cluniac monks became bishops during the eleventh century, where they became involved in promoting reform among the clergy.

Cluny, while reaching out to society in some ways, also sought to keep itself separate. Its initial foundation charter had specified independence from outside control (Chapter 10). Although such independence was not unusual in the tenth

The Third Abbey Church of Cluny   The third and largest abbey church of Cluny was consecrated in 1095 by Pope Urban II and largely completed by 1130. It is built in the Romanesque style and was the largest church in western Europe prior to the building of St. Peters in Rome in the sixteenth century. Twelve hundred monks could process inside the building. Much of the church was destroyed following the French Revolution. This drawing is of a reconstructed model done in 1855. *Caisse Nationale des Monuments Historiques et des Sites.*

century, Cluny became unique when its exemptions were confirmed and broadened by secular rulers and also by the papacy in the tenth and eleventh centuries until Cluny was truly "free from all domination."

In 1055, Abbot Hugh convinced his brother, Geoffrey II of Semur, to found a Cluniac nunnery, since, Hugh noted, there was at that time no suitable place for highborn women to retire to lead a religious life. It was established at Marcigny by 1063 for ninety-nine nuns. Hugh and his brother appointed their sister Ermengarde as prioress. Hugh intended Marcigny as a refuge for his own mother, for wives and female relatives of other monks, and for noblewomen whose husbands had been killed or who had been repudiated by their husbands; it soon attracted a great many female relatives of nobles, royalty, and high church officials. Contemporaries were amazed at Marcigny's severe standards. Some of the nuns enclosed themselves in cells like anchoresses, and all wore thick veils symbolic of their death to the world and their preparation for burial and resurrection. Such strictness set a new standard for nuns.

As the prestige of Cluny grew, an alliance developed between the papacy and Cluny. In a remarkable eulogy of Cluny in 1080, Pope Gregory VII referred to the

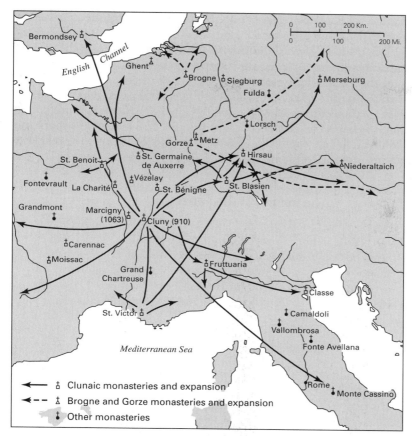

Map 11.2 **Expansion of Cluny and Other Reforming Monasteries, c. 950–1100**
The most important monastic reform movement in the tenth and eleventh centuries
was that of Cluny, but it was not the only one. Gorze and Brogne spread their styles
of monastic reform in the Low Countries and in Germany, and individual monasteries, such as Fontevrault and Grandmont, were also famous reform centers.

excellence of Cluny in terms of its spiritual fervor, its service to God, and the saintliness of its abbots. He knew of no monastery on earth that was its equal, and he
guaranteed its full immunity and liberty from all commotion or attack.[6] Gregory's
praise of Cluny was based partly upon his belief that Cluny, having been placed under the special protection of Saints Peter and Paul, was especially beholden to the
papacy more than all other monasteries.

PAPAL REFORM AND MONASTIC RENEWAL

Cluny provided a model of reform for the papacy. The "eleventh-century papal reform" or "Gregorian Reform" are neat labels for a movement that was never very

organized and was not only Pope Gregory's doing; but it had a profound impact on Europe. It began with an initiative of the Emperor Henry III (1039–1056). Very quickly, however, a group of clerical reformers took the lead, asserting the superiority of ecclesiastical authority over secular rulers. They also responded to growing hostilities toward the long-standing custom of clerical marriage, growing concern with abuses surrounding the sale of ecclesiastical offices, and a desire to reverse the negative papal image then current. As the papacy worked to reform itself and to extricate the Church from the authority of kings, princes, and local lords, monastic reforms also proliferated. These reform movements succeeded because the religious impulses of the time supported them.

The Reform of the Papacy

In 1046, Emperor-elect Henry III attended a papal synod at Sutri on his way to be crowned in Rome. Perhaps hoping to be crowned by unsullied papal hands, he presided over the deposition and resignation, respectively, of Popes Sylvester III (1045) and Gregory VI (1045–1046), both of whom allegedly bought their offices and had been thrust into power by feuding Roman noble families. Days later, in Rome, Henry deposed Benedict IX (1032–1044, 1045), a scandalously immoral pope who had been elevated to the throne by his father's faction.* Henry then received the rank of patrician, which gave him the right to involve himself in papal elections. Henry, a ruler who used his power to push reform, nominated several German popes, the most important of whom was Leo IX (1049–1054). Although some reforming actions preceded Leo, the effective beginning of a renewed papacy can be traced to Leo and his entourage.

Leo surrounded himself with reforming activists, including northern Europeans (most notably the monk Humbert of Silva Candida, soon to be a cardinal†), Peter Damian a monk from northern Italy, and Hildebrand, also an Italian monk who had been in northern exile and was to become pope. They all agreed on the need for moral reform of the clergy, the enhancement of papal primacy, and the importance of rooting out simony—that is, the buying or selling of offices and sacraments of the Church.

Among Leo's first acts were orders for the Roman clergy to separate from their wives (who were then made slaves in the papal palace) and for prostitutes in Rome to be placed in convents. Besides setting a new moral tone, Leo's program included reviving and centralizing the papal bureaucracy. One result was an enhanced secretarial office (the chancery) that produced significantly more letters and documents, particularly under Hildebrand when he became Pope Gregory VII. Under Leo, Hildebrand became financial administrator for the papal patrimony (the land and dues, mostly in central Italy, held directly by the papacy). Papal decretals (papal decrees regarding church doctrine or law) and papal legates (representatives who

---

* Benedict had refused to recognize the election of Sylvester III and had abdicated in favor of Gregory VI but had never been formally deposed.

† Cardinals were the bishops, priests, and deacons of the churches of Rome. Consequent to the reform of the papacy, they were to have greatly added importance in the governing of the papacy.

could act in the papal name) became instruments of reform. Hildebrand, for example, was sent to France as legate to investigate a controversy regarding the status of Christ's body and blood in the bread and wine of the Eucharist.

Leo traveled north to promote reform, most notably at Reims in northern France in 1049. There, in the presence of the relics of St. Remi at the high altar, Leo publicly invalidated the ordinations of every prelate present who had purchased his office. The synod at Reims also prohibited ecclesiastical appointment without election by clergy and people and condemned clerical marriages. The papacy of Leo IX took on more imperial overtones, as papal propagandists appealed to the authority of the forged Donation of Constantine (see Chapter 5) to support a concept of the apostolic see as an "earthly and heavenly empire." Peter Damian called for a compilation of canon law concerning the authority of the Holy See. Cardinal Humbert used papal decrees, papal letters, and the decisions of church councils to assert papal claims in southern Italy and papal primacy over the patriarch in Constantinople. He delivered a papal excommunication of the patriarch in 1054 that climaxed a schism between the Greek and Roman churches that has lasted until today.

Perhaps the most significant reform initiated by Leo and developed by subsequent popes was to integrate the cardinals into the papal administration. Under Pope Nicholas II, in 1059, a papal election decree made the cardinal bishops the primary electors of the pope. This took the appointment of the pope out of the hands of the Roman nobility and diminished the possibility of popes designating successors on their deathbed, although it still allowed for approval by the German emperor. In the following decades the cardinals grew to become the principal papal advisors and heads of the papal administration. By the mid-twelfth century, they were formally instituted into the College of Cardinals.

Pope Gregory VII (1073–1086)

In 1073, Hildebrand, one of the leading reformers, was elected pope by a tumultuous gathering of clerks and with the "acclamation of very many crowds of both sexes and various orders." Although his election was not in accord with the 1059 decree, he assumed the papal mantle and the title of Pope Gregory VII. Gregory was born in Tuscany in humble circumstances but brought up in Rome. His family married into one of the new urban aristocratic families whose money came from banking and whose policies opposed those of the older noble Roman families. He was therefore something of an upstart, socially. Gregory was a monk, raised at St. Mary's on the Aventine in Rome, but not a Cluniac. He had few social or political obligations except to the papacy, where he had served all his adult life and to which he was passionately committed.

Gregory brought to the papacy a forceful and charismatic personality, but one that was tinged with fanaticism and militancy. Peter Damian called him "Holy Satan" and compared him to a tiger tensed to leap,[7] while Hugh of Cluny secretly wondered about his ambitiousness. Gregory vigorously pursued the goals of clerical celibacy, an end to simony, and the exaltation of the papacy in both the spiritual and temporal spheres.

The idea that priests should abstain from sexual intercourse derives from at least the fourth century, although, if married, they were not forced to leave their wives;

celibacy was required of those in major clerical orders (the orders of priest, deacon, subdeacon). But these requirements were rarely enforced. In the tenth century some bishops were married, while marriage among lower-ranked clergy and ecclesiastical administrators was common. English literature from the eleventh century continues to refer to the priest's wife, and Milanese clergy, who were attacked as fornicators by reformers, defended their marriages sometimes in street fights. The Scandinavians, only recently converted to Christianity, petitioned Gregory VII for exemption from clerical celibacy. At the end of the eleventh century, synods in Hungary asked only that bishops and priests live in moderation with their wives. Treatises defending married clergy began to appear.

The reformers had to move slowly to eradicate clerical marriage. In the archbishopric of Mainz in 1074, "it required no small effort to uproot a custom [clerical marriage] that had been implanted over so long a period, and to reform an aging world according to the principles of the early church."[8] The archbishop of Mainz, attempting to enforce celibacy, found his life threatened. In 1081 the Emperor Henry IV was able to rally the bishops of Germany around him against the pope in part because they were under pressure from their clergy to defend the legitimacy of their marriages.

The reformers, following a long tradition of concern over this issue, wanted to prohibit clerical marriage. This would prevent ecclesiastical property being passed from father to son. They also argued that family responsibilities were not consistent with the dedication of a man to God, and that virginity (or at least celibacy) was superior to the married state in God's eyes. They especially promoted the purity of the priesthood, particularly the need for ritual purity during Communion. One historian has suggested that, "It was from the first a question of hands; hands that perform a sacramental function must be chaste."[9] It is no coincidence that the attack on clerical marriage occurred alongside a growing emphasis upon the real presence of Christ in the mass. Implicit, and sometimes explicit, in the stress on purity was the view that women were impure. The vituperative labeling of women as whores or worse, degraded women in general but particularly the wives of clergy, who were threatened with loss of family and of sustenance and even with enslavement. Some of the strongest language comes from Peter Damian:

> I speak to you, o charmers of the clergy, appetizing flesh of the devil, that castaway from paradise, you, poison of the minds, death of souls, venom of wine and of eating, companions of the very stuff of sin, the cause of our ruin. You, I say, I exhort you women of the ancient enemy, you bitches, sows, screech-owls, night-owls, she-wolves, blood-suckers, . . . Come now, hear me, harlots, prostitutes, with your lascivious kisses, you wallowing places for fat pigs, souches for unclean spirits, demi-goddesses, sirens, witches, devotees of Diana, if any portents, if any omens are found thus far, they should be judged sufficient to your name. For you are the victims of demons, destined to be cut off by eternal death. From you the devil is fattened by the abundance of your lust, is fed by your alluring feasts.[10]

It is probable that wives and families of married clergy, as well as the clergy themselves, swelled the ranks of hermits in the late eleventh and twelfth century and helped popularize double monasteries where whole families might retire.

The move to abolish clerical marriages was perhaps the most successful initiative of the reform. Nonetheless, as late as 1110 a penitential manual of Burchard of Worms decreed that "those who despised mass and communion with married priests are all to do penance," while there were still married clergy in early thirteenth-century England (and in Spain, Scandinavia, and Poland even later). Still, by the year 1200 it was less common to find married clergy, and ecclesiastical legislation inveighed against concubines instead.

Another of Gregory's goals was an all-out attack on simony. While some reformers argued that simony invalidated an ordination or an office and others argued that it did not, all were agreed that it was an abuse. Gregory's approach was a harsh one, directed at church leaders. In 1073, he excommunicated Godfrey, archbishop of Milan, who was accused of simony. In a letter to papal supporters in Milan, Gregory wrote: "As you well know . . . Godfrey had the audacity to purchase, like any vile wench, that church which once . . . shone forth among the churches of Lombardy . . . that is to say, he prostituted the bride of Christ to the Devil and befouled her with the criminal heresy of Simony."[11]

Eleventh-century writers debated Gregory's definition of simony as heresy . Was an individual who had acquired an ecclesiastical office through purchase or through favors a heretic? Ultimately the church's answer to this question would be no,* but for Gregory, the answer was yes, since those who failed to follow God's will were disobedient, and disobedience, for Gregory, was heretical. In 1102, at a church council in Rome, Pope Paschal II (1099–1118) carried Gregory's ideas forward when he also declared disobedience heretical.

A derivative of the concern with simony was lay investiture, in which the king or emperor would present the symbols of sacred power (the staff and ring) to the clergy-elect. The ruler would then say "Receive the Church" and in return receive homage from the prelate for the properties belonging to the see or abbey. This symbolic exchange represented real control by secular rulers over ecclesiastical appointments; it often included simony, and it undercut obedience to the church by insisting on loyalty to the emperor, king, or prince.

In the past, historians have labeled the eleventh-century church reform movement "the investiture controversy," a misleading title because the reform focused on many issues, of which investiture was only, somewhat belatedly, one of them. In 1058, Cardinal Humbert's *Three Books against Simoniacs* had inveighed against the lay disposition of churches, but it was not until Gregory VII's papacy that lay investiture became an active issue. And Gregory's struggle was not simply about investiture. It was a struggle over control between Church and Empire. According to one historian, Gregory wished "to snatch [the Church] from servile oppression, or rather tyrannical slavery, and restore her to her ancient freedom."[12] Control of the priesthood by the secular power, especially the German emperor, limited ecclesiastical freedom and contributed to the abuse of simony. Thus, the attack on lay investiture was part of an overall effort to strengthen ecclesiastical authority by wresting clerical appointments from the hands of lay rulers, an effort that had begun with the campaign against simony and reform of papal elections.

---

* Heresy is defined by canon law as views that are "contrary to holy scripture, publicly avowed and obstinately defended." This normally applies to doctrine rather than practice.

The lay ruler, however, had good reasons for wanting control. Churchmen, who were literate, handled many administrative tasks for rulers. They controlled land and knights' services that were crucial to the functioning of government and the success of military campaigns; it seems obvious that a ruler, and especially the emperor, would want to handpick such men. The incident that provoked the struggle was the imperial appointment of the archbishop of Milan.

Milan had a tradition as an imperial stronghold, but the papal reform program was making inroads. By 1075, the situation was explosive. The city had passed into the hands of a commune led by a religiously and politically militant group called the Patarenes. Henry IV (king of Germany and next emperor) insisted on naming his candidate to the archbishopric of Milan. Gregory responded by excommunicating Henry and supporting the Patarenes—two very dramatic moves. For a year pope and king fought. Gregory had an advantage since all Christians courted excommunication by being in contact with an excommunicated ruler. In the end, Gregory prepared to travel to Germany to oversee Henry's deposition from the throne. At that moment Henry seized the initiative. He crossed the Alps in the dead of winter with his wife and child and found Gregory snowbound at the castle of Canossa in January 1077. As Gregory described it, "for three days he [Henry] remained before the castle gate, without any royal ornament, pitiful in appearance, barefoot and clad in woolen garments, and he continued tearfully to beg for apostolic help and consolation." Gregory, who was accompanied by two of his strongest supporters, Abbot Hugh of Cluny and Countess Matilda of Tuscany, had to decide. As priest and pope, he was being asked to show mercy. As politician he was being asked to give up a diplomatic ace in the sleeve. Lifting the excommunication jeopardized the deposition. In the end, Gregory yielded to his priestly role. "Overcome at last by the earnestness of his penitence and by the prayers of all who were present, we released him from the bonds of excommunication and received him . . . into the bosom of holy mother Church."[13]

Gregory never again regained the political advantage, although the example of the German king kneeling before the pope diminished the sacral role of kingship and reinforced a papal prerogative to judge princes. The issue of lay investiture remained to be solved in the twelfth century. At the Concordat of Worms, in 1122, then Emperor Henry V renounced lay investiture, but the papacy agreed that the election of prelates could take place in the emperor's presence, that he could settle disputed elections and grant the *regalia*. This continued to give the ruler a decisive role.

Gregory, more than any previous pope, exalted the papacy over all other authority. He insisted on controlling and disciplining bishops and abbots through letters, legates, and excommunications. He was willing to appeal to monks and laity in order to bring the higher clergy to heel. This technique, in addition to Gregory's willingness to listen to appeals from lower courts and to demand that church officials attend him in Rome, led a Synod of Worms in 1076 to charge that Gregory had "robbed the bishops of every power" and turned over "the control of ecclesiastical affairs to the ravening frenzy of the mob."[14]

Gregory divided society into two orders: clergy and laity. His efforts to purify the clergy and separate them from lay influence stemmed from his belief in the

King Henry IV at Canossa, 1077   This image shows King Henry IV of Germany kneeling in supplication to Matilda, countess of Tuscany who was a staunch ally of Pope Gregory VII. Henry is also appealing to Abbot Hugh of Cluny, who appears to be lecturing Henry. This image, from a Life of Matilda at the Vatican, suggests the subordinate relationship of royal power to the Church and to a countess who was a reformer and papal supporter. *Christel Gerstenberg/Corbis.*

superiority of the spiritual realm, for "if you [the Pope] can judge the angels who guide all haughty princes, what can you [not] do to their servants? Now let kings and all princes of the earth learn how great is your power, and let them fear to neglect the commands of your Church."[15] Gregory's superior attitude toward the rulers of Europe denied traditional beliefs in the divine power of kings and emperors. In his *Dictatus Papae* Gregory claimed the authority to depose secular rulers (See Medieval Voices). As part of his apostolic power of loosening and binding in heaven and on earth, Gregory absolved Henry IV's subjects of any loyalty to their king. In excommunicating Henry IV, Gregory tried to deprive him of his office while at the same time denying him spiritual benefits. One of his justifications for this action derived from the historical example of St. Ambrose, as bishop of Milan, excommunicating the emperor Theodosius (Chapter 2). In marked contrast to the late Roman view of the emperor, however, Gregory considered the emperor to be below the rank of even the lowliest member of the clergy. He wrote:

> Who does not know that kings and princes derive their origin from men ignorant of God who raised themselves above their fellows by pride, plunder, treachery, murder—in short, by every kind of crime—at the instigation of the Devil, . . . Does anyone [therefore] doubt that the priests of Christ are to be considered as fathers and masters of kings and princes and of all believers? What king or emperor has the power through his office to snatch any Christian from the might of the Devil . . . the lowest exorcist has greater power than the highest emperor."[16]

Just as the Church had been subject to domination by the laity, so Gregory, by reversing the relationship of lay and clerical authority, now claimed lordship over

MEDIEVAL VOICES

Two Papal Statements Regarding the Relationship Between Pope and Emperor

The most systematic exposition of Gregory VII's program comes from a series of headings, called the Dictatus Papae, *bound into a selected collection of his papal letters. They may have been titles for canons (ecclesiastical laws or rules) that were not legally promulgated or fully developed at the time. Included here are those titles that touch on the relationship between imperial and ecclesiastical authority. They make it clear that Gregory envisioned an imperial and universal papacy that was superior to all worldly authority.*

#1   That the Roman Church was founded by God alone.

#2   That the Roman Pontiff alone is rightly to be called universal.

#8   That he [the Pope] alone may use the imperial insignia.

#9   That the Pope is the only one whose feet are to be kissed by all princes.

#10   That his [the Pope's] name alone is to be recited in churches.

#11   That his [the Pope's] title is unique in the world.

#12   That he [the Pope] may depose Emperors.

#27   That the Pope may absolve subjects of unjust men from their fealty.

A far more influential collection of canons, cited subsequently by canon lawyers to a far greater degree than Gregory's pronouncements and therefore perhaps more indicative of the actual course of ecclesiastical reform, are the *Seventy-Four Titles*. Focusing much more on reform within the Church, this collection includes the following excerpt on imperial authority from a letter written by Pope Gelasius I (492–496) to the Byzantine Emperor Anastasius I (491–519). This famous exposition of the relations between papal and royal power, while placing the Church above the emperor in the spiritual sphere, nonetheless preserves royal authority within its own sphere:

There are two powers by which this world is chiefly ruled, august emperor: the sacred authority of the pontiffs and the royal power. And of these the responsibility of priests is weightier in so far as they will answer for the kings of men themselves at the divine judgment. So, most clement son, you know that, even though you surpass the human race in dignity, nevertheless you piously bow your head to those who have charge of divine affairs and seek from them the means of your salvation, and thus you realize that, in the order of religion, you ought to submit yourself to them rather than rule, and that in these matters you should depend on their judgment rather than seek to have them bend to your will.

Source: Brian Tierney, ed. *The Crisis of Church & State 1050–1300* (New York: Prentice-Hall, 1964) 49–50; John Gilchrist, *The Collection in Seventy-Four Titles: A Canon Law Manual of the Gregorian Reform* (Toronto: Pontifical Institute of Mediaeval Studies, 1980) 199–200.

southern Italy, the islands of Sardinia and Corsica, Provence, Denmark, Saxony, Kievan Rus, much of eastern Europe, parts of Spain, and England. He also expected loyalty from other European rulers such as Godfrey of Lorraine, Welf of Bavaria, William of Burgundy, and Matilda of Tuscany.

In 1080, Gregory VII excommunicated Henry IV for the second time, after Henry repeatedly failed to implement papal policy in Germany. Henry responded by appointing, with the support of the German clergy, an antipope at Ravenna and then marching on Rome. In 1084, the German army virtually imprisoned Gregory. On Easter day, 1084, Henry IV received the imperial crown from the hand of the antipope. Shortly thereafter Gregory was rescued by the Normans who proceeded to ransack Rome. Gregory was no longer safe in his own city. He died at Salerno in 1085, reported as saying: "I have loved righteousness and hated iniquity, therefore I die in exile."[17] Although Gregory may have died defeated, the reform movement carried on into the twelfth century along lines he had delineated.

The relationship between papal reform and eleventh-century monasticism has been much debated by historians. Gregory VII rose from monastic orders to become pope at a time when this was not the norm. He once confided to Hugh of Cluny that he did not trust either bishops or secular rulers to assist the papacy in reforming the Church. He relied instead on monks. We have already seen that a special relationship evolved between the papacy and Cluny. The popes routinely placed monasteries under Cluny's care. Cluny included prayers for the pope in its masses, and Gregory VII was always careful to request those prayers. Cluniac monks began to fill positions in the papal curia and in episcopal sees. Gregory often used Abbot Hugh as papal legate and appears to have consulted him on ways to convert Muslims. He worked with Hugh to organize French knights to fight in Spain. Cluniac monasteries and bishops supported pilgrimages to Compostela and became involved in the papal effort to replace Hispanic Christian rites with Roman rites. Eventually several Cluniac monks became popes, including Urban II (1088–1099), who proclaimed the first crusade. But it is possible that Cluny's greatest significance for the Gregorian reform was the model it provided of liberty from outside interference, a founding principle for the papal reform.

Reformed Religious Orders

Despite the growth of monasticism, of which Cluny is the most prominent example, criticism of monasteries had begun to mount. Contemporaries noted that monasteries amassed lands and churches, involved themselves in lawsuits, and took on responsibilities as overlords. Abbots were often wealthy, lived separately from the other monks, and were sometimes guilty of simony. It had become common practice for monks (or their families) to pave the way into a monastery with a gift of land or some other benefit to the brethren. Cluny's expansion, in particular, was accompanied by some abuses. Recruitment became more indiscriminate. In 1060, it was decreed that Cluny could admit excommunicated monks, while many novices (monks in training) were admitted too quickly, with insufficient training. Contemporaries and church councils criticized Cluny for relaxing rules with regard to fasting and clothing and for demanding little reading and almost no manual labor. Peter Damian noted, in a visit to Cluny in 1063, that the monks spent so much time in choir that they had less than one-half hour for other activities. Descriptions of the Cluniac liturgy give the impression of a liturgical marathon. Contemporaries commented on Cluny's elaborate ceremonies, rich buildings, and wealth, some of which came from a princely annual gift of 2,000 gold dinars from King Alfonso VI of León-Castile (1072–1109).

Many time-honored practices of Benedictine monasticism also came under attack. One of these was child oblation, whereby a child was given to a monastery, educated there, often trained to sing in the choir, and expected to become a monk or nun (Chapter 5). This deeply rooted custom offered an avenue for wealthier families to place surplus children—girls for whom a suitable marriage was not possible or boys who could not be supported from family estates. The fact that these children might be placed against their will, possibly unable to leave as adults, seems abusive to the modern mind. But it was more humane than child abandonment, and it reflects a society where family strategies were a more important value than individual choice and where children were trained to accept parental choices. Hildegard of Bingen (1098–1179), abbess, mystic, and preacher, was the tenth child of a noble family that placed her in an anchoress cell at a monastery at age eight "as a tithe." Children might be given to monasteries to be cared for in order to facilitate parents' spiritual vocations, if one or both decided to enter a religious house, become a hermit, live a life of poverty, or go on pilgrimage. Children were also given to monasteries as a kind of spiritual insurance; the family hoped to reap the reward of prayers and intercessions. And children might be placed in monasteries because it was evident, early on, that they had educational potential or spiritual leanings.

Despite these reasons, more and more individuals began to see child oblation as an abuse. Hildegard of Bingen warned that offering a child to a monastery before he or she had reached the age of reason was a form of bondage. Ulrich, a monk at Cluny in the second half of the eleventh century, complained that parents "after they have a houseful, . . . of sons and daughters, or if they have any who are lame or crippled, deaf and dumb or blind, hump-backed or leprous, or who have any defect which would make them less desirable in the secular world, they (the parents) offer them as monks . . . so that they themselves are spared having to educate and support them."[18] Monasteries gradually limited the number of oblates, and canon law began to discourage parents from committing their children. Whereas at the beginning of the eleventh century, close to 200 oblates resided at Cluny, by the end of the twelfth century child oblation had nearly disappeared there. This became possible partly because the religious revival combined with population growth produced more adults entering the monastic life, thus lessening dependence on child oblation for replenishing members of a monastery.

The first to refuse admittance to children were the reformed monastic orders that grew out of the eremitical movement. One of the earliest was Vallombrosa, near Florence, in Italy. The founder, John Gualbert of Florence, was looking for an eremitical-style retreat, although he wanted it within the context of a religious community governed by the Benedictine rule. The land, buildings (simple huts and a hospice), books, and other necessities were given and governed by the abbess of San Ellero about 1038. As the fame of its austerities grew (strict silence and isolation, no churches or altars, extreme poverty and fasting), Vallombrosa gained independence (1055) and other reformed monasteries attached themselves to it, eventually producing a centralized, uniform, reformed order.

North of the Alps, Stephen of Muret (c. 1045–1124) established a reformed monastery, later located at Grandmont in Limoges, which by 1170, had sixty houses under its jurisdiction—all devoted to a life of continuous prayer based on the gospel. The men who entered rarely left, not even to visit family, preach, or minister; nor could they receive land. Their commitment to poverty and seclusion was severe. Similarly, Bruno of Cologne (c. 1030–1101) settled in a remote corner of France near Grenoble (Grande Chartreuse), leading to the establishment of the Carthusian order of hermit-monks. Devoted to following the poor Christ, they lived in separate cells, observed silence, prayed, read, and did manual labor. The Carthusians eventually spread throughout Europe, retaining their simplicity and popularity into modern times. Carthusians became particularly well known for their love of books, libraries of vernacular texts, and tradition of copying manuscripts.

The most famous order of reformed Benedictine monks was based at Cîteaux in Burgundy. The founder of Cîteaux was Robert of Molesme who, in 1075, led a group of hermits to found the reformed monastery of Molesme in Burgundy. By 1098, its fame had attracted donations of land and churches, serfs, revenues, and whole villages, as well as prestigious recruits and forty dependent monasteries. The resulting tension between Robert's desire to maintain a simple, disciplined, and humble life and the now abundantly gifted and more complex life at Molesme was too severe, and Robert, with companions, seceded to form a stricter community at Cîteaux.

Cîteaux was intended to be a new kind of monastery. The Cistercians (as these monks, dressed in white, are called) described themselves as "new soldiers of Christ" and "poor men with Christ the pauper." Austere and situated far from urban centers, life was difficult at Cîteaux and apparently not very attractive. This changed in 1112 when Bernard of Fontaine, son of a Burgundian aristocratic family, joined the order with an entourage of followers and relatives (see Medieval Portrait). Following this remarkable, large-scale conversion, and perhaps due in part to it, colonies of Cistercian monasteries for both men and women were founded rapidly all over Europe (see Map 11.3). Bernard became abbot of one of these colonies, Clairvaux, which itself attached or founded at least sixty-eight other monasteries.

Cîteaux, while claiming restoration of primitive Benedictine customs, was an original and compelling new order. Cistercians denied themselves everything but the most simple buildings, dress, and food; they refused to accept tithes or rents and, at first, rejected books. They wore undyed wool, built simply and founded their monasteries in underpopulated but usually beautiful and ultimately economically rich areas. They were committed to humble pursuits, rejecting the liberal arts and attempting to avoid acting as lords of peasants. Love and labor, not logic or lordship, became their focus. Their commitment to manual labor and admittance of large numbers of lay brethren (usually artisans and peasants) as workers enabled them to turn wastes into vineyards and sheep pastures, while, at the same time, assuring salvation to the illiterate. Over time, the Cistercians became great

MEDIEVAL PORTRAITS

Bernard of Clairvaux

Bernard of Clairvaux (1090–1153) joined the monastery of Cîteaux at age twenty-three. A man with extraordinary charisma, he was made abbot of Clairvaux in 1115. He spent the years from 1116 to the 1130s building Clairvaux to its full complement of 700 monks and dozens of dependent monasteries. In 1128, Bernard wrote his treatise, "Praise of the New Militia," in support of the Knights Templar, a religious-military order founded to help crusaders in the Holy Land (see Chapter 12). Bernard was the primary preacher of the Second Crusade in 1147; he was instrumental in galvanizing the French and the Germans and in preventing a recurrence of any massacres of Jews. When the crusade failed, Bernard received much criticism and responded with a searching moral inventory of himself, the crusaders, and the age.

His written works run to 3,500 pages, including 547 letters. He involved himself in nearly every debate of his time. Bernard was an adviser to popes, particularly to Pope Eugenius III (1145–1153) who had been a monk at Clairvaux, and to Kings Louis VI and VII of France and a correspondent with other leaders. Throughout his life he preached against heretics and freely criticized his contemporaries, especially the Cluniacs and even the Pope.

A man whose prose was poetic and whose forceful preaching prompted mothers to hide their sons from him for fear they would be attracted to join him, Bernard suffused his polemics with profound scriptural knowledge and a theology of love. His most famous work, unfinished at his death, is his "Commentary on the Song of Songs."

Although Bernard was invited to become a bishop or archbishop (from which position he might have attained the papacy), he resisted ecclesiastical promotion, remaining a simple monk. By 1175, he had been declared a saint. Bernard's righteous, fervent style was linked with a sense of intense personal struggle and introspection. A mystic and contemplative, he was also an activist. Delicate in health, he was courageous and domineering. An intellectual, grounded in classical literature and the Church fathers, he distrusted reason. He profoundly influenced the twelfth century by promoting his devotion to the Virgin Mary and was to become, in Dante's *Divine Comedy,* the final guide who leads Dante directly to the Virgin at the height of heaven.

entrepreneurs. The medieval equivalent of a multinational corporation, they consolidated and managed estates, harvested quantities of wine, fish, grain, or wool (depending upon local resources), developed mining, dominated markets and, in some cases, controlled retail prices. Their primitive simplicity, systematic and rational organization, and aggressive and ruthless economic exploitation had a paradoxical quality. They lived lives of military harshness, were aggressive and precise in their organization, but they did it all with voices of friendship, introspection, and spiritual sweetness.

Cistercian rigor shunned contact with women, and much of the early narrative evidence ignores women. Despite this, Cistercian monasteries for women were established from the very beginning, and the leading founders, including Bernard of Clairvaux, founded or affiliated themselves closely with houses of nuns. A number of nunneries were incorporated into the Cistercian order by the mid-twelfth

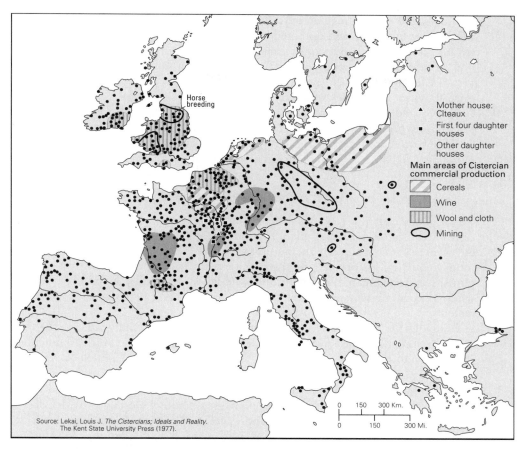

Horse
breeding

Mother house:
Cîteaux

First four daughter
houses

Other daughter
houses

Main areas of Cistercian
commercial production

Cereals

Wine

Wool and cloth

Mining

0   150   300 Km.

0   150   300 Mi.

Source: Lekai, Louis J. *The Cistercians; Ideals and Reality.*
The Kent State University Press (1977).

Map 11.3   Cistercian Expansion, c. 1100–1500   Compared with the Cluniacs (see Map 11.2), the Cistercians expanded their influence further and faster, reaching east into eastern Europe, further north, and into southwest Spain. This map shows the main areas of Cistercian productivity, which was on a large scale; their products were marketed all over Europe. While Cluny often reformed older monasteries with identities independent of Cluny, the Cistercians mostly founded new monasteries and retained greater control over them.

century, and by the thirteenth century the foundation and incorporation of nunneries outpaced any new foundations for monks. By the end of the thirteenth century, the number of women within the Order probably equaled that of men, and the number of communities of nuns exceeded those of monks.

The canons regular were another sort of reformed clergy. They emerged as part of the Gregorian effort to separate church from secular society and clergy from their wives, and they proliferated in the twelfth century. The canons regular were a hybrid order, something between a monastery of monks in clerical orders and clergy living communally. They renounced private property, adhered to celibacy, and either served in cathedral or collegiate churches or performed other, socially engaged activities (running hospitals or schools). While Cistercians were the most organized of orders, the canons regular were the most diffuse and flexible of orders. They adopted an annotated and doctored version of a rule St. Augustine had once written for his sister's religious community.

One community of canons regular was the Premonstratensians, founded by Norbert of Cleves in 1122. Norbert's emphasis was on preaching, conversion, and pastoral activism. The clergy and laity led by Norbert carried his reform spirit into Germany and among Germans in Slavic and Hungarian lands. The Premonstratensians originally welcomed communities of women, by the thousands according to one chronicler, but by about 1140 they began to reverse themselves. Citing moral dangers, the general chapter outlawed the further reception of sisters in 1198.

Women in Religious Orders

The role of women in religious orders in medieval Europe has been, traditionally, subsumed into the history of men. A good example is an eleventh-century necrology written for Marcigny by the nun Elsendis which, until recently, was credited to monks. But the history of communities of women, of great interest on its own terms, has been much restored through the labors of twentieth-century scholars, while the achievements of women religious, often long neglected, have been resurrected.

Religious life held a variety of attractions for women. In convents they had access to literate skills they might have been denied in the secular world. Thus, they could learn to read (and possibly write) Latin. Sometimes they joined convents to be with other family members. Nunneries also provided an alternative to marriage—to the pains of childbirth and the possibility of a dominant husband. They offered freedom from the drudgery of managing a household and provided actual and psychological space for spiritual and devotional growth. Sometimes networks of spiritual women developed, and convents became breeding grounds for mystics, saints, and visionaries. Convents could nurture charitable activities and leadership skills. Nuns cared for the sick and the needy, possibly taking on community roles once performed by priests' wives, and their moral authority allowed them to discipline unruly neighbors and to exert legal power in the community.

Alternatively, women sometimes entered convents because of illness or fear of death or violence; or they were forced into nunneries to free their inheritances or lessen their family's financial burdens. In twelfth-century England, the anarchy under King Stephen (and the danger to women of rape and misuse) contributed to an explosion of houses for women. In 1130, there were twenty houses for women; by 1165, there were more than one hundred. The founders were widows, husbands using their wife's dowry lands, and, less commonly, bishops.

But women religious (nuns) were often at a disadvantage. They were not always welcomed by male monastics. Although the relatively free association of male and female was characteristic of the eleventh-century reform movements, by the mid-twelfth century this changed sharply, and a new tone of misogyny emerges. Men now found the close association with women morally problematic and the expense and time involved in overseeing them burdensome. Women were therefore excluded in some new orders, set at a distance, or suppressed in orders that had originally welcomed them. They were also written out of their histories. This lack of support left women religious dependent upon the bishops, who, increasingly, came to visit and regulate their convents.

Nuns faced more economic difficulties than did the monks. Despite aristocratic exceptions, such as Fontevrault, which was generously endowed by the ducal family of Anjou, many female convents had a hard time making ends meet. They did it by accepting private property (against their vow of poverty), holding schools, accepting entry gifts, or even by sending nuns out to earn money. Because female convents were less numerous, and less wealthy, they tended to remain open mainly to the well-to-do; from those families they received gifts on entry and continued to accept oblates throughout the Middle Ages.

Also, women religious could expect to be more cloistered than the men were. As the effort to enforce celibacy began to be successful, women appeared as sexually dangerous and more in need of enclosure. Also medieval people saw women as dependent (and men as more autonomous) and allowed them fewer options. Despite this, many examples exist of twelfth-century women religious who made an impact on society, such as Hildegard of Bingen (1098–1179).* Hildegard, who came from the German nobility but spent her life in monastic surroundings, was one of the great intellects of the twelfth century and one of the most impressive female writers of her age. A mystic and visionary, she began writing in her forties, in response to what she considered a command from God. With the aid of a secretary, Hildegard produced a large and varied corpus of Latin writings, including works on medicine, cosmology, natural history, and theology—works that are encyclopedic in scope. She was, in addition, an artist-illuminator and a talented and innovative writer of liturgical songs. She produced one of the earliest liturgical dramas in European history. Her works are full of images (both painted and literary) of powerful women (personifications of Wisdom, the Church, the Synagogue, and images of the Virgin) and her theology is suffused with the language of mothering and of virginity. Her writing was done against a backdrop of physical pain (she was bedridden much of her life) and administrative burdens. An individual with a powerful personality and a visionary with prophetic powers, she impressed contemporaries. She corresponded with emperors and popes, struggled successfully for independence for her nuns, and occasionally balked at ecclesiastical authority. Her prestige was such that she could undertake preaching tours, visit and advise monasteries, and reprimand those in authority, including popes and emperors, with impunity.

HERETICAL MOVEMENTS AND THE PERSECUTION OF MINORITIES

Among Hildegard's sermons are several that warn against heretics. The religious ferment of the period was beginning to spill over into heresy. Between the seventh and eleventh centuries, the historical record offers few instances of heresy in the

* Another such leader of nuns was Heloise, whose story is told in Chapter 15.

European Christian West. From about 1010 to 1050, however, heretics began to be noticed in northern Italy (Milan and Ravenna), south of Paris (Orléans and Aquitaine) and further north (Châlons, Goslar, Cambrai, Liège). Some of the heretics were learned individuals; others were illiterate. Some transmitted their heresies to small groups, some to the masses. Based on the sources available, it is difficult to discern how widespread these heresies were or how coherent, but they did sometimes reach popular levels, attracting peasants and artisans. They seem, generally, to have derived from a desire to live an apostolic life; they sometimes manifested extreme hostility to the flesh, and they expressed an awareness of New Testament ideals and the extent to which the Church had strayed from those ideals—a kind of disillusioned apostolic idealism. In some cases the heretics denied the sacraments of matrimony or baptism, or the status of the Holy Trinity.

Ecclesiastical responses were mixed. Some heretics were treated gently by authorities or by the people; others were quickly killed. In one case the heretics were hanged because they refused to kill a chicken. Churchmen tended to describe heretics in terms similar to those used by the Church fathers. Bishop Roger of Châlons (c. 1045) incorrectly labeled the heterodox peasants in his territories as Manichean, a heresy which he knew, from reading St. Augustine, encompassed radical rejections of the material universe, including the human Christ.

By the twelfth century (somewhere between 1120 and 1140), Manichean missionaries did begin to infiltrate the West from Bosnia, Bulgaria, and Byzantium. They were first noticed in Cologne in 1143 but spread rapidly through the Rhineland, into southern France, northern Italy, and the mountains of Spain. They were clearly distinguishable from earlier heretics who mainly wanted a return to New Testament ideals. Claiming to be members of an ancient church, they rejected the Catholic Church altogether, preaching that it (like the world at large and even portions of scripture) was the product of an evil god. Their belief in two gods—an evil and a good god—is called dualism. Manicheans believed that their souls were made up of a spiritual purity and lightness imprisoned in an evil material universe. They sought escape through fasting, celibacy, and even starvation or suicide. Efforts to combat this dualistic heresy (called Catharism from the term "cathari" meaning "pure ones") eventually resulted in the use of inquisitorial methods in the thirteenth century (Chapter 16).

Historians have been intrigued with the reasons for these heresies. Medieval commentators tended to attribute heresy to the devil, thereby making it easier to do violence to heretics. Modern historians have offered more mundane explanations. The same religious impulse that promoted reform produced a more critical stance toward the Church that could easily spill over into heresy. Personal piety and a desire to return to the gospel motivated the earliest recorded instances of heresy in the eleventh century; in that respect the motivations were similar to those of the eremitical movement. Similar to the hermits, these early eleventh-century heretics likewise seem to be drawing from a growing awareness of the New Testament, derived either from their own reading or from preaching based on scripture. Whether directly or indirectly, these heretics testify to a society where texts were increasingly accessible. In the final analysis, however, the heretics were more radical in their rejection of aspects of the Catholic Church and the material world.

And when reform resulted in compromise, as it did on the issue of lay investiture; when simony was not irrevocably wiped out; and when some priests continued to be unchaste, even if unmarried, the ensuing disillusionment sometimes led to heresy. It was probably this disillusionment, as much as any missionary efforts, that produced the dramatic Cathar reaction. As one historian notes, "The more loudly the ideals of the apostolic church were proclaimed, the more vividly its [the Church's] shortcomings were advertised."[19]

Heresy also often emerges when religious authority defines itself, which the medieval Church did, increasingly, between 1050 and 1200. Gregory VII and Cardinal Humbert both argued that married or simoniacal priests were disobedient and therefore heretical. They urged the faithful not to attend their masses. This revolutionary appeal to the laity to judge, boycott, or otherwise attack unreformed clergy, however, encouraged disobedience from below and skirted the edge of the heresy of Donatism (Chapter 2). Thus, new definitions and demands created a situation where heresy and disobedience became confused, and the Church may have looked to some as though it had become a revolutionary innovator.

It has sometimes been argued that heresy flourished because it was particularly attractive to women, whose position in society had been damaged by the campaigns against married clergy and by the misogynist attitudes of many reformers. In fact, while women were occasionally involved in these heretical movements as patrons and also as disciples, no convincing evidence exists that women were any more attracted than men to heretical movements.

On the other hand, just as the Church began to see women as more dangerous and heresy as more definitive, it also began to sense danger in other groups. John Boswell argues that homosexuals were increasingly stigmatized through the twelfth and thirteenth centuries as a result of the exaltation of purity and reactivity to sexuality that characterized the Gregorian reform. By the twelfth century, accusations of homosexuality (or sodomy) became an acceptable basis for persecution.

Heretics were commonly described in terms of disease, and their influence on others was often couched in sexual terms. Eon de l'Etoile, an insane heretic who preached in the 1140s and believed that he was divine, was referred to by others as "a pestiferous man." The Cathars were characterized as a plague, infecting or contaminating regions. Tanchelm, a heretical preacher in the Low Countries in the early twelfth century, was thought to have seduced his followers. Guibert of Nogent, a twelfth-century abbot, accused heretics of meeting by night for orgies and of ritually killing the resulting children. Given these responses, it is not surprising to discover that diseased persons, particularly lepers, whose affliction was thought to be sexually transmitted, began to be singled out and isolated.

Beginning in the eleventh century, leper hospitals were built throughout Europe; rules and regulations were established that separated lepers from society, and medieval literature shows a growing concern about the threat of leprosy. When the legendary King Mark wanted to punish Isolde for her adultery with Tristan, the romance records that the most horrendous punishment he could imagine was to subject her to the sexual assaults of lepers. And when the bubonic plague emerged in Europe in the fourteenth century, lepers as well as Jews became the scapegoats for a traumatized society that had long since stigmatized them.

Jews, whose position in western Europe had always been subject to periodic persecution and marginalization, suffered renewed attacks in the eleventh century. They were more and more excluded from craft and merchant guilds and increasingly associated with moneylending, materialism, and the devil. Some of them were among the *nouveaux riches* in a society where wealth and avarice had negative, even sinful, connotations. Some might have been victims, to some extent, of the conflict between pope and emperor, since the emperor traditionally protected Jews. They were secluded in ghettos, accused of ritual child murder for the first time in 1144 (and many times thereafter), later exploited and expelled by the rulers of France and England, and, in 1215, singled out by the Church which decreed that all Jews wear distinguishing clothing. With respect to all of these groups—heretics, lepers, Jews, and homosexuals—R. I. Moore has raised the question as to why Europe would have become, in the eleventh and twelfth centuries, a society that persecuted? Part of the answer rests with the religious revival and papal reform. As religious enthusiasm grew, religious doctrine became more elaborated and the established Church more closely regulated and defined. By the twelfth century, the Church had taken a new, dominant and more activist role in medieval society, demanding greater conformity and decrying moral impurity. Therefore, it is not surprising that dissent and deviance from the norm (whether religious, sexual, or in terms of health) should take on heretical overtones and that the official responses were often intolerant.

Summary

Beginning around the turn of the millennium, European Christians began to assess their ecclesiastical institutions and to find them wanting. A combination of popular desires for religious renewal, reform-minded emperors, the example and influence of reformed monasteries, and a growing reform element within the Church hierarchy worked together to pressure the papacy to clean house. In so doing, ecclesiastical reformers sought to separate the church from lay authority, while at the same time attacking the twin problems of simony and clerical marriage. The resulting, almost revolutionary conflicts that ensued threatened imperial authority, promoted a more ascetic monasticism as a solution for individual men and women, and focused attention on those who were perceived as disobedient to the Church and not in conformity with its doctrines. Insofar as the Church did not succeed in conforming to apostolic norms, however, it fueled heretical ideas. Religious authorities responded with accusations of consorting with the devil and by turning to persecution. The combination of religious fervor linked with persecuting zeal was soon to produce the crusades—a form of holy war that directed the considerable energies of the peoples of Europe toward the enemies without and then, in the form of crusades at home, toward the enemies within.

NOTES

1. Benedicta Ward, *Miracles and the Medieval Mind: Theory, Record and Event 1000–1215* (Philadelphia: University of Pennsylvania Press, 1982) 120
2. Victor and Edith Turner, *Image and Pilgrimage in Christian Culture* (New York: Columbia University Press, 1978).

3. J. Mansi, *Sacrorum Conciliorum* (Florence, 1759–1798) xix, c. 827, canon i.

4. Henrietta Leyser, *Hermits and the New Monasticism* (New York: Macmillan, 1984) 26; Latin text in D. G. Morin, "Rainaud l'ermite et Ives de Chartres: un épisode de la crise du cénobitisme au XIe-XIIe siècle," *Revue Bénédictine,* vol. 40 (1928): 99–115.

5. Noreen Hunt, *Cluny Under Saint Hugh 1049–1189* (Notre Dame, Ind.: University of Notre Dame Press, 1968) 125; *Patrologia Latina,* 159, 951.

6. Latin text in Cowdrey, *The Cluniacs and the Gregorian Reform* (Oxford: Clarendon Press, 1970) 272–273.

7. Uta-Renate Blumenthal, *The Investiture Controversy: Church and Monarchy from the Ninth to the Twelfth Century* (Philadelphia: University of Pennsylvania Press, 1988) 116.

8. Lampert of Hersfeld, *Annales,* ed. G. Pertz, *M.G.H., Scriptores,* vol. V, 218.

9. Ronald Knox, "Finding the Law: Developments in Canon Law During the Gregorian Reform," *Studi Gregoriani,* IX (1972) 425

10. Anne Llewellyn Barstow, *Married Priests and the Reforming Papacy: The Eleventh-Century Debates* (New York: The Edwin Mellon Press, 1982) 60-61; *Patrologia Latina,* 145, 410ff.

11. *The Correspondence of Pope Gregory VII: Selected Letters from the Registrum,* trans. Ephraim Emerton (New York: Columbia University Press, 1932) 11–12

12. I.S. Robinson, *The Papacy, 1073-1198: Continuity and Innovation* (London: Cambridge University Press, 1990) x.

13. *The Correspondence of Pope Gregory VII,* 111–112

14. I.S. Robinson, "'Periculosus Homo': Pope Gregory VII and Episcopal Authority,"*Viator* (1978): 103.

15. *The Correspondence of Pope Gregory VII,* 152.

16. *Ibid.,* 166–175.

17. Christopher Brooke, *Medieval Church and Society* (New York: New York University Press, 1972) 68.

18. John Boswell, *Kindness of Strangers: The Abandonment of Children in Western Europe from Late Antiquity to the Renaissance* (New York: Pantheon Books, 1988) 181.

19. R.I. Moore, *The Origins of European Dissent* (London: Allen Lane, 1977) 81.

~

CHAPTER 12

The Crusades

By the end of the eleventh century, the reforming papacy had become an aggressive, crusading papacy. Medieval Christian Europe after 1095 is dominated by the ideology and actuality of crusades—organized military expeditions called for by the papacy in response, initially, to an appeal from Byzantium and directed primarily toward the capture of Jerusalem and the defeat of Muslim kingdoms in the eastern Mediterranean. This movement, in which an expanding western Christian culture came into conflict with Islam, provided the West with a cause that touched nearly everyone and moved many to travel to the East. Its initial success and subsequent failures altered the strategic balance in the Mediterranean by weakening Byzantium, strengthening some Italian city-states (particularly Genoa and Venice), and creating European outposts in the Holy Land. New military orders and new heroes emerged from these expeditions. But the final defeat of the Christians in the East profoundly and negatively affected the prestige of the papacy and highlighted divisions between European powers.

ORIGINS OF THE CRUSADES

Shifting conditions in the Islamic world brought new threats to the Christian East as the Seljuk Turks, newly converted to Islam, attacked the Greeks. Byzantium, traditionally a bulwark against Islamic expansion, began to falter and, in the 1090s, called upon the West for help. Western Christendom was already primed for an aggressive, religious response that quickly took the form of crusading Holy Wars.

The Changing Mediterranean World

In the second half of the eleventh century, Muslims and Christians divided the Mediterranean Sea between them, but the division was unstable. Since the seventh century, Muslims had conquered the Holy Land, the Middle East as far as northwest India, North Africa, much of Spain, Sicily, Crete, and parts of southern France. By the eleventh century, however, the Muslim world was on the defensive. Christians were putting pressure on Islamic powers in the Spanish peninsula; the Byzantines had recaptured Crete; Normans expelled Muslims from Sicily; and the Genoese took Sardinia and invaded North Africa. Islam was also itself divided—between ethnic groups (Arabs, Persians, Kurds, and Egyptians among others), between Sunni and Shi'ite Muslims, and between three religious leaders—the Abbasid caliph in Baghdad; the Fatimid, Shi'ite caliph in Cairo; and the Umayyad caliph in Spain. By 1009, the caliphate in Spain had collapsed, as Muslim Spain disintegrated into politically fragmented kingdoms governed by what historians call "party kings." The other two caliphs had become figureheads for a series of military dictators of Iraqi, Iranian, Kurdish, Armenian, or Turkish extraction. A further source of instability for Muslim rulers was the large number of protected minorities (Jews and Christians) who were tolerated but restricted, some of whom might welcome the overthrow of Islamic rulers.

Then, in the mid-eleventh century, an aggressive group of newly converted Muslims appeared. These were Seljuk Turks from Central Asia, who in short order conquered (but could not unify) nearly the whole of Iran, all of Mesopotamia, Syria, and Palestine. Their military chiefs took the title of sultan (political leader) conferred by nearly powerless caliphs who remained the religious leaders.

The Seljuks threatened the Byzantine Empire, which was weakening within and without after a century of expansion. Poor imperial leadership combined with a growing landed aristocracy and the disappearance of a free peasantry resulted in marked inequalities in the distribution of wealth. Emperors who tried to prevent such a concentration of power ended up provoking civil war and losing their thrones. Partly as a result of these economic inequities, the Byzantine army was becoming a mercenary army, heavily dependent on foreign troops. Any prospects of preserving a more balanced economy, an independent army, and a free peasant class were lost.

The year 1071 was especially devastating to the Byzantines. In that year the Normans captured the last Byzantine stronghold in southern Italy and within a decade attacked the mainland of Greece. Simultaneously, Pechenegs, who had disrupted the Balkans since the 1030s, invaded from the Danube region. And then the Seljuk Turks defeated the Byzantine army at Manzikert. They captured the emperor himself and overran much of Anatolia (modern-day Turkey), Byzantium's richest, most powerful province. The Sultan Alp-Arslan, who led the Turks, gained immortal fame at Manzikert, although the Seljuks were unable to follow up the victory by incorporating Anatolia into their empire. With no effective Byzantine or Muslim rule, Anatolia became an arena into which Turkish tribes could flow unimpeded. Among the victims of this anarchy were western pilgrims, whose mistreatment raised alarms in the West, at the same time that Byzantine defeats created an opening for the West. The response came in the form of the Crusades, a kind of Holy War.

Growth of a Crusading Ideal

The concept of a Christian holy war has roots that go back to the early fifth century when St. Augustine first provided Christians with a rationale for justifiable wars. By the ninth century, western Christians believed that physical force on behalf of a Christian God was not only justified but sanctified. An individual who died in Christ's defense was a martyr.

At first, secular rulers conducted campaigns against both Muslims and pagans, although the Church might encourage their armies with prayers and perhaps with banners and financial support. Carolingian court scholars justified Charlemagne's various wars against Muslims, pagans, and Christians alike, while clergymen were encouraged to participate in his campaigns. Ninth-century writers encouraged wars in defense of Christianity. Popes Leo IV (847–855) and John VIII (872–882) made promises of everlasting life to Christians who died defending the Church against pagan Vikings and "heathen" Muslims. In the 1060s, the papacy was granting a lifting of penance and remission of sins to armies fighting in Spain against the Muslims. From there it was a small step to the idea that Christ, through his representative, the Pope, sanctioned aggressive wars against the foes of Christendom.

Pope Gregory VII (1073–1085) is considered the originator of the crusading idea. Gregory believed that it was his right to call feudal troops to papal service. In 1074, for example, Gregory wrote to William, count of Burgundy, ". . . we beg and require of your prudence and your zeal that you bring together a military force to protect the freedom of the Roman Church and if need be that you come hither with your army in the service of St. Peter."[1] Gregory planned to lead an army against rebellious Normans and then against the excommunicated French king, Philip I. But he also planned to take an army eastward to defend Byzantium, appealing "to all those who wish to protect the Christian faith." He hoped to reunite the Eastern Church with Rome, and he may have had the liberation of Jerusalem in mind. Gregory expected personally to accompany the army, leaving the Church in the charge of the emperor-elect. Because of growing tensions with Henry IV (Chapter 11), however, Gregory shelved the expedition, referring, regretfully, in one of his letters to the "masses of Christians being slaughtered in the East without succour." In the meantime, however, he had encouraged several scholars in his reforming circle to gather scattered passages justifying God-sanctioned warfare from the writings of St. Augustine and other Church fathers. These authorities helped to justify Gregory's offer of remission of sins to those soldiers fighting on behalf of the papacy, even against Christian enemies.

Another factor that contributed to crusading fervor was the growing popularity of fighting saints. St. James of Compostela supposedly led Christians to victory against Muslims in Spain. Stories about St. George on his horse, armored and protecting Christians, circulated. One of the most popular epic poem of the period, the *Chanson de Roland* (*Song of Roland*), tells the tale of Christian, Frankish warriors dying in battle against pagan (sic) Muslims. When Roland, victorious, dies, "God sent him his angel Cherubim and Saint Michael . . . [and] St. Gabriel: they bear Count Roland's soul to Paradise."[2] Included in other epic poems about

Charlemagne was the legend that Charlemagne had captured Jerusalem, expelling the "pagans." Crusaders thus believed they were following in Charlemagne's footsteps when they marched East. Based on this legend, people believed that Islamic powers were illegitimately holding Jerusalem, which they thought had once and rightly been part of Charlemagne's empire. A society that venerated warrior saints, sang the exploits of Roland and Charlemagne, and supported a militarized papacy, was a society ready for religious war.

The Crusades were preceded by the growing popularity of pilgrimages to Jerusalem, which began to take on the character of armed marches. Even before the First Crusade, pilgrims wore special insignia and may have taken an oath before departing. As the Turks overran Anatolia, pilgrims encountered greater obstacles—tolls, decayed facilities, and physical danger—and needed more protection. By the First Crusade, little difference existed between the Church's efforts to protect pilgrims going to Jerusalem and its support of crusaders marching to free the Holy Land. Indeed, for the first century of the Crusades, both groups were called pilgrims. It is this fusion of armed forces with pilgrimage to Jerusalem that forms the basis for the Crusades of the Middle Ages (see Map 12.1).

Papal crusades carried with them certain privileges and benefits. All crusaders' homes, families, and wealth were under ecclesiastical protection; no one could collect interest on debts or go to court against them in their absence. They were exempt from tolls and immune from certain taxes. The papacy promised spiritual rewards, called indulgences (remission of sins and of the penance for sins).* Religious communities helped finance crusaders by mortgaging and buying crusaders' lands, accepting their properties as pledges, and protecting family members left behind. They promoted the crusade through preaching and offering to remember crusaders with special liturgical intercessions. The privileges offered by the Church gave the crusader a path to salvation and special status as a knight of Christ or vassal of St. Peter. Given all this, it is not surprising that Crusades attracted crowds.

Some historians have argued that the Peace of God movement (Chapter 11) also prepared Europeans for the crusade. Certainly, as part of the preparation for these crusading expeditions, the Church took care to extend provisions for peace throughout Europe, as it attempted to refocus the violent energies of warriors beyond Europe. A further factor may have been younger sons with limited inheritance rights who might have been attracted by the prospect of material gains (which, for most crusaders, were not realized); and some people might have gone in response to demographic pressures and recent famines in Europe. Overall, however, the primary reasons people went on crusade were religious, penitential, and righteous, related to their sense of sinfulness, anxiety over the next life, and the ideology of holy war.

---

* During the First and Second Crusades, confusion emerged between indulgences that promised remission of penance for sins (i.e. the penalty enjoined by the church) and those that promised remission of sins (i.e. the extinction of the sin itself). Popular opinion seems to have understood these indulgences, from the beginning, as offering instant access to heaven.

THE FIRST CRUSADE, 1095–1099

In March of 1095, Alexius I Comnenus, the Byzantine Emperor, sent representatives to a Church council in Piacenza, Italy. Under discussion may have been a reunion of the Greek and Roman churches, but Alexius's envoys were particularly interested in obtaining mercenary soldiers to combat the Turks. They exaggerated the danger that Jerusalem was in, expecting that an appeal for relief of the holy city would have greater propaganda value to western knights than aid to Constantinople.

The Call and the Response

Eight months later, at a council in Clermont, France, Pope Urban II (1088–1099) called for a crusade. What exactly he said is debated; the positive response he generated is unambiguously clear. There are five primary descriptions of Urban's speech, none of which record his actual words and all of which differ. Historians mainly agree that, in a highly propagandistic way, Urban described Turkish mistreatment of Christians and the defiling of Christian churches.* His emphasis was on liberating the Church and recapturing Jerusalem, rather than on helping the Byzantine Empire. Urban appealed to rich and poor alike. He purposefully appealed to the French and Norman barons and deliberately excluded the German Emperor Henry IV and King Philip I of France (who were excommunicated at the time), as well as King William Rufus of England, whose vehement anticlericalism made him a poor candidate for the appeal. In addition, Spain was preoccupied with the *reconquista,* and northern Italy with its place in the empire. Urban preached a restoration of peace in the West and the redirection of Christian energies toward material and spiritual rewards in the East. In his appeal Urban linked pilgrimage with bearing arms—the essence of a crusade.

Urban seems to have envisioned an army of trained knights under the command of men nominated by himself. The crusaders were to take a vow, to be ceremonially blessed, to wear the sign of the cross, and to be accompanied by a papal legate. Urban set the start date, planned the itinerary, and probably meant to join the expedition once it arrived in the Holy Land. What he got instead was a mass movement—an overwhelming response that quickly got out of hand.

Urban's call to arms was preached throughout much of Europe, with Urban himself preaching extensively. Urban also expected bishops to preach the crusade, but more effective preaching was done by poorer, less official preachers such as Robert of Arbrissel, the founder of Fontevrault Abbey, and Peter the Hermit. Peter was an unattractive, stumpy man with few and filthy clothes who mesmerized his hearers, establishing peace and giving alms wherever he went. "Whatever he did or said," according to Guibert of Nogent," seemed like something almost divine. Even the hairs of his mule were torn out as though they were relics."[3] Peter carried a

---

* The reports of Turkish attacks on Christians were exaggerated. It was not Turkish practice to persecute conquered "unbelievers." Although there were always tensions between Muslim and Christian, most eastern Christians had few problems with the Turks and may have preferred them to the Byzantines.

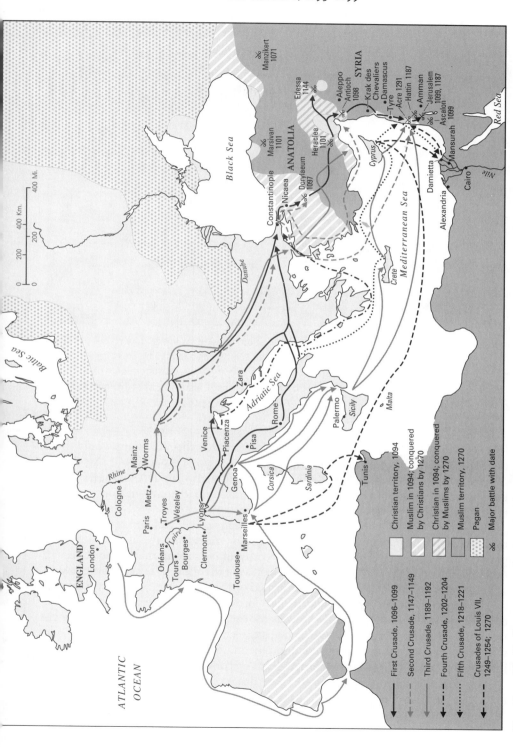

Map 12.1   The Mediterranean at the Time of the Crusades, 1096–1291   The first two crusades mainly went overland, although some of the leaders of the First Crusade crossed the Adriatic. Subsequent crusaders found it more expedient (and less dangerous) to go by sea. The Fourth Crusade never got beyond Constantinople, and the last crusades (1218–1270) focused on Egypt and North Africa.

A Crusader Takes the Cross   This manuscript illustration from the twelfth century shows the identification of crusaders with pilgrims. The crusader, who is receiving a crusading cross from a bishop, is also wearing a pilgrim's purse and carrying a pilgrim's staff. Crusaders were often called *peregrini* (pilgrims) in the written sources of the time. This image also illustrates the important role of the Church in implementing the crusades. *Bibliotheque Municipale, Besancon, France.*

letter, said to have fallen from heaven, prophesying that the Christians would drive the infidels from the Holy Land. He played on apocalyptic expectations that the recapture of Jerusalem would herald the coming Judgment Day. Tens of thousands of men, women, children, knights, and clerics set out immediately, without papal authorization and without organized military escort.

At the outset, some of these crusading groups engaged in violent anti-Semitic actions, including the murder of Jews in some of the towns through which they passed (see Medieval Voices). The Jewish communities along the Rhine River (in towns such as Cologne, Mainz, and Worms) were the most affected. These Jewish communities were relatively newly established, involved in trade, uneasily tolerated by the burghers of the towns, and usually protected by higher authorities. The combination of crusading zeal, cash needs for the journey, and the economic rivalries of some of the Christian burghers helps explain these violent outbreaks. While some of the attacks on the Jews were unpremeditated, others were planned assaults intended to force individuals to choose death or conversion.

The Jewish communities involved chose death, sometimes self-inflicted. These massacres were a watershed in European Jewish history. For the Jews, they set an example of self-martyrdom in response to persecution. They contributed significantly to the already deteriorating toleration of Jewish communities, pushing them

MEDIEVAL VOICES

The First
Crusaders
Massacre
Jewish
Communities
Along the
Rhineland

Here are two accounts, the first by a Jewish chronicler and the second by a Christian commentator, of the massacres of Jewish communities on the eve of the First Crusade:

(1) For then rose up . . . the arrogant, the barbaric, a fierce and impetuous people, both French and German. They set their hearts to journey to the Holy City, which had been defiled by a ruffian people, in order to seek there the sepulcher of the crucified [one] and to drive out the Muslims who dwell in the land and to conquer the land. They put on their insignia and placed an idolatrous sign on their clothing—the cross—all the men and women whose hearts impelled them to undertake the pilgrimage to the sepulcher of their messiah . . . exceeded the locusts on the land—men, women, and children. . . .

It came to pass that, when they traversed towns where there were Jews, they said to one another: "Behold we journey a long way to seek the idolatrous shrine and to take vengeance upon the Muslims. But here are the Jews dwelling among us, whose ancestors killed him and crucified him groundlessly. Let us take vengeance first upon them. Let us wipe them out as a nation . . ."

(2) Emicho [of Leiningen, a knightly leader of the popular crusade] and the rest of his band held a council and, after sunrise, attacked the Jews [of Mainz] in the courtyard with arrows and lances. When the bolts and doors had been forced and the Jews had been overcome, they killed seven hundred of them, who in vain resisted the attack and assault of so many thousands. They slaughtered the women also and with the point of their swords pierced young children of whatever age and sex. The Jews, seeing that their Christian enemies were attacking them and their children and were sparing no age, fell upon one another—brothers, children, wives, mothers and sisters—and slaughtered one another. Horrible to say, mothers cut the throats of nursing children with knives and stabbed others, preferring to perish thus by their own hands rather than be killed by the weapons of the uncircumcised.

Source: Excerpt from Robert Chazan, *European Jewry and the First Crusade,* (Berkeley: University of California Press, 1987) 67, 70. Reprinted by permission of The Regents of University of California.

into the margins of European society. More and more the Jews were pictured as Christ-killers who were damnably associated with wealth and privilege. Less protected and increasingly unacceptable, European Jews became subject to periodic massacres and greater alienation in much of western Europe.

Progress of the First Crusade

Historians usually divide the First Crusade into two separate movements: the People's (or popular) Crusade and the Barons' (or official) Crusade, although contemporaries did not see such a clear division. The first wave of (people's) crusaders, led mainly by Peter the Hermit, arrived in Constantinople in August 1096. Anna

Comnena, the Greek emperor's daughter, described the hordes of men, women, and children who joined the crusade:

> He (Emperor Alexius) had no time to relax before he heard a rumour that count-less Frankish armies were approaching. He dreaded their arrival, knowing as he did their uncontrollable passion, their erratic character and their irresolution, . . . [as well as] their greed for money, . . . which always led them, it seemed, to break their own agreements without scruple. . . . What actually happened was more far-reaching and terrible than rumour suggested. . . . Full of enthusiasm and ardour they thronged every highway, and with these warriors came a host of civilians. . . . There were women and children, too, who had left their own countries. Like trib-utaries joining a river from all directions they streamed towards us in full force.[4]

Undisciplined, hungry, and occasionally destructive, this People's Crusade experi-enced suffering and defeat. Once they reached Turkish territory, the majority were massacred after having themselves tortured and killed the people they encountered. Few of these crusaders made it to the Holy Land. A contemporary account of the First Crusade, the *Gesta Francorum* (*Deeds of the Franks*), written in a simple and unadorned style, perhaps by a knight, describes the end of this crusade. First Turk-ish armies destroyed one group of Christians:

> Peter the Hermit, however, had gone off to Constantinople a little before this happened, for he could not control such a mixed company of people who would not obey him or listen to what he said. The Turks [then] fell upon his men and killed most of them—some they found asleep, others naked, and all these they slaughtered. . . . Those who managed to escape fled. . . . Some leapt into the sea, and others hid in the woods and mountains.[5]

The second (official) wave of crusaders was more organized. They traveled after the summer harvest and were therefore less in need of supplies. They were better re-ceived by the Byzantines (who were, by this time, more prepared to deal with such a horde). And they were led by a decidedly talented group of military leaders, in-cluding Godfrey of Bouillon, duke of Lower Lorraine; Bohemund of Taranto (son of Robert Guiscard); Baldwin of Boulogne; Robert, duke of Normandy; Robert, count of Flanders; and Raymond, count of Toulouse. In addition, the religious and strategic leadership of the papal legate, Bishop Adhemar of Le Puy, gave a measure of unity to the ranks of Normans, Franks, Provençals, Italians, and others.

After negotiations with Alexius in Constantinople, the barons' army took Nicaea, defeated the Turks near Dorylaeum (the modern town of Eskishehir), crossed Anatolia, and took and established Edessa (modern Urfa) as an inde-pendent principality. By then, however, horses were dying in the heat, supplies had diminished, and desertions mounted. They were unable to take the city of Antioch, which had unusually strong ramparts, until after a siege of seven and a half cruel months; then they found themselves besieged inside it. At this low point the report of a miraculous discovery of the lance that had pierced Christ's side raised spirits. Despite the fact that many crusaders had already seen such a lance in

Constantinople (and indeed, another lance was in the possession of the German imperial court!), most chose to believe the sign. Lance in hand, they proceeded to battle; the Muslims, themselves divided and dispirited by desertions, fled.

The subsequent disorganization of the Turkish and Arab rulers in Syria and Palestine allowed the crusaders to march to Jerusalem and breach its walls on July 15, 1099. The massacre of Muslims and Jews that followed is described in the *Gesta Francorum:*

> . . . so our men entered the city, chasing the Saracens and killing them up to Solomon's Temple, where they took refuge. [Our men] killed whom they chose, and those they chose they saved alive. On the roof of the Temple of Solomon were crowded great numbers of pagans (sic) of both sexes, to whom Tancred and Gaston of Bearn gave their banners [to protect them].
>
> After this our men rushed round the whole city, seizing gold and silver, horses and mules, and houses full of all sorts of goods, and they all came rejoicing and weeping from excess of gladness to worship at the Sepulchre of our Saviour Jesus. . . . Next morning they went cautiously up on to the Temple roof and attacked the Saracens, both men and women, cutting off their heads with drawn swords. Some of the Saracens threw themselves down headlong from the Temple. . . . No one has ever seen or heard of such a slaughter of pagans, for they were burned on pyres like pyramids, and no one save God alone knows how many there were.[6]

They followed this conquest with the swift defeat of an Egyptian relief army and a massacre of inhabitants in the city of Ascalon.

Consequences of the First Crusade

The consequences of this victory were enormous. Above all, the crusaders had captured Jerusalem after over four centuries of Muslim rule. Now they had to hold it. In order to do so they set up three, and eventually four, territories which historians call the Latin Kingdoms of the East. Contemporaries called them *Outremer,* or, "the land beyond the sea," and the Muslims, who referred to all crusaders as Franks (Franj), called them the Frankish states. These states—Edessa, Antioch, Jerusalem, and Tripoli—were ruled independently, for the most part, of the authority of the papacy or the Byzantine emperor. Gradually, from 1099 to about 1130, the crusaders gained control over the coastal cities and conquered more of the interior, erecting a line of fortifications from Amman to Aqaba.

Another consequence of the First Crusade was growing suspicion and hatred of Byzantine Greeks. Emperor Alexius, while helpful to the crusaders in Constantinople and Asia Minor, was rightly suspicious of western loyalty (even though he had exacted loyalty oaths from the crusaders and promises to return former Byzantine territories to Byzantine sovereignty). The crusaders considered those oaths broken when Alexius did not aid them at Antioch or later, en route to Jerusalem. The chroniclers took up this anti-Greek attitude. The author of the *Gesta Francorum* calls the emperor a "fool as well as a knave." Guibert of Nogent, writing ten years later, was even harsher, calling the emperor a foul tyrant, deceiver, and usurper, an attitude that many shared.[7] In general, Latin Christians refused to acknowledge Byzantine overlordship in the East, and Latin ecclesiastical officials took over from ousted Greek patriarchs and priests—all of which increased tensions between Greeks and Latins. Various of the crusaders began to talk about a conquest of Constantinople, and in 1106 Bohemund, having returned to Europe, raised an army for this purpose (his invasion was, however, unsuccessful). This idea was to be raised again and again until the Fourth Crusade, when western armies succeeded in capturing Constantinople.

In the euphoria of victory, as a kind of postscript to the First Crusade, new waves of crusaders headed East. A crusade estimated as ranging between 50,000 and 160,000* from Lombardy, Germany, Burgundy and Champagne arrived in Constantinople in 1101, to be totally defeated by the Turks in northern Anatolia. Similar disasters befell another French army and then a third army led by William, duke of Aquitaine, Welf of Bavaria, and Ida, countess of Austria. The unrealistic zeal of these crusaders can be measured by their lack of coordination and good sense en route and by their goals, one of which was the conquest of Baghdad, a city of some two million people, well beyond the strategic reach of the crusaders. Some of them did get to Baghdad, but only as captives.

In the first crusade many women joined the pilgrim armies. Chroniclers of the First Crusade tell us very little about them. We know that they died in large numbers (drowning in a capsized ship or perishing of heat and thirst in Asia Minor), participated in the battle of Dorylaeum (as water-carriers), and helped in the siege of Archas, between Antioch and Jerusalem. But when things went badly at Antioch, women were blamed and cast out of the army, "the married as well as the unmarried, lest perhaps defiled by the sordidness of riotous living they should displease the Lord."[8]

Many women also set out on the crusade of 1101. Ida, the widowed countess of Austria, was either killed or captured in the defeat of her army in Asia Minor. In legend, she was captured and married to a Muslim, by whom she had a child, Zengī, a leader who was to recapture Edessa from the Christians in 1144.

Unlike Ida, most aristocratic women who went on crusade accompanied their husbands. Since canon law required wives to give consent before their husbands went on crusade, and since the Church worried about adultery, an obvious solution was for wives to accompany husbands. Even so, older wives, with wealth and retainers, were more welcome than younger wives, whose reputations were liable to damage. All women, no matter what their social status, were officially considered unarmed pilgrims rather than crusaders. By the time of the Third Crusade (1189–1192), unarmed pilgrims were discouraged from joining up, but this does not seem to have successfully stopped the women. More than one Muslim source for the Third Crusade talks of Frankish women riding into battle, armed and dressed in men's clothing, while western chroniclers depict women constructing siege works and working as washerwomen. In 1301, a group of Genoese noblewomen

---

* Accuracy of statistics was not a characteristic of the Middle Ages. As a result, many medieval historians refuse even to guess at the numbers involved.

received papal endorsement to go on crusade, not as soldiers but as helpers to the fighting men.[9]

One result of these massive responses was a loss of control on the part of the papacy. Urban II had proven unable to prevent the People's Crusade from starting out. The papacy was also unable to prevent the massacres of the Jews; it could not stop the old and the sick from joining the march or exercise close control over women, priests, and monks who went. It was unable to influence the establishment of independent, secular kingdoms, and its subsequent efforts to convince eastern Christians (Armenians, Nestorians, Greek Orthodox, Maronites, Copts, and Jacobites) to become Catholic were only marginally successful. Papal control over the Fourth Crusade (1204), when Christians attacked Christians, was virtually nonexistent. In the end, the western Church was unable to prevent the downfall of the Latin kingdoms.

LIFE IN THE HOLY LAND

The Latin kingdoms in the Holy Land were outposts of western Europe, and, despite intensive settlement in areas already occupied by Christians and opportunities for material gain and social advancement, the Frankish migration was never able to match the numbers of Turks that flowed into the Levant. At most perhaps 140,000 to 250,000 western Christians settled there, while the total number of Frankish knights in *Outremer* at any one time rarely exceeded 2,000. In addition, appeals West for recruits were rarely answered in time or in sufficient numbers. Therefore manpower was always a problem, especially when the crusading kingdoms were faced with a more unified Islamic response.

Frankish society in *Outremer* depended on the ruling families, their baronial peers, and crusading knights who held landed fiefs or cash "rents" in return for military service. But these knights, unlike those who lived in western Europe, became urban-dwellers, living off revenues from rural and urban properties. They were governed by kings or queens and by a High Court that gradually took on the character of a Parliament. Except in the territories of Jerusalem and Acre and other areas with a substantial local Christian population, western peasants, artisans, and merchants who traveled to the East settled in the older towns, new villages, or near fortified sites, becoming bourgeoisie or wealthy agriculturists and building castles and manor houses, roads, bridges, irrigation systems, and, in general, a flourishing agricultural base.

Although western Christians respected many of the eastern monasteries and saints, they also established a Catholic hierarchy in the Holy Land at the expense of the Greek Orthodox church. It was an unbalanced hierarchy, with numerous bishops and few parish churches. The Church in *Outremer* also remained largely unreformed, dominated by secular rulers and therefore, in the eyes of a reforming papacy, corrupt.

Except in Jerusalem (where only Christians were allowed to reside), both Muslims and Jews retained an independent status. They kept their own churches,

MEDIEVAL VOICES

An Educated
Arab
Comments on
Franks He Has
Met in the
Holy Land

Usama ibn Munqidh, a Syrian Arab who wrote his anecdotal autobiography in the twelfth century, gives an example that illustrates the varying degrees of understanding between Franks and Moslems. Although some intermixing did occur, Usama's overall portrait of the relationship between the two cultures is discouraging:

There are some Franks who have settled in our land and taken to living like Muslims. These are better than those who have just arrived from their homelands, but they are the exception, and cannot be taken as typical. I came across one of them once when I sent a friend on business to Antioch, which was governed by . . . a friend of mine. One day he said to my friend: "A Frankish friend has invited me to visit him; come with me so that you can see how they live." "I went with him," said my friend, "and we came to the house of one of the old knights who came with the first expedition. This man had retired from the army, and was living on the income of the property he owned in Antioch. He had a fine table brought out, spread with a splendid selection of appetizing food. He saw that I was not eating, and said: 'Don't worry, please; eat what you like, for I don't eat Frankish food. I have Egyptian cooks and eat only what they serve. No pig's flesh ever comes into my house!' So I ate, although cautiously, and then we left. Another day, as I was passing through the market, a Frankish woman advanced on me, addressing me in her barbaric language with words I found incomprehensible. A crowd of Franks gathered round us and I gave myself up for lost, when suddenly this knight appeared, saw me and came up. 'What do you want with this man?' 'This man,' she replied, 'killed my brother Urso . . .' The old man scolded the woman. 'This man is a merchant, a city man, not a fighter, and he lives nowhere near where your brother was killed.' Then he turned on the crowd, which melted away, and shook hands with me. Thus the fact that I ate at his table saved my life."

Source: Excerpt from *Arab Historians of the Crusades,* trans. Francesco Gabrieli (Berkeley: University of California Press, 1957) 78–80. Reprinted by permission of The Regents of University of California.

schools, and laws and were not taxed to support the Latin Church. Perhaps because the Europeans were a minority, they could not afford to be too intolerant of the majority population.

The Christians had limited cultural interchange with Muslims and Jews, although they might hunt, eat, or trade together, and sometimes Muslim scribes were utilized. Occasionally Muslims and Christians would intermarry, but most mixed marriages were between western and eastern Christians. Westerners adopted some Middle Eastern customs, dress, and cuisine, and incorporated some Middle Eastern luxuries (for example, silk and taffeta) as well as more frequent use of baths and perfumes. They also adopted the use of slaves (see Medieval Voices).

In general, however, little mutual understanding existed between cultures. Muslims and Christians misunderstood each other's religion. Muslims, while accepting Christians as People of the Book (i.e. as believers in the Old and New Testaments), thought of them as polytheists who worshiped a trinity of gods. Nor could they understand the idea of a God born of woman. Western Christians showed little interest in Islam as a religion. Although accurate information was available in the West from the early twelfth century, many western Christians viewed Muslims as pagan idolaters and Muhammad as a lapsed Christian and unscrupulous, false prophet. Although some of the Frankish nobility were literate, few showed interest in the Greek or Islamic intellectual traditions. The educated Frankish clergy set up some schools at cathedral centers. They occasionally learned Arabic, but they established no university and translated few books. Indeed, they destroyed a number of libraries. Although they produced some legal treatises and a few histories, such as William, archbishop of Tyre's *History of Deeds Across the Sea,* they failed to establish significant intellectual links between East and West.

The Muslim Middle East, with its great size and advanced civilization, remarked relatively little on the presence of the crusaders and often focused far more on conflicts among Muslim factions than on Frankish "unbelievers." When Muslim chroniclers did describe the Franks, they generally found them courageous but uncultivated, unreliable in their commitments, and uncouth in their bearing.

The crusaders did, however, build impressive citadels, the most famous of which is Krak des Chevaliers, probably the finest such building in the world. It is likely

Krak des Chevaliers   The most famous crusading castle in the Levant, Krak des Chevaliers, is on a hill overlooking the trade routes that lead from Homs to the Mediterranean. Krak was taken from the Arab prince of Homs by the count of Tripoli in 1109 and given to the Knights Hospitallers in 1141. They repaired and strengthened it, building it to its present size, with two rings of walls and a massive entrance on the south side (to the right of this photograph). The complex is steep on three sides except for the south, which is the most vulnerable.The Mamluks took Krak des Chevaliers in 1271, only twenty years before they took Acre. *Jean-Louis Nou/AKG London.*

that the crusaders learned a great deal from Byzantine and Syrian fortresses, and that this may have influenced subsequent castle building in the West—for example the castles built by Edward I in Wales. The churches they constructed, which are recognizably western in architecture and ornamentation, also suggest Syrian and Byzantine influences.

Commercial relations were important; Frankish control of the seaports along the eastern Mediterranean coast (from Antioch to Ascalon) gave the crusading states a military lifeline to the West and opened trading routes to the East for the Venetians, Genoese, and Pisans. Spices, perfumes, gold, precious stones, dyes, medicines, silks, cottons, and damasks all brought high prices in Europe. In the end, however, the trade that flowed through ports such as Alexandria, Palermo, or Constantinople far outweighed trade flowing through the crusading ports in the Holy Land. Perhaps the most important maritime transport to the crusading ports was that of pilgrims.

Frankish women who settled in the newly won territories were often viewed negatively by Muslims, who were unaccustomed to seeing women so much in public. Among the European population, however, women had relatively high status. They were in demand as wives, and the laws of inheritance in *Outremer* allowed women to hold property and political power. In fact, women were often heirs in a society where men frequently died in battle. The Kingdom of Jerusalem, for example, experienced four successive descents of the crown through the female line. Women also ruled the principality of Antioch from time to time.

A significant aspect of the crusading kingdoms was their ability to generate popular new religious orders. The Carmelite Order of white friars, for example, originated among a group of hermits who settled on Mount Carmel in Palestine and sought to imitate the lifestyle of the Old Testament prophet Elijah. The patriarch of Jerusalem drew up their rule in the early thirteenth century. After being displaced from the Holy Land in 1240, they became one of the four orders of friars in Europe.

By far the best known orders originating in the Latin kingdoms were the military orders—most importantly the Hospitallers, Templars, and Teutonic knights. These standing military organizations, dedicated to protecting Christians in the Holy Land, became a military necessity when large-scale immigration from the West did not materialize.

The Templars are perhaps the most famous. Archbishop William of Tyre described their beginning in 1119:

> In the same year, certain noble men of knightly rank, devoted to God, religious and God-fearing, professed the wish to live in chastity, obedience and without property in perpetuity, binding themselves in the hands of the lord patriarch to the service of Christ in the manner of regular canons. . . . Since they did not have a church, nor a settled place to live, the king [Baldwin II of Jerusalem] conceded a temporary dwelling to them in his palace, which he had below the Temple of the Lord [i.e. Solomon's Temple], . . . The first element of their profession . . . was "that they should protect the roads and routes to the utmost of their ability

against the ambushes of thieves and attackers, especially in regard to the safety of pilgrims."[10]

In 1128, the Knights Templar received official recognition in the West. They were praised by Bernard of Clairvaux, who helped draft their Rule at the Council of Troyes in 1129. Bernard described the Templar knight: "Without doubt, fortified by both arms (armor and faith), he fears neither demon nor man. Nor indeed is he afraid of death, he who had desired death. . . . If the cause of the fighting is good, the consequence of the fighting cannot be evil."[11] Generally they were recognized as a lay order of knights. No young children (oblates) were allowed and there was no role for women in the order. The Templars adopted white vestments with red crosses. They practiced great secrecy and had a strict hierarchy under absolute obedience to a Grand Master.

The Templars were allowed to hold property and accumulate privileges both in the East and the West. Their numerous strongholds and international connections aided the transfer of goods and funds from the West for support of the Latin Kingdoms. By 1290, the Templars had become an enormously wealthy corporation, controlling much of the circulation of funds coming from the West, lending and keeping on deposit huge sums, and answerable only to the papacy. The Templars believed that they descended from the Maccabees, Jewish restorers and defenders of the Temple of Solomon in the second century B.C. Modern-day Freemasonry, with legendary roots in the building of the Temple of Solomon, secret practices, and elaborate initiation rites, has strong parallels with the Templars. Some have mistakenly sought the origins of freemasonry among the Templars.

The Order of the Hospital of St. John of Jerusalem began with the first Catholic hospital in the Holy Land, a wealthy foundation built in 1070 to lodge and care for pilgrims. With 2,000 beds, lavish food, and separate wards for men and women, it attracted generous gifts from pilgrims. Eventually the Hospitallers took on a military aspect, perhaps in imitation of the Knights Templar. They gained land and castles in both East and West and an independent status directly under the pope. Despite an international military character and growing wealth, care of the poor and infirm remained central to the mission of the Hospitallers, and many existing hospitals were assimilated to the order.

By 1200, a third military order, the Teutonic Knights, had formed around a hospice and hospital for German-speaking pilgrims in the Holy Land. These knights quickly transplanted their activities to eastern Europe, however, and became a spearhead for German expansion into Transylvania and later Prussia. Eventually whole kingdoms in the Baltic lands were under the control of the Teutonic knights. Although all these orders differed in particulars, their primary responsibilities were to supply fighting forces and to build, defend, and repair strongholds.

The continued existence of a Catholic authority in the Holy Land depended on maintaining fortified towns and castles for defense and as garrisons. The Franks had conquered the Holy Land by means of sieges, and this remained the primary mode of fighting on both sides. Both Christians and Muslims employed catapults, roll-up towers and battering rams, tried to cut off food and water supplies, and tunneled under walls to weaken foundations. Besieged and besiegers hurled stones, Greek fire, quicklime, beehives, or heads or other body parts. The Muslims transmitted messages from place to place by drums, smoke signals, and passenger pigeons.

The Frankish castles were in naturally inaccessible places and required enormous skill to build, rebuild, or overthrow. Besides holding the major towns and castles, the Franks also had to maintain field armies, as they faced Turkish and Arab soldiers in ground skirmishes and full-scale battles. Turkish cavalries were a particular problem. Their mounted archers darted in and out, rarely standing still for a cavalry

Crusaders at the Siege of Nicea, 1097   The barons in the First Crusade, after crossing into Asia Minor, attacked Nicaea, the heavily fortified capital of the Turkish sultanate. The siege ended with a Turkish surrender and the Byzantines in command. Sieges were often brutal, with psychological as well as physical methods employed. In this instance the crusaders are using a traction trebuchet (powered by crews pulling on ropes) to hurl the heads of Turkish warriors back onto the ranks of the Turkish defenders. *Bibliotheque Nationale, Paris.*

charge. The Franks, on the other hand, were usually well enough armored (with cloth and hauberks, helmets and shields) that they might be struck by ten to twenty arrows, porcupine-fashion, and still survive. The more dangerous possibility was the impact of arrows upon the horses. Frankish knights were therefore usually surrounded by foot soldiers (with a ratio of perhaps one knight to seven foot soldiers) who used bows (especially the murderous crossbow), spears, pikes, axes, and short swords to fend off Muslim lancers, archers, and swordsmen. Once they decided to break from the cover of the foot soldiers, the massed charge of Frankish knights was usually terrifyingly effective, but it depended on a solid enemy formation as a target. If the Franks did not gain the field in the initial charge, it was difficult for them to regroup quickly, making them susceptible to being picked off one by one.

Sometimes the Muslims had the advantage because of terrain, such as at the crucial Battle of Hattin (July 4, 1187) when the Frankish army went, unwisely, into the desert of Galilee. There they faced heat and thirst, burning scrub that directed heat and smoke their way, and a Muslim army that greatly outnumbered them. Thousands of Frankish soldiers—the bulk of the army—were slaughtered or captured. As a consequence, the Christians lost Jerusalem, which, except for a brief period from 1229–1244, remained lost to western control until 1917. They also lost a portion of the True Cross that had been recovered at Antioch in 1099; the victors paraded and mocked it in Damascus.

Although the crusaders had a land military, they lacked sea power. Yet their conquests, except for Edessa, consisted of territories with access to Mediterranean ports. Thus, relations with the western sea powers (the Pisans, Genoese, and Venetians) became crucial for supplying the crusaders and for transporting new recruits to the Holy Land. Italian merchant communities therefore negotiated grants that gave them privileged enclaves. With their trading exemptions and commercial rivalries, they became a source of strength and of discord in the crusading states.

All in all, the European dominance of the Holy Land from 1099 until the fall of Acre in 1291 was a military occupation. A small military aristocracy, constantly in need of manpower, governed and exploited a native population that offered only a measure of loyalty and received only a measure of security.

As the crusaders consolidated their hold on the Holy Land, they created the conditions for their demise. Early in the twelfth century, a call for *jihad* (literally "striving" to advance Islam) began in Muslim intellectual and religious circles and gradually spread to the military. The result was the emergence of three extraordinary military leaders—Zengī, the ruler of Aleppo and conqueror of Edessa in 1144, his son Nūr-al-Dīn, and Salāh al-Dīn (Saladin). Saladin (1137–1193), the legendary Islamic liberator of Jerusalem, was born into a Kurdish warrior family. He was trained in the household of Nūr-al-Dīn and made vizier of Egypt in 1169 where he fortified Cairo and developed his own army. With the death of the last Fatimid ruler of Egypt, Saladin united Muslim Egypt with Syria and Iraq, returning Egypt to Sunni allegiance under the caliphate in Baghdad. Saladin was helped in reuniting Islamic forces by strategic deaths among other Muslim leaders and strategic mistakes on the part of the Christians, especially at Hattin. Saladin quickly became a legend among the Franks, who pictured him as a chivalrous, virtuous pagan. Muslim chroniclers were divided in their opinions, some emphasizing Saladin's

Twelfth-Century Walls of Cairo Built by Saladin   Saladin, a Kurdish military leader in Egypt, overthrew the Fatimid (Shiite) Caliphate in Cairo that had been established since the tenth century and returned Egypt to a Sunni Muslim allegiance. Saladin then joined Egypt and Syria by defeating the Zengid rulers in Syria. He was primarily responsible for the Christian defeat that led to the Muslim retaking of Jerusalem in 1187. Saladin fortified the defenses of Cairo and began to build a citadel complex for the ruler of Egypt in Cairo, which by that time was probably the largest city in the Mediterranean world. Western writers remembered Saladin as a worthy opponent of Richard the Lion-Heart. *Carmen Redondo/Corbis.*

effective leadership against the Christians and others stressing his self-interested manipulation and defeat of other Muslims.

SUBSEQUENT CRUSADES AND REACTIONS AGAINST CRUSADING

The rise of more aggressive, united Islamic leadership threatened the crusaders' conquests. In 1144, Zengī took Edessa. Europeans mounted the Second Crusade in response. The strategic mistakes of that crusade, however, played into the hands of Nūr-al-Dīn, who was poised to strike in Aleppo. In addition, the Frankish states became more and more isolated from Byzantium, potentially one of their most effective allies. Then, Saladin's unified forces, following the Battle of Hattin, took Jerusalem, and Europe responded with the Third Crusade. In 1204, the Fourth Crusade conquered Byzantium but did not reach the Holy Land. After 1204, Jerusalem returned to Christian control for one brief period (from 1229–1244)—the result of negotiations, not of armed threats. The history of the crusading movement in the thirteenth century is largely one of unfulfilled expectations and growing criticism.

The Second and Third Crusades

The Second Crusade is usually associated with the Cistercian leader, Bernard of Clairvaux. As a monastic reformer, preacher, and moral authority, perhaps only Bernard had sufficient prestige to push for a crusade after Edessa fell in 1144. The result was a papal bull in 1145/6 calling for an expedition to be led by King Louis VII of France. Bernard was given authority to preach it in France, but his enthusiasm and preaching soon spilled over into Germany, England, and Spain. Conrad III, king of the Germans, joined after hearing one of Bernard's compelling sermons.

The ensuing crusade was a disaster. Taking the overland route, through Constantinople, Conrad III's army was decimated by the Turks in Asia Minor. A shattered German army waited for Louis VII, whose own army was suffering from starvation and harassment by the Turks. At one point the army became split in mountainous terrain, and the Turks, taking advantage of this weakness, nearly captured Louis. Only a part of the army reached Antioch. For a variety of reasons, Louis decided against an attack on Nūr-al-Dīn in Aleppo, which might have enabled them to retake Edessa. Instead he moved to Jerusalem, making a collective decision with the barons and also with Conrad (who had finally arrived in Jerusalem) to attack Damascus. The decision to besiege Damascus was unwise by most accounts. Damascus, ruled by an independent Muslim ruler, had been in alliance with Christian Jerusalem. Some *Outremer* Franks may have undermined Louis's expedition since it was not in their interest to weaken Damascus. And Nūr-al-Dīn's army was fast approaching, with the prospect of squeezing the Franks between the well-defended city and an upcoming Muslim army. For whatever reasons, the siege failed almost before it began. Louis did, however, force the ruler of Damascus into the hands of Nūr-al-Dīn, who later took the city, uniting Muslim Syria and making himself champion of a renewed and militant Islam.

The failure of a crusade with papal backing, preached by Bernard of Clairvaux, and led by two kings elicited recriminations in every quarter. The Greeks, in particular, were blamed for not giving the armies sufficient support. Other commentators blamed the devil; some pinpointed preachers such as Bernard, while others blamed the wickedness of the crusaders. Eleanor of Aquitaine, Louis VII's wife, who had accompanied the crusade, was criticized for contributing to the disasters in Asia Minor and for taking to a luxurious and, commentators thought, lascivious style of living in Antioch.

Following this failure, no large-scale crusades were successfully mounted until the Third Crusade, which was authorized in 1187, following the loss of Jerusalem. Three rulers led the Third Crusade: Richard I (the Lion-Hearted) of England, the Emperor Frederick I of Germany, and Philip II of France. More than the previous crusades, this one was marked by an emphasis on Christian sinfulness and the coming of the Last Judgment (see Medieval Voices).

Frederick I's army was first to leave, crossing overland to Constantinople, with the Greeks (now in friendly communication with Saladin) constantly blocking the

MEDIEVAL VOICES

A Song
Calling for a
Crusade After
the Loss of
Jerusalem
in 1187

What David through the spirit once foretold,
God doth at length conclude;
The Saracens (so His purposes unfold)
With foul oppression hold
In bondage lewd
The holy Sepulchre where he was laid
Who for our sinful sakes was crucified:
A bitter price He paid
Who freely died
A death unmerited, suffering on the Rood!
God will arise, resistless in His splendor,
And crush the hostile host;
Though He permit the Sepulchre's surrender
Let Saracens not boast.
And God shall aid His soldiers, those of us
Signed with the Holy Cross
And warranted by that sign miraculous.
He sends the valorous
Who take the Cross
For saving of their souls a time of grace;
Therefore let every man of us confess
His sins before God's face
And, ransomless,
Beg heaven's ransom in the sign o'the Cross.
God will arise! . . .

Source: From "A Call to the Crusade," *The Goliard Poets: Medieval Latin Songs and Satires,* trans. George F. Whicher (New York: New Directions, 1949) 157. Copyright © 1949 by George F. Whicher. Reprinted by permission of New Directions Publishing Corp.

way. Despite this, Frederick passed through Asia Minor in good order but drowned in the River Saleph (modern Göksu) in Cilicia. This unexpected drowning death of the German emperor while on crusade sparked apocalyptic expectations. Some thought that the Emperor Frederick was the Anti-Christ; others thought that he was the last universal emperor (an idea that developed in the West by the eighth century) who would destroy the enemies of Christ and purify the Church. His arrival in Jerusalem at the altar of the Holy Sepulchre was to have initiated the end of the world. Instead, his army split up, some going home, some proceeding to Acre.

The armies of Richard I and Philip II sailed to the Holy Land where they both participated in a successful siege of Acre. Richard and Philip then argued, and Philip, who had been repeatedly humiliated by Richard and who was, in any case, more concerned with France than with *Outremer*, went home. Richard's subsequent victories over Saladin were impressive; he recaptured parts of Palestine, with the dramatic exception of Jerusalem, which he consequently refused to visit.

Medieval stories of the crusade of Richard the Lion-Hearted were a mixture of reality and legend. He was said to have presented King Arthur's sword Excalibur to Tancred, ruler of Sicily, conquered Cyprus on the way to Acre, and found a piece of the True Cross outside Jerusalem. One of the more gruesome aspects of his legend was his alleged proclivity for eating the flesh of Muslim prisoners. He supposedly overcame Saladin in personal combat and slew, single-handedly, hundreds of Muslims. On his return home he was captured crossing Austrian territory incognito. A hungry lion was placed in his cell, whose heart he tore out—hence his sobriquet Lion-Hearted. He was discovered when a minstrel visited castle after castle, singing the first line of a song he and Richard had composed. When he reached the right castle, Richard responded. Most, but not all, of this was legend.

In reality Richard was a great military leader, although he could be ruthless. When negotiations broke down with Saladin over Acre, Richard had nearly 3,000 Muslim prisoners killed. He was a formidable opponent in battle, a brilliant strategist, and he conquered Cyprus and won back a significant portion of the Holy Land. But his capture by the Austrians on his return trip cost England 100,000 marks in ransom. Richard died in 1199; Saladin had died six years before (in 1193), leaving Frankish Syria and some of Richard's conquests in Palestine intact. This restored but diminished Latin kingdom was now centered on the port cities of Acre and Tyre and governed by Count Henry of Champagne.

Thirteenth-Century Crusades

In 1198, a young and ambitious new Pope, Innocent III (1198–1216), proclaimed a crusade. In a letter to the patriarch of Jerusalem, Innocent declared his support for reclaiming Jerusalem and his willingness to assume leadership of the effort. This Fourth Crusade took shape slowly. England and France were at odds; Germany was divided between two claimants to the imperial throne, while Spain continued to focus on the conquest of Muslim territory in the peninsula. With princely leadership preoccupied elsewhere, Innocent sought to reassert papal direction over the Crusades, but the results were dramatically different from what he envisioned.

Since there was little response to his initial call for crusade, Innocent tried various financial and spiritual incentives—imposing a crusading tax on the clergy, placing chests in parish churches for crusading alms, and offering full remission of sins for those who contributed money or participated directly in the crusade. In violation of canon law and marital rights, he allowed men to depart on crusade without their wives' consent. Eventually, the rulers of Champagne and of Blois (coming from a French family with a long crusading history) committed themselves and enlisted others from Flanders, northern France, and Italy.

This crusade differed dramatically from previous crusades. Learning from the overland disasters that had plagued earlier crusades, these barons negotiated sea transport. But because they overestimated the response (and the number of ships required), they found themselves deeply indebted to the Venetians, with whom they had signed a contract. The Venetians, led by their wily, old, nearly blind, and enormously respected Doge, Enrico Dandolo, offered to join the crusade. But they were more interested in gaining control over seaports on the Adriatic and repaying the Greeks for having arrested and imprisoned thousands of Venetian merchants in 1171 than in recapturing Jerusalem. Since the crusaders themselves had no love lost for Byzantium, and since they were in financial arrears to the Venetians, they acceded to Venetian plans. In doing so, however, they ignored a papal bull forbidding them to attack Christians. The result was a crusade in 1204 that ended in the conquest of Constantinople, the overthrow of the Byzantine Empire, and the unification of the Eastern and Western churches. The city of Constantinople, one of the most magnificent cities in Christendom, was burned and sacked. Churches were looted, works of art and manuscripts destroyed or sold, and relics snatched. The four bronze horsemen that used to stand above the portals of San Marco in Venice were stolen from the Hippodrome. "In this unspeakable fashion," notes one historian, "the Latin Empire of Constantinople replaced the Byzantine Empire until 1261."[12]

The Fourth Crusade has generated much debate, then and since, largely because the crusaders, by targeting Constantinople, attacked and killed Christians. Geoffrey de Villehardouin, marshal of Champagne and a leader and chronicler of the Fourth Crusade, was a statesman-historian who set out to justify the crusade and his own role in it. By boldly asserting that this conquest was a success justified by God, Villehardouin vilified those who did not follow the Venetians, those who defected along the way, and those who criticized its objectives. He also downplayed a papal excommunication of the Venetians. According to Villehardouin, the crusading knights and the Venetians were brave, good, and honorable; those who deserted were cowardly and justifiably met a bad end in the Holy Land.

In the final analysis, the Fourth Crusade produced a weak and unsustainable Latin kingdom centered on Constantinople that drew men and resources away from the Holy Land. By the 1220s, it was already on the verge of collapse; the Greeks took Constantinople back by 1261.

In 1218, a Fifth Crusade tried to outflank Muslims in the Holy Land by invading the Egyptian Delta. It ended in disaster, having been grossly mismanaged by the papal legate. The German Emperor Frederick II then negotiated the return of Jerusalem to Christian authority in 1229, but in 1244 a new group of Islamic Turks invaded Syria, retaking Jerusalem and holding it, this time until the British, under General Allenby in World War I, entered Jerusalem in 1917.

Two subsequent crusades (1245 and 1270) led by Louis IX of France resulted, respectively, in Louis's capture and his death (Chapter 16).

Criticism of Crusading

Criticism of the crusading enterprise spread in the thirteenth century. The Fourth Crusade had been a problem, and although Pope Innocent III had not supported its goals, some critics blamed the results on papal sinfulness. Guilhem Figueira, in his poem "D'un sirventes far," ranted, "Rome, you do little harm to the Saracens, but you massacre Greeks and Romans. In hellfire and perdition you have your home, . . . Where, Rome, do you find that one should kill Christians?" In addition, Innocent promoted crusades within Europe—against pagans in the eastern Baltic regions, against heretics, and against Christians who were politically unacceptable. Early in his papacy, Innocent declared a crusade against Markward of Anweiler, who was attempting to usurp the Sicilian crown, and he authorized crusades against Albigensian heretics in southern France (Chapter 16). This Albigensian crusade lasted from 1209 until 1229, when southern France was violently annexed to the north. As one song, from the year 1228, notes: "They (the clergy) prefer war to peace, malice and sin please them so much. I would have enjoyed going on the first crusade, but nearly all I see of this one [the Albigensian Crusade] repels me."[13] At the second council of Lyons in 1274, Humbert of Romans prepared a three-part work for preachers who were encountering criticisms of the crusades; some thirteenth-century sermons suggest that audiences were questioning the extent to which God was on the Christian side.

The Children's Crusade of 1212 also reflects concern with the changing direction crusading efforts were taking. Actually the first of several children's crusades, it is the one we know most about. It was evidently motivated by the idea that the meek, the childlike, and the poor might succeed where the proud had failed. Thousands of boys and girls followed Stephen, a French shepherd boy "seeking God," while thousands of German youths followed a boy from Cologne named Nicholas. Many children, teens, and some adults left plows, flocks, and families despite official and parental efforts to stop them. Wealthy children brought servants with them; others were entrusted to clergy. A chronicler at Cologne called it "a miraculous affair, indeed more than miraculous, for nothing of the sort had ever been heard of in the world." An annalist at Marbach labeled it a "useless expedition of children and stupid adults," a venture undertaken "without the balance of reason or the force of counsel." Many on the journey died, were sold into slavery, or raped. Some returned impoverished and disgraced after God failed to let them "pass through the seas with dry feet [to] recover the Holy Land and Jerusalem." The Church refused them passage from any Italian port; in France, royal decrees commanded their return. Possibly, although the accounts may be legendary, some took ship at Marseilles and Pisa, only to be shipwrecked or sold into slavery. Of the many thousands who left home few returned. The psychological impact on Europe of the loss of these youths is incalculable and perhaps fed resentment against the Church for its failures in the crusading effort.

In 1251, the continuing problem of the Crusades produced another popular movement known as the Shepherds' Crusade. Attracted by the preaching of a wandering monk from Hungary who claimed to have a letter from the Virgin Mary, thousands of shepherds and cowherds (again, mostly young people) from northern France and the Low Countries united, armed with crude weapons, to join the crusade of Louis IX. At first townsfolk, and even the Queen Mother in Paris, welcomed them, but they became more violent as they moved south. By the time they reached Tours, Orléans, and Bourges, they were attacking clergy, scholars, and Jews. The remainder of the story told by the chroniclers is a sordid account of violence turned against the shepherds. In Bourges, Bordeaux, Marseilles, Aigues Mortes, and England, the remaining bands of crusaders were caught, killed, and dispersed.

Another indicator of declining interest in the Crusades is the extent to which the military orders came under criticism. They were failing to attract men, lands, and monies, and were no longer as admired for their courage and austerity. Legends arose that implicated the military orders in the defeat of the Second Crusade at Damascus. Although they died in large numbers at the battle of Hattin, and had fought bravely in the Third Crusade, their decision not to take Jerusalem in 1197 (perhaps rightly, since they did not think they had the resources to hold it) redounded negatively on them. On the other hand, they had acquired enormous resources throughout Europe, becoming moneylenders and bankers for many. As a result, many Christians believed that the military orders had sufficient wealth to carry on the struggle against Muslims without reinforcements or additional monies. In fact, the military orders had limited resources, large responsibilities, and insufficient manpower.

The orders were also harmed by papal and royal policies. The pope, for example, would have been happy to use their services in Sicily. The kings of Castile tried to lure them to Spain to fight in the frontier wars against Islamic rulers, and the Teutonic Order did, by the 1220s, shift its activities to northeastern Europe where pagans still dominated. There the Teutonic knights made large territorial conquests as they mostly killed rather than converted the pagans.

The military orders were susceptible to criticism from those who believed that holy work did not include waging war or killing pagans and Muslims. Others believed that the Crusades were failing because the crusading orders had become corrupt and sinful. The military orders exacerbated the situation by fighting among themselves. They parted company over issues of strategy—for example, whether it was best to ally with the sultan in Damascus or the sultan in Egypt—and this affected the level of support they could offer crusaders. When Acre fell in 1291, many in the West blamed the crusading orders.

By the second half of the twelfth century, the recruitment of crusaders was accompanied by increased financial demands for crusading taxes and a burgeoning bureaucracy to handle them. People believed that crusading taxes went into pockets at home rather than abroad. One song, "Bien me deusse targier," from 1188, goes: ". . . No, no matter how much I desire, I would not stay here with these tyrants who have taken up the cross so that they may tax clerks, citizens and soldiers. Greed has made more Crusaders than has faith. But this cross that they bear will not be their salvation. . . . You who tax the crusaders, do not spend in this way the proceeds of this tax."[14] In Germany, Walther von der Vogelweide wrote a poem on the papal chests set up in parish churches which says, in part, "I believe that little of the silver will come to help God's land, for priests seldom share great treasure."[15]

It became more difficult to enforce crusading vows, to determine who had made such vows, or to force the monetary redemption of vows. Crusading preachers pressed their hearers, even the infirm, the poor, and women, to make a vow, receive the indulgence, and then redeem it by paying cash. In Cornwall in the year 1200, for example, a list of those who took crusading vows includes a tailor, a blacksmith, a shoemaker, two chaplains, a gamekeeper, a merchant, a miller, two tanners, and four or five women.[16] Clearly, not all of them would go on crusade, especially since the Church was now actively encouraging only fighting men to go. Instead they were encouraged to redeem their vows for a price, including interest if they waited too long.

The Crusades were becoming increasingly professional, sometimes employing mercenaries (which strained financial resources) or accepting armed criminals doing penance. This growing professionalization and bureaucratization of the crusades, combined with military failure, the loss of Jerusalem, and the redirecting of crusades toward enemies at home convinced many that the Church was sinful and the Holy War profoundly un-Christian. Although King Louis IX was determined to recover the Holy Land, mounting two campaigns into North Africa to that end (Chapter 16), and Pope Gregory X (1271–1276) made heroic efforts to reform abuses and resurrect crusading zeal, these efforts failed. Increasingly, contemporaries promoted alternative efforts. By the thirteenth century, Catholic Europe sent out extensive preaching missions. The orders of friars, especially, advocated both crusade and mission, recognizing, on the one hand, that conversion was far more likely to occur in regions governed by Christians, while, on the other hand, arguing that military strength alone would not win converts.

THE LARGER IMPACT OF THE CRUSADES

Direct cause and effect between the Crusades and subsequent developments are difficult to prove. Some results are more obvious than others, such as the growth of bureaucracy, both ecclesiastical and secular, to handle the finances associated with crusading. Some historians have suggested that men absent on crusades allowed women, especially aristocratic women, to take on more responsibilities at home. At the level of royalty, women such as Blanche of Castile in France, Marie of Champagne, and Eleanor of Aquitaine in England, functioned as regents in the absence of sons and husbands. Below this level, it is difficult to prove this and evidence from England suggests that the absence of husbands on crusade left some women vulnerable to economic and sexual depredations.[17]

The massacres of the Jews that occurred during the First Crusade were a watershed in European Jewish history, particularly in setting an example of self-martyrdom as a response to persecution, in marginalizing the Jewish communities, and in promoting the process of self-identification (as Christians) that made Jews more unacceptable in European society.

The idea of sending missionaries into Muslim territories developed alongside the Crusades. While the First Crusade focused on the liberation of oppressed Christians and the recovery of Jerusalem, in subsequent crusades conversion became a more explicit goal. Overall, however, it cannot be shown that the Crusades, or the missions, produced any large number of converts from Islam.

The Crusades did not initiate trading networks with the Middle East, which were already extensive. But the Crusades became part of a process of more aggressive exploration, trade, and colonization. The Italian city-states (especially Venice, Pisa, and Genoa) benefited in varying degrees from the Christian dominance of the eastern Mediterranean and from crusading needs for transportation and supplies. The trade in slaves, arms, spices, textiles, dyes, medicine, metals, porcelain, rugs, glassware, and a host of other items made Italian merchants rich and increased the circulation of money throughout western Europe. New methods in banking and credit, new technologies of mapmaking, the construction of wind mills, new methods of sailing and shipbuilding, new agricultural products, and new terms were introduced to the West from the East, to which the Crusades contributed at least in part.

It has been suggested that improved military methods and technologies were a result of crusading warfare. Siege techniques (mining and sapping walls), the use of Greek fire, the crossbow and certain elaborations in castle fortifications might have been influenced by Muslim and Byzantine military methods, although these influences are debated and more research needs to be done. The Muslim technique of transmitting messages by carrier pigeon was certainly picked up in the West, as was the use of heraldic emblems on banners and shields, common in the Middle East.

The Crusades created rivalries among crusading parties, the Italian city-states, military orders, and the Latin kingdoms themselves. In the Second Crusade, rivalries between the French and the Germans undermined the expedition; the Third Crusade was marked by Richard I's disputes with Philip of France, with the duke of Austria, and with the Christian rulers at Antioch and Acre. The Fourth Crusade was marked, of course, by direct conflict with Byzantium. While these rivalries may have aided the development of national identities in the West, they also aided the downfall of the Christian kingdoms in the East.

In the end the crusaders were expelled from *Outremer*, leaving the Holy Land to Muslim rule and a Byzantine Empire in collapse. Although the initial Crusades helped restore parts of Asia Minor to the Greeks and restored the Holy Land to the Latin Christians, the Muslim offensive always resumed and the Christian responses were increasingly inadequate. The First Crusade provoked a call for *jihad*, first led by Zengī, Nūr-al-Dīn and Saladin and then by a united Mamluk State (1250–1517). The Mongols and a consolidated Mamluk regime in Egypt brought an end to *Outremer* in 1291 with the fall of Acre; the Ottoman Turks destroyed Byzantium in 1453 with the capture of Constantinople.

These setbacks did not end the crusading impulse in the West. Scholars in Paris and Spain hatched grand schemes. Popes continued to call for crusades and to levy crusading taxes. When Prince Henry the Navigator of Portugal began to promote the Portuguese exploration of Africa in the fifteenth century, his letters conveyed a crusading fervor. And Christopher Columbus carried red crusading crosses on his white sails, brought an Arabic interpreter with him, and described his journey as an expedition intended to convert "the sect of Mahomet and of all idolatries and heresies."

Summary

The crusading movement has been treated as a whole in this chapter—from its initial conceptualization by Pope Gregory VII in the eleventh century to the capture of Constantinople in 1453, thereby breaking through the chronological bounds of Part IV of this textbook.

No European ruler during this period could ignore the demands of the crusades for men and money, although it was the reputation of the papacy that tended to rise and fall with the ups and downs of affairs in *Outremer*. Crusading legends, songs, and sermons entered popular culture, and many people followed the path to the

Holy Land and returned to tell their story. The Crusades put Europeans into sustained contact with Islam—a monotheistic religion resistant to conversion and impelled by its own version of Holy War. Gradually Europeans saw Islam as a far greater threat to Christianity than paganism. It was Islamic polities more than internal problems or technological bottlenecks that placed constraints on western expansionism from the eleventh century forward. As the contested boundaries between Christianity and Islam shifted back and forth, however, the West could not sustain its hold on the Holy Land. European Christian monarchs became less and less willing to send resources overseas, as they attended more and more to strengthening and expanding their own kingdoms externally and consolidating control internally.

NOTES

1. *The Correspondence of Pope Gregory VII: Selected Letters from the Registrum,* trans. E. Emerton (New York: Columbia University Press, 1932) 22.
2. *The Song of Roland,* trans. Frederick Goldin (New York: W.W. Norton, 1978) 120.
3. Guibert of Nogent, *The Deeds of God through the Franks: a translation of Guibert of Nogent's Gesta Dei per Francos,* trans. and ed. Robert Levine (Woodbridge, Suffolk: Boydell Press, 1997) 47–48.
4. *The Alexiad of Anna Comnena,* trans. E.R.A. Sewter (Baltimore: Penguin, 1969) 308–309
5. *The Deeds of the Franks (Gesta Francorum) and other Pilgrims to Jerusalem,* ed. Rosalind Hill (London: Thomas Nelson and Sons Ltd., 1962) 4–5.
6. *The Deeds of the Franks,* 91–92
7. *The Deeds of the Franks,* 17; Guibert of Nogent, *The Deeds of God,* 38–39 and elsewhere.
8. Fulcher of Chartres, *A History of the Expedition to Jerusalem 1095–1127,* ed. H.S. Fink and trans. F. R. Ryan (Knoxville: University of Tennessee Press, 1969) 95.
9. Anthony Luttrell, "Englishwomen as Pilgrims to Jerusalem: Isolda Parewastell, 1365," *Equally in God's Image: Women in the Middle Ages,* ed. Holloway, Bechtold and Wright (New York: Peter Lang, 1990) 187.
10. William of Tyre, *History of Deeds Done Beyond the Sea,* trans. Babcock and Krey, vol. 1, book 12, ch. 17 (New York: Columbia University Press, 1943).
11. "Liber ad Milites Templi: de laude novae militiae," ed. J. Leclercq and H. M. Rochais. *S. Bernardi opera,* vol. 3 (Rome: Editiones Cistercienses, 1963) I, 1–2
12. Aziz Atiya, *Crusade, Commerce and Culture* (Bloomington: Indiana University Press, 1962) 84.
13. Elizabeth Siberry, *Criticism of Crusading 1095–1274* (Oxford: Clarendon Press, 1985) 165.
14. Richard Crocker, "Early Crusade Songs," *The Holy War,* ed. T.P. Murphy (Columbus: Ohio State University Press, 1976) 88.
15. Siberry, *Criticism of Crusading,* 129.
16. Christopher Tyerman, *England and the Crusaders 1095–1588* (Chicago: University of Chicago Press, 1988) 171.
17. Tyerman, 209–211.

~

CHAPTER 13

The Development of Government, 1050–1200

At the height of the Crusades, the Church benefited. Not only did the Church gain moral authority, but the use of councils and legates, preaching tours, crusading taxes, and the administration that grew alongside the Crusades enhanced its public authority. A stronger papacy offered a model of government to European political leaders who, by the end of the eleventh century, were crafting new bases of authority and strengthening instruments of government. No one form of secular rule prevailed. The period from 1050 to 1200 was one of ferment and formation, where a mélange of notions of personal lordship, kingship, civil law, imperial traditions, local custom, and communal values jostled uncomfortably with papal primacy and ecclesiastical law. Out of this competition between authorities emerged several strong monarchies, a single imperial authority, a powerful ecclesiastical hierarchy, and numerous other political organizations, from city-states, to towns, to counties, and duchies. Many of these developments were disorderly. Wars of succession and of conquest, civil wars, revolts, and violence accompanied developing expertise in law, greater administrative capabilities, and a growing interest in ideas of monarchy, empire, authority, and liberties. In exploring this dynamic, this chapter focuses primarily on England, the German Empire, and France—the three Christian kingdoms that dominated Europe politically by 1200. It will, however, also examine patterns of authority in Spain, Italy, and Scandinavia as well as in those western and eastern states (Ireland, Scotland, the kingdoms of eastern Europe, and the principalities of Rus) that were threatened by fragmentation or by overbearing neighbors.

AUTHORITY AND CONSTRAINT: EMPERORS, KINGS, COMMUNAL VALUES, AND LAWS

The most powerful political discourse on secular rule centered on the positions of king and emperor. Often the distinction between the two was not clear. The

Germanic tradition of kingship is difficult to trace before the fifth and sixth centuries, but by then Visigothic, Ostrogothic, Burgundian, and Frankish kings were making laws, convening church councils, appointing bishops, and waging war. As we have seen in Chapter 3 they sometimes encroached upon the authority of the Byzantine emperor, but they never appropriated the imperial title. This changed dramatically on Christmas day in the year 800, when Charlemagne took the title of Roman emperor, conferred by Pope Leo III. From then on (with a hiatus in the tenth century) a western ruler claimed to be Roman emperor. As a result, Roman imperial ideas were reintroduced into western society.

One rationale for Charlemagne's imperial coronation was the belief that the Byzantine throne was empty, having been seized in 797 by a woman, the Empress Irene. Pope Leo III, along with others, argued that a woman could not be emperor. Even when the throne returned to a man, western commentators asserted that an irreparable break had occurred in the Byzantine imperial line. They argued, additionally, that the imperial title at Constantinople was forfeit due to the usurpations, unorthodoxy, and lack of piety of the emperors. The Byzantines, while willing to recognize Charlemagne as a co-emperor and "spiritual brother" (but *not* as Roman Emperor), maintained that Constantine had transferred the empire to the East and that they held exclusive rights to it. Therefore, according to Byzantine thought, only the emperor in Constantinople could bestow the authority of kingship on lesser rulers. When western rulers failed to apply to the East for their titles, they were considered to have detached themselves from the one universal empire.

In the West, the imperial title was transferable and not affixed to a particular location. Prior to the twelfth century, Anglo-Saxon kings had occasionally called themselves emperors; Spanish rulers in the kingdom of León-Castile took the title of emperor, aspiring to rule over other kings on the peninsula; and the Ottonian rulers of Germany successfully asserted their right to the Carolingian title of Roman emperor. By the twelfth century, though, western Europeans generally agreed that the only legitimate western emperor was the Roman emperor, crowned by the pope in Rome, and that, although English, Spanish, and French kings might fancy themselves candidates for emperor, German kings had a traditional right to the throne.

The imperial throne descended through election and also by birthright. Normally the German princes (both secular and ecclesiastical) met in a Diet (public assembly) and chose the most appropriate candidate among those with royal bloodlines. By 1078, German princes were demanding the right to elect an emperor independent of hereditary principles; in 1125, with the election of Lothar III—which enjoyed the support of the papacy—they succeeded in doing so. Gradually, the electoral committee changed from a Diet including all imperial princes to a much smaller circle of seven electors. In 1257, only the archbishops of Cologne, Mainz, and Trier; the king of Bohemia; the count palatine of the Rhine; the duke of Saxony, and the margrave of Brandenburg voted; this precedent became the basis for the electoral college.

After this election (technically to the position of king of Germany), the emperor-elect was crowned emperor by the pope. This papal role was a double-edged sword. A papal crowning symbolized the divine authority of the emperor, but it also enabled the Church to argue that it conferred the authority and was therefore superior to the empire. Gregory VII (see Chapter 11) claimed the power to depose an emperor and release his subjects from obedience. Innocent III (see Chapter 16) claimed authority to decide among candidates in a disputed imperial election and to govern the empire during a vacancy. But, while the pope might make an emperor, the pope did not crown kings, and political authority in medieval Europe was more often a matter of kingship than of emperorship.

Medieval kingship was, for the most part, considered divinely ordained. When William the Conqueror was crowned king of England in 1066, both his coronation oath and the liturgy affirmed his divine authority. The Capetian kings of France considered that they ruled by the grace of God; their kingship was treated as sacred and surrounded by religious symbols (see Chapter 10). The German kings, whether emperor or not, were pictured as Christlike, communicating directly with God and receiving their crown from the hand of the Father. Europe was rife with kings— kings of Poland, Hungary, Bohemia, Norway, Denmark, León, Castile, Sicily, and Aragon, as well as Irish provincial kings and even, up to the thirteenth century, kings of the Hebrides and the Isle of Man. In the ninth and tenth centuries, the sons of territorial Viking kings, even if they themselves were landless and little more than pirates, called themselves kings. By the eleventh century the sanctity of many (but not all) medieval kings was symbolized by being crowned and anointed by a member of the clergy (usually an archbishop).

Despite their sacred character, medieval Christian kings and emperors had many constraints on their power. For one, there was no agreed-upon method of succession. Only gradually, and with the support of the Church, did hereditary succession of a king's oldest son become the norm. In the eleventh and twelfth centuries, it was possible for a brother or nephew to succeed to the throne, a widowed ruler's wife or a council of barons to rule as regents, or a member of a particularly powerful noble family to claim the throne. As a result, struggles for succession were common, and aristocratic support and consent were crucial. Those monarchies that survived and grew were those that could depend upon the loyalty of nobility. As a legendary model, in the *Song of Roland* the Emperor Charlemagne did not act without the consent of the peers of the realm. The importance of the Norman barons for the successes and failures of the Anglo-Norman rulers from 1066 to 1154 is evident to any student of English history. The German emperor was elected by and answerable to the princes. Kings consulted their councils; for example, Louis IX of France routinely consulted his barons while on crusade in the 1240s. As lord of his barons, a king was constrained by the need to maintain a consultative relationship (usually through some sort of council), to adhere to lord-vassalage duties (usually the duty of protection in exchange for military and financial support), and to fulfill any oaths to which he had assented at his coronation. Misconduct on the part of a ruler (for example, violating a pledge to his followers) was an indication of tyranny and an invitation to rebellion.

John of Salisbury (c. 1120–1180), an English commoner who rose to prominence in the Church, argued that princes who were tyrants should be criticized, corrected, and even killed. His treatise, *Policraticus,* is commonly considered the first theoretical study of politics in medieval Europe. In it he presents a portrait of princes as subject to God and to those who act in His place (e.g. the pope), obedient to law, bound by oaths of fidelity to protect their men, and concerned for the health of the body politic. Such rulers show moderation in their actions and extend respect and liberty to each member in the community. Monarchs who oppress their people or the Church were likely to be overthrown by God, perhaps by means of human hands.

Medieval Christian kings were also constrained by the claims of the Church. Their responsibilities included defending the Church and orthodoxy, crusading for Christ, protecting the undefended, and rendering God's justice on earth. In practical terms, this meant that the Church expected rulers to support crusading policies, protect church lands, and enforce ecclesiastical decisions where issues such as marriage, peace and violence, oaths, or heresy were concerned. Thus, the Emperor Otto III (996–1002), whose court consciously rivaled the ostentation of Byzantium, nonetheless called himself "the slave of Jesus Christ." Louis VII, carrying the sacred symbols of French royalty into battle in the Second Crusade, took on the persona of a humble monk when the crusade failed. And Henry II of England, majestic in his kingship, salvaged his authority vis-à-vis the Church by submitting to penance and flagellation at the tomb of Thomas Becket, the archbishop of Canterbury murdered by Henry's men.

Kings and emperors were also constrained by divine law. Medieval writers were fond of citing biblical models of behavior: Kings David and Solomon as good rulers and King Saul as an example of a wicked ruler punished by God. One of the theoretical bases for ecclesiastical claims over secular authority came from scripture (Luke 22: 38). As Christ prepared for Gethsemane, his apostles said, "Lord, here are two swords!" And Christ responded, "That is enough!" These two swords were understood, allegorically, as the swords of secular and spiritual power. While it was generally agreed that the priesthood could not appropriate both swords, it was also generally agreed upon by twelfth-century writers (most of whom were clerical) that the spiritual sword was superior to the secular or temporal sword. Although John of Salisbury (and also Otto of Freising, another important twelfth-century writer on politics) promoted cooperation between church and state, they were inclined to allow the Church power over the secular sphere. John of Salisbury used the following, popular analogy: The prince is subject to God just as the head is ruled by the soul.

Medieval kings were both bridled and empowered by law. The growth of public authority, particularly monarchy, in twelfth-century Europe depended upon the growing effectiveness of legal powers. These derived from expanding courts, the presence of trained jurists, and greater dependence on written laws and legal procedures. The rediscovery of Roman law was crucial to the formation of a more homogenized, less particularized, European legal tradition. In the 1070s, a single surviving text of Justinian's sixth-century *Digest* was discovered. Together with the briefer *Codex* and elementary *Institutes* of Justinian* it formed the basis for a school of legal studies at Bologna, Italy, whose influence spread rapidly through western

---

* The *Institutes* is an introductory text to the basic points of law in the sixth century legal reforms of Emperor Justinian. It had been available in western Europe throughout the Middle Ages. The *Codex,* a summary of imperial ordinances revised under Justinian, had also been available earlier. The Justinian *Digest,* a far more complex work that preserves the theories of classical jurists on basic issues of the law, had not been cited in the Latin West since the early seventh century. Its rediscovery in the eleventh century was crucial to the revival of Roman law.

Europe. By the 1150s, the emperor Frederick I Barbarossa was able to appeal to Roman law and to the Bolognese jurists for support in establishing his authority as emperor in northern Italy. Roman law as interpreted in the twelfth century, however, imposed limits on the ruler's will through higher norms—natural law (based on universal reason) and customary laws that had been approved by usage. At the local level a ruler's authority was limited by practice. Throughout Europe, disputes were usually settled in county, manorial, urban, shire, seigneurial, or mercantile courts, following the judgment of peers and local officials based on civil or customary law, or, in England, the precedents set by royal justices and juries at common law.

Simultaneously with the revival of Roman law came the developing study of ecclesiastical (canon) law, which, insofar as it represented divine law, placed further constraints on rulers. The collecting and harmonizing of past and present ecclesiastical legislation became an intellectual discipline in its own right. A significant number of administrators in the Roman curia as well as in secular governments were trained in both Roman civil and in canon law, and more and more justices brought a professional training to the courts.

Legally and in other respects, the ecclesiastical hierarchy was a model for civil service. Its dependence on written records, search for written precedents, growth of administrative departments (chancery, consistory, chamber of finance), of dioceses, parishes, and ecclesiastical courts were in advance of secular governments. While developing a hierarchical model of government, the papacy simultaneously promoted communal movements in many Italian cities, and oversaw the emergence of electoral forms of government in its own councils and in some of the new monastic movements, such as the Cistercians, where elected abbots attended general chapters to legislate for the entire order.

Authority of any kind was tempered by a tradition of communal decision making, deeply held communal values, and custom. We have already seen that Germanic society depended upon cooperation and communal decision making (see Chapter 3). In the more feudal areas of Europe, the nobility were expected to cooperate with their vassals and to respect past custom in their relationship with them. Added to this was Roman law and history, which invoked the idea of the *respublica* (the common good or the common profit of the people). As a result, medieval people had both a legal and a customary basis for asserting their rights.

The twelfth century saw the emergence of communes, leagues, and guilds. The merchants of the city of Laon, for example, organized a commune early in the twelfth century to provide self-government and to protect their liberties. They paid a substantial fee to Louis VI for their privileges. When faced with a recalcitrant episcopal overlord, they murdered him in his own hall. In Champagne in the 1170s, villagers began to buy franchises that allowed them free disposal of their properties, freedom to move, and freedom from tolls and military service. Some of these communities gained degrees of self-government, electing their own officials and solving local disputes. In Germany the merchants, tradesmen, and artisans of various cities (such as Lübeck, Magdeburg, Nürnberg, and Vienna) created legal protections that enabled them to elect city councils, establish law courts, and build up a military force. These models of self-government spread to other German cities and, by the thirteenth and fourteenth centuries, to eastern Europe.

French and German communities came somewhat late to the communal movement, which had been established already in Flanders and Italy for several generations. In Flanders, in particular, wealthy wool towns such as Bruges, Ypres, Ghent,
and St. Omer played one lord against another, to each town's economic and political advantage. In 1128, William Clito (son of Robert Curthose, duke of Normandy) needed the support of these towns, so he issued charters guaranteeing
mercantile rights and a free citizenry (see Chapter 9). In Italy the growth of communal government was explosive. In Milan, Genoa, Pisa, Mantua, and any number of northern Italian towns, town councils emerged claiming to represent the
people in a struggle for power with military and ecclesiastical elites. These communes derived from communities within the towns—mercantile associations or
representatives of city districts. In Milan, an eleventh-century chronicler described
them as "very strong in their aspiration for liberty, desiring wealth but more anxious to be free."[1] Communal leaders began to set up magistrates, to call popular assemblies, and to draft documents that gave legal force to their "republic." They
found justification for their position in Roman law texts that defined republics as
communities of citizens and citizens as, by nature, free and equal.[2] John Bassiani
(d. 1192), commenting on Roman law, wrote "that the vigor of both law and custom derives from the will and judgment of the people."

By the 1140s, Roman ideas of civic democracy (combined with antipapal sentiment) sparked a popular revolt in Rome itself. The Romans resuscitated the Senate
and the ancient Roman formula of "the Roman Senate and People" (*Senatus Popu-
lusque Romanus*). They called for ecclesiastical reform and invited the German ruler
to receive the imperial crown directly from them rather than from the pope. Frederick Barbarossa, who believed that his crown descended from God rather than
pope or senate, had one of the popular leaders killed in 1155, and the movement
collapsed. This Roman revolution was perhaps the most radical communal movement of the twelfth century; it was different insofar as it harked back to Roman antiquity, but it was typical in its appeal to liberty based on custom and law.

As kings, aristocrats, and city-states expanded their authority outward from
core territories to the peripheries, they encouraged migration to outlying areas by
offering freedom. The liberties and privileges offered colonists, whether east of
the Elbe, on the Spanish or Sicilian frontiers or in the crusading kingdoms, bound
rulers to respect land ownership (including the right to buy, sell, rent, or inherit), self-
government, and independent courts.

The result of these various developments was the continuing consolidation of
states that had been emerging since the tenth century, although some European
states were more successful than others. Medieval states* are characterized by increasingly centralized administrative, military, and judicial functions in addition to
ideologies that legitimated state authority (see Chapter 10). In these states the ruling elite was no longer based primarily on kinship relations but was linked to the
provision of administrative and military services. Close relationships with the ruler
depended on loyalty and service to the state on the part of elites, and protection of
landholdings and rewards for service on the part of the ruler.

---

* "State" is defined here as a unified political entity with a definite territory and a central ruler.

This growing sophistication of the state depended upon the spread of literacy (particularly Latin literacy) and the habit of preserving written records. Michael Clanchy, in his book *From Memory to Written Record,* details the proliferation of documents and the rise of a literate mentality in twelfth and thirteenth-century England. Access to books, to schools, to clerks, and to writing materials all expanded alongside archives, written inquests, and the number of civil servants. One consequence of this growth of governmental service, literate culture, and public authority may have been to diminish the role of women in the public sphere. The more formalized the processes of government, the less likely female involvement was. This has led historians to suggest that, as public authority widened in the twelfth century, the role of women diminished. Certainly, as royal power consolidated and lines of authority were drawn, female rulers had little part in the process.* John of Salisbury's explanation for the reason why women did not rule derived from his understanding of Virgil's *Aeneid.* He condemned Dido for loving Aeneas and ruling Carthage frivolously, leading to the ruin of her city.

> You may learn from the example of Dido. For with how much frivolity was Aeneas admitted, how much favour was soon found for an unknown man, an exile, a fugitive . . . persuasive words paved the way for the man's [Aeneas's] entrance . . . a more elaborate banquet was planned for capturing the devotion of all, stories followed the banquet, which was accompanied by hunting and a multiplicity of frivolous luxuries. This engendered lewdness and led to the abandonment of the city to flames and to a perpetual reason for hostility. This is the end of the rulership of women.[3]

In fact, between 1200 and 1450 few women were queens in their own right. One exception was Margaret, the seven-year-old "Maid of Norway," heir to the Scottish throne in 1286. She died at age seven on her way to Scotland, the last of a Scottish royal dynasty that had ruled since the early eleventh century.

ANGLO-NORMANS, CIVIL WAR, AND THE ANGEVIN EMPIRE

Within this context of kingship, constraint, and the growth of public authority, several powerful monarchies developed in the eleventh and twelfth centuries. The most organized and commanding new kingdom to emerge was an Anglo-Norman† state

---

* This does not mean that there were not some strong female rulers. Matilda of England and Eleanor of Aquitaine will be treated in this chapter. Other strong women-rulers were duchesses or regents, including Matilda of Tuscany, Adela of Blois, Adela and Marie of Champagne, Margaret of Navarre and Sicily, and two queens—Urraca of León-Castile and Melisende of Jerusalem. One might note the unusual privilege given to the duchy of Austria by Frederick Barbarossa—the privilege of hereditary succession through both the male and female line.

† Historians generally call the period of English history from 1066 to 1154 the Anglo-Norman era.

in England that straddled the continent and gave way, after a period of civil war, to an entity that historians have labeled the Angevin Empire. A combination of a solid alliance between the king and the Anglo-Norman barons, a generally good working relationship with the Church, and a willingness to enhance the role of central administration through the use of writs, laws, and courts made the reigns of William I, Henry I, and Henry II notable in the history of medieval state-building. The story of this state begins, however, with Anglo-Saxon England.

The Norman Conquest

One of the most centralized kingdoms in eleventh-century Europe was the Anglo-Saxon kingdom of England (at least south of Yorkshire). When King Edward the Confessor died in 1065, however, there were three claimants to the throne: Earl Harold Godwineson, the leading English candidate; Duke William of Normandy, to whom Edward perhaps once pledged the throne; and Harold Hardrada, king of Norway. When Harold Godwineson was crowned king, the other two claimants organized invasions. Harold Hardrada struck first, in the north. Rallying an army, Harold Godwineson marched to Yorkshire and defeated the Norwegian invasion in a stunning victory at Stamford Bridge. Then hearing that William had landed, he force-marched his army 260 miles back south.

The armies must have been very evenly matched, despite the fact that the English fought on foot while the Normans had horses. The hilly terrain and the English position at the foot of a ridge offset the advantage of the Norman cavalry. Harold, however, may have been at a psychological disadvantage. William had received a papal blessing, consecrated relics, and a papal banner before embarking; Harold, in contrast, had been declared excommunicate, making this something of a religious war. The battle began at 9 A.M. and lasted until dusk, at which time the Anglo-Saxon shield-wall was breached and Harold was slain at the foot of his standard.

The Norman Conquest of England has always excited debate and controversy. At various times in English history, William has been seen as a tyrant and the Norman Conquest the "yoke" of a foreign power; at other times, William's conquest has been seen as the origin of English greatness.

One immediate effect of the invasion was the widespread destruction of towns and lands and the brutal suppression of English resistance. The Anglo-Saxon nobility, both ecclesiastical and secular, were overthrown and replaced by the conquerors (Normans, along with Bretons, French, and Flemish warriors). William claimed the entire island (including Scotland and Wales) as his demesne; he then rewarded his followers by parceling out perhaps four-fifths of England and southern Wales. To secure his power William built castles at strategic points (some forty were built in the first ten years) using forced labor. William ruled the Church, attending councils, appointing (mostly Norman) bishops, and promoting continental reform measures, particularly the introduction of canon law.

William adopted the already sophisticated Anglo-Saxon administration, although the Anglo-Saxon language was replaced with Latin and French. In particular, he

King Harold of England Killed at the Battle of the Hastings, 1066   The Bayeux tapestry depicts the death of Harold in cinematic fashion. It first shows Harold struck by an arrow in the eye or forehead and then slashed in the leg as he falls. The Latin inscription reads, "King Harold has been killed." Note that the Normans are on horseback, while the English are on foot. The tapestry shows chain mail, long shields, stirrups, swords, axes, and spears. The bottom edge has images of Normans collecting battle gear and clothing from dead English soldiers. The Bayeux tapestry was directed by a Norman patron and stitched by needlewomen, perhaps at a nunnery in southeast England. *Musée de la Tapisserie de Bayeaux by permission of the Town of Bayeaux/Art Resource, NY.*

retained the administration of taxes and minting of coins, presumably because they proved so successful in bringing wealth into the king's coffers. William may also have retained Anglo-Saxon modes of military recruitment (see Chapter 7) while simultaneously introducing fixed quotas from tenants-in-chief. He introduced stricter laws governing access to the forests and expanded the forest jurisdiction to cover one-fourth of England; he also oversaw the gradual replacement of Anglo-Saxon cathedrals and abbeys with Norman buildings. Overall, William introduced a more hierarchical, centralized, and feudal set of relations between the king, his barons, and their vassals.

In 1068–1069, England north of the Humber revolted, partly because William taxed it heavily and partly because he understood the politics of the north so poorly. In response, William's troops slaughtered families, burned villages, and destroyed crops, plows, tools, and livestock. This "harrying" of the north was so effective that parts of it remained a wasteland for decades.

In 1086, William instituted a countrywide survey of resources. This survey, which produced what was called the *Domesday Book,* was done by two sets of investigators, one checking on the other. The Anglo-Saxon Chronicle commented that there was not one ox, cow, or pig left off the record. The information garnered was linked to a very heavy tax that then followed. It was also a record of the landholdings and judicial struggles over land as they were known prior to 1066 and then after the Conquest. It therefore records the tremendous changes in ownership in the wake of the Norman Conquest.

In 1087, William the Conqueror was succeeded in Normandy by his oldest son, Robert Curthose (r. 1087–1106), and in England by his second son, William Rufus (r. 1087–1100). Unity between the two kingdoms was only reestablished when Duke Robert went on crusade, leaving William in charge of Normandy. William Rufus was at the height of his power when he was killed by an arrow* while hunting.

Henry I (1100–1135)

Henry, William Rufus's younger brother, raced to Winchester to secure the treasury and the crown, but Henry was in an insecure position. He had not been designated by William, nor crowned by an archbishop, and some thought he might be implicated in his brother's death. His reign was quickly troubled by baronial rebellion and battles with the king of France, with Count Fulk of Anjou, and with his brother Robert of Normandy, whom he captured in 1106 and imprisoned until Robert's death.

Despite these initial problems, Henry I had a long and successful reign. This was due, in large part, to his abilities as a warrior, administrator, and judge of character and circumstances. Henry moved quickly to placate the church. William Rufus had sent Anselm, the archbishop of Canterbury, into exile. Henry recalled him and within the next few years hammered out an agreement on investiture. While the archbishop would invest bishops and abbots with the ring and staff, the king would invest them with temporal power. This solution to the investiture controversy foreshadowed the imperial compromise reached at Worms in 1122. Henry became a generous patron of the Church, but he exercised a heavy hand, convening councils, appointing bishops, and imposing discipline on the clergy. Gradually reform measures took hold. Ecclesiastical censures of married clergy and simony began to have an impact; the church grew in numbers of clergy and of churches; and, despite Henry's controlling presence, it began to establish its own court system and to settle jurisdictional issues internally.

Henry created a cadre of "new" men around him who would serve him loyally in battle and support him financially and administratively, and he worked to dissipate tensions between older Norman families and the newer beneficiaries of royal patronage. Loyalty became a byword. Henry generously and consistently rewarded his followers. And he pleased many of his magnates by consulting them often, reuniting England with Normandy under one ruler in 1106, and inaugurating three decades of relative peace. To those who crossed him, on the other hand, his justice was harsh and his punishments cruel (e.g. life imprisonment or mutilation by castration and blinding). As C. Warren Hollister puts it, "historians . . . while agreeing that the peace was long, have been less certain that the prince was good."[4]

---

* Contemporaries suspected that the hand was that of Walter Tyrel, who was handsomely rewarded soon after by Henry I.

Twelfth-century England saw the development of administrative procedures and the government use of literate men who were comfortable with written records. Much of this took place under Henry I, who was himself literate, and who seems to have had a talent for administration; many of his administrative innovations were inspired by ecclesiastical models. Under Henry, the Exchequer was established. The Exchequer (still the name used in England for the treasury department) was originally a checkerboard tabletop, similar to an abacus, that allowed financial officials to calculate, at a glance, sums received and sums due. Everyone, whether literate or not, could see and agree on the calculations. Receipts were then given in the form of notched sticks (especially helpful for the illiterate) while the king's clerks made a record on parchment. Although many of Henry's officials traveled with him, following the itinerant style of any twelfth-century monarch, some stayed put at Westminster, which began to develop as the seat of English government.

Henry made increasing use of the Chancery (the royal writing office), sending out peremptory writs (personal commands, for example, to his sheriffs or justiciars). The writ described a complaint and instructed an official to act, thereby initiating legal proceedings. It was not free, but available for purchase to all freemen.

Henry was considered a great king in his time. He was labeled "the peaceful king," "the Lion of Justice," and praised for restoring ancient laws and protecting the Church. He was much respected (and feared) by continental rulers. As a result, he was able to marry his daughter, Matilda, to the emperor Henry V, and his son William to the daughter of King Louis VI of France.

Civil War under King Stephen (1135–1154)

The great tragedy of Henry's life was the drowning death of William, his only legitimate son, in the wreck of the White Ship in 1120. On a clear evening, within sight of land, the ship, filled with revelers (many of them young people from the Anglo-Norman aristocracy) and steered by a drunken sailor, suddenly crashed and sank, leaving only one survivor. Although Henry had more than twenty illegitimate children, he had only one remaining legitimate child—Matilda. Despite designating her as his successor and requesting that the magnates swear an oath to support her, Henry could not force acceptance of a female monarch in twelfth-century England. A woman did not usually lead troops to battle, and most of the nobility did not relish swearing fidelity to a female. As a consequence, when Henry I died unexpectedly in 1135 (a glutton, he died eating lamprey eels), the Anglo-Norman magnates broke their oaths and supported the kingship of Stephen of Blois, Henry's nephew.

In the next few years, Matilda was able to gain a stronghold in the west of England. The civil war that followed developed into a stalemate. Stephen's initial strengths dissipated in the course of the struggle. His loss of Normandy to Matilda's second husband, the count of Anjou, was crucial, but he also alienated many early supporters by his vacillating behavior, his ill treatment of the Church, and his dependence upon favorites. Under Stephen's reign, bishops were excommunicated, relations with the papacy deteriorated, England was placed under interdict, and whole districts were plundered, villages burnt, and people oppressed. The Anglo-

Saxon Chronicle reported that, "men said openly that Christ and his saints slept."[5] Finally, Stephen agreed to disinherit his surviving son and recognize Henry, Matilda's oldest son (b. 1133), as his successor. Though Matilda never ruled England, her persistence and daring ultimately led to success on behalf of her son, Henry.

Henry II (1154–1189)

When Henry II came to the throne in 1154, he was twenty-one. He had recently married Eleanor, the heiress of the duchy of Aquitaine and repudiated wife of Louis VII of France. He was already count of Anjou and duke of Normandy. As a result of the marriage and of Henry's accession to the English crown, Henry and Eleanor now controlled much of the westernmost portion of Europe (see Map 13.1). Henry was the first of the Plantagenet rulers of England, so-called because the sobriquet of his father, the count of Anjou, was *planta genista* or broom plant. He, Eleanor, and their sons and successors (Richard I and King John) all became the substance of legend. They appeared larger than life to their contemporaries, and they are still the subject of plays, films, and books. Henry is largely remembered for his relationship with Eleanor, his role in the martyrdom of Thomas Becket, and his success in developing a more rational, centralized administration in England.

Eleanor, who had given Louis VII two daughters, produced five sons and three daughters for Henry. She and Henry gradually grew apart, perhaps because of Henry's many affairs, but more likely because beginning about 1163 he excluded her increasingly from political involvement. In 1168, Eleanor left England to take control of her duchy. Although her court at Poitiers offered music, poetry, stories, and gossip, political concerns were always foremost for Eleanor, particularly the conquest of Toulouse and the advancement of her children. In 1173, she backed a revolt of her sons against their father, with the result that, for most of the time from 1174 until Henry's death in 1189, she was held in close confinement in England. According to one of the more negative legends regarding Eleanor, it was at this time that she poisoned or otherwise tortured and killed Rosamund Clifford, one of Henry's mistresses.

Henry's relationship with Thomas Becket also became the stuff of literature and legend. Thomas Becket, who was originally Henry's chancellor, was a man noted for his competence, his loyalty to Henry, his intelligence, and his lavishness. He had risen from a Norman London merchant family and a career as a clerk to become Henry's right-hand man. When, against the advice of others, Henry named him archbishop of Canterbury in 1162, Becket, who had previously been adept at asserting royal control over the Church, reversed himself. Sometimes unsurely, but inevitably, he began to cross Henry on issues where Henry wished to assert authority over the Church. Henry wanted to reduce the jurisdiction of ecclesiastical courts; Becket moved to protect his clergy. Henry stood behind the "ancient" customs of Henry I; Becket stood behind the liberty of the Church. As their positions hardened, Becket went into exile (1164–1170). On his return, four of Henry's knights murdered him near the altar of Canterbury Cathedral on December 29, 1170.

Becket presents a puzzle to historians, who cannot seem to penetrate his motives.

Map 13.1   The Angevin Empire at the Time of Henry II, c. 1170   This map illustrates the balance of power between King Henry II of England and King Louis VII of France c. 1170. Henry and Eleanor's inherited or acquired territories far overshadowed the French royal domains. Except for England, however, much of what Henry controlled consisted of various counties and duchies with the potential to break away. By 1204 Henry's youngest son, King John I of England, had lost most of the Angevin territories on the continent.

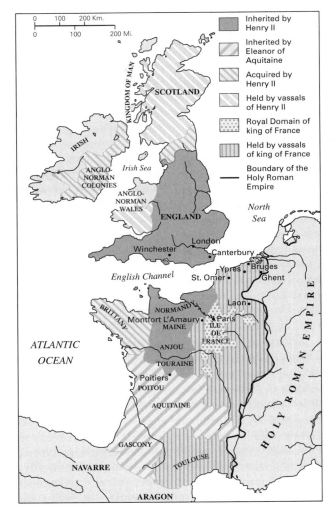

Although many of his letters are extant, he does not reveal himself. Although many who knew him wrote biographies, it is difficult to separate Becket's legend from his life. Contemporaries had strong reactions. Some saw him as a traitor; others saw his death as a martyrdom on behalf of the Church. The papacy quickly declared Becket a saint. In the end, Henry was forced to perform penance at Becket's tomb.

Henry's reputation has never fully recovered from his treatment of Eleanor and his conflict with Becket. Historians, however, have partially rehabilitated it. They note, for example, that those who knew Henry were impressed with his inexhaustible energy.

> From morning to night he is engaged unceasingly on affairs of state. He never sits down except when he mounts his horse or takes a meal and he frequently rides in one day a journey four or five times the length of a normal day's ride. It is very

difficult to find out where he is or what he will do during the day for he frequently changes his plans. . . . in this way, while other kings are resting in their palaces, he is able to take his enemies by surprise and off their guard and he inspects everything, taking particular care to judge those whom he had made judges of others.[6]

With this energy (and a great deal of intelligence) Henry strengthened the English monarchy and maintained his personal empire against all opponents, including his sons.

Although Henry did not weld the disparate parts of his empire into a unified whole, he did a remarkable job of asserting royal authority. He did this in part by building or rebuilding royal castles throughout his territories. He was also an effective besieger of castles. In England, in particular, Henry centralized and strengthened an already effective administration. Although he had inherited a long tradition of national taxes, his government updated royal records, instituted new procedures, and recovered lost revenues. Continuing the policies of his grandfather, Henry I, he brought men who were literate, numerate, and upwardly mobile into government service. The local authority of sheriffs, while more and more harnessed to royal needs, expanded. He permanently established the royal court at Westminster, with fixed procedures and standardized writs. Juries were used more systematically, and more jails were built.

Sometime in the 1160s, Henry also instituted regular, organized circuit courts. These tours of inspection by the king's justices looked into all manner of complaints as well as into all payments made (of whatever sort) in the king's absence. In particular, these judicial tours (called eyres) could be used to investigate cases of disseisin, or land seizures. Henry instituted a new process with regard to recent land seizures known as an *assize of novel disseisin.* A swift decision as to the facts of the case was produced by a jury of recognition, whose role was to restore the land to the ousted possessor, if warranted, or to reject his claim, if not warranted. The disseisor of the land then had to go through a prescribed legal procedure to determine whether he had a right to the land he had tried to seize. This determination of a right of property possession involved a duel or perhaps an ordeal by fire or water. In 1179, however, Henry instituted the trial jury, called a "grand assize," to replace judicial ordeals. The grand assize, consisting of twelve law-worthy knights of the neighborhood who best knew the truth of the matter, instituted a public inquiry and rendered a decision.[7] It took the question of judicial right entirely out of the arena of knights deciding an issue by force and put it in the hands of sheriffs, juries, and justices. This has traditionally been considered the origin of English common law. As a model of procedural remedy, it was quickly applied to a variety of other disputes.

Before Henry died, a *Treatise on the Laws and Customs of England,* traditionally assigned to Ranulf de Glanvill, appeared. It is a guide to civil proceedings in the royal courts, described by its modern editor as the first textbook of the common law. Another procedural manual, written by Henry's treasurer, Richard fitz Nigel, provided a guide to the Exchequer. Both treatises document Henry's administrative reforms. After Henry's death, the English government continued to function well, even though his son Richard I was absent most of his ten-year reign.

MEDIEVAL VOICES

Marie de France Presents Her Lais to the King, Probably Henry II

One of the writers who frequented the court of Henry II was Marie de France (fl. c. 1180s). We know almost nothing about Marie beyond her name. Her education (she knew Latin, French, and English) was that of a noblewoman, and it has been suggested that she may have been a half sister to Henry II and perhaps also an abbess. Among her works are several French Lais, *taken from Breton stories that were popular at the time and transformed into rhymed romances where love's logic is examined and the role of the lady is brought alive. Marie begins her collection of* Lais *with a prologue that addresses her patron and defends her work.*

Whoever has received knowledge
and eloquence in speech from God
should not be silent or secretive
but demonstrate it willingly. . . .
He who would guard himself from vice
should study and understand
and begin a weighty work
by which he might keep vice at a distance,
and free himself from great sorrow.
That's why I began to think
about composing some good stories
and translating from Latin to Romance;
but that was not to bring me fame:
too many others have done it.
Then I thought of the *lais* I'd heard.
I did not doubt, indeed I knew well,
that those who first began them
and sent them forth
composed them in order to preserve
adventures they had heard.
I have heard many told;
and I don't want to neglect or forget them.
To put them into word and rhyme
I've often stayed awake.
In your honor, noble King,
who are so brave and courteous,
repository of all joys
in whose heart all goodness takes root,
I undertook to assemble these *lais*
to compose and recount them in rhyme.
In my heart I thought and determined,
sire, that I would present them to you.

MEDIEVAL VOICES (Continued)

> If it pleases you to receive them,
> you will give me great joy;
> I shall be happy forever.
> Do not think me presumptuous
> if I dare present them to you.
> Now hear how they begin.

Source: Excerpt from *The Lais of Marie de France,* trans. R. Hanning and J. Ferrante (Durham, N. C.: Labyrinth Press, 1978) 28–29. Reprinted by permission of Labyrinth Press, a division of Baker Book House Company.

Although Henry has been acknowledged for regularizing and rationalizing English customary law, he also had wide-ranging, albeit less well known, intellectual and cultural interests. Like Eleanor, whose cultural patronage has been widely noted, he patronized writers. A number of letter collections and Latin treatises, mostly on law and history, were produced around Henry's court. Several Latin translations of Arabic scientific treatises were dedicated to Henry. John of Salisbury sent his *Policraticus* as well as an educational treatise entitled *Metalogicon* to Becket when Becket was Henry's chancellor. Several of Henry's officials wrote Latin treatises critical of the life of court officials.

The origins of French vernacular literature are more Angevin than French. A French compilation of the stories of Renart the Fox was written at Henry's court. Jordan de Fantosme wrote a flattering chronicle of one of Henry's campaigns in French verse. Marie de France, one of the great female authors of the Middle Ages, probably produced her lais, a collection of short romantic tales, in Angevin England (see Medieval Voices). Chrétien de Troyes, author of *Lancelot, Yvain,* and *Percival,* may have begun his literary career in Angevin circles at the start of Henry's reign. One of the earliest versions of the legend of Tristan and Ysolt, by Thomas of England, comes from the Angevin context. Wace, another contemporary, transmitted the Arthurian stories from Latin into French. His *Roman de Brut* became the prototype of medieval English histories, and his description of a courtly King Arthur, including the story of the round table, was to influence all subsequent generations. Layamon, the English poet who rewrote Wace into English, was writing when Henry died and dedicated his work to Eleanor.

Provençal troubadours (poets and songwriters) frequented the courts of Henry II, his son Henry, Eleanor, and Richard. Richard himself wrote lyrics, and his brother, Geoffrey of Brittany, joined in a musical debate with a trouvère.* In addition to these troubadour songs, Latin two- and three-part polyphony developed during Eleanor and Henry's time, much of it inspired by the exile, death, and canonization of Thomas Becket. The various accessions, deaths, triumphs, and tragedies of Eleanor, Henry, and their children occasioned music at every turn.

---

* Trouvères were poets who wrote in troubadour style but in French rather than Provençal.

Also, an Angevin fashion may have developed in both manuscript and stained glass illumination that was cross-continental and classical in style.

When Henry died in 1189, deserted by his sons and outmaneuvered by Philip II of France, he left a wealthy, powerful inheritance intact to Richard, his oldest surviving son. In comparison, neither the French nor the German rulers had as much authority over their aristocracy; nor did they have administrative procedures that were as effective (see Medieval Voices).

THE GERMAN EMPIRE, 1106–1190

One of the central issues for German historians has been the failure of Germany to achieve unification until the nineteenth century. For many German historians, part of the reason lies in the ruins of the medieval German empire (see Map 13.2). Certainly one can ask why the German rulers did not create a centralized and effective governmental apparatus, why they did not develop a dependable tax base, and why hereditary kingship did not prevail?

The Impact of the Investiture Controversy

German rulers did not command a land base such as William the Conqueror secured when he invaded England in 1066. They depended very heavily for their power on the knight services and revenues that came to them from bishoprics and monasteries under royal patronage. By 1073, no less than fifty-three counties were under ecclesiastical control; these provided the bulk of the imperial army and income. It is not an exaggeration to say that the power of the German emperor *depended* upon his ability to nominate officials to positions in the Church.

The German Empire was therefore particularly vulnerable to ecclesiastical reform, especially the attack on lay investiture initiated by Gregory VII and pursued by subsequent popes. The reform program demanded an end to lay investiture. The accommodation that emerged, which allowed lay rulers to be present at an election (and therefore to influence it) and permitted ecclesiastical officials to pay homage to lay rulers for their temporal holdings, was not reached in Germany until the Concordat of Worms in 1122. Even then, it was negotiated more between the princes and the Church than between the emperor and the Church.

In the course of the struggle over investiture, Henry IV (1056–1106) was excommunicated twice by Gregory VII and thrice by successive popes. An excommunicated ruler is a weak ruler, in danger of being deposed by his enemies. And Henry had many enemies. At various times, he found himself at war with the Saxons, the papacy, Italian rulers and cities, German princes and prince-bishops, an antiking, and even his two sons.

Henry's position was also weakened by the penance he performed before the pope at Canossa in 1077. Although Henry gained immediate political advantage by being reinstated in the Church, he lost authority. The traditional Germanic concept of kingship was a sacred one. The king (or emperor) was anointed by God, to be deposed by God. Gregorian ideology, however, saw the king as a removable official, subordinate to the needs of the Church. By the time of the Emperor Lothar

MEDIEVAL VOICES

The Death of Henry II: A King Brought Low?

Henry II died on July 6, 1189, in retreat before King Philip II of France and his own son, Richard. Upon his deathbed, reading the terms of a peace agreement, Henry discovered that his youngest and favorite son, John, was also among those who had taken the opposite side. This account, written by Gerald of Wales, uses Henry's death to make a strong moral point. Another text, the Gesta Regis Henrici Secundi *describes the treatment of Henry's body somewhat differently, noting that "he lay in state robed in royal splendour."*

When he discovered that this [the treason of his son John] was indeed the case, he sank back upon his bed and, turning his face to the wall and groaning aloud, cried, "Now let all things go as they will, I care no longer for myself or for anything else in the world." And, as those who were present have borne witness positively, nothing provoked more the gravity and violence of his disease, nothing hastened his death more than this sudden and unexpected grief. . . . When the corpse was laid out on the ground, all and sundry indulged their greed, as at such times they are wont to do, so that for some while the body was exposed naked and without any clothing, until a certain lad ran up and covered it as best he could. . . . On the morrow, when the body was carried to the high altar for burial, there was scarcely to be had, as was fitting, a ring for his finger, a sceptre for his hand or crown for his head; in a word scarcely any insignia of royalty but what had been begged for the purpose. . . . amidst his many treasures, both in England and across the sea, greater by far than was wont, he died a pauper; and that he who had heaped up riches as high as a tower and deep in the bowels of the earth, and had acquired the widest realms, yet knew not for whom he gathered them, should have left them crammed with gold and silver to the man [his son, Richard] he hated most in all the world.

Source: English Historical Documents, ed. D.C. Douglas, vol. 2 (Eyre & Spottiswoode, 1963): 409, 413–415.

III (1125–1137), the papacy was arguing that Lothar had received his imperial crown as a fief from the papacy. The pope's Lateran palace sported a portrait of Lothar leading the papal horse and holding the pope's stirrups—a sign of Lothar's vassalage.

Germany, 1106–1152

German imperial power was also compromised by the failure of German rulers to establish a right to hereditary succession. This had never been a strong tradition in Germany, although the German monarchs did succeed one another, son following father, for a century from 1024 to 1137. Henry IV, in his effort to secure hereditary succession, first had his son Conrad and then his son Henry, after Conrad's death, crowned in his lifetime. Unfortunately, both sons revolted against Henry in conjunction with enemies among the nobility. When Henry V finally succeeded Henry IV, in 1106, he was beholden to the aristocracy and wearing a weakened crown.

Map 13.2   Germany, Italy, and Eastern Europe, c. 1200   In the year 1200, the Holy Roman Empire claimed authority over Germany, Burgundy, northern Italy (down to the Papal States and including Corsica and Sardinia) and was involved in eastern Europe. Although Bohemia and Pomerania functioned as independent territories, they were under imperial authority. The heir to the Kingdom of Sicily at this time was the two-year old orphaned son of the Emperor Henry VI and the heiress of Sicily. He was to become Emperor Frederick II in 1215. With Sicily and the Empire combined in one person, imperial territories surrounded the Papal States.

And then Henry V died childless. In the election that followed, the nobility seized control, which was possible because Matilda, the wife of Henry V (and mother-to-be of Henry II of England), handed the imperial regalia over to the archbishop of Mainz. The archbishop then skillfully organized opposition to Frederick II of Swabia (of the Hohenstaufen family), the best hereditary claimant to the throne. Duke Lothar of Saxony (of the Welf family) (1125–1137) was then elected by a diet held in the presence of—and under the influence of—the clergy. At his election he agreed that the nobility had a right to elect whomever they wished and the pope had the right to confirm the election. Lothar was a pious man and a papal supporter who spent much of his reign combating and appeasing those who had better hereditary claims to his throne. Although Lothar succeeded in repelling his enemies and strengthening German (and Saxon) power along Germany's northern and eastern borders, he was also pulled by papal demands into Italian affairs, thereby dividing his energies. Lothar had no direct male heir but on his deathbed designated Henry the Proud of Saxony, his son-in-law, as heir. The princes and church leaders, however, repudiated Henry and elected a Hohenstaufen (Conrad III). This divided Germany into two camps: the Welf (the ruling family of Saxony) and the Hohenstaufen (the ruling family of Swabia), representing the northeastern and the southwestern territories of Germany respectively.

Conrad became the ruler of all of Germany but, unlike the Angevins, the German king did not maintain separate administrative structures for the various territories. The imperial household remained the administrative center of the entire empire, but it had no teeth. The real power rested increasingly with the aristocracy, who had weaker bonds of loyalty or no traditional feudal relationship with the ruler. In addition, while nonnoble subjects may have recognized the emperor's sovereignty, they were effectively governed by local nobles at the county level.

Henry V had tried to institute inquests similar to the Domesday survey in England, and in 1124–1125 he proposed a general imperial tax. The princes and the Church rejected these initiatives. While the emperor could, in theory, mobilize an army, in practice the council of princes levied soldiers. As a result, parts of the empire lost touch with the emperor. Although Italian bishops were supposed to visit the person of the emperor to pledge their fealty, they did so less and less often. Only when the emperor traveled through Italy, usually on his way to being crowned emperor in Rome, could he effectively confer titles, institute offices, and install prelates. Between 1100 and 1150, virtually no German imperial presence existed in Italy. Italian clergy and Italian cities flourished more and more independently.

Even when German rulers wished to make their presence felt in southern Europe, they faced obstacles. For much of the early twelfth century, the south German dukes were hostile or in revolt. After overcoming their resistance, German rulers then faced the Alps, which had only a handful of secure passes into Italy. In the Lombard plain of northern Italy, by the end of the eleventh century, cities were banding together to form the first urban league in medieval history. Milan, Cremona, Piacenza, and Lodi formed a communal pact against Henry IV. The formerly imperial duchy of Tuscany was in the hands of the Marquesa Matilda (d. 1115), a strong papal supporter, linked by marriage after 1089 to enemies of the emperor, and a supporter of Henry's rebellious son Conrad.

If we then add to this mix of fractured politics, decentralized power, and beleaguered authority, revolts from Saxony in the north, conflicts with the French to the west, and uneasy relations with unsettled and sometimes unchristianized peoples on the eastern frontier, it is not surprising that the German Roman emperors failed to establish the foundations of a modern nation-state.

At moments imperial political supremacy looked possible: In 1103 (just before his son's revolt), Henry IV was able to proclaim a general peace of the empire, and in 1137, it looked as though Henry the Proud (of the Welf Saxon dynasty), ruler of Tuscany, Bavaria, Saxony, and parts of Sicily, might succeed to the throne rather than the weaker Hohenstaufen Conrad III (r. 1138–1152). It was the rule of Frederick I (Hohenstaufen) from 1152 until 1190, however, that illustrates best the strengths and the weaknesses of the German Empire.

Frederick I (1152–1190)

Frederick Barbarossa (Redbeard) was designated emperor by his uncle, Conrad, who passed over his own eight-year-old son. Frederick descended from the Salian, Staufen, and Welf families, thereby uniting the leading noble and royal German families and offering hope of healing a divided Germany. Through skillful negotiations and land grants, Frederick was able to command support from the princes and to minimize the role of the papacy in his election.

Frederick was a warrior-emperor, a tireless traveler and campaigner who spent ten years of his reign in Italy and died while on crusade. While not highly literate in Latin, he appreciated Germanic culture, literature, history, and architecture. He had an exalted sense of his role as emperor and a courtly presence, but he was also a mediator who consulted his nobles and practiced the art of the possible in politics. Through it all, he kept a larger goal in mind, although historians cannot agree whether that goal was a Hohenstaufen state, a unified German state, or both.

Frederick Barbarossa promoted a sacred and nearly mythological role for himself, and he forcefully asserted his moral and judicial authority. He also worked to establish feudal relationships of dependent loyalty with leading German lords. His attempt to consolidate power, however, was defeated by competition with the papacy for authority, the strength and independence of the nobility, the fragmentation of the empire's focus in different directions, and the failure to create controlling administrative structures.

Frederick saw himself as embodying all the great imperial traditions. Imperial chroniclers emphasized Frederick's Carolingian genealogy; Charlemagne's palaces were restored, and Frederick campaigned to have Charlemagne canonized. The chroniclers, particularly his uncle, Bishop Otto of Freising, also stressed his Ottonian roots and a mythological genealogy that allowed the German people to trace descent not only from Rome and, indirectly, Troy, but also from Alexander the Great and Old Testament priest-kings. Frederick added to that a heightened religious and moral sense of his position. He was the first to call the Roman Empire "holy"; he surrounded himself with liturgies on all important occasions that exalted his divine status. Frederick's strong sense of justice was emboldened by the revival of Roman law and its claim that the emperor was the lord of the world. This strengthened his

Portrait of Frederick Barbarossa
This gilded bronze casting is a twelfth-century portrait traditionally thought to be that of Frederick Barbarossa. It shows his characteristic beard with, however, stylized, classically inspired hair. The portrait suggests that the German ruler is the legitimate successor of the Roman caesars; it has been debated as to whether this is an idealized imperial portrait rather than an actual representation of Frederick. If it is a portrait, it is the first representative portrait done in the West since Carolingian times. It is often called a reliquary, but Frederick was actually buried at Antioch after dying *en route* to the Holy Land; his body was subsequently moved to Tyre. Because Frederick died on crusade, he was popularly considered a martyr. *AKG, London.*

legal position vis-à-vis the papacy as well as against the increasingly powerful and independent northern Italian towns.

During his long rule, Frederick strengthened the empire in many ways. He consolidated royal power internally by building castles, founding towns, and expanding his personal domain (particularly by marrying the heiress of Burgundy). He also began to develop an administrative apparatus similar to that emerging in England, although it did not succeed to the same extent. From 1157 to 1167, he utilized the services of Rainald of Dassel, his chancellor and the archbishop of Cologne, who was everything to Frederick that Henry II had wanted Becket to be. Rainald brought skilled officers into the government and established high standards of competence in correspondence, legal initiatives, and official accountability. Frederick was able to proclaim a general peace throughout Germany, to influence ecclesiastical elections and politics, to establish imperial offices throughout northern Italy, and to maintain a sufficiently strong army to exercise military dominance. As a result, Frederick's imperial authority reached beyond Germany. Kings of Denmark, Bohemia, and Hungary received their crowns from Frederick and treated him as their lord.

Frederick's reign, for all its imperial promise and propaganda, had major problems that he never resolved. The most divisive continued to be the competition with the papacy for authority and power. Frederick's strategies varied from cooperation to co-option (by electing an antipope) to coercion (running the pope out of Italy). One of Frederick's manifestoes states: "In the chief city of the world [Rome] God has, through the power of the empire, exalted the Church; in the chief city of the world the Church, not through the power of God, we believe, is now destroying the empire. It began with a picture [the picture of Lothar holding the pope's stirrup]. . . . We shall not endure it, we shall not submit to it; we shall lay down the crown before we consent to have the imperial crown and ourself thus degraded. . . ."[8]

Despite Frederick's stance, he could not sustain two decades of conflict with the papacy. He signed a peace treaty with the pope in 1177, and by the time Frederick died some bishoprics had become independent princedoms; others were under the control of German princes, especially the duke of Saxony. Still others were in the papal camp, and even the imperial monasteries and bishoprics now exercised a greater degree of independence.

In addition, the emperor had few effective means of controlling the German princes, who were more and more successful at securing hereditary succession within their duchies. Many of their lands were allodial, that is to say, held freely, without owing services to the emperor. And nobility in the eastern territories were able to expand their holdings by promoting missionary activities, crusading efforts, and colonizing among Slavic and Hungarian territories. The Babenberger family in Austria, raised to ducal status by Frederick, was given enormous privileges and freedom because of their strategic frontier position vis-à-vis the Hungarians. In the north the dukes of Saxony built a power base that was, in many ways, more cohesive than the Hohenstaufen holdings in Swabia and Burgundy.

While all of this was occurring, Frederick focused on Italy. This southward focus made sense for a family whose lands were just above the Alps and for an emperor whose vision was Roman, but it pulled Germany in different directions. While Frederick poured his energies into reestablishing direct imperial rule in northern Italy, the German population was expanding toward the east. German colonists were draining marshes, cutting down forests, establishing bishoprics, and building towns in Mecklenburg, Silesia, Pomerania, and Brandenburg. From the Baltic town of Lubeck, the Danes and Germans attacked the Slavs, destroying the remnants of their pagan sanctuaries and occasionally still enslaving them. Eventually northern German princes established themselves as the overlords of a number of West Slav principalities.

In contrast to the successes of the north German princes and colonists moving eastward, Frederick faced a nearly intractable situation in northern Italy. The growth of Venice, Milan, Pisa, Genoa, and a hundred other, smaller Italian towns had made northern Italy an attractive commercial prize. For Frederick they offered taxable wealth that might enable him to fund his military and combat the growing power of the German nobility. But the citizens of these towns did not appreciate the intrusion of German imperial officials. As a result, they formed leagues, culminating in the Lombard League that defeated Frederick's army at the battle of Legnano in 1176. The papacy also had aspirations in northern Italy, which it hoped would provide a buffer against the Germans. Finally, a briefly reinvigorated Byzantine Empire was gaining a foothold near Ravenna. Although Frederick was a determined, sometimes brutal warrior, his Germans were often reluctant followers, unenthusiastic about leaving their homes to fight a foreign and commercial people. In 1167 in Rome, a malarial epidemic hit the army, making them even more recalcitrant.

Another weakness of the German Empire was the rudimentary nature of its administrative apparatus. The emperor was assisted by three chancellors (for Germany, Italy, and Burgundy), various counselors, relatives, and personal retainers. There were only four court offices, and they usually went to one of the princes. In the chanceries, the emperor was highly dependent upon a few clerics, whose literacy was essential. More and more, Frederick tried to move *ministeriales,* lower born laymen, into imperial offices and into his household, but this effort was viewed unkindly by the higher nobility, and was never done as effectively as in England. As a result, Frederick had fewer court officials or local imperial officials to carry through court policy, and insufficient hereditary lands to provide him with the kind of wealth English kings enjoyed. In order to ensure his command of revenues and knights, Frederick depended increasingly upon feudal lines of authority. In the end, historians have argued, vassalage, which came later to Germany than to either England or France, may have inhibited rather than enhanced the centralizing tendencies of the German Empire; in any case, it probably came too late. Where the English kings were able to match authority with power, the German emperors never developed the power to match their authority. It was the princes who gained more and more power, although authority continued to rest in the imperial crown.

Frederick died in 1190, rather ignominiously, drowning in Asia Minor while on crusade. But legends engendered by Frederick continued to survive. In Frederick's lifetime, the troubadours and poets who lived at the Hohenstaufen court and sang about the glorious deeds of the Germans, praised Frederick above all. In Frederick's reign the *Ring of the Nibelungs,* which reflects an epic oral tradition going back to the Merovingians, was written down and reworked to reflect the renewed glory of the Hohenstaufen warrior-elites. Otto of Freising's laudatory *Deeds of Frederick Barbarossa* painted Frederick as the prince of peace and the greatest of German emperors. A poem entitled *The Play of Antichrist,* written about 1160, portrayed the emperor as the savior of the West. When Frederick led the Third Crusade overland in 1189, popular expectations were that he would take Jerusalem, place his crown on the altar of the Holy Sepulcre, and initiate the coming of the Antichrist and the Last Judgment. Instead, he never reached the Holy Land. In legend Frederick was to become a world emperor who would lead Christians against the Antichrist and preside over a golden age. By the sixteenth century, the legend portrayed Frederick as alive, deep in Kyffhauser Mountain, sleeping an enchanted sleep that would be broken when he arose to become the savior of Germany.*

---

* After World War I there was a revival of Frederick's legend that led to the establishment of the Kyffhauser Bund. After World War II, the *Play of Antichrist* also saw a revival in Germany.

THE CAPETIANS, 1060–1179

The German emperor, who claimed overlordship over much of Europe, rarely asserted this claim vis-à-vis France. The Angevin kings generally accepted the French king as overlord for their continental holdings, despite the fact that the Angevin territorial reach dwarfed the Capetian lands. This respect for French kingship derived from its association with Charlemagne as well as the sacral character given French kingship (see Chapter 10).

French kings traced their descent ultimately from Troy but more immediately from Charlemagne. Writers of the time portrayed French kings as the defenders of holy Church, and it was they who offered a home in exile to Pope Alexander II in his struggle with the German emperor and to Becket in his struggle with Henry II. The First Crusade was proclaimed on Frankish soil, and the Greeks and Arabs characterized all crusaders as "Franks" even when they were not. Robert Bartlett has shown that most of the ruling families in twelfth-century Europe had Frankish connections.[9] The Capetian kings' special association with the abbey of St. Denis enabled both Louis VI (1108–1137) and Louis VII (1137–1180) to fight under its banner and to portray themselves as the vassals of a saint.

Despite extensive influence and a charismatic and sacral heritage, the Capetians controlled only a small amount of territory, and their power was circumscribed. The Capetian kingdom was surrounded by more or less independent duchies and counties: Toulouse, Burgundy, Blois, Champagne, Flanders, Normandy, Brittany, Anjou, Aquitaine, and others. Most of these were greater in extent and some, such as Champagne, Toulouse, and Aquitaine, had famous courts that attracted poets and writers, which enhanced their importance.

The Capetians did have some advantages, however. Partly because of their limited demesne, they were less itinerant than other rulers. They were better able, therefore, to consolidate their position in Paris, a city ideally located to take advantage of the growing trade and situated within one of the most fertile agricultural regions of the north. Paris was, by the early twelfth century, to become a great intellectual center as well, which meant that the Capetians had no difficulty attracting legal and administrative expertise. Since the Capetians were scarcely able to assert their authority over a wide area, they could concentrate on curtailing the power of castellans, governors or wardens of castles, within the Ile de France, upon whom they successfully enforced a vassal status. Beyond the Ile de France, they worked to assert their royal powers of charter-granting, arbitration, justice, and castle building—all to a more or less successful degree. And finally, in contrast to the succession crises of other lands, where dynasties died out, civil wars ensued, or lands were parceled out between sons, the Capetians, time after time, were succeeded by competent sons, anointed and ruling a unified, expanding kingdom.

The reign of Philip I of France (1060–1108) is not well documented and did not result in significant strides in French power. Philip is best known for his marital misadventures, for which he was excommunicated three times by reform-minded bishops and popes. While a variety of political motives may have been involved, the actual conflict revolved around Philip's renunciation and dismissal of his queen,

Bertha, in 1092, after twenty years of marriage and the birth of one son, Louis, in 1081. He then married Bertrade of Montfort, the countess of Anjou, who deserted her husband Fulk IV of Anjou. Although Bertrade was accepted as queen within France, the papacy and members of the French clergy never concurred and accused Philip of adultery as well as incest (she was a distant cousin). Philip, on the other hand, felt that he needed more than one legitimate son to secure the Capetian succession to the throne; Bertrada was apparently an enchanting woman, and she had already proven herself fertile; in addition, she controlled a strategic fortress on the Norman border. Although she and Philip finally agreed to separate in 1104, they continued to live together until his death, and in 1106 they were welcomed to Anjou by Fulk, her former husband. Contemporary writers are uniformly hostile to Bertrada, partly because her stepson, Louis, who had no reason to like her, became the next king. Abbot Suger, writing over thirty years later, called her "a clever shrew" and accused Philip of being "carried away by lust for the married woman he had carried off."[10] Georges Duby, who has told the story of Bertrada and Philip several times, argues that this debate crystallizes two conflicting eleventh-century viewpoints. One is the traditional Carolingian and aristocratic viewpoint of the king as divinely appointed, above the clergy, following the traditions of his Germanic forebears for whom repudiation of a wife was acceptable, particularly given the overriding need for a secure succession. The other is the ideology of ecclesiastical reform wherein temporal power is subject to spiritual power, particularly in the moral sphere and where, according to scripture and canon law, a man cannot repudiate a legitimate wife nor marry someone who is already married and a close kinswoman.

It was during the reigns of Louis VI and VII that France began to emerge. Walter Map reported that when Louis VI (the Fat) was young, he "was unable to go outside the gates of Paris to the third milestone without the leave or escort of the neighbouring princes, and not one of them either kept or feared his orders."[11] In fact, however, Louis affected a dramatic change in the power of his kingship. He was an aggressive defender of royal rights. He increased the number of royal charters, conducted numerous successful campaigns against unruly castle-holders in his demesne, and insisted upon his power as overlord, strengthening his rights at every turn. Despite all this, between his accession and the death of his son Louis VII, there were only marginal gains in territory. Louis VII is supposed to have consoled himself that "we French have only got bread and wine and a contented mind."[12]

Both Louis VI and VII created an administrative structure that was responsive to their needs. They relied on knights of lowly birth and clerks whose rewards derived from their loyalty to the king. The kingdom's economic strength came from the increased cultivation of vineyards and open fields throughout the Ile de France and the growing demand for French produce. French coinage began to replace the coins of local dukes and counts. Nor did either Louis miss the opportunity to establish fairs in their territory and invest in business partnerships. As a result, Louis VII's annual estimated income of £60,000 was ample, and since his landholdings were compact, his territories were easier (and cheaper) to administer than those of the Angevins or the Germans.

Louis VII, more than his father, traveled to promote his royal presence and extended royal privileges and protection. He also made a point of protecting church lands. Increasingly, nobles and ecclesiastical leaders from as far afield as Toulouse began to appeal to him for help or to pay him homage. Louis VII asserted his power skillfully, rarely taking on vested interests directly, but offering himself as a haven of justice and a natural lord. Suger, abbot of St. Denis (1081–1151), friend and advisor of his father, and one of the great political minds of the twelfth century, helped him in this. Suger saw the importance of a loyal and orderly administration, built upon the links between St. Denis and French royalty; he maintained the regency while Louis VII was on crusade, and held a vision of the French king as the king of kings.

Suger was able, through skillful management of resources, to minimize the negative impact of the disastrous Second Crusade (Chapter 12), but no one could protect Louis VII from the consequences of his personal life: the end of his marriage with Eleanor of Aquitaine and his failure, for most of his life, to have a son and heir. After the annulment of the marriage between Eleanor and Louis and Eleanor's hasty marriage to Henry II, her inheritance, the duchy of Aquitaine, went to Henry, whose holdings now dwarfed those of the Capetians. It took Louis three marriages before God "would bestow a child from us who after us would reign as king and would govern the kingdom. And that ardent desire, that God would give us progeny of the better sex, inflamed also us, who had been terrified by a multitude of daughters. . . ."[13] In 1165, Louis's only son, Philip, was born, and his reign (r. 1179–1223) was to see the kingdom of France extend to nearly its present size (see Chapter 16).

The reigns of Louis VI and VII are notable also for the quality of their queens. Louis VI's wife, Adelaide of Maurienne, was paid great honor and must have been a woman of great vitality. Her reign, according to Marion Facinger, "marks the high and the turning point of . . . queenship—of free sharing in the royal power as a matter of right."[14] She was essentially Louis's royal partner—signing charters, commanding court business, taking part in delicate negotiations and significant policy decisions, traveling with Louis—and also giving him at least eight sons. Her successor, Eleanor of Aquitaine, although far more famous, was more circumscribed in her role as queen of France. Louis VII never treated her as an equal partner, despite (or perhaps because of) her status as ruler of Aquitaine, and subsequent queens never regained a partnership status.

MONARCHIES ON THE FRONTIERS OF EUROPE

The monarchies that had emerged on the peripheries of Europe in the tenth century in the wake of the period of invasions did not develop stability in this period. Their instabilities were sometimes due to succession struggles, sometimes to overweening nobles, and sometimes to troubled relations with threatening neighbors. Christian Spain, for example, after several decades of peace with Muslim Spain, began an aggressive conquest against the Muslims. The Christian north had changed since the tenth century, with a growing peasant population moving into more southern agricultural areas, a revived and reforming Church, stronger territorial kingdoms, and a newly emerging nobility that was highly mobile and conversant with mailed, cavalry shock techniques. It was King Alfonso VI of León-Castile-

Galicia (1065–1109) who laid the foundation for the gradual Christian takeover of Spain. He was the first to mint coins, and he began to establish a court and chancery. He benefited from tributes exacted from the fragmented kingdoms of al-Andalus. His kingdom, at its greatest extent, more than doubled its previous territory. In 1085, Alfonso captured Toledo, which then became the largest city in Christian Spain, and pushed Christian Spain to the Tagus River. Alfonso had help. Pope Gregory VII claimed Spain as a papal possession and encouraged French armies to campaign against the Muslims. By the 1090s, Rodrigo Díaz *(El Cid)* held Valencia. After being exiled by Alfonso VI from León-Castile, *El Cid,* single-handedly, with only those troops he could entice and reward, defied Chrstian and Muslim kings, counts, and emirs to build a princedom for himself in Valencia. Although *El Cid*'s exploits in eastern Spain have been distorted by legend, the larger-than-life quality of his adventures was real. In legend, at any rate, he remained loyal to the king who had exiled him.

Alfonso called himself "Emperor of all of Spain," asserting Leonese authority over the rest of the peninsula. This empire-in-the-making was cut short by a Muslim revival when the Islamic leadership invited into Spain the Murābits, the name given a warring, fundamentalist Berber tribe from North Africa. Yūsuf ibn-Tāshufin, the Murābit emir, soon took over Muslim Spain and nearly recaptured Toledo. In 1102, the Murābits took Valencia from El Cid 's family's hands. Spain emerged nearly evenly divided between the Christian kingdoms and the Murābit kingdom (with its affiliated kingdom of Zaragoza). In the Christian territories a revitalization of trade (through the port of Barcelona and over the Pyrenees) took place, and churches and monasteries were built and enlarged. Tribute from Islam fueled the economy as did tolls and newly-founded mints. The importance of the Christian nobility and episcopacy developed as the wealth of Christian Spain multiplied.

Alfonso VI married his daughter and heir, Urraca, to Alfonso I, king of Aragon and Navarre, hoping to unite most of Christian Spain. The marriage did not work, however, and the union fell apart. Alfonso I did, however, conquer the Muslim kingdom of Zaragoza in a victory as significant for the Christians as that of the earlier conquest of Toledo. Urraca's son, Alfonso VII (r. 1126–1157), raised the imperial aspirations of León-Castile to their medieval heights. Crowned emperor in 1135, he sought to unite León-Castile with Aragon. Instead, an independent union of Aragon-Catalonia, as well as a kingship in Portugal emerged. These various kings, aided by bands of mounted French and Spanish warrior-raiders,* competed with one another while they pushed the border between Christian- and Muslim-controlled territories south significantly in the remainder of the twelfth century; the complete Christian domination over Spain had to wait, however, until the fifteenth century.

Most other kingdoms on the frontiers of Christian Europe (with the notable exception of Ireland) were recent converts to or conquests for Christianity. In one of the great adventures of an adventuring era, gangs of Norman warriors led by Robert

---

*In 1147 the capture of Lisbon by the king of Portugal was aided by the arrival of crusading ships full of English, French, German and Flemish soldiers.

Monreale Cathedral in Norman Sicily   The Norman ruler, King William II (r. 1166-1189), built this new church between 1174 and 1189 and dedicated it to the Virgin. Its gold mosaics, dome, and image of Christ Pantocrator over the altar illustrate strong Byzantine influence on the construction. Its mosaic design is one of the most ambitious in existence. Arches, ceilings, arcades, and columns within the church reflect Arab influences, while it also incorporates Norman and Italian styles. This eclecticism was typical of Norman art and architecture in southern Europe. *Macduff Everton/Corbis.*

Guiscard and his brother Roger took parts of southern Italy from the Byzantines and Sicily from the Arabs by the end of the eleventh century (see Chapter 11). The success of Norman Sicily (called the Kingdom of Two Sicilies) rested on Norman acceptance of a multireligious, multicultural mix of Latins, Greeks, Jews, and Muslims. They preserved and encouraged Sicilian economic development (for example, the manufacture of silk), architecture (an arresting assortment of Arabic, Byzantine, and Romanesque-Gothic forms), and culture. Ptolemy's *Almagest* and his *Optics* and Plato's *Meno* and *Phaedo* were translated from Greek or Arabic into Latin. Geographers, mathematicians, doctors, and scholars went to the court at Palermo. The traditions of government and kingship were more Byzantine than western. Roger II, the Great (r. c. 1113–1154), the first Norman crowned king of Sicily, was more Greek and Arabic in training and culture than Latin. He exercised power over Church and state, over orthodox Greeks as well as Roman Catholics. He functioned as a priest-king to whom papal claims of authority meant little. The sophistication and wealth of Roger's government probably outclassed that of any other European ruler. His power extended to North Africa and all of southern Italy and aimed at the throne in Constantinople. It was an exotic, vibrant, expansive state that did not retain its independence long. In 1194, the Emperor Henry VI, the son of Frederick Barbarossa, claimed Sicily for the German Empire.

Further north, Ireland saw a succession of high kings from the eleventh century forward, although they never instituted central structures. The high kingship was often contested, although the Irish had a strong traditional belief that they had always had a national kingship, a fact which Gerald of Ireland reported when he wrote one of the first descriptions of Wales toward the end of the twelfth century. At the local level, however, Ireland continued to be divided into tribal units based on ancient Celtic traditions—perhaps more archaic than any other region within Europe. By the time that Gerald wrote, the Irish were menaced and partly occupied by the Angevin rulers of England. In 1167, Dermot MacMurrough, in revolt against Rory O'Connor, the high king, asked for support from the English, thereby opening Ireland to English invasion and settlement. Since, militarily, the Irish had primitive arms and little protection by way of fortresses, they were no match for the English. Ireland became divided between English and Irish areas, although the efforts of the English to assert feudal and administrative control over medieval Ireland were never successful.

In Denmark, Norway, and Sweden the expansion of Christianity went hand in hand with the establishment of united monarchies. As royal authority united the kingdoms, confiscated properties of those disinclined to obey were often given to the churches. Churches that were funded and built by the rulers were considered royal property, although this was less true in Sweden where royal authority was slower to develop and became a point of contention as the reform effort influenced the north by the twelfth century. At first the bishops formed part of a ruler's retinue before settling down into seats by the twelfth century, at which time the Scandinavian bishops successfully promoted the canonization of Scandinavian kings by Rome, and archbishops introduced coronation rites. Despite this symbiotic relationship between religion and ruler, Scandinavian societies remained more aristocratic than monarchical. The leading men of both Denmark and Sweden continued to elect the king, and only in Norway did the Church's effort to promote hereditary succession of the ruler succeed. The power of the ruler continued to depend upon support from the magnates of the kingdoms, who often met in assemblies.

In the monarchies of eastern Europe, as in Scandinavia, the ecclesiastical hierarchy evolved together with a monarchical polity, with the Church promoting kingly saints and royal pilgrimage centers. The continuing vitality of paganism provided an ongoing rationale for the alliance of ruler and religion. The last pagan stronghold on the southern Baltic coast (the island of Rugen) only gave way in 1168, while Prussia and Lithuania were not converted to Christianity until the thirteenth and fourteenth centuries. The eastern European kingdoms—Poland, Bohemia, Hungary, Bulgaria, Serbia and Rusland—struggled over issues of centralization, independence, royal succession, and the role of princes, nobles, and freemen in the political arena. Polish rulers had worn a crown intermittently in the eleventh century, but after 1138, when the kingdom was divided among several dukes and princes, the monarchy collapsed. For the next two centuries, called the period of fragmentation, Polish territories remained decentralized and in the hands of a variety of princes and dukes who had to constantly adjust to the authority of the German emperor and other neighboring authorities as well as the demands of powerful families within their own territories. Bohemia was bedeviled by struggles among royal claimants in the absence of any strict law of succession and in the presence of the active political involvement of nobles and freemen. Bohemia waxed and waned, losing territories, becoming a fief of the German Empire, but also annexing Moravia. There were efforts at regularizing the succession of the ruling family, the Přemyslides, who took the title of king by 1085, but they were not entirely successful, and the danger of fragmentation remained very real. By 1114, however, the Bohemian ruler had become one of the electors within the German Empire and by 1200 the Přemysl ruler Otakar I (r. 1192–1230) reasserted unity, with the city of Prague at the center of the polity. It was the next three centuries, however, that were to see the greatest growth of Bohemia.

Hungary also experienced dynastic rivalries, some of them murderous, over royal successions. In the process it was in danger of losing territories and of being absorbed into the German political sphere. Unlike with Bohemia, however, this did not happen. Instead, Hungary was able to expand into Transylvania, unite with Croatia, and annex Bosnia. Hungary also sought ports and access to the Adriatic where it came into conflict with Venetian political and commercial interests. The kings of Hungary, while consulting the growing numbers of landed magnates, retained considerable authority, independence, and power and did not need to balance royal and communal interests to the degree that both Poland and Bohemia did. Hungary, deriving prestige from growing demographic and economic strengths and from relatively peaceful relations with its neighbors, emerged by the end of the twelfth century as a state of importance.

Bulgaria, which had become part of the Byzantine Empire in the tenth century (Chapter 8) revolted against the Byzantines in 1185/86. The Second Bulgarian Empire (also called the Empire of the Vlachs and Bulgarians) that emerged was founded and led by three brothers (the Asen brothers) who were of Vlach/Romanian background. It reached its apogee of power in the early thirteenth century and dominated Macedonia and Albania along with other Balkan territories. Bulgaria, having briefly turned to a Roman Catholic allegiance, returned to the Eastern Orthodox Church and received its own patriarch.

Two decades prior to Bulgaria's reemergence, an independent Serbian state was also established. It was founded by Stefan Nemanja (r. 1167–1196); his son and successor was crowned by the Roman Catholic papal legate while he also received a crown from the Byzantines. Serbia, like Bulgaria, stayed within the orbit of the Eastern Orthodox Church.

At the very outer eastern reaches of Europe, the polity known as Rus expanded in the twelfth century as towns developed, episcopal centers multiplied, trading networks thickened and spread, and literate culture expanded. But the central role that Kiev had played in the late tenth and in the eleventh century was less in evidence. While Kiev retained a preeminent role, the proliferation of royal princes, each with his own territorial base, created a kind of federation of princely powers tied by loose and shifting alliances. While the culture of eastern orthodox Christianity and the Slavic language spread to create a kind of cultural hegemony, it was not yet possible to speak of a Russian state.

Summary

In the twelfth century, questions of political authority preoccupied the people of Europe to a degree unknown since Roman times. Imperial authority was better defined. Struggles between secular and ecclesiastical authority occurred at every turn. Rules of succession were of crucial concern, as struggles for succession bedeviled many kingdoms. Kings and emperors (but rarely queens or empresses) jockeyed for power with princes, counts, and communal authorities, asserting themselves in legal, military, economic, and administrative arenas. Underlying all these developments was a growth in government—the emergence of skilled administrators, protobureaucrats who governed the courts and raised revenues to pay for the castles that allowed rulers to translate authority into power.

While none of these governments was ever completely unified, and the evolving bureaucracies remained rudimentary, we can nonetheless begin to discern, particularly in England and in France, those elements that were to undergird the growth of European states. In contrast, the imperial aspirations, papal claims, and the relative strength of the German princes worked against a strong and centralized German kingdom. And centrifugal forces in the rest of Europe (e.g. the expansion of the Angevins into Ireland, the French and Spanish pushing against the frontier with Muslim Spain, the eastward pressure of German peoples and succession crises in eastern Europe) destabilized some of the frontier kingdoms that had emerged in the tenth century.

NOTES

1. Giovanni Tabacco, *The Struggle for Power in Medieval Italy: Structures of Political Rule,* trans. R.B. Jensen (Cambridge: Cambridge University Press, 1989) 184.
2. John Mundy, "In Praise of Italy: The Italian Republics," *Speculum* (1989): 821.
3. John of Salisbury, *Policraticus,* trans. C. Nederman, book 6, ch. 22 (Cambridge: Cambridge University Press, 1990).
4. C. Warren Hollister, *Monarchy, Magnates and Institutions in the Anglo-Norman World* (London: The Hambledon Press, 1986) 171.
5. *Anglo-Saxon Chronicle,* trans. Garmonsway (New York: Dutton, 1954) 264–265.
6. Letters 14, 41, and 66 in *Petri Blesensis archidiaconi opera omnia,* ed. J.A. Giles (Oxford: 1846–47), trans. in Charles Petit-Dutaillis, *The Feudal Monarchy in France and England* (London: Kegan Paul, Trench, Trubner & Co., 1936) 109.
7. W.L. Warren, *Henry II* (Berkeley: University of California Press, 1973) 353.
8. Karl Hampe, *Germany under the Salian and Hohenstaufen Emperors,* trans. R. Bennett (Totowa, N. J.: Rowman and Littlefield, 1973) 169.
9. Robert Bartlett, *The Making of Europe: Conquest, Colonization and Cultural Change 950–1350,* ch. 2 (Princeton: Princeton University Press, 1993).
10. Suger, *The Deeds of Louis the Fat* (Washington, D.C.: Catholic University of America Press, 1991) 81.
11. *Walter Map's "De Nugis curialium,"* trans. M.R. James, rev. C.N.L. Brooke and R.A.B. Mynors (New York: Oxford University Press, 1983) 442–443.
12. Map, *ibid,* 450–451.
13. Royal charter announcing the birth of Philip, quoted in Andrew Lewis, *Royal Succession in Capetian France* (Cambridge: Harvard University Press, 1981) 65.
14. Marion Facinger, "A Study of Medieval Queenship: Capetian France 987–1237," *Studies in Medieval and Renaissance History,* V (1968): 28.

~

CHAPTER 14

The New Learning, 1050–1200

By the second half of the eleventh century, the intellectual horizons of Europe were expanding. The investment in bureaucracy and courtly culture made by many European rulers and described in the last chapter could not have occurred without the growth of educational institutions and the rise of an intellectual elite willing to become administrators, lawyers, and clerics. In addition, the Gregorian reform put greater value on the literacy of the clergy. So did the challenge of heresy, to which the Church responded, in part, by written word. Simultaneously, new translations of philosophical and scientific works began to enter Europe via Arabic and Jewish intermediaries. Then, in the early twelfth century, a new institution of learning, the university, emerged. This chapter explores the intellectual influences, debates, and mental constructs of the twelfth century. It examines universities, curricula, student life, and the role of women in the world of learning. And finally, it traces the ways in which this intellectual renaissance affected the larger society.

THE RISE OF SCHOOLING

A new and influential intellectual elite emerged in eleventh- and twelfth-century Europe. It was a product of the growing demand for literate skills, the prospect of social mobility, the growing cultural sophistication of Europe's upper classes, and the cultural influences entering from outside. This intellectual elite was largely homegrown, rooted in a growing educational network. By the twelfth century, more and more opportunities arose for learning Latin grammar, intellectual concern for logic as a method of learning developed, and an institution new to Europe—the university—emerged.

Demands for an Educated Elite

Part of the reason for this intellectual renaissance rests with the Gregorian reform. Essential to this reform was the production of letters, the collection of canon law, and the establishment of an administrative network. Also, moral concerns and doctrinal disputes called for an examination of scriptural, theological, and philosophical texts. Thus, the demands of the reform effort promoted schooling and literacy. Under Pope Gregory VII, a Roman synod in 1079 decreed that all bishops institute the teaching of liberal arts in their cathedrals. By the time of the Third Lateran Council in 1179, the Church required all cathedrals, as well as other churches and monasteries that previously had supported teachers, to maintain schools for clergy and poor scholars.

The decline of slavery, growing wealth, urbanization and social complexity of society opened avenues of social mobility (see Chapter 9). An educated man, even the son of a serf, could aspire to a rewarding career in a royal, episcopal, or noble household. He could enter the clergy, perhaps gaining a paid position and further promotion. He might earn fees by teaching. The twelfth century became an age of ambition, and avarice began to take precedence over pride in commentaries on the seven deadly sins.

The commercial quickening of Europe placed a premium on literate skills as well. Merchants needed to record transactions and handle simple accounting. Although this did not require Latin grammar, it helped to have had training in elementary reading, arithmetic, and the use of the abacus. And the professionalization of government that developed in some areas of Europe in the twelfth century (see Chapter 13) relied on trained manpower. The administrator who could correspond with churchmen, render accounts, and act prudently (perhaps based on his readings of ancient authors) was in demand.

A further factor that promoted learning was the rise of cultural centers in southern Italy, Sicily, and Spain and the transmission of manuscripts through those centers. Cities such as Palermo, Córdoba, and Toledo were culturally rich; they had libraries and scholars in touch with Arabic, Greek, and Jewish intellectual traditions. Beginning around 1050, Arabic, Jewish, and Greek sources began to become more available in the West. One of the first translators was Constantine the African (from Carthage), who probably studied in Cairo and then (c. 1085) retired to the monastery of Monte Cassino in southern Italy where he translated, from Arabic into Latin, some twenty medical works, including those of Hippocrates and Galen. Books on the astrolabe and the quadrant, dependent on Arabic works, became available in Europe.

The introduction of the abacus into Europe, an important step on the road to numerical literacy, took place at the same time. Its use spread rapidly and led to the introduction of Arabic numerals.* Arabic numbers left few documentary traces when they entered Europe around 1200, but it is likely that some intellectuals,

---

* Roman numerals are based on a primitive system of addition and subtraction (i.e. CCXLIII = two 100s + 50 - 10 + 1 + 1 + 1). They preclude the possibility of multiplication, and they do not incorporate the concept of zero or of place holding.

Medieval Methods of Counting This late medieval woodcut shows, on the right side, a form of abacus or counting board that was common in the Middle Ages. The numbers formed in this illustration are 1241 and 82. The figure at the counting board is Pythagoras, while the far left figure, according to the scroll, is Boethius, who is calculating using Hindi-Arabic numbers. Medieval writers believed that Boethius invented these numbers. In fact, they were introduced into Europe from India via Arab culture and through the writings of Leonardo Fibonacci (see Chapter 17). Their use was increasingly widespread by the fourteenth century. Behind the two male figures stands "Arithmetica," who is holding two texts and has numbers representing geometrical progressions on her gown. *Museo delle Terme, Rome, Italy/Scala/Art Resource, NY.*

accountants, and merchants were already familiar with them. Handbooks on arithmetic, using Arabic numbers, were certainly common in the thirteenth century. In 1225, Leonardo Fibonacci, a Pisan growing up in North Africa who travelled throughout the Mediterranean world, composed one of the most brilliant mathematical treatises of any age, tackling quadratic equations and using irrational numbers. He could not have done so without Arabic numbers.

These developments were mirrored in other fields of learning. Adelard of Bath (c. 1080–c. 1150) traveled East among Greek and Arabic speakers, returning to England to translate Arabic works on astrology, the astronomical tables of al-Khwarizmi (whose name gave rise to "algorism"), and the *Elements* of Euclid. From Sicily came translations of Ptolemy's *Almagest* and *Optics* and a variety of Euclidean texts. Aristotle's New Logic* (his *Prior Analytics, Posterior Analytics, Topics,* and *Sophistical Refutations*) appeared in Latin as did his *De generatione et corruptione,* the *Metaphysics,* and most of his books on natural philosophy. In the second half of the twelfth century, Toledo and other urban centers in Spain that had been recently captured from the Muslims, attracted Christian translators who produced Latin

---

* Two of Aristotle's books on logic (*Categories* and *On Interpretation*), which had been translated by Boethius in the sixth century, were known, together with Boethius's other writings on logic, as the Old Logic. Boethius may also have translated the other logical treatises of Aristotle, but no uncontested translations by him have survived.

versions of Arabic texts in science (particularly in astrology, astronomy, alchemy, mathematics, optics, and magic) and in philosophy.[1] Jewish intellectuals familiar with the texts, sometimes after translating them into Hebrew often helped Christian translators. In addition Jewish works in both Arabic and Hebrew were translated into Latin.*

These translators tackled a substantial body of philosophy written by Arabic scholars that reflected centuries of discussion and absorption of Greek philosophy. These philosophers, al-Kindī, al-Fārābī, Ibn Sīnā (Avicenna), al-Ghazālī, and Ibn Rushd (Averroës) debated free will and predetermination, creation and eternity, causality, Aristotelian logic, the role of reason, the nature of the soul, and substance and accidence—issues that would occupy the minds of thirteenth-century western philosophers and theologians. With the exception of Averroës (who was not translated until the thirteenth century), the works and ideas of these philosophers became available in Latin in the twelfth century.

The lively interest in translated scientific and philosophical texts meant that there were readers capable of understanding these problems. These readers were no longer mainly monks and cathedral canons, but an entirely new intelligentsia that had been trained in Latin grammar. Latin was taught in most monasteries, in cathedral schools, and in royal and aristocratic households. Some grammar may also have been taught at the university level, as universities emerged in the twelfth century. But one of the more significant developments of the time was independent Latin grammar schools that depended on nothing more than the presence of a teacher and boys† able to pay the fees. These schools began to appear even in small towns and rural areas—in small numbers in the twelfth century and in larger numbers in the thirteenth century—enabling even boys from poor and modest families to gain an education.

The Curriculum

The medieval curriculum was loosely based on the seven liberal arts. School texts described it this way: "Grammar speaks; dialectic teaches truth; rhetoric adorns words; music sings; arithmetic counts; geometry measures; astronomy studies stars."[2] The first three arts (grammar, dialectic, and rhetoric, called the *trivium*) focus on the art of words and were taught in schools and universities and sometimes in households by tutors. The *quadrivium* (music, arithmetic, geometry, and astronomy) encompassed the numerical sciences but was not necessarily part of secondary or university training.

Medieval education began with reading and song (learning the Latin liturgy) at the elementary level but quickly moved to Latin grammar. Latin grammar was described as training in the "the art of right expression," but it was not an easy training for schoolboys, for whom Latin was a second, rather foreign, language; it

---

* The most prolific translator was Gerard of Cremona (d. 1187). Working with a team of Arabic (and sometimes Hebrew) speakers in Toledo, Gerard produced Latin versions of works in mathematics, geometry, optics, the science of weights, astronomy, astrology, alchemy, geomancy and divination, medicine, surgery, Ptolemy's *Almagest*, and philosophical and logical works of Aristotle.

† There is no evidence that girls attended Latin grammar schools, although they sometimes received an elementary reading education.

The Liberal Arts Portrayed in Stone
These twelfth-century sculptures on the west doorway of Chartres Cathedral are part of a series that represents the seven liberal arts. Along the lower level are Pythagoras, the mathematician, and Donatus, the grammarian. Donatus was a late antique Latin grammarian whose introductory grammar text was the basis for learning Latin in the Middle Ages. Above Donatus is a schoolmaster who is portrayed as a woman because of the feminine form of the noun "grammatica." In fact, it would have been highly unusual for a woman to teach grammar. On the top left is the figure of Musica. *Photo Marburg.*

required much memorization and repetition. By the time they left grammar school, boys of twelve and fourteen would have learned vocabulary, the parts of speech, and word order, and they would have begun reading standard Latin authors such as Virgil or Cicero. The goal was to develop an ability to write and speak Latin, perhaps even to engage in competitive disputations. The training they received was thought to discipline the mind and soul, and it enabled some students to go on in logic, rhetoric, philosophy, or the study of scripture, medicine, or law.

Dialectic was sometimes equated to the study of logic, and sometimes intended in the narrower sense of using arguments in disputation. It was, after grammar, the most important of the seven liberal arts and formed the basis for the first few years of university education. It offered a methodology of learning—by question and answer, by disputation, by developing arguments—that we call "scholasticism." At first its study depended upon Boethius's books on logic as well as on Peter Abelard (1079–1142), whose teaching and writings on logic galvanized a generation of scholars. Around 1140, John of Salisbury lamented the popularity of dialectic at Paris and the extent to which students were concentrating on it to the exclusion of other disciplines. By the end of the twelfth century, the remainder of Aristotle's works on logic were available in Latin.

Rhetoric, the art of speaking persuasively, focused on style, diction, and composition and was based on the study of Ciceronian or pseudo-Ciceronian texts. The usefulness of rhetoric had declined in the late western Roman Empire, since, with the decline of civic life, there was less need for political oratory and the arguments of lawyers. Although widespread attention was paid to classical (i.e. oratorical) rhetoric in the schools of Europe from about the tenth century to the early thirteenth century, it was eventually reduced to a branch of logic. Nonetheless, several other kinds of rhetoric survived and flourished. The art of writing poetry, which was partly a grammatical and partly a rhetorical exercise, revived. The science of letter writing, called the *ars dictaminis,* flourished. Textbooks on how to write letters appeared, along with extensive collections of model letters. The high point of the *ars dictaminis* was reached in mid-thirteenth century Italy where, at the University of Bologna, it was studied as a separate discipline with its own faculty. Another derivative of rhetoric was the art of preaching. Manuals for preachers began to be written about the year 1200. They quickly acquired a standard format that emphasized illustrative examples, moral content, and a rather simple, unadorned style that valued clarity.

Beyond the trivium was the quadrivium. In the eleventh century, instruction in music, astronomy, geometry, and arithmetic tended to be practical, taught through apprenticeships and using instruments such as the abacus or the astrolabe. By the twelfth century, however, with the infusion of Arabic texts, study of the quadrivium divided between theory and practice, with an increased emphasis on books. The more theoretical elements of the quadrivium found their way into the curriculum of higher education.

Math was divided into computation and number theory. Computation was used in business, but in the academic sphere math tended to be absorbed into philosophy or theology or used as an adjunct to astronomy or geometry. The formal study of music was concerned with musical ratios and harmonies with the divine, but in the twelfth century the creative focus in music was in the area of artistic practice. Music composition and performance occurred outside academia, in monasteries, cathedrals, and noble households. New modes of liturgical composition emerged (the growing use of polyphony, the emergence of liturgical drama) as did new forms of music based on secular songs and instruments (like the lute) of eastern origin. Astronomy was a requirement in the university curriculum, and most students would have read Ptolemy's *Almagest* or a twelfth-century treatise on *The Sphere* by an Englishman named John Holywood (both of which teach that the earth is round and not flat). Geometry was a more practical science, involving land surveying, the measurement of volume and weight of goods, mapmaking, cathedral building, or the construction and use of such practical devices as the astrolabe and the compass. Geometry was taught more commonly through apprenticeships than at the university.

The liberal arts were supplemented in the twelfth and thirteenth centuries by the study of newly recovered books on natural philosophy, especially Aristotle's works. Aristotle's corpus entered European intellectual life accompanied by Arabic commentaries, particularly those of Avicenna (980–1037) and Averroës (1126–1198). Avicenna, who wrote his great *summa* or summary (entitled the *Canon of Medicine*) at Baghdad early in the eleventh century, interpreted Aristotle's metaphysics within a neo-Platonic context. He offered a theological reading of Aristotle that emphasized God's illumination of man through a universal active intellect (a kind of supranatural entity) that imparted reason to man's soul. He also postulated a world governed by a hierarchy of cause and effect with God as the perfect, complete, and final cause.

One hundred and fifty years later, in Spain, Averroës edited and commented on Aristotle's works. He was critical of the way in which his predecessors, especially Avicenna and al-Fārābī, had understood Aristotle's thought. In his discussions of free will, causality, epistemology, and intelligence, he became the unrivaled interpreter of Aristotle's works. Following Aristotle's emphasis on reason, he argued for the importance of reason and the crucial role of philosophy in interpreting the truths of revelation. For Averroës there could be no contradiction between the truths of scripture (as embodied in the Qur'an) and those of philosophy, and he rejected an earlier, influential attack on the role of philosophy in theology that had been mounted by al-Ghazālī. Although Averroës's ideas were rejected in Islamic Spain (where he was sent into exile for a while), they, along with Avicenna's *Canon,* had an enormous impact in Europe as Aristotle's works began to dominate the arts curriculum in the first half of the thirteenth century. In the statutes that regulated the University of Paris in 1215, all of Aristotle's logical writings were required. On the other hand, in 1210 the arts faculty had been forbidden to teach Aristotle's natural philosophy and metaphysics with their Arabic commentaries. Despite this and subsequent bans of Aristotelian philosophy and metaphysics, lectures on these topics continued until, by mid-century, they had become an integral part of the liberal arts course.

Besides the liberal arts, medieval universities offered three professional courses of study—law (both civil and canon law), medicine, and theology—although not every university offered all three.

The Rise of the University

The intellectual life of the twelfth century is marked by a shift from cathedral schools to the university. From the ninth through eleventh centuries many cathedrals had become teaching centers. Their attraction depended upon a bishop and a community of canons who supported (or were themselves) scholars whose learning was well regarded and some of whom were willing to teach. A first-class library, with Christian and classical Latin texts, was also essential. However, no institutional structure or no agreed-upon curriculum existed. As a result, schools rose and fell in esteem, in numbers of students, and in the quality of the teachers. There seems to have been a concentration of such schools from Belgium to northern France, down the Rhine and into Germany, from Tours to Laon, Liège to Orléans, and Mainz to Magdeburg. Liège Cathedral, for example, supported (either directly or indirectly) a school for clerics and one for lay students in the cathedral, six diocesan grammar schools, and two monastic schools. The most famous cathedral school was at Chartres. Its original importance was due to Bishop Fulbert (d. 1029) who taught grammar, arithmetic, astronomy, some medicine, and theology. Most importantly, he introduced a rational approach to theological issues, relying on reasonable argument rather than arguments based on authority, revelation, or miraculous in-

MEDIEVAL VOICES

Teaching
Methods at
Chartres
Cathedral in
the Twelfth
Century

In his Metalogicon, *which is a discussion of educational practices and ideals, John of Salisbury describes the teaching methods of Bernard of Chartres, who taught at Chartres in the first half of the twelfth century. This excerpt describes the teaching of grammar and rhetoric. John is clearly speaking from personal experience.*

Bernard of Chartres, the greatest font of literary learning in Gaul in recent times, used to teach grammar in the following way. He would point out, in reading the authors, what was simple and according to rule. On the other hand, he would explain grammatical figures, rhetorical embellishment, and sophistical quibbling, as well as the relation of given passages to other studies. He would do so, however, without trying to teach everything at one time. On the contrary, he would dispense his instruction to his hearers gradually, in a manner commensurate with their powers of assimilation. And since diction is lustrous either because the words are well chosen, and the adjectives and verbs admirably suited to the noun . . . or because of the employment of metaphors . . . , Bernard used to inculcate this in the minds of his hearers whenever he had the opportunity. In view of the fact that exercise both strengthens and sharpens our mind, Bernard would bend every effort to bring his students to imitate what they were hearing. In some cases he would rely on exhortation, in others he would resort to punishments, such as flogging. Each student was daily required to recite part of what he had heard on the previous day. Some would recite more, others less. . . . The evening exercise . . . was so replete with grammatical instruction that if anyone were to take part in it for an entire year, provided he were not a dullard, he would become thoroughly familiar with the [correct] method of speaking and writing. . . . He [Bernard] would also explain the poets and orators who were to serve as models for the boys in their introductory exercises in imitating prose and poetry.

Source: John of Salisbury, *Metalogicon,* trans. D. D. McGarry I, 24 (Berkeley: University of California Press, 1955) 67–68.

tervention. Chartres also became a place to study law (with Ivo of Chartres in the second half of the eleventh century) and classical humanism (under Bernard of Chartres at the beginning of the twelfth century).* Students, attracted from all over Europe, moved around among these schools (see Medieval Voices).

By the beginning of the twelfth century, the cathedral schools could not compete with the diversity of schools and teachers at Paris. The origins of Paris as an educational marketplace (and then a university) are tied to the person of Peter Abelard (1079–1142). His autobiographical account documents the teaching conditions there, and his own lectures were one of the city's chief attractions to scholars from around Europe (see Map 14.1).

* R.W. Southern, in a series of essays, has questioned whether there was a school at Chartres, demonstrating how tenuous the evidence for it is. On the other hand, its impressive library alone would have been enough to attract scholars.

Map 14.1   Intellectual Centers of Medieval Europe   The cathedral schools that were growing in numbers in the tenth and eleventh centuries gradually declined as important intellectual centers in the face of the growth in universities. By 1300 there were as many as twenty-three universities in Europe, and by 1400 over forty. The first university in central Europe was founded at Prague in 1356. German universities were founded in Vienna in 1365 and Heidelberg in 1386, while the number of universities continued to increase in Spain, France, and Italy. Universities also emerged in Scotland and Scandinavia.

Early in his career, Abelard taught briefly at the Cathedral of Notre Dame and then at Mont Sainte Geneviève on the left bank of the Seine River. From 1113 to 1119, Abelard became the *magister scholarum* at Notre Dame, the most famous school in Paris. No matter where Abelard taught, he attracted students. One of his correspondents wrote that, "No distance of land, no heights or mountains, no depths of valleys, no thief or obstacle on the way, held back anyone who hastened to you."[3] But Abelard was not the only draw. One of Abelard's Parisian rivals, William of Champeaux taught at a monastic school at St. Victor. William was described by a German student: "he offers his services to all comers free of charge and now directs a school of secular and sacred learning larger than any I have ever heard of or seen in my time anywhere in the world." And in 1141, Everard of Ypres heard Gilbert de la Porrée lecture at Paris, where he drew an audience of nearly 300.

By 1200, as many as 3,000 to 4,000 students may have been in Paris, drawn from all over Europe. By 1215, the year that the university was incorporated, as many as 100 faculty may have been teaching the liberal arts in Paris, while as many as twenty-five well-known schools existed within a hundred miles of Paris.[4]

Paris offered advantages in lodging, food, and drink (especially wine). It was also easy, in this city of rich merchants, for poor students to beg alms. By 1200, King Philip II was beautifying the city—paving the streets and building new walls, a great covered market, and a new palace (the Louvre). Scholars and masters benefited from the patronage and protection of Capetian kings, whose renown depended, in part, upon the intellectual attractions of Paris and whose nascent bureaucracy might command scholars' talents. Although the University of Paris arose, technically, from the Cathedral School at Notre Dame, in practice the teachers in Paris were fairly independent (at least they did not encounter much interference from the cathedral until early in the thirteenth century). They rented rooms, charged fees, and taught a wide variety of texts with apparently little supervision. It was possible for the students to attend various lectures, moving freely from school to school and from master to master, and to learn everything, including the liberal arts, theology, law, and medicine.

Students claimed clerical status, although many did not plan to enter the clergy. Over time, they gained various privileges, including rent-controlled buildings, exemption from tolls and taxes, and freedom from the legal jurisdiction of the towns except in the case of serious crimes. But they were often disruptive, bringing women into the student quarters, drinking, rioting, celebrating, and gambling. Some, in search of teachers, material support, and adventure, wandered from town to town living on the margins of society and forming an order of vagrants that was a kind of parody of monastic orders. Some of the most vivid portraits of students come from the songs they composed and sang:

"Go study," urges Reason.
I would obey indeed,
But when Love whispers treason,
Whose bidding should I heed?
While they pull me and shove,
I suffer, a buffer
Twixt Reason and Love
. . . .
Now one subdued to studious mood
Must pass his days in solitude—
I cannot, though I try.
No thank you, Reason! Say goodbye!
You're vanquished by the might of Venus.

Other songs praise the god of wine, the good of gluttony, and the partying that never ends. "Then everybody calls for dice, And throws a round or two for drinks; What wintry winds may blow, what breaths of ice, Scarce anybody thinks."[5]

In response to concerns about the moral accountability of students as well as about unsupervised teaching, and unregulated curricula, by the second half of the twelfth century, calls came for more control of the schools.

The term "university" comes from the Latin *universitas,* which means any corporate body with independent legal status. Between the 1140s and the 1180s, the masters at Paris organized themselves into faculties (of theology, law, medicine, and the arts). By 1209, if not before, the pope recognized their right to act as a single body, electing deputies, disciplining members, and creating statutes. But the university as a legal corporation was born out of an effort to free the masters from regulations imposed by the cathedral chancellor. In 1215, Robert de Courson, the papal legate, gave the University of Paris statutes that ensured the independence of the masters from the authority of the cathedral chancellor. These statutes effectively placed the university under papal authority, set out provisions specifying how the masters were to conduct themselves, and spelled out the curriculum. It was not until the masters went on strike from 1229–1231, physically removing themselves from Paris and teaching elsewhere, that the chancellor confirmed the university's right to govern itself.

The arts faculty at Paris was organized into four "nations" by the early thirteenth century, each with its own seal and corporate existence. The "nations" were organized around the regional origins of the masters and their students—French, Norman (including Brittany), Picard, and English (including the German students and masters). Each "nation" supervised a certain number of schools, prescribed the examinations, set fees, allocated teaching posts, and decided the organization and content of courses. Each had an elected proctor and officers. Representatives of the four "nations" then elected a rector of the arts faculty from among the proctors.

Oxford University emerged slightly later than Paris, in the second half of the twelfth century, and its origins are more obscure. Unlike Paris, it did not originate with a cathedral school. Oxford was a center for royal government and a market town, ideally situated by river and road for those heading west from London, and it was near the royal palace of Woodstock. Oxford may have become an intellectual center because it had an active archdeaconry court that attracted lawsuits and thus lawyers. It also housed several religious communities, as well as centers for business training and luxury book production. Early in the twelfth century grammar masters were in Oxford, then a theologian or two, and finally, by the 1180s, teachers in both canon and Roman civil law. It is difficult to pinpoint the emergence of an arts faculty. Lectures were available on Boethius and on Aristotle by the year 1200, although some arts faculty might have been there as early as 1167 when the struggles between Becket and Henry II made study in Paris difficult for English scholars. Oxford teachers had less jurisdictional constraints than Paris masters did; Oxford was also more integrated, and any grouping into "nations" did not have the same degree of corporate identity as at Paris, although there were ongoing tensions.* Eventually

---

* The masters at Oxford divided loosely into two "nations"—southern (English masters below the River Nene, Welsh, Irish, and continental masters) and northern (English masters north of the River Nene and the Scottish).

separate halls and colleges grew up that provided room and board and allowed the masters and students a good deal of autonomy.

In 1209, following the murder of a mistress by her lover-clerk and the revenge hanging, by the mayor, of the murderer's two roommates, the masters and scholars of Oxford vacated the town and set up rival schools in Reading and Cambridge, where the University of Cambridge was first established. Oxford reopened in 1214 (the masters from Reading and some of the masters from Cambridge returned) after the conflict was resolved. The papal legate who mediated this conflict drew up a document that established the privileges and immunities of the university. In particular, members of the university were to have special ecclesiastical status, being placed under the authority of a chancellor in the jurisdiction of the bishop of Lincoln. In effect, Oxford became self-governing under a chancellor, since the bishop was geographically removed and had only nominal rights. In 1231, the crown recognized Oxford as a corporate society, and addressed it as a body in letters. By the 1240s, the chancellor exercised civil and criminal jurisdiction, thereby giving him nearly complete control of the town.

While Oxford was known for theology and canon law and Paris for its arts faculty and theology, Bologna was famous as a school of civil and canon law. Italy had been the center for the revival of Roman law, which may have been resurrected in part because of the search for legal precedents during the papal reform. In addition, there was a legal center at Pavia, where jurists drew upon Lombard law and studied Roman law by glossing Justinian's *Institutes,* and drawing upon his *Digest* in their legal commentaries (see Chapter 13). But it was at Bologna that the study of Roman law developed most famously. Two Bolognese teachers—Pepo, who was called "the bright and shining light of Bologna," and Irnerius—taught from the 1060s until around 1130. We know almost nothing about Pepo, but Irnerius separated law and rhetoric, analyzed the meaning of the more difficult passages in the *Digest,* applied the method of disputation to the teaching of law, and attracted large numbers of students to his lectures. Like Abelard, he helped raise the status of the town to an intellectual center.

In contrast to Paris, the university at Bologna was run by the students, most of whom were somewhat older. Since many were foreigners, and laymen rather than clergy, they had no legal protection against the exploitation of landlords, teachers, and booksellers. After unsuccessfully seeking protection and privileges from the town, they organized corporations with their own proctors and rectors. The commune outlawed their organizations. In response, they left for Padua. Because of papal pressure, and out of concern for the loss of business, the commune capitulated, allowing the students to organize. Eventually the students were able to regulate the teaching of the masters—dictating the curriculum, governing faculty travel, and fining the faculty for not arriving on time, lecturing overtime, or lecturing badly.

Throughout the Middle Ages, the number of lawyers increased. In the twelfth century perhaps ten percent of those who matriculated at universities were lawyers. By the fourteenth century, this had climbed to twenty percent. In contrast, theologians constituted perhaps only five percent of all students, and their training often kept them at the university until they were nearly forty years of age. In most universities, students to the arts faculty comprised the bulk of the population. The baccalaureate in the arts sometimes took only one and a half to two and one half years and could be attained by the age of sixteen if a scholar was bright and ambitious. It required, however, another six years for the master's license in the arts, which could not be attained before the age of twenty, and an additional four years to become a bachelor of civil law (or six without the master of arts degree). The course in medicine took from six to eight years. It was, all in all, a demanding curriculum, and those students who completed it expected to find support, a position, and income for their labor.

The revolution in education that led to the emergence of universities throughout Europe was a resolutely masculine affair, perhaps because the universities inherited the monastic and clerical atmosphere that had surrounded education in previous centuries. The communal life in the universities harkened back to monastic and cathedral life, and the important presence of monks, friars, and canons at the universities underlined this connection. Finally, students at universities were given the status of clerks, with privileges and immunities similar to those of the clergy, while the papacy maintained a supervisory role over most universities throughout much of the rest of the Middle Ages.[6]

CHANGING MENTALITIES

Historians have characterized the intellectual revolution of the twelfth century as a renaissance and a "rise of humanism," and have traditionally associated it with the school at Chartres. Over the past decades, however, it has become clearer that these conceptual advances of the twelfth century were part of a widespread scholastic enterprise, well beyond the confines of a Chartrain school. Scholars focused on the natural world, a growing belief in the value of reason, an increase in the availability of education, a revival of classical letters, the discovery of Arabic scientific and theological writings, the emergence of dialectic, and an enhanced concept of man with a greater degree of self-awareness.* All of this was fundamentally new to medieval Europe, although the framework remained resolutely a Christian one.

A Conceptual Revolution

Twelfth-century scholars rediscovered Plato's work on cosmology (the *Timaeus*) and a core of neo-Platonic writings that focused on the natural world; they read newly introduced Arabic scientific and philosophical treatises, and revived interest in classical Roman texts. In general, they employed an encyclopedic approach to knowledge, summarizing and synthesizing these works. They turned especially to the study of natural philosophy in an effort to look at man's relationship to God through and in nature. The order and origins of the universe became central questions. Out of this emerged views of man as an intellectual and a creator, of the value

---

* The language of these writers is quite explicitly masculine. As a general rule, twelfth-century intellectual developments occurred in the absence of women. The debates, the institutions, the mental constructs truly did develop, as one book title puts it, in "a world made by men."

of man's power to shape his environment, and of his central role in the universe. Twelfth-century writers commented frequently on the book of *Genesis* because it offered them an opportunity to explore the natural causes of creation and changes in matter. It was a short step from there to explaining miracles and magic in terms of natural events.

Among these scholars were Thierry of Chartres, who wrote on the seven liberal arts, the creation of the world, mathematics, and medicine, and William of Conches, a grammarian and commentator on Boethius, Plato's *Timaeus,* and Macrobius. William also wrote a general survey of the physical universe, synthesizing recent translations of medical works with his own profound knowledge of the Latin classics to produce an account of the natural world based on scientific principles. Another writer was John of Salisbury, who eventually became Bishop of Chartres and wrote an educational defense of the trivium as well as his *Policraticus* (see Chapter 13). One might also add Adelard of Bath and Abelard, since they all knew one another's works and were part of the same world of thought regardless of where they taught.

Bernard of Chartres, one of the more renowned members of this group of intellectuals, described himself and his contemporaries in relation to the classical writers as "dwarfs perched on the shoulders of giants. [Hence] we see more and further than our predecessors, not because we have keener vision or greater height, but because we are lifted up and borne aloft on their gigantic stature."[7] Embedded in this quotation is the belief that Bernard and his contemporaries could indeed see further.

Logic and Christian Teaching

In addition to the focus on man, the natural world, and science, scholars began to apply reason to their texts in a fundamentally new way that we call "dialectic." Dialectic, or the art of argumentation, originated with the Socratic dialogues and the logical treatises of Aristotle. Boethius transmitted some of Aristotle's methods of argument to western Europe, but until the twelfth century, the Greek dialectical tradition was generally more influential in the Islamic world than it was in western Europe. Greek logic and philosophy passed to the Arabs through Syriac Christian translations in the eighth and ninth centuries. In the first half of the tenth century, Baghdad was the center for the study of logic and the use of dialectic in theology, philosophy, and law. By the second half of the century, the study of logic, called the grammar of reason by the Arabs, had diffused throughout the Arabic-speaking world, and handbooks and summaries of logic had become common. The most notable Arabic writers on logic were Al-Fārābī (c. 873–950), Ibn Sīnā (Avicenna, 980–1037), and Al-Ghazzālī (1059–1111), portions of whose works were then translated into Latin. Western intellectuals may have been influenced by Arabic uses of dialectic or, perhaps, the developing interest in dialectic in Europe was an independent, parallel evolution. All of which was enhanced by the general intellectual atmosphere in the twelfth century, which was combative, aggressive, and concerned to truly understand the world in relation to an exciting but sometimes confusing array of authorities.

Dialectic, as a method, was used in the formation of the canon law of the western Church (which is law drawn from past church councils, papal decrees, and the writings of the Church fathers). Gratian, considered the father of canon law, taught at Bologna in the first few decades of the twelfth century and published his *Concordance of Conflicting Canons* (also called his *Decretum*) around 1140. Based upon dialectical arguments for or against sometimes contradictory authorities, it was to become the standard collection of canon law in the Middle Ages. Civil lawyers, who had been teaching now for several generations, were quick to incorporate Gratian's dialectical methodology in their own lectures and glosses.

Dialectic also left its mark on theological studies. At first, in the eleventh century, commentaries on the Bible focused on grammar and rhetoric. But by the beginning of the twelfth century, explanations of scripture were, bit by bit, interspersed with theological questions suggested by the text. By circa 1150, the questions began to outweigh other kinds of comments.[8]

One of the very first theologians to apply reason and questioning to the Christian faith was Anselm, abbot of Bec and then archbishop of Canterbury (d. 1109). In about 1077, Anselm was asked by his monks at Bec to prove the existence of God, putting "nothing forward on the authority of scripture"[9] and using reason alone, a surprising request in an age of belief when scripture was authoritative and God's existence generally unquestioned. The result was his ontological proof of God's existence. Anselm wrote, in his *Proslogion*:

> God is that than which a greater cannot be conceived. And he who thoroughly understands this, assuredly understands that this being so truly exists, that not even in concept can it be nonexistent. Therefore, he who understands that God so exists, cannot conceive that he does not exist. . . . Even a fool understands what is meant by God when he hears the word. But if the object exists only in the mind, then another can be thought of as having real existence also, that is, it is greater (by existence) than the one than which no greater can exist. But this is a contradiction in terms. Therefore the Being than which no greater can be conceived exists both in mind and in reality.

This proof of God's existence was denied by various contemporaries of Anselm's, one of whom (the monk Gaunilo) argued that conceiving of the most beautiful of all conceivable islands does not necessitate its existence. Although Thomas Aquinas was later also to deny the validity of this proof, it has since been modified, debated, accepted, and rejected many times.

Shortly after Anselm's death, Peter Abelard wrote a treatise entitled *Dialectic* (1121–1125) in which he summarized the study of logic. In his later works, *Sic et Non (Yes and No)* and *Theologia Christiana,* Abelard applied logic to theology, dramatizing the degree to which theological authorities contradicted each other on such important themes as grace, God's existence, ethics, the Incarnation, and the Holy Trinity. His *Sic et Non* made an anthology of contradictory positions available to students. Abelard also tried to harmonize Jewish, Christian, and classical intellectual traditions and to show that Christianity could be explained rationally and acceptably to all men.

Partially because of increasing interactions between Jewish and Christian scholars, partially because of growing knowledge of Islam, more and more Christian scholars saw the need to defend Christianity rationally. While crusaders defended Christendom with arms, Christian intellectuals could defend it with reason. One of the greatest intellectual blocks to conversion for both Jews and Muslims was the idea of God as a Trinity. Both religions emphasized God's unity, and the Christians seemed, to them, idolaters worshipping three rather than one God. It was Peter Abelard who tackled the Trinity as an object of reasoned argument. ". . . we are obliged to endeavor to understand rationally the doctrines which we believe; and especially the fundamental doctrine of the Trinity."[10] In his *Theologia* he sought to reconcile ideas of the generation of the Son or the procession of the Spirit, the wisdom of the Son, and the love of the Holy Spirit with the undivided substance of God. He further argued that he could find prefigurations of the Trinity in Plato.

Abelard brought the dialectic method into the classroom, encouraging his students to question authority. "This questioning excites young readers to the maximum effort in inquiring into the truth . . . by doubting we come to inquiry; through inquiry we perceive the truth. . . ."[11] Among the various problems Abelard included in his treatise *Sic et Non* was the following: "That faith is to be supported by human reason et contra."

Abelard excited students with his eloquence, intellectual agility, and careful attention to the meaning of words and concepts. This concern for words and concepts involved Abelard in a controversy over "universals" that had occupied intellectuals for the preceding half century. Do universal concepts, for example the generic concept of a rose, independent of any individual roses, have substance? Are they real or unreal? Would such a universal term exist independent of any particular instance of it, i.e. any particular rose? One extreme position on this question (the nominalist position) argued that only the individual rose was real; the universal (generic) rose was merely a word. Another, opposing position (the realist position, derived ultimately from Platonic notions of ideal forms within the divine mind) argued that the universal (the generic rose, or ideas of man, or the good) was the real entity. An individual thing, whether a particular rose, man or a specific good, is only a variant of a larger reality. Abelard's view, called conceptualism, was that universals exist in the mind (both the human and divine mind in different ways) as "mental words" or "patterns of things" but not as sensible objects. ". . . we in no wise hold that universal nouns are . . . , as for example the name of the rose when there are no longer roses, but it would still, nevertheless, be significative by the understanding, . . . otherwise there would not be the proposition: there is no rose."[12]

Another of Abelard's writings was his *Ethics* where he developed some ideas derived from his own teachers—that sin comes from intention more than from the physical act. What is natural is not sinful, unless the will consents to evil. Virtue is therefore a mental habit.

In general, debates over scripture directed the medieval scholar/teacher toward logic and reason but not toward history and languages, which are needed for biblical scholarship. Most commentators on the Bible, for example, did not know Hebrew or Greek, and could not therefore teach a scholarly, historical perspective on the Bible. Therefore, some Christian scholars found that they learned from intellectual contacts with Jewish scholars. In one text Abelard says that he has heard a Jewish scholar commenting on a text from the book of Kings, while other scholars consulted the Jews and learned from them. One of Abelard's pupils noted the love of learning among the Jews, in contrast, he suggested, with the Christians:

> If the Christians educate their sons, they do so not for God, but for gain, in order that the one brother, if he be a clerk, may help his father and mother and his other brothers. . . . But the Jews, out of zeal for God and love of the law, put as many sons as they have to letters, that each may understand God's law. . . . A Jew, however poor, if he had ten sons would put them all to letters, not for gain, as the Christians do, but for the understanding of God's law, and not only his sons, but his daughters.[13]

And Abelard's *Dialogue Between a Christian, a Philosopher, and a Jew* shows an appreciation for Jewish scriptural arguments.

Abelard encountered intellectual and personal hostility through most of his life, culminating in condemnations at the Councils of Soissons (1121) and Sens (1140). At Sens, Abelard's chief adversary was Bernard of Clairvaux, who was offended by Abelard's intellectual presumption and his application of reason to matters of faith. Bernard wrote to Rome, "the secrets of God are being eviscerated, questions about the most sacred matters are being heedlessly discussed. . . . So human ingenuity usurps everything for itself, leaving nothing to faith."[14] Bernard believed that Abelard was ambitious and proud, a "contriver of heresies" and, perhaps most importantly, that he drew "the multitude after him and has a people that believe in him."[15] Contemporaries complained that he had brought down upon France a horde of disputatious students who resembled the Egyptian plague of croaking frogs. After the Council of Sens, Pope Innocent II declared Abelard heretical with regard to his views on the Trinity, the Incarnation, and the doctrine of sin, but he especially condemned him because he sought to discuss the Christian faith in public and had won so many followers. Bernard had complained about the impact of Abelard's ideas: "the faith of simple folk is laughed at, the mysteries of God forced open, the deepest things bandied about in discussion without any reverence. . . ."[16] As for Abelard, he died in 1142 while resting at the abbey of Cluny on his way to Rome to appeal the verdict of heresy. And after 1150, it was the rediscovery of Aristotle's logical works that became crucial for the continuing development of the dialectical method, while many of Abelard's works were forgotten.

A Growth of Self-Awareness

The twelfth century also saw a developing self-awareness not apparent in western Europe since the fourth century when Augustine wrote his *Confessions*. Its expression in the poetry of the troubadours and in the literature of courtly love (see Chapter 17) is considered the beginning of modern literature and the origin of modern concepts of love. It also expressed itself in a sense of individualism and a new psychological awareness.

Self-examination was central to the monastic revival of the twelfth century. When Bernard of Clairvaux preached to his monks on the steps to take in confession, his first precept was "Know thyself." And in a letter to Pope Eugenius III about 1150, Bernard wrote, "Begin by considering yourself—no, rather, end by that . . . For you, you are the first; you are also the last."[17] Bernard's concern with self was not as sophisticated as that of today's modern psychologist. He was concerned, primarily, that his monks know their own sinful proclivities. He was unaware of the complexity of the task of "knowing thyself," and his own efforts to present himself through his letters and sermons betray rich psychological depths of which Bernard himself seems unaware. Nonetheless, his precept to his monks placed attention to self as essential (and preliminary) to knowledge of God and the possibility of salvation.

Aelred of Rievaulx, a Cistercian monk and teacher from northern England, asked, "How much does a man know, if he does not know himself?" And Guibert, abbot of Nogent, who wrote one of the first comprehensive autobiographies in medieval Latin (c. 1115), wrote that,

> No preaching seems to me more profitable than that which reveals a man to himself, and replaces in his inner self, that is in his mind, what has been projected outside; and which convincingly places him, as in a portrait, before his own eyes. . . . Whoever has the duty of teaching, if he wishes to be perfectly equipped, can first learn in himself, and afterwards profitably teach to others, what the experience of his inner stuggles has taught, which is much more abundant than we can express, according to the way successes and failures which he has experienced have impressed themselves on his memory.[18]

The monk Otloh of St. Emmeram (1010–1070), in his autobiographical account, revealed deep psychological anguish over life issues similar to those of St. Augustine: Should he become a monk? Ought a Christian to read pagan classics? How reliable is scripture? Does God exist? What is the nature of suffering? "If Almighty God existed, or had any power," he wrote, "such great confusion and disorder would certainly not be apparent in everything."[19] Finally, another early autobiography (c. 1150) was that of Herman, a converted Jew from Cologne who became a Premonstratensian canon. Herman detailed the difficult course of his own spiritual search and the various personal encounters that led to his conversion.

The most famous autobiography of the twelfth century is the *History of My Adversities* by Abelard, written in 1132 to 1133. In it he details the story of his rise and fall, from his early years as a proud, ambitious intellectual to his sad isolation at St. Gildas, a monastery in Brittany. In his early years, Abelard challenged his teachers, besieging Paris intellectually until he had become famous, a renowned philosopher and theologian, a poet, and a cultural icon. In his early forties, however, he consciously set out to discover sexuality; he chose as his object Heloise, a young woman who was younger, perhaps much younger, than Abelard and who was known for her learning. He became her tutor, her lover, and the father of her child. Under pressure from her uncle, Fulbert, and against Heloise's better judgment, the two got married, although the marriage was to be kept secret for the sake of Abelard's career. For various reasons, mistrust developed between Abelard and Fulbert, to the point that Fulbert had Abelard forcibly castrated. Wounded, both bodily and spiritually, Abelard constrained Heloise to enter a convent, while he became a monk at the royal abbey of St. Denis outside Paris. Abelard returned to teaching and writing but soon alienated the monks at St. Denis and then quarreled with old enemies, leading to his condemnation for heresy at an ecclesiastical council at Soissons in 1121.

> And so, I took myself off to a lonely spot I had known before in the territory of Troyes, and there, on a piece of land given me, by leave of the local bishop, I built a sort of oratory of reeds and thatch and dedicated it in the name of the Holy Trinity. . . . No sooner was this known than the students began to gather there from all parts, hurrying from cities and towns to inhabit the wilderness, leaving large mansions to build themselves little huts, eating wild herbs and coarse bread instead of delicate food, spreading reeds and straw in place of soft beds and using banks of turf for tables.[20]

Still badgered by the Church, and feeling intensely persecuted, Abelard sought further escape by accepting an appointment in 1126 as abbot of a remote monastery in his native Brittany. The monks, however, were murderous; they tried to poison Abelard and to waylay him on the road. "But now," Abelard concludes, "Satan has put so many obstacles in my path that I can find nowhere to rest or even to live; a fugitive and wanderer, I carry everywhere the curse of Cain, forever tormented by . . . quarrels and forebodings without and within."[21]

Abelard's efforts at self-analysis and self-justification were not, however, always sensitive to others, and this is particularly true of his treatment of his relationship with Heloise, which he regarded entirely as a matter of lust. Heloise, who received a copy of the autobiography via a third person, was offended and wrote to Abelard. Her letters, which show a high degree of self-awareness, complain of Abelard's neglect and speak plainly of her continuing physical desire for him. She characterizes her religious life as hypocritical and her attitude toward God as accusatory. "O God—if I dare say it—cruel to me in everything! . . . Of all wretched women I am the most wretched, and amongst the unhappy I am unhappiest. The higher I was exalted when you preferred me to all other women, the greater my suffering over my own fall and yours. . . ."[22]

In response to Heloise's appeals, Abelard became spiritual advisor to Heloise's community of nuns, sending them letters of direction, Latin hymns, sermons, and a commentary on the book of Genesis. When Abelard died, his body was brought to Heloise, and the two of them now rest together in the famous Père Lachaise cemetery in Paris.

Abelard and Heloise Conversing This manuscript illustration shows Abelard (as a monk) and Heloise (a nun) talking, presumably about the letters of direction, sermons, and advice that Abelard gave to Heloise in her capacity as prioress of the nunnery of the Paraclete. This is the earliest illustration of the two lovers and spiritual companions. It comes from a fourteenth-century manuscript of the *Le Roman de la Rose* (see Chapter 17). The *Roman de la Rose,* written more than a century after Abelard's death, was the first to mention the letters that the two exchanged. *Musée Condé, Chantilly/The Bridgeman Art Library.*

BOOKS AND LITERACY

The growth of self-awareness, so poignantly demonstrated by Heloise, was grounded in bookishness. The increasing number of libraries and growing literate skills affected both men and women, albeit differently, and helped make possible a new aristocratic culture that valued the intellect and culture as much as the life of arms.

The Spread of Books

Books and libraries were readily available in the twelfth and thirteenth centuries—much more so than people today assume. Books, written primarily on parchment, had traditionally been housed in monastic and ecclesiastical libraries. As a popular saying of the twelfth century put it, "A monastery without a library is like a fortress without an armory." The larger monastic libraries held collections of 500 to 700 codices, each of which might include a number of different works. Most monasteries had copyists producing volumes for their library, but they also borrowed books and sometimes loaned their own books to outsiders—to bishops, clergy, and even lay people for study and for copying. Monastic and ecclesiastical libraries may have had open access for guests. By the end of the thirteenth century, however, some of the oldest and greatest monastic libraries, such as Monte Cassino in Italy, were in disarray. Books had been pawned or loaned and not returned; monks no longer cared to copy books, instead employing paid scribes or buying books. Books were now available through the newer university libraries, private libraries, the bookseller, and the stationer as well as in the libraries of reformed monastic orders.

Among those reformed orders, the Carthusians, in particular, were famous for their libraries and zealous in their production of books. Every novice received writing tools, and the order's strict vows of silence gave the written word all the more importance in their mission. Carthusian libraries were famous not simply for the numbers of their books, but also because they were rich in vernacular texts which, by the fourteenth century, they were loaning to outsiders.

The most impressive university library was that of the Sorbonne in Paris. In 1290, the collection contained 1,017 volumes. Forty years later, the nearly 2,000 volumes were divided into a main reading room (with stacks) where the standard books were chained to desks and a smaller, circulating library that contained duplicates and lesser used materials. Students who wanted to borrow a book from the small library only had to ask. The librarian kept a record of the borrowers, along with the title and call number of the manuscript, but sometimes the borrowers lost the books (see Medieval Voices).

Students, then like today, copied their own notes and collected their own libraries; it was common for students to buy portions of texts and lectures from professional scribes and booksellers. Gradually various colleges, halls, or houses of study also collected libraries.

By the end of the thirteenth century, professional men (doctors and lawyers especially) and even middle-class men and women might have a small library. Richard de Bury, a fourteenth-century bishop of Durham who was a famous book lover and collector (to the point that every room in his house was stacked with books), found books in the homes of parish priests and schoolteachers of "rude boys" in rural areas of northern England. A German schoolmaster, Hugo von Trimberg (1235–1313), boasted that he had collected 200 books, which he would use to support himself in his old age by loaning them for fees or selling them to pupils.[23] Parishes began to develop small libraries, with books chained up front for all to use. And town officials began to establish municipal public libraries.

Although many of the books were in Latin, especially those used in the monastic and university libraries, increasingly through the twelfth century, romances, histories, family chronicles, saints' lives, and a variety of devotional works began to be written in the vernacular. This was a turning point in the history of lay literacy. Romances, especially in French, were read to aristocratic lay audiences. Women as well as men participated in these activities. Chrétien de Troyes, in his French romance *Yvain,* describes a "well-bred maiden, mild and beautiful, not yet sixteen" who read a long romance to her father and mother, the lord and lady of the castle.[24] Constance Fitz-Gilbert, an aristocratic Anglo-Norman of the twelfth century, read poems privately, in her room. Treatises were addressed to women, such as Chrétien de Troyes' romance *Lancelot,* written for Marie of Champagne.

MEDIEVAL VOICES

A Set of
Library
Regulations
from the
Fifteenth
Century

Although the following rubrics for library regulations are late (1431, from Angers), they reflect the earlier practices of university libraries. Each rubric tells what the specific rules will be about. Other than the fact that many of the more valuable books were chained to prevent theft, and that we no longer correct our library book collections, many of these issues are a matter of concern in today's university libraries.

On not drawing out chained books and volumes of the library without obtaining the permission in writing of the rector and college.

On visiting the library each year at the close of the university and checking up its inventory and putting it away with the keys of the reading desks in a chest.

On not whispering or making a noise or disturbance in the library and on excluding those doing this.

On preferring members of the teaching staff to all others and giving them the place in the library which they want.

On not bringing or keeping women in the library building as occasion for sin.

On not stealing anything from the library and to whom it is permitted to correct its books and to whom not.

On copying lectures and the charges therefor and conversion of them to the perpetual use of the library.

On charging for the books and quaternions [small booklets] of the library before they are loaned out and marking them with a sign manual.

To whom the unchained books and quaternions of the library may be loaned and to whom not, and of the method of doing this and raising the salary of the custodian.

On demanding a fine from those who keep books or quaternions of the library more than thirty days.

Source: University Records and Life in the Middle Ages, ed. Lynn Thorndike (New York: Columbia University Press, 1944) 320–321.

The nobility now commissioned both Latin and vernacular books, creating private libraries. Ingeborg, the spouse of Philip II of France, expressed her love of books through collecting, copying, and commissioning them. It is difficult to know just how literate some of these aristocratic patrons were. One cautionary example is that of Count Baldwin II of Guines (fl. 1150–1190), an educated man with an impressive library who never learned to read. Clerks read his books to him.

Women and Literacy

Medieval women, particularly from wealthier families, often had access to books, as we have seen above with regard to the reading of romances. Literacy, for women, was largely a reading literacy. It was not common for women to write, except perhaps in the convents.

Women in convents had access to Latin literature. One of the more impressive convent libraries must have been at Gandersheim in Saxony, where the tenth-century nun Roswitha was familiar with Virgil, Lucan, Horace, Ovid, Terence, and perhaps Plautus, Prudentius, Sedulius Scottus, Fortunatus, Martianus Capella, and Boethius.[25] We have already mentioned the learning of Hildegard von Bingen in the twelfth century (see Chapter 11). The twelfth-century convent at Notre Dame de Saintes had a school, a library, and literate nuns who were expected to read the Church fathers, biblical commentaries, monastic contemplative writings, and other works.[26] By the late thirteenth and the fourteenth century, however, the use of Latin in nunneries became problematic—perhaps sufficient for the nuns to sing the liturgy and read scripture at meals but little else. Convent libraries were more likely to have devotional literature in the vernacular. This loss of Latin (and the learning that went with it) was due, in part, to the exclusion of nuns from universities where, by the fourteenth century, most monasteries sent their monks, however briefly. Even so, some convents still made impressive contributions, albeit in the vernacular. Religious women, for example, were responsible for keeping and passing on the German mystical writings of Meister Eckhart and Heinrich Suso, two of the most important mystics of the fourteenth century. St. Katherine's convent in Nuremberg had holdings of some 600 German manuscripts, mostly prayer and devotional books, sermons, and ascetic literature.

Nuns also copied manuscripts, often with artistic decorations that were particularly valued. In 1139, Pope Innocent II wrote in gratitude to the nuns of Admont in Germany for their gift of a saintly biography they had copied. One of the most famous copyists was the nun Diemud of Wessodrunn who produced at least forty-five manuscripts between 1080 and 1120, mostly liturgical and theological works. And the illuminations that Hildegard of Bingen painted to illustrate her own manuscripts became famous in the twentieth century.

Nuns wrote letters, exchanged poems, composed charters, kept accounts of sermons (usually in the vernacular), and wrote biographical accounts of other nuns and female saints. The thirteenth-century convent of Helfta in Germany produced three learned female mystics whose multivolume works of revelations and prayers circulated widely. Heloise, by all reports, received a very high-level conventual education in Latin, the Latin classics, and the works of the Church fathers. On three occasions Abelard credits her also with knowledge of Greek and Hebrew, noting that she is "alone at this time adept in the experience of the three tongues."[27] She has gained fame from the few surviving Latin letters she wrote as well as the learned debates she conducted with Abelard, who recounted them in his autobiography.

Not all nuns were expected to know how to write, which was a separate, more difficult skill, requiring special training. Official business could be written by professional clerks or by clergy. Hildegard of Bingen, who produced plays, treatises, and prophecies that made her one of the most important and influential authors of the twelfth century, may have dictated rather than written her works. Writing ability, particularly for a laywoman, was sometimes seen as dangerous—a way for her to communicate surreptitiously with a lover. As late as the fourteenth century, in a collection of letters from the Paston family in England, it appears doubtful that the wives knew how to write. Only one, Margaret Paston, signed her name and that very shakily with an unpracticed hand. Whereas women often left books to others in wills, they never wrote their own wills. And while there are numerous portraits of women reading, there are very few of a woman writing at her desk.

Literacy and Society

Clearly, in the twelfth and thirteenth centuries, literacy and books had become increasingly common among aristocratic and professional classes. One result was the rise of a schoolroom-trained, combative elite whose entrance into administrative ranks offered a challenge to the culturally dominant roles of monasteries and the lay aristocracy. These "new men" began to take an increasing interest in patronage and the use of literate skills. Alexander Murray has documented the emergence of a professional elite by way of what he calls the language of separation. Twelfth- and thirteenth-century philosophers and lawyers asserted the superiority of their skills by labeling competitors as well as social inferiors with intellectually pejorative names—rustics, ignoramuses, fools, vulgar. As the *Carmina Burana* puts it. "The illiterate man is like a brute, since he to art is deaf and mute."[28]

Contemporaries began to take quite seriously the dictum that an illiterate king is a crowned ass, and royal patronage became an important factor in encouraging the twelfth-century renaissance. The first known patron of French literature was Matilda, the wife of Henry I of England (1088?–1118) (see Medieval Portrait). Henry II and Eleanor of Aquitaine, as well as Frederick I were also artistic patrons (see Chapter 13), but the role of patron was not confined to royalty. Heloise's numerous requests to Abelard provoked many of his later writings, including 133 hymns. Countess Matilda of Tuscany, who was learned in Latin, patronized the writing of her own biography and that of one of the bishops of Lucca. She spent her life with politics, studies, and religious devotions, leaving a large library of books to the Church at her death in 1115. Educated women dominated the courts of Europe in the twelfth century, patronizing poets, romance writers, chroniclers, and the production of psalters and other devotional works. In the thirteenth and fourteenth centuries, women were also among some of the earliest and most important patrons of university colleges and other educational institutions.

Among the aristocratic and the wealthy it became increasingly common to employ tutors in the households. By the end of the twelfth century, the tools of literacy—books, the ability to read, use of the vernacular as a language of culture, and even an acquaintance with writing skills—were no longer exceptional among the aristocracy. The French romance of Flora and Blancheflor, for example, shows aristocratic children reading Ovid.

It is much less clear that a learned literacy, whether in Latin or the vernacular, and access to books was common among middling or poorer people. M. B. Parkes has coined the phrase "pragmatic literacy" to describe the writing and reading skills needed by those who kept records for commercial, administrative, or legal reasons. Practical treatises and reference works on the law, on estate management, and on accounting practices were drawn up for local officials, some of whom could have

MEDIEVAL PORTRAITS

Matilda of Scotland, Wife of King Henry I of England

Matilda of Scotland (d. 1118), a descendant of Anglo-Saxon and Scottish rulers, married Henry I of England in 1100 after leaving the English convent where she had been educated in Latin learning. Whether she had been veiled while there was a matter of some importance. She testified that her aunt had once put a black hood on her head but that she had thrown it off; in addition, her father, seeing her once with a hood, had also torn it off. And if she had worn one, it was more for fear of the Normans than for piety's sake. Her determination to be married to Henry was respected by the ecclesiastical hierarchy.

More learned than her husband, and an active participant in governing, Matilda was also a patroness of writers, builders, and musicians. Based largely in Westminster, she issued charters in her own name, attested other charters, administered her dower lands, and served as regent when Henry was on the continent. The emerging establishment of Westminster as the administrative and ceremonial center of the kingdom occurred around her and because of her. She founded a leper hospital and a priory in and around London and sponsored construction of bridges and bathhouses. She patronized the historical writings of William of Malmesbury, received letters and poems, supported artisans in needlecraft and metalwork, commissioned the writing of *The Voyage of St. Brendan* and a biography of her mother, St. Margaret of Scotland, and promoted musicians and musical performances at court. Writers praised and celebrated her, crediting her with bringing peace to the land and helping promote justice in the laws. She appears to have been a strong-willed queen, active in gaining permission to leave the monastery, a co-equal with her husband in the government of the realm, and a patroness of culture and learning.

Source: Eadmer, *History of Recent Events,* trans. G. Bosanquet (London: Cresset Press, 1964) 126–131; Lois L. Honeycutt, "Proclaiming her dignity abroad: The Literary and Artistic Network of Matilda of Scotland, Queen of England 1100-1118," *The Cultural Patronage of Medieval Women,* ed. June Hall McCash (Athens: University of Georgia Press, 1996) 155–174.

come from the peasant class. Sample business letters and contracts in the vernacular were available for reference. Acquaintance with pragmatic literacy became more common, albeit still not the norm, in the twelfth century at all levels of society.

A further indication of the growth of literacy in the period from 1100–1250 is the creation of ecclesiastical and governmental archives. Clearly document writing underwent an enormous increase after 1100. By the year 1200, we have nearly 200 letters extant per year from the papal archives, 120 from English royal archives, and perhaps sixty per year from the French government. And these are only the surviving records. By 1200, tax records were being made in quadruplicate in England, with copies sent to the collector, the sheriff, and the baronial steward in the counties, all three of whom were laymen. "The initiative in using documents came from the king and gradually made its way down the social scale—to most barons by 1200, to knights by 1250, to peasants by 1300."[29] This does not mean that the peasants were able to write, but that they were able to use the services of clerks to participate in a written culture and to preserve their rights through written records.

Even the documents themselves began to change shape, as finding aids allowed scholars and bureaucrats better access to the written text. Cross-referencing, indices, chapter titles, paragraphing, punctuation, and alphabetized reference books all begin to emerge in the twelfth and thirteenth centuries. Perhaps just as scholars had begun to understand that they could manipulate the natural world through reason or the political and social hierarchy through learning and ambition, so did they begin to understand that they could manipulate the written page itself.

Summary

The process by which a society moves from reliance on oral transmission of ideas to written record is one of the most significant of all transitions. It has been argued that it changes the way people think, as they become more logical, more self-aware, and more systematic in their approach to the world around them.* Whether or not there is such a causal connection, it is the case that medieval Europeans made a large step toward literacy in the twelfth and thirteenth centuries, as schools developed and new ideas began to circulate through the transmission of texts. As the number of translations into Latin from Greek, Arabic, and Hebrew texts grew, Europeans expanded their understanding of science, natural philosophy, and logic while they promoted and patronized education, literacy, and the production of books. As a result, a new intellectual elite emerged to take its place in Church, government, and society, while literate tools became available even to craftsman and the sons of peasants.

NOTES

1. Marie-Thérèse d'Alverny, "Translations and Translators," *Renaissance and Renewal in the Twelfth Century*, ed. R.L. Benson and Giles Constable (Cambridge: Harvard University Press, 1982) 452–454.
2. David L. Wagner, ed., *The Seven Liberal Arts in the Middle Ages* (Bloomington: Indiana University Press, 1983) 60.
3. Stephen C. Ferruolo, *The Origins of the University* (Stanford: Stanford University Press, 1985) 20.
4. R.W. Southern, "The Schools of Paris and the School of Chartres," *Renaissance and Renewal in the Twelfth Century*, ed. R.L. Benson and Giles Constable (Cambridge: Harvard University Press, 1982) 119.
5. *The Goliard Poets,* trans. George F. Whicher (New York: New Directions, 1965) 179–181, 271.
6. A. B. Cobban, *English University Life in the Middle Ages* (Columbus: Ohio State University Press, 1999) 2–3.
7. John of Salisbury, *Metalogicon,* trans. D. D. McGarry (Berkeley: University of California, 1955) 167.
8. Beryl Smalley, *The Study of the Bible in the Middle Ages,* 3rd ed., rev., ch. 2 (Oxford: Blackwell, 1983).
9. R. W. Southern, *Saint Anselm* (Cambridge: Cambridge University Press, 1990) 118.

---

* This is not to deny the complexity and the richness of oral culture or to suggest that an increased organizational capacity is somehow better.

10. G. Bosworth Burch, *Early Medieval Philosophy* (New York: King's Crown Press, 1951) 70–71.

11. Introduction to *Sic et Non: a critical edition,* ed. B.B. Boyer and Richard McKeon (Chicago: Chicago University Press, 1977).

12. Richard McKeon, ed. and trans. *Selections from Medieval Philosophers,* vol. 1 (New York: Scribner's Sons, 1929) 254.

13. Smalley, 78–79.

14. Ferruolo, *The Origins of the University,* 57.

15. Otto of Freising, *The Deeds of Frederick Barbarossa,* trans. C.C. Mierow (New York: Norton, 1953) 85.

16. A. Victor Murray, *Abelard and St. Bernard: A Study in Twelfth-Century "Modernism"* (Manchester: Manchester University Press, 1967) 50–51.

17. Bernard of Clairvaux, "De consideratione," III, 6., *Patrologia Latina,* vol. 182, col. 0745–0746.

18. Colin Morris, *The Discovery of the Individual, 1050-1200* (New York: Harper & Row, 1972) 67; *Patrologia Latina,* vol. 156, col. 27B–28C.

19. Otloh of St. Emmeran, "Libellus de suis tentationibus, varia fortuna et scriptis," *Patrologia Latina,* vol. 146, col. 0029–0050.

20. *The Letters of Abelard and Heloise,* ed. Betty Radice (Harmondsworth: Penguin, 1974) 88–89.

21. Ibid., 102.

22. Ibid., 129.

23. Karl Christ, rev. Anton Kern, trans. and ed. Theophil M. Otto, *The Handbook of Medieval Library History* (Metuchen, N. J.: Scarecrow Press, 1984) 304.

24. ll. 5121–5133.

25. Eileen Power, *English Medieval Nunneries c. 1275 to 1535* (New York: Biblo & Tanner, 1964) 238.

26. Penelope Johnson, *Equal in Monastic Profession* (Chicago: University of Chicago, 1991) 144.

27. Joan M. Ferrante, "Women's Role in Latin Letters from the Fourth to the Early Twelfth Century," in *The Cultural Patronage of Medieval Women,* ed. J. H. McCash (Athens: University of Georgia Press, 1996): 100n22.

28. A. Murray, *Reason and Society in the Middle Ages* (Oxford: Clarendon Press, 1978) 241.

29. Michael Clanchy, *From Memory to Written Record* (Cambridge: Harvard University Press, 1979) 56.

PART V

~

The Height of Medieval Culture, 1100–1300

CHAPTER 15

~

Medieval Society, 1100–1300

In Chapter 9, the Dark Ages, the feudal system, and the three social orders were examined as popular constructs that have been used to explain medieval society. Such paradigms, however, fail to capture the great variety of social life in medieval Europe. This is certainly true for 1100 to 1300. During this period, knightly culture flourished, towns expanded, and peasant society begins to emerge in all its facets in the documents. The clergy was becoming an essential component of society at all levels, and Christian Europeans were developing a more sophisticated understanding of Judaism and Islam as well as confronting new pagan forces such as the Mongols. This chapter will examine various aspects of medieval society. Just as medieval writers sought to capture the essence of their society with their paradigm of the three social orders, so does this textbook (indeed any textbook) seek to organize medieval society around societal differences in order to dissect and better understand it. In this case these categories include peasants, aristocracy and townsfolk; laypersons and clergy; Christians and non-Christians; men and women; children and adults; in the final analysis, however, the dynamism and mobility of the Middle Ages defeat all our best efforts to place medieval society into neat frames of reference.

PEASANT SOCIETY

Peasants are rural people involved with agricultural and craft production whose work in the Middle Ages supported other elements of society, for example, the state, lords, merchants, and townfolk. In the twelfth century, John of Salisbury called peasants the feet of the state: "These are the laborers, constantly attached to the soil . . . the artisans who work in wool or wood, iron or brass . . . those who are charged with the care of maintaining us."*[1]

---

* John of Salisbury was of the opinion that magistrates must do what is to the advantage of the humbler people and avert injuries to them, as he put it, "[that] the republic might put shoes, as it were, on its workers."

Peasant society was not uniform. There were wealthy peasants, middling-level peasants, and poor peasants who were fortunate if they could rent a cottage and hire out their labor. For example, Barbara Hanawalt mentions one very poor peasant in England in 1279 who was a vagrant, had no home, and in dying, left only two possessions: a coat and a cow.[2] In eastern Europe and parts of Scandinavia there were still peasants who were pagans, while many agricultural laborers and villagers in parts of Spain and Sicily were Muslim. Many peasants were unfree, and the term usually used to describe them is "serfs."* Other peasants were legally free, although, as members of the lower social class, they remained dependent. Some peasants were craftsmen; they might be carpenters or leather-workers. Peasants might make money by brewing and innkeeping, selling produce at market, carting goods, or spinning cloth in their homes. It is very difficult to generalize about medieval peasants at any time, as their status might change from generation to generation depending upon individual talents as well as social, political, and economic shifts.

Constraints Placed on Peasants

In many parts of Europe (for example, the Loire valley, Champagne, and Burgundy in France, across Spain, Normandy, southern Italy, much of England, and parts of eastern Europe), peasants were burdened by various kinds of servitude to lords and, increasingly toward the end of this period, by duties to the state or the monarchy. Some of the constraints on peasants were associated with the land itself. Other constraints were legal and economic and associated with the person rather than the land. Some constraints were a matter of social attitude in a hierarchical society where superiors lorded it over lower classes.

Many lords of manors held reserve or demesne land (land directly exploited by the lord). Demesne included plowed fields, meadows, woods, wastelands, roads, and bridges. One way of managing these lands was to require serfs to work the fields, build the bridges, and repair the roads. In compensation, peasants might receive a boon of food, but they also lost the time and labor needed for their own lands. In the twelfth century, lords tended to replace these forced services with money rents and to hire workers, but whenever the price of labor went up, lords would be tempted to reimpose labor services.

Serfs could not leave the lord's domain, marry their daughters, or educate their sons without the lord's permission. This permission often involved a fine that was paid at the lord's court, where serfs were subject to the lord's justice. The unfree status of serfs was hereditary, and lands and goods held by them belonged, in the final analysis, to the lord. Thus, when a serf died, it was common to provide a heriot, that is, a death duty (usually one of his best beasts), to signify that the serf held his goods at the lord's behest. Serfs were also subject to arbitrary taxes demanded by the

---

* The term "serf," which comes from the Latin "servus" meaning slave, was never that common in England, where "villein" was preferred. The word "serf" began to disappear in France during the twelfth and thirteenth centuries. In the Macon region of France, "serf" had gone out of use by the end of the twelfth century except as an insult. Instead, the word "villein" began to be customary, which arose from a fusion between free and unfree peasants. It developed a somewhat negative connotation, evolving into the English word "villain."

lord that, once exacted, could become customary. Even as many of these servile conditions diminished, as they did throughout much of western Europe by the fourteenth and fifteenth centuries, peasants might still be constrained to use the lord's mill for grinding flour or his oven for baking bread. This enabled the lord to maintain a monopoly over essential economic services, even if the peasants were legally free.

There were other parts of Europe where the peasants were comparatively freer, albeit still of an inferior class. There were no lords (or lordship) in Frisia. Throughout Germany many peasants held land freely. The same was true in southern France, where remnants of Roman law, which provided for free land tenure, still had influence. In northern Italy, partly because of the number of cities and the peculiarities of the elite (more urban, with no regular military service), servitude among the peasantry was disappearing by the tenth century and practically unknown by the late-twelfth century. In parts of Spain also, where peasants were needed to colonize areas newly conquered from the Muslims, they enjoyed substantial freedoms. An enormous variety of freedoms and regulations existed in eastern Europe, where a more uniform serfdom emerged only toward the end of the Middle Ages. In England, peasants were free of obligations or legal constraints in whole regions. In the West Midlands, for example, fifty to seventy-five percent of all peasant tenants held their lands with hereditary rights or for life. In the north, where people lived in scattered villages and hamlets and practiced more of a pastoral than a grain economy, lordship was a patchwork affair. This was also true for peasants in marginal areas (e.g. the fens) or along the borders with Scotland and Wales. The map of serfdom and freedom was constantly in flux and the terms applied to peasants often unclear, even to contemporaries. As a result, historians will continue to research and debate the conditions of medieval peasantry. One can conclude, however, that even when legally free, peasants remained dependent on those of higher status and may never have felt entirely free to take control of their own lives.

Slavery, while no longer a common condition in medieval Europe, was not unknown. Scandinavian society depended upon slaves until the fourteenth century; slavery continued in the Balkans throughout the Middle Ages, as did the buying and selling of slaves throughout the Mediterranean, especially in port cities such as Genoa. Perhaps as early as the eleventh century, black sub-Saharan slaves were sold via North Africa to households in Muslim Spain. By the fourteenth century, Christian households in southern Europe were using domestic, mostly female, slaves captured from the Crimea. A recent study by Susan Stuard argues that, while by the twelfth and thirteenth centuries slaves were no longer used for agricultural production throughout most of Europe, there was never a time when female slaves (*ancillae*) were not present in the households of some of the wealthier families.

Peasants who were not free, especially men, could and did gain their freedom. One way was through geographical mobility. Peasants who moved into newly colonized lands to help clear them received their freedom in exchange. In order to compete with the attractions of newly opened lands, some lords offered benefits to those who stayed. Unfree peasants who received permission (or those who simply ran away) might move into towns, where, it was proverbially said, "town air made free." This was not necessarily so. William Jordan has noted that serfs frequently lived in towns.[3] They might act as free individuals, but they were not legally free. In 1257, 366 serfs of the Abbey of St. Pierre-le-Vif in Sens (France) paid £6,000 *parisis* for their freedom, even though many of them had been living in urban areas for over a generation.[4]

The number of manumissions (releases from slavery or serfdom) in the twelfth and thirteenth centuries increased dramatically as the upper classes, needing money for building, paying debts, and expensive living, negotiated for ready cash. Such manumissions were also viewed as an act of charity. In some cases, whole villages were given charters of freedoms and privileges (franchises) for large sums of money, which might burden them with debt for years. Between 1177 and 1350, there were 280 enfranchisement charters in Lorraine alone. In the Paris region between 1246 and 1280, charters were issued for sixty villages.[5] It was a large-scale movement that made headway by dint of mass pressure and offers of cash. Buying these charters became possible because peasants were becoming part of a growing market economy; they needed freedom to trade; they had the cash to pay for it and the organizational ability to demand it.

Children of serfs might gain freedom by getting an education and entering the clergy or a lay profession, where they could move up the social scale. Although evidence of such social mobility is difficult to document in the twelfth century, people believed this was possible. Twelfth-century English people told the legend of Earl Godwin of Wessex (the father of King Harold) who they believed had risen from being the son of a shepherd to the most powerful man in the kingdom. In 1126, the provost of Bruges and his brother, the castellan of Bruges, were thought to have had a servile background, although this circumstance was used to attack them.[6] Suger, the abbot of St. Denis (d. 1151), who ruled France while Louis VII was on crusade, described himself as "of humble origins." Robert Grosseteste, a thirteenth-century bishop of Lincoln, may have been born a villein.[7] Judith Bennett, writing the biography of the peasant Cecilia Penifader of Brigstock (c. 1295–1344), cites Cecilia's brother, William, a peasant who left the village for ten years of education, returning as a *magister* and village cleric.[8] Enough boys of rural background were attending the university in fourteenth-century England for vacations to be arranged around the planting and harvesting of crops. Once educated, these boys might become priests, secretaries, clerks, stewards, or bailiffs in charge of a lord's property. The literate were readily employed, whatever their social origins.

Freedom was sometimes demanded and fought for. Rural communities in northern Italy, for example, organized successfully in the eleventh and twelfth centuries to demand hunting rights and rights in the common lands and pastures, while French villages in the twelfth and thirteenth centuries fought for exemptions from obligations to lords and autonomy in running their affairs. Rights were often difficult to obtain; they might be gotten in stages, at great cost, and sometimes violently. In the fourteenth century, villagers throughout southern England asserted their freedom by purchasing copies of parts of the Domesday Book relating to their holdings. With the help of literate individuals (perhaps lawyers, gentry, and clerks) and with large sums of money, they withdrew their services, arguing unsuccessfully in court that these services were not documented in 1086.[9]

Family Life and Economy

Throughout medieval Europe, peasants generally lived in nuclear families, although in the southern Mediterranean extended families were common. Usually an older grandparent maintained a separate household, as did a married brother or sister; occasionally a grandparent or unmarried aunt or uncle lived with the nuclear family. More common, because of high death rates, was a stepparent or a single parent in the household. Wealthier peasant households might have a servant or two living with them, but generally, household size was small, perhaps five individuals.

Peasants did not have large numbers of children. Death rates among children were high (twenty to forty percent would not reach their fifth birthday), and some form of contraception might have been practiced. Children required a significant economic investment; they did not help in any serious fashion with household and farming tasks until they were seven or eight years old, and if a peasant family decided to educate a child, (usually from age seven on), the investment could be substantial. Prior to age seven, children required nurturing and watching; few peasant women could afford wet nurses or hire servants as babysitters. Children played, just as children do today, got in trouble, and caused their parents grief. Contrary to the assertions of some historians, medieval parents seem to have had tender feelings toward their children and did not take their loss lightly.

On the other end of the age scale, someone was considered old who had reached age sixty, although it was difficult to know one's birth date. Perhaps ten percent of a medieval population was over fifty. (Once past early adulthood for men or childbearing years for women, an individual had a good chance of living into old age.) Retired peasants often stayed on their own land, perhaps living in a smaller residence; they might make arrangements with relatives and neighbors to see that they were provided for. Wealthier peasants might hire a caretaker, and many peasants belonged to religious guilds that gave them benefits. Few peasants had access to the hospitals or monasteries that functioned as retirement homes for people higher up the social ladder.

By the twelfth century, most peasants lived in villages with broad streets, homes that were sometimes two stories high, and dirt floors that were cleaned every day. Although villages might smell, and people often shared their homes with animals, most people valued cleanliness. Sometimes life was noisy: church bells rang; blacksmith shops were full of racket; people hawked their wares; and children and animals roamed the streets.

Medieval peasant society was not a self-sufficient frontier society; it depended upon markets and artisans to supply what the individual household did not produce. Although thread might be spun at home, cloth was usually bought at the market. Even bread and ale might be bought rather than baked or brewed at home. And although many peasant households had a vegetable garden, a croft with fruit trees, and places to keep pigs, geese, or rabbits, they still bought some of their food at market stalls.

Villages developed and solidified between 1100 and 1300. Open-field farming became more common, requiring communal decisions with regard to labor, materials, and produce. The collective use of woods and pastures encouraged group ef-

Peasants Celebrating with Music and Dancing This late medieval manuscript from the Bodleian Library at Oxford includes an illustration of peasants dancing in a circle. This round dancing was traditional and was performed with a singer while the dancers marked time with their steps and sang the choruses. In this instance, the singer is outside the circle and off to the right. One of the musicians is playing the bagpipes while another strikes a percussion instrument. Country dances often took place in the churchyard, a practice that the Church tried to discourage. A sense of community in a village arose around the games and dances as villagers took time from their work. *Bodleian Library, Oxford.*

forts. Muslim peasant communities in Valencia and al-Andalus built impressive irrigation systems and governed them on a communal basis. Peasant communities regulated water usage, held public assemblies and local legal proceedings, and helped govern parish churches.

The parish church increasingly became a community focal point. By the twelfth century, parish boundaries began to take on forms recognizable to modern society, and the parish church's role in the lives of its parishioners began to develop, faster in some regions, more slowly in others. The villagers often had a hand in choosing parish curates and clerks, and in maintaining the lights, books, ornaments, and fabric of the building. Peasants attended the parish church for baptisms, masses, festivals, processions, funerals, and sermons. Sometimes schooling took place there, and, increasingly, marriages were celebrated at the church rather than in the home. The parish rector or vicar also, of course, collected dues and tithes from parishioners.

Marriage was often based upon economic rather than romantic considerations. Although peasants did marry for love, often the dowry or inheritance was a crucial concern. One way a man could better his circumstances was through an advantageous marriage, perhaps to a widow. There are also examples of lords forcing peasants to marry spouses chosen for them by a local jury. Should they refuse, they owed heavy fines.[10]

Once married, women were an economic asset, essential to maintaining the home economy. They helped in the fields and with the animals, brought in supplemental incomes from spinning wool, brewing ale, making butter and cheese, growing vegetables and herbs, marketing, taking in lodgers, lending money, and so forth. They earned income as casual wage-laborers. They also gathered fruits, nuts, herbs, and hunted small game. Despite their crucial economic role, peasant women held no official positions in their communities such as membership on juries or churchwarden for the local church.

Most peasant women could expect to spend their lives as married women and then perhaps as widows. They were highly unlikely to enter a nunnery, although occasionally they became anchorites, attached to a parish church. If they hired themselves out as servants (perhaps as dairymaids), this was usually a temporary position until marriage. Unmarried women outside the religious sphere were uncommon in rural medieval society, although there are occasional examples of single female peasant landholders or single women living with parents. Single women might move to an urban area where they could gain a livelihood as a live-in servant, laundress, or spinster (someone who spun cloth); if poor, they might just as easily go into prostitution.

Attitudes Toward the Peasants

Medieval writers of the twelfth and thirteenth centuries were not kind to peasants. A thirteenth-century preaching manual by Jacques de Vitry warned the wealthy not to despise the humble, for they can be dangerous.[11] Villeins and serfs were represented in the literature as ugly and dirty. In the song "Garin le Lorrain," a villein was described with "hair bristling, face as black as coal. He went for six months without bathing; none but rain water ever touched his face." Medieval comic tales pictured the peasant as ridiculous, badly formed, filthy, and repulsive. "They have one squint eye and the other is blind. They have a shifty look. They have one good foot and the other twisted."[12] On the other hand, Benedict of Sainte-More, writing in the twelfth century, had a somewhat more sympathetic view. "It is the [laborers] who enable the others to live, who nourish and sustain them; and yet, they endure the severest tempests, snows, rains, tornadoes; they till the earth with their hands, with great pain and hunger. They lead a thoroughly wretched life, poor, suffering, and beggarly" (see Medieval Voices).

Harsh attitudes toward peasants by the middle and upper classes prompted mistreatment and promoted sexual domination, if not brutality. When Andreas Capellanus wrote his, perhaps tongue-in-cheek, book of advice on seducing women, he noted, very briefly, that, "If you should, by some chance, fall in love with some of their [farmers'] women, be careful to puff them up with lots of praise and then, when you find a convenient place, do not hesitate to take what you seek and to embrace them by force."[13] The late thirteenth-century collection of love lyrics, nature poems, and drinking songs entitled the *Carmina Burana,* includes this episode:

> There I came, the day was fateful, For the nymph [a shepherdess] was far from hateful . . . ; But no sooner was I heeded Then the bleating flock stampeded, And she ran and bleated too in pretty fright. So she neared the sheepfold, screeching,

MEDIEVAL VOICES

A Thirteenth-
Century Tale
About a
Peasant Who
Visits Town

Medieval fabliaux, or comic tales, often tell us about people's attitudes toward those of other social classes. The following tale, in French from the thirteenth century, illustrates the prejudice that medieval people held regarding peasants, especially their lack of cleanliness. This particular anecdote also concludes that once a peasant, always a peasant no matter how far one rises.

Once upon a time there lived near Montpellier a peasant who used to load two donkeys with the manure he had collected for spreading on the land. One day, having loaded his donkeys, he speedily set out with them for the town, driving them along with some difficulty and with frequent shouts of "Gee up there!" After a while he turned into the street where the apothecaries were. Their apprentices were busy pounding away at their mortars, mixing spices. Now, as soon as the peasant smelled those spices, he couldn't have walked another step, not even if you had given him a hundred silver marks; he simply fainted on the spot, and fell down like a dead man. Then great was the consternation of the passers-by, who exclaimed, "Mercy on us! Just look, that man has dropped dead!"—and they couldn't think why. . . .

A local worthy, who had been in the street when it happened, came forward and said to the bystanders, "Gentlemen, if any of you would like to see this good man recover, I'll cure him, for a consideration." A townsman at once said to him "Cure him right now, and you shall have twenty shillings from my pocket." "Certainly," the other replied. He took the pitchfork with which the peasant used to urge on his donkeys, lifted up a forkful of manure and held it close to his nose. As soon as the peasant got a whiff of the manure and lost the scent of the spices, he opened his eyes and jumped to his feet, saying that he felt perfectly all right. In his delight at being thus cured, he swore he would never pass that way again, if he could avoid it.

In the light of this anecdote I would like to remind you that he who puts aside all pride acts sensibly and reasonably. No man should be false to his origins.

Source: Excerpt from *Medieval Comic Tales,* trans. Richard et al. (Totowa, N. J.: Rowman and Littlefield, 1973) 3–4. Reprinted by permission of Boydell & Brewer Ltd.

While I followed her beseeching. . . . Then we somehow fell to wrestling, And from struggling passed to nestling—There was never lovelier queen in tattered gown. . . .[14]

THE RISE OF A KNIGHTLY CULTURE

Those who fought on horseback, the knights of medieval Europe, rose in status in the High Middle Ages, breaking into the ranks of the aristocracy by the twelfth century. They evolved a chivalric ethos that justified and idealized a career based on war.

Older Aristocracy

Between the ninth and eleventh centuries, relatively few families were noble, and they were very rich, with large, dispersed landholdings, several castles, and the power to command and punish. Most of these elite families could trace their ancestry back generations and often to the blood of local ruling families or crowned kings.

By the twelfth century, a number of developments had weakened these "county families," as they have been called. The deaths of male heirs, often because of their military calling, jeopardized family lines, especially when the heiress was attractive prey to upstart young men. High birth rates sometimes resulted in the breakup of blocks of land, and a fall in income convinced some aristocrats to intermarry with wealthy merchant families.

Sometimes the families simply died out. The following example illustrates just how quickly this could happen. Henry, castellan of Bourbourg (d. 1151), had twelve children, seven of whom were sons; two entered the Church; two others died accidentally; a fifth was blinded in a tournament. The eldest son was married twice but had no heir. The seventh son then became castellan, but his only male child died in infancy in 1194. The whole inheritance reverted to the only granddaughter on the paternal side.[15] By the thirteenth century, only a few old aristocratic family lineages remained intact. Competing for their places were masters of castles who did not have the same ancestral glory but who gained power through military might, and then created aristocratic lineages for themselves, sometimes out of whole cloth, calling themselves lords and knights.*

The Rise of the Knight

Knights were mounted combatants, militarily superior to other unmounted fighting forces, serving a lord or king. By the eleventh century in France and the twelfth century in Germany, knights had begun to rise in the social ladder. Their growing wealth and expanding control over peasants and local justice, as well as their access to revenues and armed retainers, raised their stature. The number of knights holding castles and fiefs (called lordships) by the twelfth century was so large that historians speak of a revolution.[16]

As early as the eleventh century, these knights, whether involved with the Peace or Truce of God, going on crusade, or joining crusading orders, were being exalted by the Church. Preachers promoted the ideal of a *miles Christi* (soldier of Christ), and models of soldier-saints (e.g. St. George, St. James of Compostela) captured the popular imagination. Lengthy songs (called *chansons de geste*) lauded knightly deeds, and clerks chronicled their campaigns and pushed their reputations. The medieval Church justified the role of the knight in protecting the unprotected and pursuing the Church's enemies. The chivalric warrior, or knight of God, became

---

* A significant exception to the link between nobility, land, and military service occurred in Hungary where nobility was linked with allodial (freehold) lands rather than with military service. In addition, lands in Hungary were passed on to all sons. The result was that the number of nobles was quite large, and some of them held so little land that they lived more like peasants than nobility.

part of an elite order within medieval society, similar in some ways to a monastic order or the priesthood.

The knights of medieval Europe became a coherent group with their own values and sense of superiority. They hunted, feasted, and celebrated in ways that marked them off increasingly as nobility, and by the twelfth century less and less distinction existed between those ancient noble families of distinguished ancestry and the newer class of knightly warriors. One of the most famous of all medieval knights was William Marshal (1145–1219), the fourth son of an Anglo-Norman knight of no great lineage. His rise to regent and advisor to kings rested primarily upon his skill as a warrior, the monies he gained from knights he captured and ransomed in tournaments, and the reputation he enjoyed for loyalty. At age forty, as a gift from King Henry II, he was given the Duchess of Pembroke as a bride and the title that went with her. His biographer, describing this remarkable rise to power, influence, and prestigious title, stressed the bonds of loyalty between knights, their esprit de corps, and their pride in the exercise of arms.

Chivalric Ideals and Realities

The values by which knights lived blended martial, aristocratic, and Christian elements, values shared by knights all over Christian Europe, with the possible exception of northern Italy. By the twelfth century, the greater noblemen and knights, those with hereditary fiefs and castles, began the practice of wearing heraldic devices* that identified them as belonging to an elite group. The *ordo* (way of living) of knighthood required discipline and training. Young boys began learning to use arms and to ride horses in battle at age seven. The use of a couched lance required high levels of skill, and the cavalry charge in battle required an ability to maneuver on horseback that could only be learned with practice. It became common, therefore, for young men to leave the household of their parents to live with another family, preferably a family of higher social status, to receive training in horsemanship and other martial arts, in etiquette, and sometimes in letters. This practice (called "fosterage") made it difficult for poorer men, without connections, to receive training for knighthood. In addition, the growing cost of equipment (armor, lance, sword, war horses, saddles, etc.) became an effective barrier to upstarts. One of the most famous knightly romances from the twelfth century is that of Percival, a crude Welsh lad with no apparent knightly ancestry, who was trained by one of the great nobles of King Arthur's court. But Percival's noble origins were only disguised, and his natural prowess on horseback was remarkable, allowing him to defeat great knights and abscond with their equipment (see Medieval Voices).

By the twelfth century, knightly status was conferred by dubbing a knight on the shoulder with the flat end of the sword, nearly always for service on the battlefield. Whereas earlier knighting was informal, and to some degree less significant, in the twelfth century a ritual evolved that is illustrated in the knighting of Geoffrey of Anjou in 1228 on the eve of his marriage to Matilda, daughter of King Henry I of England and widowed empress. Geoffrey was given a ritual bath and then dressed in a

---

* Heraldic devices were hereditary insignia that identified a warrior in battles and tournaments.

Training in Knightly Skills   This illustration shows young boys building up their skills in knightly exercises. The youth on the left is approaching a quintain (target) that moved when one hit it with a lance. This helped the tilter build his skills in aiming his lance and in moving quickly, so that the quintain did not come around and hit the tilter. In this case the youth is practicing without a horse, while the young boy on the right is riding a mock horse pulled by others and practicing with an immobile target. *Bodleian Library, Oxford.*

tunic of gold and purple cloth, and given gold spurs. A shield was hung around his neck, and Henry I girded on the knight's sword. Thirty young men were made knights at the same time and given gifts of horses and arms. Feasting and a tournament followed.[17]

Mass knightings occurred quite often, either at court, in battle, or sometimes on pilgrimage. Eventually the Church played a larger role. The aspiring knight might spend a night's vigil in a church and hear mass in the morning. The priest might give him a light blow on the shoulder, along with God's blessing. Or the priest might bless the sword, place it on the altar, and admonish the neophyte knight to fulfill his Christian duties. But the Church never achieved complete control over the ceremony. It remained a military rite whose goal was to imbue knights entering the profession of arms with a sense of high purpose. The late thirteenth-century romance of Durmart le Galois describes a chivalric knight:

> A knight must be hardy, courteous, generous, loyal and of fair speech: ferocious to his foe, frank and debonaire to his friend. . . . see to it that you so conduct yourselves that you have a good right to the name. He has a right to the title of knighthood who has proved himself in arms and thereby won the praise of men. Seek therefore this day to do deeds that will deserve to be remembered, for every new knight should make a good beginning.[18]

The literary portrait of Durmart le Galois, full of high ideals, masks a reality that was often brutal and less than idealistic. Knighthood was a violent calling. A knight's power over those of lesser degree could be physically abusive with little recourse.* The violence they visited on others was also visited on themselves. It was not uncommon for knights to die in tournaments, in battle, and in ordeals. Wars were brutal, even though knights were protected to some extent by armor. At the

---

* A novel that depicts this aspect of knighthood well is Ken Follett's *Pillars of the Earth.*

MEDIEVAL VOICES

The Education of a Knight in the Twelfth Century

Chrétien de Troyes wrote the epic tale of Percival; or, the Story of the Grail *in the 1180s. It is the story of a noble Welsh youth raised in a rural setting far from the court of King Arthur, protected by his widowed mother from knightly life (and its attendant dangers) and ignorant of courtly manners. When he finally visits Arthur's court and begins his journey to becoming the best knight in the world, he is taken in hand by Gornemant of Gohort, who teaches him to use weapons and to act in a chivalric manner. The two passages quoted here describe Percival's education, emphasizing physical expertise and military equipment as well as the more chivalric elements of a knight's training.*

The nobleman unfurled the banner
and taught the youth the proper manner
for holding shields, by holding it
in front of him a little bit,
touching the horse's neck, and laid
the lance in rest. With spurs to aid,
he pricked the horse, a charger worth
a thousand marks. No horse on earth
could match his spirit, strength, and speed.
The lord was excellent indeed
at using lance and horse and shield,
equipment he had learned to wield
in boyhood, and the youth was thrilled,
because the lord was highly skilled.
When finished with the exercise
performed before the young man's eyes,
a drill at which the lord excelled,
he rode back to the youth and held
his lance raised, coming to inquire,
"Tell me, my friend, if you desire
to learn to check and spur a steed
and use a lance and sword at need?"
At once the youth began to say
he would not live another day
or have great wealth and lands to claim
until he learned to do the same.
. . . .
The nobleman bent down and fastened
the right spur on the young man's foot,
as was the custom: he must put
the spur on the new knight who made him.

MEDIEVAL VOICES (Continued)

The squires were there as well to aid him
while he was arming the new knight
at any need, however slight.
The lord attached the sword in place.
He gave the young knight an embrace
and said he's given with the sword
the highest honor of Our Lord,
an order made by God's decree,
and it was knighthood, chivalry:
that such an order must remain
without deceit, without a stain
"Dear brother, bear my words in mind.
If it should happen that you find
you're fighting with another knight
who proves unequal to your might,
I want to urge you and command,
once that you have the upper hand,
and he no longer holds his own
and pleads that mercy now be shown,
then you must show him clemency:
don't slay the knight intentionally.

. . . .

Friend, also do as I beseech:
if you find men or women, maybe
an orphan or a noble lady
who seem in any way distressed,
give help and counsel, do your best,
if your assistance will suffice,
and if you have some good advice.
One more thing you should realize,
a lesson you must not despise
or ridicule in any way:
go frequently to church and pray
to Him who made creation whole,
so He'll have mercy on your soul,
and in this temporal condition,
so He will keep you as His Christian.

Source: Perceval, or, The Story of the Grail, trans. Ruth H. Cline (New York: Pergamon Press, 1983) 43, 47–49.

battle of Hattin (1187), where Saladin killed and captured the Christian forces and regained Jerusalem, perhaps 2,000 knights died.* Tournaments, which began to emerge about the year 1000, were also dangerous. They originated as mock wars, or mêlées, that ranged over a wide area set aside in the countryside. The knights divided into two teams and fought ferociously for the sake of reputation and ransom, and many of them died. Although the Church tried to outlaw tournaments numerous times between 1130 and 1316, it was never successful. Indeed, tournaments became wildly popular throughout Europe. Gradually the mêlée, which had little pageantry and was essentially a rough and tumble man's world, evolved toward a more formally organized spectator sport with rules, defined spaces, and more emphasis on the popular one-on-one jousts using tilts, a low barrier between the two combatants. This evolution was complete by the early fifteenth century, thereby reducing, but not eliminating the possibility of losing one's life.

When an aristocratic family left no sons, the inheritance usually descended to the surviving daughters. This happened with some regularity given the high death rates among males† as well as the number of sons who went into the clergy. Occasionally a substantial inheritance might fall, intact, to a daughter. This occurred in Aquitaine in 1137 when Duke William X of Aquitaine died, leaving his eldest daughter, Eleanor, as heir. She became a magnificent prize, first linked in marriage with Louis VII of France and then, after the annulment of that marriage, captured and wedded by Henry Plantagenet (see Chapter 13).

Sometimes daughters received a portion of the inheritance, or perhaps a part of their mother's dowry. At the time of marriage, however, that property generally became marital property, and the husband gained control over it. Although he could not sell it without his wife's consent, the husband could treat the property as though it were his own. There were exceptions to this, of course. Both Eleanor of Aquitaine and Isabel of Pembroke retained control of their inheritances after marriage. Married women sometimes held urban property in their own name; in those parts of Europe where Roman law was still in effect, women could continue to hold property separately after marriage, and in many instances, husbands gave part of the marital property to their wives.

Marriage, particularly among the upper classes, was a political calculation based on class and wealth. Upper-class women were not expected to choose their husbands, although occasionally they were independent enough to flout social conventions and dynastic needs. If a young woman lost her parents, her feudal lord could intervene and select a partner for her, based on his own best interests. Noble women tended to marry young. It was not exceptional for the daughter of an aristocratic family to be betrothed (and sometimes married) as a child, although the Church argued against such practices. Once married, the wife, as a young girl, might go to live in the household of her husband, to be trained in household duties by his family.

---

* The total number of Christian forces may have been close to 20,000, most of whom were either killed or captured. Muslim sources give figures of 30,000 to 40,000.
† It is estimated that forty-six percent of all men died violently after the age of fifteen.

Prior to the twelfth century, marriage was not a primary concern of the Church. Older customs, which allowed for marriage of children, the repudiation of a wife, and abduction of a bride, continued to be practiced. The father of the groom rather than a priest might perform the marriage, as an 1194 account of the marriage of the eldest son of the count of Guines describes. In this case, the pair were married in bed, with clergy sprinkling the couple with holy water and censing the bed, while the father bestowed the marital blessing.[19] Clearly this ritual was designed to focus on fertility and to fulfill family inheritance strategies. By the twelfth and thirteenth centuries, however, the Church was beginning to take control of the marriage process. Canon law prohibited the marriage of girls younger than twelve. It required consent, outlawed abduction, and substituted repudiation with divorce and annulment. The Church also tried to outlaw clandestine marriages and to enforce the public calling of banns (the announcement, by the priest, of an intended marriage). It believed that marriage, as a sacrament, should be conducted by a priest at the entrance of the parish church.

Aristocratic wives often had many children, sometimes as many as ten to twelve. Count Baldwin of Guines, who married the heiress of Ardres in the mid-twelfth century, gave her ten children until she died, totally exhausted, in childbirth. He, like many other aristocrats, also had a large number of illegitimate children. These children were normally sent out to wet nurses for the first year or two. From at least age seven onwards, they would usually be sent to other households for raising. In the interim, nurses and tutors would care for them. This made it difficult for noblewomen to have any degree of close involvement in their children's upbringing, and it raises questions about the extent to which they felt affection for their children. Guibert of Nogent's mother doted on him as a child but left his training to an abusive tutor; then she entered a nunnery when he was twelve, prompting him to write, "She knew for certain that she was a cruel and unnatural mother." On the other hand, Matilda, the wife of William the Conqueror reportedly said of her rebellious oldest son: ". . . do not wonder that I love my first-born with tender affection. By the power of the most High, if my son Robert were dead and buried seven feet in the earth . . . and I could bring him back to life with my own blood, I would shed my life-blood for him."[20]

The maternal role of women of all classes tended to be ignored in the Middle Ages, despite the idealization of motherhood epitomized by the Virgin Mary. Literature, theology, and canon law rarely refer positively to it, at least until the late Middle Ages. It does not appear to have been a source of pride or interest among the upper classes. Instead, the aristocratic woman's role focused on household management—supervision of the servants, budget management, and provisioning the household. Women were expected to spend time embroidering. They also knew how to ride, hunt, dance, and perhaps to sing and tell stories. They might spend time with games or reading romances (or hearing them read). Many aristocratic women were known for their piety, and some learned enough Latin to follow the services. A wife might manage the estate when the husband was away and, on occasion, defend the house or castle from attack, and it was unusual, but not unknown, for a women to don armor (like Joan of Arc) and ride astride a horse. In general, the life of the wife in a castle of the twelfth and thirteenth centuries required hard work, often at close quarters with the men of the household, and it carried with it the constant danger of death in childbirth. A twelfth-century poem written, possibly, by a woman in the form of a dialogue, puts it this way:

> Lady Carenza of the lovely, gracious body,
> give some advice to us two sisters,
> and since you know best how to tell what's best,
> counsel me according to your own experience:
> shall I marry someone we both know?
> or shall I stay unwed? that would please me,
> for making babies doesn't seem so good,
> and it's too anguishing to be a wife.
> Lady Carenza, I'd like to have a husband,
> but making babies I think is a huge penitence
> your breasts hang way down
> and it's too anguishing to be a wife.
> . . . .
> Perhaps I should be a nun?
> Yes, I'll renounce this world.
> For having babies is too much pain.
> And it's too anguishing to be a wife.[21]

THE EMERGENCE OF AN URBAN SOCIETY

The economy of twelfth and thirteenth-century Europe, and especially Italy, was increasingly commercial. It was the age of the newly rich, of usury (charging excessive interest on loans), of credit and banking, and new kinds of contracts. In parts of Europe, older, aristocratic values based on kinship, courage, and courtesy began to give way to mercantile, moneyed values. The thirteenth-century Italian poet, Cecco Angiolini, wrote:

> Preach what you will, Florins* are the best of kin: Blood brothers and cousins true, Father, mother, sons, and daughters too. . . . The French and the Italians bow to them, so do noblemen, knights and learned men. Florins clear your eyes and give you fires, turn to facts all your desires. And into all the world's vast possibilities. So let no man say, I'm nobly born, if he have not money. Let him say, I was born like a mushroom, in obscurity and wind.[22]

Georges Duby has characterized this shift as a transition from a gift economy to a profit economy. Money began to be viewed as a tool rather than as a treasure to be given to the Church in exchange for prayers or to one's vassals in exchange for loyalty. Peasants began to market their goods for cash, hoping to bring in a surplus.

* In 1252 Florence, imitating Islamic governments in Spain and the Sicilian crown, began to mint gold coins, called "florins." They derived their name from the name of the city.

Landlords were increasingly asking for money rents rather than goods and services. Urban centers and market fairs saw money flow freely, raising issues of profit, interest, and usury. Schoolmasters charged fees for their services, and John of Salisbury complained that scholars, and particularly lawyers, were only concerned with the riches they could get for their wisdom. This suggests the beginning of new attitudes. Although many ecclesiastical writers believed that neither time nor knowledge could be sold, since they both were gifts from God, increasingly both time and knowledge became commodities to be conquered, manipulated, and used profitably.

A Moneyed Economy

Twelfth- and thirteenth-century Europe witnessed the beginnings of an urban, capitalist economy. Previously Europe had been on the periphery of the more developed, more urbanized cultures of Byzantium and Islam, but between the eleventh and thirteenth centuries old towns expanded and new towns were being established everywhere. By the fourteenth century, Ghent had expanded from 80 to 644 hectares. Florence, which grew to a population of over 100,000, extended its city walls three times between the twelfth and thirteenth centuries. In northern Italy, it was now unusual for a peasant to be more than twenty-five miles from any substantial town. In England, royal policy produced more than 120 new, planned cities by the end of the thirteenth century, and small villages everywhere grew into marketing towns, sometimes with a fair.[23]

Eastern Europe became increasingly market oriented between 1150 and 1300. Princes and bishops in Poland, Bohemia, Hungary, Transylvania, Silesia, Pomerania, and Mecklenburg began to give up their traditional markets for chartered market towns with urban liberties and citizen guilds that attracted German merchants, who ran the towns and paid rent to the prince. The privileges that accompanied these charters were known as "German city law." These chartered towns eventually extended from Lübeck along the Baltic all the way to Novgorod and then south into the towns of Bohemia and Hungary and east to Kiev. In Poland, for example, there may have been 250 market centers by the end of the twelfth century. The trade between them and beyond the bounds of Poland included silver from the mines, salt, furs, amber, cod and herring, cloth, and grains.

Murābit control of Muslim Spain (see Chapter 13) enhanced trade between Spain and North Africa (see Map 15.1). Grain, gold, and ivory from North and sub-Saharan Africa were traded for the textiles, leather goods, and other crafts of Spain. This growth in trade brought prosperity and a growing number of urban centers to al-Andalus.

Trade was particularly vital in Italy where cities and banking proliferated, merchants were effective middlemen, and the economy was diversified. New credit mechanisms arose as well as innovative forms of partnership arrangements, and a greater availability of gold and silver coins. Shipbuilding, a specialty of Venice, is a good example of a capitalized industry that helped the Italians dominate the trade routes of the Mediterranean. Each ship necessitated investments of from 2,500 to 7,000 lire each. Many individuals (sometimes as many as a hundred) made these

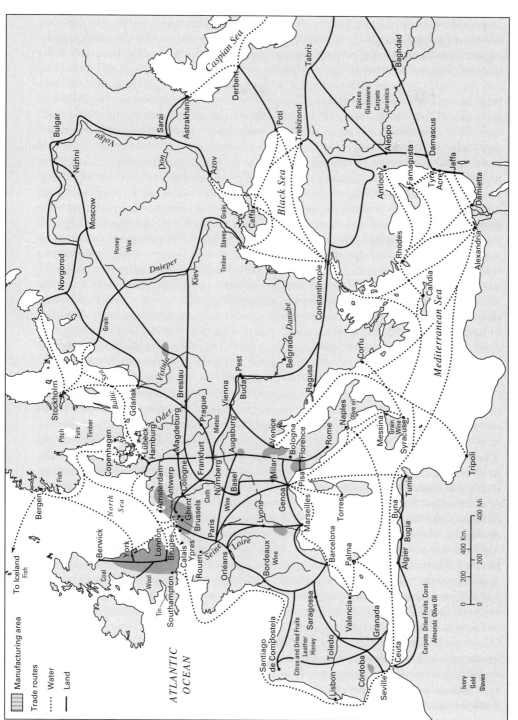

Map 15.1 Major Towns and Trade Routes, c. 1250 By 1250 the sea route along the Atlantic coast of Europe had opened up. The European crusading outposts (Tyre, Acre, and Jaffa) added strength to the already dominant position of Genoese and Venetian merchants in the eastern Mediterranean. Merchants from Pisa, Barcelona, and Valencia competed with the Genoese in the western Mediterranean.

investments and expected their capital to multiply. The merchandise that traveled on the ships, especially if it was compact and valuable (spices, jewels, relics, luxury cloths, slaves) could bring in enormous profit. New types of contracts evolved to allow for the distribution of labor, investment capital, and profits. The *commenda* was popular: one party invested labor and the other (who bore the burden of any loss) the capital. Sea loans, which guaranteed a certain level of interest or profit but also carried full liability, were used until they were declared usurious in the thirteenth century. Other commercial arrangements emerged as well. Marine insurance was invented. Checks and credit from banks, techniques that had been developed earlier by Jewish and Arab merchants in North Africa, became central to Italian banking. Double-entry bookkeeping emerged by the end of the thirteenth century; one line item usually listed the profits given to good works in the name of God.

The Italians not only developed credit, loans, and commercial contracts, they also produced moneylenders, pawnbrokers, deposit banking, and merchant banks. The first known loan made by a moneylender in medieval Europe was, ironically, to the papacy in Rome in the eleventh century at twenty percent interest. It was the Lombards in Italy who developed the greatest reputation as pawnbrokers, although others in Europe (the Cahorsins in southern France, for example) were also notorious pawnbrokers. Pawnbrokers often lent money at forty to fifty percent interest, a clearly usurious rate. Deposit banking was an offshoot of money changing. Wealthy individuals who chose to deposit their money in a bank for a certain time period were guaranteed a return of perhaps ten to twelve percent, but the bank then lent out the money, for shorter terms, at perhaps thirty percent interest. The large Italian banks of the thirteenth and fourteenth centuries (the Bardi and Peruzzi family banks of Florence, for example) were merchant banks. They had huge capital reserves—more, in some instances, than the annual revenues of the king of England—and agents in urban centers throughout Europe. Such banks might invest in industry, commerce, and shipbuilding. The typical Italian merchant banker was "involved in complex and far-flung operations, spanning the Hanseatic region or, better, the Mediterranean. . . . His techniques had grown increasingly specialized, and his tentacles stretched all the way from China, visited by Marco Polo, to Bruges and London, where he had established himself or installed his brokers."[24]

Many twelfth-century ecclesiastical reformers argued against Christians who earned interest through investments, deposit banking, or money loans. Not only did this appear to be profiting from time, it was also destroying Christian community. Usury between Christians and non-Christians, however, was exempt from these concerns, and this put more and more pressure on Jewish merchants, especially in northern Europe, to become moneylenders.

Social Mobility and Stratification

Wealthy urban tradesmen regularly took children from poorer urban and rural families as apprentices. Migration from rural areas or small towns to larger towns was, therefore, common. It was possible for a young man to begin life with very little, to invest his labor in the transport of goods, to reinvest the profits, and to become rich within his lifetime. Walter Map, a clerk and storyteller at the court of Henry II of England, tells the tale of Sceva and Ollo:

alike in age . . . boys of low birth, [who] acquired at the same time a small capital, and in our days became first hawkers of small commodities, and then by continued success of large ones. From packmen they rose to be carriers, from being carriers to be masters of many waggoners, and always remained trusty partners. With the growth of their trade . . . the love of money grew as great as grew the wealth.[25]

One concrete example from the fourteenth century was Dick Whittington, who migrated to London, began as an apprentice and rose to wealth as a merchant, becoming mayor of London.*[26] The Italian Francesco Datini, poor and orphaned by the plague in 1347, moved to Avignon and then Prado to pursue a mercantile career. At his death he left an enormous fortune to charity.

Merchants were a socially mobile group, but it was difficult for a merchant family to maintain itself, or its connection with trade, over more than two or three generations. Urban death rates were high, and birth rates were low; as a result families sometimes died out. Francesco Datini, for example, had only one surviving child—an illegitimate daughter. Sometimes the surviving sons of wealthy merchants became knights or entered a profession (especially law) or the clergy; they were successful but separated from trade. In Italy, where merchants often entered the political arena, it was not uncommon to suffer exile (and the loss of one's goods) for being on the losing side in a political struggle. Daughters might enter a nunnery or marry into an aristocratic family. Less wealthy merchant families had fewer options for their children, who often stayed within their father's trade. In general, entries and exits into and out of the merchant class were frequent. A significant exception was the Jewish families, particularly outside Spain, who had few professional or economic options beyond trade and money lending.

Merchants throughout Europe were usually literate, more so in the thirteenth than the twelfth century. They wrote letters and kept accounts and diaries. They had to read commercial documents, letters of exchange, and manuals of business practices. Jewish merchants were nearly all literate in Hebrew as well as other languages. Townswomen were less likely to know how to write, but among the upper and middle classes, it was not unusual for them to read the vernacular and perhaps a bit of Latin. Schools were housed in the homes of wealthy merchants in Ypres in the thirteenth century. In the 1330s, Giovanni Villani estimated, perhaps optimistically, that 8,000 to 10,000 boys and girls were learning to read in Florence, while another 1,000 to 1,200 boys were learning the abacus. Cities, towns, and hamlets across northern Italy had schools by the thirteenth and fourteenth centuries. Milan had nearly 100 grammar teachers at the end of the thirteenth century; the names of eighty grammar masters have survived from Bologna between 1265

* His saga gave rise to the children's story that he had arrived penniless, with only a cat. In fact, he arose from a rural family of moderate means.

and 1328. Many merchant families hired tutors or sent their children to local priests to learn to read and write. Towns also had abacus teachers to train merchants, clerks, accountants, and artisans.

Guilds and Confraternities

Most Christian merchants, craftsmen, and tradesmen in the cities and towns of the Middle Ages belonged to a guild, a professional association that governed the standards and behavior of the trade; Jews and Muslims (indeed any non-Christians) were excluded from these guilds. The earliest municipal documents from England are guild documents from the twelfth century. In Italy even the smaller cities had twenty to thirty guilds by the thirteenth century. Guilds regulated working hours, wage rates, apprenticeship contracts, and the quality of work produced. They looked to the interests of their members, tending to be exclusive and monopolistic. The more prestigious guilds took on a role in city government, while less powerful guilds might foment discontent and group protests. The relationship between guilds and town government fluctuated from place to place and decade to decade, but often the governors of leading guilds were also town officials.

Only rarely would a woman (usually a guild member's widow) have a leadership role, but women as well as men might belong to guilds and train boy and girl apprentices. In the thirteenth century, *Livre des Métiers,* a book detailing the guild regulations of Paris, Etienne Boileau listed 100 guilds, six of which had only female members and eighty of which included both men and women in the membership. Women worked at an astonishing variety of professions, as silk weavers, brewers, innkeepers, laundresses, teachers, butchers, chandlers, ironmongers, net makers, bookbinders, and so forth. They might run ale houses, taverns, or inns; prepare foods for sale at a cook shop; or market textiles and other products in shops. But they were usually paid less well and worked less regularly than the men. Sometimes they helped their husbands at market, in a shop, or in a craft at home. On the other hand, women were not as restricted to one trade as men were, sometimes starting out as domestic servants but then progressing to brewing or keeping a shop. A female brewer might also be an innkeeper, for example.

Merchants, craftsmen, and women might also belong to a confraternity, a religious guild that promoted community, good works, and piety. Most religious confraternities celebrated a particular saint's feast; they also provided mutual support among members (witnessing in court, assisting families in hardship, paying funeral expenses). Religious guilds established schools, participated in charitable works, and founded chantries for masses for the dead. Women sometimes played prominent parts in these associations; occasionally they founded them. These confraternities developed especially in the thirteenth century. In Florence, between 1224 and 1300, twenty such confraternities were established. In their membership, they rejected the ties of neighborhood, kinship, and even social class. Insofar as they concerned themselves with penitential activities, liturgical singing, the commemoration of the dead, and the veneration of saints, they provided a way for laity to express piety and perform religious rituals relatively free of clerical supervision.

Confraternities and guilds contributed greatly to the rituals of urban life. On particular feast days, members might go in procession to the parish church or cathedral. If a religious guild was one of the *disciplinati* (confraternities of flagellants), members might engage in public flagellation—beating themselves with whips until the blood flowed, in imitation of Christ's passion. In northern Europe, particularly in fourteenth-century England, both religious and craft guilds took part in civic plays associated with Corpus Christi day. The carpenters' guild might, for example, build the cross and direct the crucifixion scene. Guilds held tournaments and gave public banquets. These urban rituals reinforced ideas of unity and hierarchy within the towns.

Urban Life and the Government of Towns

The eleventh and twelfth centuries experienced the rise of municipal communes, in which the governing authority of a town was in the hands of its leading citizens. This took place especially in France, Italy, and the Low Countries. Communes sought independence from any sort of seigneurial lordship, whether that of a count, a local knight, or an ecclesiastical lord (bishop, archbishop, or abbot). Urban independence did not, however, mean that these towns became democracies. Although notaries, lawyers, and other writers in twelfth-century Italy promoted ideas of liberty and republicanism, in practice urban political power was predominately the power of an economic elite. Women were excluded, as were servants and slaves; and many poor artisans could not enroll as freemen or citizens.

On the other hand, women could own, inherit, or sell property more easily within a town than in the countryside, as laws governing the descent of urban land were more flexible than the rules of hereditary descent in the countryside; they might have their own bakery or mill, for example, or they might rent out properties. Middle class townswomen had a measure of economic freedom; they depended more on markets and peddlers for their goods than was possible for women in the countryside, and they may have had servants to help with the time-consuming household tasks of cooking and cleaning.

Although the rituals of urban life emphasized unity, in reality disunity was frequent with several sources of conflict. In the rise of communes, it was common for the citizenry to collide with seigneurial authorities, whether ecclesiastical or lay. Sometimes strife arose between town officials and churchmen, who might have peculiar, vested interests that did not coincide with civic interests. In university towns, disputes occurred between students and townsfolk. There were conflicts between richer and poorer guilds, between guild masters and journeymen, between citizens and noncitizens. In a few industries (cloth making in Flanders and Florence; shipbuilding in Venice) a large, volatile mass of workers was employed—something close to an urban proletariat—who could riot or rebel. And in the Mediterranean cities of the fourteenth and fifteenth centuries, the slave population was seen as a potential domestic enemy.

The physical environment of medieval towns is not easy to recreate. The use of aerial photography since the 1940s has made it possible to discern the layout of many villages, but the remains of most medieval towns are obscured by modern construction. Painstaking archaeological digging is the major means of recovery. Most medieval towns were overcrowded by the thirteenth century, while more spacious suburbs developed in some cities, and everywhere city walls expanded. In the center of the city, streets were narrow and houses tall (three to four stories). It was standard for household production to take place on the first floor, the living quarters to occupy the second and third floors, and the servants' quarters to be on the fourth floor. A fire would be maintained in a central room. Windows were oiled parchment; glass was still rare in the fourteenth century. Floors were strewn with rushes (not carpets), and tapestries or panels of linen cloth hung on the walls to keep out the cold. Furniture would be sparse, even in the homes of the better off, and several members of a family might share a bed. The very wealthiest townsfolk might have feather beds, silk hangings, and platters and cups of gold and silver.

People lived in sections of the city, usually grouped by trades. Most cities had walls and city gates that would be closed at night. Towns had open-air places for fairs, a surfeit of churches (some older cities had forty to fifty parish churches), and lots of noise from town criers, animals, blacksmiths, bells, and children playing. Neighborhoods were crowded, and children spun tops, played hoops, ran races, and played ball in narrow streets where they might also encounter unruly adolescent apprentices, pimps or prostitutes, cock fights, gambling, and riots. The streets were alive with peddlers, servants, and people of every social complexion, wearing clothes of many colors and fabrics. There might be minstrels, pageants, and parades, with occasional sermons at designated places, or perhaps a public execution. Towns were lively, although life could be fragile within them.

Medieval cities were always at risk for fires, since most homes were built with wood. Only the most substantial of merchants could afford a stone house. Towns were also subject to floods, and they were breeding places for disease. Keeping the refuse out of the town and the pigs off the streets was a constant concern for town governments, and it appears that they did not succeed very well. As a result, mortality rates could be very high, and most towns depended on immigration from the countryside in order to maintain their population.

THE CLERGY

Clergy formed a separate class within society. Andreas Capellanus, a twelfth-century French chaplain and author, called them "the noblest class of all."

> A clerk's nobility . . . is not derived from his ancestors, nor can the secular power deprive him of it, but by God's grace alone . . . is it granted, and by His gift is it given, and by God alone may the privileges of this kind of nobility be annulled if His commands are violated.[27]

Despite Andreas's emphasis on God's role, it was the bishop or pope who ordained clergy and promoted them through the ecclesiastical ranks. The lowest ranks were the clerks in minor orders, beginning with the tonsured (boys entering school were usually tonsured) and moving on to the positions of doorkeeper, exorcist, reader, and acolyte (see Chapter 5). Clerks at this level were allowed to marry and not required to be celibate. By the thirteenth century, not only priests, but in fact all clergy in major orders (subdeacons, deacons, and priests) were required to be celibate.

The members of the Church hierarchy described above might be either regular or secular clergy (see Chapter 5). In the early Church, regular clergy were monks and nuns, but by the thirteenth century they also included canons and friars—clergy who lived a communal life and were vowed to lives of celibacy, poverty, and obedience, and, in the case of monks and nuns, were cloistered. "Some persons choose to live a life which is austere and secluded from other men. . . . Such persons as these are called the regular clergy, because they all have certain rules by which they are compelled to live."[28] Since Chapters 5 and 12 examine monastic orders and Chapter 17 describes the friars, we will mention here only the orders of canons (Augustinians, Premonstratensians, and Victorines, for example). Canons were priests who adopted a rule to live communally and under a vow of celibacy. They were less cloistered than monks and less involved in a life of prayer and meditation. They could, according to canon law, take on the cure of souls, and they often engaged in charitable activities (teaching schools, visiting the sick).

Secular clergy took no vows of poverty and needed income, usually from benefices, to live. Prior to the thirteenth century, the line between secular clergy and laity was flexible. Those in minor orders, who might be married, sometimes held benefices within the Church. Nor was there a distinctive form of dress to separate these clergy from laity. This changed under Pope Innocent III (1198–1216), who decreed that a married man could not hold a benefice, while the Fourth Lateran Council (1215) detailed the distinctive clothing that clergy had to wear.

Beneficed clergy drew their incomes from the revenues of the Church. The rector of a parish church received the tithes of parishioners as well as extra income from land, altar fees, and various services. Sometimes the rector of a church was an institution (most commonly, a monastery). Sometimes the rector was absent. In these cases a vicar or a curate served the parish, earning perhaps one third of the tithes. Many vicars were quite poor.

Below the vicar were unbeneficed clergy (chaplains, deacons, and clerks), who made their living saying masses, acting as scribes, teaching children, carrying holy water, as a reader in the parish—all for a small stipend and for alms. Above the vicar were the parish rector, deans, archdeacons (who administered the ecclesiastical court system), cathedral canons and dignitaries, and the bishop or archbishop of the diocese.

Bishops and archbishops were the magnates of the Church. Although their position in the early Church had given them enormous power (see Chapter 5), by the thirteenth century they were somewhat more constrained by the growth of an ecclesiastical hierarchy, the growing power of the papacy, and the fact that many of the reformed monasteries had been given exemptions from episcopal oversight. Bishops often lived worldly lives, administering their dioceses, providing hospitality, and sometimes advising popes and princes. Some bishops lived more austerely, attending conscientiously to their many responsibilities: ordaining and disciplining

Parish Church at Iffley in England

St. Mary's parish church in Iffley, Ox-
fordshire, is one of the best preserved
twelfth-century village churches in England. It was built between 1170 and
1180 in a Romanesque, pre-Gothic
style. A local patroness, Juliana de St.
Remy, has been credited with funding
its construction. The church has elaborate decorations, with extensive
sculptures which, for some reason,
remained unfinished. The west end,
pictured here, was restored in the
nineteenth century. In the thirteenth
century a cell for a recluse seems to
have been added to the church.
Michael Holford.

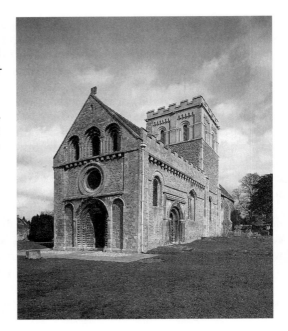

clergy; seeing to the buildings, books, and services of all parish churches within
their jurisdiction; overseeing ecclesiastical courts; instituting clergy into benefices;
visiting and inspecting diocesan churches and monasteries; summoning synods;
disseminating canon law and papal decrees; granting licenses; and performing certain liturgical and ceremonial functions, including for some archbishops, the
crowning of the king. Eudes Rigaud, archbishop of Rouen from 1247 to 1276, left
us the first detailed set of episcopal visitation records from France. In 1248, he
found that the canons at Rouen Cathedral "violated their ordinances by talking in
the choir. Clerics wander about the church and gossip with women while the service is being celebrated. The statute concerning the processional into the choir is not
observed. The Psalms are too briskly run through and sung without pauses. . . .
When they ask permission to go out they give no reason for their going." Several
masters were accused before the archbishop of incontinence, frequenting taverns,
dicing, and engaging in trade.[29]

The parish rector or vicar was the clergyman most people encountered on a daily
basis. He had cure (or care) of souls, performing five of the seven sacraments that
the Church had adopted at Fourth Lateran Council: penance, Eucharist, marriage,
baptism, and extreme unction. The other two sacraments (confirmation and ordination) were reserved to bishops. Bishop Robert Grosseteste of Lincoln described
the work of pastoral care in a sermon in 1245 at the Council of Lyons:

> . . . the work of pastoral cure consists not only in the administration of the Sacra-
> ments and the saying of canonical hours and celebration of the masses, . . . but

also in the veracious doctrine of a life of truth, in terrific condemnation of vices, . . . It consists also in the feeding of the hungry, in giving drink to the thirsty, in clothing the naked, in receiving guests, in visitation of the sick, and prisoners, and especially of one's own parishioners to whom belong the temporal goods of the churches. The people should be instructed and informed by the examples of these works in the holy exercises of an active life.[30]

The ordinary lay parishioner would have recourse to the parish for baptisms, confession and absolution, masses, and funerals. Weddings also were sometimes conducted at the church door. The parish priest helped with the sick and was present at the deathbed. He might oversee the collection of tithes and the education of a clerical apprentice. Most parish clergy rarely gave sermons, perhaps four times a year, but it was incumbent upon them to teach the main tenets of Christianity to their parishioners, particularly the Ten Commandments and the Lord's Prayer. Worshipers attended mass standing on straw-covered floors or kneeling on cushions and sitting on stools. Pews did not yet exist.

A certain amount of decorum was expected of people who headed to church. The poet, Robert of Blois, advised women,

> If you are going to the church, walk straight with dignity and do not trot or run, or idle either. Salute even the poor. . . . Especially in church one must watch one's countenance, for one is in the public eye, which notes evil and good. Kneel courteously, pray with care and do not laugh or talk too much. Rise at the moment of the (reading of) the Gospel, cross yourself at beginning and end. At the offering, hold yourself well. Rise also, hands joined, at the elevation, then pray on your knees for all Christians. If you are too weighed down by illness or pregnancy, you may read your psalter seated.[31]

A parishioner might visit the church to pray at a chapel dedicated to a particular saint. Should a lay person shirk church, keeping a tavern or running a business on Sunday, for example, he or she might be brought before an ecclesiastical court. Should a parishioner refuse to pay tithes or other customary dues to the parish or engage in a variety of moral sins (blasphemy, adultery, oath breaking, prostitution, defamation, eating on fast days), the vicar might accuse him or her before a church court. In these various ways, the parish church provided a focus, not only for pious devotion but also for teaching the basics of the Christian religion to parishioners, extending social services, and regulating the moral and ecclesiastical life of parishioners.

NON-CHRISTIANS AND NON-LATINS

Although much of Europe had been Christianized by the High Middle Ages, a significant number of non-Christians lived within Europe as well as on the peripheries of Christian Europe. In the lower Danube, along the Black Sea, another pagan Turkish people, called the Cumans, entered Europe. They mingled with Hungarian society, although their clothing clearly signified their nomadic, pagan presence. By the early thirteenth century, fearing the oncoming Mongols, the Cumans migrated farther west, submitting to the Hungarian king and to Christian conversion. Prior to the Mongol invasions Muslim and Jewish merchants were also common in Hungary, as were orthodox Christian Byzantine merchants, monks, and scholars. Along the Baltic coast and to the northeast of Germany lived large numbers of pagan peoples—Oborites, Polabians, Liutizians, Rugians, Prussians, Lithuanians, Latvians, Estonians, and Finns. They had a prosperous trade in furs, slaves, and amber, and they often raided their Christian neighbors. Most of them converted to Christianity by the fourteenth century at the latest.

Further south Muslims under Muslim rule and Mudejars (Muslims living under Christian rule) constituted a significant population in the Spanish peninsula. Muslim merchants were commonly seen in Italy, and a large Muslim population remained in southern Italy and Sicily. The twelfth-century Norman kingdom housed a complex mix of peoples—Arabs, Jews, Byzantines, Normans, and Lombards. The mélange of architectural styles, languages, and customs have suggested to historians that the Norman kingdom witnessed perhaps the greatest degree of cultural intersection of any part of Europe, although tensions were obvious. Lombards and Normans remained proud of their independent identify; Muslims in western Sicily often defied the government; and intermarriage between Christians and non-Christians continued to be uncommon. By the early thirteenth century, by which time the Norman kingdom had passed by inheritance to the Hohenstaufen of Germany, non-Christian subjects faced greater discrimination: Marriage with non-Christians was outlawed, Jews were ordered to dress distinctively, and Muslims were attacked and deported.

The Jewish communities in the southern Mediterranean were long standing, many having migrated there in Roman times. Long-distance trading in the early Middle Ages had brought Jewish merchants into eastern Europe and along the coast of North Africa. And by the turn of the eleventh century, small numbers of Jewish families had moved into the northwest of Europe, into the heartland of the Carolingian Empire, along the Rhineland, and then into England (into towns like London, Norwich, and York). These communities flourished with the growing economic prosperity of these regions, and they soon produced their own schools, scholars, merchants, craftsmen, and money lenders. Unlike in earlier centuries, however, they were restricted from holding lands, confined to urban areas, and increasingly pushed to specialize in money lending. They were protected by the crown, although, in the final analysis, this protection did not suffice in the wake of growing anti-Jewish prejudice from the eleventh century forward.

Summary

Medieval society was hierarchical and still largely agricultural; the peasants who worked the fields formed its backbone. The crops they produced fed the other segments of society. At the top were nobles and knights, who developed a commitment to the ideal of chivalric behavior that they did not always demonstrate in practice. The growing towns housed craftsmen and merchants. Craft workers formed guilds and confraternities that they used both to protect themselves economically and to further cement social bonds. The role of women at all these levels was significant but constricted by societal expectations and legal restraints. The clergy became increasingly defined as a group distinct from lay members of society in this period, and the Church imposed rules of behavior and dress that emphasized these differences. This was similarly true for non-Christian minorities within Europe, who gradually were pushed to the margins of European society.

While these were the main groups of medieval society, group membership was not rigidly defined. Knights gained increasing prestige during these centuries and, in fact, came to be viewed of equal status with nobility, especially as the numbers of the old aristocratic families dwindled. Merchants gained wealth and power in the increasingly monetary economy, but merchant families were fluid and often did not last more than a few generations. Even peasants were not a monolithic class, and across Europe and time, they varied in the degree of serfdom that they suffered or freedom that they enjoyed. The clergy drew from all these lay groups—peasants, townsfolk, knights, nobles, and women; all provided people to the Church, enabling it to grow. From slaves to lords, from peasant women to abbesses, from stipendiary priests to archbishops, medieval society was becoming more complex. But it was still the peasant who formed the base of this society, and the lord, whether ecclesiastical or lay, who demanded subservience and benefits from more dependent classes.

NOTES

1. John of Salisbury, *Policraticus,* trans. C. Nederman (Cambridge: Cambridge University Press, 1990) book 6, ch. 20.
2. Barbara Hanawalt, *The Ties That Bound: Peasant Families in Medieval England* (New York: Oxford University Press, 1986) 57.
3. W. C. Jordan, *From Servitude to Freedom: Manumission in the Sénonais in the Thirteenth Century* (Philadelphia: University of Pennsylvania, 1986).
4. Jordan, *From Servitude to Freedom,* ch. 3.
5. Rodney Hilton, *Bond Men Made Free* (New York: Viking Press, 1973) 83.
6. Galbert of Bruges, *The Murder of Charles the Good, Count of Flanders,* trans. J. B. Ross (New York: Harper, 1967) 97–98.
7. George Homans, *English Villagers of the Thirteenth Century* (New York: Russell & Russell, 1960) 252.
8. Judith M. Bennett, *A Medieval Life: Cecilia Penifader of Brigstock, c. 1295–1344* (Boston: McGraw Hill, 1999) 49–50.
9. Rosamund Faith, "The 'Great Rumour' of 1377 and Peasant Ideology," in *The English Rising of 1381,* eds. R. H. Hilton and T. H. Aston (Cambridge: Cambridge University Press, 1984) 43–70.
10. Henrietta Leyser, *Medieval Women: A Social History of Women in England 450–1500* (New York: St. Martin's Press, 1995) 121.
11. Achille Luchaire, *Social France at the Time of Philip Augustus* (New York: F. Ungar Publishers, 1957) 394.
12. Luchaire, 398.
13. Andreas Capellanus, *The Art of Courtly Love,* trans. J.J. Parry (New York: Columbia University Press, 1960) 150.
14. *The Goliard Poets: Medieval Latin Songs and Satires,* trans. G. F. Whicher (Norfolk, Conn.: New Directions, 1949) 215. For more on the rape of rural women, see Kathryn Gravdal, *Ravishing Maidens: Writing Rape in Medieval French Literature and Law* (1991).
15. Georges Duby, *The Chivalrous Society* (Berkeley: University of California Press, 1977) 109.

16. Thomas Bisson, "Medieval Lordship," *Speculum* 70 (1995): 749.

17. Maurice Keen, *Chivalry* (New Haven: Yale University Press, 1984) 42.

18. *Li Romans de Durmart le Galois,* ed. E. Stengel (Tübingen: H. Laupp, 1873), lines 12129–12137, 12144–12153, quoted in Keen, *Chivalry,* 80.

19. Georges Duby, *Medieval Marriage* (Baltimore: Johns Hopkins University Press, 1978), ch. 3.

20. Orderic Vitalis, *Historiae Ecclesiasticae Libri Tredecim,* ed. Auguste Le Prévost, 5 vols., ch. 2 (Paris, 1838–1855) 382–383; *Self and Society in Medieval France: The Memoirs of Guibert of Nogent* ed. J. F. Benton (New York: Harper & Row, 1970) 74.

21. Meg Bogin, *The Women Troubadours* (New York: W. W. Norton) 144–145. For some of the variant ways to read this poem, see *Songs of the Women Troubadours,* ed. and trans. Bruckner, Shepard, and White (New York: Garland Publishing, 1995) 178–179.

22. Lauro Martines, *Power and Imagination* (New York: Knopf, 1979) 79.

23. Maurice Beresford, *New Towns of the Middle Ages: Town Plantation in England, Wales, and Gascony* (New York: Praeger, 1967).

24. Jacques Le Goff, *Time, Work and Culture in the Middle Ages,* trans. A. Goldhammer (Chicago: University of Chicago, 1980) 34.

25. Walter Map, *De Nugis Curialium: Courtier's Trifles,* ed. and trans. M. R. James (Oxford: Clarendon Press, 1983) 393.

26. C. M. Barron, "Richard Whittington: The Man Behind the Myth," *Studies in London History,* ed. A.E.J. Hollaender and W. Kellaway (London: Hodder and Stoughton,1969) 197–208.

27. Andreas Capellanus, *The Art of Courtly Love,* 141–142.

28. S.P. Scott, C.S. Lobingier and J. Vance (trans.), *Las Siete Partidas,* vol. 1 (Chicago: Commerce Clearing House, 1931) 112, quoted in Malcolm Barber, *The Two Cities* (London: Routledge, 1992) 32.

29. *The Register of Eudes of Rouen,* trans. S. Brown (New York: Columbia University Press, 1964) 39–40.

30. E. Brown, *Fasciculus Rerum Expetendarum,* vol.2 (London, 1690) 253, quoted in R.A.R. Hartridge, *A History of Vicarages in the Middle Ages* (New York: Barnes & Noble, 1930) 77.

31. Charles-Victor Langlois, *La vie en France au moyen âge* (Paris: Slatkine, 1984) 195–199.

CHAPTER 16

~

Church and State in the Thirteenth Century

Historians often describe the thirteenth century as the time when European medieval culture reached its highest expression. Some of the most memorable and remarkable popes, emperors, kings, and princes—like Pope Innocent III, the Emperor Frederick II, St. Louis IX of France, Alfonso X (the Wise) of Léon-Castile, and Chingis Khan (whose rule reached into eastern Europe); reigned during this period. It was a century of papal monarchy and state-building, Gothic cathedrals and the coming of the friars, and of an influx of Arabic learning and the intellectual contributions of Thomas Aquinas, Bonaventure, and Roger Bacon, among others; it was a time of scientific advances, global explorations, and great vernacular literature. It was also a century of significant casualties for Europeans. The line of Hohenstaufen emperors ended, and the German empire weakened; heretics faced more organized repression, and, in the process, northern France took the southern (Provençal) region by force. Mongols terrorized eastern Europe; Muslims retook the Holy Land; wars between papal and imperial forces damaged both Italy and Germany; and the French and English fought.

This chapter begins by examining an increasingly powerful papacy, whose authority provoked particularly violent conflicts with the German Empire, which, by the 1270s, had lost leadership and credibility in the struggle. Declining imperial authority was paralleled by centralizing states elsewhere in Europe, particularly in western Europe—England, France, and Spain. Eastern Europe in the 1230s confronted the invading Mongols, a new and destructive enemy. The inability of the Church to stop or convert the Mongols added to a growing disillusionment with the Church, fueled by popular discontent over crusading ineffectiveness. Heresies flourished in this climate. To strengthen the preaching and proselytizing of the Christian religion both within and without Christendom, Pope Innocent III authorized a new kind of religious order—the mendicant orders of friars. These friars, in addition to preaching widely, spearheaded inquisitorial proceedings against heretics in parts of Europe. In the course of these developments, the Church had at its disposal a complex, centralized bureaucracy at Rome and an effective, European-wide hierarchy of clergy that enabled it to pressure rulers and promote its agenda.

POPE AND EMPEROR

Papal authority extended its reach through various administrative and legal mechanisms as well as through church councils and crusades. As it did so, a kind of papal monarchy developed. This stronger papacy proved a particular problem for the German Empire, as the popes claimed the right to decide disputed imperial elections and to administer the empire during imperial vacancies. The resulting clash between pope and emperor weakened the German throne, exacerbated divisions in Italian politics, and left the papacy victorious but mired in secular politics.

Papal Monarchy

The thirteenth-century papacy rested on a greatly enhanced administrative structure. By 1200, the Church had nearly completed placing parish churches throughout Europe. In so doing it controlled a hierarchy that began with the local parish curate, vicar, or rector, and then moved up to rural deans, archdeacons, bishops, archbishops, and cardinals, and included abbots and their monks, cathedral chapters, and unbeneficed clergy—all of whom became increasingly subject to the papacy (see Chapter 15). Rome sent legates to enforce its will, and reserved more and more benefices throughout Europe for its own appointments. This structure enabled the papacy to collect taxes and tithes from around Europe. The administration of its own lands in the papal states and elsewhere also added to its wealth.

Increasingly, clergy came to Rome to be ordained and to plead for promotion. Bishops traveled to Rome to make their submission or to attend church councils. Even laymen visited Rome to request dispensations or to pursue legal claims. As a result, the pope required an expanded administrative staff. Under Innocent III, the papal registers were also organized, and he established fixed rules for dealing with documents.

Through his use of church councils the pope could consult with leading representatives of the Church, utilizing a form of representative rule that enhanced papal power. In addition, after having struggled with contested elections to the papacy in the twelfth century, the college of cardinals fashioned a form of election that depended upon a majority vote of those present. Thus, through the thirteenth century, the process of succession to the papacy was remarkably stable.

The papacy had also grown as a legal construct. This growth depended, in part, on the establishment of ecclesiastical courts throughout the dioceses of Europe. And these courts rested on a body of ecclesiastical law called canon law. This church law had been effectively pulled together by lawyers and administrators in the wake of the Gregorian reform, and particularly in the 1140s by Gratian, a law teacher at Bologna, in his *Decretum,* an authoritative concordance of canon law (see Chapters 11 and 14). This concordance did not, however, answer all questions. Increasingly, legal disputes came directly to the pope who, in conjunction with his cardinals and with lawyers, resolved points of law, settled appeals, and issued written decisions (called decretal letters). By 1209, Pope Innocent III began to publish formal law books, authorized for use in the schools.

As the papal administration became more complex and legalistic, canon law writers developed a theory of papal monarchy, describing the Roman Church as the "*monarcha omnium ecclesiarum,*" the ruler of all the churches. Based upon ideas originating with Gregory VII and developed in Gratian's *Decretum,* canonists followed two principles: 1) the pope was morally superior to all men and accountable for the state of their souls, and 2) the papacy was juridically superior to the state and could enforce its power through ecclesiastical sanctions (excommunication, interdicts),* including depriving a ruler of his or her office.

A pope often associated with papal monarchy is Innocent III (1198–1216). Innocent III was thirty-seven years old when he became pope—the youngest cardinal in the college of cardinals. He came from Rome and had studied in Rome, Paris, and Bologna. He was a product of the schools, a scholar of theology perhaps with legal training, and one of the most prolific producers of papal decrees. On the day of his consecration as pope, Innocent put forward a quasi-divine claim to power: "Now you see, what kind of servant he is who commands the household, truly the vicar of Jesus Christ, the successor of Peter, Anointed of the Lord, . . . who is the mediator between God and man, placed below God but above men, who is less than God, but greater than man."[1] Innocent also characterized himself as the "Ordinary Judge of all" and one who had "plenitude of power."

Upon becoming pope, Innocent proclaimed the Fourth Crusade. Crusading fervor had lessened, however, and it took four years before the armies set out. Innocent sought to keep control of this crusade, and thus he called on towns, counts, and barons—but not kings. But his control failed (see Chapter 12). The most dramatic result, the capture and sacking of Constantinople in 1204, appalled Innocent, who stated that, after what had happened, the Greeks had every right to treat the Latins like dogs.[2] The resulting ecclesiastical unification of East and West, however, served papal purposes. In the end, this imposition of the Roman Church on the Greeks lasted less than sixty years.

Innocent initiated contacts with schismatic Armenian and Maronite Christians in the East, with Christians in Muslim-held Jerusalem and Alexandria, and with the schismatic Serbian, Ruthenian, and Bulgarian churches, all of whom he hoped to reunite with the Catholic Church. He subsequently bent his efforts toward mounting the Fifth Crusade to liberate Christians in Jerusalem and Egypt.

Innocent also launched crusades within Europe, the most notorious of which was the Albigensian Crusade, named after the town of Albi, a center of Cathar

---

* Excommunication cuts a Christian off from the body of the Church. Although excommunication has an evolving history since the days of the early Church, during the Gregorian reform it became a weapon for coercing individuals to obey church decrees rather than simply for enforcing doctrine. An excommunicate was deprived of all ecclesiastical rights, including the company of other Christians. Interdict is closely linked with excommunication, although it is usually applied to groups of persons or a region rather than a single individual. An interdict normally prevented access to the sacred functions of the Church, although baptism and extreme unction would not have been withheld.

heresy in southern France (see Chapter 11). In 1209, frustrated by the failure of rulers in southern France to proceed against this rapidly growing heresy and also reacting to the 1208 murder of the papal legate in southern France, Innocent declared a crusade. He released the subjects of heretical rulers from obedience and offered the land to Catholics. The crusading army—financed by papal levies—was led by the abbot of Cîteaux as papal legate, and by Simon III, count of Montfort (d. 1218). The townspeople of Béziers, Carcassonne, Lavaur, and Muret (whether orthodox or heretical) were massacred; tens of thousands were killed. Many citizens and peasants of southern France were disinherited and despoiled, and the culture of southern France was devastated. When the war ended in 1229, northern France annexed the south. In the Treaty of Paris of 1229, the defeated leaders of the south agreed to the restoration of the Catholic Church, the establishment of the University of Toulouse as a center of orthodox teaching, and the suppression of heretics. (Every lord was committed to tracking heretics down, and every parish was to have a team of heretic hunters.)

In 1215, Innocent III called the Fourth Lateran Council.* Its primary purposes were to promote aid to the Holy Land and to combat heresy within Christendom. The Council consolidated preparations for the Fifth Crusade, which had been declared in 1213. It condemned heresy in southern France and declared the heretics' lands forfeit. It excluded the suspect count of Toulouse from ruling forever and transferred his territories to Simon de Montfort. The Council also initiated inquisitorial judicial procedures and promoted pastoral reforms. In addition, Fourth Lateran imposed upon all Christians the duty of confessing annually during Lent and of receiving the Eucharist. It insisted that bishops preach or supply preachers, examine clergy carefully before ordaining them, and appoint masters to teach at cathedrals. Fourth Lateran established seven sacraments (baptism, ordination, extreme unction, marriage, penance, Eucharist, and confirmation) and confirmed the doctrine of "transubstantiation" for the operations of the Eucharist.† With regard to marriage, impediments beyond the fourth degree of consanguinity were lifted,‡ clandestine marriage prohibited, and the use of church banns promoted. The Council established procedures for episcopal elections and mandated that ecclesiastical positions not remain vacant over three months. It legislated in secular affairs, excommunicating the barons rebelling against King John in England, ratifying the election of Frederick II as Holy Roman Emperor, and upholding the excommunication of the former Emperor Otto IV. Finally, it put Jewish communities under curfew during Easter week, blamed them for blasphemies against Christians, and required them, along with Muslims, to wear distinctive clothing. These are only a

---

* This Council was attended by over 400 bishops, the largest number to date of any church council. Also attending were over 800 abbots, priors, chapter representatives, and lay dignitaries.

† "Transubstantiation" is the doctrine that a miraculous change occurs during the priestly consecration of the Eucharist, and the elements of bread and wine, although keeping their original physical appearance, are physically transformed into the body and blood of Christ.

‡ Initially the Church prohibited marriages in which marital partners were related within seven degrees, that is to say, if their great-great-great-great-great grandparents were siblings. Most individuals could not reconstruct their genealogies this far back, and most of the European nobility, were they able to do so, would most likely have discovered that they were related within seven degrees of consanguinity.

portion of the decisions taken at the Fourth Lateran Council, all completed in less than three weeks!

Finally, Innocent reenergized the struggle between church and state. Relations between church and state had stabilized in the twelfth century with the accommodation on lay investiture at the Concordat of Worms (see Chapter 11).* Innocent III, however, clashed with King John of England (r. 1199–1216) when Innocent refused to accept John's appointee as archbishop of Canterbury. Innocent placed England under interdict from 1208 to 1213 until John, under pressure from a French invasion and from his own barons, surrendered England to Innocent as a papal fief.

But the most dramatic conflict occurred between Innocent and the German emperors. As background for understanding the conflict, it is significant that Innocent had consolidated the papal states, gaining Spoleto, Ancona, and parts of south Tuscany and exercising stronger papal control over Rome itself. This greatly expanded papal territory in central Italy needed protection from attack coming from either north or south. Innocent sought especially to preserve the independence of Sicily in the south, keeping it in subjection to the papacy. When Emperor Henry VI died in 1197, Sicily was separated from Germany and inherited by Constance, Henry's wife, and their three-year-old child, Frederick. This resulted in the reestablishment of the Sicilian kingdom as a papal fief, and when Constance died in 1198, Frederick's legal guardian was the pope (see Map 16.1).

Meanwhile, in Germany, the imperial election was in dispute. Philip of Swabia (a Hohenstaufen and related to Frederick) and Otto of Saxony (a Welf) were elected by separate groups of princes. Historian Karl Hampe calls this "unhappy double election . . . the most fatal event in the medieval history of Germany."[3]

Innocent sought to mediate this disputed imperial election. In so doing, he asserted a papal right to decide imperial elections in the case of a dispute. Innocent argued that imperial elections were conducted under papal auspices, based on papal superiority and the historical fact that the papacy had "translated" royal power from Childeric to Pepin and from Byzantium to Charlemagne. Should an emperor be deficient, either in the mode of his election or in his functioning (e.g. in defending the Church, fighting heretics, keeping treaties and oaths, or waging war), the papacy reserved the right to depose him.

Innocent favored Otto, who was willing to agree to papal demands for territory in Italy. In 1201, Innocent wrote to the German electors that, by virtue of the disputed election, the papacy, by authority of God and St. Peter, had the decisive vote. Otto duly became emperor. But in 1208, Philip of Swabia was murdered, allowing Otto to renege on his promises to Innocent and to invade Italy. Innocent excommunicated Otto, securing Frederick of Sicily's election and coronation as emperor in 1215. Frederick II (r. 1215–1250) promised Innocent that he would separate Sicily from Germany and yield it to the pope. Innocent died before this came about, however, and Frederick never relinquished control of Sicily.

Innocent, then, met with several failures. Of all the schismatic groups he hoped to attract into the Catholic fold, only the Armenians and the Maronite Christians

---

* The major exception to this was Thomas Becket's struggle to preserve ecclesiastical liberty in the face of what he considered Henry II's overbearing policies.

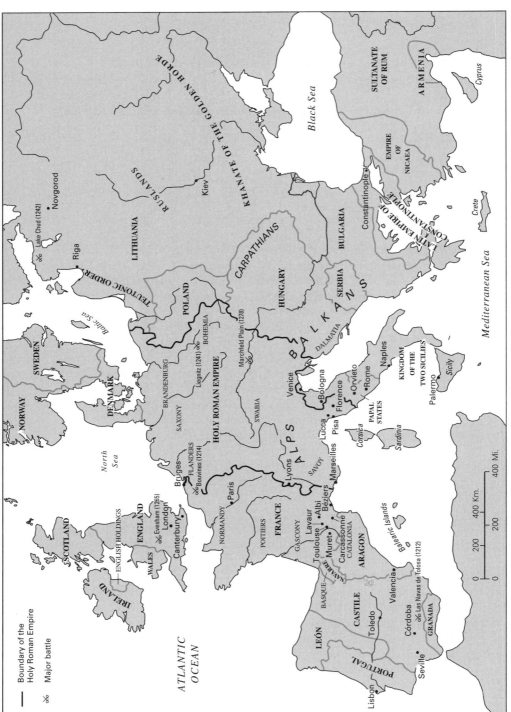

Map 16.1   Political Divisions of Europe, c. 1250   By 1250 the Christian rulers of Spain had captured most of Spain except Granada; the Byzantine Empire, under Latin domination in Constantinople, had broken apart. Serbia was beginning its expansion into a dominant position in the Balkans, and a new power along the Baltic, the Teutonic Order, had emerged. The Mongols had destroyed Kievan Rus, while western Europe was beginning to take the shape of the modern nation-states of today. The Holy Roman Empire, under Frederick II joined Sicily, northern Italy, and Europe.

responded positively. The Fourth Crusade got out of his control and never arrived in the Holy Land. The ensuing unification of Greek and Roman Christians only exacerbated hatred for one another. The Fifth Crusade, never launched while he lived, was a dismal failure. When Innocent died in 1216, most schismatic churches were still schismatic, Jerusalem and Egypt were still unliberated, and the union of Greeks with the West was a forced legal and political union that did not endure. Similarly, with the election of Frederick II as emperor (a seeming triumph for Innocent), Innocent crowned one of the greatest enemies the medieval Church would ever know. On the other hand, for better or for worse, Innocent did initiate the Fourth Crusade, lead a fight against heresy, call one of the great church councils (Fourth Lateran), and dominate the politics of his age.

The Holy Roman Empire and Italian Politics

Innocent's meddling in imperial politics created divisions within Italy. The split between Otto and Frederick (and later between the papacy and Frederick) gave rise to two parties, called Guelph and Ghibelline. By the beginning of the fourteenth century, many Italians were no longer sure how this split originated. Cardinal Napoleone Orsini (1263–1342) concluded that he really did not understand what a Guelf or a Ghibelline was, while Pope Benedict XII (1334–1342) commented, apropos of Guelfism, that "Italian politics are extremely changeable. Italians want one thing one day and one another."

In fact, the term "Guelf" comes from Welf, the German noble family to which Otto belonged, while "Ghibelline" was an Italian rendering of "Waiblingen," the castle of the Hohenstaufen dukes of Swabia. The terms appear after 1215 when Frederick II and the papacy first clashed. Areas of Italy that became Guelf were generally understood as propapal; those that became Ghibelline were generally understood as proimperial. If a town was Guelf (for example, Florence), a traditional enemy (for example, Lucca and Pisa) might naturally become Ghibelline. A slight tendency arose for Guelphism to be associated with popular rule, but not always (for example, Ghibelline Pisa had popular rule; Guelph Orvieto was ruled by nobles). Affiliation became a matter of habit and tradition, and some Italian cities (Venice and Rome) were committed to neither side, as was true of some popes. These divisions, however poorly understood or however historically generated, were to rend Italy well into the fourteenth century.

The ruler who galvanized the Ghibellines was Frederick II. Orphaned at age four, Frederick had been passed around among the Sicilian barons, growing up under chaotic conditions in the streets of Palermo where he imbibed a mix of Muslim, Norman, Byzantine, and Italian cultures. His character, a combination of steely determination and misanthropy, fascinated his contemporaries and continues to fascinate historians. According to the chronicler Matthew Paris, who met him, he was the "greatest of the princes of the world—the bewilderment of the world and the initiator of great change."[4] In evaluating Frederick, keep in mind that the surviving evidence for his reign is mainly propaganda. Few chronicles or administrative registers survive.

Classical Statue of the Emperor Frederick II   This photo, which shows the head of a half-length bust of Frederick II, illustrates the neoclassical style typical of the monuments associated with Frederick II. Frederick focused on the restoration of Roman imperial authority during his reign. This can be seen in his coinage, the rhetoric that surrounded his rule, his seals, and the sculpture and architecture he patronized. Most of the monumental achievements of his reign have disappeared or are in ruins like this statue. *Museo Civico, Barletta, Italy/ Giraudon/Art Resource, NY.*

Frederick knew six languages, devoured ideas, and wrote books and poetry. He was among the first to write Italian vernacular poetry; indeed, Dante labeled him the father of Italian poetry. His library had Latin, Greek, Hebrew, and Arabic works; he patronized lawyers, rhetoricians, and artists and promoted the translation of Arabic texts in medicine, mathematics, optics, astronomy, and astrology. An expert horseman and skilled in arms, Frederick was much attached to animals (he collected a menagerie and wrote on falconry). The bent of his mind was scientific, proceeding by reason and proofs in nature. He applied these principles to animal breeding and to farming; he corresponded with the mathematician Leonardo

Fibonacci (see Chapter 17) and with Muslim scholars and attracted the polymath Michael Scot to his court. Regarding religion, one Arabic commentator observed that, one saw from the way he spoke "that he was a materialist and that his Christianity was simply a game to him."[5] A story, perhaps apocryphal, goes that he had a condemned criminal shut up in a barrel so that observers might detect the soul leaving the barrel when he died. The results led the emperor to doubt the existence of the soul. It was alleged that he called Christ an imposter along with Moses and Muhammad, and he was accused of calling people fools who believed in the virgin birth.

Frederick was an efficient administrator who took a previously sophisticated and centralized state in Sicily and southern Italy, which had, however, been neglected during the papal regency, and crafted an even more sophisticated, imperial, and centralized program of government. He appointed judges, notaries, and lawyers himself, restricted the bearing of arms, increased taxes, imposed royal monopolies, developed the bureaucracy, asserted greater control over towns, and then summoned people twice a year so that he could gather tax information and they could voice their grievances. He founded the University of Naples to educate men for his service, and he published a law code, the *Liber Augustalis,* that exalted royal authority.

Frederick was less successful in Germany. There, despite some efforts to replicate Sicilian administrative reforms, Frederick ended by offering massive concessions to the German princes in order to gain their support for his Italian policies. Then, when the papacy deposed Frederick in 1245, many German princes revolted against him. Bohemia, while nominally under imperial authority, gained authority and autonomy, electing its own rulers after 1212, while other princes usurped what few imperial rights there were. The German imperial government had no administrative center, and the empire remained a cultural and linguistic hodgepodge without effective leadership.

Despite the weakness of his authority in Germany, Frederick presented himself as Caesar-Augustus, and also as the Son of God, the Messiah, the son of justice. His propagandists called his kingdom a new Holy Land and his birthplace, Jesi, the new Bethlehem. The proclamations that issued from his court, couched in elaborate rhetorical flourishes, proclaimed that he was divine justice, God's representative on earth, whose right came from God alone. Through marriage he was also king of Jerusalem, crowned in Jerusalem amid general expectations that such an event portended universal Christian rule and the beginning of a new age.

Given the rhetoric it is not surprising that he had conflicts with the papacy, which excommunicated him in 1227 and 1239, preached a crusade against him, and deposed him at the Council of Lyons in 1245 for perjury, breach of the peace, sacrilege, and suspicion of heresy. Pope Innocent IV (1243–1254) justified this deposition by drawing upon the ideas of Gregory VII and Innocent III and the examples of their depositions of Henry IV and Otto IV, but he went further. Innocent IV argued that in moral matters, and in all matters of defect, negligence, ambiguity, and emergency, the Church had the right to act. Indeed, biblical history showed that God governs man and that divine law requires the subjection of God's chosen people to the priesthood. Innocent then launched a propaganda campaign and crusade against Frederick, promising the soldiers absolution of sins for partici-pating. Frederick responded to the crusade and the defamation campaign by killing relatives and friends of the pope and invading central and northern Italy. The strug-gle ended with Frederick's sudden death from dysentery in 1250. Within eighteen years afterwards the Hohenstaufen lineage was wiped out, after which the imperial throne remained vacant for a generation.

In a final footnote to this story of imperial decline, Sicily, for which Frederick had fought so ferociously, was offered by the papacy to Charles of Anjou, younger brother of the king of France. Charles's army moved south, defeating and killing the Hohenstaufen ruler (Manfred, Frederick II's illegitimate son). Angevin rule was not well received by the Sicilians, however. In 1282, they rose up, massacred the French, and invited the king of Aragon into the kingdom. Twenty years of war between Angevins and Aragonese resulted; royal estates fell into the hands of the Sicilian aristocracy, and the long-term destruction of Sicilian society and its economy began.

EMERGING NATION-STATES: FRANCE, ENGLAND, AND SPAIN

While the conflict between papal and imperial forces and between Guelphs and Ghibellines tore Italy apart and placed the Holy Roman Emperor in a disadvanta-geous position vis-à-vis the German princes, other states within Europe (most no-tably England, France, and Spain) were uniting behind one ruler and centralizing their kingdoms.

France

The Capetian monarchy of France, small in size, benefited from its location (cen-tered on Paris), the sacred character of its kingship, and a dynastic continuity dat-ing from the late tenth century. Between 1179 (the coronation of Philip II) and 1270 (the death of Louis IX) and largely because of the character of these two rulers, France expanded its territories to resemble modern France (see Map 16.2).

Philip II (r. 1179–1223), called Philip Augustus for his achievements, was a re-markable architect of royal power. The only son of Louis VII and born late in his life, Philip was considered a God-given child—an idea further strengthened when as a young boy he was lost in the forest and later found unharmed, and again when a desperate pilgrimage by Louis to Becket's shrine in England seems to have healed Philip from a deadly sickness. Philip II was fourteen when his father died, and yet within his first decade as ruler, he so successfully manipulated tensions between the older Angevin king, Henry II, and Henry's sons that he provoked war between them. Thereafter, he enlarged his realm, increased his treasury, and enhanced the administrative capacity of the kingdom. When he died, he had roughly dou-bled the size of his domain and multiplied the royal annual income twenty-two times over what his father had received. He left a surplus in the treasury that

Map 16.2   The Growth of the French Monarchy, 1180–1314   From modest beginnings (see Map 13.1) northern France expanded impressively under Philip II
(Augustus). Normandy, in particular, was taken by the French after more than
300 years in the hands of the Normans, Anglo-Normans, and Angevins. Poitou
was conquered by Louis VIII during the Albigensian Crusade, and Toulouse
and Languedoc were annexed by France in 1271. Brittany became a royal fief
under Philip II, but effective control of Brittany was not yet possible.

supported the reigns of his son Louis VIII (r. 1223–1226) and grandson Louis IX
(r. 1226–1270).[6]

Philip was served by powerful political instincts, administrative talents, a good
relationship with the Church, good fortune in the deaths of his enemies, and a
somewhat avaricious temperament. Initially overshadowed by both the Angevin
and German empires, Philip benefited when Richard I was captured and imprisoned on his return from the crusades. Since, technically, Richard was no longer on
crusade, Philip was no longer constrained from attacking his lands. The enmity

that ensued when Richard was released from captivity was cut short when Richard died unexpectedly at age forty-one at a siege in southern France. This left the Angevin empire in the hands of Richard's younger brother, John; while a crafty military opponent, John was capricious, sometimes lethargic, and often tyrannical. The results were all to Philip's benefit, as he seized most of the Angevin holdings on the continent.

Philip's opportunities began in 1202 when John married Isabella of Angoulême, antagonizing the French lord to whom she was betrothed and allowing Philip to declare John, who was a vassal to Philip for some of his territories, disobedient. In 1203, John lost further moral high ground—and the lordship of Brittany—by the murder (perhaps committed by John personally) of his young nephew Arthur of Brittany. In 1204, Philip seized Normandy. John subsequently lost Anjou and Maine, the original homeland of Angevin power, thereby losing direct access to Poitiers and Gascony. Then in 1214, Philip won the battle of Bouvines against a coalition of English allies, including the Emperor Otto IV. This famous battle, in which the larger, allied army was routed completely, ended John's chances of reconstituting the Angevin empire.* By 1216, Philip's son Louis invaded England, taking London and most of eastern England with the support of some English earls and bishops. The invasion failed when John died before Louis could secure the English crown for himself. The English crowned John's heir, Henry III, instead.

Philip II reached outside his royal domains constantly, controlling the marriages of heiresses, widows, and wards in the surrounding territories of Champagne, Blois, Flanders, and Brittany and gaining territorial concessions for himself in the process. He encouraged nobility outside his domains to apply to his royal court for redress and to render him homage and fealty. He inventoried his rights and insisted upon them, while maintaining his own freedom from homage to anyone (even the emperor). Philip also intervened to help churchmen and towns in conflict outside his domain. He issued charters of liberties or privileges that extended his influence and, usually, strengthened his purse. Through his son, Louis, Philip intervened, somewhat reluctantly, in the south to support the Albigensian Crusade. This ultimately brought the territories of Toulouse into the hands of the French crown via the 1229 Treaty of Paris. By 1271, for the first time since the age of Charlemagne, France's borders reached the Mediterranean. In addition, agreements were reached over borders with Spain; the French state was taking a more modern shape.

Much relating to this process of expansion was written down. Philip was the first French king to develop a central accounting bureau and permanent archives. He created a small circle of advisors—clerks and lesser but literate nobles—while reducing the role of powerful hereditary nobles within his household and his government. He appointed salaried royal officials (*baillis*)—knights who acted as itinerant justices, collected royal revenues, executed royal policy, and reported regularly to the king and his advisors. As a result, Philip was able to execute commands efficiently and without interference from powerful local interests—for example, with his expulsion of the Jews and expropriation of their debts in 1191. Throughout, he remained generally on good terms with the Church, going on the Third Crusade

---

* It also provided the papacy with its opportunity to depose Otto and crown Frederick II as emperor.

(briefly) in 1190, mostly permitting free elections of bishops and abbots (which, in any case, tended toward his interests), and negotiating compromises in struggles between lay and ecclesiastical jurisdictions. If Philip was not overly generous with the Church, his forbearance looked attractive relative to the heavy-handed policies of the Angevins.

Finally, Philip benefited from the legends and symbols surrounding his kingship—the holy oil at his coronation at Reims, the symbolic connection with St. Denys (where he was to be buried with much splendor), and a growing identification with ancient French and Trojan heroes. This gave the Capetians a heritage independent of the Roman Empire but with imperial echoes as is suggested by Philip's title "Augustus."

Though Philip Augustus was the real builder of French monarchy, it was his grandson Louis IX who has captured the imagination of posterity. This is partly because Louis epitomized the aspirations of the age—joining intense religious concerns with a passion for justice—but also because Jean de Joinville, a noble from Champagne, dictated an account of Louis. Jean portrayed Louis as an intense human being, a saint-king, and a personal friend, both fallible and admirable. As a result, Louis is the first medieval ruler we feel we really know.

In the early years of Louis' reign, his regent-mother, Blanche of Castile, had problems with restive barons, particularly in the south of France, anxious to reassert the power they had lost as France expanded. Blanche's strength and skill as a ruler, followed by Louis' decision to go on crusade in 1247 (and take most of the barons with him), settled them down. Louis intended to take the largest army ever East, but he mainly attracted the French. The Germans were too preoccupied with the conflict with Pope Innocent IV; the English were too recently smarting from French defeats; and the pope (who had declared a crusade against Frederick II) was reluctant to see Louis take warriors away from Europe. By the force of his vision and the resources of the French treasury, Louis led an army of perhaps 15,000 men (including 2,500 to 2,800 knights) overseas to Egypt, the center of Muslim power in the eastern Mediterranean. Louis planned to follow in the footsteps of the Fifth Crusade, which had landed at Damietta in the Egyptian delta, and of St. Francis of Assisi, who had disembarked at the same spot on his missionary travels to Egypt. Damietta fell to the crusaders almost immediately, but the ensuing effort to reach Cairo foundered, allowing the Egyptians time to mount a counterattack that destroyed the French army. Louis, and many others, were captured. After expensive negotiations, Louis ransomed himself and others, gave up Damietta, and stayed on in the Holy Land with a remnant of his army. His mother, Blanche, governed during his absence, continuing to strengthen France internally while at the same time supporting the Crusade financially. In 1254, however, the death of his mother and financial necessity brought Louis home. Louis had spent much in this crusade, and he had gained very little. Although he led another abortive crusade (this time to North Africa in 1270), it was the effective end of the crusading movement. The city of Acre, the last Christian stronghold in the Holy Land, fell to the Mamluk rulers of Egypt in 1291.

Given the dimensions of this catastrophe, how did Louis become one of France's most noteworthy kings, canonized seventeen years after his death? The French chroniclers report that Louis faced imprisonment with great strength of character

Louis IX's Royal Chapel (Sainte Chapelle) in Paris   This image of the interior of Sainte Chapelle looks toward the apse and the relic platform. King Louis IX of France had this royal chapel and reliquary built in the center of Paris to house the Crown of Thorns, a fragment of the True Cross, and other relics bought from the Frankish Byzantine emperor Baldwin II. Built in the 1240s, Sainte Chapelle is remarkable for its stained glass windows and its sculptures, as well as for an architectural lightness that gives the building a feeling of a jewel set in stone. *James Stanfield/ National Geographic Image Collection.*

and was perfectly willing to be martyred; Muslim sources do not deny this. Louis's decision to stay on in the Holy Land, while criticized by many who felt he was needed in France, showed remarkable loyalty to those Frenchmen still unransomed as well as to the larger crusading cause. Louis's willingness to take full responsibility for the crusade's failure brought him to a kind of religious conversion. On his return, he was a more austere king, committed to piety and deeply concerned with justice. As a result, he pushed for independent investigators to examine the royal administration of the *baillis,* to correct abuses, and to hear appeals. He strengthened local government, reinvigorated the administration of Paris, and better defined the royal role in finances. Louis also traveled incessantly to render justice, and he made himself available to plaintiffs, in legend and perhaps in reality, under an ancient oak tree at Vincennes or sitting in the public gardens in Paris. Out of this developed the French *Parlement,* the king's law court.

Louis now sought peace more conscientiously, mediating between the king of England and his enemies, in the imperial-papal conflict, and between French barons. He would not war within Europe, and within France outlawed trials by combat and private wars. His treatment of the Jewish communities, after his return, was more thoughtful and less harsh than that of Philip or of himself prior to the crusade. Louis tried, in every way possible, to make his title "Most Christian King" a reality. In so doing, he gained the support of the French people to such an extent that he was able to dominate the French church and stand up to the papacy. By humbling himself, he made himself into an unassailable religious leader, enhancing the French perception of themselves as a chosen people and their king as an independent source of religious legitimacy.

England

England's thirteenth-century rulers did not serve her as well. John (d. 1216), a king abhorred by many (including some modern historians), was followed by his son Henry III (r. 1216–1272), also considered by many to have been an inadequate king, and his grandson, Edward I (r. 1272–1308), a stronger ruler but one also plagued with problems. With the defeat of John's allies at Bouvines, English kings settled down to rule a more insular kingdom, although they retained parts of southwestern France. Within the British Isles, however, John successfully invaded Ireland. Edward conquered the independent northern Welsh kingdoms and tried to subdue Scotland.

Thrown back on less extensive resources, England in the thirteenth century struggled with the nature of political power, the role of the community, and the emergent sense of being English and insular rather than Angevin and continental.

Angevin tendencies toward willful rule heightened under King John. By 1214, the barons of England had multiple grievances against him, including his mistreatment of heirs and their lands, his mistreatment of their wives,* his demands that barons serve in armies outside England or pay uncustomary sums of money for relief from such service, his extension of royal rights in the forests, and his use of Jewish moneylenders to extract interest from the barons. Added to this were the complaints of Stephen Langton, archbishop of Canterbury, who did not trust the king's intentions with regard to the Church. For ten years, from 1204 to 1214, John applied his considerable talents as an administrator to squeezing as much money as possible from church and state in support of the recovery of Angevin lands on the continent. Historians can follow this process in detail because John, who distrusted most people, committed much of it to writing.

In 1214, when John's allies lost the battle of Bouvines, John was simultaneously deserted by his Poitevin knights in the south of France. He returned to England to start over, once again employing quasi-legal methods to raise revenues. But this time the barons, towns, church leaders, and much of the English community had had enough. In May 1215, a group of barons, mostly from northern England, renounced their homage to John. Others, including Stephen Langton, quickly joined

---

* John was adulterous and sometimes pursued the wives and daughters of his barons. He could be harsh on others, however, and at one point seized the concubines of the clergy, holding them for ransom. His control over the wives of his men can be gleaned from the following entry in his archives, quoted in W. L. Warren's biography (p. 190): "The wife of Hugh Neville promises the lord king two hundred chickens that she might lie one night with her husband."

them, and together they forced John to sign a document called the Magna Carta. The Magna Carta is considered the founding document of English liberties. But it is a peculiar document, dealing with a variety of grievances in sixty-one clauses with no clear-cut order. Underlying the specific concessions that John agreed to at Runnymede on June 15 were, however, larger principles that placed the king under the law, guaranteed the liberties of the different social orders, and asserted the need for consent to taxation. Although Pope Innocent III immediately declared the Magna Carta "illegal and unjust . . . a shameful and demeaning agreement," the document was reissued, slightly revised, through the thirteenth century, thereby gradually achieving the status of law (see Medieval Voices).

A concept of taxation with consent developed in the thirteenth century along with a new institution, the Parliament.* Continuing military campaigns, the impact of inflation, and the insufficiency of customary revenues all produced intermittent financial crises for the crown. Increasingly, the crown levied taxes not just on knights' holdings but on the property of all individuals, whether baron, serf, clergy, or laity. These financial "aids" were not customary and were to be used for specific purposes; as a result, those paying began to feel that they should have a say in those purposes. Negotiations with Henry III over taxes produced the first Parliaments in the 1230s, in which he agreed to redress grievances and reconfirm the Magna Carta in exchange for income. Parliaments, threats to revolt, and occasional actual revolts (as in 1233 and 1258–1265) characterized relations between Henry III and the aristocracy. English barons were dissatisfied with Henry's foreign policies (which tended to ignore Normandy and focus on grandiose schemes in southern France, Sicily, and Germany). They did not like the prominence of non-English advisors in the king's council, Henry's tendency to assert personal rule, or the increasingly poor state of royal finances. These grievances gave the barons and then the knights and towns of England increasing leverage in a struggle to control the king's actions through a baronial council and through Parliaments.

In 1255, Henry III agreed to an absurdly high payment to the papacy for the sale of Sicily to his son. Irrespective of whether the papacy had the right to sell Sicily out from under the Hohenstaufen, England could not afford the price. By 1258, the barons revolted, led by Simon de Montfort IV. Simon, who became a legendary tragic figure and was later credited with founding the House of Commons, spearheaded reforms, creating a governing council that worked closely with a small, elected Parliament. These arrangements did not last, and Simon was killed in the battle of Evesham in 1265. But the sentiments of his supporters lived on and are nicely expressed in the Song of Lewes, a poem written in support of the revolt: ". . . the community of the realm should advise and let it be known what everyone feels, for their own laws are most familiar to them. Nor are all the people of a country such fools as not to know more than others about the customs of the realm which have been passed down from father to son."[7]

---

* The English Parliament is not to be confused with the French Parlement. The Parlement was a court of law, while England's Parliament, which began as a Council of Barons, became a legislative and tax-granting institution.

MEDIEVAL VOICES

King John, Under Pressure from the Church and Barons of England, Signs the Magna Carta at Runnymede in 1215

The following selections from the Magna Carta focus on some of the freedoms it guaranteed and the process by which a Parliament should be called.

John, by the grace of God, king of England, lord of Ireland, duke of Normandy and Aquitaine, and count of Anjou, to the archbishops, bishops, abbots, earls, barons, justiciars, foresters, sheriffs, stewards, servants, and to all his bailiffs and liege subjects, greeting. . . .

In the first place we have granted to God, and by this our present charter confirmed for us and our heirs forever that the English Church shall be free, and shall have her rights entire, and her liberties inviolate; . . . We have also granted to all freemen of our kingdom, for us and our heirs forever, all the underwritten liberties, to be had and held by them and their heirs, of us and our heirs forever.

. . . the city of London shall have all its ancient liberties and free customs. . . . And for obtaining the common counsel of the kingdom . . . , we will cause to be summoned the archbishops, bishops, abbots, earls, and greater barons, severally by our letters; and we will moreover cause to be summoned generally, through our sheriffs and bailiffs, all others who hold of us in chief, for a fixed date, namely, after the expiry of at least forty days, and at a fixed place; and in all letters of such summons we will specify the reason of the summons. And when the summons has thus been made, the business shall proceed on the day appointed, according to the counsel of such as are present, although not all who were summoned have come. . . .

No freemen shall be taken or [and] imprisoned or disseised or exiled or in any way destroyed, nor will we go upon him nor send upon him, except by the lawful judgment of his peers or [and] by the law of the land. To no one will we sell, to no one will we refuse or delay, right or justice. . . .

Wherefore it is our will, and we firmly enjoin, that the English Church be free, and that the men in our kingdom have and hold all the aforesaid liberties, rights, and concessions, well and peaceably, freely and quietly, fully and wholly, for themselves and their heirs, of us and our heirs, in all respects and in all places forever. . . .

Source: From *The Great Charter: Four Essays on the Magna Carta* (New York: Mentor, 1965) 110–142. Copyright © 1965 by American Council of Learned Societies. Used by permission of Pantheon Books, a division of Random House, Inc.

Henry's son Edward I (r. 1272–1308) was a more respected king, with a record of military victories, but similar tensions (over financial exigencies, liberties, and the king's right to govern with or without adequate council) dominated his reign. Edward campaigned constantly—in Gascony, Wales, and Scotland. He was more successful than his father in negotiating baronial support for his armies, perhaps because he generally fought closer to home. But by 1297, the costs put the crown once more in debt, sparking another revolt against military service and taxes levied without due consultation. Under the circumstances, it is not surprising that during Edward's reign Parliament became a more regular feature of English politics, with representation from the shires and the towns as well as from ecclesiastical and baronial leaders.

In the struggles between crown and community, England's foreign population suffered. Hatred was directed against those around the king from Poitiers or Savoy, against Italian merchants (who were loaning monies to the crown, collecting monies for the papacy, and dominating the wool trade), but particularly against the Jews, who were expelled from England after having been wrecked financially by Edward I.

Jews were the property of the crown. As a result, John had been able to collect the debts owed them and force payment to the crown. The Jewish community was also subject to arbitrary taxation which rose to extravagant heights under Henry III (20,000 marks in 1241/42 and 60,000 in 1245); this destroyed the wealth of the great Jewish moneylenders and forced many Jewish families to leave England. Little liquid wealth was left to extract when the Jews were finally expelled in 1290. The crown now took all their assets, and Parliament, in apparent gratitude for the expulsion, granted Edward the taxes he needed.

One other group of foreigners was highly resented by the English—papal tax collectors and papal appointees to benefices. When King John put England under the protection of Innocent III, he also opened it to papal intrusion. And the thirteenth-century papacy required money and positions to support its territorial struggles in Italy, its ongoing crusading efforts, and its expanding bureaucracy. By 1253, the Church in Italy was receiving 50,000 marks per year from England. Papal tax collectors, Italian merchants, and Italian clergy were not safe, however, in a more nationalist and xenophobic England. For example, in the 1230s papal appointees were kidnapped and held for ransom, their properties destroyed, and their messengers attacked by a group of terrorists led by a Yorkshire knight and folk hero who, like Robin Hood, robbed prelates and fought for English liberty.[8]

Spain

At the beginning of the thirteenth century, Spain was a medley of competitive kingdoms: the Christian kingdoms of León, Castile, Portugal, Aragon, and Navarre and a number of Muslim kingdoms under the rule of the Almohad, fundamentalist Berbers from North Africa. Pope Innocent III, who encouraged resumption of a crusade against the Muslims, broke the uneasy truce between Christians and Muslims. In 1212, Alfonso VIII (r. 1158–1214) of Castile defeated the Almohad in a spectacularly decisive battle at Las Navas de Tolosa, and Muslim political control of the south began to break apart. In 1232, James I of Aragon (r. 1213–1276) captured Majorca, and by 1238 he had taken Valencia. In 1236, Ferdinand III of Castile (r. 1217–1252) captured Córdoba; by 1238, the great Muslim city of Seville was in Castilian hands. The Portuguese had also been moving south, so that by the death of Ferdinand III, Muslim rulers held only the southern littoral of the peninsula, to which they clung for another 240 years (see Medieval Voices).

MEDIEVAL VOICES

A Plea for Help from the Muslims of Seville in 1247

Ferdinand III of Castile was able, with the breakup of Almohad power in Spain, to unify León and Castile in 1230 and take Córdoba in 1236. A decade later he besieged Seville for a year and a half. The following excerpts are from an Arabic chronicle of the siege, followed by a poem by Abu Musa Harun b. Harun designed to elicit help from the emir in North Africa:

In the year 645 [1247] the Christians encircled the city of Seville and laid siege to it by land and sea. . . . They captured a large number of the inhabitants and seized some of their children in ships, with which they maintained a very tight blockade. They kept up a bombardment from mangonels and destroyed all amenities, both small and great, except what was in the houses of a few rich people, . . . the people became dismayed, and staggered around like drunkards even though they weren't drunk; a great many died of starvation. Resigning any hope of corn or barley, the people began to chew skins; the fighting men among the general populace and the ranks of the army perished.

When the siege at Seville reached extremes of severity, and support from other towns was nonexistent, and [the Sevillians] became squeezed in the grip of the enemies of God, the infidels, they turned to the Amir of the Believers al Mu'tadud bi'llah al-sa'id and all the Muslims of western North Africa, beseeching their help and letting them know of the terrible struggle and the severe and excruciating distress that had overtaken them. [The people of Seville tried] to waken their desire to come to their help and incited them to wage Holy War against the infidels, enemies of God. Among their words was an ode which would delight the hard of heart and which the unmoveable mountains would respond to:

O Hims (Seville) . . . The guardians of the Trinity have risen up; forestall them and rouse your thoughts from headless slumber.

How many captives have come to have their feet bound in fetters, shattered, complaining of abasement?

And how many a suckling babe continues to be cast down, snatched away from his mother, and has been weaned in the waves (i.e. thrown in the water)? . . .

Conquering the Peninsula is one of the customs of your forefathers; so plant your feet in our land to spread guidance.

There is no excuse for leaving it and abandoning it to the unbelievers. Time, and you within in, are not sterile.

Is there anyone who will answer our call, and give us a lifeboat in the swelling sea of disasters?

Nothing remains in us but dying breaths; all of us, [though] in existence, are like the nonexistent. . . .

In the year 646 [1248] the accursed tyrant (Ferdinand III) gained control of the city of Seville—may God restore it to Islam!—after its inhabitants, from the prevalence of famine and the dearth of food, had drained the cup of death.

Source: Excerpts from Charles Melville and Ahmad Ubaydli, *Christians and Moors in Spain,* vol. 3: Arabic sources 711–1501 (Warminster, Eng.: Aris & Philipps, 1992) 144–149. Reprinted by permission of Aris & Philipps Ltd.

As Christian Spain expanded, its population grew. In contrast, in Muslim Spain and throughout North Africa, population was beginning to decline. As Muslim cities shrank, cities in Christian territories expanded. Demographic vitality mirrored economic vitality. Wines, fruits, olives and olive oil, textiles (especially wool), and fish were transported down the river basins and throughout the countryside by cart and pack animal. Italian merchants frequented Seville and Lisbon en route to England, France, or Flanders, while Basque and Catalan sea captains captured trade routes in the western Mediterranean and along the Atlantic seaboard. The Aragonese kings moved into the Mediterranean to capture the islands of Majorca, Minorca, Sardinia, and, by the 1280s, Sicily.

The nobility and the Church benefited most of all. The highest nobility became rich indeed, amassing lands that sometimes stretched across the peninsula, while the lesser nobility (*hidalgos*)* found avenues for enriching themselves in warfare and the colonization of new lands. The Catholic Church now could count forty-four bishoprics and innumerable monasteries, friaries, and military orders, including some native Spanish orders.

Kings, still primarily concerned with warfare against the Muslims, gradually instituted court structures, legal codes, and tax collections (farmed out to the Jews). The government of Alfonso X, the Wise (r. 1252–1284) of Castile illustrates this trend. Under Alfonso the official language of government became Spanish, and the court began to produce extensive records, helped by the introduction of paper (cheaper and easier to produce than parchment). Alfonso employed university-trained bureaucrats and counselors, thereby antagonizing the barons. New law codes, based on Roman law, began to supplant oral custom and memory, a development that was troubling to a people used to the flexibility of frontier life. The principle of absolute rule in Roman law undercut older notions of a king acting in consultation with his barons. So as in England, when royal expenses outran revenues, *cortes* (assemblies representing the nobles, clergy, and townsfolk) forced the government to be more consultative. Alfonso complicated matters by seeking the Holy Roman imperial crown, reviving claims to parts of France, expending vast sums of money in a sometimes arbitrary fashion, and disinheriting his son. By 1282, his son, his family, the military orders, the nobles, and many cities rebelled. Alfonso, a man of great talent and generosity, ended his reign deprived of sovereignty, and declared incompetent.

Alfonso X had made his court a center for learning, attracting some of the greatest writers of the thirteenth century—Ramon de Penyafort (1175–1257) in canon law; Ramon Lull (d. 1315) a mystic, love poet, novelist, scholar, philosopher, and missionary to Islam (see Chapter 17); and Arnold de Villanova (c.1235–1311/13), doctor and scholar in Arabic, Hebrew, Latin, and Spanish. Translators at Alfonso's court turned Arabic and Hebrew works into Spanish. Chroniclers wrote histories of the Arabs and of Spain; troubadour songs and literary tales of the Virgin (the *Cantigas de Santa Maria*) were written and performed to please the court. Most notably, Alfonso oversaw collections of law codes in Spanish, particularly the collection of some 2,700 legal formulations and essays on legal philosophy called the

---

* From *hijos de algo*, literally, sons of something.

Siete Partidas. Within the Christian framework of these statutes, Alfonso exhibited a notable toleration of Jewish religious practices and a protective stance toward Jewish economic interests. This contrasts with the prejudicial dismissal of Muslims, whose mosques, for example, were not allowed in Christian towns.

PRESSURES ON THE PERIPHERY OF EASTERN EUROPE

Throughout eastern Europe, western settlers (first Frisian and then German) were invited to leave their homelands to develop towns and clear forests and swamps in the east. The movement of German settlers, in particular, from the eleventh century on is of the greatest importance. German migrants into Silesia, for example, bolstered Silesian independence from Poland. Germans brought their own laws, institutions, customs, and language, and their presence greatly strengthened east-west trading networks. This German frontier migration (called the *Drang nach Osten*) was accompanied, in part, by German military and political operations into Slavic territories such as those mounted by the lords of Brandenburg or by the Teutonic Order of Knights. The weight of Germany gradually shifted eastward, a movement that has shaped the relations between Germany and eastern Europe into modern times.

By the thirteenth century, eastern Europe consisted of a series of kingdoms all jockeying for prominence, with some of the larger, established kingdoms (Poland and Hungary in particular) experiencing fragmentation and diminished royal authority in the face of a rising aristocracy.

Poland, while expanding its influence in the pagan Baltic region, had disintegrated into five squabbling duchies, leaving it ripe for a partition of sorts. In 1229, the Teutonic Knights (see Chapter 12) arrived along the Baltic. They were an aggressive, colonizing force to Poland's north, and, although they were ostensibly crusading against pagan Prussian slavs, Christian slavs also felt threatened. By 1300 the Teutonic Order had conquered the Prussians and established a state extending northeast of Poland. In 1308 they took Gdańsk, Poland's major port on the Baltic. Poland was also threatened on the east by the pagan Lithuanians, on the west by the margraves of Brandenburg, and on the southwest by the kingdom of Bohemia. By 1300 a Bohemian ruler was crowned, briefly, as king of Poland.

Although little studied, one of the kingdoms to emerge on Poland's frontier was the pagan kingdom of Lithuania. The Lithuanians were highly resistant to Christianity, forming an enclave for other Baltic peoples who resisted Christian baptism. Protected by marshes, lakes, and vast forests, and lacking large urban centers, the Lithuanians were not easily invaded. Strengthened by trade, by new leadership, and by recruits among other pagans, they advanced into Rus and Polish territories and captured the port of Riga from the Teutonic Knights. By 1300, the Lithuanian rulers Traidenis (d. 1281/82) and Gediminas (d. 1341/42) established foundations for a Grand Duchy that dominated north-central Europe, Belorus, and the Ukraine until the sixteenth century.

Bohemia under the Přemysl dynasty (895–1306) appeared to be on the verge of creating a large central European empire at the expense of Poland, Austria, and Hungary. One medieval chronicler noted that King Otakar II of Bohemia (d. 1278) planned to extend his kingdom from the Baltic to the Adriatic Sea and to the limits of the world. He certainly had his eye on the German imperial crown. Rudolph of Hapsburg, the first Hapsburg ruler of Austria, stopped Otaker with the defeat of the Bohemians and death of Otakar at a battle on Marchfeld Plain in 1278.

The great Hungarian kingdom under the Árpád line of rulers was less secure. From the end of the eleventh century until the fourteenth century (when the Angevin dynasty came to the throne), the Hungarians saw dynastic instability and the rise of powerful baronial families. When the last Árpádian ruler died in 1301, huge baronies ruled, semi-independent from royal authority and under almost no central control. By the thirteenth century, Cuman Turks had migrated to Hungary from the east. The Hungarians also had to worry about aggression from the German Empire and from Venice along the Dalmatian coast.

In the midst of these shifting political allegiances and threats to unity, the economy of eastern Europe was flourishing. The eastward colonization of Germans changed the character of cities throughout eastern Europe. German traders and artisans not only brought skills with them, they brought along legal protections and privileges. These privileges, known as German city law, allowed the Germans to rule themselves. They had their own quarter, their own courts, their own elected city council, and sometimes their own military forces. Eventually these privileges extended to all the inhabitants of a city and to other cities. The movement of goods and peoples via long-standing east-west trade routes into and out of eastern Europe quickened in the first half of the thirteenth century, although routes through the Balkans diminished after the Latin conquest of Constantinople in 1204. Traditional products, such as furs, amber, and honey were supplemented by the growing demand for bulk resources, particularly timber and grain. Timber, shipped as logs or as partially manufactured boards, made up for the increasingly depleted forests of western Europe, while grain shipments through the Baltic fed areas of western Europe that were no longer self-sufficient. In exchange, salt, cloth, and metal goods flowed east. Silver mines in Bohemia and later in Silesia created economic wealth, and cities such as Prague, Cracow, Gdańsk, eastern German cities such as Lübeck and Hamburg, and Kiev in Rus (until the Mongol conquest) grew in wealth and population. After the Mongol invasions, trade out of eastern Europe shifted course, flowing through Caffa and other Black Sea ports in the south and through Novgorod and Moscow in the north. Commerce that had traditionally gone through Kiev and into eastern Hungary virtually ceased.

Over the centuries, southeastern Europe had been subject to attack from nomadic tribes, such as the Huns, Avars, and Magyars, crossing the steppes. In the first half of the thirteenth century, the Mongols threatened Europe. Sweeping into Rus in the 1230s and eastern Europe in 1240/41, they devastated towns, wiped out whole populations and positioned themselves to advance into western Europe.

The Mongols initially succeeded due to the leadership of Chingis Khan (1162?–1227). Chingis, in line to be chief of his subclan, spent his childhood in the wild with his mother and siblings, constantly threatened by rivals. This difficult survival honed his leadership skills, and he emerged from the wilderness to defeat his enemies, confederate the Mongol tribes, begin the conquest of China, overrun central Asia, eastern Iran, and the Rus steppes, and create a Turkic-Mongol Empire with palaces in China and pastures for horses on the Hungarian plain.

Chingis led a huge, efficiently organized army (100,000 to 200,000 men). He had a mobile cavalry rigorously equipped for traveling, and a corps of engineers that excelled at siegecraft. He also surrounded himself with advisors of genius—men who knew how to keep lines of communication open, to plan military strategy, and to administer conquered territories. He was systematic and cold-blooded in his battles. He, his followers, and successors were driven by a belief that they had been charged with a divine mission of world conquest. The peoples they encountered in this mission had two choices—submit or be destroyed. When insulted (if envoys were abused or if a Mongol leader was killed) or defied, he was willing to wipe out whole populations. Each Mongol soldier was required to bring back an ear from every victim, to be counted by the bagful, and scarcely anyone escaped a Mongol massacre. As a result, Chingis created a psychology of terror that aided his drive westward.

The Europeans most severely affected by the Mongol invasion were the Rus. In the winter of 1237/38, the Mongols, led by Batu, the grandson of Chingis, and Sübödai, one of the great Mongol generals, attacked, destroying nearly every major city. The city of Kiev, with a population of perhaps 30,000, fell in 1240. Only Novgorod, in the northwest, remained untouched, saved by spring thaws that hampered the movement of Mongol cavalry.

Archbishop John of Plano Carpini, passing through Kiev, reported that "we came across countless skulls and bones of dead men lying about on the ground. Kiev had been a very large and thickly populated town, but now it has been reduced almost to nothing . . . scarce two hundred houses there and the inhabitants are kept in complete slavery."[9] For the next 250 years, however, the Mongols mostly stayed at some distance, mainly exacting tribute. They tolerated Orthodox Christianity and did not impose their laws, language, or institutions. Still, great damage had been done, and some of the more despotic characteristics of later Russian history (autocratic rule, the seclusion of women, and the regimentation of social classes) may have been partly the result of Mongol influence (although Byzantine influence as well as internal pressures can also explain these developments).

For the most part the northeastern Rus princes, including Alexander Nevsky (1219–1263), prince of Novgorod, reached an accommodation with the Mongols, submitting to their authority and thereby preserving what was left of Kievan Rus. This accommodation with the Mongols allowed the Rus led by Alexander Nevsky to defend their territories successfully from the Swedes (twenty-six battles), the Teutonic knights (eleven battles), the Lithuanians (fourteen battles) and the Norwegians (five battles). Alexander won a famous battle on frozen Lake Chud in Estonia against the Teutonic knights* and was subsequently canonized by the Russian Orthodox Church. Although Novgorod survived, it was the princes of Moscow, who provided armed guards for the Mongols and collected the Mongol tribute, who particularly benefited and were able to expand their cities and extend their power.

After the fall of Kiev, the Mongols turned against Poland and southern Hungary in a brilliant pincer movement that made it impossible for the defending armies to know where to place their defenses. With little resistance, Cracow was burned

---

* This epic battle is depicted by Sergei Eisenstein in his film *Aleksandr Nevskii,* produced in Russia in the Soviet period.

and Hungary overrun. The Hungarian army was completely destroyed, thousands were captured, villages were deserted, and an estimated twenty to fifty percent of the population died. When another European army confronted the Mongols in 1241 at Liegnitz, it was destroyed. The Mongols were poised to reach the Adriatic and to strike at the heart of Europe, and it is questionable that the European powers could have stopped them. Fortuitously, Chingis Khan's son and successor, Great Khan Ogodai, died in 1241, and the Mongol army in the west was withdrawn until the succession crisis was over. The Mongols returned to harass eastern Europe, but the large campaigns that followed were directed toward Islam, resulting in the destruction of Baghdad in 1258, the overthrow of the Abbasid caliphate,* and the subjugation of the Seljuk Turks.

Although Europeans expressed mostly fear and revulsion in the face of what they perceived as a barbaric, cruel, and treacherous people, there were reasons for being more positive. By the second half of the thirteenth century (after the election of Mönke, grandson of Chingis, as Great Khan), the Mongol Empire became a marvel of efficient administration. It promoted trade and enforced peace, allowing for the passage of great wealth east and west and enriching Italian merchants in particular. Moreover, envoys from the papacy, King Louis IX, and Emperor Frederick II sought alliances with the Mongols against the Muslims, and the possibility, sometimes viewed as a probability, was entertained that the pagan Mongols would convert to Christianity. As a result, individual friars were sent as negotiators and missionaries. Two of them, John of Plano Carpino and William Rubruck, wrote reports. Neither one was optimistic about the possibility of a Mongol conversion, although they both noted the presence of Christians in the Mongol court. These Christians were not orthodox from Rome's point of view; they were Nestorian Christians whose communities were scattered throughout the Orient, and they were often jealous of their positions and worked to undermine western Christians.

Later in the century Marco Polo reported that the Mongol ruler Kublai Khan

> . . . sent for all the Christians and desired them to bring him the book containing the four Gospels. After treating the book to repeated applications of incense with great ceremony, he kissed it devoutly and desired all his barons and lords there present to do the same. . . . Being asked why he did so, he replied: "There are four prophets who are worshipped and to whom all the world does reverence. The Christians say that their God was Jesus Christ, the Saracens Mahomet, the Jews Moses, and the idolaters Sakyamuni Burkhan. . . . And I do honour and reverence to all four, so that I may be sure of doing it to him who is greatest in heaven and truest.[10]

Marco Polo, however, concluded that the khan favored Christianity and suggested that if Catholic preachers had been sent to the khan he would have become a Christian. In the end, the West failed to send the requisite clergy and did not ally with the Mongols when they descended upon Syria and Palestine against the Muslims. In the early fourteenth century, the Mongols of Central Asia converted to Islam.

---

* Surviving members of the caliphal family fled to Egypt where a reconstituted caliphate was established under the Mamluks.

It is interesting to speculate what might have happened if the West had strengthened its position in the eastern Mediterranean in alliance with the Mongols, or if the papacy had responded to Kubilai Khan's request, relayed by Marco Polo, for 100 Christian missionaries. Instead, the West neither allied with nor defeated the Mongols; they did not convert them or mount a crusade against them. The weak response on the part of the Church, in addition to the failure of the crusades, and the ongoing struggle between church and state worked at cross-purposes to the more exalted papal claims to power.

WEALTH, THE APPEAL OF POVERTY, AND RESPONSES TO HERESY

Papal power, which was severely tested in the thirteenth century by the emperor, the failing crusades, and the intrusion of pagan Mongols into Christendom, rested not only on legal claims, religious authority, administrative reach, and political ploys but also on economic wealth. By the beginning of the thirteenth century, in part because of its involvement in financing the crusades and in part because of its growing ties to Italian bankers, the papacy had developed the most sophisticated financial network in Europe. The great wealth of the Church in Rome was now nearly proverbial, as the following acrostic suggests:

*R*adix
*O*mnium
*M*alorum
*A*varitia or "ROMA: Avarice is the root of all evil."

Ecclesiastical groups outside Rome also flourished in this economy. Cistercian monasteries, in particular, originally committed to an evangelical poverty, became the beneficiaries of growing demand for their products. One example suffices. In the early twelfth century, Les Dunes in Flanders was a small hermitage on a desolate sand dune twenty-five miles west of Bruges. By 1138, the small house associated itself with the Cistercians and recruitment skyrocketed. Simultaneously, the economic center of Flanders shifted to Bruges. By about 1250, the monastery had 120 monks, 248 *conversi* who made up a skilled labor force of weavers, fullers, tanners, skinners and shoemakers, and a fleet of ships. At the end of the thirteenth century, Les Dunes held 25,000 acres, and it was a contemporary jest that the sand dunes had become a mound of silver.[11]

The Pursuit of Poverty: Waldensians, Joachimites, and Friars

In the face of such wealth, thirteenth-century writers thought that avarice, rather than pride, had now become the worst of the seven deadly sins. Stories of saints who lived lives of heroic poverty became increasingly popular. One of the more popular was that of St. Alexis. The son of wealthy Roman parents, he supposedly left home on his wedding day and moved to the Holy Land as a beggar. Returning, he spent the last seventeen years of his life as a beggar, unrecognized, under the staircase of his father's house.

In the 1170s, Peter Waldo, a wealthy merchant-usurer from Lyons, heard the story of St. Alexis preached by a street performer. It so affected him that he decided to follow the scriptural dictum: "Go sell what thou hast and give to the poor and thou shalt have treasure in heaven." He began to preach a message of poverty and organized a following, called the Poor Men of Lyons (or Waldensians, followers of Peter Waldo), who preached and practiced poverty. Simultaneously, Joachim, abbot of the Cistercian abbey of Fiore in Calabria, wrote powerful criticisms of the spiritual delinquency of the age. His reforms at Fiore stressed poverty, and his prophetic voice envisioned an apocalyptic third age of the Holy Spirit, following the ages of the Father and of the Son, when peace, love, liberty, ideal monasticism, and apostolic poverty would prevail. By the 1180s, Peter Waldo and his followers were declared heretical for disobeying papal injunctions against preaching. Although Joachim's experiment at Fiore was praised, one of his treatises (although not his person) was declared heretical at the Fourth Lateran Council.

In the second decade of the thirteenth century, however, Pope Innocent III lent papal support to two new orders, the Franciscan and Dominican friars,* both of which were committed to apostolic poverty. Like the Waldensians, they were also committed to preaching.

The first to be founded was the Franciscan Order (also called the Order of Friars Minor). Francis, son of a wealthy merchant of Assisi, underwent a spiritual crisis in his twenties, at which point he gave up his ideal of becoming a knight and repudiated his father's desire for him to work as a cloth merchant. Instead Francis began to exhibit strange behaviors. Meeting a leper in the road, he got off his horse, kissed the leper, and gave him money. He began to give his clothing away and to distribute alms to beggars. Praying before a cross in the church of San Damiano, Francis heard a voice say three times: "Francis, go and repair my house, which, as you see, is falling completely into ruin."[12] Francis, who was not highly educated and tended to be very literal in his approach to spiritual matters, quickly began to repair the church of San Damiano, offering for this task his father's goods. In a dramatic scene in the middle of Assisi, Francis's father denounced his son who, in response, took off his clothes and handed them to his father. The bishop of Assisi wrapped Francis, now naked, in his cloak, symbolically taking him into the folds of the Church. Francis quickly began to gather followers who were impressed with the austerities of his life as well as with the charismatic message he preached. By 1209/10, Francis had written up a simple rule; that same year Pope Innocent III confirmed the order and the rule.

The early lives of St. Francis are filled with legends such as his preaching to the birds or taming the wolf of Gubbio. These stories testify to Francis's aversion to money. In one story, he reprimands a brother for desiring to pick up a sack of

---

* Derived from *frere* and *frater*, meaning "brother"; St. Francis preferred that members of his order be called "little brothers" or *fraticelli*.

An Early Portrait of St. Francis of Assisi   This famous portrait of St. Francis was done by Cimabue (c. 1240–c. 1302). It is part of a larger composition of the Madonna enthroned with Child and with Angels that is in the lower church of the basilica of St. Francesco in Assisi. Possibly painted about 1278/80, it was repainted in the nineteenth century. The image shows Francis with the wounds of the stigmata on his hands. This "portrait" is perhaps as close as we can come to what Francis may have looked like. Many of the greatest artists of the turn of the fourteenth century painted cycles of murals relating to the life of St. Francis.
St. Francesco, Assisi, Italy/Art Resource, NY.

money, at which point the money turns into a snake. In another story, to punish a brother who had picked up a coin, Francis has him put it between his teeth and deposit it on a dung heap. In the surviving rules for the Franciscan order from 1221 and 1223, the brethren were strictly forbidden to touch coins. Nor were they allowed buildings, clothing (beyond the bare necessities), or even books (beyond those needed for liturgical purposes). They were to take no heed for the morrow, begging or working for their food on a daily basis and saving nothing for the following day. For this reason, they were called mendicants or beggars.

This severe, even revolutionary commitment to poverty attracted an enormous following. Between 1210 and 1217, sufficient recruits were made that the order divided into eleven provinces (six in Italy, two in France, one each in Germany, Spain, and the eastern Mediterranean). By 1300, there were 1,400 convents throughout Christendom. The Franciscans also attracted female converts who became the Order of Poor Clares, and Francis created a tertiary order for laymen and women who did not want to become friars but were committed to a life of peace (not bearing arms), simplicity (two meals a day; not attending games or spectacles; fasting, praying, and practicing charity), and liturgical practice (hearing mass frequently, attending funerals, etc.) (see Medieval Voices).

Brother Masseo, one of Francis' earliest disciples, is quoted as asking Francis: "Why you? Why you? Why you? Why does everyone run after you and seem to long to see you, and hear you, and obey you? You aren't handsome to look at, and

MEDIEVAL VOICES

A Monastic
Rule Written
by St. Clare
of Assisi,
1195–1253

Clare, canonized by the Church in 1255, heard Francis of Assisi preach when she was about fifteen years of age. In 1212, she committed herself to a life of poverty under the guidance of Francis and his friars. She and her followers, who became the Poor Ladies of Assisi, practiced an enclosed, monastic form of life following the Benedictine rule. Clare spent the rest of her life directing her nuns, often from the sick bed, and fighting to gain papal approval of a rule she wrote for her followers that guaranteed commitment to the highest poverty. In 1252, Pope Innocent IV confirmed Clare's rule with its emphasis on poverty, seclusion, silence, simplicity, manual labor, and obedience. The following selection is from Chapter VI of the Rule of Saint Clare:

Not Having Possessions. 1. After the Most High Celestial Father saw fit to enlighten my heart by His grace to do penance according to the example and teaching of our most blessed Father Saint Francis, shortly after his own conversion, I, together with my sisters, voluntarily promised him obedience. 2. When the Blessed Father saw that we had no fear of poverty, hard work, suffering, shame, or the contempt of the world, but that, instead, we regarded such things as great delights, moved by compassion he wrote for us a form of life as follows: "Since by divine inspiration you have made yourselves daughters and servants of the most high King, the heavenly Father, and have taken the Holy Spirit as your spouse, choosing to live according to the perfection of the holy Gospel, I resolve and promise for myself and for my brothers always to have that same loving care and special solicitude for you as [I have] for them." 3. And that we might never turn aside from the most holy poverty we had embraced [nor those, either, who would come after us], shortly after his death he wrote his last will for us once more, saying: "I, brother Francis, the little one, wish to follow the life and poverty of our most high Lord Jesus Christ and of His most holy mother and to persevere in this until the end; and I ask and counsel you, my ladies, to live always in this most holy life and in poverty. And keep most careful watch that you never depart from this by reason of the teaching or advice of anyone." 4. And just as I, together with my sisters, have been ever solicitous to safeguard the holy poverty which we have promised the Lord God and the Blessed Francis, so, too, the Abbesses who shall succeed me in office and all the sisters are bound to observe it inviolably to the end: 5. that is to say, they are not to receive or hold onto any possessions or property [acquired] through an intermediary, or even anything that might reasonably be called property, 6. except as much land as necessity requires for the integrity and the proper seclusion of the monastery; and this land is not to be cultivated except as a garden for the needs of the sisters.

Source: "A Monastic Rule written by St. Clare of Assisi," from *Francis and Clare: The Complete Works,* trans. Regis J. Armstrong and Ignatius C. Brady (New York: Paulist Press, 1982) 218–219. Reprinted by permission of Paulist Press. www.paulistpress.com.

you don't know very much, and you aren't noble; so how does it happen that everyone runs after you?" Francis answered, "Because I am so base, God chose me as his instrument."[13] But historians would answer this question differently and at much greater length.

St. Francis certainly had an intense, charismatic personality. His asceticism was extreme, but it was combined with an intense love of all God's creation. His commitment to poverty was severe, but mixed with great tenderness. Above all, he saw the world as a manifestation of Christ, and he lived his life as an imitation of Christ. He loved trees because of the cross. He loved light because Christ was the light of the world. He experienced the stigmata* (in 1224 at La Verna) identifying with Christ's passion. This devotion to Christ, this *imitatio Christi,* had an epic quality about it that appealed to all Europe.

Francis lived the life he preached, and his integrity was palpable. His days consisted of fasting, constant prayer and bodily mortification, public confession, abasement, and total abhorrence of money. He distanced himself from all women, even those who sought to become Franciscans, by placing them in a separate, highly cloistered order. He did not concern himself with doctrinal issues and eschewed intellectual pursuits (his own Latin was rudimentary, and he wrote very little). In his preaching he told stories and used himself as an exemplum.

Francis had a genius for promoting popular piety. The creche scene (a living reenactment of the scene at Bethlehem stable), which he initiated at Greccio in the winter of 1223, gained immediate popularity. His preferred benediction, "The Lord give you peace," and his emblem signifying the Lamb of God were to become regular features of modern Catholicism. His preaching (and that of his followers) worked to transform crusading ideals and the program of the *militia Christi* into something more humane—a life of renunciation and peace at home and of missionary fervor abroad. Francis tried several times to go to the Holy Land and preach; he succeeded in 1219, traveling to Syria and to Egypt where he preached to the sultan. His followers were soon to have missions in China, India, and Southeast Asia as well as in Islamic lands.

The intensity of Francis' commitment to poverty was balanced by his obedience to the Church. He was fortunate in his patrons—the bishops of Assisi and of Ostia—the latter the head of the college of cardinals, an intimate advisor to popes, and then pope himself. Francis's respect for the clergy was enormous. In his humility, he refused to take orders beyond that of deacon, and in his rule insisted that friars subordinate themselves to the humblest parish priest. Above all, however, Francis succeeded because Innocent III could see the need for an orthodox order committed to poverty and preaching. The papacy used the Franciscan order as an instrument for reaching out to those areas of Europe, particularly southern France and northern Italy, populated by growing numbers of heretics and those disillusioned by the power and wealth of a Church that no longer seemed to mirror New Testament ideals.

---

* These are marks that sometimes bleed that resemble the wounds of Jesus Christ on the cross. St. Francis is the first clearly documented case of an individual with these marks. There are currently some seventy known cases of this phenomenon.

The Dominican order of friars, founded a few years later by St. Dominic de Guzman, from its beginning was more clearly intended as a preaching order against heretics. Dominic had the support of Spanish clergy as well as the bishop of Toulouse and the cardinal-bishop of Ostia. From the outset the Dominicans emphasized the need for theological training. Unlike the Franciscan rule, which was original, the Dominicans (called the Order of Preachers) took the rule of Augustinian canons. The character of the Dominican order was more institutionalized, with a system of elections and a hierarchy of committees concluding with a general chapter that met once every three years. Every Dominican friar had a voice in the election of those who represented him and was then bound by the decisions of his representatives. This electoral form was built upon the system of general chapters used by the Cistercians and required by the Fourth Lateran Council. According to Rosalind Brooke, in the hands of the Dominicans it was, "the most mature constitutional system known in the thirteenth century."[14] It became a model for evolving constitutionalism in the Italian city-states as well as for the emerging representative institutions in the European kingdoms.

The active preaching and begging of the friars and their lack of a cloistered life or of any significant temporal holdings differentiated them sharply from previous monastic orders, while their commitment to missionary activity and to peace separated them from the military orders. But their effective organization, which was European-wide, made them ideal candidates for spearheading inquisitorial proceedings against heretics.

Heresy and the Development of an Inquisitorial Process

By the end of the twelfth century, two heresies were spreading throughout much of Europe. The followers of Peter Waldo had created a separate church that emphasized popular preaching, use of vernacular scripture, and repudiation of the institutional Catholic Church. And the Cathars, first noticed in the Rhineland area, had spread from Spain to Bosnia and were particularly numerous in southern France, northern Italy, and southern Germany. The Cathars had their own writings, simple liturgies and ceremonies, and bishops and missionaries. The sect was organized into those who were hearers (or sympathizers), those baptized into the religion (the believers), and those who adhered to all the demands of a radically ascetic and antimaterialistic religion (the *perfecti* or elect, who were also the ministers and teachers). Both Cathars and Waldensians rejected the sacraments and discipline of the Catholic Church, but, while the Waldensians adhered to scripture, the Cathars rejected the Old Testament (as the creation of an evil god), the human Christ and therefore the incarnation, the virgin birth, and the resurrection. Not only were the Cathars more organized and widespread than previous heretical groups, they were more radical in their rejection of Catholicism.

Reactions to these doctrines were disparate. Locally, mob justice or fanatic pursuit by self-designated heretic hunters might result in the death of presumed heretics. Secular authorities legislated against heretics. Peter of Aragon banished all heretics under threat of death at the stake. Emperor Frederick II penalized them with banishment, confiscation of property, and death. But it was the reaction of the

Church that people now remember and associate, in a peculiarly powerful way, with the Middle Ages.

The thirteenth-century use by the Church of an inquisitorial process was preceded by the revival of Roman law, which, from the fourth century on, had condemned heretics and provided a wide range of harsh penalties, especially confiscation of property. It was also preceded between the eleventh and thirteenth centuries by a rich theological and ecclesiastical literature that discussed and defined heresy. Over this same time period, a new legal procedure evolved, known as *inquisitio.* This allowed cases to be brought into court, not as a result of an accusation (an action by a plaintiff), but as a result of an official judicial inquiry. In 1229, for example, Louis IX of France ordered all royal officials to search for heretics. Similarly, a papal bull of 1184 and the Fourth Lateran Council of 1215 commanded bishops to seek out heretics in their jurisdictions.

In a papal bull of 1231, Pope Gregory IX gave official permission to the Dominican friars to ferret out heresy. The penalties they could impose included death, although they had to turn heretics over to the secular power for execution. The court-initiated inquisitorial proceedings became more formal under Innocent IV. The Dominicans, and later the Franciscans, were asked to administer them in conjunction with the local bishop.

The friars were considered suitable for this task because they answered to the papacy alone. They could also provide skilled theologians who could, as Pope Gregory IX put it, confound the deceits of the heretics. For reasons of protection, the names of witnesses were concealed from suspected heretics, and trials were secret. Since it was illegal to aid heretics, no lawyers could be found to defend them. Since partial proofs of guilt were insufficient in capital crimes, a confession was desirable and torture justifiable when other forms of full proof failed. Although the number of heretics killed in medieval Europe is not large by modern standards (between 1,000 and 2,000), the number of people who lost their goods or their reputations was much higher. And the inquisitors, who kept extensive records over time and place, could cast a shadow of doubt over the orthodoxy of families for generations. Despite the relative efficiency of inquisitorial investigations, however, heretical communities continued to hang on in the mountains between Spain and France, the hill towns of northern Italy, Alpine communities, and in parts of eastern Europe.

Summary

The thirteenth century saw dramatic differences in its leaders, particularly evident in the dominant personalities—Pope Innocent III as an authoritative leader of the Church; St. Francis of Assisi and his radical commitment to poverty; Emperor Frederick II as an excommunicate ruler and reluctant crusader; and Louis IX of France as a saintly, crusading king. In addition, the histories of Europe's kingdoms were so varied that it is difficult to distinguish a trend. France and England, and to a lesser extent Spain, grew in organizational effectiveness, while the German Empire did not. Sicily, a model of centralized government under Frederick II, was in decline by the end of the century. French royal power grew at the expense of the English and the Provençals, but the thirteenth-century struggle was but a prelude to the wars between England and France that followed. The expansion and unification of Christendom under papal auspices that Innocent III sought at the beginning of the thirteenth century produced contrasting results. The Christian powers of eastern Europe were battered by succession crises, the growing power of the nobility, and Mongol invaders. The ongoing Christian conquest of Spain was balanced by crusading defeats in the eastern Mediterranean. The definitive defeat of the Hohenstaufen emperors did not guarantee the success of papal monarchy, and it left a legacy of destruction for Italy. Autocratic politics contrasted with constitutional developments, first in the Church (with its ecumenical councils and its practice of representative government within monastic and mendicant orders) and later in the secular political sphere, resulting in, for example, the Magna Carta and an English Parliament. Ecclesiastical wealth and temporal politics sat uneasily beside a desire for apostolic poverty that expressed itself in both heterodox and orthodox ways. In the midst of expanding Christian missions, there were heretical challenges at home, a pagan Mongol presence in the East, and a pagan Lithuanian Empire in the northeast. This dynamic context, with its successes and disappointments, stimulated the intellectual and cultural life of Europe, however, as literate and illiterate alike came in contact with a wider, more complex world.

NOTES

1. Helene Tillmann, *Pope Innocent III* (Amsterdam: North Holland Publishing, 1980) 21.
2. Tillmann, 266.
3. Karl Hampe, *Germany under the Salian and Hohenstaufen Emperors,* trans. R. Bennett (Totowa, N. J.: Rowman & Littlefield, 1973) 236.
4. Matthew Paris. *Chronica Majora* (Cambridge University, Corpus Christi College ms 16) f. 245r.
5. David Abulafia, *Frederick II: A Medieval Emperor* (New York: Oxford University Press, 1988) 186.
6. John W. Baldwin, *The Government of Philip Augustus,* ch. 1 (Berkeley: University of California Press, 1986).
7. Michael Clanchy, *England and its Rulers 1066–1272* (Totowa, N. J.: Barnes and Noble, 1983) 280.
8. Clanchy, 246–247.
9. *Mission to Asia,* ed. Chrisopher Dawson (New York: Harper & Row, 1955) 29–30.
10. *The Travels of Marco Polo,* trans. Ronald Latham (New York: Penguin, 1959) 119.
11. The story of Les Dunes is told by R.W. Southern, *Western Society and the Church in the Middle Ages* (Harmondsworth, Eng.: Penguin, 1970) 265–269.
12. Thomas of Celano, "The Second Life of St. Francis," *St. Francis of Assisi. Writings and Early Biographies,* ed. Marion A. Habig (Chicago: Franciscan Herald Press, 1972) 370.
13. "The Little Flowers of St. Francis," *St. Francis of Assisi. Writings and Early Biographies,* 1322–1323.
14. Rosalind Brooke, *The Coming of the Friars* (London: George Allen and Unwin, 1975) 98.

~

CHAPTER 17

High Culture and Popular Culture in the Thirteenth Century

Although Europe lost its foothold in the Holy Land, and much of Rusland was under Mongol domination, the thirteenth century was nonetheless a century of European expansion. Christian forces took the islands of the western Mediterranean and most of the Spanish peninsula; Italian, Catalan, and Spanish merchants controlled more Mediterranean routes than had been the case for western Europeans since late Roman times. The Venetians occupied ports and islands in the eastern Mediterranean, while the Genoese moved into the Black Sea. With the twelfth-century invention of the compass, sea-routes along the Atlantic coast opened up. Trade was ongoing through the Baltic Sea and with Iceland and annual contacts with Greenland developed. The first documented expedition attempting to cross the Atlantic since Viking times occurred in 1291 when two brothers from Genoa sailed west towards India. (They did not return.) Mongol control of the east European steppes, central Asia, and much of China allowed missionaries and merchants, like Marco Polo, to venture east to China, south Asia, and southeast Asia.

As new wealth flowed into Europe, towns grew in population and in their ability to dispose of and consume goods. Aristocratic and royal courts became centers for culture and patronage. New wealth poured into the Church, some of which was used in the program of building cathedrals. An intellectual expansiveness accompanied the geographical widening of horizons and growing material well-being, as western thinkers came into contact with the entire corpus of Aristotle's surviving works and with Arabic science, medicine, and natural philosophy.* In addition, a lively cultural milieu developed with a rich vernacular literature, a reawakened interest in drama, art, and architecture, and a vigorous popular culture. The increasingly self-conscious and aggressive Christianity of the thirteenth century, however, also promoted intolerance toward non-Catholic cultures.

* We use the term "Arabic" rather than "Islamic" advisedly. Although Muslim Arabic writers on science considered that their learning came from God, and they were all steeped in the Qur'an, no such thing as an Islamic science exists. And some Arabic scholars were Christian. Also, "Arabic" science included much that came from Chaldea, the Greeks, Persia, India, and Egypt and was not, strictly speaking, either Arabic or Islamic.

ENCOUNTERS WITH "THE OTHER"

There was a gulf between the East and the Latin West in the thirteenth century, and that gulf was nowhere so apparent as in relations between Byzantium and the West. Although pockets of cross-cultural exchanges existed in Sicily and in Hungary (where Greek communities settled), and although the Venetians considered Byzantium their commercial backyard, the prejudice of Latins against Greeks was pronounced, as was the distaste of Byzantines for the Latins. Volatile feelings produced violence—Greek arrests and massacres of Latins in 1171 and 1182, the Norman sack of Thessalonica in 1185, and the conquest of Constantinople by Latins in the Fourth Crusade. Culturally, little borrowing and less understanding took place. While Byzantine scholars pursued studies of classical Greek philosophy and literature (Plato and Homer in particular), western thinkers had no Homeric texts and only partial access to Plato, since Greek was not understood by most Latin scholars. On the other hand, learned Greeks had a limited grasp of Latin culture. Contacts with Byzantium were mainly mercantile and diplomatic, except during the period of Latin rule (1204–1261), which bred even greater hatred between Latins and Greeks.

In the wake of the 1204 conquest of Constantinople, the count of Flanders became emperor in Constantinople. The Roman Church insisted upon Greek obedience to the pope, although it did not force changes in the Greek rites. The pope also took Byzantine monasteries under his special protection. Nonetheless, few Greek Orthodox prelates were willing to take the oath of submission; most went into exile. This made it easier for the Latin conquerors to expropriate church properties. As a result, Greek hatred of the West deepened to such an extent that one historian argues that the expulsion of the Latins in 1261 is the beginning of the Greek nation. When the Byzantine Emperor, Michael VIII (Paleologus), agreed at the Council of Lyons in 1274 to renewed Roman domination of the Greek Church in return for aid against the Turks, Byzantium reacted so negatively that the agreement was retracted. In the end, the Greek people seemed to prefer Turkish to Roman rulers, and the West, which wanted allies against Islam, never overcame its suspicions sufficiently to ally successfully with the Greeks.

As described in Chapter 16, the Mongols were potential allies. But western views of the Mongols were a confusion of negative and hopeful images. Writers reported that the Mongols were the precursors to Antichrist, or that they came from the land of Gog and Magog mentioned in the biblical Book of the Apocalypse. Others saw them as deliverers sent by God (see Medieval Portraits).

Although numerous thirteenth-century texts described the Mongols, none is more famous than that of Marco Polo. Written about 1298 when he was in a Genoese prison, Marco shared his notes and dictated his story to a fellow prisoner, a romance writer named Rustichello of Pisa. Although the account is mixed with a dash of romance and epic battle descriptions, in the main it is a sober account of one man's twenty-year journey through central Asia, China, around southeast China, through southern India, and into the Persian Gulf. Marco traveled with the eye of an administrator trusted by the khan and with the acumen of a merchant-seaman interested in locating commercial sources of goods. Marco's attitude toward the

---

MEDIEVAL PORTRAITS

The Search for Prester John

In the 1140s, Europeans heard rumors of a Christian kingdom in the Orient. Bishop Otto of Freising wrote that "[the] Bishop of Gabul from Syria . . . said that a few years ago a certain John, king and priest of the people living beyond the Persians and Armenians in the extreme Orient, professing Christianity, though of the Nestorian persuasion, marched in war against the . . . kings of the Medes and the Persians, and conquered their capital. . . ." A bit later a letter in Arabic allegedly from Prester John, written to the Byzantine emperor, appeared in which he detailed his kingdom of the "Three Indies," describing unlimited wealth, magical mirrors that made one invisible, exotic animals, and men with eyes in front and back. As a result, the pope sent three emissaries to Prester John, although they did not know quite where to go.

Legends usually have some historical basis, and the origin of the Prester John legend probably comes from the fact that several tribes of Turks and Mongols in the eastern steppes of Asia converted to Nestorian Christianity in the eleventh century. Even some western Mongol tribes and the Khitan rulers of China were influenced by Nestorianism. When the northern Khitan Empire in China fell, one of the rulers, Ye-lu Dashi, led a united army of tribes into Persia, defeating the Seljuks in 1141 and finally settling in Turkestan. Although Ye-lu Dashi was not himself Christian, he was surrounded by Christians and may have been the origin of the Prester John legend.

Europeans looked long and hard for Prester John's kingdom, convinced for some time that the Mongols were associated with it, sometimes imagining that it was in China or perhaps India. By the time the Portuguese began to explore the west African coast in the fifteenth century, one of their goals was to find the kingdom of Prester John in that continent, and they thought they had found it in Ethiopia. For centuries the hope lived that Prester John's kingdom, with its wealth and magic, would join with the West to push back Islam and reconquer the Holy Land.

Mongols was tolerant and full of admiration.* He was also tolerant of "idolaters," primarily Buddhists and Hindus, praising their austerity and humaneness, their monks and their yogis. He mentions Nestorian Christians without much concern for doctrinal differences. He was, however, prejudiced against Muslims. His *Description of the World* details, with obvious pleasure, the overthrow of the caliph in Baghdad in 1258 by the Mongol army. He describes Muslims as wicked, treacherous, and sinful, "dogs" not fit to lord it over Christians. As for Islamic doctrine, he reports that "the accursed doctrine of the Saracens [is that] every sin is accounted a lawful act even to the killing of any man who is not of their creed."[1] Marco Polo's account

---

* He mentions, for example, the Mongol manufacture of powdered milk when on campaigns; he describes in great detail and with much admiration their establishment of a pony express system of communication and their use of paper money.

was widely read, translated into many languages, and well thumbed by Columbus, who set out to find the lands Marco Polo described. Although Marco Polo may have opened men's eyes to the East, his description of Muslims fed western prejudices.

The characteristic thirteenth-century European view was anti-Islamic, and one of the more interesting questions is why attitudes toward Islam were so harsh. Prior to the Crusades, views of Islam did not differentiate Muslims significantly from pagans. In the epics, especially those associated with Charlemagne, Muslims were described as idolaters and Muhammad as a magician. While this may have been the popular view, more learned commentators and attentive western travelers knew better by the thirteenth century. Westerners now had access to two Latin translations of the Qur'an; they could read biographies of Muhammad translated from Arabic sources; and they understood that Muslims revered Jesus and Mary as well as the Old Testament prophets, although they denied the Trinity, the Incarnation, and the use of religious images. They knew that Muslims insisted on God's oneness; that Muhammad had successfully fought paganism and given Islam a developed theology of the afterlife; and that Muhammad was a prophet but not divine.

Nonetheless, many (although not all) Christian treatments of Islam presented damning, distorted information. The most obvious line of attack was Muhammad himself, who was variously portrayed as lascivious, ambitious, money-grubbing, political, and ready to war or rob. Christians seem to have assumed that by attacking Muhammad's character they would discredit his revelations. They also argued that his revelations met his personal needs, that he tricked people into believing them, and that he died an unnatural death. None of these arguments would convince Muslims (and some would outrage them), so it is difficult to know what audience, other than Christians, the writers had in mind.

Travelers in the Middle East were often impressed with the kindness, generosity, strict adherence to religious duties, and honesty of Muslims, while they were offended by the call to prayer, the Muslim acceptance of several wives, and Muslim rejection of asceticism and celibacy (except during Ramadan). It was confusing for Christians, because many Islamic practices and beliefs seemed close to Christianity, and yet Muslims were unbaptized. Many believed that an apostate or heretical Christian monk had originally taught Muhammad and that Muslims were therefore Christian heretics or schismatics. It was galling that Islam had somehow achieved territorial and religious control over formerly Christian areas such as Syria, Egypt, North Africa, and by the end of the thirteenth century, the Holy Land once more.

The Church discouraged Muslim-Christian interactions within Europe. Canon law required Muslims living within Christian territories to wear distinctive clothing; no Christians could be their servants, nor could Christians eat with them. They could not serve in public office nor engage in trade with fellow Muslims outside Christendom. These intolerant attitudes contrast with the toleration western intellectuals extended to Arabic writings rapidly being disseminated throughout Europe.

Like Muslims, the position of Jews in twelfth and thirteenth century Europe was precarious. Jews had been marginalized in earlier centuries, but, with some exceptions, they were generally not endangered. Their role as merchants in a less-developed era made them economically valuable. Especially during Carolingian times, some Jewish families maintained estates and led fairly secure professional and personal lives.

By the twelfth and thirteenth centuries, Jewish communities in the Rhineland and in France were developing sophisticated intellectual, scholarly communities. They gained access to legal texts, rabbinical commentaries, and biblical exegetical works from centers of Judaic studies in the Middle East and in Spain. But, as they mastered Talmudic sources, produced commentaries and glosses, and developed their own dialectical methodology, they were simultaneously pushed to the economic margins. As Christian Europe gained in wealth and Christian merchants and bankers increased in numbers, Jewish merchants became dispensable. This, combined with increasingly harsh ecclesiastical strictures against Jews, made it more difficult for Jewish families to earn a living.

We have already seen the extent to which Jewish communities suffered during the First Crusade (see Chapter 12). The vulnerability of the Jewish populations of Europe became especially apparent in 1182 when Philip II of France expelled them from the royal domain, particularly Paris. Although they were allowed to return in subsequent years, the French king and nobility allowed occasional massacres of Jews in their lands. Massacres of English Jewish communities also occurred, particularly one in the city of York in 1190. In both kingdoms, Jews were taxed at the will of the ruler; they were shunted away from agriculture, crafts, and mercantile activities, and forced to act as moneylenders and pawnbrokers. The Third Lateran Council (1179) curbed Jewish economic autonomy and limited Jewish interactions with Christians. The Fourth Lateran Council (1215) called for Jews to wear distinguishing clothing and deprived them of public office. Following the Fourth Lateran, papal legates pushed for the introduction of distinctive emblems such as red or yellow circular patches; they were heeded in England and France but only slowly in Spain, Italy, and eastern Europe. Finally, England in 1290 and France in 1306 expelled all Jewish people and forced them to settle elsewhere (in central and eastern Europe, Provence, Navarre, northern Italy, and Spain). Spanish Jewish communities continued to enjoy a relatively secure position, although this changed radically by the fifteenth century. Medieval Poland became a haven for western European Jewry. They were welcomed as part of an overall effort to attract immigration from the West.[2]

As the economic and political position of Jews deteriorated, cultural attitudes dehumanized, and indeed demonized, them. At the intellectual level, the increased reliance on reason to support Christian doctrine led some scholars to conclude that the Jews were unreasonable and unspiritual. At the popular level, a theme developed in the twelfth century that had enormous staying power in European popular culture—the rumored murder of a Christian child by Jews. It was first associated with accusations concerning the death of a young boy, William of Norwich, in England in 1150; soon this legend of Jews murdering innocent children was believed throughout Europe. Even Chaucer, who generally took a tolerant albeit ironic attitude toward the culture of his day, included this anti-Jewish tale when he wrote his *Canterbury Tales* in the 1380s.

The growing hostility toward perceived "outsiders" also affected heretics, usurers, lepers, homosexuals, and finally witches (see Chapter 19). To give just one example, John Boswell has argued that homosexuals began to suffer from the later twelfth to the fourteenth century. This is reflected in thirteenth-century law codes. Except in Germany, and in the Kingdom of Naples under Frederick II, homosexuality was proscribed and the death penalty (by castration, dismemberment, and burning) prescribed. By 1300, homosexual priests could be disbarred and handed over to secular authorities for judgment. In the theological treatises of the time, homosexuality was increasingly defined as a sin against nature.

INTELLECTUAL TRENDS

A transformation took place in the intellectual life of Europe between the twelfth and thirteenth centuries due largely to the recovery of Aristotle's works and the transmission of Arabic philosophical writings and Greek and Arabic scientific writings. The impact of Aristotle's writings was very deep. His *Politics* and *Ethics* opened men's eyes to moral and political theories independent of Christian norms. His scientific writings offered an empirical approach to the natural world that was fundamentally new. The enormous extension of knowledge these texts offered provoked some of the greatest minds of the century to consider how to assimilate them or on what grounds to reject them. Aristotle (and his Arabic commentators) had a great impact on the theological and philosophical minds of the high Middle Ages, particularly on Thomas Aquinas, Bonaventure, and Moses Maimonides. In addition to Aristotle's work, a flood of newly translated Greek and Arabic texts in science and medicine entered Europe. The assimilation of these works laid the groundwork for the breakthrough advances in medicine and science that one normally associates with early modern Europe.

The Recovery of Aristotle

Between 1140 and 1280 all of Aristotle's surviving philosophical, metaphysical, scientific, political, ethical, and poetical works were translated into Latin. Aristotle's works, a vast encyclopedia of ancient knowledge, challenged Christian learning and provided a contrast to its neo-Platonic heritage. Aristotle's focus was on the material world, which he approached in a comprehensive, logical fashion and with an empirical, inductive eye. He described, categorized, and analyzed animals, plants, human anatomy, geology, the physics of sublunar motion, planetary motion, human reasoning, chemical interactions, change and causation, light, vision, and how we know. He denied Plato's world of forms and the idea that men know truth intuitively. Instead, using logic and observation, he first examined the physical world and then derived conclusions about the soul and the spiritual world. Using analogies and extrapolating from causality in the material world, Aristotle postulated the existence of a First Mover as the cause of the universe. This First Mover was unchanging and its impact on the cosmos deterministic. Aristotle considered both Mover and universe to be eternal and necessary. In addition, he considered man's intellect (as opposed to his body) eternal and incorruptible, relating, in a way he did not define, to the Intellect of the First Mover. For Christians, steeped in the biblical story of creation and a world where miracles happened, many of these ideas were unacceptable.

Aristotle's works were difficult to understand. They derive from notes composed for or copied from his lectures and were never polished for publication. Therefore, western intellectuals had recourse to Arabic commentators who made Aristotle more comprehensible. These commentators, however, reinterpreted Aristotle within the context of neo-Platonism and Islamic concepts of God (which made Aristotle's notion of God seem somewhat more Christian and less pagan).

The two greatest Arabic commentators on Aristotle were Avicenna [Ibn Sīnā (980–1037)] and Averroës [Ibn Rushd (1126–1198)]. Much of Avicenna's work was translated into Latin in twelfth-century Spain, while Averroës' commentaries were largely translated at the court of Frederick II in the 1220s. Avicenna defined God not simply as the First Mover but as the underlying cause of all existence. By positing that there is only one necessary Being, the cause of all possible being who was also pure intelligence, perfect goodness, and perfect beauty, Avicenna transformed Aristotle into more of a metaphysician than he was and his ideas into a framework more acceptable to a Muslim or Christian thinker. On the other hand, Avicenna also argued that God created only the first being, who in turn produced the next and so on, making the world an emanation rather than a direct creation of God.

Averroës, known as "The Great Commentator" for his passage-by-passage analysis of Aristotle, helped Europeans through a difficult set of texts. He described God as pure act and emphasized the mixture of potentiality and actuality in the material world. Averroës' interpretation of the relationship of the potential and active within man's intellect (in which the active element was lodged in a transcendent single mind through which all men think) and his acceptance of Aristotle's view of the world as eternal caused problems for Christian thinkers. Averroës believed that the human soul, after the death of the body, is reabsorbed into the single, unified intellect, losing all individuality. In addition, he argued that the world was predetermined, without free will or the possibility of miracles. These opinions, as well as the prevailing empiricism in Aristotle's works, meant that their reception in the Christian West was not without problems.

In 1215, Aristotle's *Metaphysics* and many of his works on nature were proscribed at the University of Paris. Between 1215 and 1240, while ecclesiastical authorities deliberated whether to allow the teaching of Aristotle's natural philosophy and metaphysics, European thinkers derived most of their knowledge of Aristotle from Avicenna.* It is not until the 1240s that treatises appeared showing a direct understanding of Aristotle and interest in Averroës. In this same decade Roger Bacon (c. 1220–1292), the great English Franciscan thinker, began to lecture at Paris on Aristotle's scientific works. By 1255, the arts faculty at Paris, acting independently of ecclesiastical authorities, had adopted a curriculum that was predominantly Aristotelian. Aristotle's *Physics* and his *Metaphysics,* his works *On the*

---

* There is one significant exception—that of Robert Grosseteste, the chancellor of Oxford (c. 1168–1253), who knew Aristotle well and who translated some of his works directly from the Greek.

Heavens, Generation and Corruption, Meteorology, On the Soul, On Animals, etc. along with both the "Old Logic" and the "New Logic" (see Chapter 14) were all required. Moral philosophy soon included Aristotelian texts: the *Nicomachean Ethics* and *Politics.* If the students did not care to read all of these often difficult texts, they had recourse to summaries, textbooks, and commentaries that synthesized and sometimes simplified the material. The teachers in the arts faculties throughout Europe, however, would have had to know Aristotle very well by the second half of the thirteenth century. Surviving manuscripts of Avicenna and Averroës show that they were being read alongside Aristotle (see Medieval Portrait).

Bonaventure and Aquinas

The two thinkers who best epitomize the intellectual trends of the thirteenth century are the Franciscan St. Bonaventure (1221–1274) and the Dominican St. Thomas Aquinas (1224/25–1274). Both had to come to grips with the new trends in the arts curriculum, but they did so in radically different ways. Before looking at them, however, we will examine how the friars moved into the universities in the first place.

The Dominicans, whose main mission was preaching, emphasized education from their origin and set up schools of grammar and theology in every province of their order. Their eventual involvement in the theology faculties of the universities is, therefore, not surprising. For Franciscans to hold university chairs in theology was more surprising. St. Francis was averse to learning (which he thought led to pride) and only allowed books for divine office. He believed that the profoundly loving heart, steeped in prayer, had an intuitive grasp of scripture and needed only to follow Christ's example. The extent to which his idealism failed can be grasped by the fact that, even before his death, Franciscan friars were attending theological lectures at various universities.

It was one thing to attend lectures, and another to give them. The friars were not welcomed into the theological faculties for several reasons. When the university faculties went on strike (as Paris did in 1229 and 1253), the mendicants refused to leave, preferring to obey their superiors rather than the decisions of their fellow teachers. Also, with direct privileges from the papacy, the friars were viewed as papal intruders within the university. Further, they had not been trained at the university and had not necessarily studied arts, a prerequisite for theology. Finally, the secular masters were in danger of being outnumbered. At Paris by 1252, they held only six out of twelve chairs in theology and were rapidly losing their voting power. As a result, a battle developed between the secular masters and the mendicants, resulting in a full-fledged attack on mendicant privileges and principles. The papacy intervened on behalf of the friars, and four of the chairs in theology at Paris were, as a result, reserved for the friars. In 1256, Pope Alexander IV ordered Paris to give chairs to two mendicant theologians—Bonaventure and Thomas Aquinas.

Although Bonaventure never formally took his chair as doctor of theology (having been made Minister General of the Franciscan Order at the same time), he wrote numerous treatises and taught classes at the Franciscan house in Paris. Bonaventure, born in Italy but a student at Paris in the 1240s, reacted against the

MEDIEVAL PORTRAITS

Moses Maimonides

Moses Maimonides (1135–1204) was born in Muslim Spain to a Jewish family. His family left Spain due to the repressive fundamentalism of the Almohades and traveled to North Africa, Palestine, and finally Egypt, where Maimonides rose to a prominent position as court physician. He was learned in philosophy, theology, and law, and influenced by Muslim philosophers (Fārābī, Ibn Bājjah, and Averroës in particular), the Judaic tradition, and Greek philosophy, particularly Aristotle. As chief rabbi of Egypt, he gained political, religious, and intellectual prominence in Jewish communities throughout Europe and the Middle East. In the history of Jewish medieval thought, he has a pivotal and profound position, parallel to that of Aquinas in Christian philosophy and theology. He wrote rabbinic books, a codification of Jewish law, and a system of ethics, but the work for which he is most famous is his philosophical *Guide for the Perplexed,* written in 1197.

Scholars do not agree on how to read Maimonides, what his theological ideas were, or even who his intended audience was. Maimonides argues that language cannot begin to describe God (who is of a radically different nature than language can grasp), and that, therefore, no positive attributes can be posited of God. Maimonides has a realistic view of what the intellect (and reason) can or cannot understand. Therefore, he is unwilling to assert that the world is created or even what its nature is, since we cannot demonstrate the truth of such theories. Maimonides is critical of Jewish theologians who assert supernatural forces; he insists on following reason and being skeptical of imaginative reconstructions. Maimonides struggled with the role of prophecy in religion, an issue that became central to his thinking. The ability to prophesize, for Maimonides, was a natural phenomenon, only available to individuals disciplined by intellectual and moral virtue. His ideas had enormous implications for his understanding of the role of Muhammad, of many Old Testament prophets, and also, possibly, of Christ.

Maimonides also believed that the Bible presents truth in different ways, depending upon the audience and what "truths" they need to maintain their faith. Thus, he argued, a Jew who is a faithful follower of the Law will read the Bible differently than a mystic or an intellectual. All these various readings have "truth" in them. Maimonides' skepticism and his empiricism, his attack on theologians, and his radical views on prophecy and the Bible meant that he had to argue elliptically at times. His work influenced scholastics like Thomas Aquinas in the thirteenth century, mystics such as Meister Eckhart in the fourteenth century (see Chapter 19), and many modern thinkers.

growing authority of Aristotle. Bonaventure did not accept Aristotle's views in theology, metaphysics, or the physics of the cosmos, although he respected his authority in questions of nature. He attacked Aristotle's reliance on reason and any suggestion that natural philosophy was a science separate from theology. For Bonaventure, theology governed all, just as Christ was the master of all. Reason, focused on finite objects, could never provide the certitude of truth that faith and

Holy Scripture did. Bonaventure argued that man's knowledge of God is innate, and that man's goal, to seek happiness, peace and knowledge, can only be obtained by seeking God. Therefore, exploration of the natural world, while interesting, is unnecessary for man's higher purposes and often produces error. He believed that Aristotle and Averroës erred when they asserted that the world was eternal or that the soul was not individual. Bonaventure believed that a direct, mystical illumination of the soul was the highest form of knowledge and that the physical world offered analogies, symbols, and mirrors of God but not proofs of His existence. This theory, of God's reflection in the material world, is labeled "exemplarism."

Bonaventure's theology, best expressed in his treatise *The Soul's Journey to God*, was mystical in its goal of seeing God rather than demonstrating His existence. It was an intellectual achievement of the first order—comprehensive, consistent, highly learned—although it might appear irrational to those who do not share Bonaventure's faith in Christian theology or his direct experience of God. Perhaps for this reason Bonaventure's writings have not been as influential as the synthesis that his contemporary (and adversary), Thomas Aquinas, offered.

Thomas Aquinas became acquainted with the writings of Aristotle and Averroës early in life. As a teenager, he studied at Naples, where Averroës had been translated less than two decades earlier. Subsequently Thomas studied with the Dominican scholar Albert the Great (c.1206–1280) at Cologne. Albert, called "The Great" because of his vast erudition in all fields (scientific, philosophical, and theological), sought to make Aristotle's natural philosophy intelligible and useful to the Latin world. In so doing, he accepted Aristotle's work on its own terms and argued for the intrinsic value of scientific knowledge and research. Thus, when Thomas returned to lecture at Paris from 1252 to 1259 and again from 1269 to 1272, he was steeped in Aristotle, Aristotle's Arabic commentators, and a scientific methodology based on observation.

Thomas wrote approximately 100 separate works, filling more than fifty volumes in a modern edition. Witnesses to his life remarked on his astonishing powers of concentration. At the height of his career he was dictating and writing three to four works simultaneously. It is reported that he dictated in his sleep, and, in any case, he did not sleep much. Often he forgot to eat. In December 1273, Thomas was suddenly struck while at mass, whether with a stroke or some mystical experience, no one knows. He put away his writing instruments, stating "All that I have written seems like straw to me," and died three months later.

Included among the intellectual achievements of Thomas Aquinas is his *Summa contra Gentiles,* a reasoned exposition of God and the Christian religion intended for missionaries working among Muslims and schismatic Christians. His *Summa Theologiae* is a systematic exposition of God's existence and His attributes, the Trinity, the procession of creatures from God, man's goal of moving God-ward, and Christ and the sacraments. As a guide to Catholic theology it is unsurpassed and has, for centuries, provided instruction to parish priests, confessors, and theologians. Thomas also produced commentaries on Aristotle that were meant to replace those of Averroës.

Aquinas was a thoroughgoing Aristotelian in methodology. He began with sense experience and did not believe that we have innate ideas or that forms of things preexist. He rejected the notion that God's existence was self-evident, arguing that knowledge of God comes from examining His effects. Thus, his famous five proofs of God's existence (from motion, from causality, from the relationship of the possible to the necessary, from the grades of nature, and from the governance of things)[3] all begin with man's experience of the external world and are designed to be convincing even to pagans. Higher knowledge that cannot be derived from reason and sense experience cannot be proven. Thus, for Thomas, the creation of the world, the Incarnation of Christ, or the nature of God cannot be proved; these must be accepted on faith.

Thomas's doctrines were based on his distinction between *esse* and *essentia* (being and essence), both of which derive from God; this allowed him to develop a metaphysics based on Aristotelian and Averroistic notions of act and potency. God, for Thomas, is pure act and *Esse Subsistens,* i.e. in Him being and essence are identical; there is no potentiality in God. It is He who is the creative cause and final end of creation. All creatures receive being (*esse*) from God, but the *esse* and *essentia* of creatures are not identical. Creatures cannot be pure being. They require the ability to operate—that is they cannot subsist outside nature. The only exception is the rational soul of man, which can exist separate from the body, albeit in an incomplete form. Completion requires the resurrection of the body.

Both Bonaventure and Thomas Aquinas viewed man as God's greatest creation, but God apparently rejoiced more in man than woman, for, according to Bonaventure, the divine image of God is clearer in the body of a man than in the body of a woman. Woman is relatively imperfect, although not absolutely imperfect, since nature requires both male and female. A woman's imperfections, however, render her less dignified, less powerful, and with less authority to govern.

Thomas Aquinas, following Aristotle, held that women were imperfect, undeveloped men.

> As regards the individual nature, woman is defective and misbegotten, for the active force in the male seed tends to the production of a perfect likeness in the masculine sex; while the production of woman comes from a defect in the active force or from some material indisposition, or even from some external influence.[4]

As a result, man and woman in marriage have the relationship of master to servant. Aquinas also followed Aristotle in asserting that, in the act of procreation, the male was the active, form-giving principle, the female the passive receptacle. Bonaventure, following the opinion of Greek physicians and of Avicenna, taught that women were cocreators in the act of generation.

The differences between the philosophies of Bonaventure and Aquinas became more pronounced in the last decade of their lives, as Bonaventure's disciples entrenched behind a revived Augustinianism, while the Aristotelian-Averroistic tendencies of Aquinas were expressed more radically by some members of the arts faculty.

Averroës, in addition to the theories described above, had also asserted that when reason leads to truths that contradict theological truths, these two truths coexist, representing different levels of truth. This position (called the theory of double truths) was never, as far as we know, defended by any masters at Paris. But Siger

MEDIEVAL PORTRAITS

Ramon Lull: A Failed Attempt to Integrate Reason and Faith and to Promote Christian Missions

Ramon Lull (1232?–1316) grew up on the island of Majorca, among a mix of Muslims, Jews, and Christians; he lived an aristocratic, worldly life at the royal court. At age thirty he experienced an insistent vision of Christ that would not leave him until he dedicated his life to God. Lull gave up his wealth, position, family, and various *amours* and began the program that would dominate his life—the conversion of Jews and Muslims to Christianity by writing books and establishing monastic schools where future missionaries could learn needed languages (Hebrew and Arabic). With his intellectual curiosity and driving desire to convert, he produced over 200 surviving works containing a philosophical-theological system that aimed to offer a key to all knowledge and a methodology for proving the truth of Christianity and particularly the Trinity. Lull began with the concept of God and then described the various divine attributes (which he called dignities) in a way that could be considered orthodox by all three religions. Lull then went on to postulate the generative power of God, relating it, through a highly ordered scheme, to His manifestations in the created world. Creation thus becomes a mirror of divine perfection—a view that is uncompromisingly platonic. As he examined the structure of that relationship between being and becoming, Lull created a trinitarian logic that he believed mirrored the real world. Letters and figures, analogies and congruences expressed that logic, which he called a combinatory art. Lull's "logic," which he thought could be applied to all knowledge, made little impact on Muslims. Nor was he any more successful with his project for schools, despite nearly fifty years of petitioning popes and princes for support.

   Lull understood Islam as perhaps no other western thinker did, and he carried on his campaign without rancor or harshness. He believed in free, not forced, conversions, and disapproved of missionary efforts that focused on disproving Islam rather than proving Christianity. Although he supported the Crusades at times, most of Lull's writings advocate a return to the missionary methods of the apostles.

of Brabant (c. 1240–1284), the most prominent of the "Latin Averroists" at Paris, did expound on a unified intellect and the eternity of the world and certainly preferred a philosophical mode of inquiry to a theological one. In response, attacks mounted against the errors of the philosophers, culminating in the bishop of Paris's condemnation, in 1277, of 219 propositions drawn, in part, from Aristotle, Averroës, Avicenna, and Maimonides, among others. A few propositions from Aquinas were also condemned, along with a hodgepodge of ideas from astrology, magic, moral philosophy, and even courtly love literature—in a word, almost anything heard on the streets of Paris that sounded anti-Christian. Gordon Leff concludes, that "After 1277 [philosophy had to withdraw]—away from revelation and into the natural world where reason could have full play. 1277 was not the beginning of modern science . . . but it was the beginning of the end of . . . the harmonizing of faith and natural reason."[5] (See Medieval Portrait).

Medieval Science

In the thirteenth century, Europeans established a tradition of science and medicine that rested on the shoulders of earlier Greek and Arabic contributors. In medicine the West benefited from the works of Hippocrates as well as some of the (100+) treatises written by Galen, a second century A.D. Greek physician whose work summed up and extended Greco-Roman achievements. These translations from the Greek were accompanied by translations from Arabic medicine, whose practitioners had fully absorbed the Greco-Roman heritage and had developed their own dynamic medical tradition. By the thirteenth century, Avicenna's *Canon of Medicine* and works by Rhazes, Haly Abbas, and Hunayn ibn Ishàq were translated into Latin and brought a more sophisticated level of medicine to Europe. Also by the thirteenth century, faculties for teaching medicine were established at universities in Montpellier, Paris, Oxford, Padua, and Bologna. By the fourteenth century, students could witness dissections of the human body, at least in the Italian universities.

Medicine, although increasingly informed by book learning and associated with universities, had always been practiced at the village level by women using herbs, midwifery, and traditional knowledge. This popular medical tradition continued alongside the professional, although we know less about it. Women were not, however, always excluded from more learned levels of doctoring. The most famous of those women was Trotula, a twelfth-century doctor from Salerno whose existence is shadowy but who appears to have written a work of practical medical remedies and perhaps also one on gynecology. By the twelfth and thirteenth centuries, midwives might be attached to hospitals, where they gave shelter, food, and medical attention to the sick. Such hospitals developed in Byzantium in the early Middle Ages and in Islam by the ninth century. They were probably introduced into the West by the Knights Hospitallers at the time of the Crusades.

Doctors and surgeons in the Middle Ages accepted a theory of four bodily humors: blood (which was hot and moist), phlegm (cold and moist), black bile (hot and dry), and yellow or red bile (cholera, which was cold and dry) (see Introduction). Women were at a disadvantage in this physiological system. Their bodies tended toward the cold and moist, an unpleasant combination that made them timid and phlegmatic. Angry or melancholic people had an excess of black bile; cheerful persons had too much blood, hence a sanguine personality. Astrological influences counted, as did the particular combination of the four elements (air, fire, water, and earth) in each individual's makeup. A balance of humors was part of good health, and doctors often focused on sensible measures—a balanced diet, more exposure to the sun, more water, more (or less) exposure to the planet Venus. On the other hand, bloodletting or vomiting sometimes was recommended to achieve balance. And some medicinal remedies included ingredients such as ground-up snake flesh or animal feces. In general the study and practice of medicine depended upon wisdom passed down through books or by word of mouth. It was not yet an experimental science.

The same was true for other sciences—botany, biology, zoology, physics, chemistry, and mathematics. As with medicine, most treatises on these subjects came from Greek and Arabic writers. Mathematics, in particular, benefited from the introduction of Arabic numerals, concepts of zero and negative numbers, the use of equations, and the beginnings of algebraic computations. Leonardo Fibonacci (c. 1170–c. 1240), who grew up among Pisan merchants in North Africa, became one of mathematic's great theorists. He studied with Arabic teachers, traveled to Greece, Egypt and Syria, and was active at the court of Frederick II. In 1202, he published his *Liber Abaci,* which provided an extensive introduction to Hindu-Arabic numerals and to speculative issues regarding the properties of numbers. In his writings he discussed root extraction, indeterminate equations, second- and third-degree equations, congruent numbers, and number sequences, including what is called the Fibonacci sequence.

Two sciences, in particular, came close to, but did not succeed in becoming experimental: physics and optics. In the field of physics, medieval scholars focused on the study of motion. In doing so they described, mathematically and with graphs, the relationship between time and velocity. They also developed a theory of impetus, defined as a quality impressed upon a body when it is moved and measured by the velocity and the denseness of the moving object.

And they studied optics—how the eye works, how we see, what light is, how light refracts and reflects, what causes rainbows, what the color spectrum is, how mirrors work. The greatest influence in this field was Alhazen (Ibn al-Haytham, c. 965–c. 1040) whose treatise on optics was translated into Latin around 1200. Following his work, various western thinkers such as Robert Grosseteste, Roger Bacon, John Pecham (all Englishmen), and a Polish scholar named Witelo came close to pronouncing a quantum theory of light, examined the workings of the rainbow and of crystals, and mathematically described how light breaks into colors and radiates from a single point. All of these "experiments" (really, observations) could be done with minimal technology. Some advances did occur. Sometime in the thirteenth century eyeglasses were invented; in the fourteenth century, the pinhole camera appeared. Nevertheless, breakthrough experiments with light require more sophisticated equipment than was available to medieval men. In general, the science of optics remained descriptive and not experimental.

One of the most famous scientists of the thirteenth century was Roger Bacon (c. 1220–1292), who became legendary as a magician and a visionary. People remember his suggestions that man can build flying machines or self-propelled boats. (Indeed, he claimed that they had already done so.) In his own time, Roger Bacon was not much mentioned, and most of our information comes from what he has to say about himself—the difficulties he had being taken seriously, the impediments to his writing, his unfavorable opinions of fellow intellectuals. Bacon's great contribution was to exalt the role of science. For Bacon, all knowledge was beautiful, utilitarian, and cohesive. He believed one universal science existed that included revelation and prophecy but required observation for verification. This universal science, which brought together ancient and Arabic authorities, astrology, alchemy, mathematics, medicine, and all philosophy and theology, could be verified through experience and applied to man's use and the extension of Christianity. Bacon's "science" was not experimental in a modern sense, but his vision of the significance of science, and his conclusion that the science of pagans and of Arabs was part of God's revelation, illustrates a broad-minded and highly empirical frame of mind.

THE CULTURE OF LAY SOCIETY

Thus far medieval intellectual culture was primarily a culture of clerics. Yet, during the twelfth and thirteenth centuries a vigorous lay (nonclerical) culture began to develop. As universities grew in numbers and accessibility,* a Latin education became available to individuals who might not enter the clergy. In addition, vernacular languages began to be written down. French, Provençal, German, Spanish, Italian, and even some English began to be used for family histories, genealogies, epics, romances, and poetry. Lay audiences, long entertained by minstrels and jongleurs who memorized their fare, began to read romances or have them read publicly. Poetic recitations of great military deeds gave way to written epics.

Epics and Romances

Perhaps the most famous epic poem of the period, written down in the twelfth century, was the *Song of Roland*. The historical episode underlying the *Song of Roland* was the defeat of Charlemagne's rearguard by the Basques at Roncevaux Pass in the Pyrenees in 778. It is difficult to understand why such an ignominious defeat should have become such a famous legend. In the twelfth-century version, Roland (leader of the rearguard), although dying on the battlefield, is undefeated; the enemy has shifted from Basques to Saracens (Muslims); Charlemagne returns for revenge, defeats the enemy, and gives the martyred Franks a Christian burial. Historical defeat has been turned into legendary victory, and in the process, the knightly values of courage, loyalty to lord, and the rightness of Christianity are affirmed.

Another great epic cycle, the William of Orange cycle of twenty-four poems, was also written down in the twelfth century. William of Orange, a soldier and ruler from Narbonne in southern France, was a contemporary of Charlemagne's son Louis. His epic cycle stresses the loyalty and family pride of the heroes, the despicable nature of the Saracens, unworthiness of the northern French, and the vacillating weakness of both king and pope. In "Aliscans," William travels to France to seek the aid of Louis against Saracens who have killed his nephew and ravaged his land. While he is gone, his wife Guiborc, a converted Saracen, defends Orange with her ladies, all armed as warriors. Although the trip to France is successful and William returns with reinforcements, King Louis had proven to be cowardly and his queen a whore and a glutton. "Aliscans" expresses intolerance of other religions ("if a man heeds not the Christian messages . . . he has no right to live"[6]), extreme views of women (either heroic or evil), and southern prejudice against the northern French.

These epics from France and Provence were mirrored in England by stories of the legendary King Arthur. Whether or not Arthur ever existed, by the ninth

---

* By the end of the thirteenth century, perhaps twenty universities were in Europe, mostly in France, Italy and Spain. England had two (Oxford and Cambridge). Germany and eastern Europe had no universities at all; the earliest was the University at Prague (in Bohemia) founded in 1348.

century legendary sites were linked with his name and people believed that Arthur had fought certain battles, including the historical battle of Mons Badon. By the early twelfth century, Arthur's fame had spread to Italy, Brittany, and France.

Two twelfth-century authors wrote down the stories of Arthur in ways that captured the attention of their contemporaries. Geoffrey of Monmouth (c.1100–1155) came from a Breton family that settled in southern Wales after the Norman conquest. About 1136, he published *The History of the Kings of Britain.* Largely fictional, the book is a pastiche of local legends and classical sources all shaped to Geoffrey's purposes, which included promoting peace (in a time of civil war), denying Canterbury's historical importance, attacking Rome, exalting Brittany's role in British history, and portraying strong female rulers in pre-Roman Britain. A large portion of Geoffrey's *History* is devoted to the story of King Arthur and to prophecies attached to the name of Merlin. Over the years scholars have debated the extent to which Geoffrey was aware of Welsh tales of Arthur. It appears that, although Geoffrey twisted stories to his liking and disguised his sources, he was very much aware of Welsh (and probably also Breton) tales of Arthur. The Arthur he describes is a great king who combined the forces of the British Isles to conquer most of Europe, only to be thwarted at the gates of Rome by the treachery of his nephew Mordred. Returning to Britain to fight Mordred, Arthur falls in battle and is carried away to the isle of Avalon to heal his wounds. This fable, which many of Geoffrey's contemporaries believed to be historical, was translated from Latin into French by the Norman poet Wace, who added a good many elements, including a round table at Arthur's court.

A generation later (in the 1170s and 1180s), Chrétien de Troyes (whose name is most likely a pseudonym—"the Christian from Troyes") transformed the Arthurian stories into romantic epics written in French octosyllabic couplets. Perhaps because Chrétien was French, Arthur is no longer an imperial-minded king. The geographical locale of Arthur's kingdom is vague, and the focus is on the knights of his court (Lancelot, Gawain, Kay, Yvain, and Percival). Women are also prominent; Guinevere, Arthur's wife, is the model of a powerful queen. In one of his most famous romances, *Lancelot or the Knight of the Cart,* written for Marie de Champagne, daughter of Eleanor of Aquitaine and King Louis VII, Chrétien integrates chivalry with the troubadour theme of adulterous love. Lancelot worships, woos, defends, and beds Guinevere, who is imperious and capricious. Lancelot is expected to be obedient. "A love is obedient, and once that he is wholly hers he does whatever she prefers. . . ."[7] In contrast, Chrétien's other romances stress virtuous, and often married, love. One of his central themes is the spiritual maturation of the protagonist, who starts as superficial and self-centered, but through crisis deepens his love and learns to serve society. In his final, unfinished romance (*Percival or the Story of the Grail*) Chrétien presents, for the first time in European written literature, the story of Percival, the fisher-king, and the search for the Holy Grail.

Chrétien's romances, especially *Percival,* became a lodestone for future authors who enlarged and recast them in poetry or prose. Thus, the Holy Grail became a stone (in Wolfram von Eschenbach's *Parzival,* written in German about 1210), a chalice holding Christ's blood (Robert de Boron's French story *Joseph d'Arimathie,* written c. 1195, or the anonymous *Perlesvaus,* written in French c.1210), or the dish from which Christ ate the Last Supper (the prose *Quest of the Holy Grail,* written in French between 1215 and 1230). The prose *Quest* adds the character of Galahad, son of Lancelot and Elaine (daughter of the fisher-king). It tells of Galahad's arrival at Camelot, the quest for the Holy Grail, the numerous adventures of Arthur's knights, the failure of Gawain and Lancelot to achieve the adventure, and the visions of the Grail given to Percival, Bors, and Galahad, the latter the very figure of Christ. When Galahad leaves England for the Holy Land (where he dies, accompanying the Holy Grail heavenward), Malory* notes "for this night it [the Grail] shall depart from the realm of Logres [England], and it shall nevermore be seen here."[8]

Courtly Love

"Courtly love," like the love of Lancelot for Guinevere, is a much debated term generally associated with the troubadours of Provence. On the surface, their poems all seem quite similar. The courtly lover usually loves a lady who is a paragon of beauty and virtue. He was born to serve her, but is being denied his reward due, perhaps, to too many spies, too great a distance, too much jealousy on the part of the husband, too much anger or coldness from the lady. Occasionally the lover is granted what he longs for, but more often the love is unrequited. The consequence for the lover may be a series of love-tests, duels on behalf of the beloved, or emotional suffering. A particularly popular, but somewhat despairing love poem was one by Lord Jaufre Rudel (fl. mid-twelfth century), whose later "vida"[†] alleges that he fell in love with the countess of Tripoli sight unseen and died in her arms on pilgrimage to the Holy Land.

> When the days are long in May,
> I enjoy the sweet song of the birds far away,
> and when I am parted from their song,
> and parting reminds me of a love far away:
> I go bent with desire, head bowed down;
> then neither the song nor the hawthorn's flower
> pleases me more than the winter's ice.
>
> . . . .
>
> Sad and rejoicing I shall part from her,
> when I have seen this love far away:
> but when I shall see her I do not know,
> our lands are very far away:
> there are many ways and roads,

---

* Around 1470 Thomas Malory, an English knight, rewrote this tale in English. From Malory it descended to the twentieth century, where it was retold in books (by T. H. White and Marion Zimmer Bradley, for example), in film, and in plays (*Camelot*). This quotation comes from Malory's version of the *Quest.*

† "Vidas," or lives, were brief biographies of troubadour poets. The minstrels who sang their songs passed on the information. The "Lives" often tell of romantic episodes that cannot be proven historically.

and I am no prophet

. . . .

but as it it pleases God!

I shall have no pleasure in love
if it is not the pleasure of this love far away,
for I do not know a gentler or a better one
anywhere, not close by, not far away:
her worth is so true, and perfect, so
that there, in the kingdom of the Saracens,
I wish I were a prisoner for her.[9]

Many of these poems have hidden meanings, however. Other interpretations place Jaufre's song in a crusading context, giving the "love far off" layers of meaning. It is not only a woman, but also the city of Jerusalem and perhaps even God. The poetry has an ambiguity, an enigmatic quality. The loved one is never named and has no personal qualities; often the poetry barely masks another purpose, sometimes sexual, or, in this case, crusading. The poet usually seems more interested in his own emotional state than he is in the love he is courting, and it is never clear how sincere the poet (or the lover) is. Women who wrote troubadour poetry (twenty are known) sometimes cited the lack of sincerity of such lovers. The countess of Dia, in the twelfth century, wrote:

Of things I'd rather keep in silence I must sing:
so bitter do I feel toward him
whom I love more than anything.
With him my mercy and fine manners are in vain,
my beauty, virtue and intelligence.
For I've been tricked and cheated
as if I were completely loathesome.[10]

The best known female poet was Marie de France (1160?–1215?), who wrote lais, animal fables, and a translation of *St. Patrick's Purgatory*. The women she crafted in her lais were independent-minded, motivated by love more than social convention and by compassion more than honor or glory (see Chapter 13).

Fabliaux, Comic Tales, and Proverbs

Courtly love poems and romances tended to be idealized, stylized, and elitist. Other, more realistic genres of literature appealed to a wider audience. Comedic tales, mock epics, short poems and stories, as well as popular proverbs were all well established in the oral tradition and were being written down by the early thirteenth century.

The greatest mock epic is the vernacular "Roman de Renart" which chronicles the adventures of the trickster, Renart the Fox. The tales tell of clever animals making fun of society and provoking obscene, comic situations. Similar tricksters in medieval popular culture include Richeut, the crafty prostitute who teaches her son to be a seducer of women, and "Till Eulenspiegel," who uses linguistic traps and a disrespectful sense of humor to dupe priests and townsfolk. His signature was often the excrement he left behind.

Shorter comic poems in verse (known as *fabliaux* in French) were set among towns and villages and peopled with rich, overbearing peasants; upstart servants; pretentious townsfolk; impoverished nobility; lover-priests; gullible fools; and lusty women. They tell of tricksters and adulterers, magic and morals, and are interlaced with practical pieces of wisdom such as "Don't fly before you have wings;" "Who wants everything loses everything;" "If you have a pretty wife, don't harbor clerks."[11] The language of these tales is often vulgar, with explicit references to sex and bodily functions. They convey a plain sense of humor that offers insight into the texture of medieval life.

Ballads, such as the ballads of Robin Hood, began to circulate in the thirteenth and fourteenth centuries. And proverbs were popular. In England many proverbs circulated under the name of King Alfred, including such commonplaces as "A wise child is his father's joy" or "A child is better unborn than unbeaten" and "a fools' arrow is soon shot." Proverbs made their way into children's schoolbooks. In English, some of these include: "Far from the eye, far from the heart," "Better friend in court than penny in purse," and "A burnt hand dreads the fire."[12]

The Romance of the Rose

One of the most popular vernacular texts was the thirteenth-century *Romance of the Rose,* written in French. It is an ungainly work—composed by two separate authors over more than forty years (1230s–1270s), with all the attendant differences in style and intent. The second part, written by Jean de Meun, is overly long, full of scholastic-style speeches by characters such as Reason, The Old Woman, The Friend, Nature, and Genius. Little action takes place, although the Lover does, in the end, graphically rape the Rose, his apparent goal through almost 400 pages in a modern edition. Embedded in this text (which has survived in over 200 manuscripts and early printed copies) is a treatise attacking kingship; a treatise on free will; a diatribe against women; ideas about language, love, sex, sin, and marriage; and a debate over natural versus unnatural love. The *Romance* does not address religion. Rather, it appears to advocate natural love, albeit with lots of warnings about women and the difficulties of marriage. Part of the appeal of the text is the ambiguous message it conveys, since the authors' views are filtered through various characters, not all of whom agree. Jean de Meun tells the reader that the real meaning of the text is hidden and will be explained later in glosses* (which he never did).

By the fourteenth century, the *Romance of the Rose* was being read by all of literate French society—the aristocracy, bourgeoisie, clergy, and scholars. At the beginning of the fifteenth century, Christine de Pizan, the first independent female

---

* A *gloss* is an explication or an amplification of a word or part of a text, similar in function to this footnote. In medieval texts, glosses are usually written in the margins of a page.

writer, vigorously attacked Jean de Meun as a misogynist, and the debate that ensued has lasted until today.

RELIGIOUS CULTURE

An individual whose library included *The Romance of the Rose* might also have religious readings—lives of the saints, liturgical books, moral treatises, and perhaps even mystical writings. Religious concerns were no longer confined to a spiritual elite in monasteries or hermitages or to the clergy, separated from the laity by their literacy and ordained status. Literacy, particularly in the vernacular but also in Latin, was spreading to laity, whose interests were infused with the religiosity of the culture. Even if one did not read, lay men and women would be impressed with the magnificent cathedrals built in the twelfth and thirteenth centuries. If they were prominent townsfolk or substantial landowners they may have contributed personally to the construction, while tithes and profits from all laity financed cathedrals. Laity could watch liturgical dramas and "mystery" plays that retold, in popular form, stories from scripture. They heard sermons and participated in pilgrimages and might be attracted to even more radical forms of popular religious expression. The popular religious manifestations of thirteenth-century Europe were rich and varied, but they sometimes evolved independent of the Church, a circumstance with the potential to undercut the value of more official forms of religious expression.

Religious Drama, Songs, and Art

One of the most popular books produced in thirteenth-century Europe was Jacobus de Voragine's *Legenda Aurea* (Golden Legend). It is a lively retelling of the stories of saints and their miracles, organized according to the church calendar. Written about 1260, it was quickly translated into all the major European vernaculars. Those who could not afford it were likely to find it in their parish church, chained and available for clergy and laity alike. The *Golden Legend* provided stories for many medieval plays and subject matter for much medieval art.

Other themes, besides saints' tales, were popular. Hildegard von Bingen's great musical drama, the *Ordo Virtutum* (dated c. 1151), became the ancestor of morality plays that focused on the struggle between vices and virtues for the salvation of a single soul. Church liturgies dramatized scenes that reenacted Christ's passion, birth, or resurrection. Jacopone da Todi (c.1236–1306) was a Franciscan friar whose poetry was written in a rough but expressive dialect form sometimes disdained by others, but his poem "Donna del paradiso" was the first dramatic verse in Italian and the predecessor of Italian opera. Written for three voices and a chorus, it tells the story of Christ's passion through his mother Mary, a messenger, the people, and Christ himself. For many listeners, this may have been the first time they heard long passages from scripture in their own language rather than in Latin. It became popular immediately and was used by groups of lay people (for example, the tertiary orders of the Franciscans) as part of their Good Friday services. Eventually other voices were added, the staging became more elaborate, and modern drama began to emerge.

By the thirteenth century, lay people also gathered in churches to sing lauds or hymns of praise to the Virgin Mary and songs of repentance. At first they were simple songs, repetitive chanting of biblical verses, but they soon evolved into popular ballads and marching songs. Most of these surviving songs have no known author, but one of the more popular, written by an Italian named Garzo, goes like this: "Whoever wishes to disdain the world/ should always think of death./Death is fierce and hard and strong;/it breaks walls and splinters door. /It is such a common fate/ that no one can escape it."[13]

Paintings on church walls and, particularly in Italy, fresco painting was another common way of expressing religious devotion. Although much of the history of fresco painting belongs to the Renaissance, it was also popular in the thirteenth century and is best expressed in the art of Cimabue (fl. 1272–1302), a Florentine artist influenced by early Christian and Byzantine mosaic art. Cimabue created a greater sense of human space in his monumental altarpieces and wall paintings. He refined the Byzantine use of gold while simultaneously giving his figures more solidity and greater complexity. Few works from Cimabue survive, and several attributed to him were destroyed in an earthquake in 1997 that damaged the basilica of St. Francis in the town of Assisi.

In much of Europe, and particularly in the north, painting gave way to the art of sculpture and stained glass, particularly in Gothic cathedrals where walls gave way to windows and facades became more decorative. In the twelfth century, sculptors worked with the cathedral facade, carving designs into the pillars so that the sculptures look very much like part of the pillar itself. But by the thirteenth century, sculptors worked independently, carving thousands of images that were then placed in niches and crannies of cathedrals. At Reims Cathedral in France, for example, the 3,000 statues carved for the fabric were numbered in order to match them to their niches. These sculptures took on increasingly lifelike forms, as the sculptors themselves became more important and more in demand.*

Medieval Architecture

Twelfth and thirteenth-century Europe witnessed a building boom of cathedrals, churches, and castles that surpassed, in millions of tons of stone quarried, the amount used in ancient Egypt for the pyramids. The Romanesque and Gothic cathedrals that dot Europe represent one of the greatest ages for building that the world has ever known. Beauvais cathedral, the tallest cathedral built, is over fourteen modern stories high inside the nave. The spires that adorn some cathedrals rise to thirty or forty stories.

It has often been noted that medieval cathedrals represent a form of scripture written in stone. They signify the Heavenly Jerusalem, dwelling place of the

---

* It is a mistake to assume that medieval builders were anonymous. Especially by the thirteenth century, it was common for an architect or master mason to leave his name or his portrait engraved in the church. Stone carvers also left their marks. And many inscriptions that once were visible have disappeared.

saved—facing Jerusalem in the east, built in a cruciform pattern, with the western (entry) portal depicting the Last Judgment and responding to the words from John 10:9: "I am the door: by me if any man enter in, he shall be saved." The main part of the cathedral, the nave where the people stood, derives its name from Latin *navis,* a ship or ark, symbol of the Church, wherein the people are saved. The master masons who constructed these buildings used geometrical designs and mathematical ratios that, though simple, had heavenly significance. They played with ratios involving the number seven (representing the seven days of creation), six (a perfect number since it is the sum of one, two and three, as well as double the Trinity) or nine (triple the Trinity). The western end of most cathedrals is squarish, representing two by two, or four, signifying the material world. The eastern end, incorporating circular patterns, represents God who, like the circle, is without beginning or end.

Between the end of the eleventh and the beginning of the thirteenth centuries, the great Romanesque churches began to give way to a different style of architecture that we call Gothic. Romanesque churches had thick walls, horizontal lines, extremely heavy stone ceilings (or alternatively flat, wooden ceilings), with rounded arches, and paintings for decoration. In contrast, Gothic churches had lighter ceilings, thinner walls, outside buttressing, and high, ribbed vaults that strove for structural lightness. Gothic architecture emphasized verticality, using pointed

Interior Nave of St. Denys, the Royal Monastic Church Outside Paris   This nave, constructed in the decades after the death of Abbot Suger, faces a choir that Suger had built in the 1140s, in just over three years time, and in which he integrated novel features that were to define the Gothic style. The choir had more delicate piers and more light entering through larger stained glass windows than previous churches. The rounded barrel vaults were replaced with pointed, ribbed arches. The new church made it possible to accommodate the crowds that came on pilgrimage, and the choir included an ambulatory and nine altars that visitors could stop at. The result was a more sublime, airier feeling with a greater emphasis on verticality. *Robert Holmes/Corbis.*

arches, elongated shafts, multiple spires, vaulted roofs, larger arcade and window openings, and decorated flying buttresses. Additional elements one associates with Gothic churches are the elaborate sculptures, rose windows and other stained glass, rather than wall paintings. These responded more to the symbolic meaning of the church than to architectural necessity, although stained glass brought more (divine) light into the interior, contributing to the "lightness" of the building.

Abbot Suger, who wrote about his rebuilding of St. Denys Abbey outside Paris in the 1130s and 1140s, emphasized the importance of light. "The dull mind rises to truth through that which is material, and, in seeing this light, is resurrected from its former subversion." In this, he was influenced by reading pseudo-Dionysius's *On Celestial Hierarchy,* which stressed that material things (as true lamps) lead us to the true light where Christ is the true door. Suger, who wanted to open St. Denys both to God as divine light and to the people, was proud of his achievement. Inside the church he had engraved: "The heart of the sanctuary glows in splendour. That which is united in splendour, radiates in splendour. And the magnificent work inundated with a new light shines. It is I, Suger, who have in my time enlarged this edifice. Under my direction it was done."[14]

St. Denys is the first "Gothic" cathedral, although elements of the Gothic style, such as the ribbed vaults, can be found earlier (for example, at Durham in England). Indeed, any straightforward development of style is not to be found. Multiple masters often worked on one church; master masons were mobile and could work on several buildings; it took decades (and sometimes centuries) to finish these buildings and many builders tended to incorporate archaic, conservative, popular, or experimental elements as the situation demanded. St. Denys, however, does reflect a series of revolutionary choices made by Abbot Suger. Clustered piers, pointed arches, high ribbed vaults, arches springing from shafts, three large sculpted west portals, two western towers, a round window on the west end, ambulatories at the east end, continuous bands of windows, outside buttresses—all these new elements in a royal church ensured that they would be diffused and copied throughout northern France and then the rest of Europe. By the thirteenth century, the classic Gothic style, perhaps best represented by Chartres Cathedral, triumphed.

Medieval churches were built by and for the community. Paid for by donations, tithes, and the profits from fairs and ecclesiastical lands, they were built by laborers and craftsmen who went where the wages were and who gradually organized themselves into guilds. Churches were intended for everyone, and everyone used them— for the liturgy, as pilgrimage sites, for ceremonial occasions, for burials, for sermons, as a meeting place, as schools, even as a gaming area for children. At Amiens, the entire population of the town (c. 8,000 people) could fit in the cathedral. The stained glass windows at Chartres, paid for by guilds, sanctified everyday work with their portraits of butchers, bakers, carpenters, wine merchants, and water carriers. Wooden carvings under the choir seats or sculpted heads at the joins of arches represent scenes of animals, musicians, peasants, or the builders themselves. The medieval church, and particularly the cathedral, represented not only the heavenly city; it represented and served all. While the sculpture program, overall architectural design, and the liturgy were conceived by men steeped in scripture, the

The Gothic Cathedral at Chartres Chartres Cathedral, pictured here, was rebuilt beginning in 1194. The cathedral is 45 feet tall at the clerestory (third floor, top window) level. Its famed stained glass windows (for example, the rose window on the south side pictured here) allow light to flood into the interior. Because of the windows, the walls are less solid; the pillars and pointed, ribbed vaults reach upward. To strengthen this taller, more open church, the builders at Chartres were the first to reinforce an entire cathedral with flying buttresses. Chartres set the pattern for the high Gothic style that would dominate Europe in the thirteenth century. The sculptures around the portals at Chartres are also famous (see Chapter 14). *Archivo Iconografico, S. A./Corbis.*

representations of common people and the multiple uses of the space mirrored the world of less literate souls.

Popular Religion

As in earlier centuries, popular religion in thirteenth-century Europe still centered on relics. St. Denys housed the severed head of its martyred saint; Chartres held the blue tunic of the Virgin that she wore at the birth of Christ. Relics were so popular that people paid to see, touch, or petition them. The thirteenth century saw an enormous increase in the number of relics in Europe. In part this was due to the conquest of Constantinople in 1204 and the subsequent dispersal of its wealth of relics. It was also due to the miraculous (and not so miraculous) multiplication of relics, a practice the Church tried to discourage.

New relics meant new pilgrimage centers. The most famous new site was Canterbury, the scene of Thomas Becket's martyrdom in 1170. Because the murder was so dramatic and the miracles occurring at his tomb so numerous and well publicized, Canterbury quickly became a rival to Compostela and even Rome. In the six years after Becket's death, the monks at Canterbury counted 665 pilgrims who experienced miracles, mostly cures. These pilgrims were from all classes: Twenty-six percent were knights, and the rest middle- and lower-class individuals. A French pilgrim possessed by the devil visited St. Denys only to discover that St. Denys "had left to his colleague St. Thomas the business of curing the sick . . . in order that a new and relatively unknown martyr might make his name." Ten years later, however, Thomas's shrine was passé and new sites (with new relics or holy objects) were considered more efficacious.

Newer forms of popular piety emerged in the thirteenth century in competition with pilgrimages and relics. Three of these were the rise of spiritual "revolutionaries" with apocalyptic expectations and radical ideas on poverty, the emergence of flagellant groups, and the growing popularity of the worship of the body of Christ.

St. Francis had offered a radical example of poverty, but even before he died, the Franciscan order had relaxed its strictures on property. By 1230, the order had become rich from many pious gifts. Eventually a compromise developed by St. Bonaventure and a papal bull issued by Nicholas III in 1274 allowed the Order to enjoy the fruits (i.e. income) from property without holding legal title (which remained in papal hands). While technically adhering to poverty, members of the order were able to live quite comfortable lives.

Some friars remained committed to Francis's extreme ideals on poverty, however. This group, called "Spirituals" (as opposed to "Conventuals"), was also influenced by the prophetic writings of Joachim of Fiore (Chapter 16). Joachim had predicted the coming of a third age (the age of the Holy Spirit) led by a new order of monks. Spiritual Franciscans saw Francis as the herald of this new age. Based upon Joachim's writings, they expected the year 1260 to inaugurate it. Although 1260 proved disappointing, the Joachimite doctrine survived and spread through the writings of spiritual Franciscans of the next generation.

The apocalyptic expectations of the year 1260 were only part of a broad pattern of thirteenth-century apocalyptic beliefs. Antichrist was expected; a messiah would come. In France in 1251, a Hungarian monk-preacher named Jacob summoned the poor, especially shepherds, to go to the Holy Land and free the Holy Sepulchre. The movement, nearly an army, was called the *Pastoureaux,* although people from all occupations joined. They were well received until they began to attack clergy and show contempt for the sacraments. When a royal edict outlawed the movement, they dispersed, to be hunted down through France and as far as England.

Nine years later, in the midst of wars between the Guelfs and Ghibellines in Italy, a new mass movement arose at Perugia. Masses of people, led by priests, processed from town to town flogging themselves with leather whips and metal prongs, demanding peace, and urging others to join this dramatic public penance. Wildly popular, the movement eventually settled down, and groups of flagellants, called *disciplinati,* formed confraternities attached to a particular church where they practiced this form of discipline on a regular basis.

The flagellant movement spread north, particularly to southern Germany and the Rhineland, where hundreds of penitents marched, singing and in uniforms. They claimed to be in possession of a heavenly letter that spelled out God's desire to punish his sinful people. It stated that anyone who joined a flagellant procession for thirty-three and a half days was more likely to be forgiven by God. The letter warned, in the manner of chain letters that circulate today, that if any member of the clergy omitted to pass on this divine message his people would be eternally damned.[15] In Germany this movement took on anticlerical and heretical overtones and was suppressed.

This emphasis on blood and on processions manifested itself in another form of popular piety—the worship of the Corpus Christi, the body of Christ. In the twelfth and thirteenth centuries, the Eucharist rose in importance in Christian worship. Communion was required at least once a year. The Eucharist, which entailed the transubstantiation of bread and wine into the body and blood of Christ, became increasingly elaborate.

At the beginning of the thirteenth century, Juliana of Cornillon (c. 1193–1258), a mystic from near Liège, heard Christ ask her to institute a new feast celebrating his body. After many starts and stops, the papacy declared a universal feast of Corpus Christi in 1264.[16] Miri Rubin argues that the establishment of this moveable feast, which was so different from the usual commemoration of saints, was a reflection of growing clerical power and the emphasis the Church was placing on the sacraments. By 1300, the feast of Corpus Christi had been incorporated into liturgies, into the names of new foundations, and into the sermon literature. By the fourteenth century, any number of religious and guild fraternities were dedicated to Corpus Christ. They promoted activities associated with the Eucharist—processions and, by the 1370s, street dramas. The Eucharistic host began to function as a relic itself. It bled; it cured the sick; it went on display and in procession, to the point where some religious authorities began to request that it be kept indoors and not be carted about the neighborhood.

This focus on Christ's body also gave rise to heresies—the idea that Christ's body could not have been eaten as bread, that he would not put himself in the hands of unworthy priests, that his body was in heaven and remains there. The polemical literature that ensued forms an important backdrop to the Reformation of the sixteenth century and is part of the breakdown in authority of the medieval Church that will be the subject of Chapter 19.

Summary

The dynamism of the thirteenth century is apparent at every level—in the Church, the universities, in the political arena, and among the laity. The richness of the intellectual contributions, leavened with the influx of Aristotle's works and the many texts of Arabic and Greek provenance, was matched by productions in other cultural spheres. Historians have sometimes seen cathedrals as books written in stone, and the greater sophistication in the sculptures and stained glasses of thirteenth-century cathedrals lends itself to this kind of conclusion. The emphasis on religious as well as secular themes in cathedral decorations was mirrored by a vibrant lay culture that was both worldly and devotional. New forms of popular piety appeared, some of them well beyond the bounds of ecclesiastical control. Taken as a whole, both the high and the popular culture of the thirteenth century threatened to move beyond acceptable limits, sometimes provoking harsh reactions in the form of ecclesiastical censure, the growing use of the inquisitorial process, and intolerance of the "other." The conflicting impulses that developed were to become exacerbated in the fourteenth century as economic and demographic upheavals and political crises mounted. Despite growing tensions, however, thirteenth-century Europeans absorbed new influences and produced new forms of thought and devotional practices that opened up a wider world for many; that openness to new experiences and new ideas survived the difficulties to come.

NOTES

1. *The Travels of Marco Polo,* trans. R. Latham (New York: Penguin, 1959) 134.
2. Mark R. Cohen, *Under Crescent and Cross: The Jews in the Middle Ages* (Princeton: Princeton University, 1994).
3. *Summa theologiae,* Ia, q.2, a.3.
4. *Summa theologiae,* I, q.92, a.1.
5. Gordon Leff, *Paris and Oxford Universities in the Thirteenth and Fourteenth Centuries* (New York: Wiley, 1968) 237–238.
6. *The Song of Aliscans,* trans. Michael A. Newth (New York: Garland, 1992) 33 (ll. 1058–1060).
7. *Lancelot, or the Knight of the Cart,* trans. R. Cline (Athens, Ga.: Georgia University Press, 1990) ll. 3798–3800.
8. *Malory. Complete Works,* 2nd ed., ed. Eugène Vinaver (London: Oxford University Press, 1971) 603.
9. Margaret Switten, "Singing the Second Crusade," *The Second Crusade and the Cistercians,* ed. M. Gervers (New York: St. Martin's Press, 1992) 67–76; Frederick Goldin, *Lyrics of the Troubadours and Trouvères: An Anthology and a History* (Garden City, N.Y.: Anchor Books, 1973).
10. Meg Bogin, *The Women Troubadours* (New York: Norton, 1980) 85.
11. Charles Muscatine, *The Old French fabliaux* (New Haven: Yale University Press, 1986) 103–104.
12. B.J. Whiting, *Proverbs, Sentences and Proverbial Phrases from English Writings Mainly before 1500* (Cambridge: Belknap Press, 1968); Nicholas Orme, "Early School Note-Books," in Orme, *Education and Society in Medieval and Renaissance England* (London: Hambleton Press, 1989) 83–84.
13. George T. Peck, *The Fool of God: Jacopone da Todi* (Tuscaloosa: University of Alabama Press, 1980) 67.

14. *Abbot Suger on Abbey Church of St. Denis and its Art Treasures,* ed. and trans. E. Panofsky, 2nd edition (Princeton: Princeton University Press, 1979) 48–51.
15. Norman Cohn, *The Pursuit of the Millennium* (New York: Oxford University Press, 1970) 129–130.
16. Miri Rubin, *Corpus Christi: The Eucharist in Late Medieval Culture,* ch. 3 (Cambridge: Cambridge University Press, 1991).

PART VI

~

The Later Middle Ages, 1300–1492

CHAPTER 18

∾

Economic and Political Crisis, 1300–1450

At the beginning of the fourteenth century, France, Germany, and Spain were expanding on the continent. Italian city-states dominated Mediterranean sea-lanes and were sailing the Atlantic route to northern Europe and beginning to control the Italian countryside. England, in the capable hands of King Edward I, was aggressively moving into Scotland and Wales. Aragon in eastern Spain was developing a seaborne empire that extended into Greece. Eastern Europe had consolidated into the kingdoms of Hungary, Poland, and Lithuania (soon to be joined), Bohemia, and the lands of the Teutonic Order. The pope in 1300 was asserting the most far-reaching claims over the kings of Europe and demanding obedience. These expanding populations, dynamic economies, and efforts of overreaching rulers were unsustainable, however.

By 1450, France was exhausted from plague, the Hundred Years' War, and the depredations of mercenary soldiers and had to rebuild. England was on the eve of a civil conflict ("The War of the Roses"), and the papacy was trying to rebuild after an extended residency at Avignon and a schism among the cardinals and the papacy itself. Population was at its lowest point in perhaps two hundred years. In terms of climate, Europe was experiencing a "Little Ice Age," and, to add to the unsettling picture, eastern Europe was threatened by the Ottoman Turks. Simultaneously, however, the elements for an economic revival were in place, nation-states were taking shape, new technologies of war were making knights obsolete, a cultural renaissance in Italy was in full swing, much of eastern Europe was in a golden age, and Europe was on the cusp of a worldwide expansion.

This transitional period from 1300 to 1450, so perplexing in its simultaneous contraction and dynamism, has been characterized by one historian as the "waning" of the Middle Ages, while another has labeled it an "age of ambition." It is sometimes described as a time of decline; it is also labeled the age of the Italian Renaissance. Often seen as a time of intellectual dissolution (from the high point of the great contributions of the thirteenth century), it was also a period of expanding education and of lively intellectual centers. An era of papal decline, it simultaneously experienced growing piety, mysticism, and parish investments; a time of war, it witnessed rising nations and city-states; a time of economic contraction, it saw increases in per capita income and a wealthier peasant class. But the first fifty years began inauspiciously, culminating in an epidemic of bubonic plague.

EUROPE IN CRISIS, 1300–1348

In the half century prior to the outbreak of plague, western Europe appears to have contracted economically and demographically. Climate became colder; famines and bankruptcies occurred; politics were remarkably unstable.

A Colder Climate Brings Famine

From growing evidence of expanding Alpine and polar glaciers, reports of ice floes in the sea-lanes between Scandinavia, Iceland, and Greenland, and the freezing of the Thames River, historians conclude that a Little Ice Age occurred between 1300 and the late 1400s. Colder and stormier weather handicapped agriculture, reducing cultivation at a time when Europe's population density (which in some areas was not exceeded until the twentieth century) was pressing hard upon available resources. Living standards stagnated, and more and more peasants worked marginal lands or turned to day labor.

While no one debates the climate changes, historians have had much debate regarding the extent of economic hardship and demographic crisis in the early fourteenth century. Evidence for it is inconclusive and sometimes contradictory;* still, most historians agree that a crisis was mounting. Certain economic indicators— falling rents, empty tenement houses in towns, and decreasing agricultural cultivation—support this interpretation. Active land sales, especially in rural areas, suggest distress sales by the poor. By the 1290s, there were scattered harvest shortfalls. Some people died of famine. Cold winters, rainy summers, and poor harvests were reported in northern Europe around 1300. Between 1315 and 1320 harvests failed throughout the north, forcing people to eat "strange diets"—dogs, cats, horses, and, reportedly, human beings. Troops were needed to control the markets; perhaps five to ten percent of the population perished. People were further battered by livestock losses from rampant diseases, and then, by the early 1320s, by drought and further harvest failures. Only in the mid-1320s was there a return to normalcy, though scattered famines continued in the 1330s and early 1340s.

---

* Few documents exist from this period to allow historians to calculate population statistics. The occasional census, as in Tuscany, and sometimes manor rolls give demographic information on a small regional basis. As a result, attempts to analyze death, replacement, and fertility rates are problematic. Medieval historians have to depend upon indirect indices for determining demographic trends—indications of land pattern use, evidence for land sales, comments from chroniclers, wage rates, and trade patterns.

Financial and Political Insecurity

Financially, western Europe was in a precarious position by the 1340s. England declared bankruptcy, refusing to pay its Italian creditors. As a consequence, the three leading banking houses of Florence collapsed by 1345/46. The downfall of the last crusading stronghold (Acre, which fell to the Mamluks in 1291), and the closing down of routes into East Asia also hurt the European economy. Turkish invasions, Mongol attacks, and a more effective papal ban on trade with Muslims (particularly between 1323 and 1344) diminished commerce between West and East. And piracy was a growing problem in the Mediterranean. In response to these disruptions, European merchants pulled back from their trade in low cost items to concentrate on luxury items, whose higher prices balanced out the growing risks and diminishing markets.

While trade became more difficult, internal security was also worsening. Notorious in this respect was the government of Edward II of England (r. 1307–1327). His father, Edward I (r. 1272–1307), had been a strong king though he wasted resources on overly ambitious wars with France, Wales, and especially with Scotland. At the time of Edward's death, the English were overburdened with war taxes, and justice had devolved into the hands of aristocratic commissioners and often capricious local justices of the peace. Edward II was not the king to set it right. He did not enjoy governing, much preferring to hunt and to spend time with countryfolk. He also had his favorites (first Piers Gaveston from Gascony, and then the two Hugh Despensers, father and son), giving rise to concerns on the part of contemporaries and speculation on the part of modern historians that Edward was homosexual. In 1312, Edward's barons seized and beheaded Gaveston, embittering Edward. Subsequent baronial efforts to force reforms on Edward provoked civil war from 1321 to 1322. In addition, Robert Bruce, lord of Annandale and future king of Scotland, led the Scots to rebel, decisively defeating Edward's army at the Battle of Bannockburn in 1314. Finally, Edward's queen Isabella with her lover and her young son rebelled and invaded England in 1326, overthrowing Edward. Given all this, it is no surprise that government under Edward was lax, justice notably corrupt, and criminal violence rampant (see Medieval Portrait).

One cause of the violence was the custom of maintenance, where magnates gave livery (clothing with identifying colors and badges) to armed bands. The wealthy found these bands useful for subverting justice (for example, by threatening jurors and parties to lawsuits) and conducting local feuds. People tended to carry weapons with them—knives, swords, or longbows, depending upon one's social status—thus intensifying the violence. Corrupt royal courts sometimes responded by outlawing individuals, depriving them of basic legal rights and property, perhaps for unfair reasons. These outlaws sometimes organized their own bands. In the 1320s and 1330s, two well-known gangs were active in England—the Coterels and the Folvilles. Led by members of the gentry class, they were employed by abbots and higher officials to do their dirty work. It proved difficult to bring such gangs to justice; local juries were either protective of them or threatened by them.

The Robin Hood legends most likely emerged from these conditions. They appear to have some historical basis, possibly originating as early as the thirteenth

MEDIEVAL PORTRAITS

William Wallace and Robert Bruce

Every history of Scotland highlights the unexpected death of King Alexander III (r. 1249–1286), whose fall over a cliff in the middle of a stormy night precipitated a political crisis. The subsequent death in 1290 of Alexander's only direct heir (Margaret of Norway) opened the kingship to two claimants, John Balliol and Robert Bruce, and to the aggressive opportunism of Edward I of England. While acting as an impartial overlord in the choice between Balliol and Bruce, Edward prepared a legal and historical claim to the Scottish throne and bolstered his military, administrative, and judicial presence in southern Scotland. In the end John Balliol was chosen king. He was, by all accounts, an earnest ruler, and not, as legend has it, Edward's puppet. But Edward proceeded to humiliate him, declared English sovereignty over Scotland, and inserted his followers into government and church and his military into the countryside. Acts of Scottish resistance followed. In retaliation Edward massacred the townsfolk of Berwick and removed the Stone of Destiny—on which Scottish kings were crowned—to Westminster.

The resulting Scottish rebellion was led, in large part, by William Wallace (c. 1270–1305), the younger son of a lesser noble who had been killed by the English in 1291. Wallace is a rather shadowy figure with all the elements of which legends are made. He was an impressive person—6'7" tall, a warrior of uncommon skill and strength, with an ability to lead men and to reconcile factions. While he was an effective guerilla leader, he also won the more traditional battle at Stirling Bridge, where Scottish foot soldiers decimated the English cavalry. Wallace was Guardian of Scotland briefly; but in the end he was betrayed, captured, and brutally executed by the English.

Subsequent to Wallace's death, Robert Bruce (1274–1327) emerged as an anti-English leader and the most obvious heir to the throne. An early supporter of Wallace, he had also, as prudence may have dictated (Bruce owned lands in England), gone over to the side of Edward in 1302. Therefore, partisans of Wallace are not always praising of Bruce. In the final analysis, however, it was Robert Bruce who led the guerilla forces that undid Edward's occupation. Only seven months after Wallace's execution, Robert Bruce was crowned King Robert I of Scotland. Enthroned by Isabel of Fife, as head of her kin, at Scone, he immediately had to fight for his crown. The losses were grim, including three of his brothers, and his own survival was often perilous. Bruce was finally aided by the death of Edward I, the sluggishness of Edward II, and by his growing popularity among the people and preachers of Scotland. In 1314, he devastated an English army at Bannockburn and ruled Scotland forcefully until his death.

century, although the weight of evidence points to Edward II's reign. By 1400, they were popular throughout England. Historians have located a place—probably Barnesdale in Yorkshire rather than Sherwood Forest. They have identified a likely sheriff, a candidate for Robin's knightly friend Richard at Lee, and a Long John. They have located the priory where Robin Hood was said to have been bled to death, and they believe that the abbot of St. Mary's York was corrupt, as the legend suggests. Several candidates for Robin have been found, but there is no agreement

Fourteenth-Century Longbow and Crossbow This image, which comes from a fourteenth-century English manuscript, shows the two most common bows used in medieval warfare. The crossbow (on the right) was heavier and slower to load and shoot, but sufficiently powerful to penetrate armor. The other bow is what is traditionally called a longbow. In 1252, in England, all men with property worth more than 40 shillings were to possess one. It was not until the campaigns of Edward I, however, that the longbow overtook the crossbow as a weapon of choice. The longbow was as powerful as the crossbow, but it was faster, more flexible, and could kill at a range of 300 yards. When archers with these bows were massed together in large numbers, their impact on the opposing army could be devastating. *The British Library, London/Bridgeman Art.*

on which might be the real Robin, or whether Robin was a composite. Experts do agree that there was no Maid Marian, who first appears in sixteenth-century versions of the legend.

Problems with public order, the continuous state of warfare between England and Scotland, and periodic hostilities with France strained English resources. Economic problems arising from the famine of 1315/20 and violent fluctuations in the English money supply made things worse. By the time Edward III (r. 1327–1377) imposed unprecedented demands for resources to fight France in the Hundred Years' War, the economy was far less able than before to sustain such pressure.

Across the English Channel, France was suffering under the government of Philip IV, "The Fair" (r. 1285–1314). Philip brought the French monarchy to a height of power and influence, but he did so at great cost. He fought expensive, unsuccessful wars with Flanders, Gascony, and Aquitaine. He increased the size of the bureaucracy and expanded the role of the royal courts. Needing money, he imposed the first general taxes in French history and manipulated the currency to his benefit. He expelled the Jews in 1306, confiscating their properties. Philip intervened much more directly in people's lives than any previous French king. He called the first meeting of the Estates of the realm to ratify his often unpopular decisions, and he actively encouraged propaganda in favor of royal authority and the needs of the body politic. His most recent historian concludes that under Philip IV, the balance of loyalty swung toward the secular, sovereign state.[1] In this sense, his reign is the beginning of the modern state. At his death, he left his subjects poorer than when he ascended the throne. The French barons, who had grown to hate his ministers, forced their resignation under his son, Louis X.

Philip expanded upon the traditionally sacred image of French kingship. His propagandists proclaimed a kingship that was uniquely sacred, held directly from God, and imperial in scope. All subjects, including the clergy, owed him obedience and service. His sacred status stood at some variance, however, with his unscrupulous means. Two episodes were particularly problematic—his attack on the authority of the papacy in the person of Pope Boniface VIII (see Chapter 19) and his condemnation of the Knights Templar.

At the beginning of the fourteenth century, the Knights Templar transferred many of their assets from the Holy Land to France where they already held extensive properties and functioned as the king's bankers. In a secret and highly efficient operation in October 1307, Philip had the members arrested. Accusing them of heresy, blasphemy, and sexual deviance, and using torture and threats of burning, he extracted confessions of wrongdoing. A few, including the Grand Master, Jacques de Molay, retracted their confessions and were burned. The papacy acquiesced in Philip's actions, albeit unhappily. Pope Clement V (1305–1314) insisted, however, that Temple property be transferred to other orders, and Philip gained relatively little in the end.

After Philip IV's death, his line died out. (Contemporaries related it to a curse placed on the king by Jacques de Molay.) Between 1314 and 1328, his two sons and grandson died without male heirs; the French throne was up for grabs. Although it went to Philip of Valois, Philip IV's nephew, Edward III of England had a good claim to it. In passing the throne from Capetian to Valois, the French overlooked the claims of female Capetians. They argued that an ancient Frankish rule called the Salic Law prevented them from accepting a king through female descent. In truth, no records of any such law exist before a claim to this effect was made in 1317. Edward III, technically the closest surviving male descendant of Philip IV through his mother Isabella (Philip's daughter), asserted his rights to the throne anyway, thereby initiating what came to be called The Hundred Years' War.

Italy suffered disruption as well, as the Guelf-Ghibelline struggles intensified in the 1320s and 1330s. Political conditions in Naples and Sicily became chaotic, where French, Germans, Aragonese, and the Angevin rulers of Hungary* all intervened at various times, destroying both economies and unleashing a plague of mercenary soldiers. By the 1340s, republics throughout Italy gave way to more authoritarian regimes. From 1300 to 1450, Milan, the largest city, was in the hands of the Visconti family, ruthless, aggressive military leaders who nearly destroyed Florence in 1400. Clearly the first half of the fourteenth century was an unsettled

---

* After the death of King Ladislas IV of Hungary in 1290, his sister Marie of Hungary, the wife of Charles II of Naples, had the best claim to the throne. It was not until 1308, however, that her grandson, Charles-Robert, was finally accepted as ruler by the Hungarians. Because he descended from the Angevin rulers of Naples, he and his son Louis the Great (r. 1342–1382) are called the Angevin rulers of Hungary.

period for western Europe, and it culminated in the first visitation of the second pandemic of bubonic plague.*

THE BLACK DEATH

The fourteenth-century plague we call "The Black Death" was one of the greatest natural disasters mankind has endured. Bubonic plague is spread by the bacillus *Pasteurella pestis,* which can be transmitted by fleas that reside on rodents (rats, squirrels, and marmots, for example). During an epidemic, it can also spread from person to person by coughing. This pulmonary or pneumonic form of the plague is invariably fatal: People die from it within two days but often within hours. The bubonic form, transmitted by fleas, kills more slowly—after four or five days—and is less lethal, with a death rate of around sixty percent of those infected.[†] It produces, as one medieval chronicler put it, a "swollen and dropsical mass of inflamed lymphatic glands," called buboes. The buboes are painful; the blood turns black; there is internal hemorrhaging and a disoriented nervous system. A medieval Welsh lament described

> . . . death coming into our midst like black smoke, a plague which cuts off the young, a rootless phantom which has no mercy for the fair countenance. Woe is me of the "shilling" in the armpit; it is seething, terrible . . . a head that gives pain and causes a loud cry . . . a painful angry knob. . . . Great is its seething, like a burning cinder, a grievous thing of an ashy color . . . seeds of black peas, broken fragments of brittle sea-coal . . . the early ornaments of black death. . . .[2]

The Plague Spreads Throughout Europe

The plague entered Europe in 1347. It seems to have originated in the steppe of central Asia, provoked by an overpopulation of marmots, the movement of Mongols, or an earthquake that forced rodent populations out of their burrows. Although the accuracy of the story is suspect, Italian chroniclers thought the plague entered Europe when Genoese soldiers and sailors, defending the Black Sea port of Caffa, were infected. They fled in ships, first to Messina in Sicily and then to Genoa. The people of Messina allowed them to dock, but seeing the deaths, forced them back to sea. However it arrived, the plague spread through Italy in 1347. By January 1348, it reached southern France. By June and August, it traveled to Paris, and early in 1349 it crossed the channel to England. Scandinavia was devastated in 1350; it reached the northern states of Rusland in 1352 (see Map 18.1).

Giovanni Boccaccio wrote the most famous account of this plague in the introduction to his *Decameron* (1350). Boccaccio stressed the rapidity and enormity of

---

* The first pandemic occurred in the sixth century, devastating the empire of Justinian (see Chapter 4) and depopulating the West.
† Early in the twentieth century a vaccine was discovered that cures bubonic plague if administered early enough.

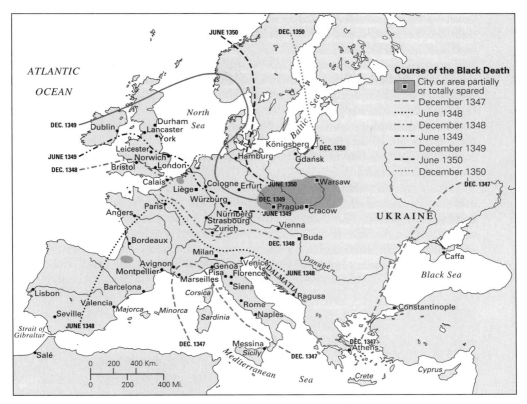

Map 18.1   The Spread of Bubonic Plague, 1347–1350   Although bubonic plague spread mainly through trading routes, very few rural areas escaped completely and some were devastated. Milan was spared largely because its rulers barricaded houses with the victims inside. The progress of the plague was rapid, reaching the eastern Baltic shores by 1350; it had already reached the Ukraine in 1347.

the deaths and the extent to which society broke apart in the face of such "cruelty of heaven and of man." Relatives deserted relatives; husbands deserted wives; parents deserted children. Thieves made off with the bodies and their goods; funeral services became an impossibility; people took corpses from their homes and set them out in the street to be carted away. Boccaccio concludes, "It was come to this, that a dead man was then of no more account than a dead goat would be today."

The Church met the onslaught with prayers and processions. Soon, however, it was clear that processions spread the plague, and they were stopped. Church bells, usually rung at funerals, rang so continuously they had to be silenced. Bodies outnumbered the available graveyards, so new burial grounds were hastily consecrated. The laity were counselled to confess to one another in the absence of a priest. While some priests may have fled, many clergy did their duty. In England, forty to forty-five percent of the beneficed clergy died. The Church responded by ordaining huge numbers of new, sometimes barely literate clergy. In fact, the Church could do little to protect people, and many concluded that plague was God's punishment for their sins and those of the Church.

The medical establishment could do little either. Doctors did not understand the causes or methods of transmission of bubonic plague. Some thought it was spread by a poisonous miasma in the air, or caused by astrological alignments or earthquakes or transmitted by the looks of sick people. Some thought that the wells had been poisoned (perhaps by Jews or lepers). Doctors urged people not to breathe the noxious air, to eat certain herbs and spices, purge or bleed themselves and, in general, keep their bodily humors balanced. The most helpful recommendations were quarantines and flight.*

Some long-term responses to the crisis proved useful. Medical training became more professionalized, with greater emphasis on anatomy, surgery, and more hands-on medicine. Many towns and hospitals hired public doctors, regulating their activities. As early as 1347, some Italian towns created boards of public health with authority to impose quarantines, improve sanitary conditions, supervise city doctors, report cases of plague, and collect information on the dead. Eventually these preventive measures worked, but most were not in place between 1347 and 1350.

Impact of the Plague

Overall an estimated thirty to fifty percent of the population of Europe died in this pandemic. Ecclesiastical records are filled with references to orphans, widows, and widowers. A great many intellectuals of the time died, although mortality among academics was relatively low (estimated at fifteen percent at Oxford University, for example). Francesco Petrarch lost his beloved Laura. Geoffrey Chaucer, who was six at the time, lost many of his relatives but (atypically) neither parent. Twenty-eight percent of the cardinals of the Church died, as did 25 archbishops and 207 bishops. Humans, however, are amazingly resilient, and by 1360 population levels were recovering. Marriage and birth rates were high and mortality low. But plague returned in 1361 and again in 1369, each time killing another ten to twenty percent of the population. It then entered a cycle in which it recurred approximately every twenty years well into the fifteenth century. The population of western Europe lost its ability to recover and declined for over a century.

In the panic of plague, two groups, lepers and Jews, were vulnerable to scapegoating. Lepers were shunned and counted as among the dead; they lived out their lives in leper hospitals and colonies. During the plague, they not only died in great numbers due to their already weakened conditions, they were also killed under sus-

---

* One writer, Ibn al-Khatīb in Spain, recognized the infectious nature of the plague. He noted that it arrived with contaminated merchants and that the nomads, who were relatively isolated, were less affected. In contrast, many Islamic religious scholars believed that individuals could not escape God's will and should not try, and that those who died were martyrs.

picion of poisoning the air or the water supply. Following this, lepers and leprosy disappeared from Europe.*

Jewish communities suffered especially. By 1351, 60 major and 150 smaller Jewish communities were destroyed and over 350 separate massacres had taken place. Nearly all Jewish communities in Germany were gone; survivors migrated to Poland, Lithuania, and the principalities of Rusland where they were offered protection and where they remained until the twentieth century. Responsibility for these massacres rests partly with a revived flagellant movement, particularly in Germany. Highly organized and highly inflammatory, these groups passed by the thousands through towns and villages, scourging themselves. They sang hymns of Christ's passion and were generally viewed as martyrs and men of God. Becoming increasing militant, they turned against the clergy, the Jews, and the well-to-do, until in October 1349 Pope Clement VI required their suppression.

Although we can see some of the immediate psychological and religious effects of plague, long-term effects are less clear. To some degree, historians have to guess. In the Middle Ages death was a public occurrence. People believed that you died as you lived, and chroniclers often wrote of the saintly deaths of saintly individuals. A violent or unquiet death suggested some hidden sin. In the plague, however, innocent children died painfully alongside seasoned sinners. Even saints died in agony. The result may have been a sense that the world was less rational than previously thought and less just—or, possibly, people saw it as more sinful, worthy of such pain. Archbishop Zouch of the English city of York wrote in a 1349 circular letter to his clergy, "This, surely, must be caused by the sins of men who, made complacent by their prosperity, forget the bounty of the Most High Giver." Matteo Villani, a Florentine chronicler, wrote, "Having to begin our treatise by recounting the extermination of humankind. . . . My mind is stupified as it applies itself to write the sentence that divine justice with great compassion sent on mankind, worthy by corruption of sin of the final judgment."[3]

Another possible conclusion was that the Church, by its sinfulness, helped bring on the plague. As a result, people may have turned away from it. This is suggested by the growth of private religiosity and anticlericalism, and by the development of new heresies. It is not that Europeans became irreligious. Rather, they began investing in local parish churches rather than in cathedrals, joining religious confraternities governed by laymen, bequeathing monies to schools or to local recluses, and reading vernacular devotional works on their own. One of the more popular devotional books, written in the fifteenth century by Thomas à Kempis, a monk from the Low Countries, was *The Imitation of Christ*. It provides guidance for individual examination of the soul in preparation for death. Written in dialogue form, with Christ as an interlocutor, it is still one of the more popular works of Christian devotion ever written.

---

* Various theories explain the disappearance of leprosy in Europe by 1400. One theory argues that pulmonary tuberculosis, which was on the increase, offered a degree of immunity to leprosy. Another argues that consumption of vitamin C increased. Perhaps it was also the high death rate of lepers and the new health measures, one of which was to burn the clothes of the dead.

Can one discern the impact of plague upon the literature and art of the time? Perhaps. Treatises on the "Art of Dying" became popular, and the theme of death appeared in manuscript illuminations, frescoes, and tomb sculpture. *Transitio* tombs appeared that illustrated an individual both alive and in an advanced state of physical decay, sometimes with the words, "I was that which you are and what I am that will you be." And finally, the theme of the dance of death developed, particularly in France. It commonly included a skeletal figure of death leading the living in a dance to their deaths.

In terms of literature, Boccaccio's *Decameron* includes plague as a background frame for the hedonistic stories told by ten young men and women fleeing the morbidity of Florence. But his work is unusual in its extended description of plague. Thirty to forty years later William Langland, in *Piers Plowman,* mentions the plague but seems more concerned with the moral inadequacies of government and clergy. Geoffrey Chaucer, who lived through several visitations of the plague, rarely mentions it. Some of the leading mystical writers of the time, Catherine of Siena and Julian of Norwich, who, as children, witnessed the plague of 1348, do not talk about it. Therefore, one is left to ask: Were flights into mysticism, the ironic detachment of Geoffrey Chaucer, or the anticlericalism in Chaucer, Langland, and Boccaccio consequences of a fundamental disillusionment that arose from the experience of rampant death? We cannot say.

URBAN AND RURAL ECONOMIES AND THE POLITICS OF REVOLT

However difficult it is to determine the short-term impact of the plague, conclusions about the long-term economic impact of the plague are not easily reached either. Overall, recovery from the 1348 visitation seems to have been substantial. Not until plague returned in the 1360s, 1370s, 1390s, and into the next century did demographic decline become pronounced and long term. The shifting economies may, however, have contributed to the atmosphere of discontent that led to a significant number of revolts in the fifty years after the plague.

Post-Plague Economies

By the early fifteenth century, vacant holdings and uncultivated acres became common features of the western European landscape. In England, two thousand to three thousand late medieval deserted villages have been discovered. In most cases these were small, poor villages whose survivors may have moved to larger, more prosperous places. In other cases, agricultural areas reverted to pasture for sheep. All indications from wills, inventories, land sales, and building styles suggest that, by the fifteenth century, rural areas throughout much of Europe were losing population but gaining wealth.

Some rural folks migrated to towns and cities. Urban areas like London, Paris, Florence, and Cologne depended upon migration for population replacement. As a result, most urban areas continued to thrive until the fifteenth century, at which time depopulation was sufficiently extensive that some towns, such as York and Bruges, declined markedly. To some extent these declines were balanced by the continued vitality of older trading centers like London and Milan, by the emergence of newer towns, like Amsterdam, and by the economic boom now being experienced in the towns of eastern Europe. Clearly, in the wake of plague, wealth shifted around quite a bit.

Not surprisingly, depopulation eventually put pressure on wage rates. Wages did not rise immediately following 1347/48. The English Parliament tried to guarantee the availability of workers by quashing higher wages and preventing job mobility. The rapid replacement of some of the diminished population also dampened wage rises. Finally, inflation in most parts of western Europe made any real wage rate gains difficult. Real wages and per capita income rose by the late 1370s, however, when sustained demographic decline set in. By then the dearth of skilled artisans enabled them to demand higher prices and better wages. Long-term scarcity of workers increased the labor value of women, laborers, and farmers. Members of the artisan and bourgeois classes were able to dress better, consume more, and build bigger houses. Bourgeois houses in some towns began to feature large chambers, libraries, maids' quarters, bathrooms, fireplaces, mirrors and glass windows, cellars, halls, and even chapels. These newly rich could also afford an education for their children.

The nouveaux riche were not always well received. Henry Knighton, a canon at Leicester, complained in 1388 of "the elation of the lesser folk in dress and accoutrements in these days . . . so that one person cannot be discerned from another in splendor of dress or belongings, neither poor from rich and powerful nor servant from master."[4] As a result, governments throughout Europe passed laws, called sumptuary laws, that attempted to regulate personal extravagances and conspicuous consumption. The combination of labor scarcity, wage laws, and sumptuary laws aggravated social tensions.

Revolts and Rebellions

A remarkable number of revolts and rebellions occurred throughout late medieval Europe. Prior to the Black Death, a serious revolt took place in Flanders between 1323 and 1328. After the Flemish reconquered Flanders from the French at the famous Battle of Courtrai (1302), they were not going to accept pro-French policies from the count of Flanders. Abusive taxes and corrupt officials were also threatening them. The peasants and urban workers who revolted were well organized, with a hierarchy of assemblies and a rough form of republicanism. They succeeded in throwing out corrupt officials and replacing them with their own people, preventing tax collections, and defeating the count's army several times. By the end of the revolt, they had moved beyond concern with a heavy-handed state and had begun to question the entire notion of privilege. In 1328, however, knights invading from France destroyed them. Although thousands died in the aftermath, the urban guilds, particularly the cloth guilds, succeeded in overthrowing pro-French mercantile interests and gaining access to seats in town government. While they never controlled the towns, they did strengthen their political and economic position.

This revolt, notable for its level of organization and its comparative success, was one of many revolts in the fourteenth and fifteenth centuries. In Germany, for example, it is estimated that there were sixty separate peasant revolts between 1336 and 1525. From 1347 to 1351, the people of Rome, led by an upstart named Cola di Rienzo, usurped the city government and tried to reconstitute elements of the ancient Roman Republic. Among the most violent of the late medieval rebellions was the 1358 French "Jacquerie," so-called because of the derogative term "Jacques" given to French peasants. Over the course of two weeks, rural artisans, clerks, clergy, and bourgeoisie from the Loire and Seine valleys in the heart of France revolted. Their action appears to have been part of a larger movement, emanating from Paris, of townsfolk destroying neighboring castles and of nonnobles attacking nobles. Both the uprising and its put-down were sudden, bloody events that shocked Europe. Froissart, a late fourteenth-century Flemish chronicler wrote, unsympathetically: "These mischievous people thus assembled without captain or armor, robbed, burnt and slew all the gentlemen that they could lay hands on, and forced and ravished ladies and damsels and did such shameful deeds that no human creature ought to think on any such, and he that did most mischief was most praised. . . ."[5]

Twenty years later, in 1378, the dye workers of the city of Florence (called *ciompi* from their dye-colored feet) rebelled. Their revolt followed nearly forty years of riots and insurrections in Florence and neighboring towns. In contrast with revolts in northern Europe, the peasants in the countryside were not involved. Although the ciompi were initially successful, the coalition government they created fell in 1382. When the ruling oligarchy returned to power, they destroyed the guilds the ciompi had created.

Perhaps the best-known revolt took place in England in 1381. In May and June peasants and artisans in southern England revolted. Their rebellion spread to urban areas, especially London, and then north, destroying manors and manorial court rolls; attacking royal officials, justices, and tax-collectors; and targeting selected persons and properties (for example, the archbishop of Canterbury was beheaded and Savoy House, belonging to the king's uncle John of Gaunt, was burned). Finally, however, the rebels were disbursed and their leaders killed.

The causes and goals of this particular revolt have been much debated. Underlying it was the frustration of common people who were not benefiting from an economy with scarce labor and cheap land. Rather than allow rents to go down and wages to go up, landlords had tried to reinforce servile tenures and recuperate rents. From the 1350s, Parliament legislated wage ceilings. In the late 1370s, Parliament imposed a highly regressive poll tax that was collected not once, but three times. These inequities spurred an ideological commitment to equality best expressed in the succinct words of John Ball, a priest-leader of the revolt: "When Eve delved and Adam span, who was then the gentleman?" As a result, the rebels rose with clearly defined grievances and goals and did a reasonable job of destroying the instruments of their oppression, whether written records or particular individuals. Although the rebels honored the monarchy, they attacked lordship and landlords, asking for an end to servitude. They voiced hatred of lawyers, petitioning the king to behead "all lawyers, escheators and others who had been trained in the law." And they asked that government once again be regulated by the decrees of the common people.[6]

Some historians have argued that these revolts represent a crisis in feudalism or the first sign of proletarian struggle. Some have argued that they were spontaneous uprisings. It is noteworthy that women did not seem to play a strong role, perhaps because they were doing better economically. In general, although the revolts were fairly well organized and on occasion voiced an ideology of equality, they were unsuccessful overall.

FAMILY LIFE AND COURTLY CULTURE

Women were an integral part of the late medieval economy, and, at a time when labor was scarce, their work became more valuable. Women seem to have had a marked ability to move between jobs (see Chapter 15), and this may have increased after the plague. In some cities, such as Cologne, women ran their own businesses. Throughout Europe women were prominent in the textile and secondhand clothes industry; they dominated the silk industry where they had their own guilds. Sometimes they ran schools; in Paris the schoolmistresses had a guild. The growing ability of women to earn an income may partly explain the rising living standards so apparent by the end of the fourteenth century. It may also explain the larger number of single, unmarried women, the later age at which women tended to get married, and the fewer children they had, at least in northern Europe, at the end of the Middle Ages.

In southern Europe, labor shortages did not push native women into the labor market. Instead, a lively slave trade developed between the Crimean steppe and the western Mediterranean. Tartar women (and some men) were captured and transported from the Crimea to slave markets in Majorca, Genoa, Marseilles, and elsewhere. There they were sold as slave-servants to wealthy and middle-class townsfolk. Florence, for example, having lost nearly two-thirds of its population since the early fourteenth century, had a great many domestic slaves who filled the labor gap, thereby providing Florentines with more leisure and resources for investing in arts and culture.

While women played an increasingly important economic role, their legal status was limited, although this varied from place to place. In a few towns (such as Cologne and Lübeck in Germany) women had a remarkable number of freedoms. But in many jurisdictions they could not inherit, or inherited only half of what a son would inherit (see Chapter 15). While aristocratic or royal women took part in politics, most women did not and could not hold public offices, such as on city councils or in guilds. They had no voting rights, and sometimes could not represent themselves in legal cases, make or execute wills, or administer their own estates. Adulteresses were treated more harshly than adulterers, and female prostitutes were increasingly placed in controlled ghettoes. Still, women did play significant roles, as in the cases of Christine de Pizan and Joan of Arc. One example of a lesser

Women Weaving, Carding, and Spinning Wool
This image comes from a fifteenth-century manuscript of Giovanni Boccaccio's book "On Famous Women." The women are carding the wool to spin it and then weaving dyed wool. In the high Middle Ages women often worked in fabric workshops, producing a large percentage of the cloth exported throughout Europe and beyond. Gradually, however, men took over many aspects of wool production, such as dying, fulling, and weaving. They organized themselves into guilds to which women sometimes, but not always, belonged. *The Art Archive.*

known albeit influential woman is Gertrude Morneweg, a merchant's widow in the city of Lübeck who cornered the bond market early in the fourteenth century, benefiting from foreclosures of wealthy families to whom she had extended loans.[7]

Women were not included among the idealized "three orders" of medieval society, i.e., those who worked, those who prayed, and those who fought (see Chapter 9). Instead, they had a separate, parallel hierarchy: virgins at the top, then widows, with married women at the bottom. Toward the end of the Middle Ages, these values shifted somewhat as motherhood rose in esteem. Married women with children began to aspire to sanctity. Images of the Holy Family were more common, and devotion to Mary, the mother of Christ, and St. Anne, the mother of Mary, grew. More and more often Christ was portrayed as an infant or small child held by Mary or perhaps being taught by her with book in hand. Books were written for the Good Housewife, whose value was now, at least, being debated rather than denigrated or ignored.

A wife had many responsibilities. Despite the disruptions of the fourteenth century, family life in this period showed many similarities to family life in the thirteenth century. Women were in charge of the household, including the servants, children, and foster-children if the household was a large one. Most people lived in nuclear families, although at least in northern Europe those families were smaller than before—the birth rate might have dropped as low as two to three children per family, either because of the prevalence of disease or because the use of contraceptives or abstinence were limiting fertility.

Medieval families valued their children and mourned them when they died, an unfortunately common occurrence given the high death rate for children (see Chapter 15). In poorer families, the mother took the child along while she worked, while in wealthier families children were cared for by wet-nurses, servants, and babysitters. The ideal wet-nurse was expected to nourish and mother the child, empathize with its joys and sorrows, give the child daily baths and rides on her shoulder, sing lullabies, and rock it on her knee. As children grew, they played with toys (rattles, balls, rocking horses, blocks, boats, dolls, even a bicycle-like riding toy), played running games, imitated adults in their play, made swords and horses out of sticks, and constructed castles.[8] After age seven, children were thought to require instruction along with occasional beatings to modify behavior. A fourteenth-century child-rearing book ("Symon's Lesson") cautions: "Child, climb not over house nor wall, For no fruit, birds nor ball. Child, over men's houses no stones fling, Nor at glass windows no stones sling. . . . And child, when thou goest to play, Look thou come home by light of day."[9]

Medieval writers listed three stages of development: infancy (to age seven), childhood (from seven to fourteen for boys and seven to twelve for girls), and adolescence (from twelve or fourteen until marriage, sometimes as late as thirty or forty). Infants were considered dependent and were not expected to attend school or to work. Small children were rarely left alone. Should an infant lose one or both of its parents, regulations were strict with regard to the responsibilities of guardians. As children reached age seven, they might be put in school. Some girls along with boys attended primary or parish schools where they learned to read and perhaps to write; they also memorized parts of the Latin liturgy. Boys could learn arithmetic and accounting in "business" or abacus schools. As Symon said, "A child were better to be unborn than to be untaught and so be lorn."[10] Somewhere between ages twelve and eighteen, boys and sometimes girls became apprentices. A smaller percentage of boys went on to Latin grammar schools, where they learned to read and write Latin; an even smaller number went on to a university.

Schooling, which was available throughout most of Europe by the twelfth and thirteenth centuries, became more common in the fourteenth and fifteenth centuries. The son of a wealthy peasant might attend elementary school in his local parish and, if he was bright enough and had monies from family, friends, or other benefactors, might attend grammar school and a university. In Germany alone, in the last century and a half before 1500, the demand for education was such that fourteen new universities were founded. Universities emerged at Prague, Cracow, Buda and Vienna. By 1500, literacy in either Latin or a vernacular language was not uncommon, at least for boys.

Sons and daughters of the aristocracy were usually educated at home, attended by nurses, servants, and tutors, although girls might be sent to a convent. Girls learned reading and sewing. Boys learned reading, perhaps writing, Latin grammar, estate management, riding, hunting, and jousting. They also learned how to behave at the table or in the chapel, how to dance and sing or play instruments, and how to speak properly. Some courtesy manuals suggest that the level of decorum at the table was not high; they counsel against belching, feeding the dogs, or stuffing one's mouth.

It was common for wealthy families to send their children to the royal court or another aristocratic household for further training at about age thirteen. This custom tied families together socially and consolidated patronage patterns. The largest households gained prestige and influence through patronage of this sort. And sometimes, influential marriages, friendships, and careers resulted. Well-to-do sons with an eye to an ecclesiastical career might go on to a university.

In the late Middle Ages, European high society was not easy to enter. Whereas a knight in 1250 could rise through military prowess and marriage, by 1450 much more emphasis was placed on lineage, landed wealth, royal service, and education. Heraldic devices (an individual's coat of arms), an innovation in the twelfth century, became a matter of life and death in the fourteenth. Society was becoming dominated by a handful of landed magnates graced with an impressive genealogy and royal favor. Other knights and gentlemen became dependent, in turn, on their good favor. A successful courtier (a knight, scholar, or gentleman at an aristocratic or royal court) often led a circumscribed life—always alert to political danger and the court's administrative, financial, and military needs. As a result, acting decorously and speaking wisely was a way of surviving. Despite its precariousness, the culture surrounding the great courts—Naples, Burgundy, Paris, Orléans, Prague, Budapest, Milan, Castile, Westminster, and perhaps Lancaster in England—was trumpeted in books, paintings, opulent fashions, and remarkable banquets and tournaments.

Two French writers especially exalted this courtly culture—Jean Froissart and Christine de Pizan. Froissart (1337–1410), a Fleming who served the English court, wrote a chronicle of English-French relations exalting war and gallantry. He painted a picture of a valorous world where chivalry was not dead but in full bloom, where armies numbered tens of thousands, tournaments abounded, and life centered on court. He did not care to document the horrors of long sieges, the financial and administrative burdens of continuous warfare, or the unchivalric actions of court officials. His compelling nostalgic vision has shaped modern views of this period.

Christine de Pizan (c.1363–c.1429) was a transplanted Italian whose father had been invited to the French court of Charles V (r. 1364–1380). Charles was a gentle, learned king who put great store in courtly displays of wealth and patronage. He taxed the French heavily but also promoted peace, valuing his role as a wise counselor and judge. Christine grew up under his patronage and idealized Charles as "Charles the Wise."

Christine educated herself after her beloved husband died, leaving her, at twenty-five, with two children, a dependent mother, and other needy relatives. Years of battling lawyers and threading her way through court culture to retain her husband's assets taught her a great deal. In the end, she became the first author in European history to support herself on income derived from writing. Between 1399 and 1406, Christine wrote perhaps twenty books and hundreds of ballads and other lyrics. Although she began as a ballad writer, chronicling her personal tragedy and describing the loves of others, she became an important and popular political writer. A French chauvinist and a political moralist, she wanted a return to courtly, humane values and decried the decline of loyalty at the French court and the rise of private feuds. She correctly prophesied that disputes at court would lead to civil war and then, perhaps, an English invasion. Devastated by the bloody events that bore out these predictions (the duke of Orléan's murder of the duke of Burgundy in 1408, uprisings in Paris, and the French defeat at Agincourt by the English), she retreated to a convent. Only once more, in 1429, did she raise her voice in a poem praising Joan of Arc. Regarding this young girl of sixteen, whose leadership had defeated the English, Christine exalted, "we never heard tell of such an extraordinary marvel, for the prowess of all the great men of the past cannot be compared with this woman's . . . God gives [her] strength and power to be the champion who casts the rebels down. . . . What an honour for the female sex, which it seems that God loves!"[11]

Although contemporaries knew Christine best for her ballads and political trea-tises, she is known today for her defense of women. Her attack on the *Romance of the Rose* as a misogynist text became a *cause célèbre*. Although one cannot call Chris-tine a feminist, since she assumed female subordination to men socially, she was the first writer to produce a self-conscious defense of women. In her treatise, *The City of Ladies,* Reason explains that men vilify women because of Eve and also because they secretly realize that women have superior intellectual capacities and greater no-bility of nature. She then describes the achievements of famous historical and legendary women.

Christine's books were in great demand during her lifetime. Not long after her death, however, her books were lost to view until the twentieth century.

Christine de Pizan at Her Writing Desk
Christine grew up in a bookish atmo-sphere and may have known the Paris book trade very well as a result of her father's connections and the literary interests of King Charles V. Christine herself wrote prolifically; she then em-ployed numerous individuals to help copy and illuminate her manuscripts, some of whom were women. Her style of writing, her choice of topics (often political), and the lavish illustrations made her books popular among the nobility and members of the royal court who commissioned them. While female authors like Christine were growing in numbers, more often women worked with books as miniaturists, illuminators, or calligra-phers. *The British Library, London/Art Resource, NY.*

THE HUNDRED YEARS' WAR

Christine especially lamented the destruction caused by war. Europe between 1300 and 1450 was plagued by war. One reason was the weakness of certain kings, particularly those of England and France. Another was the rise of mercenary companies. Whereas military power had, in earlier centuries, been dependent upon landholders whose duty it was to fight for king or lord, by 1300 great lords and independent cities were hiring mercenary captains to fight their battles. In Italy these captains were called *condottieri*. They came from all over Europe. John Hawkwood, who fought for Florence, was an Englishman; Captal de Buch, a Gascon, fought for the English, as did a number of Flemish captains. These men-of-war provided troops that they recruited and contracted for. Unrestrained by feudal loyalties, they attended mainly to the needs of their men and their own ambitions. As a result, they changed allegiance as it suited them. The shield-motto of Duke Werner von Urslingen, a mercenary leader from the 1340s, which says, "Duke Werner of the Great Company, enemy of God, of pity, and of mercy," epitomizes a certain lack of chivalric values. These gangs of soldiers, so-called free companies, were a scourge during peacetime when, lacking income, they ravaged the countryside as compensation.

For much of the period from 1300 to the late fifteenth century, however, these mercenary bands were busy with conflicts in Italy, Germany, and Spain, with the Wars of the Roses in England, the Flemish wars, and, especially, the Hundred Years' War between England and France (see Map 18.2).

The Hundred Years' War, which actually lasted 116 years, was the longest war in European history. It is traditionally dated from 1337 to 1453. In fact, hostilities between France and England had been ongoing since the Norman conquest and certainly since Angevin times; they continued, intermittently, well past 1453, perhaps up to the Entente Cordiale just prior to World War I.

The beginning date of 1337 coincides, more or less, with Edward III's claim to the French throne. A diplomatic move, Edward's claim allowed England to resist French feudal claims on England's continental possessions; and it ultimately justified Henry V's conquest of France in 1420. Although England subsequently lost the throne, English monarchs continued to call themselves kings of France until 1803.

Edward III was also provoked when the French gave armed support to the Scots against England. And the French were promoting piracy along England's southern coast, making inroads into Flanders (an English ally who was crucial to the wool trade), and attacking Gascony, which was under direct English rule and its main supplier of wine. Once war began, Edward campaigned throughout French territories. As successes multiplied, war became an end in itself—a way of gaining glory—and England's claim on the French throne became nonnegotiable.

The two sides did not fight continuously. Military activities were episodic, from 1345 to 1347, 1355 to 1356, 1359 to 1360, 1369 to 1389, 1415 to 1444, and 1449 to 1453, at which time England lost Gascony, retaining only a continental toehold at Calais. Although the English lost the war, they won three important battles. At the battle of Crécy, in 1346, England had the smaller force, of which half

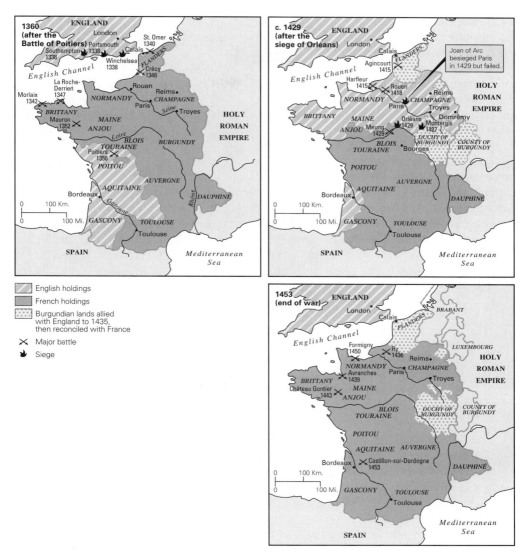

Map 18.2   The Hundred Years' War, 1337–1453   The year 1429 was the high point of the English presence in France during the Hundred Years' War. The weak rule of Henry VI of England (r. 1422–1461) and the unexpected, brief but heroic leadership of Joan of Arc (1412–1431) turned the tide against the English. By 1453 England was left with a toehold on the continent at Calais, just across the English Channel.

The Battle of Crécy, 1346   In the first major battle of the Hundred Years' War, Edward III faced a French army that was twice as large as his. The French nobility broke ranks, however, and charged the English who were ensconced on a terraced hillside with woods behind them. English archers combined with English pikemen kept their order and killed perhaps 1,500 French knights and nobles. The tightly knit formation of a block of pikemen, such as those pictured here, had been an effective instrument of war throughout the Middle Ages. *Bibliotheque Municipale, Besancon, France/ Erich Lessing/Art Resource, NY.*

were archers from Wales and Chester. The French, with perhaps forty thousand men, were an unruly mass of knights, men-at-arms, and crossbowmen from France, Germany, Bohemia, Genoa, and Flanders, all streaming toward the English and straining to outdo each other in bravery. Wave after wave, they foundered in the face of an English barrage of arrows and possibly cannonballs. "For the bowmen let fly among them at large, and did not lose a single shaft, for every arrow told on horse or man, piercing head, or arm, or leg among the riders and sending the horses mad. . . . So the knights in the first French battle fell, slain or sorely stricken, almost without seeing the men who slew them."[12] Total French losses were over ten thousand, including the blind king of Bohemia, who had ridden into battle tied to two of his knights. The English claimed five hundred dead.

Although the plague in 1348 slowed military activities somewhat, the armies were back in the field by 1356. At Poitiers, King John of France met the English under the command of Edward, the Black Prince, Edward III's oldest son.* Again

---

* Edward, the Black Prince of Wales, was considered a great warrior, having led campaigns in France and Spain, but he developed a long-term illness and died before his father. Edward's title derived from the fact that he rode black horses, wore black armor, and had a black field on his heraldic badge. Shakespeare seems to have been the first to refer to him as the Black Prince.

the French outnumbered the English, perhaps three to one. But the French cavalry charges against concealed archers and men-at-arms were worse than useless, and the English captured King John, his son, and many lords and knights, and killed perhaps two to three thousand.

For the remainder of Edward III's reign and that of his grandson, Richard II, English campaigns in France consisted of raids that ravaged the countryside and bled the French. While the French were being punished, the English were spending too much on arms. In the 1370s, Edward III aged badly, the Black Prince became too ill to fight, and English writers like Geoffrey Chaucer and William Langland nourished notions of peace. Eventually unhappiness with the government's handling of the war sparked struggles over the throne and the deposition of King Richard II in 1399 by his cousin Henry, duke of Lancaster (Henry IV, r. 1399–1413).

Henry IV's claim to the throne was weak—based on usurpation, an unclear bloodline, and parliamentary support. Consequently, he was never in a position to campaign abroad. This inaction might have risked losing French territories, except that France was being torn apart by civil war. These divisions gave the English an opening, which Henry V (r. 1413–1422) grabbed.

Henry V has been elevated into legend through Shakespeare's historical plays, *Henry IV,* parts 1 and 2, and *Henry V.* Shakespeare portrays Henry as a heroic, chivalric king. In reality, he was a brutal warrior who burned heretics at home and caused enormous suffering among the French. In 1415, Henry invaded Normandy, besieging the port of Harfleur where he lost perhaps one quarter of his army. With a weakened army of eight thousand he proceeded toward Calais until a French force of more than forty thousand stopped him. In the ensuing battle of Agincourt, the smaller English force advanced against the French. Sharpened stakes planted in a muddy field, backed by longbowmen, enabled the English to gain the upper hand in the course of little over an hour. Perhaps eight thousand Frenchmen died, and when a smaller army of French sought to restart the battle, Henry ordered all French prisoners killed, including most of the knights. England lost, at most, five hundred men. It took Henry another four years to conquer France, during which time he conducted a siege of the city of Rouen where, in December of 1418, twelve thousand old men, women, and children were expelled from the city but not allowed through English lines. They died between the two armies. In 1420, the Treaty of Troyes declared the French dauphin (the future Charles VII) a bastard, made Henry V the heir to Charles VI, and gave Catherine of Valois, Charles VI's daughter, to Henry to wed.

With the conquest completed, Henry might have gone on to capture the dauphin, but Henry died of dysentery in 1422, leaving both kingdoms to his nine-month old son, Henry VI (r. 1422–1461). The subsequent story tells, at first, of more English victories and then their gradual defeat. It also tells of the disastrous reign of Henry VI, who was never a warrior but a stubborn, childish man prone to bouts of madness.

The French cause was rejuvenated with the unlikely help of a sixteen-year-old peasant girl, Joan of Arc (1412–1431). Joan became a living standard for the French army; she led the dauphin to victory at Orléans and Meun and to his coronation at Reims in 1429. Shortly thereafter she was captured by the Burgundians, who were allies of the English, tried by the English as a heretic, and burned. She became, in her brief lifetime, the living embodiment of French patriotism. Nearly twenty years later, as the French expelled the last of the English, the Church began to hear evidence from eyewitnesses as to the sanctity of Joan's life and the seriousness of her cause. It was not until the twentieth century, however, that the papacy canonized her.

The Hundred Years' War was particularly destructive for France, although England also suffered—from Scottish raids in the north, French naval attacks on its southeastern ports, and heavy governmental demands in men and money. In northwest France, trade and commerce declined precipitously. English raids destroyed French agricultural productivity. The French monarchy sustained huge expenses building town walls, maintaining its navy, and fielding an army that, increasingly, consisted of Scottish mercenaries. These costs forced the government to levy heavier taxes, with the result that the country's wealth moved out of the hands of peasants and into the hands of government officials.

NATION-STATES AND PARLIAMENTS

The wars between France and England spurred nationalist feelings on both sides. For perhaps the first time in European history self-conscious national identities arose, facilitated by the emergence of vernacular languages. Henry V was the first English king since 1066 to speak and write English rather than French. The great literary works of the time were increasingly written in the vernacular: Dante's *Commedia*, Boccaccio's *Decameron*, Chaucer's *Canterbury Tales*, William Langland's *Piers Plowman*, Christine de Pizan's *Cité des Dames*, the *Nibelungenlied* in Germany, or the Archpriest of Hita's *Libro de Buen Amor* in Spain. At the Council of Constance in 1415, Europeans tried to sort out what a nation-state was: "Whether nation be understood as a people marked off from others by blood relationship and habit of unity or by peculiarities of language . . . or whether nation be understood as it should be, as a territory equal to that of the French nation."[13]

National sentiment was propagated through the Church. In the English diocese of Rochester in the 1370s, the bishop told his congregations that God was English and it was therefore right that Englishmen fight for their country. In 1420, the bishop of Lincoln placed copies of pro-war sermons on the door of every church in his diocese. One can also trace the growth of nationalism in the writing of national histories and the production of popular war songs.

The demands of war had repercussions on the nature of the state. European rulers began to take greater control of their armies. By the 1450s, the French had a national, standing army, no longer the preserve of the aristocracy. Loyalty to lord was being replaced by loyalty to king and country, and all free men (not just knights and nobles) were liable to render service. At the same time the aristocracy was changing from a fighting warrior class into a court nobility. A domesticated aristocracy was crucial to the success of royal power and the emerging nation-states.

Of paramount importance in this development was the declining military usefulness of cavalry charges and castles. As we have seen at Crécy, Poitiers, and

Agincourt, the undisciplined cavalry charge gave way before archers and foot soldiers. At Courtrai in 1302, the French cavalry had been defeated by Flemish foot soldiers, and, in the late fifteenth century, Swiss pikemen fended off Hapsburg knights to preserve their confederation. When guns and cannons were introduced by the mid-fourteenth century, they made castles obsolete. In 1453, Ottoman Turkish artillery battered down the walls of Constantinople, the most strongly fortified city in Christendom and one that had been taken only once before (by the crusaders) in more than 1,100 years.

New forms of warfare required rulers to find new ways to raise monies. Taxation, traditionally tied to feudal dues, became national in scope and more regular in payment. France established a national salt tax; England imposed the poll tax and taxes on moveable goods. This raised the question of consent. One model at hand was on the Spanish peninsula where kings regularly obtained consent from representative bodies (called *cortes*) for taxes and on questions of war and peace. In France in 1304, Philip IV called, for the first time, a meeting of representatives of the three estates of the realm—the nobility, the Church, and the townsfolk. Its members mainly heard the king's decisions and reported them back to their communities. This was not an exercise in constitutionalism; Philip's estates were instruments of royal propaganda. But they became less subservient after defeat by the English and worked to influence, for example, the choice of royal councilors. The national estates in France did not, in the end, become an established institution, but local estates did, although they functioned largely as judicial forums. In Sicily, assemblies attended by two representatives from every town met to discuss taxes and governance. Throughout Italy, regional and general assemblies met to discuss public matters, and the Church had, for centuries, offered a model of elections and of representative forms of assemblies and governance.

The idea of representative government, in which nominated or elected officials gave consent to taxation, made laws, and discussed politics progressed furthest in England. The English had vague memories of the community of the realm in Anglo-Saxon and Norman times. It was the Magna Carta (1215) that first called for a representative assembly (of twenty-five barons) to handle grievances. Subsequent dissatisfaction with royal policy in the 1240s and 1250s led to several assemblies that met to discuss taxation, petition the king, and consider general political business. The first "Parliament," with representatives from towns and shires, was summoned in 1265 by Simon de Montfort who was at odds with the government of Henry III. Similar parliaments followed, although no one quite knows their composition or what their procedures were. In response to the fiscal demands of the Hundred Years' War, Parliament met more frequently and for longer periods. A division between Commons and Lords evolved, and in 1376 the Commons elected a Speaker. In 1399, Henry IV appealed to Parliament to legitimize his overthrow of Richard II. In 1407, in the face of Henry's weak claim to the kingship, Commons successfully asserted its right to grant taxes. By the 1460s, documents tell of parliamentary elections and debates; Parliament had evolved into a legislative body and a political forum.

The justification for these assemblies was not primarily based on any body of political theory or of law. Although Roman law, common law, and Aristotelian ideas all underscored the sovereignty of the law, they did not offer compelling grounds for representative assemblies. Long-standing traditions of community representation existed, however, throughout Europe. These took many forms: juries, sworn associations, noble councils, meetings of the commons, urban communes, guilds and fraternities, parish associations, university governance, ecclesiastical synods, monastic general chapters, and town councils. Italian city-states, with their communal republics and governments by lot or by election, had stimulated the writing of treatises in the twelfth and thirteenth centuries supporting republican constitutions. The short-lived Roman Republic of Cola di Rienzo in the 1350s gave life to republican ideals.

Another important factor in the rise of representative assemblies was the governing practices of the Church. Early on, councils had met to delineate the Christian creed. The twelfth and thirteenth centuries witnessed the important second, third, and fourth Lateran Councils, which legislated for the entire western Church. In Italy, people had traditionally elected their priests, and throughout Europe bishops and abbots were, in theory and sometimes in reality, elected by the cathedral or monastic chapter. By the twelfth century, the newly established college of cardinals began to experiment with the mechanism for electing the pope, finally settling on election by majority vote. Monasteries, university faculties, and the fraternal orders offered models for representative government as well. The idea of representation was integral to the way the medieval church functioned. By the fourteenth and fifteenth centuries, an important body of political thought, called conciliar theory, argued that representatives in a general ecclesiastical assembly had ultimate power, even to depose a pope or declare him heretical.

STABILITY AND INSTABILITY ON THE FRONTIERS OF EUROPE

An economically expansive eastern border in flux and a western border in the Spanish peninsula where Christian powers were pushing into the western Mediterranean and Atlantic framed European developments from 1300 to 1450. In the East, the remnants of the Byzantine Empire gradually gave way to the westward moving conquests of the Ottoman Turks from Asia Minor. The gradual domination of the eastern Mediterranean by the Muslim Ottoman Empire (which was to last, albeit in a weakened form, until World War I) gave added impetus for European Christian interests to secure the western Mediterranean, and to move into the Atlantic and around the horn of Africa (see Map 18.3).

Eastern Europe

In northeastern Europe a number of powers emerged and competed. In the early fourteenth century, several German, Baltic, and Livonian cities combined under the leadership of the city of Lübeck to form an informal league that became, at the end of the fourteenth century, the more formal Hanseatic League. At its height in the early fifteenth century, the league had perhaps 150 member towns with

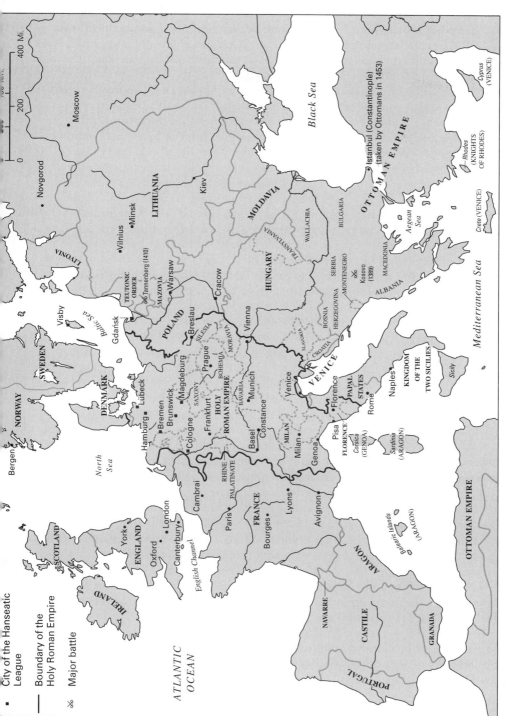

Map 18.3 Political Divisions of Europe, c. 1480 Two significant developments by 1480 are the emergence of the combined empire of Poland-Lithuania and the Ottoman Empire. Venice and Aragon had become dominant sea powers in the Mediterranean, while the Hanseatic League, an association of about 100 northern (mostly German) towns, was working to control trade in the northern seas. By the middle of the fifteenth century, however, the power of the Hanseatic League ebbed from its height in the fourteenth century, as Moscow expanded west, and Denmark, Sweden, and Norway united c. 1400.

privileged facilities in London, Bruges, Bergen, Stockholm, Novgorod, and Cracow. It was an association of mostly German merchants and shipbuilders whose network was centered on the Baltic and controlled goods flowing back and forth between England and Flanders to as far east as the northeastern Rus states. It was not a stable federation, however, as the member towns fluctuated. In addition, it fought wars with the Danes in the fourteenth century and the Swedes in the fifteenth, and was threatened when Dutch and English merchants began to compete for this northern trade, or when trade routes shifted toward more southern routes through Germany and Poland. Finally, urban leagues lost out to a consolidation of German princely powers in the fifteenth century.

The Order of Teutonic knights were another new power in the northeast. They transferred their headquarters to the southeastern Baltic shores after the loss of the Holy Land. The Teutonic Order attracted German migration eastward, founding towns, and settling German peasants in Prussia and Livonia. The emerging centrally controlled state of the Teutonic Order regulated everything in minute and uniform detail, down to the two chickens, one bushel of rye, and one of barley required in taxes from every parcel of cultivated land. The Order built castles and ran trading ventures in what one historian has described as "a state without kings or princes." But an emerging Lithuanian Empire extending from Estonia to the Ukraine stopped the Order's expansion eastward. In 1387, this empire became Christian as a consequence of a dynastic union with Poland, thereby depriving the Order of its rationale for attacking it (destroying pagans). In 1410, the combined forces of Lithuania and Poland defeated the Teutonic Order at Tannenberg in the northeast of modern Poland (see map 18.3). Battered by Poland-Lithuania throughout the fifteenth century and weakened within by opposition from the cities of Gdańsk, Torun, Köningsberg and others, and associations of knights who disliked the order's autocratic control, the Order acknowledged Polish sovereignty over its Prussian territories in 1466.

The Polish-Lithuanian union (which chose one king to govern both kingdoms in 1447) grew both economically and in terms of political preponderance, with a university at Cracow founded in 1364, newly colonized towns peopled by German immigrants, an army, royal court, and administration dominated by nobility, and an increasingly market-oriented countryside. The rate of technological change, agricultural development, growth in banking and mercantile wealth made the fifteenth century in northeastern Europe a golden age of economic well-being and cultural expression. The Polish-Lithuanian union was to last, in one form or another, until the Third Partition of Poland in 1795 placed Lithuania under Russian rule.

Further south Bohemia (including Moravia, Slovakia, and Silesia) had become part of the Holy Roman Empire. Towns in Bohemia flourished as German colonists moved in. In the fourteenth century, Prague became the home of the empire, where, in 1348, the emperor founded the first university in eastern Europe. Soon, tensions grew between the German town populations and the Slavic countryside, and these ethnic tensions were mirrored in the university. Although the initial tensions related to issues of ecclesiastical and moral reform after John Hus (d. 1415) became rector of the university, the escalating conflict exhibited antipapal and anti-German undertones. When it evolved into a full-blown religious struggle between supporters of Hus and the imperial government (see Chapter 19), the conflicts between Germans and Slavs also sharpened.

It is much more difficult to summarize developments in southeastern Europe. One origin of the twentieth-century troubles in the Balkans is the failure of some of the medieval kingdoms there (Serbia, Montenegro, Macedonia, and Moldavia) to achieve anything other than fleeting kingdoms due to being battered by neighbors, by the Byzantines, and ultimately by the Turks. The most dramatic political development in the late medieval Balkans was the military expansion of the Ottoman Turks into this area. Romania (Wallachia), not yet a consolidated state, allied with the Turks and was not conquered—due largely to its isolated and protected geography. Hungary was the only country to survive somewhat intact, and (almost) alone, it held the center of eastern Europe against the Turks. The Byzantine Empire, which might have played that role, succumbed after a thousand years of buttressing the West against eastern invaders.

The Last Centuries of Byzantium and the Rise of the Ottomans

The gradual decline of Byzantium in the late Middle Ages is of crucial importance. The conquest of Byzantium by the Latins from 1204 to 1261 weakened the empire, and it never recovered. Michael VIII Palaeologus (r. 1261–1282) was a usurper who blinded and imprisoned the legitimate heir and placed an unpopular candidate on the patriarchal seat in Constantinople. As a result, he faced dissension among the clergy and popular disapproval. In addition, Sicilian kings and Aragonese adventurers had their eyes on Byzantine lands. A hostile tsar in Bulgaria and aggressive kings of Serbia nearly succeeded in taking Constantinople.

In an effort to give himself diplomatic and political breathing space, Michael Paleologus agreed to the union of the Greek and Roman churches, effected at the Council of Lyons in 1274; he also agreed to a peace treaty with Charles of Anjou, king of Sicily. He offered marriage alliances to the Bulgarians and Serbs. None of these ploys worked for long, and they provoked hatred in Constantinople. In the East Michael was unable to recapture former Byzantine territories in Asia Minor, which were now held by the Turks and subject to Mongol invaders.

By 1300, an organized Turkish state in the northwest corner of Asia Minor appeared under the Ottomans. The Ottomans descended from a Turkic tribe that migrated into Anatolia under the Seljuk Turks. They enjoyed security, intellectual vitality, and strong government under the Seljuks up to the middle of the thirteenth century. Although the Seljuks were defeated by a Mongol army in 1243 and central Anatolia came under Mongol rule, the Turkish beys (or leaders) in the western parts of Anatolia remained protected and even strengthened by the westward migration of Turkish Muslims escaping the Mongols. As the Seljuks weakened under Mongol pressure and the Byzantine Empire constricted, the marcher territories in western Anatolia expanded. The Ottomans, from their base in the northwest (around the city of Bursa), benefited from three skilled leaders in the fourteenth century—Osman, Orhan, and Murad—and a strict policy of hereditary succession. Their form of government was well organized—based on a landed military aristocracy—and the state grew wealthy on taxes, booty, and prisoners (one-fifth of whom were reserved for the state military and bureaucracy). The Ottomans also harnessed the power of nomadic sheikhs from a variety of heterodox Turkish religious orders; these sheikhs supplied whirling dervishes (Sufi mystical brethren) who led the Ottomans to battle and added religious fervor to the conquests. Osman consolidated power in western Anatolia without much resistance and from there, Orhan and then Murad rapidly conquered Gallipoli, Thrace, Macedonia, Bulgaria, and Serbia. As a result, the Ottomans were first and foremost a Balkan empire.

Meanwhile, Byzantium, reduced in size and financially strapped, descended into political chaos. The Byzantine Empire did not have the military wherewithal to defend itself. Emperor Andronicus Paleologus (r. 1282–1321) had scrapped the navy, making Byzantine possessions beyond the walls of Constantinople sitting ducks for aggressive powers. The empire barely survived a rampage by Aragonese mercenaries (1303), civil war (1321–1355), plague (1348), sieges of Constantinople by the Genoese (1348–1349, 1351), a Serbian invasion (1348–1349), a devastating earthquake (1354), and the Ottoman seizure of the Straits of Gallipoli in the same year. From the 1360s onward, the Turks surrounded Constantinople. By 1372, the Emperor John V Paleologus had become the sultan's vassal. Serbia, in an attempt at reviving a Balkan Christian alliance, was defeated along with its allies at the hard-fought Battle of Kosovo in 1389 (see Medieval Voices). By the 1390s the Ottomans dominated Wallachia and Bosnia, leaving only Hungary as a center of resistance. They now controlled most of what had once been Byzantium.* The successful Ottoman siege of Constantinople in 1453 was scarcely more than a footnote to this conquest, however dramatic it may have seemed from the western viewpoint.

The Spanish Peninsula

While Ottoman forces were advancing into the Balkans and eastern Europe, Spanish Christian rulers were putting pressure on the sole remaining Spanish Muslim kingdom (Granada), which somehow managed to hang on until its final overthrow in 1492. North of Granada the Christian majority witnessed constant jockeying among royal claimants and among the kingdoms of Aragon, Castile, and Portugal. Finally a dynastic marriage between two cousins, Fernando of Aragon and Isabella of Castile, in 1469 united Aragon and Castile.

Under Muslim rule, the Spanish peninsula had accommodated three religions— Islam, Judaism, and Christianity. As the Christians pushed south, they had continued this irenic policy. In the fourteenth century, however, this changed. The reasons for this change are hard to fathom but a number of theories have been put forward: hysteria following the plague; preaching, particularly against the Talmud; the growing power of the Inquisition and its concern with converted Jews. Whatever the reason, the position of Spanish Jewry became precarious. In 1391, a widespread massacre killed perhaps forty percent of the estimated fifty thousand Jews, mostly in urban areas. Jews who converted under duress were called *conversos* and became objects of suspicion and of inquisitorial investigation throughout the fifteenth century and into the early modern period. In 1492, unconverted Jews were expelled. The last expulsion of Muslims was not until 1607, but Muslims within Christian Spain lived increasingly circumscribed lives—separated from Christians

---

* There was a brief Byzantine revival in the first two decades of the fifteenth century when Byzantium retrieved parts of Thrace, Thessalonica, and their position as overlord of the Turks.

MEDIEVAL VOICES

The Battle of Kosovo in 1389

The Serbian kingdom founded at the end of the twelfth century by Stefan Nemanja reached its greatest extent at the end of the thirteenth and in the fourteenth century under Kings Stefan Uroš II Milutin (d. 1321) and Stefan Dušan (1331–1355). At this point Serbia comprised modern-day Bosnia-Herzegovina, Montenegro, Albania, Macedonia, northern Greece, and Bulgaria. It was a Greek Orthodox empire of great wealth. King Milutin intermarried with the Byzantine imperial family and was poised to absorb the diminishing Byzantine Empire. King Dušan nearly took Constantinople. In response, the Byzantines sought military support from the Ottomans, who initiated a conquest of the Balkans that was to last over five hundred years. Serbia was defeated by Ottoman Turks at the battle of the Field of Blackbirds (Kosovo Polje) in 1389. The hero of that defeat, Prince Lazar, was captured and killed. He is memorialized in Serbian history and literature. By the fifteenth century folksongs about Kosovo were being sung, although they were not written down until the nineteenth century. In the interim they passed from singer to singer—a kind of underground music under the Ottomans. How much the songs changed over the centuries is impossible to know; what remains is fragmentary.

Yes, and from Jerusalem, O that holy place, A great gray bird, a taloned falcon flew! . . . he bears with him . . . a letter from the Blessed Mother. He brings it to the Tsar at Kosovo And places it upon his trembling knees. And thus the letter itself speaks to the Tsar. "Lazar! Lazar! Tsar of noble family, Which kingdom is it that you long for most? Will you choose a heavenly crown today? Or will you choose an earthly crown?" . . . The Tsar chose a heavenly kingdom, And not an earthly kingdom, He built a church on Kosovo . . . Then he gave his soldiers the Eucharist . . . Then the Turks overwhelmed Lazar, . . . And his army was destroyed with him Of seven and seventy thousand soldiers. All was holy, all was honorable And the goodness of God was fulfilled . . . Great Tsar Lazar perished on that day and with him died a good and ancient Empire—With him died the Kingdom of this Earth.

Source: The Battle of Kosovo, trans. J. Matthias and V. Vučković (Athens: Ohio University Press, 1987).

and with a limited ability to build mosques, to hear the call to prayer, or to govern themselves.

Summary

This chapter focused on the crisis years in the first half of the fourteenth century and the subsequent years of war and upheaval. The tragic impact of the bubonic plague on western Europe in the 1340s and beyond is almost incomprehensible to the modern mind. And, although economic dislocation, wars, and rebellions followed, Europeans recovered their dynamism with surprising rapidity. By 1400, per capita income had grown and social mobility, particularly through education, was benefiting the less fortunate. The aristocratic military elite transformed themselves into a more courtly class, while the demands of war allowed for something approximating the modern nation-state to begin to emerge. Parliaments developed alongside kingship. Nonetheless, the period ended with the psychologically devastating news of the fall of Constantinople to the Ottoman Turks in 1453 and the well-established presence of the Ottomans in the Balkans. Popes continued to call for crusades but to little effect. Only in the Spanish peninsula did crusading fervor continue with the fall of Granada and the gradual expansion southward and westward into the Atlantic.

Lost in the contradictions of the late Middle Ages were the overarching claims to authority on the part of the papacy. The next chapter details a declining papal power and investigates the religious and intellectual vitality characteristic of Europe by the fifteenth century. Both these developments were, in part, a response of a society that had experienced untoward tragedy and significant disruption, neither of which the Church had been able to ameliorate.

NOTES

1. Joseph Strayer, *The Reign of Philip the Fair* (Princeton: Princeton University Press, 1980).
2. William Rees, "The Black Death in England and Wales, as exhibited in Manorial Documents," *Proceedings of the Royal Society of Medicine,* vol. 16, part 2 (1923) 34; this extract is from the work of an early fifteenth-century Welsh poet, Jeuan Gethin, who lost several children to the plague.
3. Matteo Villani, "Chronica," in *Giovanni Villani Chronica con le continuazioni di Matteo e Filippo* (Torino: Einaudi, 1979) 294.
4. *Chronicon Henrici Knighton,* ed. J. R. Lumby, vol. 2 (Rolls Series, 1895, vol. 92) 299.
5. *The Chronicle of Froissart,* trans. Sir John Bourchier, vol. 1 (New York: AMS Press, 1967) 404.
6. R. H. Hilton, *Bond Men Made Free: Medieval Peasant Movements and the English Rising of 1381* (New York: Viking Press, 1973) 15; Alan Hardin, "The Revolt against the Justices," *The English Rising of 1381,* ed. R. H. Hilton and T. H. Aston (New York: Cambridge University Press, 1984) 165.
7. Edith Ennen, *The Medieval Woman,* trans. Edmund Jephcott (Oxford: Blackwell, 1989) 166.
8. Shulamith Shahar, *Childhood in the Middle Ages* (London: Routledge, 1990) 83, 104; *On the Properties of Things: John Trevisa's Translation of Bartholomeus Anglicus, De Proprietatibus Rerum,* vol. 1, gen. ed. M.C.Seymour, Book 6, ch. 9 (Oxford: Clarendon Press, 1975) 304.
9. "Symon's Lesson of Wisdom for All Manner of Children," *The Babees' Book: Medieval Manners for the Young,* ed. Edith Rickert (New York: Cooper Square Publishers, 1966) 123–125, quoted in Barbara Hanawalt, *Growing Up in Medieval London: The Experience of Childhood in History* (New York: Oxford University Press, 1993) 78.
10. *The Babees' Book,* 122, quoted in Hanawalt, ibid., 70.
11. Angus J. Kennedy and Kenneth Varty, eds., *Ditié de Jehanne d'Arc: Christine de Pisan* (Oxford: Society for the Study of Mediaeval Languages and Literature, 1977) 44–46.
12. *Chronicon of Geoffrey le Baker of Swinbrook,* quoted in H.A. Myers, *Medieval Kingship* (Chicago: Nelson-Hall Inc., 1982) 309.
13. J.A.F. Thomson, *The Transformation of Medieval England 1370–1529* (London: Longman, 1983) 76.

CHAPTER 19

~

Institutional and Intellectual Developments, 1300–1450

In 1300 the Catholic Church declared a Jubilee year, an innovative celebration that invited Christians to make a pilgrimage to Rome, to visit sacred stations within the city, and to receive full remission of sins. The popularity of this Jubilee year was enormous, and thousands responded, filling the roads to Rome. Shortly thereafter the pope, Boniface VIII, issued one of the most extreme claims for papal power ever published. Despite these assured beginnings, by 1450 the authority of the papacy had been damaged by events that were only in part within its control. Many contemporaries held, for example, that church corruption had been one reason for God's punishment of its people with plague. At the very least, the Church had not been effective in lifting the moral tone of the age. Papal prestige was hurt by the decision of Pope Clement V (1305–1314) to settle at Avignon, thereby separating the papacy from the sacred aura of Rome. Nor had the papacy been able to intervene effectively in the wars of the time or prevent rebellions, even within the city of Rome itself. Crusades no longer worked as a way for popes to galvanize support, despite the threat of Ottoman Turks close to Constantinople and in the Balkans. Then, at the end of the fourteenth century, a schism erupted in the Church. Two popes were elected by factions of the college of cardinals and supported by competing secular rulers. By 1409, there were three popes. The councils called to solve this problem concluded by contesting papal authority. Finally, new approaches to religion (some of them heretical) threatened religious certainties that had evolved through the centuries. It was a period when laity challenged clergy, and kings and intellectuals challenged the papacy. It was a time when some of the best minds were attracted to mysticism and to discovering a personal rather than institutional connection with the transcendent. Some authors of this period, especially Dante and Chaucer, reflect the uncertainties of the age as they questioned the structure of society as well as its locus of authority.

THE PAPACY, 1300–1378

The papacy in 1300 was at the height of its exalted claims to temporal power, but within the decade popes had begun to take the road to Avignon, building a base for themselves north of the Alps, divorced from their spiritual center at Rome. This "Babylonian Exile" of the papacy, as it came to be called, ushered in an era in which the papacy became known more for its materialism and its secularity than for its spirituality.

Popes Celestine V and Boniface VIII

A dramatic chapter in the history of the papacy began with the death of Pope Nicholas IV (1288–1292) and a prolonged conclave of cardinals from 1292 to 1294. Because of rivalries among the twelve cardinals, no single candidate could secure a majority vote. The conclave lingered in Rome; it split up and reunited; still no candidate emerged. Finally, in June 1294, seemingly inspired by divine guidance, the cardinals elected Peter Morrone, a holy hermit and founder of the eremitical order of Celestine monks.

It may have seemed like good timing for a saintly pope. The end of the century was approaching; Acre, the last western stronghold in the Holy Land, had just fallen. Writers and preachers were predicting the coming of the Antichrist and the rise of a messianic figure—a Last Emperor or an angel-pope. Peter Morrone (Pope Celestine V) was an unkempt and semiliterate recluse of unimpeachable morality, an ideal candidate for angel-pope. Unfortunately, he was totally inadequate as the head of a sophisticated papal bureaucracy.

After just six months, Celestine V resigned as pope, the only pope ever to do so voluntarily. During his papacy, he had established residence in Naples, where he became a pawn of the Angevin rulers. He had offered the unheard-of novelty of plenary indulgences for his pet projects; he supported the spiritual Franciscans while forcing other orders to become Celestines. He also ignored procedures and rules, "[giving] dignities, prelacies, offices, against all custom, at anyone's suggestion and the dictates of his own untutored simplicity," according to the archbishop of Genoa.[1] After his resignation, Celestine wandered around Italy for a few months, then attempted to flee but was recognized, captured, and imprisoned in Rome where he soon died. According to rumor his death (as well as his resignation) had been brought about by the next pope, Boniface VIII.

Throughout Boniface's papacy (1294–1303) people questioned his role in Celestine's demise and his legitimacy as pope. It did not help that Boniface was a wrathful, sometimes blasphemous individual, who was intent on advancing his own family and who treated cardinals and kings as his minions. On the other hand, Boniface was effective. Trained as a lawyer and a curialist, he was a master at manipulating the papal bureaucracy. As a legal expert, Boniface organized, recodified, and clarified, in great detail, old and new papal legislation. He streamlined the finances of the papacy and was tenacious about collecting old debts, fees for service, and other payments. For example, in 1302 a new abbot was elected in England's St.

Portrait of Pope Boniface VIII   This marble statue of Pope Boniface VIII is by Arnolfo Cambio (1245–1302), one of the great architects and sculptors of the late thirteenth century. Boniface was the first pope to have authentic portrait statues done of himself. A great many of them have survived. They were placed around Rome and in strategic locations throughout the papal states.   *Museo dell' Opera del Duomo, Florence, Italy/The Bridgeman Art Library.*

Alban's monastery. The abbot's costs for having his election confirmed at Rome and for a private visit with the pope were over 10,000 florins. For so huge a payment the abbot needed a loan, which papal bankers supplied. This might be considered simony, but Boniface issued a papal bull asserting that popes, as ruler of all temporal goods, can never, technically, be involved in simony. Through such steps, Boniface increased papal revenues multifold. He also spent huge sums acquiring land for family members, particularly strategic lands along the roads into Rome.

Substantial revenues came to the Church during the Jubilee year (1300). The Jubilee began as a popular movement. Suddenly, from Christmas 1299 on, huge crowds gathered in Rome, believing that they would receive forgiveness of sins. Boniface took advantage of popular expectations to proclaim a Jubilee, promising full remission of sins. Contemporaries estimated that 200,000 people flooded into Rome on a daily basis and that several millions made the pilgrimage before the year was over.

By 1300, the papacy had reached an apogee of power. It now had a separate court of appeal, a codified system of law, and a series of local ecclesiastical courts in place throughout Europe. The papacy's financial resources had grown dramatically with the institution of a crusading tax that had become, essentially, an income tax on clergy. In addition, the pope took greater control over appointments to benefices.* In a very real sense, all roads now led to Rome, but it had become an expensive journey.

Underlying all of this was an exalted view of the papacy that clashed with the growing power of kings and emerging nation-states. The conflicts that arose centered on two issues: (1) the right of princes to tax the clergy, and (2) clerical immunity from secular courts, an issue that had been at the heart of the earlier conflict between Henry II of England and Archbishop Thomas Becket.

In 1296, the French and English kings prepared to tax the clergy in their realms more heavily than usual and for an entirely secular reason—to fund a war between the two kingdoms. Boniface reacted by publishing the bull *Clericis laicos* that threatened excommunication and asserted papal power over abuses by secular rulers. Philip IV responded by cutting off monies to Rome, supporting Boniface's enemies, and attacking Boniface's right to be pope. Boniface eventually backed down. In 1303, Philip IV arrested the bishop of Pamiers on charges of blasphemy, heresy, and treason, a blatant disregard of papal authority, and Boniface responded with more threats of excommunication and one of the most overarching claims for papal power ever published, the bull *Unam Sanctam* (see Medieval Voices). In response, the French sent a force of soldiers and lawyers to arrest Boniface. He was captured in his hometown of Anagni and quite probably mistreated. Although the townsfolk rescued him, the trauma was too great for the eighty-six-year-old pontiff, who died a month later.

The Papacy Moves to Avignon

The cardinals next tried to elect someone acceptable to all parties, but the new pope, Clement V (1305–1314), from Gascony, was rarely able to resist French pressures. By 1309, Clement had settled at Avignon, a papal territory on the Rhone river close to France, which remained the seat of the papacy for the next seventy years.

Francesco Petrarch (1304–1374), the Italian poet, characterized this papal residency at Avignon as "the Babylonian Captivity of the Church," a phrase with connotations of exile (from Rome) and of Antichrist (who was to rise from Babylon). According to Petrarch, Avignon was a place of great wealth, where courtiers, merchants, and clergy crowded into over-priced quarters along narrow, fetid streets. Many commentators remarked on the wealth of the Avignon popes, particularly Pope Clement VI (1342–1352) who rode a mule with a gold bridle and golden spurs, slept on pillows lined in ermine, and practiced such extravagance that he drove the papacy, a financially healthy institution at his consecration, into debt.

---

* Benefices were ecclesiastical offices to which certain revenues were attached. A system of papal provisions allowed the papacy to provide benefices to members of its bureaucracy who were absentees and often held multiple benefices. The result was that the local needs of the church began to suffer, and local resentment against papal provisions and financial demands flourished.

MEDIEVAL VOICES

A Declaration
of Papal
Supremacy
over Temporal
Power

In November 1302, Pope Boniface VIII issued a bull entitled Unam
sanctam, *taken from the first two words of the bull "One holy, Catholic
and apostolic church. . . ." Boniface begins his bull, which was directed
particularly at Philip IV of France, by arguing for the unity of the Catholic
Church, outside of which there is no salvation. He then continues by
quoting the theory of the two swords, an argument often used in support of
ecclesiastical authority. The doctrine of the two swords (see Chapter 11)
can be used to argue that the temporal and spiritual powers are separate, or
it can be used to argue, as Pope Boniface does here, that the spiritual power
governs the temporal.*

We are taught by the words of the Gospel that in this church and in her power there are two
swords, a spiritual one and a temporal one. For when the apostles said "Here are two swords"
(Luke 22:38), meaning in the church since it was the apostles who spoke, the Lord did not reply that it was too many but enough. Certainly anyone who denies that the temporal sword is
in the power of Peter has not paid heed to the words of the Lord when he said, "Put up thy
sword into its sheath" (Matthew 26:52). Both then are in the power of the church, the material sword and the spiritual. But the one is exercised for the church, the other by the church,
the one by the hand of the priest, the other by the hand of kings and soldiers, though at the
will and suffrance of the priest. One sword ought to be under the other and the temporal authority subject to the spiritual power. . . .

Therefore, if the earthly power errs, it shall be judged by the spiritual power, if a lesser spiritual power errs it shall be judged by its superior, but if the supreme spiritual power errs it can be
judged only by God not by man, . . . Therefore we declare, state, define and pronounce that it is
altogether necessary to salvation for every human creature to be subject to the Roman Pontiff.

Source: Brian Tierney, *The Crisis of Church and State 1050–1300* (Englewood Cliffs, N.J.: Prentice-Hall, 1964)
188–189.

Great fortunes were made in Avignon, where Italian merchants gathered to cater to
the needs of a wealthy bureaucracy.

The papacy had good reasons to be at Avignon. Primary was its location, closer
to the powers of French, England, and Germany. At Avignon, the papacy was also
shielded from strife between Italian city-states and factionalism in Rome. And it
was far from the malarial climate of Rome, where summers were particularly un-
safe. When the Black Death came, the papal residence at Avignon proved an effective shield against plague also.

Of the seven popes who ruled at Avignon between 1309 and 1378, four were reformers and men of good character, but the two Clements were not strong leaders,
and a third, Pope John XXII (1316–1334), was highly controversial. An intelligent
man with a forceful, perhaps overly uncompromising personality and the talents of
an autocratic ruler, John was in his seventies when he was elected. He lived into his

nineties. His original plan was to restore a balance of power in Italy, to strengthen papal independence, and to return to Rome. He was a watchful, forceful upholder of orthodoxy who did not hesitate to use inquisitors against perceived heretics or his own perspicuity to settle matters of doctrine. And yet, somehow things went wrong. The papacy remained in Avignon, becoming wealthier, more centralized, and more efficient. John's efforts to manipulate a balance of powers in Italy provoked the antipapal League of Ferrara (1333), strengthening the Milanese. His relations with the German Empire deteriorated following a disputed imperial election in 1314. Louis of Bavaria eventually won that election, but John XXII refused to recognize this outcome and spent his entire papacy fighting Louis. In 1327, Louis, although excommunicated, was crowned emperor by a layman in Italy, allying himself with the Milanese against the pope. In 1328, in front of an assembly at St. Peter's, Louis issued a decree deposing Pope John XXII.

The pope had his troubles within the Church as well. He condemned and burned members of the spiritual Franciscans and promulgated papal bulls that undercut the Franciscan belief that Christ had embraced poverty. He refused to allow the papacy to hold property on behalf of the mendicant orders (as it had been doing). He presided over the condemnation of several leading intellectuals, most notably Marsilius of Padua, William of Ockham, and Meister Eckhart. He denied the doctrine of the beatific vision (that saints saw God's face after death and before judgment day) thereby undercutting belief in the efficacy of saints. As a result of these actions, the pope himself was declared heretical by a French national synod, the Dominicans, the Franciscans, and the imperialists. John died an isolated, embittered man in 1334. The German Empire had the last word. In 1338 the German electors declared that a king elected by a majority of their number needed no confirmation from the pope. This assertion of the independence of the empire from the papacy threatened to undo claims for papal authority that had been made since the time of Gregory VII.

By 1378, the papacy had lost credibility as a diplomatic peacemaker and as Europe's overlord. Although it had centralized the Church by taking into hand the disposal of churches, dignities, offices, and benefices, and by improving its administrative efficiency and financial base, in the process it had gained a reputation for wealth and corruption that seemed, to many, inconsistent with spiritual power. It also appeared to have become a pawn of the French. With the decline in papal prestige went a rise in power and numbers of the college of cardinals, making them a force to be reckoned with. This last development opened the way for a schism within the ranks of the cardinals and the election of more than one pope. It also opened the way for a conciliar movement that sought to place final authority in a church council rather than in the hands of the pope and cardinals.

SCHISM AND CONCILIARISM

Prior to discussing papal schism and the theory of conciliarism, it is helpful to glance once more at theories of papal power prominent in Rome circa 1300. In addition to Boniface VIII's papal bull *Unam sanctam,* another widely circulated document was a treatise entitled *On Ecclesiastical Power,* written in 1301/02 by Giles of Rome (c. 1247–1316), an Augustinian professor of theology at Paris and archbishop of Bourges. In this extended treatment of papal supremacy, Giles argues that the political sword is entirely subordinate to the spiritual and that all forms of ownership and political power are subject to the Church. The Church is embodied in the papacy, to which the entire Christian world is subject. Theology and right order demand that all material things be subordinated to the spiritual. As Giles put it, "the Supreme Pontiff, being the most spiritual man according to status and in respect of eminence of power, judges all things—that is, is lord of all things—and will himself be subject to the judgment of no one: that is, it will be possible for no one to be his lord or even his equal."[2]

Giles' ideas were almost immediately contested by John of Paris (1240/41–1306), a supporter of Philip IV and a Dominican professor of theology at Paris. John's treatise *On Royal and Papal Power* rejects what he calls the Herodian error of papal supremacy over temporal affairs. He also, however, rejects any doctrine that completely divorces ecclesiastical power from temporal power. John is one of the first thinkers to couch his argument in terms of kingship rather than empire. He argues for a natural pluralism of political society, which is, however, separate from and not subordinate to spiritual authority.

More radical was the work of Marsilius of Padua (c. 1275–1342), an Italian lawyer imbued with republican ideals. By 1323, he published *The Defender of Peace,* a radical assault on the papal position. He spent the rest of his life in the entourage of Louis of Bavaria, providing support for Louis's coronation and his deposition of the pope. Marsilius' ideas are more likely to be read today in college courses than are those of John of Paris or Giles of Rome, perhaps because of his republicanism and his sustained influence over time. In his discussion of secular power, he followed Aristotle. In his discussion of ecclesiastical power, he used scripture and canon law to argue that the Church was based on the people, that an elected general council of the Church had more power than the pope did, and that the papacy was merely an executive power. Although a large body of canon law and ecclesiastical tradition supported the authority of councils, Marsilius was the first to suggest that such councils be elected from both laity and clergy and to argue that the papacy had no authority separate from its administrative functions. In addition, he followed the spiritual Franciscans in arguing that the Church had no authority over temporal goods. His treatise caught the attention of Reformation thinkers in the sixteenth century; in the fourteenth century it caught the attention of Pope John XXII, who declared it and Marsilius heretical.

Antipapal theories were followed by antipapal actions. Aragon briefly repudiated papal lordship in 1344, as did England in 1366. The Emperor Charles IV (r. 1355–1378) began to exercise control within the empire over episcopal elections, ecclesiastical properties, and some cases in the ecclesiastical courts. In 1356, the Diet of Prague issued what is called the Golden Bull, declaring that the papacy had no rights whatsoever over the election of emperor or vacancies in the position. Rulers began to order reforms of the clergy, to found universities, and to tax the clergy. This rising state control contributed directly to the papal schism of 1378 to 1415.

In 1377, Pope Gregory XI returned to Rome briefly before he died; the new pope, Urban VI (1378–1389), turned out to be violent and abusive toward the cardinals, a majority of whom retreated to Avignon where they declared his election invalid, deposed him, and elected Clement VII (1378–1394). France and its allies declared for Clement, as eventually did Spain. England, the German Empire, Scandinavia, and much of Italy declared for Urban. Each pope excommunicated the other; they made competing appointments, taxed clergy twice, and had duplicate colleges of cardinals. Confusion reigned. Some monasteries had two abbots or two priors, and the financial demands of both sides led to a scandalous marketing of indulgences, benefices, and jubilees. It was a constitutional crisis for the Church with no ready solution. Slowly, a number of churchmen and intellectuals concluded that a general council of the Church was needed to set things right.

General councils had been crucial to the early years of the Christian church; and local, regional, and general synods and councils were common to the functioning of the medieval Church. A large body of thought existed relating to the role of councils in the Church. One of the chief conciliarist thinkers, Jean Gerson (1363–1429), chancellor of Paris University, argued that Christ had handed his authority to the Christian community, best represented by a church council than by an individual pope. Some conciliarists argued for a church of all believers; influenced by Aristotle's *Politics,* some suggested that the Church's government should be mixed—monarchy (papacy), aristocracy (cardinals), and democracy (the lower clergy and/or the laity). Others, influenced by the growing numbers of representative governments and corporate bodies in late medieval Europe, argued for a more representative form of church government. Some argued that the Church could govern itself through periodic councils without papal authorization (including deposing popes) and legislate on matters of faith as well as reform. Others focused on more moderate reforms of the papacy, without undercutting its authority. Regardless of the differences, between 1378 and the 1440s there was an increasing call for reform through a council.

In 1409, a church council at Pisa deposed both popes and elected a third, Alexander V (1409–1410). But neither of the other two popes recognized the council, and Christendom now had *three* popes, one in Avignon, one in Rome, and one in Pisa. In 1414, King Sigismund of Germany and one of the popes (John XXII, Alexander's successor from 1410 to 1415 and now labled an antipope) called a general council at Constance; it was perhaps the best attended council of the Middle Ages, and it succeeded in dispensing with all three popes (by deposition, imprisonment, and abdication) and electing Pope Martin V (1417–1431), who returned the papacy to Italy. The council also issued a decree asserting the supremacy of conciliar authority (the power of which came from Christ) and another requiring that general councils meet on a regular basis. Martin V called two further councils—at Siena (1423–1424) and at Basle (1431–1449).

The Council at Basle was the high point of conciliarism. Over five hundred bishops, abbots, cardinals, university doctors, canons, members of religious orders, and lower clergy attended the council at one point (1434). Basle tried to reform and decentralize the papacy and to negotiate unions with the Hussites and the Greek Orthodox Church. In the final analysis, the Council failed. It was undermined by the papacy and upstaged by a competitive council at Ferrara-Florence (1438–1439). In the end it also lost the support of the kings and princes of Europe. In subsequent years, the papacy claimed authority over all councils in no uncertain terms.

Many historians have suggested that the failure of the conciliar movement opened the way to the Protestant Reformation in the sixteenth century. Conciliar ideas also contributed significantly to ideas on representative government and the nature of corporate society for which the Enlightenment thinkers John Locke and Jean Jacques Rousseau are famous.

NOMINALISM, MYSTICISM AND THE *DEVOTIO MODERNA*

A crisis of authority within the Church of the dimensions experienced in the late Middle Ages had wide-ranging consequences. For William Ockham, one of the leading philosophical thinkers of the fourteenth century, it posed the question of individual responsibility in the face of what he considered illegitimate papal actions. For others, religious expression turned inward, with notable results in the production of mystical writings. Sometimes these mystics, in exalting the soul's experience of divine union, raised suspicions and drew condemnations from the Church. Others searched their souls comfortably within the bounds of orthodoxy. Another response was to create reformed, devotional communities, like the *Devotio moderna,* that were separate from church-state struggles and the corruption of the material world.

Late Medieval Nominalism

William of Ockham (1289?–1347?) was a Franciscan friar and a philosopher at Oxford. In 1324, he traveled to Avignon where, in the course of examining the papal position on poverty and the mendicants, he began his career as a polemicist. As his disillusionment with the papacy of John XXII mounted, he fled to the court of Louis of Bavaria and was subsequently declared heretical by the pope. From 1328 until his death, Ockham wrote treatises on evangelical poverty, the errors of the Church, the power of the papacy, and the problem of a pope he considered heretical. He never recanted.

Ockham was a nominalist (see Chapter 14) who argued against the reality of universal essences. For Ockham, senses and intellect can perceive only individual objects or inner experience; beyond this, one can only infer things. Universals, such as concepts of man, goodness, and justice, are signs that have meaning but not necessarily reality. Ockham was not denying the existence of universals, but he was denying that we can know them. The structure of the world as described by intellectuals, to Ockham, is the result of a linguistic consensus; it does not necessarily reflect reality.

Although Ockham's theories derive from a philosophy of language, they had theological implications. They raised doubts about proofs of the existence of God and the tenets of the Christian faith. For Ockham, none of these things can be logically proven; at most, they are probable or possible. Ockham's skepticism is the foundation of scientific inquiry, but in the realm of theology it was unsettling. Ockham placed more importance on faith and the truth of revelation through scripture than he did on rational answers to religion questions. God did not necessarily work in a logical fashion, and Ockham did not believe that God was necessarily constrained by the workings of a logical mind or the framework of theological categories and moral rules.

Ockham's radical skepticism opened the way for more faith-filled and mystical ways of approaching religion. It also opened the way for a more expansive view of God's absolute power. In theory, God could have established an irrational world, or more than one world, or a world with a different moral order. This led Ockham and others in the fourteenth and fifteenth centuries to postulate two powers of God— his absolute and his ordained power. "Sometimes we mean by God's power those things which he does according to laws he himself has ordained and instituted. These things he is said to do by ordained power. But sometimes God's power is taken to mean his ability to do anything that does not involve a contradiction, regardless of whether or not he has ordained that he would do it. These things he is said to be able to do by his absolute power."[3] While God *might* have willed any number of possibilities, he chose to create this world, the Catholic Church, the Christian religion, and a moral order. This choice was viewed as his covenant or promise to the world. Thus, while God might, at any moment, choose to create another kind of a world, in fact he would not, since he has committed himself to this one. God is not capricious. This view allowed theologians and philosophers to argue for God's absolute, possibly irrational will, while at the same time arguing that the institutional church was the product of God's ordained will and hence was not to be overthrown or questioned. Ironically, Ockham's nominalism, while radical in its implications for epistemology, could justify a traditionalist approach to salvation.

In politics, however, Ockham's views had more radical implications. Political writings preoccupied him for the last twenty years of his life. Ockham believed that Pope John XXII and his successors were heretical due to their stance against evangelical poverty and John XXII's denial of the doctrine of beatific vision. Ockham argued that even the simplest layman is bound to take action against such a pope. For Ockham, heresy was any error contrary to divine revelation. Anyone learned in scripture and following right reason had a responsibility to correct heretical error. Ockham's thought embodied a kind of radical individualism, which led Ockham to take a public stand against Pope John XXII and to support his political enemies.

Mysticism

Side by side with these currents of scholastic thought was a growing body of mystical writings. The late Middle Ages was a time of fervent mysticism. Mysticism is direct knowledge of God—a kind of contact or union with God often described by the mystic as ineffable and inexpressible. The Germans had a rich tradition of mystical writers, primarily women in convents, who wrote in the twelfth and thirteenth centuries. In fourteenth-century Germany, however, one of the greatest of all mystics emerged—Meister Eckhart (c. 1260–1329?). He grew up in a Germany that was rapidly becoming a country of walled towns and large villages where spiritual needs attracted the mendicant friars.* At an early age Eckhart joined the Dominican order where he rose to the position of Master of Theology at Paris, Dominican Provincial of Saxony, and Vicar-General of Bohemia. He was an administrator and a reformer, a spiritual advisor, a popular preacher, a teacher, and a writer of scholastic and mystical treatises. In the last few years of his life, however, Meister Eckhart came under suspicion for heresy at the papal court in Avignon.

In the midst of an active life, Meister Eckhart had become a mystic. The sermons he preached (mostly in German) transmitted his mystical insights through the use of scholastic terminology, scriptural references, and a paradoxical and poetic language. Eckhart describes God as "being and above being," "an oversoaring being and an overbeing nothingness." God is One, being, and becoming. These, according to Eckhart, are the least inadequate things one can say about God. All other attributes of God (goodness, mercy, justice, for example) are concepts that one must move beyond in order to reach God. One must even go beyond the Trinity to the Godhead, the essence of which is absolutely inexpressible. God is above all being and all distinction. But he has given being to all creatures; he created all things in the absolute beginning of his eternity, which is outside time. It does not follow, however, that the world or any individual soul is eternal. Still, the soul has a "ground," a little spark within it, which is inexpressible, in which grace gives birth to the Word. This birth of the Word (or Christ) in the soul is the center of Eckhart's mysticism. Thus man becomes the son of God and Christ dwells in us by grace. In order for this to happen, man must overcome his will and no longer be afflicted by material things. Then God's will can enter in. When this happens, the soul flows so completely into God that it knows only love; the soul thus rises higher than angels, entering into God like a drop of water in a vat of wine. According to Meister Eckhart, all humans are capable of attaining this state.

Perhaps it was Eckhart's efforts to preach to lay people and to female convents that alarmed the Church. Eckhart believed, "If we are not to teach people who have not been taught, no one will ever be taught, and no one will ever be able to teach or write. For that is why we teach the untaught, so that they may be changed from uninstructed into instructed." But, traditionally, the practice of contemplating God had been the preserve of a spiritual elite, not that of the common man or woman. Eckhart's use of the German vernacular, his nontraditional interpretations of scripture ("God made scripture fertile and sowed into it the imprint of everything anyone's mind can coax out of it."), and his attempts to provoke and startle his audience made him a popular preacher—and the papal court at Avignon nervous. Beginning in 1326, various commissions examined his writings, extracting articles they declared heretical. Meister Eckhart denied that he could be heretical, for heresy, he wrote, "depends on the will" rather than the intellect. He appealed to the papacy and submitted in advance to the papal decision, which condemned seventeen of his statements: "Lest articles of this sort and their contents further infect

* By the year 1300, there were ninety-four Dominican and perhaps two hundred Franciscan convents throughout Germany. There were also seventy-four Dominican nunneries and twenty-five houses of Poor Clares.

the hearts of the simple among whom they were preached."[4] It is not known whether Eckhart died before or after this condemnation.

Meister Eckhart had many followers and two disciples who were Dominican preachers and great mystics: Johannes Tauler (c. 1300–1361) and Heinrich Suso (c. 1296–1366). Tauler's sermons are much like Eckhart's in their concern for the union of the soul with God. Unlike Eckhart, Tauler railed against moral decline and at every moment expected the Last Judgment, especially in the wake of the Black Death. Suso, whose sense of spiritual joy is reminiscent of Francis of Assisi, wrote some of the most popular literature in the late Middle Ages (treatises entitled *The Clock of Wisdom* and *The Book of Eternal Wisdom*). Suso was extreme in his spiritual practices, mortifying his body through physical abuse and fasting. He wore, for example, underclothes with sharp nails sewed into them; he slept in this device.[5] Suso was a teacher and spiritual advisor to men and women of every rank. The nun, Elsbeth Stagel from Zurich, became his biographer and recorded his conversations and correspondence. Suso's suffering spirituality found many followers in the fourteenth century. Whether it was due to the preaching of masters like Tauler and Eckhart or the example of someone like Suso, or whether it was in response to the traumas of the age, more and more people turned to mysticism.

Among the many mystics, two women stand out, one from France, the other from England. Margarete Porete of Paris was one of the earliest and most radical of late medieval mystics. Between 1296 and 1306, the bishop of Cambrai condemned and burned her treatise, *The Mirror of Simple (Annihilated) Souls,* written in the French vernacular. Although the bishop ordered Margaret to cease circulating her work, she continued recommending it to "simple people." In response, the Inquisitor General of France appointed a commission of twenty-one theologians to examine the text while the Inquisition examined Margarete. She steadfastly refused to take an oath required of suspect heretics or even to respond to questions. For her obdurateness and her refusal to defend or explain herself, as much as for the content of her text, she was condemned and burned at the stake in 1310 in the first formal auto-da-fé of the Paris Inquisition.

Ironically, her book survived in monastic libraries, but attributed to more mainstream mystics. In the fifteenth century, it was translated into Italian, Latin, and Middle English. It was rediscovered in 1867 and republished in the early twentieth century by the Benedictines as an anonymous text. Only in 1946 did an Italian scholar, Romana Guarnieri, link the text with the author, and only in the last decade has Margarete Porete become better known.

Her treatise is written in the form of a dialogue between Love, the Soul, Reason, and the Senses; occasionally, Jesus Christ, the Church, and the author join in. Reason is the interlocutor—questioning but not understanding, amazed and clearly beyond his depth. "Reason will wonder at such language, but he has reached his limit." The way to God is not through reason but through a distinctly feminine love that has to be experienced to be understood. This path goes through seven stages, including one stage of the Dark Night of the Soul. The goal is nothingness, for the more the soul knows of God, the more it knows nothing. In this state of nothingness, "No one can find her; she is saved by faith alone; she is alone in love; she does nothing for God; she leaves nothing to God; she cannot be taught; she

MEDIEVAL VOICES

A Mystical Masterpiece of the Fourteenth Century	The Cloud of Unknowing *is one of the great devotional classics of the English language. It was written in the second half of the fourteenth century by an author who chose to remain anonymous. He or she follows a mystical path characterized by the sense of God's unknowability—the* via negativa *of mysticism. The book is written as a series of instructions from a master to a learner, with an emphasis on humility, prayer, and love. It dwells on paradoxes and describes a contemplative ascent through stages that, for most, is achieved only by discipline and hard work. For a few, however, it is a daily occurrence without seeming effort. The author cautions the disciple to be wary of counterfeit contemplatives, "for the devil has his contemplatives as God has his".*

Do not give up then, but work away at it till you have this longing. When you first begin, you find only darkness, and as it were a cloud of unknowing. You don't know what this means except that in your will you feel a simple steadfast intention reaching out towards God. Do what you will, this darkness and this cloud remain between you and God, and stop you both from seeing him in the clear light of rational understanding, and from experiencing his loving sweetness in your affection. Reconcile yourself to wait in this darkness as long as is necessary, but still go on longing after him whom you love. . . .

This work does not need a long time for its completion. Indeed, it is the shortest work that can be imagined! It is no longer, no shorter, than one atom, which as a philosopher of astronomy will tell you is the smallest division of time. It is so small that it cannot be analysed: it is almost beyond our grasp. Yet it is as long as the time of which it has been written, "All the time that is given to thee, it shall be asked of thee how thou hast spent it." And it is quite right that you should have to give account of it. It is neither shorter nor longer than a single impulse of your will, the chief part of your soul.

Source: The Cloud of Unknowing, trans. Clifton Walters (New York: Penguin, 1978) 61–62.

cannot be robbed; she cannot be given anything; she has no will." Submissive to God, loving God, being possessed by God, the soul is content in a peace of true freedom and needs no masses or sermons, fasting or prayers. Such souls can only be discerned by God and other like-minded souls. The institutional church (she calls it the "lesser Church") cannot find them. "This soul has become a high-flying eagle, soaring above the other birds. . . . there is nothing that she need fear, no comfort she needs, no hurt that can diminish her. Her generosity makes her a friend to all, in perfect charity, and she has no need to ask anything of anyone."[6]

Margarete Porete's treatise was especially popular in England where mysticism was flourishing. Of the many English mystics—Richard Rolle, Walter Hilton, St. John of Bridlington, the unknown author of *The Cloud of Unknowing* (see Medieval Voices), Nicholas Love, Richard Methley and others—perhaps the greatest was Julian of Norwich (1343–c.1419). We do not know her real name; we know little other than what she tells us in her *Book of Revelations*. When she was thirty years old, she fell so ill that she received the last rites. In rapid succession, at the moment of death, she experienced sixteen revelations. After this she was cured of her illness, becoming an anchorite (see Chapter 11) in the parish church of St. Julian of Norwich (from whence she took her name) until she died in her seventies. She wrote the first, shorter, version of her *Book of Revelations* (or *Showings*) immediately after her illness; twenty years later she expanded upon it, as she understood her experience more deeply and had read more widely. The text is a rare account of a near-death experience; the longer, later version, written in poetic prose, has been compared in style and beauty with Chaucer's *Canterbury Tales*. It is also theologically profound, "by far the most profound and difficult of all medieval English spiritual writings," according to its modern translators.[7]

Julian's *Revelations* focus especially on the excruciating painfulness of Christ's passion. Some of her revelations are quite concrete; others are statements from God or Christ, or spiritual images, such as the Godhead as a single point. In the course of describing her revelations, she treats sin, the nature of prayer, the mother aspects of Christ and God, and the nature of love. A fundamental question Julian asks is, "How can everything be well when such great hurt has come to your creatures through sin?" In response to this question, she describes God as a mother who anticipates the wishes of her child, thinking ahead to what is good for the child, although the child may not appreciate or understand it.

Devotio Moderna

In 1384, Geert Groote, an ecclesiastical reformer from the Low Countries, died. He bequeathed his home to a group called the Sisters of the Common Life. During his life he had gathered disciples in homes in the towns of Deventer, Zwolle, and Kampen. Some of his disciples were laymen and women, some were priests; among them were scholars. They appear to have fasted together, prayed together, and worked at copying devotional literature and service books for churches and monasteries. They took special pains to support scholars in town schools with room and board and to promote the priesthood as a calling for those scholars. Some historians see this movement, called the *devotio moderna* or the Brethren of the Common Life, as a point of origin for the classical and scholarly revival of the fifteenth and sixteenth centuries, especially with its emphasis on education and the copying of manuscripts. But the manuscripts they copied were traditional and devotional, and the scholars they supported went to schools already in existence.

The Brethren were responsible for founding a monastery at Windesheim in 1387, which spawned a number of new monastic foundations. And they produced one of the greatest devotional writers of the late Middle Ages, Thomas à Kempis (c. 1379–1471), who met the Brethren while at school at Deventer and eventually entered one of their monasteries. Thomas became an accomplished copyist and master of the novices. In this latter capacity he wrote a little book called the *Imitation of Christ*, a masterpiece of religious literature (see Chapter 18). The *Imitation of Christ* addresses the concerns of the novices regarding sin, humility, prayer, fear of death, faith, how to practice the virtues, the reading of holy books, and meditation on the life of Christ. It also includes a guide to the sacraments. Above all, this small book offers a path of self-knowledge, eschewing concern for worldly matters in this too transitory world. It is markedly different from the monastic literature of the twelfth century, where piety was equated more with external behavior than with introspection. This tendency toward self-examination, while not in itself mystical, was a step in that direction.

LATE MEDIEVAL HERESY AND THE BEGINNINGS OF WITCHCRAFT TRIALS

The Brethren of the Common Life developed within orthodox bounds, but other movements swept parts of Europe in the late Middle Ages that the Church considered less orthodox. While some of them (such as the Lollards and Hussites) were clearly a threat to ecclesiastical authority and power, others were not. The Church, however, seems to have deepened its suspicions, finding heresy, for example, among beguines and beghards, untraditional religious communities that drew recruits from the less well-to-do. This preoccupation with heresy also involved the Church in society's growing concern with witchcraft. The late medieval linkage of witchcraft with heresy, a linkage made by the Church, was an explosive one that laid the groundwork for the witch crazes of early modern Europe. Women were particularly vulnerable in this climate. Beguines, female lollards, and suspected witches were threatened and many suffered.

Beguines, Beghards, and the Heresy of the Free Spirit

Prior to the thirteenth century, religiously-minded women had only two options for leading a spiritual life—as a nun or an anchorite. In the thirteenth century, however, another alternative emerged—groups of lay women called Beguines joined together voluntarily to live lives of poverty and chastity while remaining in the world. This movement began in towns in the Low Countries and along the Rhine. The women were poorly organized: They took no vows, their commitment could be temporary, and they had no approved rule. Some lived in common in one house, or else each had a cottage; some lived at home. Some worked; some begged; some were economically independent. Although every class of society was represented, the beguines mostly came from the middling classes. Beguines were expected to exhibit irreproachable behavior, to engage in manual labor (perhaps weaving), to visit the sick, and to give alms to the poor. Sometimes groups of beguines lived in small, contiguous cottages called beguinages. Beguinages were an answer to a late medieval urban phenomenon—the rising number of unmarried or widowed women who had marginal places in society.

Side by side with communities of beguines were groups of men, mostly working class, who also formed voluntary communities leading lives of poverty and chastity. Called beghards, their numbers were always less than those of the beguines; they were a loose group of itinerant workers and beggars who preached, counseled others, and did charitable work.

Although approved by the Church at various times in the thirteenth century, beguines and beghards were both haunted by suspicions of heresy. Margaret of Porete was described as a beguine, and her execution for heresy tainted the movement. Another beguine was Bloemardinne of Brussels whose strong mystical bent encouraged people to believe that she walked between rows of Seraphim. According to tradition she taught others, much as Margaret had done, but from a special silver seat. Inquisitors and chroniclers associated these two women and other beguines (as well as Meister Eckhart) with a heresy that they called "The Heresy of the Free Spirit"—the belief that man can attain such perfection in this life as to gain complete freedom from the laws and obedience of the Church. Such individuals would not need moral regulation, which was only for imperfect persons. These ideas may have been taken to extremes by small groups of persons, or they may have been taken to extremes in the minds of inquisitors. In 1311, the Council of Vienne labeled beguines and beghards as heretics of the free spirit, and a number of people were imprisoned or executed. The persecution of beguines and beghards was fairly continual for the next hundred years, and most fourteenth- and early fifteenth-century papal decrees against heresy specify beguines and beghards. It is a testament to the strength of the beguinage movement that these communities managed to survive under these circumstances. Eventually the beghards adopted the third rule of St. Francis to avoid suspicions of heterodoxy. In 1415, the Council of Constance declared beguines, and other semimonastic orders, orthodox and acceptable. Concerns about heretics of the free spirit seem to have disappeared after 1415, replaced, as we shall see, with concerns for the "heresy" of witchcraft.

Waldensians, Hussites, and Lollards

The Church considered a number of other groups heretical in late medieval Europe. The Waldensians, who originated from followers of Peter Waldo of Lyons (Chapter 16), formed numerous tight-knit, secretive small groups in northern Italy, southern France, Switzerland, and parts of Germany and Austria. They believed that they constituted the real church, based on apostolic authority and scriptural authenticity. It was a Bible-based church that rejected papal authority and was led by itinerant masters who preached and taught. Although inquisitors would occasionally uncover a group of Waldensians and bring them to trial for heresy, in general the Waldensians escaped large-scale persecution. They were not to be so lucky in the sixteenth century, although some Waldensian communities, particularly those in the Alps, have survived into the twenty-first century.

Two new heresies—Lollardy and Hussitism—emerged in the fourteenth and fifteenth centuries, and are interesting in part because they took on nationalistic overtones. The first heresy was Wycliffitism or Lollardy, named after its founder John Wycliffe (c.1330–1384) or his followers (lollers, a term of disparagement that suggested that they were people who babbled). John Wycliffe has been described as a bitter man, an academician and failed politician. He came to the attention of English leaders in the 1370s with ideas of dispossessing the Church of temporal power and subordinating it to the state. This idea was attractive at a time when anti-clericalism was high, the papacy was at Avignon and suspected of being pro-French, and the government wanted revenues from the Church. The emerging forces of English nationalism at first welcomed Wycliffe's stance. But Wycliffe was also an evangelist and a determinist. He believed that the Church should embrace poverty and return to its scriptural, apostolic simplicity. He also argued that God had preordained individual salvation and that no clergy, indeed no pope, could be assured that he was one of the elect. If anything, most clergy would be among the damned! Wycliffe argued that there was an invisible community of the elect as opposed to the hierarchy of the Church, which he came increasingly to identify with the Antichrist. His writings attacked the idea of a separate priesthood, suggesting that all individuals were priests and could relate directly to God. Wycliffe believed that the Bible should be understood literally and should be accessible to laity in the English vernacular. Finally, he attacked the sacrament of the Eucharist, arguing against transubstantiation of the elements, although he did believe the Christ was somehow truly present. Given the similarity between Wycliffe's ideas and the later ideas of Martin Luther, historians have felt justified in calling this movement a proto-Reformation.

Wycliffe's followers, who at first included members of the gentry and later mostly men and women from artisan backgrounds, translated the Bible into English and established small groups of readers, sometimes called schools, that passed on his ideas in popular and debased forms throughout the fifteenth century. Eventually the ecclesiastical and political hierarchy became alarmed at his ideas and influence, which may have partially inspired the Peasants' Revolt of 1381. The archbishop of Canterbury condemned Wycliffe's works as heretical in 1411; in 1428 his body was dug up and reburied in unconsecrated ground. Throughout the fifteenth century English episcopal courts occasionally brought Lollards to trial for their unorthodox beliefs and for reading and circulating English Bibles.

Although Wycliffe's ideas became suspect in English circles, they took on an entirely different life when they were transmitted (through Anne of Bohemia, the wife of King Richard II) to the relatively new University of Prague. Here a group of radical reformers, who were already attacking ecclesiastical wealth, identified the visible church with Antichrist, and preached to the laity in the Czech vernacular rather than in German. They welcomed Wycliffe's ideas. The most famous of these reformers was John Hus (1372–1415). A dynamic preacher and lecturer, Hus was in favor of church reform and Czech control of the German-dominated university. In 1409, he became rector of the university, but as the movement grew more radical, Hus went into exile. In 1415, he traveled to the Council of Constance to present his ideas. Despite a safe conduct from the emperor, Hus was captured and burned, thereby providing religious radicals and Czech nationalists with a martyr to their movement.

The ensuing armed struggle against the emperor, who wanted to enter Prague, and the Church was perhaps the first nationalistic revolt in European history. In the Four Articles of Prague of 1420, the Hussites made the following demands: the free preaching of the Gospels, a state takeover of endowed, income-producing church lands, reception by all communicants of both the bread and the wine at communion, and freedom for the kingdom of Bohemia. The movement ultimately splintered into moderate and radical wings, as the papacy and the emperor led a series of crusades against them. The radicals in this revolt (called Taborites) advocated services in the vernacular and a priesthood of all believers, rejecting holy images, many of the sacraments and the idea of purgatory. Much of their fervor came from expectations that the Last Judgment was near. By the 1430s, Bohemia had suffered enough; at the Council of Basel, Catholics and moderate Hussites agreed on a peace that offered the Eucharist in both kinds to the Hussites and required that the clergy administer ecclesiastical property modestly. It left the ecclesiastical hierarchy intact; the nobility kept church lands they had seized, and the radicals were completely alienated. Hussitism never really died out. In 1519, when Martin Luther confronted accusations that he was a Hussite, he read the ideas of John Hus for the first time and was astonished at their similarity to his own. The Hussites became part of the Protestant vanguard in the sixteenth century.

The Rise of Witchcraft Trials

Prior to 1300 the Church took relatively little note of witchcraft, although early penitentials did describe a variety of "pagan" practices that included incantations and spells, potions for healing or for poisoning, and native practices such as leaving presents out at night for elves or placing sick children on hot roofs or inside ovens for healing. These practices, labeled superstitions in the early penitential manuals, were, by the fourteenth century being labeled heresy and witchcraft. The first accusations of witchcraft occurred at the beginning of the fourteenth century and are associated with high profile political trials—such as the trials of the Templars in Paris and the posthumous trial of Pope Boniface VIII. During the pontificate of John XXII, a spate of trials took place for sorcery and invocation of the devil. After Pope John XXII's death, the relatively few witchcraft trials for which we have records also cited sorcery and invocations of the devil. But after 1400, the number of witchcraft trials began to increase, reaching dramatic proportions by 1500 and well into the seventeenth century. At this stage, accusations of devil worship and pacts with the devil gained ground. The reasons for this have puzzled historians (see Medieval Voices).

The atmosphere of upheaval and instability certainly contributed—bubonic plague, greater social mobility, schism in the Church, corruption, wars, and danger from the Turks in eastern Europe. Some historians have cited a breakdown of family structures and increased migration between urban and rural areas. Clearly, the growing involvement of the Church in defining and prosecuting heresy contributed. Inquisitorial procedures could easily be turned against witches once witchcraft was defined as heretical. Heretics had traditionally been accused of aiding the devil. It was not that difficult to make the mental leap to the belief that an individual or individuals were actually worshipping the devil (called diabolism). Eventually, witchcraft became *the* heresy—the ultimate rejection of God and promotion of his greatest enemy. By 1486, these ideas were codified in an inquisitorial manual entitled *The Hammer of Witches,* which explained, among other things, how the devil could beget children upon witches and how women, because of their inherent weakness, were more susceptible to the devil.

MEDIEVAL VOICES

A Papal View of Witchcraft in the Fourteenth Century

In 1320, Pope John XXII's views on witchcraft were expressed in a letter issued by the cardinal of Santa Sabina to the Inquisitors of Carcassonne and Toulouse. This letter suggests that there was already widespread acceptance of the connection between witches and diabolism.

Our most holy father and lord, by divine providence, Pope John XXII, fervently desires that the witches, the infectors of God's flock, flee from the midst of the House of God. He ordains and commits to you that, by his authority against them who make sacrifice to demons and adore them, or do homage unto them by giving them as a sign a written pact or other token; or who make certain binding pacts with them, or who make or have made for them certain images or other things which bind them to demons, or by invoking the demons plan to perpetrate whatever sorceries they wish; or who, abusing the sacrament of baptism, themselves baptize or cause to be baptized an image of wax or some other material; and who themselves make these things or have them made in order to invoke the demons, or if knowingly they have baptism, orders, or confirmation repeated; then, concerning sorcerers and witches, who abuse the sacrament of the eucharist or the consecrated host and other sacraments of the Church by using them or things like them in their witchcraft and sorcery, you can investigate and otherwise proceed against them by whatever means available, which are canonically assigned to you concerning the proceeding against heretics. Indeed, our same lord amplifies and extends the power given to Inquisitors by law as much as the office of the inquisition against heretics and, by his certain knowledge, likewise the privileges in all and singular cases mentioned above.

Source: Witchcraft in Europe 1100–1700: A Documentary History, Kors and Peters, eds. (Philadelphia: University of Pennsylvania Press, 1972) 80–81.

Some historians have noticed the simultaneous emergence of the female voice (in religion, in literature, even in the social and economic arena) with the growing concern for witches. They have hypothesized that witchcraft trials, which were disproportionately against women, were a reaction to an emerging female presence. Feminist historians have sometimes seen the persecution of witches as a deliberate attack on those who threatened clerical authority. Traditional healers or midwives may have become less acceptable as the art of medicine became more professional. Some argue for an increase in mental illnesses; and still others argue for a surviving pagan cult. Some explanations are far-fetched while others have more validity, but none of the answers completely explain the persecution of witches, which remains one of the more complex and perplexing developments in European history.

Most late medieval accusations of witchcraft came from the towns. They were directed at individuals from various social levels, although preponderantly from the lower and middle classes; two-thirds of the accused were women. Witchcraft trials varied in kind and number from region to region, although some areas were free of concern with witches (for example, Spain, southern Italy, Bohemia, and Poland).

Based upon the available evidence, it is virtually impossible for the historian to decide whether witches had always existed in medieval Europe and were, finally, being noticed by inquisitors; whether the learned inquisitors, with their own ideas of witches, convinced women to confess through torture and the power of suggestion; or whether witchcraft concerns (on everyone's part) were part of a developing mass hysteria. Richard Kieckhefer has done a particularly interesting study of late medieval witchcraft. His methodology was to examine the progress of witchcraft trials from initial accusation to final disposition. In his examination of some five hundred witch trials between 1300 and 1500, he points out that the original accusations nearly always involved sorcery and almost never involved diabolism. Only after the case had been brought to court several times, and the learned inquisitors had had a chance to influence the accused and to intervene in the proceedings, was diabolism added to the charge. As a result, Kieckhefer concludes that sorcery was part of the popular tradition. People throughout medieval Europe believed in the power of sorcery and were willing to accuse others of sorcery. They were not likely to bring charges of devil worship, however. But educated examiners, faced with sorcerers, were likely to jump to the conclusion that the accused consorted with the devil. By the end of the Middle Ages, the notion that certain individuals (and particularly women) invoked and even physically embraced the devil seems to have been believed by many of the learned men of Europe. Gradually such ideas spread to the population at large. In turn, this produced beliefs such as those of a woman at Lausanne in fifteenth-century Switzerland who said that she had heard rumors that witches gathered together, ate the flesh of children, flew on brooms that they rubbed with an unguent, and refrained from making the sign of the cross.[8] Whatever the causes, the witchcraft craze resulted in the deaths of thousands.

DANTE AND CHAUCER: LITERARY ENDINGS AND BEGINNINGS

The late Middle Ages was also a period of great flowering of vernacular literature. Dante and Chaucer, two authors of great poetic stature, led Europe out of the Middle Ages and into a period that historians have traditionally labeled the Renaissance. Dante Alighieri (1265–1321), born a Florentine, wrote *The Divine Comedy* during the last decade of his life, while in exile. This poem, written in three canticles (*Inferno, Purgatorio, Paradiso*), is one of the world's great pieces of literature. It is also a stinging commentary on the times in which Dante lived.

Dante was part of a circle of poets in Florence influenced by Provençal, French, and Sicilian poetry. Dante and his fellow poets moved away from courtly love poetry toward a poetry that portrayed women as angelic and love as a spiritual experience, not simply carnal or emotional. In his first book, the *Vita Nuova* (or *The New Life*), Dante tells the story of his love for Beatrice Portinari, whom he met when he was nine years old. When she died in 1290, he was distraught. He concluded his *Vita Nuova* with these words:

> . . . if it be the pleasure of Him through whom all things live that my life continue for a few more years, I hope to write of her that which has never been written of

Dante Holding His *Divine Comedy*   In 1465 Domenico de Michelino painted this fresco within the cathedral of Florence to commemorate the two hundredth anniversary of Dante's birth. Dante stands holding his *Divine Comedy* and pointing toward Hell. Behind him is Purgatory as he envisioned it, with the earthly paradise at the top. To Dante's left is the city of Florence, and above him are the heavenly spheres of Paradise. *Art Resource, NY.*

any other woman. And then may it please the One who is the Lord of graciousness that my soul ascend to behold the glory of its lady, that is, of that blessed Beatrice, who in glory contemplates the countenance of the One who is through all ages blessed.[9]

This Dante did in his *Divine Comedy.*

Dante's life was also shaped by his involvement in Florentine politics in the 1290s and his exile from Florence in 1302. One of his earliest biographers noted that "In this (political career), fortune was so far favorable to him that no embassy was listened to or answered, no law was passed or repealed, no peace was made, no war begun, and in short no discussion of any weight was undertaken unless he first gave his opinion in regard to it."[10] By 1300, Dante had become one of the priors of Florence and was deeply involved with the major factions within the city—the White Guelfs and the Black Guelfs. By 1301, tensions had risen, complicated by a developing alliance between the Black Guelfs, Pope Boniface VIII, and the French. With Boniface VIII maneuvering in the background, the French and the Black

Guelfs captured the city in November 1301. Dante was indicted and exiled, his properties confiscated; eventually a price was placed on his head. In exile he became a fervent supporter of the emperor (then Henry VII of Luxembourg) and more and more critical of Florence, the politics of the papacy, and Philip IV of France.

In a letter to the Florentines in 1311, announcing the arrival of the emperor, Dante's anger against the Florentines spilled out: "You, who trespass every law of God and man, and whom the insatiable greed of avarice has urged all too willing into every crime . . . O you of one mind truly for evil! . . . your city . . . shall be delivered at the last into the hands of the stranger, after the greatest part of you has been destroyed in death and captivity."[11]

Dante followed this with his treatise *On Monarchy,* written about 1312 or 1313. There he used scholastic logic, scripture, and history to argue that Christ had not founded his church on Peter (indeed, he argues, Peter was too intemperate a man), nor had the Emperor Constantine authority to give imperial power over to the papacy in the Donation of Constantine. Logically, Dante argued, one monarch who is, by virtue of his universality, above greed best serves justice. The realm of this world monarch would be the direct descendent of the Roman Empire, which had been placed on earth by God and sanctified by Christ's birth. The papacy was to be limited to the spiritual sphere, without temporal power. This novel and radical treatise (foreshadowing the ideas of Marsilius of Padua) was declared heretical by the papacy. It was taken off the index of prohibited works only in the twentieth century.

Unfortunately for Dante, Henry VII died of malaria at Pisa in 1313, having failed to fulfill Dante's dream. Perhaps it was at this point in his life that Dante found himself lost in a dark woods, psychologically and politically.

"In the middle of the journey of our life I came to myself within a dark wood where the straight way was lost. Ah, how hard a thing it is to tell of that wood, savage and harsh and dense, the thought of which renews my fear! So bitter is it that death is hardly more . . ."[12] So begins his *Divine Comedy.* In this work Dante recounts his journey out of this dark wood, a journey that takes him through Hell and Purgatory to the height of Paradise. Virgil, the great Roman epic poet and author of the *Aeneid* guides the first two stages of this journey. Beatrice and then Bernard of Clairvaux guide Dante through Heaven. He tells his story in an Italian verse form he invented.

Dante's political agenda intertwines with his prophetic and spiritual message. Through the fictional device of portraying himself as a fallible but salvageable protagonist, Dante judges popes, kings, emperors, and saints, distributing them in sometimes surprising places in the afterworld, subtly reworking popular beliefs and theological commonplaces. He combines personal and political commentary with a mystical vision of the afterlife. The papacy is criticized for its involvement in temporal affairs, and Pope Boniface VIII is consigned to Hell. Beatrice appears in nearly Christ-like terms, as an intellectual guide and a merciful intercessor who does not hesitate to disagree with the views of others or to correct Dante while leading him to mystical heights. While dramatizing the horrors of hell and the pains of purgatory, *The Divine Comedy* also offered hope to repentant sinners and excommunicates. Prayers and tears, the mercy of Mary, and the intercessory role of Beatrice are privileged at the expense of the clerical hierarchy, and all of it is wrapped up in a paradoxical framework of God's intricate and immovable justice interlaced with his unfathomable and omnipresent love.

The *Divine Comedy* is written in so systematic a fashion, drawing so extensively on an encyclopedic range of medieval learning and so steeped in both Old and New Testament imagery, that many commentators have described it as one of the culminating literary accomplishments of the Middle Ages. It shares this characterization with Aquinas's *Summa Theologiae,* and, in previous generations, it was common to describe Dante's vision as Aquinas set to poetry. But Dante is more radical and subversive than Aquinas. He was also the first layman to write seriously about theological issues since Boethius wrote his *Consolation of Philosophy* in the sixth century.

Dante is extremely critical of the wealth and temporal power of the papacy. In this he appears to have been influenced by the spiritual Franciscans and his own treatment at the hands of Boniface VIII. His admiration for Virgil and his belief that the Roman Empire was divinely ordained led him to appreciate Roman, pagan culture. Thus, *Purgatorio* is filled with exemplary images from classical times, while, even in *Paradiso,* metaphors from classical mythology abound and Roman or Trojan rulers are not absent. In his respect and love for classical literature, and particularly for Virgil, Dante set the stage for the revival of classical culture that would follow in the Italian Renaissance.

In his youth, Dante was not simply a poet. According to his contemporaries, he was also an artist. In addition, Dante steeped himself in philosophy, theology, and possibly law, had read Aristotle and knew the biblical texts and the Church fathers intimately. He was knowledgeably critical of canon law and had read widely in the classical poets. Still, his Latin was medieval Latin, and later writers were critical of it for its lack of classical grace. Dante himself may not have been content with his Latin style. He chose to write his greatest works, the *Vita Nuova,* the *Banquet,* and the *Divine Comedy,* in Italian, setting the stage for the emergence of Italian as a literary language.

Finally, Dante's *Divine Comedy* creates images that are so concrete and so dramatically intense, that the reader can virtually see through his words. At times, one can almost smell Hell and hear the music of Paradise. Individuals also come alive. The great pride of a Ulysses, the anger of St. Peter, the pathos and pretty excuses of an adulterous Francesca affect Dante and the reader. Many scenes from the *Divine Comedy* have become the themes of great art. Dante's *Divine Comedy* was completed just before he died in 1321, and it was immediately popular. Over one hundred commentaries on it were written before the year 1500. It is one of the pieces of world literature most often translated into the English language.

Geoffrey Chaucer (1342?–1400) was the earliest great writer of English poetry and creator of *The Canterbury Tales.* Chaucer's family background was upper middle class, and through his career as a government bureaucrat, court poet, and diplomat, he was eventually knighted. As a child, Chaucer lived through the first visitation of bubonic plague. He witnessed its recurrence in the 1360s through the 1390s. During the Hundred Years' War, Chaucer was captured and ransomed while in France. In the Peasants' Revolt of 1381, the rebels entered London through Aldgate, passing directly under Chaucer's chambers. Chaucer visited Italy and met

Petrarch, possibly heard Boccaccio lecture, and read Dante. He was steeped in the French poetic tradition, having translated, in particular, the *Romance of the Rose.* He was at court in the difficult years toward the end of Edward III's reign and through the overthrow of Richard II by Henry of Lancaster. Chaucer had only begun to write his greatest works when the Church divided between two popes. And yet, his writings are not overtly political, nor do they have any obvious religious agenda. Through all of Chaucer's writings, particularly his *House of Fame* (written about 1379), *Parliament of Fowles* (1380), *Troilus and Creseyde* (heavily influenced by Boccaccio and written in the 1380s), and *Legend of Good Women* (1386–1394), Chaucer is concerned mostly with love and relationships between men and women. Although he is not insensitive to political and ecclesiastical issues, his views in this area tend to be subtly suggestive. Perhaps Dante's exile was an example to Chaucer, and certainly English court politics could be brutal. Chaucer was also not as willing as Dante to engage theological and spiritual issues, although one discerns more than a little anticlericalism in his texts.

   The Canterbury Tales, written over the last twenty years of his life and incomplete, are a lively, ironic description of a troop of pilgrims on their way from London to Canterbury. To entertain themselves they elect, under the guidance of an innkeeper, to tell tales—tales that are usually less than spiritual in their content. The pilgrims are a cross section of English people—from an impoverished knight to a plowman, clergy (a friar, monk, clerk, nun, prioress, parson, pardoner, summoner, and three priests) as well as laity (merchant, sheriff, cook, miller, wife of Bath, and perhaps another dozen fellow-pilgrims, including Chaucer himself). The knight and a debt-ridden merchant share company with tradesmen and craftsmen (including a dyer) whose wealth is apparent and whose wives put on airs. Clearly the display of wealth was no longer a clear indicator of social class. Morally, most of the clergy are suspect—full of trickery and hypocrisy (with the significant exception of the parson), while the lowliest layman, the plowman "Liv(ed) in peace and perfect charity, And, as the gospel bade him, so did he, Loving God best with all his heart and mind And then his neighbour as himself . . . For steadily about his work he went To thrash his corn, to dig or to manure Or make a ditch; and he would help the poor For love of Christ and never take a penny."[13] Surely this is a world upside down—where plowmen were more charitable than monks and friars, where dyers disposed of more money than merchants, and where women like the wife of Bath could lead a bawdy life and get rich doing so, rail against clerical misogyny, and preach to fellow-pilgrims.

   Just where Chaucer stands in all of this is never clear. Gently ironic, his own persona in the poem is a failed tale-teller who bores the audience. Perhaps most unsettling about Chaucer's tales and tale-tellers is that there is no standard by which they are judged. Unlike Dante, whose unflinching judgments on the people he met in his fictional journey are couched in terms of divine justice, Chaucer offers no answers and no authority. Is he subtly critiquing the knight for his mercenary livelihood? Is he critiquing knighthood as a social class? Or is his description of the knight ("a most distinguished man, Who from the day on which he first began to ride abroad had followed chivalry, Truth, honour, generousness and courtesy") to be accepted as an ideal, as many have argued? The prioress is clearly a self-centered and hypocritical lady, more concerned with her lap dogs than with true charity, but does her anti-Semitic tale suggest a deeper level of evil? Or was Chaucer himself anti-Semitic and the tale intended to be a retelling of a popular story of a local saint? Is Chaucer admiring the gumption of the wife of Bath, or does he present her tale (one where the woman successfully demands mastery in her marriage) as an ironic comment on her life? What is one to think of his retelling of the story of patient Griselda or his story of the great evils done to the legendary Queen Constance, whose mistreatment no one but a saint could endure? Chaucer gives no prescription for relationships between men and women; he merely offers an array of human behavior—a great human comedy that ends with a rather traditional sermon from the parson and a retraction from Chaucer himself where he requests his audience "to pray for me, that Christ have mercy on me and forgive me my sins: and especially for my translations and enditings of worldly vanities, which I revoke in my retractions: as . . . The Tales of Canterbury, those that tend towards sin. . . ."[4]

Summary

Chaucer's pilgrims reside in a fictional world that has no obvious, agreed-upon authority. In this respect Chaucer's literary masterpiece mirrored the loss of authority in late medieval Europe. With the papacy in exile in Avignon or in schism until 1415, with the destruction of the Hohenstaufen and the reduced authority of the Holy Roman Empire, with conflicts between papal universalism and rising nationalism, with famine, plague, and war, Europeans were no longer so certain as to their salvation. This psychological uncertainty may partially explain the new heresies, the turn to mysticism, and the growing concern with witches.

On the other hand, Chaucer drew upon and manipulated long-standing literary and cultural traditions that were scarcely disturbed by these developments. These traditions included religious as well as secular perspectives, Latin and vernacular literatures, and classical and Christian texts. When he withdrew to his study in his house over Aldgate, he was able to place his everyday experiences into this larger, more enduring context. And yet, his daily experiences gave him a nice appreciation of the military, the court, the clergy and scholars, of foreign cultures, merchants, and people on the street. His example reminds us how rich in meaning the lives of medieval men and women were, how open to experience they were, and how resilient they could be in the face of adversity.

NOTES

1. T.S.R. Boase, *Boniface VIII* (London: Constable, 1933) 45.
2. Giles of Rome, *On Ecclesiastical Power,* trans. R. W. Dyson, part I, ch. 2 (Woodbridge, Suffolk: Boydell Press, 1986) 5.
3. Steven Ozment, *Age of Reform (1250-1550): An Intellectual and Religious History of Late Medieval and Reformation Europe* (New Haven: Yale University Press, 1980) 38.
4. *Meister Eckhart: The Essential Sermons, Commentaries, Treatises, and Defense,* trans. E. Colledge and B. McGinn (New York: Paulist Press, 1981), 72, 88; *Meister Eckhart: Thought and Language* (Philadelphia: University Press, 1986) 14, 28.

5. Richard Kieckhefer, *Unquiet Souls: Fourteenth-Century Saints and Their Religious Milieu* (Chicago: University of Chicago Press, 1984) 148.

6. *A Mirror for Simple Souls,* trans. Charles Crawford (New York: Crossroad, 1981) 62–63, 124 and *passim.*

7. Julian of Norwich, *Showings,* trans. and intro. Edmund Colledge and James Walsh (New York: Paulist Press, 1980) intro.

8. Richard Kieckhefer, *Magic in the Middle Ages* (Cambridge: Cambridge University Press, 1990) 92. See also Kieckhefer, *European Witch Trials* (Berkeley: University of California Press, 1976).

9. Mark Musa, *Dante's Vita Nuova: A Translation and an Essay* (Bloomington: Indiana University Press, 1973) 86.

10. Leonardo Bruni's "Life of Dante," *The Earliest Lives of Dante,* trans. J.R. Smith (New York: Ungar, 1963) 85.

11. *Dantis Alagherii Epistolae: The Letters of Dante,* ed. and trans. Paget Toynbee (Oxford: Clarendon Press, 1920) 63–81.

12. *The Divine Comedy of Dante Alighieri,* trans. John Sinclair, vol. 1 (Oxford: Oxford University Press, 1939) 23.

13. Chaucer, *The Canterbury Tales,* trans. Nevill Coghill (New York: Penguin, 1951) prologue, 33.

Epilogue: The Italian Renaissance, 1300–1492

The term "Renaissance" is an intellectual construct, just like the term "Middle Ages." This traditional division between two eras in European history suggests a sharp break. Human history, however, is a story of change and continuity, and the danger of "periodizing" history is that the continuity is obscured. The events that have been described in this book provided an essential foundation for the literary, geographical, scientific, educational, architectural, and artistic flowering that typifies early modern Europe. And yet, one must find a stopping point, and the Italian renaissance, which many contemporaries believed was significantly different from what came before, is as good a place to stop as any.

In choosing to end here, we reiterate what we said in the Introduction—that no one in the Middle Ages would have understood that they lived in a middle period. Medieval people characterized themselves as "moderni" (modern men), carrying forward a culture grounded in antiquity. Insofar as they saw their era moving toward an end, it was the end of history, not the end of one period or the beginning of another.

It is only with the accelerated recovery of classical Roman and Greek history in the fourteenth and fifteenth centuries that Italian intellectuals began to argue that "barbarian" migrations into the late Roman Empire constituted a meaningful break with the past. They argued that their own age, by recovering this antique past, had broken with the "Gothic" centuries—a time, as they saw it, when culture was debased. Although the notion of a revival of culture was, in the first instance, an Italian construct, the French coined the term "Renaissance," which means "rebirth," in the sixteenth century. By the time of the Enlightenment, the idea of a "Renaissance" changed its meaning from a specific revival of the arts to an overarching sense of a turn toward a more rational world—away from the irrational and the religious. It was not until the nineteenth century, and particularly in the writings of historians such as Jules Michelet and Jacob Burckhardt, that the Renaissance was embraced as a distinct age with a distinctive spirit that expressed itself in every aspect of the age. Twentieth-century writers have been more skeptical. Medievalists have argued that this particular Renaissance was not unique, and others, who see the Renaissance as a phenomenon mainly restricted to male elites, have suggested that the less loaded and more inclusive term "early modern Europe" is a more satisfactory label for the post-medieval era.

Although the French liked to think of this early modern "Renaissance" as a rebirth of French culture, it was mainly an Italian phenomenon prior to 1500. It began at the turn of the fourteenth century as a rebirth of Roman classical and Italian culture, and it spread to transalpine Europe with the help of the printing press only in the second half of the fifteenth century. The Italian Renaissance never constituted a sharp break with the Middle Ages. For example, although the field of philosophy was enriched in the fifteenth century with the translations of Plato's works from Greek into Latin, the works of Aristotle dominated the curriculum well into the seventeenth century. Although new forms of art emerged, based on classical models and more sophisticated techniques, many of the subjects would have been familiar to a medieval audience. Although the period saw the revival of classical Latin, it also saw a continuation of crusading efforts.

This epilogue draws the medieval world to its close; it focuses on the Italian renaissance of culture and ends with the discovery of the New World in 1492, new political ideas, and the prospect of the Protestant Reformation, all of which fundamentally changed the worldview of Europeans.

LITERATURE

The fourteenth century saw a revival of Italian history and culture. The first generation of Renaissance artists and thinkers revived an Italian national literature, both in Italian and Latin. Accompanying this was a growing appreciation for the classical tradition (of Rome in particular) and the beginnings of the recovery of antiquity. In art, a greater naturalism and humanism represented, to some degree, a turning away from contemplative religious ideals to a worldly political and cultural activism.

The first and greatest of the fourteenth-century figures was the poet, Dante Alighieri (see Chapter 19). Dante's vision was bold. In *The Divine Comedy,* he positions himself in the company of the great poets of classical culture—Homer, Plato, Virgil, Ovid, and Lucan. He gives himself the task of envisioning his own version of purgatory and chronicling his own salvation. Dante foreshadows the Renaissance emphasis on the creative individual, whose free will enables him to reach divine heights. He describes his emotions and those of others—his pity and his anger, Beatrice's anger as she castigates him for his lustfulness. The attention to the individual and to the human side of life in Dante's work is new.

Dante also exalts the Roman Empire, which he believed was the only form of government divinely ordained and capable of achieving unity and peace. This led him to study classical Roman mythology and epic poetry. He also argued on behalf of the Italian language as a vehicle for literary expression, partly in reaction to the dominance of French culture in thirteenth-century poetry and prose.

Despite these characteristics, which are often seen as Renaissance traits, Dante was one of the greatest of medieval poets, whose vision of Heaven, Hell, and Purgatory describes an Aristotelian universe and a Christian hierarchy of souls that medieval individuals would have understood.

Dante is often considered one of the "three crowns of Florence" in the fourteenth century. The other two crowns were Petrarch (1304–1374) and Giovanni Boccaccio (1313–1375).

Although Petrarch's family came from Florence, he spent most of his life in southern France or northern Italy. In 1341, he was crowned poet laureate in Rome, where he delivered a dramatic speech in defense of poetry on the steps of the Roman capitol. This event, a conscious imitation of a classical ritual, had enormous propaganda value for the revival of interest in Roman civilization. Petrarch was a self-promoter, a pursuer of fame, but not without intense soul-searching and self-questioning with regard to his salvation. Although Petrarch was attracted to a life of monastic seclusion, he remained a man of the world. He was almost single-handedly responsible for initiating interest in the recovery of classical culture, becoming the very embodiment of classical knowledge. His Latin was modeled after Cicero, whose works he adored and whose letters he discovered. He was a walking encyclopedia of Roman history, someone people asked to identify a coin or an inscription. He produced a critical (and still impressive) edition of Livy's *History of Rome*. Spiritually he felt so akin to the ancients that he composed letters to them and discoursed with them in his writings. Fittingly, he died with his head on a volume of Caesar's writings.

Giovanni Boccaccio was a contemporary and friend of Petrarch's. Although he spent much of his youth in Naples, economic reasons forced him to return to Florence in the 1340s where he wrote most of his major works. His greatest literary success was the *Decameron,* which, except for its complex literary structure, is more traditional than innovative. It is based on medieval tales of romance, stories of vice and virtue, gossip, and bawdy adventure tales. It is sexually explicit, and its background is entirely mercantile. But many of Boccaccio's other writings contributed to the classical revival. Besides his reference works on classical mythology and his editions and discoveries of classical texts, Boccaccio was the first to try to introduce the study of ancient Greek into Florence. He also worked, with moderate success, to awaken the Florentine people to Dante's importance. Boccaccio's fame (or perhaps infamy) also rests on the attention he paid to women. Besides writing his *Decameron,* a sometimes scandalous work on sexual relations, ostensibly for a female audience, he wrote a reference text on famous women in the classical world. Unfortunately, his attitude toward women was prejudicial and his portraits of them pejorative. His most virulent invective against women, the *Corbaccio* (the Crow), offers an array of misogynist arguments, with special emphasis on the sexual appetites of women. Still, it was Boccaccio who ensured that the Italian Renaissance would be associated with Florence and who laid the groundwork for the community of scholars trained in classical learning, called humanists, who congregated in Florence by the beginning of the fifteenth century.

These humanists—who flocked to Florence, other northern Italian cities, and to Rome—are too numerous to name. They brought a new interest in classical texts, a more refined, classical Latin, a better developed sense of history, interest in an education that was more classically based and more humanely dispensed, and a patronage system that rewarded them with positions as secretaries, diplomats, tutors, and teachers. In addition to their exploration of ancient Roman culture, they revived the Greek language and Greek learning. Plato's *Republic* and most of his *Dialogues,* the writings of Polybius, the *Geography* of Ptolemy are only a few of the Greek writings that were recovered.

Most humanists were men, but a few were women. So far a group of approximately thirty women has been identified, mostly from the courts and towns of northern Italy and from ruling families or urban aristocratic and professional elites. Certain families, such as the Gonzaga family of Mantua, tended to produce learned women. But little work produced by these women survives, usually only a single treatise or oration. Women humanists did not have an easy time. They were attacked, often viciously, by male humanists, as well as by other women. They were considered unnatural and unfeminine, so not surprisingly, they were only marginally productive.

ART AND ARCHITECTURE

The literary revival was accompanied by a renaissance in painting, sculpture, and architecture. Giotto di Bondone (c. 1277–1337), a Florentine painter and friend of Dante's, has traditionally been credited with initiating this shift. Giorgio Vasari, a sixteenth-century Florentine artist, wrote in *Lives of the Artists* that ". . . it was Giotto alone who, by God's favor, rescued and restored the art, even though he was born among incompetent artists . . . Giotto not only captured his master's own style* but also began to draw so ably from life that he made a decisive break with the crude traditional Byzantine style and brought to life the great art of painting as we know it today."[1]

Giotto, whose paintings were done in fresco, had virtually no classical examples of painting to draw upon, and much of his inspiration seems to have come from trying to integrate Byzantine painting styles with surviving classical sculptural friezes. He gives a bulky, sculptural quality to his work, stressing the body enfolded in robes, people touching, clasping, with their feet solidly on the ground. Giotto's figures are no longer frontal, and they have lost much of their symbolic quality. They stand in human surroundings, reacting with human emotions. Giotto, however, did not have a perfected sense of perspective, and he paid little attention to landscape. Contemporary with Giotto were other great artists such as Duccio and Simone Martini from Siena. In sculpture, the thirteenth-century works of Nicola and Giovanni Pisano captured a remarkable integration of classical and Gothic elements that was to influence Giotto's painting.

Giotto had no immediate remarkable successors. It is not until the Florentine

---

* His master was the artist Cimabue (see Chapter 17).

Giotto's Madonna from the Altar of Ognissanti (All Saints) in Florence, 1305–1310 Giotto worked on this altarpiece not long after he finished his famous frescos for the Arena Chapel in Padua. While there are many aspects of this *Enthroned Madonna with Saints* that are similar to those done by late thirteenth-century artists, Giotto has created a different sense of space. The body of the Madonna is solid and down to earth, while the Christ child is a robust figure who is no longer symbolically portrayed but seems real blood and flesh being held by His mother. The steps and the sides of the throne suggest a depth to the painting. The alignment of the angels, one in front of the other, also suggests depth. These figures are as much human as divine. *Uffizi, Florence, Italy/ The Bridgeman Library.*

painter Masaccio (1401–1428?) that Giotto's artistic achievement was definitively superseded. Masaccio developed the technique of perspective and experimented with nudes, with emotionalism and narrative frames, with classic styles, the use of light, and naturalism to give his figures a new kind of grandeur. His few surviving paintings, especially those in the Brancacci chapel of the church of the Carmines in Florence, became a school for subsequent painters.

Between 1400 and the sixteenth century, artists vied with one another in the beauty and artistry with which they portrayed the human body. Donatello, the greatest sculptor of the early fourteenth century, was the first since antiquity to sculpt a freestanding nude. This emphasis on the body was to culminate in the works of Michelangelo.

The popularity of portraiture, from the mid-fifteenth century on, both in painting and in sculpture, also illustrates the new preoccupation with human form. Sculpted portraits, modeled on Roman busts, are extremely realistic. There are painted portraits, with heads in profile, forward, or at an angle. Patrons had themselves painted into their commissioned works. Portraits of the Madonna and child, placed in realistic, homelike settings, suggest that one might see them on the streets of any fifteenth-century town. Leonardo da Vinci, remembered for his *Mona Lisa, Last Supper,* and the *Virgin and St. Anne,* was especially intrigued by the macabre and the scientific. His notebooks are filled with designs of parts of the body. At one point he recorded the last days of a centenarian, drawing him from life, then dissecting him and drawing him in death.

Many of these paintings have an architectural quality, particularly Masaccio's *Holy Trinity,* which illustrates the new idea of buildings scaled to the size of humans according to classical proportions. According to Vitruvius, a Roman architect at the time of Caesar Augustus whose writings were particularly influential in the Renaissance, buildings should have proportions like the human body and should be built on a human scale. He emphasized visual designs that hide the underlying structure of a complex. Thus the buildings of the Italian Renaissance did not strive for the

Masaccio's Holy Trinity with Mary, John the Evangelist, and Two Donors, c. 1426–1427 This fresco was painted in the Dominican church of Sta. Maria Novella in Florence. It is generally agreed to be Masaccio's most mature work. It is a tomb painting; although it is not shown in this image there is a skeleton painted below the Trinity, and there was a tomb under the floor in front of the painting. The saying above the skeleton reads: "I was once what you are, and what I am, you also will be." The eyes of the donors and of John the Evangelist, as well as the gestures of Mary ask the viewer to look up to Christ. The painting is especially notable for Masaccio's use of perspective and the illusionistic architectural quality he gives to the setting. The design is similar to buildings designed by Brunelleschi and testify to a possible partnership between Masaccio and Brunelleschi in developing the use of perspective. The details of the figures also enhance the viewer's sense of three dimensionality. *S. Maria Novella, Florence, Italy/Art Resource, NY.*

height or immensity of Gothic cathedrals. Whereas Gothic cathedrals focused on the grandeur of divinity and on the interplay and pervasiveness of light, Renaissance architecture focused on harmony in relationship to man. Renaissance architectural theorists stressed what was pleasing to the human eye, arguing, for example, that the rounded classical arch was more pleasing than the pointed Gothic arch, which they argued was disruptive and distracting. Renaissance architecture could also, however, be monumental, as witnessed by Brunelleschi's design for the cathedral in Florence; or it could be Gothic, as was the cathedral at Milan.

PHILOSOPHY

The Italian philosophers of the fifteenth century presented a positive view of man. Man was made in the image of God; his soul partakes of God. They saw man's inventiveness as imitative of God's creativity and emphasized that God gave the world to mankind to fashion. These were not new ideas. They had been expressed by scholastics in the twelfth and thirteenth centuries and by mystics in the fourteenth. But now man's inventiveness and ability to shape his environment depended more on the extent of his intellectual freedom and less on God's grace. Such a man has no limits. His striving for virtue or for fame is natural, justified by his own divine nature as well as by classical authorities such as Plato.

Two of the most famous philosophers of the Italian Renaissance were Marsilio Ficino (1433–1499) and Giovanni Pico della Mirandola (1463–1494). Ficino argued that the soul naturally strives to transcend determinism, to become God-like by searching for those abstract qualities that are closest to divinity. For Ficino, beauty was one of those qualities. Pico della Mirandola emphasized the search for philosophic truth more than the search for beauty. He argued that man was in a unique position, capable of becoming a devil or a saint. This ability, based on free will, makes it possible for men to rise above the angels. They are the sons of God, soaring beyond angelic dignity and nearly divine themselves. His *Oration on the Dignity of Man,* written as an introductory speech to a planned disputation of nine hundred religious and philosophical theses,* puts it succinctly: "We can become what we will. . . . Let us compete with angels." Pico's *Oration* is often chosen as the defining text of Renaissance philosophy, although the largest proportion of the theses he sought to debate in 1487 are from the writings of Thomas Aquinas. Pico's

---

* Pico's nine hundred theses were an effort to integrate the fundamental truths that he thought were embedded in all the major systems of religious and philosophical thought—the Platonic, the Kabbalistic, the Aristotelian, the Christian, etc. He published these theses in Rome in 1486, inviting all scholars to a public disputation regarding them. Underlying this project was his conviction that one should not follow one school of thought exclusively. The diverse intellectual traditions all reflected part of the truth and could be integrated. He noted, "Let a hundred schools compete." Pope Innocent VIII suspended the projected disputation and established a commission to examine the theses. Three were declared heretical, three possibly heretical, and three dubious. Pico della Mirandola was forced to flee Italy.

Latin was more scholastic than classical, and his admiration for Plato was balanced with his admiration for the writings of medieval scholars such as Duns Scotus and Albertus Magnus.

Both Ficino and Pico emphasized man's unity with the cosmos as well as his ability to control his environment. With such arguments they gave legitimacy to magic (which is, after all, a form of controlling one's environment). In particular they gave legitimacy to the writings of pseudo-Hermes Trismegistus (Hermes, the thrice-great), to astrological practices, and to the Judaic kabbalistic tradition as well. Hermes, who was thought to have been an Egyptian sage who was older than Plato and contemporary with Moses, was in fact the spurious author of a rather mixed-up compilation of seventeen treatises called the *Corpus Hermeticum*. It combined astrology, theology, and philosophy to produce a kind of scientific magic. These hermetic texts, which were really written in the first three centuries A.D., argued that the entire cosmos was interrelated by laws of sympathy and antipathy. To know these laws allowed man to be reborn through this magical knowledge.

Marsilio Ficino, who translated the hermetic writings from Greek into Latin, believed strongly in astrological influences. For example, he thought that scholars were normally born under the sign of Saturn and would naturally be saturnine or melancholic. Ficino, who was also trained as a physician, reached back into ancient Greek practices to suggest certain psychological prescriptions for various disorders. The saturnine scholar, for example, should counteract Saturn's effects with the influence of the sun and of sun-like things (e.g. gold, the music of Orpheus).

The Kabbalah is an esoteric or mystical tradition that claims to represent the secret parts of the Torah. It promises a secret knowledge of the universe, in some texts leading to a transmigration of the soul. This post-Talmudic Jewish mysticism was usually taught orally, through an initiation process. The wisdom of the Kabbalah derives from a group of medieval Jewish texts (especially the twelfth-century *Book of Brightness*). It uses astrology and the magical power of combinations of numbers and Hebraic letters to explain creation and to communicate with the divine across the universe. For example, by assigning numerical values to letters in the Hebrew alphabet one could develop a kind of a code for sending messages via an angelic network. Pico della Mirandola was particularly influenced by the Kabbalah.

This willingness to experiment with the astrological, numerological, psychological, theological, and mystical in order to better one's life or soul leads, eventually, to a more scientific view of the universe. It is not too large a step from this kind of magical approach to a willingness to experiment with nature. In addition, astrology, while reawakening interest in long-dead astral cults, also provided a body of research and observations, an attentive study of climate, of the earth, and of celestial phenomena. The Italian astrologer, Paolo Toscanelli, for example, accurately calculated the paths of fifteenth-century comets. He also calculated the circumference of the globe and predicted, in a letter written to a correspondent in Portugal, that one could reach the spice lands of the Indies by sailing west. A copy of this letter was in Christopher Columbus's notebook.

GEOGRAPHY

While medieval merchants and missionaries had explored the world to the east, the fourteenth and fifteenth centuries were a time of exploration of the western seas. Around 1300 the sultan of Mali sent a large expedition westward until they encountered a massive river and turned home.[2] When the Portuguese discovered the Canary Islands in the 1340s, Giovanni Boccaccio expressed great excitement. By the early fifteenth century, the Portuguese were colonizing the Madeira Islands and the Azores and exploring the coast of Africa. Portugal became a center for the accumulation of geographical information, as did Florence. Merchant-sailors and mapmakers had extensive geographical discussions with the Greeks during a church council in Florence in the 1430s, and Florentines produced one of the most sophisticated world maps of the time. The recovery of ancient geographical information, and the expanding contacts between intellectuals and merchants undoubtedly contributed to the increasingly acceptable notion that there were islands in the Atlantic to be discovered as well as a westward route to East Asia. When Columbus discovered the New World in 1492, he was pursuing a possibility that had been proposed many times in an ocean that had already been partially explored.

POLITICS

The concern with man in relation to his environment can also be seen in the field of politics. Jacob Burckhardt, a nineteenth-century Swiss art historian, argued that Renaissance Italy had peculiar political conditions, with competitive city-states no longer restrained by pope or emperor, and political leaders whose power was based on talent (and sometimes brute force) rather than noble blood. Burckhardt argued that this produced a new consciousness of the power of the political individual.

It was certainly true that traditional political solutions had failed the Italians. More and more the city-states of Italy seemed to be at the mercy of the rule of the current strongman—the Visconti and then the Sforzas in Milan, the Medici in Florence, the pope in Rome, or intervening rulers from outside monarchies. Wars between these powers became endemic. The Italian city-states and territories of the fourteenth and fifteenth centuries had to find new solutions and new ways of preserving peace. They were therefore the first western Europeans to develop diplomacy into an art and a necessity, although they were undoubtedly influenced in this sphere by the Byzantines and perhaps by the practice of papal diplomacy. Italian rulers and political writers were the first to articulate the idea of a balance of power, an idea that helped bring peace briefly in the 1460s to the deeply divided Italian peninsula. Following a long tradition of Italian political thinkers, but enhanced by the availability of classical political writings of Plato and Polybius, Italians argued for the superiority of republics over monarchy as a form of government. As they developed their ideas on politics, the older church-state competition for authority became less relevant, and they concentrated instead on the practicalities of retaining power in the increasingly secular and dangerous political atmosphere of Renaissance Italy.

In the wake of a disastrous French invasion of the Italian peninsula in 1494, and the ups and downs of a weak Florentine Republic, we find Niccolò Machiavelli (1469–1527) musing about what some have termed a "science" of politics. Machiavelli combined a background in classical texts with extensive diplomatic experience. Machiavelli's purpose was to suggest practical means for attaining a united and strong Italy that would be proof against foreign invasion. He did this by teaching tactics derived from certain rules of political behavior. The tactics advocated in his *Prince* are usually considered amoral if not immoral but necessary given man's evil nature: One should avoid war, break faith if necessary, be feared more than loved, get rid of your opponents, and cater to the people. Machiavelli's politics, which emphasize the ability of man to shape his environment, are completely secular. Religion and the role of God are excluded or used as tools. Fortune, rather than God, is invoked. Machiavelli rails against the Church, largely because he saw it as a political obstruction to the unification of Italy. Machiavelli is the prime example of what is often regarded as a strong secular strain in the Renaissance. But the pursuit of the politically effective may not have been Machiavelli's highest good. Machiavelli was influenced not only by the classics but also by Dante. He wrote, besides the *Prince,* an *Exhortation to Penitence,* and he was a member of a religious fraternity. Machiavelli may have had a moral vision, although this is highly debated. It might be that Machiavelli was describing, rather than prescribing, in

Terracotta Bust of Machiavelli   This bust of Machiavelli, now housed in the Palazzo Vecchio in Florence, is done by an unknown artist from life. It shows a relatively young Machiavelli, most likely at a time when he was secretary and diplomat for the Florentine Republic, prior to his exile from political life under Medici rule. *Palazzo Vecchio, Florence, Italy/Art Resource, NY.*

order to warn his compatriots against the rule of princes. Or it might be that, for Machiavelli, politics was at best a salvaging operation considering the evilness of man and corruption of society. In this last sentiment, Machiavelli seems very much a medieval man.

RELIGION

Indeed there is much that remains religious in the Italian Renaissance. One needs to keep in mind that Renaissance Florence was also a city with twenty-five companies of flagellants. At the height of the Renaissance, the religious prophecies and moral politics of Girolamo Savonarola, a Dominican friar (d. 1498), captivated Florence. Pico della Mirandola was to be converted by Savonarola to a more ascetic religiosity, burning his early love poems and flagellating himself. Perhaps the paganism and secularism of the Italian Renaissance has been overemphasized. Paintings that were once considered "pagan" can no longer be seen as a repudiation of Christianity. They are a product of the Renaissance philosopher's belief in the unity of truth between Christian and pagan views of the world. Pico, who believed deeply in this unity, died in the clothing of a mendicant friar, expressing his desire to give up his wealth and preach for Christ.

The true religious skeptic (someone like Leonardo da Vinci) is an isolated figure in the Renaissance. Although more focused on man and his achievements than was the Middle Ages, this period was a time of strong religious beliefs. It was an age of great religious preachers, an age of great saints (Catherine of Siena, Catherine of Genoa, Ignatius Loyola), and of great religious painting. It was also the preparatory time for the Reformation. When Isabella and Ferdinand of Spain commissioned Christopher Columbus to sail the Atlantic, they did so in the hope that he would convert Asians to the Christian faith and that he would facilitate the Christian recovery of Jerusalem. When Christopher Columbus landed in 1492, he planted a crusading cross as he stepped off the ship and into the New World.

NOTES

1. Giorgio Vasari, *Lives of the Artists,* vol. 1 (London: Penguin, 1965) 57–58.
2. As reported by the encyclopedist Ibn Amīr Hājib. See Abbas Hamdani, "An Islamic Background to Voyages of Discovery" in *The Legacy of Muslim Spain,* vol. 1, ed. Salma Khadra Jayyusi (Leiden: Brill, 1974) 273–304.

APPENDICES

POPES AND RULERS OF THE MIDDLE AGES

Popes*

Sylvester I (314–335)
Marcus (336)
Julius I (337–352)
Liberius (352–366)
Felix II (355–365)
Ursinus (366–367)
Damasus I (366–384)
Siricius (384–399)
Anastasius I (399–401)
Innocent I (401–417)
Zosimus (417–418)
Eulalius (418–419)
Boniface I (418–422)
Celestine I (422–432)
Sixtus III (432–440)
Leo I the Great (440–461)
Hilarius (461–468)
Simplicius (468–483)
Felix III (483–492)
Gelasius I (492–496)
Anastasius II (496–498)
Symmachus (498–514)
Lawrence (498–499, 501–506)
Hormisdas (514–523)
John I (523–526)
Felix IV (526–530)
Dioscorus (530)
Boniface II (530–532)
John II (533–535)
Agapitus I (535–536)
Silverius (536–537)
Vigilius (537–555)
Pelagius I (556–561)
John III (561–574)
Benedict I (575–579)
Pelagius II (579–590)

Gregory I the Great (590–604)
Sabinian (604–606)
Boniface III (607)
Boniface IV (608–615)
Deusdedit (615–618)
Boniface V (619–625)
Honorius I (625–638)
Severinus (640)
John IV (640–642)
Theodore I (642–649)
Martin I (649–653)
Eugenius I (654–657)
Vitalian (657–672)
Adeodatus II (672–676)
Donus (676–678)
Agatho (678–681)
Leo II (682–683)
Benedict II (684–685)
John V (685–686)
Conon (686–687)
Theodore (687)
Paschal (687)
Sergius I (687–701)
John VI (701–705)
John VII (705–707)
Sisinnius (708)
Constantine (708–715)
Gregory II (715–731)
Gregory III (731–741)
Zacharias (741–752)
Stephen II (752)
Stephen III (752–757)
Paul I (757–767)
Constantine (767–768)
Philip (768)
Stephen IV (768–772)

Adrian I (772–795)
Leo III (795–816)
Stephen V (816–817)
Paschal I (817–824)
Eugenius II (824–827)
Valentine (827)
Gregory IV (827–844)
John (844)
Sergius II (844–847)
Leo IV (847–855)
Benedict III (855–858)
Anastasius Bibliothecarius (855)
Nicholas I the Great (858–867)
Adrian II (867–872)
John VIII (872–882)
Marinus I (882–884)
Adrian III (884–885)
Stephen VI (885–891)
Formosus (891–896)
Boniface VI (896)
Stephen VII (896–897)
Romanus (897)
Theodore II (897)
John IX (898–900)
Benedict IV (900–903)
Leo V (903)
Christopher (903–904)
Sergius III (904–911)
Anastasius III (911–913)
Lando (913–914)
John X (914–928)
Leo VI (928)
Stephen VIII (929–931)
John XI (931–935)
Leo VII (936–939)

* Antipopes are in *italic*.

Stephen IX (939–942)
Marinus II (942–946)
Agapitus II (946–955)
John XII (955–964)
Leo VIII (963–965)
Benedict V (964)
John XIII (965–972)
Benedict VI (973–974)
Boniface (974 and 984–985)
Benedict VII (974–983)
John XIV (983–984)
John XV (985–996)
Gregory V (996–999)
John XVI (997–998)
Sylvester II (999–1003)
John XVII (1003)
John XVIII (1003–1009)
Sergius IV (1009–1012)
Benedict VIII (1012–1024)
Gregory (1012)
John XIX (1024–1032)
Benedict IX (1032–1044,
   1045, 1047–1048)
Sylvester III (1045)
Gregory VI (1045–1046)
Clement II (1046–1047)
Damasus II (1048)
Leo IX (1049–1054)
Victor II (1055–1057)
Stephen X (1057–1058)
Benedict X (1058–1059)
Nicholas II (1058–1061)
Alexander II (1061–1073)
Honorius (1061–1064)
Gregory VII (1073–1085)
*Clement III (1080 and
   1084–1100)*
Victor III (1086–1087)

Urban II (1088–1099)
Paschal II (1099–1118)
Theodoric (1100–1101)
Albert (1101)
Sylvester IV (1105–1111)
Gelasius II (1118–1119)
Gregory VIII (1118–1121)
Callistus II (1119–1124)
Celestine (II) (1124)
Honorius II (1124–1130)
Innocent II (1130–1143)
Anacletus II (1130–1138)
Victor IV (1138)
Celestine II (1143–1144)
Lucius II (1144–1145)
Eugenius III (1145–1153)
Anastasius IV (1153–1154)
Adrian IV (1154–1159)
Alexander III (1159–1181)
Victor IV (1159–1164)
Paschal III (1164–1168)
Callistus (III) (1168–1178)
Innocent II (1179–1180)
Lucius III (1181–1185)
Urban III (1185–1187)
Gregory VIII (1187)
Clement III (1187–1191)
Celestine III (1191–1198)
Innocent III (1198–1216)
Honorius III (1216–1227)
Gregory IX (1227–1241)
Celestine IV (1241)
Innocent IV (1243–1254)
Alexander IV (1254–1261)
Urban IV (1261–1264)
Clement IV (1265–1268)
Gregory X (1271–1276)
Innocent V (1276)

Adrian V (1276)
John XXI (1276–1277)
Nicholas III (1277–1280)
Martin IV (1281–1285)
Honorius IV (1285–1287)
Nicholas IV (1288–1292)
Celestine V (1294)
Boniface VIII (1294–1303)
Benedict XI (1303–1304)
Clement V (1305–1314)
John XXII (1316–1334)
Nicholas (V) (1328–1330)
Benedict XII (1334–1342)
Clement VI (1342–1352)
Innocent VI (1352–1362)
Urban V (1362–1370)
Gregory XI (1370–1378)
Urban VI (1378–1389)
Clement (VII) (1378–1394)
Boniface IX (1389–1404)
Benedict (XIII) (1394–1417)
Innocent VII (1404–1406)
Gregory XII (1406–1415)
Alexander V (1409–1410)
John (XXIII) (1410–1415)
Martin V (1417–1431)
Clement VIII (1423–1429)
Benedict (XIV) (1425)
Eugenius IV (1431–1447)
Felix V (1439–1449)
Nicholas V (1447–1455)
Callistus III (1455–1458)
Pius II (1458–1464)
Paul II (1464–1471)
Sixtus IV (1471–1484)
Innocent VIII (1484–1492)
Alexander VI (1492–1503)

Kings of the Barbarian Successor States

Vandals

Geiseric (427–477)
Hunneric (477–484)
Gunthamund (484–496)
Thrasamund (496–523)
Hilderic (523–530)
Gelamir (530–534)

Ostrogoths

Theodoric (471–526)
Athalric (526–534)
Theodahat (534–536)
Witiges (536–540)
Hildibad (540–541)
Eraric (541)
Totila (541–552)
Teia (552–553)

Visigoths

Euric (466–483)
Alaric II (483–506)
Theodoric and Amalric
  (506–522)
Amalric (522–531)
Theudis (531–548)
Theudigisel (548–549)
Agila (549–554)
Athanagild (554–567)
Leova I (567–572)
Leovigild (570–586)
Reccared I (586–601)
Leova II (602–603)
Witterich (603–610)
Gundimar (610–612)
Sisibut (612–620)

Reccared II (620–621)
Swinthila (620–631)
Sisinand (631–636)
Chinthila (636–640)
Tulga (640–641)
Chindaswinth (641–652)
Recceswinth (652–672)
Wamba (672–680)
Erwig (680–687)
Egica (687–701)
Witiza (701–710)
Roderic (1701–711)

Lombards

Alboin (568–572)
Clepho (572–573)
Autheri (583–590)
Agilulk (590–615)
Adaloald (615–625)
Arioald (625–636)
Rothari (636–652)
Rodoald (652–653)
Aribert (653–662)
Godebert (662)
Grimoald (662–700)
Berthardi (672–688)
Cunibert (688–700)
Luitbert (700–701)
Aribert (701–711)
Ansprand (712)
Liutprand (712–743)
Hildebrand (743–744)
Ratchis (744–749)
Aistulf (749–756)
Desiderius (756–774)

The Pippinids and Carolingians

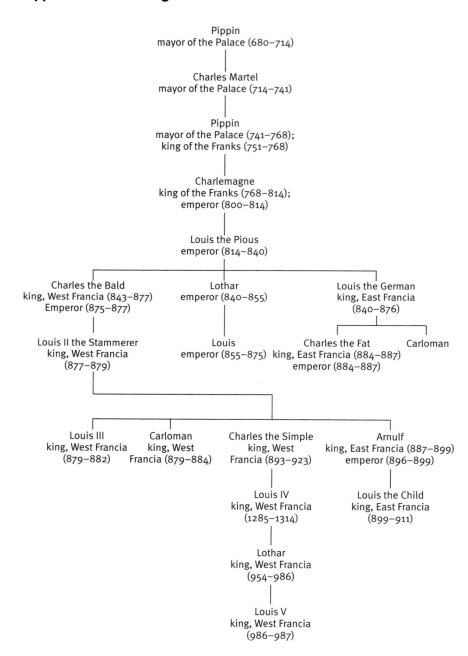

Pippin
mayor of the Palace (680–714)

Charles Martel
mayor of the Palace (714–741)

Pippin
mayor of the Palace (741–768);
king of the Franks (751–768)

Charlemagne
king of the Franks (768–814);
emperor (800–814)

Louis the Pious
emperor (814–840)

Charles the Bald
king, West Francia (843–877)
Emperor (875–877)

Lothar
emperor (840–855)

Louis the German
king, East Francia
(840–876)

Louis II the Stammerer
king, West Francia
(877–879)

Louis
emperor (855–875)

Charles the Fat
king, East Francia (884–887)
emperor (884–887)

Carloman

Louis III
king, West Francia
(879–882)

Carloman
king, West
Francia (879–884)

Charles the Simple
king, West
Francia (893–923)

Arnulf
king, East Francia (887–899)
emperor (896–899)

Louis IV
king, West Francia
(1285–1314)

Louis the Child
king, East Francia
(899–911)

Lothar
king, West Francia
(954–986)

Louis V
king, West Francia
(986–987)

The Capetian and Valois Kings of France

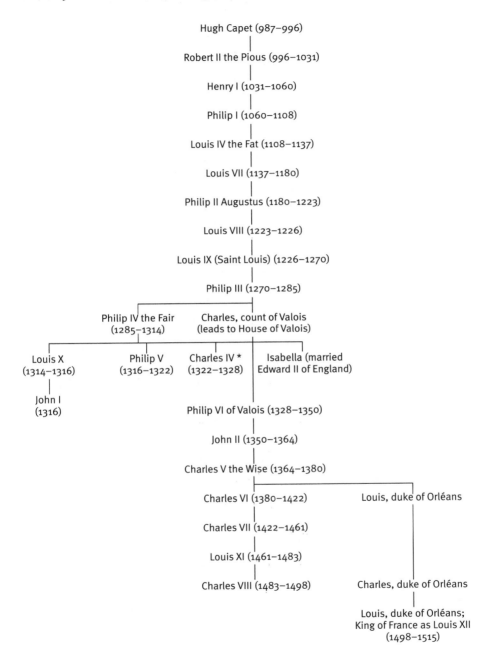

Hugh Capet (987–996)

Robert II the Pious (996–1031)

Henry I (1031–1060)

Philip I (1060–1108)

Louis IV the Fat (1108–1137)

Louis VII (1137–1180)

Philip II Augustus (1180–1223)

Louis VIII (1223–1226)

Louis IX (Saint Louis) (1226–1270)

Philip III (1270–1285)

Philip IV the Fair (1285–1314)

Charles, count of Valois (leads to House of Valois)

Louis X (1314–1316)

Philip V (1316–1322)

Charles IV * (1322–1328)

Isabella (married Edward II of England)

John I (1316)

Philip VI of Valois (1328–1350)

John II (1350–1364)

Charles V the Wise (1364–1380)

Charles VI (1380–1422)

Louis, duke of Orléans

Charles VII (1422–1461)

Louis XI (1461–1483)

Charles VIII (1483–1498)

Charles, duke of Orléans

Louis, duke of Orléans; King of France as Louis XII (1498–1515)

*End of the Capetian line of kings.

The Norman and Plantagenet Kings of England

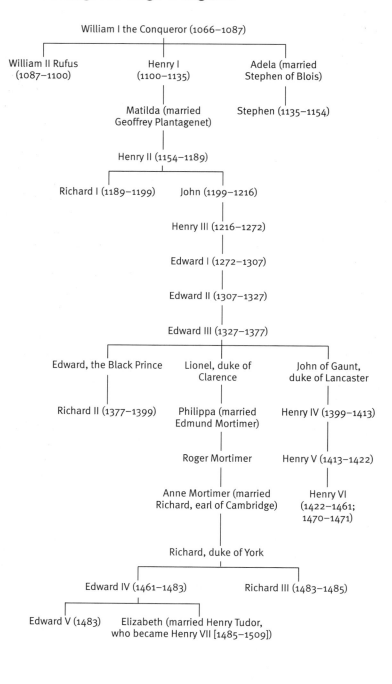

William I the Conqueror (1066–1087)

William II Rufus (1087–1100)

Henry I (1100–1135)

Adela (married Stephen of Blois)

Matilda (married Geoffrey Plantagenet)

Stephen (1135–1154)

Henry II (1154–1189)

Richard I (1189–1199)

John (1199–1216)

Henry III (1216–1272)

Edward I (1272–1307)

Edward II (1307–1327)

Edward III (1327–1377)

Edward, the Black Prince

Lionel, duke of Clarence

John of Gaunt, duke of Lancaster

Richard II (1377–1399)

Philippa (married Edmund Mortimer)

Henry IV (1399–1413)

Roger Mortimer

Henry V (1413–1422)

Anne Mortimer (married Richard, earl of Cambridge)

Henry VI (1422–1461; 1470–1471)

Richard, duke of York

Edward IV (1461–1483)

Richard III (1483–1485)

Edward V (1483)

Elizabeth (married Henry Tudor, who became Henry VII [1485–1509])

Holy Roman Emperors*

Saxon Dynasty
Henry I the Fowler (919–936) (not crowned)
Otto I the Great (936–973)
Otto II (973–983)
Otto III (983–1002)
Henry II (1002–1024)

Salian or Franconian Dynasty
Conrad II (1024–1039)
Henry III (1039–1056)
Henry IV (1056–1106)
Henry V (1106–1125)
Lothair of Saxony (1125–1137)

Hohenstaufen Dynasty
Conrad III (1138–1152) (not crowned)
Frederick I Barbarossa (1152–1190)
Henry VI (1190–1197)
Philip of Swabia (1198–1208)
 (not crowned)
Otto IV of Brunswick (1198–1214)

Frederick II (1215–1250)
Conrad IV (1250–1254) (not crowned)

The Great Interregnum (1254–1273)

Post-Hohenstaufen Succession
Rudolf I of Hapsburg (1273–1291)
Adolf of Nassau (1292–1298)
Albert I of Austria (1298–1308)
Henry VII of Luxembourg (1308–1313)
Louis IV of Bavaria (1314–1346)
(Rival) Frederick III of Austria (1314–1326)
Charles IV of Luxembourg (1346–1378)
Wenceslas of Bohemia (1378–1400)
Rupert I of the Palatinate (1400–1410)
Sigismund of Bohemia-Hungary (1410–1437)

Hapsburg Dynasty
Albert II of Austria (1438–1439)
Frederick III of Styria (1440–1493)
Maxmilian I (1493–1519)

*The addition of "Holy" to the title occurred during the reign of Frederick I Barbarossa (1152–1190).

Kings of Christian Spain

Kings of Aragon

Aznar I Galindo
  (c. 809–839)
Galindo I Aznarez
  (c. 844–867)
Aznar II Galindo (867–893)
Galindo II Aznarez
  (893–922)
Sancho II Carcés (970–994)
García II Sanchez
  (994–1000)
Sancho III Carcés el Mayor
  (1000–1035)
Ramiro I (1035–1063)

United with Navarre 1076–1134

Sancho I Ramírez
  (1063–1094)
Pedro I (1094–1104)
Alfonso I (1104–1134)
Ramíro II (1134–1137)
Petronilla and Ramón
  Berenguer IV of Barcelona
  (1137–1163)

United to Catalonia

Alfonso II (1162–1196)
Pedro II (1196–1213)
James I (1213–1276)
Pedro III (1276–1285)
Alfonso III (1285–1291)
James II (1291–1327)
Alfonso IV (1327–1336)
Pedro IV (1336–1387)
John I (1387–1395)
Martin I (1395–1412)
Ferdinand I (1412–1416)
Alfonso V (1416–1458)
John II (1458–1479)
Ferdinand II (1479–1516)

Kings of Asturias, León, and Castile

Pelayo (718–737)
Favila (737–739)
Alfonso I (739–757)
Fruela I (757–768)
Aurelius (768–774)
Silo (774–783)
Mauregato (783–788)
Bermudo I (788–791)
Alfonso II (791–842)
Ramíro I (842–850)

Ordoño I (850–866)
Alfonso III (866–910)
Kingdom divided among Alfonso's sons
Barcia I (910–914)
Ordoño II (910–924)
Fruela II (910–925)
Alfonso IV (925–931)
Ramíro II (931–950)
Ordoño III (950–956)
Sancho I (956–958)
  (960–966)
Ordoño IV
  (958–960)
Ramíro III (966–982)
Bermudo II (982–999)
Alfonso V (999–1028)
Bermudo III (1028–1037)
Ferdinand I (1035–1065)
  Castile: Sancho II
    (1065–1072)
  León: Alfonso VI
    (1065–1070)
  León, Castile, Galicia:
    (1072–1109)
  León: Sancho II
    (1070–1072)
  Galicia: García
    (1065–1072)
Urraca (1109–1126)
Alfonso VII (1126–1157)
  León: Ferdinand II
    (1157–1188)
  Castile: Sancho III
    (1157–1158)
  Castile: Alfonso VIII
    (1158–1214)
  León: Alfonso IX
    (1188–1230)
  Castile: Henry I
    (1214–1217)
Ferdinand III (*Castile*:
  1217–1252; *León*:
  1230–1252)
Alfonso X (1252–1284)
Sancho IV (1284–1296)
Ferdinand IV (1296–1312)
Alfonso XI (1312–1350)
Pedro the Cruel (1350–1366)
  (1367–1369)
Henry II (1366–1367)
  (1369–1379)

John I (1379–1390)
Henry III (1390–1406)
John II (1406–1454)
Henry IV (1454–1474)
Isabella I (1474–1504)

Navarre

Inigo Arista (c. 810–851)
García Iniquez (851–870)
Fortun Garcés (870–905)
Sancho I Garcés (905–926)
García II Sanchéz (926–970)
Sancho II Garcés (970–992)
García III Sanchéz
  (994–1000)
Sancho III Garcés el Mayor
  (1000–1035)
García IV Sanchez
  (1035–1054)
Sancho IV Garcés
  (1054–1076)
Sancho I (1076–1094)
Pedro I (1094–1104)
Alfonso I (1104–1134)
García IV Ramírez
  (1134–1150)
Sancho VI (1150–1194)
Sancho VII (1194–1234)
Thibault I (1234–1253)
Thibault II (1253–1270)
Henry I (1270–1274)
Jeanne I (1274–1304)
Louis (1305–1314)
Philip II (V of France)
  (1314–1322)
Charles I (IV of France)
  (1322–1328)
Jeanne II (1328–1349)
Charles II (1349–1387)
Charles III (1387–1425)
Blanche (1425–1441)
John (1425–1479)
Leonor (1479)
Francisco (1479–1483)
Catherine (1483–1512)

Portugal

House of Burgundy

Henry of Burgundy
  (1095–1112)
Alfonso I Henriques
  (1112–1185)

Sancho I (1185–1211)
Alfonso II (1211–1223)
Sancho II (1223–1248)
Alfonso III (1248–1279)
Dinis (1279–1325)
Alfonso IV (1325–1357)

Pedro I (1357–1367)
Ferdinand I (1367–1383)
Leonor Teles (1383–1385)

House of Avis
John I of Avis (1385–1433)

Duarte (1433–1438)
Alfonso V (1438–1481)
John II (1481–1495)
Manuel (1495–1521)

Rulers of Eastern Europe

Hungary
Árpád Dynasty
Géza (972–997)
Stephen I (997–1038)
Peter Urseolo (1038–1041, 1044–1046)
Aba Samuel (1041–1044)
Andrew I (1046–1060)
Béla I (1060–1063)
Solomon (1063–1074)
Géza I (1074–1077)
Ladislas I (1077–1095)
Coloman I (1095–1114)
Stephen II (1114–1131)
Béla II (1131–1141)
Géza II (1141–1161)
Stephen III, son of Géza II (1161–1162)
    (1165–1172)
Ladislas II (1162–1163)
Stephen V, son of Béla II (1163–1165)
Béla III (1172–1196)
Emeric I (1196–1204)
Ladislas III (1204–1205)
Andrew II (1205–1235)
Béla IV (1235–1270)
Stephen V (1270–1272)
Ladislas IV (1272–1290)
Andrew III (1290–1301)
Wenceslas of Bohemia (1301–1305)
Otto of Bavaria (1305–1307)
Charles I (1307–1342)
Louis the Great (1342–1382)
Mary of Anjou (1382–1385) (1386–1387)
Charles II (1385–1386)
Sigismund (1387–1437)
Albert of Hapsburg (1437–1439)
Vladislav I (1440–1444)
Ladislas V (1444–1457)
Matthias Corvinus (1458–1490)

Poland
Polanie (Piast) Dynasty
Piast
Siemowit
Lestek
Siemomysł (d.c. 963)
Mieszko I (c. 963–992)
Bolesław I the Brave (992–1025) crowned 1025
Mieszko II (1025–1031) (1032–1034)
Bezprym (1031–1032)
Kazimierz I the Restorer (1039–1058)
Bolesław II the Bold (1058–1079)
Władysław I Herman (1079–1102)

Zbigniew (1097–1107)
Bolesław III (1107–1138)
Seniors
Władysław II (1138–1146)
Bolesław IV (1146–1173)
Mieszko III the Old (1173–1202)
Kazimierz the Just (1177–1184)
Piast King of Poland
Przemysł II (1270–1296) crowned 1295
Premislids-Kings of Poland
(Bohemian Dynasty)
Waclaw II (1296–1305) also King of Bohemia
    and Poland (1300–1305)
Waclaw III (1305–1306)
Piast Kings of Poland
Władysław (1306–1333)
Kazimierz the Great (1333–1370)
Angevin Kings of Poland
Louis of Hungary (1370–1382)
Jadwiga (1382–1395)
Jagiellonien Dynasty
Władysław Jagiełło (1386–1434)
Władysław III (1434–1492)
Kazimierz Jagiellońezyk

Russia
Rurik Dynasty
Rurik (862?–879?)
Oleg (879?–912)
Igor (913?–945)
Olga (945–964)
Svyatoslav (964–972)
Yaropolk (973–980)
Vladimir the Saint (980–1015)
Svyatopolk I (1015–1019)
Yaroslav the Wise (1019–1054)
Izyaslav I (1054–1068) (1069–1073)
    (1076–1078)
Svyatoslav II (1073–1076)
Vsevolod (1078–1093)
Svyatopolk II (1093–1113)
Vladimir II Monomakh (1113–1125)
Mstislav I (1125–1132)
Yaropolk II (1132– 1139)
Vyacheslav (1139) (1150)
Vsevolod II Olgovich (1139–1146)
Igor II (1146)
Izyaslav II (1146–1149)
Yury I (1149–1150) (1150–1154) (1155–1157)
Rostislav I (1154–1155) (1159–1161)
    (1161)
Izyaslav III Davidovich (1157–1159) (1161)

Mstislav II (1167–1169)
Gleb (1169–1170)
1170 Kiev ceases to be the seat of the
    Grand Duke
Grand Princes of Moscow
Ivan I Kalita (1328–1341)
Simeon (1341–1353)
Ivan II (1353–1359)
Dimitry II (1359–1360) (1362–1363)
    (1363–1389)
Dimitry the Elder (1360–1362) (1363)
Vasily Dimitrievitch I (1389–1425)
Vasily Dimitrievitch II (1425–1432) (1433?)
    (1434–1462)
Yury IV (1432–1433) (1434)
Ivan III (1462–1505)
Vasily Ivanovitch III (1505–1533)

Bohemia
Přemyslid Dynasty
Vratislav I (907?–921)
Václav (921–929)
Boleslav I (929–967)
Boleslav II (967–999)
Boleslav III (999) (1003)
Vladivoj (1002–1003)
Jaromir (1003–1012)
Oldřich (1012–1034
Břetislav I (1034–1055)
Spytihněv II (1055–1061)
Vratislav II (1061–1092)
Konrád I (1092)

Břetislav II (1092–1100)
Bořivoj II (1100–1107)
Svatopluk (1107–1109)
Vladislav I (1109–1125)
Soběslav I (1125–1140)
Vladislav II (1140–1173)
Bedřich (1173) (1179–1189)
Soběslav II (1173–1179)
Konrád Ota (1189–1191)
Václav (1191–1192)
Přemysl Otakar I (1192–1230)
Václav (1230–1253)
Přemysl Otakar II (1253–1278)
Václav II (1278–1305)
Václav III (1305–1306)
House of Hapsburg
Rudolf (1306–1317)
House of Görz-Tirol
Jindřich (1307–1310)
House of Luxembourg
Jan (1310–1346)
Karel (1346–1378)
Václav IV (1378–1419)
Zikmund (1419–1437)
House of Habsburg
Albrecht (1438–1439)
Ladislav (1440–1457)
House of Poděbrad
Jiřiz Poděbrad (1458–1471)
Jagiellonians
Vladislav II (1471–1516)

Byzantine Emperors

Constantine I (324–337)
Constantius II (337–361)
Julian (361–363)
Jovian (363–364)
Valens (364–378)
Theodosius I (379–395)
Arcadius (395–408)
Theodosius II (408–450)
Marcian (450–457)
Leo I (457–474)
Leo II (474)
Zeno (474–475 and 476–491)
Basiliscus (475–476)
Anastasius I (491–518)
Justin I (518–527)
Justinian I (527–565)
Justin II (565–578)
Tiberius II Constantine
  (578–582)
Maurice (582–602)
Phocas (602–610)
Heraclius (610–641)
Constantine III, Heraclius III,
  and Heraclonas (641)
Constans II (641–668)
Constantine IV (668–685)
Justinian II (685–695 and
  705–711)
Leontius (695–698)
Tiberius III (698–705)
Philippicus Bardanes
  (711–713)
Anastasius II (713–715)
Theodosius III (715–717)
Leo III (717–741)
Constantine V (741–775)
Leo IV (775–780)
Constantine VI (780–797)
Irene (797–802)
Nicephorus I (802–811)
Stauracius (811)
Michael I Rangabe (811–813)
Leo V (813–820)
Michael II (820–829)
Theophilus (829–842)
Michael III (842–867)
Basil I (867–886)
Leo VI (886–912)
Alexander (912–913)

Constantine VII (913–959)
Romanus I Lecapenus
  (920–944)
Romanus II (959–963)
Nicephorus II Phocas
  (969–969)
John I (969–976)
Basil II (976–1025)
Constantine VIII
  (1025–1028)
Romanus III Argyrus
  (1028–1034)
Michael IV the Paphlagonian
  (1034–1041)
Michael V Calaphates
  (1041–1042)
Zoe and Theodora (1042)
Constantine IX Monomachus
  (1042–1055)
Theodora (1055–1056)
Michael VI Stratioticus
  (1056–1057)
Isaac I Comnenus
  (1057–1059)
Constantine X Ducas
  (1059–1067)
Eudocia (1067 and 1071)
Romanus IV Diogenes
  (1068–1071)
Michael VII Ducas
  (1071–1078)
Nicephorus III Botaniates
  (1078–1081)
Alexius I Comnenus
  (1081–1118)
John II Comnenus
  (1118–1143)
Manuel I Comnenus
  (1143–1180)
Alexius II Comnenus
  (1180–1183)
Andronicus I Comnenus
  (1183–1185)
Isaac II Angelus (1185–1195)
Alexius III Angelus
  (1195–1203)
Isaac II Angelus and Alexius
  IV Angelus (1203–1204)
Alexius V Murzuphlus (1204)

Latin Emperors of Constantinople

Baldwin I of Flanders
  (1204–1205)
Henry of Flanders
  (1206–1216)
Peter of Courtenay (1217)
Yolande (1217–1219)
Robert II of Courtenay
  (1219–1228)
Baldwin II (1228–1261)

Greek Emperors of Nicaea

Constantine Lascaris (1204)
Theodore I Lascaris
  (1204–1222)
John III Ducas Vatatzes
  (1222–1254)
Theodore II Lascaris
  (1254–1258)
John IV Lascaris (1258–1261)
Michael VIII Palaeologus
  (1259–1261)

Paleologus Dynasty at Constantinople

Michael VIII Palaeologus
  (1261–1282)
Andronicus II Palaeologus
  (1282–1328)
Andronicus III Palaeologus
  (1328–1341)
Michael IX Palaeologus
  (1294–1320)
John V Palaeologus
  (1341–1347, 1354–1376,
  1379–1391)
John VI Cantacuzenus
  (1347–1354)
Andronicus IV Palaeologus
  (1376–1379)
John VII Palaeologus (1390)
Manuel II Palaeologus
  (1391–1425)
John VIII Palaeologus
  (1425–1448)
Constantine XI Palaeologus
  (1449–1453)

Muslim Rulers

The Rightly Guided Caliphs
Abu Bakr (632–634)
'Umar ibn 'Abd al–Khattab
 (634–644)
'Uthman ibn 'Affan
 (644–656)
'Ali ibn Abi Talib (656–661)

The Umayyad Caliphs
Mu'awiya ibn Abi Sufyan I
 (661–680)
Yazid I (680–683)
Mu'awiya II (683–684)
Marwan I (684–685)
'Abd al–Malik (685–705)
al–Walid I (705–715)
Sulayman (715–717)
'Umar ibn 'Abd al–'Aziz
 (717–720)
Yazid II (720–724)
Hisham (724–743)
al–Walid II (743–744)
Yazid III (744)
Ibrahim (744)
Marwan II (744–750)

The Abbasid Caliphs
Abu'l–'Abbas al–Saffah
 (749–754)
al–Mansur (754–775)
al–Mahdi (775–785)
Harun al–Rashid (786–809)
al–Amin (809–813)
al–Ma'mum (813–833)
al–Mu'tasim (833–842)
al–Wathiq (842–847)
al–Mutawakkil (847–861)
al–Muntasir (861–862)
al–Musta'in (862–866)
al–Mu'tazz (866–869)
al–Muhtadi (869–870)
al–Mu'tamid (870–892)

al–Mu'tadid (892–902)
al–Muktafi (902–908)
al–Muqtadir (908–932)
al–Qahir (932–934)
al–Radi (934–940)
al–Muttaqi (940–944)
al–Mustakfi (944–946)
al–Muti' (946–974)
al–Ta'i' (974–991)
al–Qadir (991–1031)
al–Qa'im (1031–1075)
al–Muqtadi (1075–1094)
al–Mustazhir (1094–1118)
al–Mustarshid (1118–1135)
al–Rashid (1135–1136)
al–Muqtafi (1136–1160)
al–Mustanjid (1160–1170)
al–Mustadi (1170–1180)
al–Nasir (1180–1225)
al–Zahir (1225– 1226)
al–Mustansir (1226–1242)
al–Musta'sim (1242–1258)

Umayyad Rulers of Spain
'Abd al–Rahman I (756–788)
Hisham I (788–796)
al–Hakam I (796–822)
'Abd al–Rahman II (822–852)
Muhammad I (852–886)
al–Mundhir (886–888)
'Abd–Allah (888–912)
'Abd al–Rahman III
 (912–961)*
al–Hakam II (961–976)
Hisham II (976–1009 and
 1010–1013)
Sulaiman (1009–1010)
 (1013–1016)
Muhammad II (1009)
 (1010)
'Ali (1016–1018)
'Abd al–Rahman IV
 (1018–1019)

al–Qasim (1019–1021)
 (1022–1023)
Yahya (1021–1022) (1025)
'Abd al–Rahman V
 (1023–1024)
Muhammad III (1024–1025)
Hisham III (1026–1031)
Dominions divided into petty
 kingdoms

Nasrid Kingdom of Granada
Muhammad I (1232–1272)
Muhammad II (1272–1302)
Muhammad III (1302–1309)
Nasr (1309–1314)
Ismail (1314–1325)
Muhammad IV (1325–1333)
Yusuf I (1333–1354)
Muhammad V (1354–1359
 and 1362–1391)
Isma'il II (1359–1360)
Muhammad VI (1360–1362)
Yusuf II (1391–1395)
Muhammad VII (1395–1408)
Yusuf III (1408–1417)
Muhammad VIII (1417–1428
 and 1430 and 1432–1444)
Muhammad IX (1428–1430)
Yusuf IV (1430–1432)
Yusuf V (1445, 1450,
 1462–1463)
Muhammad X (1445–1445)
 (1446–1453)
Sa'd (1444–1446)
 (1453–1462)
Ali (1462–1483) (1483–1485)
Muhammad XI (1482–1483)
 (1487–1492)
Muhammad XIII
 (1485–1487)
Conquest of Granada by
 Castile and Aragon

* Declared caliph in 929.

CHRONOLOGY

Political/Military	Social/Economic	Cultural/Religious
284–306: Diocletian		303: The Great Persecution
306–337: Constantine I		328: Consecration of Constantinople
337–361: Constantius II		325: Council of Nicaea 339–397: Ambrose of Milan 342–420: Saint Jerome 354–430: Augustine of Hippo
378: Battle of Adrianople 379–395: Theodosius I		
390–450: Galla Placidia		390s: Christianity becomes official Roman religion
395–410: Alaric the Visigoth 410: Visigoths sack Rome		
		438: Theodosian Code 440–461: Pope Leo I 451: Council of Chalcedon
471–526: Theodoric the Ostrogoth		480–524: Boethius 480–550: Benedict of Nursia
481–511: Clovis I		c. 490–c.580: Cassiodorus
527–547: Theodora 527–565: Justinian I 522: Nika Rebellion 533–551: Byzantium reconquers the West		
		537: Dedication of Hagia Sophia c. 543–615: Columbanus 573–594: Gregory of Tours 590–604: Pope Gregory I
	c. 540s: Bubonic plague spreads throughout the Byzantine Empire	

		570–629: Muhammad 597: Roman mission arrives in England 600–636: Isidore of Seville
	7th century: Spread of the heavy plow from the Slavs into northern Europe	
610–641: Heraclius 623–624: Abu Bakr		622: The *Hegira*
642: Muslims conquer Alexandria 642–652 Khazar–Arab wars		632: Death of Fatima
	c. 650: General economic expansion in the West begins	
652–827: Muslim attacks on Sicily		658–739: Saint Willibrord 664: Synod of Whitby 664–656: Organization of the Qur'an c. 672–735: Bede 680–754: Saint Boniface
698: Muslims conquer Carthage	8th century: Introduction of the three–field system	8th to 10th centuries: *Beowulf* composed
710: Muslims invade Spain 714–741: Charles Martel 716: Muslims attempt to take Constantinople 722–737: Second Khazar–Arab war 730: Iconoclastic decrees 730–825: Mercian hegemony in England 732: Battle of Tours		
		735–804: Alcuin
751–768: Pippin, first Carolingian king 750: Abbasids come to power 755: Establishment of the Papal States 756: Beginning of Umayyad rule in Spain 756–774: Desiderius, last king of the Lombards 757–769: Offa		
768–814: Charlemagne		770–840: Einhardt
793: Vikings sack Lindisfarne		
		c. 800: Conversion of Khazars to Judaism

	800–1200: Warming climate in Europe 9th to 10th centuries: Height of Viking shipbuilding; use of sun compasses	c. 800: *Book of Kells* 806–882: Hincmar of Rheims c. 813: Discovery of tomb of St. James of Compostela
814–840: Louis the Pious 827: Muslims invade Sicily and take Crete 830: Vikings raids begin in the East to the Black Sea	9th and 10th centuries: Spread of water mills throughout northern Europe; spread of irrigation methods from the Levant to Spain and Sicily	
	9th century: Padded horse collar appears	840–843: Dhuoda of Uzes writes the handbook for her son 842: Oaths of Strassbourg
843–877: Charles the Bald 851: Vikings winter over off the coast of England 855: Vikings attack Seville 895: Magyars settle in Hungary 871–899: Alfred the Great 895: Magyar raids into Germany begin 899–911: Louis the Child, last Carolingian king in the East 929: Agreement to separate East and West Francia 986–987: Louis V, last Carolingian king in the West 986–987: Hugh Capet		
860s: Magyars move into the Lower Danube area and begin to raid westward		860s: Methodius and Cyril lead mission to Moravia; 865: Bulgarian Khan Boris baptized into the Orthodox Christian Church
867–954: Viking Kingdom of Yorvik in England		866: al-Kindī, philosophy and scientist at Baghdad, who introduced Greek and Indian writings to Muslims, died
895–955: Magyars attack western Europe		
896–924: Bulgarian ruler Symeon attacks Constantinople		
860, 907, 941: Rus attack Constantinople	907: Commerical treatises between Rus and Byzantines	
	10th century: Growth of woolen and linen textile manufacture; introduction of two-person, horizontal loom	

902: Arab takeover of Sicily and the Balearic Isles	10th century: Development of copper and silver mines; increased minting of coins; iron sources in Sicily and Scandinavia open up; spread of gold currency from Muslim and Byzantine mints	
907: Magyars destroy Moravia	10th and 11th centuries: Rise of castles and castellans throughout the old Carolingian Empire	
910: Rise of Shi'ite Fatimid dynasty in Kairouan, North Africa	10th and 11th centuries: Expansion of agricultural base; introduction of new crops from the Levant	910: Foundation of monastery of Cluny in Burgundy
919–1027: Expansion of Byzantium	10th and early 11th centuries: Establishment of Viking towns throughout the north; growth of towns throughout Europe	930s: Reform of the monastery of Gorze
	Late 10th and 11th centuries: Spread of Jewish communities in northern Europe	929: Restoration of Umayyad caliphate in Spain under 'Abd al-Rahman III
		10th century: Zenith of Muslim scholarship and culture in Spain; populations of perhaps 300,000 and 100,000 in Cordoba and Palermo
		950: Al-Fārābī, neo-Platonic Muslim philosopher and logician, dies in Aleppo
955: Otto I defeats Magyars at Lechfeld		
		960: Harold Bluetooth, king of Denmark converts to Christianity 960s: Monastic revival in England
962: Otto I crowned Roman Emperor by the pope		960s: Hrotsvitha of Gandersheim Polish ruler, Miezko I, converts to Christianity
965: Rus defeat and destroy the Khazars		
	980s: First Viking settlements in Greenland	
	Rise of Venetian trade	
972: Hungary united under one ruler		980–1037: Ibn Sīnā, wrote *Canon of Medicine* in Baghdad
987: Hugh Capet, founder of Capetian dynasty of France, becomes king		988: Vladimir, ruler of Kiev, baptized into Greek Orthodox Christianity

		988–1054: Introduction of Byzantine traditions into Kiev; flourishing Kievan culture
		980s into early 12th century: Peace movements throughout Europe
		995: Olaf Skotkö nung is first Christian ruler of Sweden
		997: St. James of Compostela sacked by Muslims
		999–1003: Gerbert of Aurillac becomes Pope Sylvester II
c. 1000: King Stephen of Hungary given crown by Pope Sylvester II		c. 1000: Norwegian rulers Olaf Trygvason and Olaf Haraldsson convert to Christianity; Hungarian ruler Stephen converts to Christianity
c. 1000: Height of Fatimid rule in North Africa	c. 1000: Viking discovery of the New World	c. 1000: Christianity reaches Iceland and Greenland
		1007–1092: Peter Damian, Italian reformer
1002–1018: Byzantine emperor Basil II defeats the Bulgars	Early 11th century: Beginnings of communal movement in Italy	1009: Destruction of the Holy Sepulchre by the Fatimid caliph in Cairo, al-Hākim; end of Umayyad caliphate in Spain
1014: Defeat of Vikings by Irish at the Battle of Clontarf; Brian Boru dies	Early 11th century: Disappearance of mention of slaves in Capetian archives	1010–1050: Earliest notices of heretics in Europe in the high Middle Ages
1016–1035: Danish King Canute rules England; Canute conquers Norway in 1026	Early 11th century: Knights begin to fight mock wars or mêlées	
Early 11th century: Normans begin to establish a power base in southern Italy		
1018: Bolesław of Poland receives crown from the papacy		
1018: Union of northern and southern Scotland		1030s: Increase in number of pilgrims traveling to the Holy Land 1033 mass pilgrimage
		1033–1109: Anselm of Bec and archbishop of Canterbury
1030s: Pecheneg nomads disrupt the Balkans		1046: Synod at Sutri: Emperor Henry III deposes several popes

		mid-11th century: Truce of God established
		1050s: Arabic and Greek texts become available in the West
		1049–1054: Pope Leo IX, beginning of papal reform
1050: Breakup of Fatimid North Africa into three principalities		1055: Foundation of first Cluniac nunnery at Marcigny
1050s: First raids of Seljuk Turks into Anatolia (eastern Byzantium)		1059: New papal election decree— cardinal bishops become the electors of the pope
1057–1063: Gruffydd rules a united Wales		1059–1111: Al-Ghazālī, Islamic scholar, mystic, and polemicist against neo-Platonism
		1060s–1080s: Beginning of legal studies at Bologna; Constantine the African translates Greek and Arabic medical works at Monte Cassino
1066: Norman conquest of England		
1068–1069: Revolt in northern England and the "harrying" of the north		
1071: Byzantines lose Bari, last Byzantine port in southern Italy, to the Normans		1070s: Discovery of Justinian's Digest in the West
1071: Defeat of Byzantines at the battle of Manzikert in eastern Anatolia; Seljuks, led by Alp-Arslan, capture Byzantine emperor		
1071: Pecheneg nomads attack Byzantium		1073–1085: Pope Gregory VII
		1077: Henry VI of Germany receives absolution from Pope Gregory VII at Canossa
1085: Christian capture of Toledo; border of Christian Spain pushed to the Tagus River	1080s: Milanese communal government	1080s–1189: Reign of Roger II, the Great (c. 1113–1154), cultural revival in Norman Sicily
1091: Byzantines defeat and destroy Pechenegs	1085: Communal government established in Pisa	1095: Consecration of Third Church of Cluny

1096–1099: First Crusade and capture of Jerusalem	1086: Countrywide survey of resources in England, written down in the Doomsday Book	1095: Council of Clermont and Urban II's call for a crusade to capture Jerusalem
1096: Massacre of Jewish communities along the Rhineland	Late 11th century: Introduction of silk manufacture into Norman Sicily	1098–1179: Hildegard of Bingen, mystic, prophetess, administrator, preacher 1100: Establishment of monastery of Fontevrault by Robert of Arbrissel
1101: First Crusade	12th century: Mass manufacture of horseshoes	1112: Bernard of Clairvaux enters the reformed monastery of Cîteaux 1113–1119: Peter Abelard (1079–1142), *magister scholarum* at Notre Dame in Paris
1119: Organization of the Knights Templar	12th century: Develop of professional guilds in cities and towns of Europe	1122: Investiture controversy resolution in the Concordat of Worms
1125: German princes elect Lothar III, first king elected independent of hereditary principles	12th century: Rise in Latin and vernacular literacy; growth of ecclesiastical and governmental archives	1122: Foundation of Premonstratensians order of canons regular
1128: Knights Templar receive recognition in the West; Rule drafted at Council of Troyes in 1129	Increasing number of women writers and readers; introduction of paper manufacture into Spain	1132–1133: Abelard writes *Histories of My Adversities* and Heloise responds to it with her letters
1135–1153: Civil War in England	1130–1316: The Church attempts to outlaw knightly tournaments;	1140s: Gratian, teaching law at Bologna, writes his *Decretum*, a concordance of canon law
1144: Zengī takes Edessa, one of the Latin crusading kingdoms	Opening up of ports along the eastern coast of the Mediterranean to the Genoese, Pisans, and Venetians	12th century: *El Cid* written in first half of the twelfth century; *The Song of Roland* written in the second quarter
1145–1147: Second Crusade led by Louis VII of France and Conrad III of Germany	12th–15th centuries: The Church gradually gains control over ceremony of marriage	
1140s: Revolt in Rome and attempt to establish a republic	12th century: Use of magnetic compass allowing sailing in the Mediterranean at all seasons and opening up the Atlantic to shipping	1120–1140: First notices of Manichean missions in western Europe. They were later called Cathars or Albigensians
c. 1167–1196: King Stefan Nemanja of Serbia founds the Serbian state	12th–13th centuries: Beginnings of an urban, capitalist economy	1140s: Construction of the choir of St. Denys, with a new Gothic style of architecture 1140–1280: Translation into Latin of all of Aristotle's surviving works
1177: Peace treaty between the papacy and Emperor Frederick I	1171: Arrest and imprisonment of thousands of Venetians by Byzantium	1140s–1180s: Revival of jihad by Muslims in the Levant against the crusaders

1182: Philip II expels the Jews from the royal domain	1182: Massacre of western merchants, mainly Genoese, by Byzantines	
1137–1193: Saladin Ayyubid control of Egypt and conquest of Syria	1185: Norman sack of Thessalonica	c. 1120–1180: John of Salisbury; writes *Policraticus* in the 1150s
1187: Defeat of Christians at the battle of Hattin and Muslim capture of Jerusalem	Late 12th century: Introduction of windmills into western Europe from the East	1126–1198: Ibn Rushd (Averroës), commentator on Aristotle in Islamic Spain 1160s–1180s: Cultural revival in Germany under Emperor Frederick I Barbarossa
1187–1191: Third Crusade	1177–1350: 280 enfranchisement charters issued in Lorraine alone	1168: Defeat of last pagan stronghold on southern Baltic coast
1190: Death of Emperor Frederick Barbarossa en route to the Levant in Third Crusade	12th and 13th centuries: Manumissions of slaves and serfs increase throughout western Europe	1170: Murder of Thomas Becket at Canterbury Cathedral
1198: Disputed imperial election in Germany; Pope Innocent III claims the right to decide between two claimants	12th and 13th centuries: Migration of Germans and extension of German city law into eastern Europe	1170–1180s: Chrétien de Troyes writes the first Arthurian romances
1198–1204: Fourth Crusade		1180s: Followers of Peter Waldo (Waldensians or the Poor Men of Lyons) declared heretical by the papacy
1204: Capture of Constantinople; burning and sacking of Constantinople; unification of eastern and western Christian churches		1180s: Marie de France writes her *lais* and other works
1192–1230: King Otokar I unifies Bohemia		1174–1189: Building of Monreale Cathedral in Norman Sicily
1185/86–early 13th century: Bulgar revolt against Byzantium and second Bulgarian Empire		1187: Gerard of Cremona, translator of Arabic, Greek and Hebrew texts in Toledo, dies
c. 1200: Foundation of Teutonic Knights	c. 1200: Introduction of Arabic numbers	1204: Moses Maimonides dies in Egypt
1204: Philip II of France seizes Normandy	Early 13th century: Expanded east-west trade through central and eastern Europe	1198–1216: Pope Innocent III
1214: Philip II wins the battle of Bouvines against John of England and the Emperor Otto IV	13th and 14th centuries: Rise of largescale merchant banking, especially in Italy	1209: Papal recognition of university faculty as a single body at Paris

Early 13th century: Pagan Cumans enter Hungary and submit to King of Hungary		1210: Papal recognition of the Franciscan Order of Friars Minor, headed by Francis of Assisi
1209–1229: Albigensian Crusade		
1212: Children's Crusade; defeat of Muslims in Spain at the battle of Las Navas de Tolosa		1214: Papacy establishes privileges and immunities of the university at Oxford
1215: King John of England signs the Magna Carta		1215: Fourth Lateran Council; recognition of the Dominican Order of Friars
1215: Frederick II becomes Holy Roman Emperor; rise of Guelf and Ghibelline factions in Italy		1215: Incorporation of the university at Paris
1218: Fifth Crusade; defeat in Egypt		1220s: Translation of Averroës's commentaries on Aristotle into Latin
1162?–1227: Chingis Khan creates a Turkic-Mongol empire that threatens China, the Middle East, and Europe		1170–c.1240: Leonardo Fibonacci, mathematician, published his *Liber Abaci* in 1202
1220s: Teutonic Knights shift their activities from the Levant to northeast Europe		1226: Death of Francis of Assisi; expansion of the Franciscan Order throughout Europe
		1230s–1270s: *Romance of the Rose* is written by Guillaume de Lorris and Jean de Meun
1229: Treaty of Paris that ended the Albigensian Crusade		1229: Establishment of university of Toulouse
1229: Emperor Frederick II negotiates the return of Jerusalem to Christian hands		1231: Papal bull gives the Dominicans permission to search out heretics
1232: King of Aragon captures Majorca from the Muslims 1235: King of Castile captures Córdoba		c. 1206–1280: Albert the Great, Dominican and commentator on Aristotle
1238: King of Aragon captures Valencia from the Muslims 1248: King of Castile captures Seville		1221–1274: Bonaventure, Minister General of the Franciscan Order
1230s: Mongols sweep into Rus 1240: Kiev falls 1240–1241: Mongols attack eastern Europe	1246–1280: Sixty villages receive charters in the Paris region	1224/25–1274: Thomas Aquinas, Dominican and theologian
1247–1254: Crusade of Louis IX; defeat in Egypt; Louis IX captured		c. 1220–1292: Roger Bacon

1250: Mamluks take control of Egypt from the Ayyubids		1250–1291: Revival of jihad by the Mamluks
1251: Shepherd's Crusade in France, originally organized to bring help to Louis IX in the Levant; later forcibly disbursed	1252: Florence mints the first gold coin outside Spain and Sicily	1260: High point for apocalyptic expectations based on predictions by Joachim of Fiore (d. 1201); growth of movement of Spiritual Franciscans
		1252–1284: Spain becomes a center of learning under the rule of Alfonso X, the Wise; oversees collection of law codes in the *Siete Partidas*
1257: Seven electors established for election of German king and emperor; origins of imperial electoral college	Second half of 13th century: Mongol Empire promotes trade routes between Europe and East Asia	
1258: Destruction of Baghdad by the Mongols and end of the Abbasid caliphate in Baghdad		
1261: Latin control of Constantinople ends; Byzantine Empire weak but back in Constantinople		
		1265: *Song of Lewes* written in support of Simon de Montfort's revolt against Henry III of England
1268: Charles of Anjou kills last Hohenstaufen heir to the Sicilian crown and takes control of Sicily	1268–1279: Earliest papermill in Italy, at Fabrian.	
1278: Emperor Rudolf of Hapsburg defeats an expanding Bohemia at the battle of Marchfeld Plain		1277: Bishop of Paris condemns 219 propositions in Paris
1282: Sicilian Vespers—revolt against Charles of Anjou		
1291: Fall of Acre and end of the crusader states in Outremer	1291: Genoese ship sails west to find the Indies but does not return	
	End of 13th century: Milan has nearly 100 grammar masters; names of 80 grammar masters for Bologna survive from 1265–1328	1292: Expulsion of Jews from England
		1294–1303: Pope Boniface VIII
c. 1298: Marco Polo writes his *Description of the World*, the account of his travels through the Mongol empire, China, southeast Asia, India and the Middle East		1300: First Jubilee of the Roman Church

		1302: Boniface published the book *Unam Sanctam*
c. 1300: Growth of the kingdom of the Teutonic Order along the Baltic	c. 1300: Europe reaches the height of its medieval population; beginning of a "Little Ice Age" that lasts until the late 1400s	1296–1303: Struggle between the papacy and Philip IV of France; Writings pro and con the papacy by Giles of Rome and by John of Paris
c. 1300: Lithuania emerges as a large, pagan kingdom in northeast Europe		
1302: Flemish defeat the French at the battle of Courtrai		1306: Expulsion of Jews from France
		1307: Arrest and eventual condemnation (1312) of the Knights Templar
1305: William Wallace is executed; Robert Bruce crowned king of Scotland		1305–1378: Papacy at Avignon, called the Babylonian Captivity of the Church
	1315–1320: Widespread famine in northern Europe	1310–1321: Dante writes *The Divine Comedy*
		1311–1415: Persecution of beguines and beghards
1323–1328: Revolts in Flanders	1330s: Giovanni Villani estimates that 8000–10,000 boys and girls in Florence are learning to read	1320–1324: Marsilius of Padua writes his *Defender of the Peace*, an attack on the temporal power of the Church 1327/28: Meister Eckhart condemned by the papacy for his mystical writings; Marsilius of Padua excommunicated
1328: End of the Capetian Dynasty in France; first Valois king		1328: William of Ockham leaves Avignon and begins to write against the papacy; he was subsequently declared heretical
1337: Beginning of the Hundred Years' War	1336–1525: Peasant revolts throughout Germany	1337: Giotto di Bondone, Florentine painter in the early Renaissance, dies
		1338: German electors declare that the king they elect needs no confirmation by the pope
		1341: Petrarch crowned poet laureate in Rome
	1345: England declares bankruptcy	
1346: Battle of Crécy won by the English against the French		

1347–1351: Cola di Rienzo leads a revolt in Rome and tries to reinstitute the ancient Roman Republic	1347–1352: Bubonic plague spreads through Europe, killing 30–50 percent of the population	1350: Giovanni Boccaccio writes his *Decameron*
		1348–1351: Massacres of Jewish communities
		1348: University at Prague founded
1356: Battle of Poitiers won by the English against the French; King John II of France captured	1351: English Parliament tries to stabilize wages and slow worker migrations	1356: Golden Bull published by Diet of Prague says that the papacy has no rights over imperial elections or imperial vacancies
1358: French "Jacquerie" rebellion	1360s: Bubonic plague returns	1360s: William Langland writes *Piers Plowman*
		1364: University of Cracow founded
1360s: Ottoman Turks surround Constantinople	1370s: Rising real wages and per capita income	1377: Pope Gregory XI returns to Rome from Avignon; papal schism begins 1378
1378: Rebellion of the Ciompi in Florence		1370s and 1380s: John Wycliffe writes against the temporal power of the papacy; promotes English translation of the Bible
1381: Poll tax revolt in England		1380s–1390s: Geoffrey Chaucer writes his *Canterbury Tales*
	End of the 14th century: Hanseatic League established	1390s: Lollard movement develops in England, fueled by John Wycliffe's ideas
		1370s–1390s: Julian of Norwich writes her *Revelations of Divine Love*
	14th and 15th centuries: Growth in availability of elementary and grammar education; increasing literacy	1337–1410: Jean Froissart
	14th century: Importation of slaves into southern Europe from Crimea	c. 1363–c. 1429: Christine de Pizan, writer of ballads, chivalric works, histories, defenses of women
		1387: Lithuania becomes a Christian kingdom
1389: Ottoman Turks defeat the Serbs at the battle of Kossovo		1380s: Origins of the Devotio Moderna movement in the Low Countries
1399: Richard II overthrown in England; Lancastrian Henry VI becomes king	1390s: Witchcraft trials on the increase	1391: Massacre of Jews in Spain

1410: Teutonic knights defeated by Lithuania and Poland at Tannenberg		1409: Council of Pisa; schism between three popes
1415: Henry V wins the battle of Agincourt against the French		1415: Council of Constance; John Hus burned 1415–1417: Papal schism ended
1420: Henry V declared king of France		1420–1430s: Hussite wars in Bohemia
		1426–1427: Masaccio paints the Holy Trinity in Santa Maria Novella, Florence
		1429: Joan of Arc leads the French to victory and the Dauphin to be crowned
		1423–1424: Council of Siena
		1430s: Thomas à Kempis writes the *Imitation of Christ*
		1431–1449: Council of Basle 1438–1439: competitive council at Ferrara-Florence
	1440s: Beginning of larger numbers of sub-Saharan African slaves coming into southern Europe	15th century: Height of the Italian Renaissance; revival of interest in the writings and history of the ancients; art and architecture flourish in Florence and throughout northern Italy
	1440s: Population begins to recover from decline after the bubonic plague	
1447: Union of crowns between Poland and Lithuania		1433–1499: Marsilio Ficino, translator of Plato
1453: Fall of Constantinople to the Ottoman Turks; end of Byzantine Empire		
		1486: Inquisitorial manual *The Hammer of Witches*
1492: Fall of Granada, last Muslim territory in Spain	1492: (Re-) discovery of the New World by Christopher Columbus	1492: Expulsion of Jews from Spain
		1463–1494: Giovanni Pico della Mirandola, Renaissance philosopher
1469–1527: Machiavelli, writer and observer of politics	1500s: Climate improves; end of "Little Ice Age"	1498: Savonarola burned in Florence

BIBLIOGRAPHY

Introduction

The Apocalypse in the Middle Ages, ed. Richard K. Emmerson and Bernard McGinn (Ithaca, N.Y.: Cornell University Press, 1992).

Cadden, Joan. *The Meanings of Sex Differences in the Middle Ages: Medicine, Science and Culture* (New York: Cambridge University Press, 1993).

Cipolla, Carlo. *Clocks and Culture, 1300–1700* (New York: Norton, 1977).

Dohrn-van Rossum, Gerhard. *History of the Hour*, trans. T. Dunlap (Chicago: University of Chicago, 1996).

Edson, Evelyn. *Mapping Time and Space: How Medieval Mapmakers Viewed Their World* (London: British Library, 1997).

Erickson, Carolly. *The Medieval Vision: Essays in History and Perception* (New York: Oxford University Press, 1976).

Fernández-Armesto, Felipe. *Before Columbus: Exploration and Colonisation from the Mediterranean to the Atlantic, 1229–1492* (London: Macmillan, 1987).

Grant, Edward. *Planets, Stars and Orbs: The Medieval Cosmos, 1200–1687* (New York: Cambridge University Press, 1994).

Hamdani, Abbas. "An Islamic Background to the Voyages of Discovery," in *The Legacy of Muslim Spain*, ed. Salma Khadra Jayyusi (Leiden: Brill, 1992), 273–304.

Harrison, Kenneth. *The Framework of Anglo-Saxon History* (New York: Cambridge University Press, 1976).

Harvey, P. D. A. *Medieval Maps* (Toronto: University of Toronto Press, 1991).

Henisch, Bridget Ann. *The Medieval Calendar Year* (University Park, Pa.: Pennsylvania State University Press, 1999).

Jacquart, Danielle and Claude Thomasset. *Sexuality and Medicine in the Middle Ages*, trans. M. Adamson (Cambridge: Polity Press, 1988).

Knowles, David. "The Monastic Horarium 970–1120," *Downside Review* 51 (1933): 706–726.

Landes, David. *Revolution in Time: Clocks and the Making of the Modern World* (Cambridge: Harvard University Press, 1983).

Le Goff, Jacques. *Time, Work and Culture in the Middle Ages*, trans. Arthur Goldhammer (Chicago: University of Chicago Press, 1980).

Lewis, C. S. *The Discarded Image: An Introduction to Medieval and Renaissance Literature* (Cambridge: Cambridge University Press, 1967).

Poole, Reginald L. *Chronicles and Annals* (Oxford: Clarendon Press, 1926).

———. *Medieval Reckonings of Time* (London: SPCK, 1935).

———. *Studies in Chronology and History* (Oxford: Clarendon Press, 1934).

Russell, Jeffrey Burton. *Inventing the Flat Earth: Columbus and Modern Historians* (New York: Praeger, 1991).

Visions of the End: Apocalyptic Traditions in the Middle Ages, ed. Bernard McGinn (New York: Columbia University Press, 1979).

Ward, Benedicta. *Miracles and the Medieval Mind: Theory, Record, and Event, 1000–1215* (Philadelphia: University of Pennsylvania Press, 1987).

Ware, R. Dean. "Medieval Chronology: Theory and Practice," *Medieval Studies: An Introduction*, ed. J. W. Powell, 2nd ed. (Syracuse, N.Y.: Syracuse University Press, 1992), 252–277.

Woodward, David. "Reality, Symbolism, Time, and Space in Medieval World Maps," *Annals of the Association of American Geographers* 75 (1985): 510–521.

——— and J.B. Harley. *The History of Cartography*, Vol. 1 (Chicago: University of Chicago, 1987).

Chapter 1 The Roman Foundations of Medieval Europe

Ammianus Marcellinus. *The Later Roman Empire (A.D. 354–378)*, Walter Hamilton trans. (Harmondsworth, Eng.: Penguin, 1986).

Boardman, John, Jasper Griffin, and Oswyn Murray, eds. *The Oxford History of the Roman World* (Oxford: Oxford University Press, 1991).

Bowersock, Glen Warren. *Julian the Apostate* (Cambridge: Harvard University Press, 1978).

Brown, Peter. *The World of Late Antiquity* (London: Thames and Hudson, 1971).

Bury, J. B. *History of the Later Roman Empire*, 2 vols. (New York: Dover, reprint, 1958).

Cameron, Averil. *The Later Roman Empire, A.D. 284–430* (Cambridge: Harvard University Press, 1993).

———. *The Mediterranean World in Late Antiquity*, A.D. 395–600 (New York: Routledge, 1993).

Carcopino, Jérôme. *Daily Life in Ancient Rome* (New Haven: Yale University Press, 1940).

Crook, J. A., A. Lintott, and E. Rawson, eds. *The Last Age of the Roman Republic, 146–43 B.C.,* The Cambridge Ancient History, 2nd ed., Vol. 9 (Cambridge: Cambridge University Press, 1994).

Fatham, Elaine, Helene Peet Foley, Natalie Boymel Kampen, Sarah B. Pomeroy, and H. A. Shapiro. *Women in the Classical World. Image and Text* (Oxford: Oxford University Press, 1994).

Finley, M. I. *The Ancient Economy*, 2nd. ed. (Berkeley: University of California Press, 1985).

Gibbon, Edward. *Decline and Fall of the Roman Empire,* ed. J. B. Bury, 7 vols. (New York: Macmillan, 1914).

Martianus Capella. *Martianus Capella and the Seven Liberal Arts,* trans. W. H. Stahl (New York: Columbia University Press, 1971).

Mathews, John. *The Roman Empire of Ammianus* (Baltimore: Johns Hopkins University Press, 1989).

Percival, John. *The Roman Villa. An Historical Introduction* (Berkeley: University of California Press, 1976).

Rostovtzeff, Mikhail. *The Social and Economic History of the Roman Empire*, 2nd ed., 2 vols. (Oxford: Clarendon Press, 1957).

Salway, Peter. *Roman Britain* (Oxford: Oxford University Press, 1982).

Shelton, Jo-Ann, ed. *As The Romans Did. A Sourcebook in Roman Social History*, 2nd ed. (New York: Oxford University Press, 1998).

Turpin, William. "The Law Codes and Late Roman Law," *Revue Internationale des droits de l'antiquité*, 3eme séries 32 (1985): 339–353.

Ward-Perkins, Bryan. *From Classical Antiquity to the Middle Ages* (Oxford: OUP, 1984).

Wells, Colin. *The Roman Empire* (Glasgow: Fontana, 1984).

Wickham, Chris. "The Other Transition: From the Ancient World to Feudalism," *Past and Present* 103, (1984): 3–36.

Chapter 2 Early Christianity

Augustine of Hippo. *The City of God Against the Pagans*, 7 vols. (Cambridge: Loeb Classical Library, 1957–1972).

Barnes, Timothy D. *Constantine and Eusebius* (Cambridge: Harvard University Press, 1981).

Benko, S. *Pagan Rome and the Early Christians* (Bloomington: University of Indiana Press, 1984).

Brown, Peter. *Augustine of Hippo* (New York: Dorset Press, 1967).

———. *The Cult of the Saints* (Chicago: University of Chicago Press, 1981).

———. *The Making of Late Antiquity* (New York: Barnes and Noble, 1998).

———. *Religion and Society in the Age of Saint Augustine* (New York: Harper & Row, 1972).

Chadwick, Henry. *The Early Church* (Grand Rapids: University of Michigan Press, 1967).

Dodds, E. R. *Pagan and Christian in an Age of Anxiety* (New York: W. W. Norton, 1970).

Drake, H. A. *Constantine and the Bishops. The Politics of Intolerance* (Baltimore: The Johns Hopkins University Press, 2000).

Eusebius. *The Ecclesiastical History*, 2 vols., trans. K. Lake and J. E. L. Oulton (Cambridge: Loeb Classical Library, 1928 and 1932).

———. *The Life of Constantine*, in *A Select Library of Nicene and Post-Nicene Fathers*, 2nd series, trans. E. C. Richardson (New York: The Christian Literature Company, 1890).

Gibbon, Edward. *The Decline and Fall of the Roman Empire*, ed. J. B. Bury (London: Methuen, 1909).

Haskins, Susan. *Mary Magdalen: Myth and Metaphor* (New York: Harcourt Brace, 1993).

Jones, A. H. M. *The Later Roman Empire: A Social, Economic, and Administrative Survey*, 2 vols (Norman, Okla.: University of Oklahoma Press, 1964).

Lewis, Naphtali, and Reinhold Meyer. *Roman Civilization. Sourcebook II: The Empire* (New York: Harper Torchbooks, 1955).

MacMullen, Ramsay. *Constantine* (London: Croom Helm, 1987).

Markus, R. A. *The End of Ancient Christianity* (Cambridge: Cambridge University Press, 1990).

McMullen, R. *Christianizing the Roman Empire (A.D. 100–400)* (New Haven: Yale, 1984).

Momigliano, A., ed. *The Conflict between Paganism and Christianity in the Fourth Century* (Oxford: Clarendon Press, 1963).

Noble, Thomas F. X., and Thomas Head, eds. *Soldiers of Christ. Saints and Saints' Lives from Late Antiquity and the Early Middle Ages* (University Park, Pa.: The Pennsylvania State University Press, 1995).

Reynolds, L. D. and N. G. Wilson. *Scribes and Scholars. A Guide to the Transmission of Greek and Latin Literature*, 2nd ed. (Oxford: Clarendon Press, 1986).

Seltzer, Robert M., ed. *Religions of Antiquity* (New York: MacMillan, 1989).

Chapter 3 Barbarians Enter the Empire

Ammianus Marcellinus. *Res Gestae*, 3 vols, ed. and trans. John C. Rolf (Cambridge: Loeb Classical Library, 1971).

Burns, T. S., *A History of the Ostrogoths* (Bloomington: Indiana University Press, 1984).

Collins, Roger. *Early Medieval Europe, 300–1000* (London: Macmillan, 1991).

———. *Early Medieval Spain. Unity in Diversity, 400–1000* (London: Macmillan, 1983).

Fouracre, Paul, and Richard A. Gerberding, trans. *Late Merovingian France. History and Hagiography 640–720* (New York: Manchester University Press, 1996).

Fredegar. *The Fourth Book of Fredegar with its Continuations*, ed. and trans. J. M. Wallace-Hadrill. 1960. Reprint (Westport, Conn.: Greenwood Press, 1981).

Goffart, Walter. *Barbarians and Romans, A.D. 418–554. The Techniques of Accommodation* (Princeton: Princeton University Press, 1980).

———. *The Narrators of Barbarian History* (Princeton: Princeton University Press, 1988).

Gregory of Tours. *The History of the Franks*, trans. Lewis Thorpe (London: Penguin Books, 1974).

James, Edward. *The Franks* (Oxford: Blackwell, 1991).

Liber Historiae Francorum. The Rise of the Carolingians and the Liber Historiae Francorum, trans. R. A. Gerberding (Oxford: Clarendon Press, 1987).

Matthews, John. *The Roman Empire of Ammianus* (Baltimore: Johns Hopkins University Press, 1989).

Orosius. *Seven Books of History Against the Pagans,* trans. R. J. Deferrari in *Fathers of the Church*, Vol. 50 (Washington, D.C.: Catholic University of America Press, 1964).

Pohl, Walter and Helmut Reimitz, eds. *Strategies of Distinction. The Construction of Ethnic Communities 300–800* (Boston: Brill, 1998).

Straud, Susan Mosher, ed. *Women in Medeival Society* (Philadelphia: University of Pennsylvania Press, 1976).

Thompson, E. A. *The Huns.* Revised edition (Oxford: Blackwell, 1999).

———. *Romans and Barbarians. The Decline of the Western Empire* (Madison: University of Wisconsin Press, 1982).

Wallace-Hadrill, J. M. *The Barbarian West 400–1000.* 1952. Revised (Oxford: Blackwell, 1988).

———. *The Long-Haired Kings.* 1962. Reprint (Toronto: University of Toronto Press, 1982).

Wickham, Chris. *Early Medieval Italy. Central Power and Local Society 400–1000* (Ann Arbor: University of Michigan Press, 1989).

Wolfram, Herwig. *History of the Goths,* trans. Thomas J. Dunlap (Berkeley: University of California Press, 1988).

Wood, Ian. *The Merovingian Kingdoms 450–751* (New York: Longman, 1994).

Chapter 4 Two Eastern Mediterranean Empires

Ahmed, Leila. *Women and Gender in Islam: Historical Roots of a Modern Debate* (New Haven: Yale University Press, 1992).

Cameron, Alan. *Circus Factions. Blues and Greens at Rome and Byzantium* (Oxford: Clarendon Press, 1976).

Cameron, Averil. *The Mediterranean World in Late Antiquity, A.D. 395–600* (New York: Routledge, 1993).

Cook, Michael. *The Koran. A Very Short Introduction* (Oxford: Oxford University Press, 2000).

———. *Muhammad* (Oxford: Oxford University Press, 1996).

Esposito, John. *Islam: The Straight Path* (Oxford: Oxford University Press, 1988).

Garland, Lynda. *Byzantine Empresses: Women and Power in Byzantium, A.D. 527–1204* (New York: Routledge, 1999).

Haldon, J. F. *Byzantium in the Seventh Century* (New York: Cambridge University Press, 1997).

Hambly, Gavin R. G., ed. *Women in the Medieval Islamic World* (New York: St. Martins, 1999).

Herrin, Judith. *The Formation of Christendom* (Princeton: Princeton University Press, 1987).

Hourani, Albert. *A History of the Arab Peoples* (New York: Warner Books, 1992).

Humphreys, R. Stephen. *Islamic History: A Framework for Inquiry* (Princeton: Princeton University Press, 1991).

Kennedy, Hugh. *The Prophet and the Age of the Caliphates* (New York: Longman, 1986).

McClanan, Anne. "The Empress Theodora and the Tradition of Women's Patronage in the Early Byzantine Empire" in ed. June Hall McCash, *The Cultural Patronage of Medieval Women* (Athens, Ga.: University of Georgia Press, 1996).

Mernissi, Fatima. *The Forgotten Queens of Islam* (Minneapolis: University of Minnesota Press, 1993).

Norwich, John Julius. *Byzantium. The Early Centuries* (New York: Alfred A. Knopf, 1989).

———. *A Short History of Byzantium* (New York: Alfred A. Knopf, 1997).

Obolensky, Dimitri. *The Byzantine Commonwealth. Eastern Europe, 500–1453* (New York: Praeger, 1971).

Procopius. *History of the Wars, Secret History, and Buildings*, trans. Averil Cameron (New York: Washington Square Press, 1967).

Schimmel, Annemarie. *And Muhammad Is His Messenger: The Veneration of the Prophet in Islamic Piety* (Chapel Hill: University of North Carolina Press, 1985).

Smith, Margaret. *Rabi'a the Mystic and Her Fellow-Saints in Islam* (New York: Cambridge University Press, 1928, reprint 1984).

Spellberg, D.A. *Politics, Gender, and the Islamic Past: the Legacy of 'A'isha bint Abi Bakr* (New York: Columbia University Press, 1994).

Stowasser, Barbara Freyer. *Women in the Qur'an, Traditions, and Interpretations* (Oxford: Oxford University Press, 1994).

Whittow, Mark. *The Making of Byzantium, 600–1025* (Los Angeles: University of California Press, 1966).

Chapter 5 The Early Medieval Church in the West

Benedict of Nursia. *The Rule of Saint Benedict*, ed. Timothy Fry (Collegeville, Minn.: The Liturgical Press, 1980).

Brown, Peter. *The Cult of the Saints* (Chicago: The University of Chicago Press, 1981).

———. *The Rise of Western Christendom* (Oxford: Blackwell, 1997).

Collins, Roger. *Early Medieval Europe 300–1000* (London: Macmillan, 1991).

Fouracre, Paul, and Richard A. Gerberding. *Late Merovingian France* (New York: Manchester University Press, 1996).

Gregory of Tours. *The History of the Franks*, trans. Louis Thorpe (London: Penguin, 1977).

Herrin, Judeth. *The Formation of Christendom* (Princeton: Princeton University Press, 1987).

Hillgarth, J. N., ed. *Christianity and Paganism, 350–750* (Philadelphia: University of Pennsylvania Press, 1992).

James, Edward. *The Origins of France from Clovis to the Capetians 500–1000* (London: Macmillan, 1982).

Knowles, David, and Dimitri Obolensky. *The Christian Centuries, Volume Two: The Middle Ages* (New York: Paulist Press, 1979).

Levison, Wilhelm. *England and the Continent in the Eighth Century* (Oxford: Clarendon Press, 1946).

Noble, Thomas F. X., and Thomas Head, eds. *Soldiers of Christ. Saints and Saints' Lives from Late Antiquity and the Early Middle Ages* (University Park, Pa.: The Pennsylvania State University Press, 1995).

Peters, Edward, ed. *Monks, Bishops and Pagans. Sources in Translation* (Philadelphia: University of Pennsylvania Press, 1975).

Wallace-Hadrill, J. M. *The Frankish Church* (Oxford: Clarendon Press, 1983).

Wood, Ian. *The Merovingian Kingdoms 450–751* (New York: Longman, 1994).

Chapter 6 An Early Medieval Empire in the West

The Annals of St-Bertin, trans. Janet Nelson (New York: Manchester University Press, 1991).

Collins, Roger. *Early Medieval Europe 300–1000* (New York: St. Martin's, 1991).

Dhuoda. *Handbook for Her Warrior Son. Liber Manualis,* ed. and trans. Marcelle Thiébaux (Cambridge Medieval Classics 8, 1998).

Einhard. *The Life of Charlemagne,* in *Two Lives of Charlemagne,* trans. L. Thorpe. (Harmondsworth, Eng.: Penguin, 1969).

Fouracre, Paul. *The Age of Charles Martel* (London: Longman, 2000).

Ganshof, François. *Frankish Institutions Under Charlemagne,* trans. Bryce and Mary Lyon (Providence: Brown University Press, 1968).

Gerberding, Richard A. *The Rise of the Carolingians and the Liber Historiae Francorum* (Oxford: Clarendon Press, 1987).

Godman, Peter, and Roger Collins, eds. *Charlemagne's Heir: New Aspects of the Reign of Louis The Pious* (Oxford: Clarendon Press, 1990).

Halphen, Louis. *Charlemagne and the Carolingian Empire,* trans. Giselle de Nie (Amsterdam: North-Holland, 1977).

James, Edward. *The Origins of France From Clovis to the Capetians, 500–1000* (London: Macmillan, 1982).

McKitterick, Rosamond. *The Frankish Kingdoms Under the Carolingians, 751–987* (London: Longman, 1983).

———. *The Carolingians and the Written Word* (New York: Cambridge University Press, 1989).

Nelson, Janet. *Rulers and Ruling Families in Early Medieval Europe* (Aldershot: Variorum, 1999).

The New Cambridge Medieval History, Vol. II, ed. R. McKitterick (New York: Cambridge University Press, 1995).

Riché, Pierre. *The Carolingians: A Family Who Forged Europe,* trans. Michael L. Allen (Philadelphia: University of Pennsylvania Press, 1993).

———. *Daily Life in the World of Charlemagne,* trans. Jo Ann McNamara (Philadelphia: University of Pennsylvania Press, 1988).

———. *Education and Culture in the Barbarian West from the Sixth through the Eighth Century,* trans. J. Contreni (Columbia: University of South Carolina Press, 1976).

Wallace-Hadrill, J. M. *Early Germanic Kingship in England and on the Continent* (Oxford: Clarendon Press, 1971).

———. *The Frankish Church* (Oxford: Clarendon Press, 1983).

Chapter 7 The British Isles

Asser. *Life of Alfred,* eds. Simon Keynes and Michael Lapidge (Harmondsworth, Eng.: Penguin, 1983).

Bede. *The Ecclesiastical History of the English People* (London: Penguin, 1990).

Brooke, Christopher. *From Alfred to Henry III. 871–1272* (New York: W. W. Norton, 1969).

————. *The Saxon and Norman Kings* (Glasgow: Fontana, 1967).

Campbell, James, general ed. *The Anglo-Saxons* (Oxford: Phaidon Press, 1982).

————. *Essays in Anglo-Saxon History* (London: Hambledon Press, 1986).

Collins, Roger. *Early Medieval Europe. 300–1000* (New York: St. Martin's, 1991).

Crossley-Holland, Kevin, ed. *The Anglo-Saxon World. An Anthology* (New York: Oxford University Press, reprint 1987).

Dumville, David N. *Wessex and England from Alfred to Edgar.* (Woodbridge, Suffolk: The Broydell Press, 1992).

Farmer, D. H., ed. *The Age of Bede* (New York: Penguin, reprint 1998).

Finberg, H. P. R. *The Formation of England, 550–1042* (London: Paladin Books, reprint 1984).

Herlihy, David. *Medieval Households* (Cambridge: Harvard University Press, 1985).

Hodgkin, R. H. *A History of the Anglo Saxons,* 3rd ed., 2 vols. (Oxford: Clarendon Press, 1952).

Levison, Wihelm. *England and the Continent in the Eighth Century* (Oxford: Oxford University Press, 1946).

Loyn, H. R. *The Governance of Anglo-Saxon England 500–1087* (Stanford: Stanford University Press, 1984).

Mayr-Harting, Henry. *The Coming of Christianity to Anglo-Saxon England,* 3rd ed. (University Park, Pa.: Pennsylvania State University Press, 1991).

Rumble, Alexander R., ed. *The Reign of Cnut* (London: Leicester University Press, 1994).

Sawyer, P. H. *The Age of the Vikings,* 2nd. ed. (New York: St. Martin's, 1971).

————. *From Roman Britain to Norman England* (New York: St. Martin's, 1978).

Snyder, Christopher. *An Age of Tyrants: Britain and the Britons A.D. 400–600* (University Park, Pa.: Pennsylvania State University Press, 1998).

Stenton, Frank. *Anglo-Saxon England,* 3rd ed. (Oxford: Clarendon Press, reprint 1986).

Wallace-Hadrill, J. M. *Early Germanic Kingship in England and on the Continent* (Oxford: Clarendon Press, 1971).

Whitelock, D., ed. *The Anglo-Saxon Chronicle* in *English Historical Documents,* 2nd ed. Vol. I (London: Eyre Methuen, 1979).

Chapter 8 New Influences

Ahmad, Aziz. *A History of Islamic Sicily* (Edinburgh: Edinburgh University Press, 1975).

Barford, P. M. *The Early Slavs: Culture and Society in Early Medieval Eastern Europe.* (Ithaca, N.Y.: Cornell University Press, 2001).

Bartha, Antal. *Hungarian Society in the 9th and 10th Centuries,* trans. K. Balázs. (Budapest: Akadémiai Kiadó, 1975).

Boba, Imre. *Nomads, Northmen and Slavs: Eastern Europe in the Ninth Century* (Mouton: The Hague, 1967).

Bowlus, Charles R. *Franks, Moravians, and Magyars: The Struggle for the Middle Danube, 788–907* (Philadelphia: University of Pennsylvania Press, 1995).

Clarke, Helen and Björn Ambrosiani. *Towns in the Viking Age* (New York: St. Martin's Press, 1991).

Collins, Roger. *The Arab Conquest of Spain, 710–797* (Oxford: Basil Blackwell, 1989).

———. *Early Medieval Spain: Unity in Diversity, 400–1000,* 2nd ed.(New York: St. Martin's Press, 1995).

Davies, Norman. *God's Playground: A History of Poland,* Vol. 1 (New York: Columbia University Press, 1982).

Dolukhanov, Pavel M. *The Early Slavs: Eastern Europe from the Initial Settlement to the Kievan Rus* (New York: Longman, 1996).

Dunlop, D. M. *The History of the Jewish Khazars.* 1954 Reprint (New York: Schocken, 1967).

Egil's Saga, trans. Hermann Pálsson and Paul Edwards (New York: Penguin, 1976).

Engel, Pál. *The Realm of St. Stephen: A History of Medieval Hungary, 895–1526,* trans. Pálosfalvi (London: I. B. Tauris, 2001).

Fine, John V. A. *The Early Medieval Balkans: A Critical Survey from the Sixth to the Late Twelfth Century* (Ann Arbor: University of Michigan Press, 1983).

Golden, Peter. *Nomads and Sedentary Societies in Medieval Eurasia* (Washington, D.C.: AHA, 1998).

Haldon, J. F. *Byzantium in the Seventh Century: The Transformation of a Culture* (New York: Cambridge University Press, 1990).

Jesch, Judith. *Women in the Viking Age* (Rochester, N.Y.: Boydell Press, 1991).

Kaegi, Walter E. *Byzantium and the Early Islamic Conquests* (New York: Cambridge University Press, 1992).

Roesdahl, Else. *The Vikings,* 2nd ed.(New York: Penguin Press, 1998).

——— and David M. Wilson, eds. *From Viking to Crusader: The Scandinavians and Europe 800–1200* (New York: Rizzoli International Publications, 1992).

Sawyer, Birgit and Peter. *Medieval Scandinavia* (Minneapolis: University of Minnesota Press, 1993).

Sawyer, P. H. *Kings and Vikings* (Sawyer: Methuen & Co., 1982).

Seaver, Kirsten A. *The Frozen Echo: Greenland and the Exploration of North America, ca. A.D. 1000–1500* (Stanford: Stanford University Press, 1996).

Simon, Franklin and Jonathan Shepard. *The Emergence of Rus 750–1200* (New York: Longman, 1996).

Smyth, Alfred P. *Scandinavian Kings in the British Isles 850–880* (Oxford: Oxford University Press, 1977).

The Vinland Sagas: The Norse Discovery of America, trans. Magnus Magnusson and Hermann Pálsson (Baltimore: Penguin, 1965).

Vlasto, A.P. *The Entry of the Slavs into Christendom: An Introduction to the Medieval History of the Slavs* (Cambridge: Cambridge University Press, 1970).

Chapter 9 Land and People

Bartlett, Robert. *The Making of Europe: Conquest, Colonization, and Cultural Change, 950–1350* (Princeton: Princeton University Press, 1993).

Bisson, Thomas N. "Medieval Lordship," *Speculum,* 70 (1995): 743–759.

Bloch, Marc. *Feudal Society,* 2 vols. (London: Routledge & Kegan Paul, 1961).

Bonnassie, Pierre. *From Slavery to Feudalism in Southwestern Europe* (Cambridge: Cambridge University Press, 1991).

Brown, Elizabeth A. R. "The Tyranny of a Construct: Feudalism and Historians of Medieval Europe," *American Historical Review,* 79 (1974): 1063–1088.

Clarke, Helen and Bjorn Ambrosiani. *Towns in the Viking Age* (New York: St. Martin's Press, 1991).

Duby, Georges. *The Early Growth of the European Economy: Warriors and Peasants from the Seventh to the Twelfth Century*, trans. H.B. Clarke (Ithaca, N.Y.: Cornell University Press, 1974).

Freedman, Paul. *The Origins of Peasant Servitude in Medieval Catalonia* (Cambridge: Cambridge University Press, 1991).

Gimpel, Jean. *The Medieval Machine* (New York: Holt, Rinehart and Winston, 1976).

Graham-Campbell, James. *The Viking World*, 2nd ed. (London: Frances Lincoln, 2001).

Hilton, R. H. *Bond Men Made Free* (New York: Viking, 1973).

Hodges, Richard. *Primitive and Peasant Markets* (Oxford: Blackwell, 1988).

Hodgett, Gerald A. J. *A Social and Economic History of Medieval Europe* (London: Methuen,1972).

Lewis, Archibald R., *Naval Power and Trade in the Mediterranean AD 500–1100* (Princeton: Princeton University Press, 1951).

———, *The Northern Seas: Shipping and Commerce in Northern Europe, AD 300–1100* (Princeton: Princeton University Press, 1958).

Lewis, Archibald R. and Runyan, Timothy J. *European Naval and Maritime History, 300–1500* (Bloomington: Indiana University Press, 1985).

McDonald, John and G. D. Snooks. *Domesday Economy: A New Approach to Anglo-Norman History* (Oxford: Oxford University Press, 1986).

Poly, Jean-Pierre and Eric Bournazel. *The Feudal Transformation 900–1200* (New York: Holmes & Meier, 1991).

Pryor, John H. *Geography, Technology, and War: Studies in the Maritime History of the Mediterranean, 649–1571* (Cambridge: Cambridge University Press, 1988).

Reynolds, Susan. *Fiefs and Vassals: The Medieval Evidence Reinterpreted* (Oxford: Oxford University Press, 1994).

Unger, Richard W. *The Ship in the Medieval Economy, 600–1600* (London: Croom Helm, 1980).

Wolverton, Lisa. *Hastening toward Prague: Power and Society in the Medieval Czech Lands* (Philadelphia: University of Pennsylvania Press, 2001).

Chapter 10 Rulers and Religion

Barraclough, Geoffrey. *The Crucible of Europe: The Ninth and Tenth Centuries in European History* (Berkeley: University of California Press, 1976).

Becker, Marvin B. *Medieval Italy: Constraints and Creativity* (Bloomington: Indiana University Press, 1981).

Brooke, Christopher. *Europe in the Central Middle Ages 962–1154*, 3rd ed. (New York: Longman, 2000).

Brown, R. Allen. *The Normans* (New York: St. Martin's Press, 1984).

Chibnall, Marjorie. *The Normans* (Oxford: Blackwell, 2000).

Duckett, Eleanor. *Death and Life in the Tenth Century* (Ann Arbor: University of Michigan Press, 1968).

Dunbabin, Jean. *France in the Making 843–1180* (Oxford: Oxford University Press, 1985).

Evans, Joan. *Monastic Life at Cluny, 910–1157* (Hamden, Conn.: Archon Books, 1968).

Fichtenau, Heinrich. *Living in the Tenth Century: Mentalities and Social Order*, trans. Patrick Geary (Chicago: University of Chicago Press, 1991).

Fleckenstein, Josef. *Early Medieval Germany* (Amsterdam: North-Holland Publishing, 1978).

Gatch, Milton McC. *Preaching and Theology in Anglo-Saxon England: Alfric and Wulfstan* (Toronto: University of Toronto Press, 1977).

Geary, Patrick. *Phantoms of Remembrance: Memory and Oblivion at the End of the First Millenium* (Princeton: Princeton University Press, 1994).

Hallam, Elizabeth M. *Capetian France 987–1328* (London: Longman, 1980).

Hrotsvit of Gandersheim: A Florilegium of Her Works, trans. Katharina M. Wilson (Rochester, N.Y.: D.S. Brewer, 1998).

Kreutz, Barbara M. *Before the Normans: Southern Italy in the Ninth and Tenth Centuries* (Philadelphia: University of Pennsylvania Press, 1991).

Lewis, Archibald. *The Development of Southern French and Catalan Society 718–1050* (Austin: University of Texas, 1965).

Leyser, K. J. *Medieval Germany and Its Neighbours 900–1250* (London: Hambleton Press, 1982).

———. *Rule and Conflict in an Early Medieval Society: Ottonian Saxony* (Bloomington: Indiana University Press, 1979).

Martin, Janet. *Medieval Russia, 980–1584* (Cambridge: Cambridge University Press, 1995).

Reilly, Bernard F. *The Contest of Christian and Muslim Spain, 1031–1157* (Oxford: Blackwell, 1992).

Reuter, Timothy. *Germany in the Early Middle Ages 800–1056* (London: Longman, 1991).

Richter, Michael. *Medieval Ireland: The Enduring Tradition* (New York: St. Martin's Press, 1988).

Rosenwein, Barbara. *Rhinoceros Bound: Cluny in the Tenth Century* (Philadelphia: University of Pennsylvania Press, 1982).

Searle, Eleanor. *Predatory Kinship and the Creation of Norman Power, 840–1066* (Berkeley: University of California Press, 1988).

Tabacco, Giovanni. *The Struggle for Power in Medieval Italy: Structures of Political Rule* (Cambridge: Cambridge University Press, 1989).

Whittow, Mark. *The Making of Byzantium, 600–1025* (Berkeley: University of California Press, 1996).

Chapter 11 Religious Revival and Reform

Barstow, Anne. *Married Priests and the Reforming Papacy* (New York: E. Mellen, 1982).

Berman, Constance H. *The Cistercian Evolution: The Invention of a Religious Order in Twelfth-Century Europe* (Philadelphia: University of Pennsylvania Press, 2000).

Blumenthal, Uta-Renate. *The Investiture Controversy: Church and Monarchy from the Ninth to the Twelfth Century* (Philadelphia: University of Pennsylvania Press, 1988).

Boswell, John. *Kindness of Strangers: The Abandonment of Children in Western Europe from Late Antiquity to the Renaissance* (New York: Pantheon Books, 1988).

Cowdrey, H. E. J. *The Cluniacs and the Gregorian Reform* (Oxford: Clarendon Press, 1970).

Elkins, Sharon K. *Holy Women of Twelfth-Century England* (Chapel Hill: University of North Carolina Press, 1988).

Flanagan, Sabina. *Hildegard of Bingen, 1098–1179* (New York: Routledge, 1989).

Glaber, Rodulfus. *The Five Books of the Histories*, ed. and trans. John France (Oxford: Clarendon, 1989).

Head, Thomas and Landes, Richard, eds. *The Peace of God: Social Violence and Religious Response in France around the Year 1000* (Ithaca, N.Y.: Cornell University Press, 1992).

Hunt, Noreen. *Cluny under Saint Hugh 1049–1109* (Notre Dame, Ind.: University of Notre Dame Press, 1968).

Johnson, Penelope. *Equal in Monastic Profession: Religious Women in Medieval France* (Chicago: University of Chicago, 1991).

Lackner, Bede. *The Eleventh-Century Background of Cîteaux* (Washington, D.C.: Cistercian Publications, 1972).

Lambert, Malcolm. *Medieval Heresy: Popular Movements from the Gregorian Reform to the Reformation*, 2nd ed.(Oxford: Blackwell, 1992).

Lawrence, C. H. *Medieval Monasticism: Forms of Religious Life in Western Europe in the Middle Ages*, 2nd edition (London: Longman, 1989).

Le Goff, Jacques. *The Birth of Purgatory* (Chicago: University of Chicago, 1984).

Lekai, Louis J. *The Cistercians: Ideals and Reality* (Kent, Ohio: Kent State University Press, 1977).

Leyser, Henrietta. *Hermits and the New Monasticism: A Study of Religious Communities in Western Europe 1000–1150* (New York: St. Martin's, 1984).

Melczer, William. *The Pilgrim's Guide to Santiago de Compostela* (New York: Italica Press, 1993).

Moore, R. I. *The Formation of a Persecuting Society* (Oxford: Blackwell, 1987).

———. *The Origins of European Dissent* (London: Allen Lane, 1977).

Newman, Barbara. *Sister of Wisdom: St. Hildegard's Theology of the Feminine* (Berkeley: University of California Press, 1987).

Robinson, I. S. *The Papacy 1073–1198: Continuity and Innovation* (Cambridge: Cambridge University Press, 1990).

———. *Authority and Resistance in the Investiture Contest* (Manchester: Manchester University Press, 1978).

Russell, Jeffrey Burton. *Dissent and Reform in the Early Middle Ages* (Berkeley: University of California Press, 1965).

Sumption, Jonathan. *Pilgrimage: An Image of Medieval Religion* (Totowa, N.J.: Rowman and Littlefield, 1975).

Tellenbach, Gerd. *The Church in Western Europe from the Tenth to the Early Twelfth Century* (Cambridge: Cambridge University Press, 1993).

Thompson, Sally. *Women Religious: The Founding of English Nunneries after the Norman Conquest* (Oxford: Clarendon Press, 1991).

Turner, Victor and Edith Turner. *Image and Pilgrimage in Christian Culture* (New York: Columbia University Press, 1978).

Voice of the Living Light: Hildegard of Bingen and Her World, ed. Barbara Newman (Berkeley: University of California Press, 1998).

Warren, Ann. *Anchorites and Their Patrons in Medieval England* (Berkeley: University of California Press, 1985).

Wilkinson, John. *Jerusalem Pilgrims: Before the Crusades* (Warminster, Eng.: Aris & Phillips Ltd., 1977).

Chapter 12 The Crusades

Alexiad of Anna Comnena, trans E.R.A. Sewter (Baltimore: Penguin, 1969).

Arab Historians of the Crusades, ed. F. Gabrieli (Berkeley: University of California, 1957).

Brundage, James A. *Medieval Canon Law and the Crusader* (Madison: University of Wisconsin, 1969).

Bull, Marcus. *Knightly Piety and the Response to the First Crusade: The Limousin and Gascony c. 970–c. 1130* (Oxford: Clarendon Press, 1993).

Chazan, Robert. *European Jewry and the First Crusade* (Berkeley: University of California, 1987).

Christian Society and the Crusades, 1198–1229: Sources in Translation, including the Capture of Damietta by Olive of Paderborn, ed. E. Peters (Philadelphia: University of Pennsylvania, 1971).

Dickson, Gary. "The Advent of the *Pastores* (1251)," *Révue Belge de Philologie et d'Histoire*, 66 (1988): 249–267.

Ellenblum, Ronnie. *Frankish Rural Settlement in the Latin Kingdom of Jerusalem* (Cambridge: Cambridge University Press, 1998).

Erdmann, Carl. *The Origin of the Idea of Crusade*, trans. M. Baldwin and W. Goffart (Princeton: Princeton University Press, 1977).

Forey, Alan. *The Military Orders from the Twelfth to the Early Fourteenth Centuries* (Toronto: University of Toronto Press, 1992).

Fulcher of Chartres. *A History of the Expedition to Jerusalem 1095–1127*, ed. H.S. Fink, trans. F. R. Ryan (Knoxville: University of Tennessee, 1969).

Gervers, Michael, ed., *The Second Crusade and the Cistercians* (New York: St. Martin's Press, 1992).

Gesta Francorum: The Deeds of the Franks and the Other Pilgrims to Jerusalem, ed. Rosalind Hill (London: Thomas Nelson and Sons, 1962).

Guibert of Nogent. *The Deeds of God through the Franks: A Translation of . . . Gesta Dei per Francos*, ed. and trans. Robert Levine (Rochester, N.Y.: The Boydell Press, 1997).

Holt, P. M. *The Age of the Crusades* (London: Longman, 1986).

Housley, Norman J. *The Later Crusades, 1274–1580: from Lyons to Alcazar* (Oxford: Oxford University Press, 1992).

Joinville, Jean and Geoffroi de Villehardouin. *Chronicles of the Crusaders*, trans. M. R. B. Shaw (Baltimore: Penguin, 1963).

Kedar, Benjamin. *Crusade and Mission: European Approaches toward the Muslims* (Princeton: Princeton University Press, 1984).

Lyons, Malcolm Cameron and D. E. P. Jackson. *Saladin: The Politics of the Holy War* (Cambridge: Cambridge University Press, 1982).

Mayer, Hans Eberhard. *The Crusades*, 2nd ed.(New York: Oxford University Press, 1988).

Nicholson, Helen. *Templars, Hospitallers and Teutonic Knights: Images of the Military Orders, 1128–1291* (Leicester: Leicester University Press, 1989).

Odo of Deuil. *De profectione Ludovici VII in Orientem. The Journey of Louis VII to the East* (New York: W. W. Norton, 1948).

Porges, Walter. "The Clergy, the Poor, and the Non-Combatants on the First Crusade," *Speculum*, vol. 21 (1946): 1–23.

Powell, James M., ed. *Muslims Under Latin Rule 1100–1300* (Princeton: Princeton University Press, 1990).

———. *Anatomy of a Crusade, 1213–1221* (Philadelphia: University of Pennsylvania Press, 1986).

Prawer, Joshua. *The World of the Crusaders* (New York: Quadrangle, 1972).

———. *Crusader Institutions* (Oxford: Oxford University Press, 1980).

Queller, Donald. *The Fourth Crusade: The Conquest of Constantinople 1201–1214* (Philadelphia: University of Pennsylvania, 1977).

Raedts, Peter. "The Children's Crusade of 1212." *Journal of Medieval Studies*, vol. 3 (1977): 279–323.

Richard, Jean. *The Crusades, c. 1071–c. 1291*, trans. J. Birrell (Cambridge: Cambridge University Press, 1999).

Riley-Smith, Jonathan. *The Crusades: A Short History* (New Haven: Yale University Press, 1987).

———. *The First Crusaders*. (Cambridge: Cambridge University Press, 1997).

————. *The First Crusade and the Idea of Crusading* (Philadelphia: University of Pennsylvania, 1986).

————. *What Were the Crusades?* (Totowa, N.J.: Rowman and Littlefield, 1978).

Riley-Smith, Jonathan, ed. *The Oxford Illustrated History of the Crusades* (Oxford: Oxford University Press, 1995).

Setton, Kenneth M., ed. *A History of the Crusades*, 6 vols. (Madison: University of Wisconsin, 1955–1990).

Siberry, Elizabeth. *Criticism of Crusading 1095–1274* (Oxford: Clarendon, 1985).

Smail, R.C. *Crusading Warfare, 1097–1193*, 2nd ed. (Cambridge: Cambridge University Press, 1995).

Chapter 13 *The Development of Royal Government*

Barlow, Frank. *Thomas Becket* (Berkeley: University of California Press, 1985).

Benson, Robert L. "Political *Renovatio*: Two Models from Roman Antiquity," in R. L. Benson and Giles Constable, eds. *Renaissance and Renewal in the Twelfth Century* (Cambridge: Harvard University Press, 1982): 339–386.

Brett, M. *The English Church under Henry I* (Oxford: Oxford University Press, 1975).

Brown, Elizabeth A. R. "Eleanor of Aquitaine: Parent, Queen, and Duchess," *Eleanor of Aquitaine: Patron and Politician*, ed. William W. Kibler (Austin: University of Texas Press, 1976): 9–34.

Burns, J. H., ed. *The Cambridge History of Medieval Political Thought c. 350–c. 1450* (Cambridge: Cambridge University Press, 1988).

Chambers, Frank McMinn. "Some Legends Concerning Eleanor of Aquitaine," *Speculum*, vol. 16 (1941): 459–468.

Chibnall, Marjorie. *The Empress Matilda: Queen Consort, Queen Mother and Lady of the English* (Oxford: Blackwell, 1991).

Clanchy, M. T. *England and its Rulers 1066–1272* (New York: Barnes and Noble, 1983).

————. *From Memory to Written Record, England 1066–1307*, 2nd ed. (Oxford: Blackwell, 1993).

Davis, R. H. C. *King Stephen 1135–1154* (Berkeley: University of California Press, 1967).

Derry, T. K. *A History of Scandinavia* (Minneapolis: University of Minnesota Press, 1979).

Douglas, David C. *William the Conqueror* (Berkeley: University of California Press, 1964).

Dunbabin, Jean. *France in the Making 843–1180* (Oxford: Oxford University Press, 1985).

Evergates, Theodore. *Feudal Society in the Baillage of Troyes under the Counts of Champagne, 1152–1284* (Baltimore: Johns Hopkins University Press, 1975).

Facinger, Marion F. "A Study of Medieval Queenship: Capetian France 987–1237," *Studies in Medieval and Renaissance History*, vol. 5 (1968): 3–47.

Fuhrmann, Horst. *Germany in the High Middle Ages c. 1050–1200*, trans. T. Reuter (Cambridge: Cambridge University Press, 1986).

Gillingham, John. *The Angevin Empire*, 2nd ed. (London: Arnold, 1984).

————. *Richard I* (New Haven: Yale University Press, 1999).

Green, Judith A. *The Government of England under Henry I* (Cambridge: Cambridge University Press, 1986).

Hallam, Elizabeth M. *Capetian France 987–1328* (London: Longman, 1980).

Hamp, Karl. *Germany under the Salian and Hohenstaufen Emperors*, trans. R. Bennett (Totowa, N.J.: Rowman and Littlefield, 1973).

Haverkamp, Alfred. *Medieval Germany 1056–1273*, 2nd ed., trans. Braun and Mortimer (Oxford: Oxford University Press, 1992).

Heer, Friedrich. *The Holy Roman Empire* (New York: Praeger, 1968).

Hollister, C. Warren. *Monarchy, Magnates and Institutions in the Anglo-Norman World* (London: The Hambleton Press, 1986).

John of Salisbury. *Policraticus*, trans. C.J. Nederman (Cambridge: Cambridge University Press, 1990).

Kapelle, William. *The Norman Conquest of the North: The Region and Its Transformation, 1000–1135* (Chapel Hill: University of North Carolina, 1979).

Kuttner, Stephan. "The Revival of Jurisprudence," in *Renaissance and Renewal in the Twelfth Century*, ed. R. L. Benson and Giles Constable (Cambridge: Harvard University Press, 1982): 299–323.

Lewis, Andrew W. *Royal Succession in Capetian France: Studies on Familial Order and the State* (Cambridge: Harvard University Press, 1981).

Munz, Peter. *Frederick Barbarossa* (Ithaca, N.Y.: Cornell University Press, 1969).

Myers, Henry A. *Medieval Kingship* (Chicago: Nelson-Hall, 1981).

Newman, Charlotte. *The Anglo-Norman Nobility in the Reign of Henry I* (Philadelphia: University of Pennsylvania Press, 1988).

Norwich, J. J. C. *The Kingdom in the Sun, 1130–1194* (London: Longman, 1976).

———. *The Normans in the South, 1016–1130* (London: Longman, 1967).

O'Callaghan, Joseph F. *A History of Medieval Spain* (Ithaca, N.Y.: Cornell University Press, 1975).

Otto of Freising. *The Deeds of Frederick Barbarossa,* trans. C. C. Mierow (New York: Columbia University Press, 1966).

———. *The Two Cities: A Chronicle of Universal History to the Year 1146 A.D.,* trans. C.C. Mierow (New York: Columbia University Press, 1928).

Pacaut, Marcel. *Frederick Barbarossa*, trans. A. J. Pomerans (New York: Charles Scribner's Sons, 1970).

Reynolds, Susan. *Kingdoms and Communities in Western Europe, 900–1300* (Oxford: Clarendon Press, 1984).

Robinson, I. S. *Henry IV of Germany 1056–1106* (Cambridge: Cambridge University Press, 1999).

Smith, Denis Mack. *Medieval Sicily* (New York: Viking, 1968).

Suger, Abbot of Saint Denis. *The Deeds of Louis the Fat,* trans. Cusimano and Moorhead (Washington, D.C.: The Catholic University of America Press, 1992).

Turner, Ralph V. *Men Raised from the Dust: Administrative Service and Upward Mobility in Angevin England* (Philadelphia: University of Pennsylvania, 1988).

von Caenegem, R.C. *The Birth of the English Common Law* (Cambridge: Cambridge University Press, 1973).

Warren, W. L. *Henry II* (Berkeley: University of California Press, 1973).

Wood, Michael. *Domesday: A Search for the Roots of England* (London: BBC Books, 1986).

Chapter 14 The New Learning

Abelard. *Dialogue of a Philosopher with a Jew and a Christian* (Toronto: Pontifical Institute of Medieval Studies, 1979).

Baldwin, John W. *Masters, Princes and Merchants: The Social Views of Peter the Chanter and His Circle*, 2 vols. (Princeton: Princeton University Press, 1970).

———. *Scholastic Culture of the Middle Ages 1000–1300* (Lexington, Mass.: D.C. Heath, 1971).

Benson, Robert L. and Constable, Giles, eds. *Renaissance and Renewal in the Twelfth Century* (Cambridge: Harvard University Press, 1982).

Brundage, James A. *Medieval Canon Law* (New York: Longman, 1995).

The Cambridge History of Later Medieval Philosophy, eds. Norman Kretzmann, Anthony Kenny, Jan Pinborg (Cambridge: Cambridge University Press, 1982).

Carre, Meyrick H. *Realists and Nominalists* (Oxford: Oxford University Press, 1946).

Chenu, M.D. *Nature, Men, and Society in the Twelfth Century* (Chicago: University of Chicago Press, 1968).

Christ, Karl. *The Handbook of Medieval Library History* (Metuchen, N.J.: Scarecrow Press, 1984).

Clanchy, M. T. *Abelard: A Medieval Life* (Oxford: Blackwell, 1997).

————. *From Memory to Written Record: England 1066–1307* (Oxford: Blackwell, 1979; rev. 1993).

The Cosmographia of Bernardus Silvestris, trans. W. Wetherbye (New York: Columbia University Press, 1973).

Dales, Richard C. *The Intellectual Life of Western Europe in the Middle Ages,* 2nd rev. ed. (Leiden: Brill, 1992).

The Didascalicon of Hugh St. Victor, trans. Jerome Taylor (New York: Columbia University Press, 1961).

Fakhry, Majid. *A History of Islamic Philosophy,* 2nd ed. (New York: Columbia University Press, 1983).

Ferruolo, Stephen. *The Origins of the University: The Schools of Paris and their Critics 1100–1215* (Stanford: Stanford University Press, 1985).

A History of Twelfth-Century Western Philosophy, ed. Peter Dronke (Cambridge: Cambridge University Press, 1988).

Jaeger, Stephen. *The Envy of Angels: Cathedral Schools and Social Ideals in Medieval Europe, 950–1200* (Philadelphia: University of Pennsylvania Press, 1994).

John of Salisbury. *Policraticus,* trans. Cary J. Nederman (Cambridge: Cambridge University Press, 1990).

Le Goff, Jacques. *Intellectuals in the Middle Ages* (Oxford: Blackwell, 1993).

The Letters of Abelard and Heloise, trans. B. Radice (Harmondsworth, Eng.: Penguin, 1974).

Luscombe, D.E. *The School of Peter Abelard* (Cambridge: Cambridge University Press, 1969).

Morris, Colin. *The Discovery of the Individual,* reprint (Toronto: University of Toronto Press, 1987).

Murphy, James J. *Rhetoric in the Middle Ages* (Berkeley: University of California Press, 1974).

Murray, Alexander. *Reason and Society in the Middle Ages* (Oxford: Clarendon Press, 1978).

Murray, A. Victor. *Abelard and St. Bernard* (Manchester: Manchester University Press, 1967).

Powell, James M. *Albertanus of Brescia: The Pursuit of Happiness in the Early Thirteenth Century* (Philadelphia: University of Pennsylvania Press, 1992).

Radding, Charles M. *The Origins of Medieval Jurisprudence* (New Haven: Yale University Press, 1988).

————. *A World Made by Men: Cognition and Society, 400–1200* (Chapel Hill: North Carolina Press, 1985).

Rescher, Nicholas. *The Development of Arabic Logic* (Pittsburgh: University of Pittsburgh Press, 1964).

Self and Society in Medieval France: The Memoirs of Abbot Guibert of Nogent (1064?–c.1125), trans. John F. Benton, reprt (Toronto: University of Toronto Press, 1984).

Semaan, Khalil I., ed. *Islam and the Medieval West* (Albany: State University of New York Press, 1980).

Southern, R. W. *Saint Anselm: A Portrait in a Landscape* (Cambridge: Cambridge University Press, 1990).

———. *Platonism, Scholastic Method and the School of Chartres* (Reading, Eng.: University of Reading, 1979).

Steenberghen, Fernand Van. *Aristotle in the West* (Louwain: Nauwelaerts, 1970).

University Records and Life in the Middle Ages, ed. L. Throndike (New York: Columbia University Press, 1944).

Webber, Teresa. *Scribes and Scholars at Salisbury Cathedral c. 1075–c. 1125* (Oxford: Clarendon Press, 1992).

Weintraub, Karl Joachim. *The Value of the Individual: Self and Circumstance in Autobiography* (Chicago: University of Chicago, 1978).

Chapter 15 Medieval Society

Bartlett, Robert. *The Making of Europe: Conquest, Colonization and Cultural Change 950–1350* (Princeton: Princeton University Press, 1993).

Bean, J. M.W. *From Lord to Patron: Lordship in Late Medieval England* (Philadelphia: University of Pennsylvania Press, 1989).

Bennett, Judith. *Women in the Medieval English Countryside: Gender and Household in Brigstock Before the Plague* (Oxford: Oxford University Press, 1994).

Bisson, Thomas. "Medieval Lordship." *Speculum* 70 (1995): 743–759.

The Broadview Book of Medieval Anecdotes, compiled by Richard Kay (Lewiston, N.Y.: Broadview, 1988).

Brooke, Christopher. *The Medieval Idea of Marriage* (Oxford: Oxford University Press, 1989).

Brown, Elizabeth A. R. "The Tyranny of a Construct: Feudalism and Historians of Medieval Europe." *American Historical Review* 79 (1974): 1063–1088.

Duby, Georges. *The Chivalrous Society,* trans. Cynthia Postan (Berkeley: University of California Press, 1977).

———. *Medieval Marriage: Two Models from Twelfth-century France,* trans. E. Forster (Baltimore: Johns Hopkins University Press, 1978).

———. *William Marshal: The Flower of Chivalry.* trans. Richard Howard (New York: Pantheon, 1985).

Ennen, Edith. *The Medieval Woman,* trans. Edmund Jephcott (Oxford: Blackwell, 1989).

Evergates, Theodore, ed. and trans. *Feudal Society in Medieval France: Documents from the County of Champagne* (Philadelphia: University of Pennsylvania Press, 1993).

———. *Feudal Society in the Baillage of Troyes under the Counts of Champagne, 1156–1284* (Baltimore: Johns Hopkins, 1975).

Ferrante, Joan. *Woman as Image in Medieval Literature, from the Twelfth Century to Dante* (New York: Columbia University Press, 1975).

Fossier, Robert. *Peasant Life in the Medieval West,* trans. Juliet Vale (Oxford: Blackwell, 1988).

Goldin, Frederick. *The Mirror of Narcissus in the Courtly Love Lyric* (Ithaca, N.Y.: Cornell University Press, 1967).

The Goliard Poets, trans. George F. Whicher (Norfolk, Conn.: New Directions, 1965, c. 1949).

Gorecki, Piotr. *Economy, Society, and Lordship in Medieval Poland 1100–1250* (New York: Holmes & Meier, 1992).

Hanawalt, Barbara. *The Ties That Bound: Peasant Families in Medieval England* (Oxford: Oxford University Press, 1986).

Herlihy, David. *Medieval Households* (Cambridge: Harvard University Press, 1985).

Hilton, R. H. *English and French Towns in Feudal Society: A Comparative Study* (Cambridge: Cambridge University Press, 1992).

———. *A Medieval Society: the West Midlands at the End of the Thirteenth Century* (London: Weidenfeld and Nicolson, 1967).

Homans, George. *English Villagers of the Thirteenth Century* (New York: Russell & Russell, 1960, c. 1941).

Jordan, William C. *The French Monarchy and the Jews: from Philip Augustus to the Last Capetians* (Philadelphia: University of Pennsylvania Press, 1989).

———. *From Servitude to Freedom: Manumission in the Sénonais in the Thirteenth Century* (Philadelphia: University of Pennsylvania, 1986).

Karras, Ruth Mazo. *Common Women: Prostitution and Sexuality in Medieval England* (Oxford: Oxford University Press, 1996).

Keen, Maurice. *Chivalry* (New Haven: Yale University Press, 1984).

Labarge, Margaret Wade. *Women in Medieval Life: A Small Sound of the Trumpet* (London: H. Hamilton, 1986).

Le Goff, Jacques. *Time, Work and Culture in the Middle Ages* (Chicago: University of Chicago Press, 1980).

Leyser, Henrietta. *Medieval Women: A Social History of Women in England 450–1500* (New York: St. Martin's Press, 1995).

Lyrics of the Troubadours and Trouveres: an Anthology and a History, trans. F. Goldin (Garden City, N.Y.: Anchor Books, 1973).

Miller, Edward and John Hatcher. *Medieval England: Rural Society and Economic Change 1086–1348* (London: Longman, 1980, c. 1978).

Power, Eileen. *Medieval Women,* ed. M. M. Postan (Cambridge: Cambridge University Press, 1975).

Reynolds, Susan. *Fiefs and Vassals: The Medieval Evidence Reinterpreted* (Oxford: Oxford University Press, 1994).

———. *Kingdoms and Communities in Western Europe, 900–1300* (Oxford: Clarendon Press, 1984).

Shahar, Shulamith. *Childhood in the Middle Ages* (London: Routledge, 1990).

Songs of the Women Troubadours, ed. and trans. Bruckner, Shepard, and White (New York: Garland Publishing, 1995).

Wood, Charles. *The Quest for Eternity: Manners and Morals in the Age of Chivalry* (Hanover, N.H.: University Press of New England, 1983).

Chapter 16 Church and State in the Thirteenth Century

Baldwin, John W. *The Government of Philip Augustus* (Berkeley: University of California Press, 1986).

Bennett, R. F. *The Early Dominicans* (Cambridge: Cambridge University Press, 1937).

Brooke, Rosalind B. *The Coming of the Friars* (London: George Allen and Unwin, 1975).

Clanchy, Michael. *England and Its Rulers 1066–1272* (New York: Barnes and Noble, 1983).

Duby, Georges. *The Legend of Bouvines: War, Religion and Culture in the Middle Ages* (Berkeley: University of California Press, 1990).

Francis and Clare: The Complete Works, trans. R. J. Armstrong and I. C. Brady (New York: Paulist Press, 1982).

Holt, J. C. *Magna Carta* (Cambridge: Cambridge University Press, 1965).

Jordan, William C. *Louis IX and the Challenge of the Crusade: A Study in Rulership* (Princeton, N.J.: Princeton University Press, 1979).

Martin, Janet. *Medieval Russia 980–1584* (Cambridge: Cambridge University Press, 1995).

Mollat, Michel. *The Poor in the Middle Ages: An Essay in Social History* (New Haven: Yale University Press, 1986).

Moore, R. I. *The Origins of European Dissent* (London: Allen Lane, 1977).

Moorman, John. *A History of the Franciscan Order* (Oxford: Clarendon Press, 1968).

Peters, Edward. *Inquisition* (Berkeley: University of California Press, 1989).

Prestwich, Michael. *English Politics in the Thirteenth Century* (New York: St. Martin's Press, 1990).

———. *War, Politics and Finance under Edward I* (Totowa, N.J.: Rowman and Littlefield, 1972).

Reilly, Bernard F. *The Medieval Spains* (Cambridge: Cambridge University Press, 1993).

Robson, Michael. *St. Francis of Assisi: The Legend and the Life* (London: G. Chapman, 1997).

St. Francis of Assisi: Writings and Early Biographies, ed. Marion A. Habig, 4th rev. ed. (Chicago: Francsican Press, 1991).

Saunders, J. J. *The History of the Mongol Conquests* (Philadelphia: University of Pennsylvania Press, 2001, c. 1971).

Sayers, Jane. *Innocent III: Leader of Europe 1198–1216* (London: Longman, 1994).

Shannon, Albert Clement. *The Popes and Heresy in the Thirteenth Century* (Villanvova, Pa.: Augustinian Press, 1949).

Slattery, Maureen. *Myth, Man and Sovereign Saint: King Louis IX in Jean de Joinville's Sources* (New York: Peter Lang, 1985).

Southern, R.W. *Western Society and the Church in the Middle Ages* (Harmondsworth, Eng.: Penguin, 1970).

Stacey, Robert C. *Politics, Policy, and Finance under Henry III, 1216–1245* (Oxford: Clarendon Press, 1987).

Strayer, J.R. *The Albigensian Crusades* (New York: Dial Press, 1971).

Sumption, Jonathan. *The Albigensian Crusade* (Boston: Faber, 1999, c. 1978).

Tillmann, Helene. *Pope Innocent III,* trans. W. Sax (Amsterdam: North Holland Publishing Company, 1980).

Warren, W. L. *King John* (Berkeley: University of California Press, 1978).

Chapter 17 High Culture and Popular Culture

Clanchy, Michael. *From Memory to Written Record: England, 1066–1307,* rev. ed. (Oxford: Blackwell, 1993).

Cohen, Mark R. *Under Crescent and Cross: The Jews in the Middle Ages* (Princeton, N.J.: Princeton University Press, 1994).

Cohn, Norman. *The Pursuit of the Millennium* (Oxford: Oxford University Press, 1970, c. 1951).

Daniel, Norman. *The Arabs and Mediaeval Europe,* 2nd. ed. (London: Longman, 1979).

———. *Islam and the West: The Making of an Image,* rev. ed. (Oxford: Oneworld, 1993).

Dunlop, Ian. *The Cathedrals' Crusade: The Rise of the Gothic Style in France* (New York: Taplinger Co., Hamish Hamilton, 1982).

Easton, Stewart C. *Roger Bacon and His Search for a Universal Science* (New York: Columbia University Press, 1952).

Geoffrey of Monmouth. *History of the Kings of Britain,* trans. Lewis Thorpe (Baltimore: Penguin Books, 1966).

Gies, Joseph and Frances. *Leonard of Pisa and the New Mathematics of the Middle Ages* (Gainesville, Ga.: New Classics Library, 1969).

Gilson, Etienne. *The Philosophy of St. Bonaventure* (New York: Sheed & Ward, 1940).

Gimpel, Jean. *The Cathedral Builders* (New York: Grove Press, 1983).

Guillaume de Lorris, and Jean de Meun. *The Romance of the Rose,* trans. Charles Dahlberg (Princeton: Princeton University Press, 1971).

Gumilev, L.N. *Searches for an Imaginary Kingdom: The Legend of the Kingdom of Prester John,* trans. R. E. F. Smith (Cambridge: Cambridge University Press, 1987).

Hillgarth, Jocelyn. *Ramon Lull and Lullism in Fourteenth-Century France* (Oxford: Clarendon Press, 1971).

James, John. *Chartres: The Masons Who Built a Legend* (London: Routledge & Kegan Paul, 1982).

Jordan, William C. *The French Monarchy and the Jews: from Philip Augustus to the last Capetians* (Philadelphia: University of Pennsylvania, 1989).

Lancelot or the Knight of the Cart, trans. Ruth Cline (Athens, Ga.: Georgia University Press, 1990).

Leaman, Oliver. *Moses Maimonides* (New York: Routledge, American University in Cairo Press, 1990).

Lindberg, David C. *The Beginnings of Western Science* (Chicago: University of Chicago Press, 1992).

Luscombe, David. *Medieval Thought* (Oxford: Oxford University Press, 1997).

Martindale, Andrew. *Gothic Art* (Oxford: Oxford University Press, 1967).

McGinn, Bernard. *The Calabrian Abbot: Joachim of Fiore in the History of Western Thought* (New York: Macmillan, 1985).

Moorman, John. *A History of the Franciscan Order from its Origins to the Year 1517* (Oxford: Clarendon Press, 1968).

Morgan, David. *The Mongols* (Oxford: Blackwell, 1986).

Muscatine, Charles. *The Old French Fabliaux* (New Haven: Yale University Press, 1986).

Peck, George T. *The Fool of God: Jacopone da Todi* (Tuscaloosa, Ala.: University of Alabama Press, 1980).

Percival or the Story of the Grail, trans. Ruth Cline (Athens, Ga.: Georgia University Press, 1985).

The Quest of the Holy Grail, trans. P. M. Matarasso (Harmondsworth, Eng.: Penguin Books, 1971).

Rubin, Miri. *Corpus Christi: The Eucharist in Late Medieval Culture* (Cambridge: Cambridge University Press, 1991).

Selected Works of Ramon Llull. 2 vols., ed. and trans. Anthony Bonner (Princeton: Princeton University Press, 1985).

Stow, Kenneth. *Alienated Minority: The Jews of Medieval Latin Europe* (Cambridge: Harvard University Press, 1992).

Topsfield, L.T. *Chrétien de Troyes: A Study of the Arthurian Romances* (Cambridge: Cambridge University Press, 1981).

Torrell, Jean-Pierre. *Thomas Aquinas,* trans. R. Royal (Washington, D.C.: Catholic University Press, 1996).

The Travels of Marco Polo, trans. Ronald Latham (Harmondsworth, Eng.: Penguin Books, 1958).

von Simon, Otto. *The Gothic Cathedral* (Princeton: Princeton University Press, 1956).

Weisheipl, James A. *Friar Thomas D'Aquino: His Life, Thought and Works* (Garden City, N.Y.: Doubleday, 1974).

West, Delno. *Joachim of Fiore: A Study in Spiritual Perception and History* (Bloomington: Indiana University Press, 1983).

Wilson, Christopher. *The Gothic Cathedral: The Architecture of the Great Church 1130–1530* (London: Thames and Hudson, 1990).

Chapter 18 Economic and Political Crisis

Allmand, Christopher. *The Hundred Years War* (Cambridge: Cambridge University Press, 1989).

Atkinson, Clarissa. *The Oldest Profession: Christian Motherhood in the Middle Ages* (Ithaca, N.Y.: Cornell University Press, 1991).

Barrow, G. W. S. *Robert Bruce and the Community of the Realm of Scotland* (Edinburgh: Edinburgh University Press, 1988).

Black, Antony. *Political Thought in Europe 1250–1450* (Cambridge: Cambridge University Press, 1992).

Boase, T. S. R. *Death in the Middle Ages* (New York: McGraw-Hill, 1972).

Brehier, Louis. *The Life and Death of Byzantium* (Amsterdam: North Holland Publishing Co., 1977).

Campbell, Bruce M.S., ed. *Before the Black Death: Studies in the "Crisis" of the Early Fourteenth Century* (Manchester: Manchester University Press, 1991).

The City of Scholars: New Approaches to Christine de Pizan, ed. Margaret Zimmerman and Dina de Rentiis (New York: W. de Gruyter, 1994).

Curry, Anne. *The Hundred Years War* (New York: St. Martin's Press, 1993).

Ennen, Edith. *The Medieval Woman,* trans. Edmund Jephcott (Oxford: Blackwell, 1989).

Fourquin, Guy. *The Anatomy of Popular Rebellion in the Middle Ages* (Amsterdam: North Holland Publishing, 1978).

Goldberg, P. J. P. *Women, Work, and Life Cycle in a Medieval Economy: Women in York and Yorkshire c. 1300–1520* (Oxford: Clarendon Press, 1992).

Goldberg, P. J. P., ed. *Women in England c. 1275–1525: Documentary Sources* (Manchester: Manchester University Press, 1995).

Hanawalt, Barbara A. *Crime and Conflict in English Communities, 1300–1348* (Cambridge: Harvard University Press, 1979).

————. *Growing Up in Medieval London: The Experience of Childhood in History* (Oxford: Oxford University Press, 1993).

————. *The Ties That Bound: Peasant Families in Medieval England* (New York: Oxford, 1980).

Hillgarth, Jocelyn. *The Spanish Kingdoms, 1250–1516,* 2 vols. (Oxford: Oxford University Press, 1976–1978).

Hilton, R. H. *Bond Men Made Free: Medieval Peasant Movements and the English Rising of 1381* (New York: Viking Press, 1973).

Horrox, Rosemary, trans. and ed. *The Black Death* (Manchester: Manchester University Press, 1994).

Jordan, William C. *The Great Famine: Northern Europe in the Early Fourteenth Century* (Princeton: Princeton University Press, 1996).

Keen, Maurice. *Chivalry* (New Haven: Yale University Press, 1984).

————. *English Society in the Later Middle Ages 1348–1500* (London: Penguin, 1990).

Köprülü, M. Fuad. *The Origins of the Ottoman Empire,* trans. G. Leiser (Albany: State University of New York, 1992).

Lucas, Angela M. *Women in the Middle Ages: Religion, Marriage and Letters* (New York: St. Martin's Press, 1983).

Mackay, James. *William Wallace: Brave Heart* (Edinburgh: Mainstream, 1995).

Mollat, Michel and Philippe Wolff. *The Popular Revolutions of the Late Middle Ages* (London: Allen & Unwin, 1973).

Neillands, Robin. *The Hundred Years War* (New York: Routledge, 1990).

Nichol, David M. *The Last Centuries of Byzantium 1261–1453* (New York: St. Martin's Press, 1972).

Orme, Nicholas. *From Childhood to Chivalry: The Education of the English Kings and Aristocracy 1066–1530* (London: Methuen, 1984).

Platt, Colin. *King Death: the Black Death and its Aftermath in late Medieval England* (Toronto: University of Toronto Press, 1996).

Strayer, Joseph. *The Reign of Philip the Fair* (Princeton: Princeton University Press, 1980).

TeBrake, William H. *A Plague of Insurrection: Popular Politics and Peasant Revolt in Flanders, 1323–1328* (Philadelphia: University of Pennsylvania, 1993).

Thomson, John A. E. *The Transformation of Medieval England 1370–1529* (New York: Longman, 1983).

Tuck, Anthony. *Crown and Nobility 1272–1461: Political Conflict in Late Medieval England* (Oxford: Basil Blackwell, 1986).

Warner, Marina. *Joan of Arc: The Image of Female Heroism* (New York: Knopf, 1981).

Willard, Charity Cannon. *Christine de Pizan: Her Life and Works* (New York: Persea Books, 1984).

Ziegler, Philip. *The Black Death* (New York: Harper & Row, 1969).

Chapter 19 Institutional and Intellectual Developments

Ancelet-Hustache, Jeanne. *Master Eckhart and the Rhineland Mystics* (London: Longman, 1960).

Anderson, William. *Dante the Maker* (Boston: Routledge, 1980).

Barraclough, Geoffrey. *The Medieval Papacy* (London: Thames and Hudson, 1968).

Black, Anthony. *Council and Commune: The Conciliar Movement and the Fifteenth-Century Heritage* (Sheperdstown: Patmos Press, 1979).

———. *Monarchy and Community: Political Ideas in the Later Conciliar Controversy* (Cambridge: Cambridge University Press, 1970).

———. *Political Thought in Europe 1250–1450* (Cambridge: Cambridge University Press, 1992).

Boase, T. S. R. *Boniface VIII* (London: Constable, 1933).

Chaucer, Geoffrey. *The Canterbury Tales* (New York: Penguin, 1951).

Clark, James M. *The Great German Mystics: Eckhart, Tauler and Suso* (Oxford: Basil Blackwell, 1949).

Colish, Marcia. *Medieval Foundations of the Western Intellectual Tradition 400–1400* (New Haven: Yale University Press, 1997).

Dante. *Monarchia,* trans. Prue Shaw (Cambridge: Cambridge University Press, 1995).

Dante's Inferno, Purgatorio and Paradiso, trans. John D. Sinclair (Oxford: Oxford University Press, 1961).

The Earliest Lives of Dante, trans. J.R. Smith (New York: Ungar, 1963).

Giles of Rome on Ecclesiastical Power, trans. by R. W. Dyson (Woodbridge: The Boydell Press, 1986).

Howard, Donald. *Chaucer: His Life, His Works, His World* (New York: E. P. Dutton, 1987).

John of Paris. *On Royal and Papal Power,* trans. A.P. Monahan (New York: Columbia University Press, 1974).

Kieckhefer, Richard. *European Witch Trials: Their Foundations in Popular and Learned Culture, 1300–1500* (Berkeley: University of California Press, 1976).

———. *Magic in the Middle Ages* (Cambridge: Cambridge University Press, 1990).

———. *Repression of Heresy in Medieval Germany* (Philadelphia: University of Pennsylvania Press, 1979).

———. *Unquiet Souls: Fourteenth-Century Saints and Their Religious Milieu* (Chicago: University of Chicago Press, 1984).

Knowles, David. *The English Mystical Tradition* (London: Burns & Oates, 1961).

Lambert, Malcolm. *The Cathars* (Oxford: Blackwell, 1998).

———. *Medieval Heresy: Popular Movements from the Gregorian Reform to the Reformation* (Oxford: Blackwell, 1992).

Leff, Gordon. *Heresy in the Later Middle Ages: the Relation of Heterodoxy to Dissent c. 1250–c. 1450,* 2 vols. (Manchester: Manchester University Press, 1967).

Lerner, Robert. *The Heresy of the Free Spirit in the Later Middle Ages* (Berkeley: University of California Press, 1972).

Leuschner, Joachim. *Germany in the Late Middle Ages,* trans. Sabine MacCormack (Amsterdam: North-Holland Publishing Co., 1980).

Marguerite Porete. *The Mirror of Simple Souls,* trans. and intro. Ellen L. Babinsky (New York: Paulist Press, 1993).

Marsilius of Padua. *Defensor Pacis,* trans. Alan Gewirth (Toronto: University of Toronto Press, 1980).

McDonnell, Ernest W. *The Beguines and Beghards in Medieval Culture* (New Brunswick, N.J.: Rutgers University Press, 1954).

McGinn, Bernard and Edmund Colledge, eds. *Meister Eckhart: The Essential Sermons, Commentaries, Treatises and Defense* (New York: Paulist Press, 1981).

———. *Meister Eckhart and the Beguine Mystics* (New York: Continuum, 1994).

McGrade, A. S. *The Political Thought of William of Ockham: Personal and Institutional Principles* (Cambridge: Cambridge University Press, 1974).

Mollat, G. *The Popes of Avignon* (Edinburgh: New York: Harper & Row, 1963).

Oakley, Francis. *The Western Church in the Later Middle Ages* (Ithaca, N.Y.: Cornell University Press, 1979).

Ozment, Steven. *The Age of Reform 1250–1550: An Intellectual and Religious History of Late Medieval and Reformation Europe* (New Haven: Yale University Press, 1980).

Post, R. R. *The Modern Devotion* (Leiden: E.J. Brill, 1968).

Russell, Jeffrey Burton. *Dissent and Order in the Middle Ages: The Search for Legitimate Authority* (New York: Twayne, 1992).

Strayer, Joseph. *The Reign of Philip the Fair* (Princeton: Princeton University Press, 1980).

Tierney, Brian. *Foundations of the Conciliar Theory* (Cambridge: Cambridge University Press, 1955).

Ullman, Walter. *A Short History of the Papacy in the Middle Ages* (London: Methuen, 1972).

William of Ockham. *A Letter to the Friars Minor, and Other Writings*, ed. McGrade and Kilcullen (Cambridge: Cambridge University Press, 1995).

INDEX